THE TENTH (IRISH) DIVISION

Printed and bound by Antony Rowe Ltd, Eastbourne

MULES IN THE ANZAC SAP

THE TENTH (IRISH) DIVISION IN GALLIPOLI

BY

BRYAN COOPER

MAJOR, GENERAL LIST NEW ARMIES
FORMERLY 5TH SERVICE BATTALION THE CONNAUGHT RANGERS

WITH AN INTRODUCTION BY
MAJOR-GEN. SIR BRYAN MAHON, D.S.O.

WITH APPRECIATIONS BY
MR. ASQUITH
MR. BALFOUR
SIR EDWARD CARSON
MR. JOHN REDMOND

HERBERT JENKINS LIMITED
3 YORK STREET ST. JAMES'S
LONDON S.W. 1 ○ ○ MCMXVIII

" So they gave their bodies to the common weal and
received, each for his own memory, praise that will never
die, and with it the grandest of all sepulchres, not that in
which their mortal bones are laid, but a home in the minds
of men, where their glory remains fresh to stir to speech or
action as the occasion comes by."—*Thucydides.*

" It seems as if this poor Celtic people were bent on
making what one of its own poets has said of its heroes
hold good for ever : ' They went forth to the war but they
always fell.' "—*Matthew Arnold.*

PRINTED BY BURLEIGH LTD., AT THE BURLEIGH PRESS, BRISTOL, ENGLAND

TO

THE GLORIOUS MEMORY

OF THE

OFFICERS, NON-COMMISSIONED OFFICERS

AND MEN

OF THE

TENTH IRISH DIVISION

WHO LAID DOWN THEIR LIVES IN

GALLIPOLI

AND

TO THOSE WHO MOURN FOR THEM

APPRECIATIONS

Major Cooper's narrative of the exploits of the 10th Division in the Gallipoli Campaign is a moving and inspiring record, of which Irishmen everywhere may well be proud.

I trust that it will be widely read in all parts of the Empire.

(Sd.)   H. H. ASQUITH

This war has been fruitful in deeds of splendid bravery and heroic endurance ; but neither in bravery nor endurance have the 10th Division in the Gallipoli Campaign been surpassed by any of their brothers-in-arms who have been fighting in Europe and Asia for the cause of civilisation and freedom.

(Sd.)   ARTHUR JAMES BALFOUR

Dear Bryan Cooper,

I am very glad that you have undertaken to record the splendid services of the 10th Division in Gallipoli. Their magnificent bravery in the face of almost insurmountable

difficulties and discomforts stands out amongst
the countless acts of heroism in this war, and
I think it particularly apt that the history
of the actions of these brave Irishmen in the
campaign should be recorded by a gallant
Irish officer.

Yours sincerely,

(Sd.)   EDWARD CARSON

I have been asked to write a short Foreword
to the following pages, and I do so with the
utmost pleasure.   By the publication of this
little book, Major Bryan Cooper will be per-
forming a most valuable service, not only to
his own country, Ireland, but to the Empire.

The history of the 10th (Irish) Division is, in
many respects, unique.   It was the first Irish
Division raised and sent to the Front by Ireland
since the commencement of the War.   Not
alone that, but it was the first definitely Irish
Division that ever existed in the British Army.

Irish Divisions and Irish Brigades played a
great part in history in the past, but they were
Divisions and Brigades, not in the service of
England, but in the service of France and other
European countries and America.

The creation of the 10th (Irish) Division,
therefore, marks a turning point in the history
of the relations between Ireland and the
Empire.

In many respects, the 10th (Irish) Division, notwithstanding the extraordinary and outstanding gallantry that it showed in the field, may be said to have been unfortunate. No Division in any theatre of the War suffered more severely or showed greater self-sacrifices and gallantry. And yet, largely, I fancy, by reason of the fact that its operations were in a distant theatre, comparatively little has been heard of its achievements ; and, for some reason which a civilian cannot understand, the number of honours and distinctions conferred on the Division has been comparatively small. And yet we have the testimony of everyone, from the Generals in Command down, that the Division behaved magnificently, in spite of the most terrible and unlooked-for difficulties and sufferings.

Before they went into action, their artillery was taken from them, and they landed at Suvla and Anzac without a single gun.

They were a Division of the new Army entirely made up of men who had no previous military experience, and who had never heard a shot fired. Yet, the very day they landed, they found themselves precipitated into the most tremendous and bloody conflict, exposed to heavy shrapnel and machine-gun fire, on an open strand, where cover was impossible.

To the most highly trained and seasoned troops in the world, this would have been a trying ordeal; but, to new troops, it was a cruel and terrible experience. And yet the testimony all goes to show that no seasoned or trained troops in the world could have behaved with more magnificent steadiness, endurance, and gallantry. Without adequate water supply —indeed, for a long time, without water at all, owing to mismanagement, which has yet to be traced home to its source—their sufferings were appalling.

As Major Bryan Cooper points out, it is supposed to be a German military maxim that no battalion could maintain its morale with losses of twenty-five per cent. Many of the battalions of the 10th Division lost seventy-five per cent., and yet their morale remained unshaken. The depleted Division was hastily filled up with drafts, and sent, under-officered, to an entirely new campaign at Salonika, where it won fresh laurels.

Another cruel misfortune which overtook them was, that, instead of being allowed to fight and operate together as a Unit, they were immediately split up, one Brigade being attached to the 11th Division, and entirely separated from their comrades.

There has been some misapprehension created, in certain quarters, as to the constitution of this 10th Division and its right to call itself an Irish Division. Major Bryan Cooper sets this question at rest. What really occurred was, that, quite early in the business, when recruiting for the 10th Division was going on fairly well in Ireland, for some unexplained reason, a number of English recruits were suddenly sent over to join its ranks. They were quite unnecessary, and protests against their incursion into the Division fell upon deaf ears. As it happened, however, it was found that a considerable number of these English recruits were Irishmen living in Great Britain, or the sons of Irishmen, and, when the Division went to the Front, Major Bryan Cooper states that fully seventy per cent. of the men, and ninety per cent. of the officers, were Irishmen. That is to say, the Division was as much entitled to claim to be an Irish Division in its constitution as any Division either in England, Scotland, or Wales is entitled to claim that it is an English, Scotch, or Welsh Division.

Men of all classes and creeds in Ireland joined its ranks. The list of casualties which Major Bryan Cooper gives is heart-breaking reading to any Irishman, especially to one like myself, who had so many personal friends who fell gallantly in the conflict.

Irishmen of all political opinions were united in the Division. Its spirit was intensely Irish. Let me quote Major Bryan Cooper's words :—

" It was the first Irish Division to take the field in War. Irish Brigades there had often been. They had fought under the Fleur-

de-Lys or the Tricolour of France, and under
the Stars and Stripes, as well as they had done
under the Union Jack. But never before in
Ireland's history had she seen anywhere a
whole Division of her sons in the battlefield.
The old battalions of the Regular Army had
done magnificently, but they had been
brigaded with English, Scotch, and Welsh
units. The 10th Division was the first
Division almost entirely composed of Irish
Battalions who faced an enemy. Officers
and men alike knew this, and were proud of
their destiny. As the battalions marched
through the quiet English countryside, the
drums and fifes shrieked out 'St. Patrick's
Day' or 'Brian Boru's March,' and the dark
streets of Basingstoke echoed the voices that
chanted 'God Save Ireland,' as the Units
marched down to entrain. Nor did we lack
the green. One Unit sewed shamrocks into
its sleeves. Another wore them as helmet
badges. Almost every Company cherished
somewhere an entirely unofficial green flag,
as dear to the men as if they were the regimental colours themselves. They constituted
an outward and visible sign that the honour of
Ireland was in the Division's keeping, and the
men did not forget it."

The men who had differed in religion and
politics, and their whole outlook on life, became

brothers in the 10th Division. Unionist and Nationalist, Catholic and Protestant, as Major Bryan Cooper says—" lived and fought and died side by side, like brothers." They combined for a common purpose : to fight the good fight for liberty and civilisation, and, in a special way, for the future liberty and honour of their own country.

Major Bryan Cooper expresses the hope that this experience may be a good augury for the future.

For my part, I am convinced that nothing that can happen can deprive Ireland of the benefit of the united sacrifices of these men.

I congratulate Major Bryan Cooper on his book. The more widely it is circulated, the better it will be for Ireland and for the Empire.

J. E. REDMOND

St. Patrick's Day, 1917

B

INTRODUCTION

I HAVE been asked to contribute a short introduction to this account of the doings of the 10th (Irish) Division in Gallipoli.

I commanded the Division from the time of its formation until it left Gallipoli Peninsula for Salonika, and I am extremely glad that some record has been made of its exploits. I do not think that the author of this book intends to claim for the Division any special pre-eminence over other units ; but that he puts forward a simple account of what the first formed Irish Service Battalions suffered and how creditably they maintained the honour of Ireland.

Memories in war-time are short, and it may be that the well-earned glories of the 16th and Ulster Division have tended to obliterate the recollections of Suvla and Sari Bair. (The Division has also the distinction of being the only troops of the Allies that have fought in Bulgaria up to date.)

In case these things are forgotten, it is well that this book has been written, for never in history did Irishmen face death with greater courage and endurance than they did in Gallipoli and Serbia in the summer and winter of 1915.

During the period of its formation the Division suffered from many handicaps. To the difficulties which are certain to befall any newly created unit were added others due to the enormous strain that the nation was undergoing ; arms and equipment were slow in arriving ; inclement weather made training difficult, and for sake of accommodation units had had to be widely separated in barracks all over Ireland. All these difficulties were, however, surmounted, partly by the genuine keenness of all ranks, but in the main by the devoted work of the handful of regular officers and N.C.O.'s who formed the nucleus of the Division.

No words can convey how much was done by these men, naturally disappointed at not going out with the original Expeditionary Force. They nevertheless threw themselves whole-heartedly into the work before them, and laboured unceasingly and untiredly to make the new units a success, they were ably seconded by retired officers who had rejoined, and by newly-joined subalterns, who brought with them the freshness and enthusiasm of youth.

Nor were the men behindhand. Though the monotony of routine training sometimes grew irksome, yet their eagerness to face the enemy and their obvious anxiety to do their duty carried them through, and enabled them to become in nine months well-trained and disciplined soldiers.

When they reached Gallipoli they had much to endure. The 29th Brigade were not under my command, so I cannot speak from personal knowledge, but I believe that every battalion did its duty and won the praise of its generals.

Of the remainder of the Division I can speak with greater certainty. They were plunged practically at a moment's notice into battle, and were placed in positions of responsibility and difficulty on a desolate sun-baked and waterless soil, where they suffered tortures from thirst. In spite of this, and in spite of the fact that they were newly formed units mainly composed of young soldiers, they acquitted themselves admirably. No blame or discredit of any kind can possibly be attached to the rank and file of the 10th Division. Whatever the emergency, and however great the danger, they faced it resolutely and steadfastly, rejoicing when an opportunity arose that enabled them to meet their enemy with the bayonet.

Ireland has had many brave sons ; Ireland has sent forth many splendid regiments in past times ; but the deeds of the men of the 10th (Irish) Division are worthy to be reckoned with any of those of their predecessors.

(Sd.)   BRYAN MAHON

AUTHOR'S PREFACE

THIS book (which was written in haste during a period of sick leave) does not profess to be a military history; it is merely a brief attempt to describe the fortunes of the rank and file of the Tenth (Irish) Division. The Division was so much split up that it is impossible for any one person to have taken part in all its actions; but I went to Gallipoli with my battalion, and though disabled for a period by sickness, I returned to the Peninsula before the Division left it, so that I may fairly claim to have seen both the beginning and the end of the operations. I have received great assistance from numerous officers of the Division, who have been kind enough to summarise for me the doings of their battalions, and I tender them my grateful thanks.

I must also thank Mr. H. Hanna, K.C., for allowing me to inspect part of the proofs of his forthcoming book dealing with "D" Company of the 7th Royal Dublin Fusiliers. I owe Mr. Hanna a further debt of gratitude for his kindness in allowing the reproduction of the sketches of "The Salt Lake," "Anafarta

Plain," and "'D' Company in the Trenches," which were executed by Captain Drummond Fish, of the Royal Irish Rifles, for his book. Captain Fish has also very kindly allowed me to use three more of his sketches, which, though deprived of the charm of colour possessed by the originals, give a far better idea of the scenery of Gallipoli than can be obtained from any photograph. Having shared the life led by Captain Fish's battalion in Gallipoli, I cannot help admiring the manner in which he managed to include a paint-box and a sketch-book in the very scanty kit allowed to officers. I must further express to my comrade, Francis Ledwidge, who himself served in the ranks of the Division, my sincere gratitude for the beautiful lines in which he has summed up the object of our enterprise. In them he has fulfilled the poet's mission of expressing in words the deepest thoughts of these who feel them too sincerely to be able to give them worthy utterance.

In dealing with the general aspect of the Gallipoli Expedition, I have tried to avoid controversial topics. As a general rule, I have followed the version given by Sir Ian Hamilton in his despatch, which is still the only official document that exists for our guidance. I am conscious that the book, of necessity, has omitted many gallant deeds, and has dealt with some units more fully than with others.

I can only plead in extenuation that I found great difficulty in getting detailed information as to the doings of some battalions, and that to this, rather than to prejudice on my part, is due any lack of proportion that may exist. It is by no means easy for an Irishman to be impartial, but I have done my best.

BRYAN COOPER

March 1*st*, 1917

P.S.—Since this was written Francis Ledwidge has laid down his life for the honour of Ireland, and the world has lost a poet of rare promise.

CONTENTS

CONTENTS

APPENDICES

LIST OF ILLUSTRATIONS

THE IRISH IN GALLIPOLI

Where Aegean cliffs with bristling menace front
The treacherous splendour of that isley sea,
Lighted by Troy's last shadow ; where the first
Hero kept watch and the last Mystery
Shook with dark thunder. Hark ! the battle brunt !
A nation speaks, old Silences are burst.

'Tis not for lust of glory, no new throne
This thunder and this lightning of our power
Wakens up frantic echoes, not for these
Our Cross with England's mingle, to be blown
At Mammon's threshold. We but war when war
Serves Liberty and Keeps a world at peace.

Who said that such an emprise could be vain ?
Were they not one with Christ, who fought and died ?
Let Ireland weep : but not for sorrow, weep
That by her sons a land is sanctified,
For Christ arisen, and angels once again
Come back, like exile birds, and watch their sleep.

FRANCIS LEDWIDGE

FRANCE
24th February, 1917

THE TENTH (IRISH) DIVISION

THE TENTH (IRISH) DIVISION
IN GALLIPOLI

CHAPTER I

THE FORMATION OF THE DIVISION

" The Army, unlike any other profession, cannot be taught through shilling books. First a man must suffer, then he must learn his work and the self-respect which knowledge brings."—Kipling.

WITHIN ten days of the outbreak of the War, before even the Expeditionary Force had left England, Lord Kitchener appealed for a hundred thousand recruits, and announced that six new divisions would be formed from them. These six divisions, which were afterwards known as the First New Army, or more colloquially as K.1, were, with one exception, distributed on a territorial basis. The Ninth was Scotch, the Eleventh North Country, the Twelfth was recruited in London and the Home Counties, and the Thirteenth in the West of England. The exception was the Fourteenth, which consisted of new battalions of English light infantry and rifle regiments. The Tenth

B

Division in which I served, and whose history I am about to relate, was composed of newly-formed or " Service " battalions of all the Irish line regiments, together with the necessary complement of artillery, engineers, Army Service Corps, and R.A.M.C. They were distributed as follows :—

29TH BRIGADE.

5th Service Battalion, Royal Irish Regiment.
6th ditto Royal Irish Rifles.
5th ditto The Connaught Rangers.
6th ditto The Leinster Regiment.

The 5th Royal Irish Regiment afterwards became the Divisional Pioneer Battalion, and its place in the 29th Brigade was taken by the 10th Hampshire Regiment.

30TH BRIGADE.

6th Service Battalion, Royal Dublin Fusiliers.
7th ditto ditto
6th Service Battalion, Royal Munster Fusiliers.
7th ditto ditto

31ST BRIGADE.

5th Service Battalion, Royal Inniskilling
Fusiliers.
6th ditto ditto
5th Service Battalion, Royal Irish Fusiliers.
6th ditto ditto

It will be seen that the 29th Brigade consisted of regiments from all the four provinces of Ireland, while the 30th Brigade had its depôts in the South of Ireland, and the 31st in Ulster.

The Divisional Troops were organised as follows :—

ARTILLERY.

54th Brigade R.F.A.
55th   ,,   R.F.A.
56th   ,,   R.F.A.
57th (Howitzer) Brigade R.F.A.
Heavy Battery R.G.A.

ENGINEERS.

65th Field Company R.E.
66th   ditto   R.E.
85th   ditto   R.E.

10th Divisional Signal Company.
10th Divisional Train.
10th Divisional Cyclist Company.
30th Field Ambulance, R.A.M.C.
31st   ditto
32nd   ditto

A squadron of South Irish Horse was allocated as Divisional Cavalry, but this only joined the Division at Basingstoke in May, and was detached again before we embarked for Gallipoli.

Fortunately, one of the most distinguished of Irish Generals was available to take command of the Division. Lieut.-General Sir Bryan

Mahon was a Galway man who had entered the
8th (Royal Irish) Hussars from a Militia
Battalion of the Connaught Rangers in 1883.
For ten years he served with his regiment,
acting as Adjutant from 1889 to 1893, but
recognising that British Cavalry were unlikely
to see much active service, he transferred to the
Egyptian Army in the latter year. He served
with the Cavalry of this force in the Dongola
Expedition in 1896, and was awarded the
D.S.O. For his services in the campaign,
which ended in the capture of Khartoum, he
received the brevet rank of Lieutenant-Colonel.
He next commanded the mounted troops which
achieved the defeat and death of the Khalifa,
and for this he was promoted to Brevet-Colonel.
He was then transferred to South Africa, where
he commanded a mounted brigade and had the
distinction of leading the column which effected
the relief of Mafeking, being created a Companion
of the Bath for his services on this occasion.
After the South African War he returned to
the Soudan as Military Governor of Kordofan.
His next commands were in India, and he had
only vacated the command of the Lucknow
Division early in 1914. While holding it in
1912 he had been created a K.C.V.O.

At the time he took over the 10th Division
he was fifty-two years of age. His service in
Egypt and India had bronzed his face and sown
grey in his hair, but his figure and his seat on a

LIEUT.-GENERAL SIR BRYAN MAHON, K.C.V.O., C.B., D.S.O.

horse were those of a subaltern. He scorned display, and only the ribbons on his breast told of the service he had seen. A soft cap adorned with an 8th Hussar badge, with a plain peak and the red band almost concealed by a khaki cover, tried to disguise his rank, but the manner in which it was pulled over his eyes combined with the magnificent chestnut he rode and the eternal cigarette in his mouth, soon made him easily recognisable throughout the Division.

Experienced soldier as he was, he had qualities that made him even better suited to his post than military knowledge, and in his years in the East he had not forgotten the nature of his countrymen. The Irish soldier is not difficult to lead : he will follow any man who is just and fearless, but to get the best out of him, needs sympathy, and this indefinable quality the General possessed. It was impossible for him to pass a football match on the Curragh without saying a pleasant word to the men who were watching it, and they repaid this by adoring their leader. Everything about him appealed to them—his great reputation, the horse he rode, his Irish name, and his Irish nature, all went to their hearts. Above all, he was that unique being, an Irishman with no politics, and this, in a Division that was under the patronage of no political party, but consisted of those who wanted to fight, was an enormous asset.

Fortunately, the Infantry Brigadiers had also some knowledge of Irish troops. Brigadier-General R. J. Cooper, C.V.O., who led the 29th Brigade, had commanded the Irish Guards. Another Irish Guardsman, Brigadier-General C. FitzClarence, V.C., commanded the 30th Brigade at the time of its first formation, but he was soon afterwards called to France to command the 1st Brigade in the Expeditionary Force, and met his death at the first battle of Ypres. His place was taken by Brigadier-General L. L. Nicol, who had done the bulk of his service in the Rifle Brigade, but had begun his soldiering in the Connaught Rangers. The 31st Brigade was commanded by Brigadier-General F. F. Hill, C.B., D.S.O., who had served throughout a long and distinguished career in the Royal Irish Fusiliers. The Divisional Artillery was at first under the command of Brigadier-General A. J. Abdy, but when this officer was found medically unfit for active service, he was replaced by Brigadier-General G. S. Duffus.

I must now describe the actual formation of the Division, and in view of the fact that it was the beginning of one of the most gigantic military improvisations on record, it may be desirable to do so in some detail.

Fortunately there were some regular cadres available. In the first place, there was the Regimental Depôt, where usually three regular officers were employed, the senior being a major. In almost every case he was promoted to temporary Lieutenant-Colonel, and given the command of the senior Service Battalion of his regiment. The other two officers (usually a captain and a subaltern) were also transferred to the new unit. Then, again, the Regular Battalion serving at home before embarking for France was ordered to detach three officers, and from ten to sixteen N.C.O.'s. In many cases these officers did not belong to the Regular Battalion, but were officers of the Regiment who had been detached for service with some Colonial unit, such as the West African Frontier Force, or the King's African Rifles. Being on leave in England when war broke out, they had rejoined the Home Battalion of their unit, and had been again detached for service with the New Armies. Where more than one Service Battalion of a regiment was being formed, the bulk of these officers and N.C.O.'s went to the senior one.

There was yet another source from which Regular Officers were obtained, and those who came from it proved among the best serving in the Division.

At the outbreak of the War all Indian Army officers who were on leave in England were ordered by the War Office to remain there and were shortly afterwards posted to units of the First New Army. Two of the Brigade-Majors of the Division were Indian Army officers, who, when war was declared, were students at the Staff College, and nearly every battalion obtained one Indian officer, if not more. It is impossible to exaggerate the debt the Division owed to these officers. Professional soldiers in the best sense of the word, they identified themselves from the first with their new battalions, living for them, and, in many cases, dying with them. Words cannot express the influence they wielded and the example they gave, but those who remember the lives and deaths of Major R. S. M. Harrison, of the 7th Dublins, and Major N. C. K. Money, of the 5th Connaught Rangers, will realise by the immensity of the loss we sustained when they were killed, how priceless their work had been.

A certain number of the Reserve of Officers were also available for service with the new units. It seemed hard for men of forty-five or fifty years of age who had left the Army soon after the South African War, to be compelled to rejoin as captains and serve under the orders of men who had previously been much junior to them, but they took it cheerfully, and went through the drudgery of the work on the barrack square without complaining. Often their health was unequal to the strain imposed upon it by the inclement winter, but where they were able to stick it out, their ripe experience was most helpful to their juniors.

The battalions which did not secure a Regular Commanding Officer got a Lieut.-Colonel from the Reserve of Officers, often one who had recently given up command of one of the regular battalions of the regiment. Besides officers from the Reserve of Officers, there were also a considerable number of men who had done five or six years' service in the Regular Army or the Militia and had then retired without joining the Reserve. These were for the most part granted temporary commissions of the rank which they had previously held. A few were also found who had soldiered in Colonial Corps, and eight or ten captains were drawn from the District Inspectors of the Royal Irish Constabulary. These united to a knowledge of drill and musketry a valuable insight into the Irish character, and as by joining they forfeited nearly £100 a year apiece, they abundantly proved their patriotism.

It will thus be seen that each battalion had a Regular or retired Regular Commanding Officer, a Regular Adjutant, and the four company commanders had as a rule had some military experience. The Quartermaster, Regimental Sergeant-Major, and Quartermaster-Sergeant were usually pensioners who had rejoined, while Company Sergeant-Majors and Quartermaster-Sergeants were obtained by promoting N.C.O.'s who had been transferred from the Regular battalion. The rest of the cadres

had to be filled up, and fortunately there was
no lack of material.

For about a month after their formation the
Service Battalions were short of subalterns, not
because suitable men were slow in coming
forward, but because the War Office was so
overwhelmed with applications for commissions
that it found it impossible to deal with them.
About the middle of September, however, a rule
was introduced empowering the C.O. of a
battalion to recommend candidates for temporary second-lieutenancies, subject to the
approval of the Brigadier, and after this the
vacancies were quickly filled. Some of the
subalterns had had experience in the O.T.C.,
and as a rule these soon obtained promotion,
but the majority when they joined were quite
ignorant of military matters, and had to pick
up their knowledge while they were teaching
the men.

About the end of the year, classes for young
officers were instituted at Trinity College, and
a certain number received instruction there,
but the bulk of them had no training other
than that which they received in their battalions. They were amazingly keen and anxious
to learn, and the progress they made both
in military knowledge and in the far more
difficult art of handling men was amazing.
Drawn from almost every trade and profession,
barristers, solicitors, civil engineers, merchants,

medical students, undergraduates, schoolboys, they soon settled down together and the spirit of *esprit de corps* was quickly created. Among themselves, no doubt, they criticised their superiors, but none of them would have admitted to an outsider that their battalion was in any respect short of perfection. I shall never forget the horror with which one of my subalterns, who had been talking to some officers of another Division at Mudros, returned to me saying, " Why, they actually said that their Colonel was a rotter ! " Disloyalty of that kind never existed in the 10th Division. The subalterns were a splendid set, and after nine months' training compared well with those of any regular battalion. They believed in themselves, they believed in their men, they believed in the Division, and, above all, in their own battalion.

I must now turn to the men whom they led. Fortunately, the inexperience of the new recruits was, to a large extent, counteracted by the rejoining of old soldiers. It was estimated that within a month of the declaration of war, every old soldier in Ireland who was under sixty years of age (and a good many who were over it) had enlisted again. Some of these were not of much use, as while living on pension they had acquired habits of intemperance, and many more, whose military experience dated from before the South African War, found the in-

creased strain of Army life more than they
could endure. However, a valuable residue
remained, and not only were they useful as
instructors, and in initiating the new recruits
into military routine, but the fact that they
had usually served in one of the Regular
battalions of their regiment helped to secure
a continuity of tradition and sentiment, which
was of incalculable value. In barracks these
old soldiers sometimes gave trouble, but in the
field they proved their value over and over
again.

Of the Irish recruits, but little need be said.
Mostly drawn from the class of labourers, they
took their tone from the old soldiers (to whom
they were often related), and though comparatively slow in learning, they eventually
became thoroughly efficient and reliable soldiers.

There was, however, among the men of most
of the battalions, another element which calls
for more detailed consideration. Except among
old soldiers and in Belfast, recruiting in Ireland
in August, 1914, was not as satisfactory as it
was in England, and in consequence, Lord
Kitchener decided early in September to transfer
a number of the recruits for whom no room
could be found in English regiments to fill up
the ranks of the 10th Division. The fact that
this was done gave rise, at a later date, to some
controversy, and it was even stated that the
10th Division was Irish only in name. This

was a distinct exaggeration, for when these
" Englishmen " joined their battalions, it was
found that a large proportion of them were
Roman Catholics, rejoicing in such names as
Dillon, Doyle, and Kelly, the sons or grandsons
of Irishmen who had settled in England. It
is not easy to make an accurate estimate, but
I should be disposed to say that in the Infantry
of the Division 90 per cent. of the officers and
70 per cent. of the men were either Irish or
of Irish extraction. Of course, the 10th Hampshire Regiment is not included in these cal-
culations. It may be remarked that there has
never, in past history, been such a thing as a
purely and exclusively Irish (or Scotch) battalion.
This point is emphasised by Professor Oman,
the historian of the Peninsular War, who states :
" In the Peninsular Army the system of territorial names prevailed for nearly all the regiments, but in most cases the territorial designa-
tion had no very close relation with the actual
provenance of the men. There were a certain
number of regiments that were practically
national, i.e., most of the Highland battalions,
and nearly all of the Irish ones were very
predominantly Highland and Irish as to their
rank and file : but even in the 79th or the
88th there was a certain sprinkling of English
recruits." (" Wellington's Army," p. 208.)
Before leaving this subject it should be noted
that the Englishmen who were drafted to the

Division in this manner became imbued with the utmost loyalty to their battalions, and wore the shamrock on St. Patrick's Day with much greater enthusiasm than the born Irishmen. They would have been the first to resent the statement that the regiments they were so proud to belong to had no right to claim their share in the glory which they achieved.

At first, however, they created a somewhat difficult problem for their officers. They had enlisted purely from patriotic motives, and were inclined to dislike the delay in getting to grips with the Germans; and being, for the most part, strong Trades Unionists, with acute suspicion of any non-elected authority, they were disposed to resent the restraints of discipline, and found it hard to place complete confidence in their officers. They also felt the alteration in their incomes very keenly. Many of them, before enlistment, had been miners earning from two to three pounds a week, and the drop from this to seven shillings, or in the case of married men 3s. 6d., came very hard. The deduction for their wives was particularly unwelcome, not because they grudged the money, but because when they enlisted they had not been told that this stoppage was compulsory, and so they considered that they had been taken advantage of. However, they had plenty of sense, and soon began to realise the necessity of discipline, and understood that their officers, instead of being mercenary tyrants, spent hours in the Company Office at the end of a long day's work trying to rectify such grievances as non-payment of separation allowance. Regimental games helped them to feel at home. Some of them soon became lance-corporals, and before Christmas they had all settled down into smart, intelligent and willing soldiers. One English habit, however, never deserted them : they were unable to break themselves of grumbling about their food.

The Division contained one other element to which allusion must be made. In the middle of August, Mr. F. H. Browning, President of the Irish Rugby Football Union, issued an appeal to the young professional men of Dublin, which resulted in the formation of "D" Company of the 7th Royal Dublin Fusiliers. This was what is known as a " Pals " Company, consisting of young men of the upper and middle classes, including among them barristers, solicitors, and engineers. Many of them obtained commissions, but the tone of the company remained, and I know of at least one barrister who had served with the Imperial Yeomanry in South Africa, who for over eighteen months refused to take a commission because it would involve leaving his friends. The preservation of rigid military discipline among men who were the equals of their officers in social position was not easy, but the breeding and education of the " Pals " justified the high hopes that had been formed of them when their Regiment was bitterly tested at Suvla.

The Royal Artillery, Royal Engineers, Army Service Corps, and the Royal Army Medical Corps recruits who came to the Division were, for the most part, English or Scotch, since no distinctively Irish units of those branches of the service exist. Generally speaking, they were men of a similar class to the English recruits who were drafted into the infantry.

A detailed description of the training of the Division would be monotonous and uninteresting even to those who took part in it, but a brief summary may be given. The points of concentration first selected were Dublin and the Curragh, the 30th Brigade being at the latter place. At the beginning of September, the 29th Brigade were transferred to Fermoy and Kilworth, but the barracks in the South of Ireland being required for the 16th (Irish) Division, two battalions returned to Dublin, the 6th Leinsters went to Birr, and the 5th Royal Irish to Longford. The latter Battalion soon became Pioneers and were replaced by the 10th Hampshires, who were stationed at Mullingar. The 54th Brigade, Royal Field Artillery, were at Dundalk, and the remainder of the Artillery at Newbridge and Kildare. The Engineers, Cyclists, and Army Service Corps trained at the Curragh, the Signal Company at Carlow, and the Royal Army Medical Corps at Limerick.

Naturally, the War Office were not prepared for the improvisation of units on such a large scale, and at first there was a considerable deficiency in arms, uniform, and equipment. Irish depôts, however, were not quite so over-whelmed as the English ones, and most recruits arrived from them in khaki, although minor articles of kit, such as combs and tooth-brushes were often missing. The English recruits on the other hand, joined their battalions in civilian clothes, and were not properly fitted out till the middle of October. The Royal Army Medical Corps at Limerick also had to wait some time for their uniform.

The Infantry soon obtained rifles (of different marks, it is true) and bayonets, but the gunners were greatly handicapped by the fact that the bulk of their preliminary training had to be done with very few horses and hardly any guns. Deficiencies were supplied by models, dummies, and good will ; and considering the drawbacks, wonderful progress was made. Another article of which there was a shortage was great-coats, and in the inclement days of November and December their absence would have been severely felt. Fortunately, the War Office cast aside convention and bought and issued large quantities of ready-made civilian overcoats of the type generally described as " Gents' Fancy

c

Cheviots." Remarkable though they were in appearance, these garments were much better than nothing at all, and in January the warmer and more durable regulation garments were issued. The men also suffered a good deal of hardship at first from having only one suit of khaki apiece, for when wet through they were unable to change, but they recognised that this discomfort could not be instantly remedied, and accepted it cheerfully.

Until the end of 1914, the bulk of the work done by the Infantry consisted of elementary drill, platoon and company training and lectures, with a route march once or twice a week. A recruits' musketry course was also fired. Plenty of night operations were carried out, two evenings a week as a rule being devoted to this form of work. The six battalions in Dublin were somewhat handicapped by lack of training ground, as the Phœnix Park became very congested. This deficiency was later re-medied to a certain extent by certain landowners who allowed troops to manœuvre in their demesnes ; but considerations of distance and lack of transport made this concession less valuable than it would have been had it been possible to disregard the men's dinner hour.

Side by side with this strenuous work the education of the officers and N.C.O.'s was carried on. The juniors had everything to learn, and little by little the news that filtered through from France convinced the seniors that many long-cherished theories would have to be reconsidered. It gradually became clear that the experience of South Africa and Manchuria had not fully enlightened us as to the power of modern heavy artillery and high explosives, and that many established tactical methods would have to be varied. We learnt to dig trenches behind the crest of a hill instead of on the top of it ; to seek for cover from observation rather than a good field of fire ; to dread damp trenches more than hostile bullets. We began, too, to hear rumours of a return to mediæval methods of warfare and became curious as to steel helmets and hand grenades.

Had these been the only rumours that we heard, we should have counted ourselves fortunate. Unhappily, however, in modern war there is nothing so persistent as the absolutely unfounded rumour, and in K. 1 they raged like a pestilence. We were all eager to get the training finished and settle to real work, and our hopes gave rise to the most fantastic collection of legends. The most prevalent one, of course, was that we were going to France in ten days' time, usually assisted by the corroborative detail that our billets had already been prepared, but this was run close by the equally confident assertion on the authority of a clerk in the Brigade Office, " that we were destined for

Egypt in a week." It is to be hoped that after the War, some folk-lore expert will investigate legends of the New Armies. If he does so, he will be interested to find that France and Egypt were almost the only two seats of War which the Division as a whole never visited.

In the New Year, battalion training began, carried out on the occasional bright days that redeemed an abominable winter. At the beginning of February it was proposed to start brigade training, and in order to enable the 29th Brigade to concentrate for this purpose, various changes of station were necessary. Accordingly, the whole 29th Brigade moved to the Curragh, where one battalion was accommodated in barracks and the other three in huts. In order to allow this move to be carried out the 7th Royal Dublin Fusiliers, the Reserve Park Army Service Corps and the Divisional Cyclist Company were transferred to Dublin where they were quartered in the Royal Barracks.

Brigade field days, brigade route marches and brigade night operations were the order of the day throughout February, and a second course of musketry was also fired. Early in March the Divisional Commander decided to employ the troops at the Curragh in a series of combined operations. For this purpose he could dispose of two infantry brigades (less one battalion), three brigades of Royal Field Artillery, the heavy battery (which joined the Division from Woolwich about this time), three field companies of Royal Engineers, while on special occasions the divisional Signal Company were brought over from Carlow and the Cyclists from Dublin. He could also obtain the assistance of the two reserve regiments of cavalry which were stationed at the Curragh.

Though we criticised them bitterly at the time, these Curragh field-days were among the pleasantest of the Division's experiences. By this time the battalions had obtained a corporate existence and it was exhilarating to march out in the morning, one of eight hundred men, and feel that one's own work had a definite part in the creation of a disciplined whole. The different units had obtained (at their own expense) drums and fifes, and some of them had pipes as well. As we followed the music down the wet winding roads round Kilcullen or the Chair of Kildare, we gained a recollection of the hedges on each side bursting into leaf, and the grey clouds hanging overhead, that was to linger with us during many hot and anxious days.

As a rule, these combined operations took place twice in the week. For the rest of the time ordinary work was continued, while on the 16th of April, Sir B. Mahon held a ceremonial inspection of the units of the Division which were stationed at the Curragh, Newbridge and Kildare. The infantry marched past in " Battalion Mass," and the artillery in " Line

Close interval." At this time, too, Company Commanders began to mourn the loss of many of their best men who became specialists. As mules, Vickers guns, signalling equipment, etc., were received, more and more men were withdrawn from the Companies to serve with the regimental transport, the machine-gun section, or the signallers. The drain due to this cause was so great that the Company Commander seldom saw all the men who were nominally under his command except on pay-day. While this process was going on the weaklings were being weeded out. A stringent medical examination removed all those who were considered too old or too infirm to stand the strain of active service, and they were sent to the reserve battalions of their unit. Men of bad character, who were leading young soldiers astray, or who, by reason of their dishonesty, were a nuisance in the barrack-room, were discharged as unlikely to become efficient soldiers. But on the whole there was not much crime in the Division. A certain amount of drunkenness was inevitable, but the principal military offence committed was that of absence without leave. This was not unnatural under the circumstances. Men who had not fully realised the restraints of discipline, and had been unable to cut themselves completely adrift from their civilian life were naturally anxious to return home from time to time. If they could not obtain leave, they went without it ; when they got it, they often overstayed it, but their conduct was not without excuse.   One man who had overstayed his pass by a week, said in extenuation, " When I got home, my wife said she could get no one to plant the land for her, and I just had to stay until I had the garden planted with potatoes." And there is no doubt that in most cases of absence the relations of the absentee were responsible for it.   It was not easy for men who had been civilians four months before to realise the seriousness of their offence while they saw the Division, as they thought, marking time, and knew that their homes were within reach, and officers were relieved when at the end of April units received orders to hold themselves in readiness to move to a point of concentration near Aldershot.

This point of concentration proved to be Basingstoke, and by the end of the first week in May the whole Division was assembled there. As we journeyed we read how the 29th Division had charged through the waves and the wire, and effected its landing at Cape Helles, and how against overwhelming odds the Australians and New Zealanders had won a foothold at Gaba Tepe. At that time, however, our thoughts were fixed on France.

At Basingstoke we were inspected and watched at work by the staff of the Aldershot Training Centre, and were found wanting in some respects. In particular, we were unduly ignorant of the art and mystery of bombing, and many hot afternoons were spent in a labyrinth of trenches which had been dug in Lord Curzon's park at Hackwood, propelling a jam tin weighted with stones across a couple of intervening traverses. Bayonet-fighting, too, was much practised, and the machine-gun detachments and snipers each went to Bordon for a special course. In addition, each Brigade in turn marched to Aldershot, and spent a couple of days on the Ash Ranges doing a refresher course of musketry.

The most salient feature, however, of the Basingstoke period of training was the Divisional marches. Every week the whole Division, transport, ambulances and all, would leave camp. The first day would be occupied by a march, and at night the troops either billeted or bivouacked. On the next day there were operations : sometimes another New Army division acted as enemy, sometimes the foe was represented by the Cyclists, and the Pioneer Battalion. As night fell, the men bivouacked on the ground they were supposed to have won, occasionally being disturbed by a night attack. On the third day we marched home to a tent, which seemed spacious and luxurious after two nights in the open. These operations were of great value to the staff, and also to the transport, who learned from them how difficulties which

BASINGSTOKE. A HALT

MUSKETRY AT DOLLYMOUNT

appeared insignificant on paper became of paramount importance in practice. The individual officer or man, on the other hand, gained but little military experience, since as a rule the whole time was occupied by long hot dusty marches between the choking overhanging hedges of a stony Hampshire lane. What was valuable, however, was the lesson learnt when the march was over. A man's comfort usually depended on his own ingenuity, and unless he was able to make a weatherproof shelter from his ground sheet and blanket he was by no means unlikely to spend a wet night. The cooks, too, discovered that a fire in the open required humouring, and all ranks began to realise that unless a man was self-sufficient, he was of little use in modern war. In barracks, the soldier leads a hard enough life, but he is eternally being looked after, and if he loses anything he is obliged to replace it at once from the grocery bar or the quartermaster's store. On service, if he loses things he has to do without them, and in Gallipoli where nothing could be obtained nearer than Mudros and everything but sheer necessities had to be fetched from Alexandria or Malta, the ingrained carelessness of the soldier meant a considerable amount of unnecessary hardships. It would be too much to say that these marches and bivouacs eradicated this carelessness, but they did, at any rate, impress on the more thoughtful some of the difficulties to be encountered in the future.

The monotony of training was broken on the 28th of May when His Majesty the King visited and inspected the Division. The 31st Brigade was at Aldershot doing musketry, but the 29th and 30th Brigades and the Divisional Troops paraded in full strength in Hackwood Park. His Majesty, who was accompanied by the Queen, rode along the front of each corps and then took up his position at the Saluting Point. The troops marched past : first the Infantry in a formation (Column of Platoons) which enabled each man to see his Sovereign distinctly, followed by the Field Ambulances, the squadron of South Irish Horse, and the Artillery, Engineers and Army Service Corps. On the following day, His Majesty inspected the 31st Brigade as they were marching back from Aldershot to Basingstoke.

This inspection was followed by another one, as Field-Marshal Lord Kitchener, who had been unable to accompany His Majesty, paid the Division a visit on June 1st.

It would be superfluous to describe both these inspections, since the same ceremonial was adopted at each, and since the 31st Brigade was absent on the 28th May, an account of the parade for Lord Kitchener may stand for both occasions. The inspection took place in an open space in Hackwood Park, the infantry being drawn up, one brigade facing the other two on the crest of a ridge, while the mounted troops in an adjoining field were assembled on a slope running down to a small stream. The scene was typically English ; here and there a line of white chalk showed where a trench had broken the smooth green turf, and all around, copses and clumps of ancient trees, in the full beauty of their fresh foliage, spoke of a land untouched for centuries by the stern hand of war. Soon very different sights were to meet the eyes of the men of the 10th Division, and at Mudros, and on the sun-baked Peninsula, many thought longingly of soft Hampshire grass and the shade of mighty beeches.

Though the sun shone at intervals, yet there was a chill bite in the wind, and the troops who had begun to take up their positions at 10 o'clock were relieved when at noon the Field-Marshal's cortège trotted on to the review ground, and began to ride along the lines. The broad-shouldered, thick-set figure was familiar, but the face lacked the stern frown so often seen in pictures, and wore a cheerful smile. Yet he had good reason to smile. Around him were men—Hunter, Mahon, and others—who had shared his victories in the past, and before him stood the ranks of those who were destined to lend to his name imperishable glory. He, more than any other man, had drawn from their homes the officers and men who faced him in Hackwood Park, and trained and equipped them, until at last, after ten months' hard and strenuous work, they were ready to take the field.   He looked on the stalwart lines, and all could see that he was pleased. After he had passed along the ranks, he returned to the saluting point, and the march past began.   The Division had no brass bands, but each unit, in close column of platoons, was played past by the massed drums and fifes of its own Brigade.   First came the Royal Irish, swinging to the lilt of " Garry Owen," in a manner that showed that their C. O. and Sergeant-Major were old Guardsmen.   Then followed the Hampshires, stepping out to the tune that has played the 37th past the saluting point since the days of Dettingen and Minden. Then again the bands took up the Irish strain, and the best of drum-and-fife marches, " St. Patrick's Day," crashed out for the Connaught Rangers.   Then came a sadder note for the Leinsters' march is " Come Back to Erin," and one knew that many of those marching to it would never see Ireland again.   But sorrowful thoughts were banished as the quick-step of the Rifles succeeded to the yearning tune. After the Rifles had passed, the music became monotonous, since all Fusilier Regiments have the same march-past, and by the time the rear of the 31st Brigade had arrived, one's ears were somewhat weary of the refrain of the " British Grenadiers."   At a rehearsal of the Inspection, the Dublin Fusiliers had endeavoured to vary the monotony by playing " St. Patrick's Day," but the fury of the Connaught Rangers, who share the right of playing this tune with the Irish Guards alone, was so intense that it was abandoned, and Munsters and Dublins, Inniskillings and Faugh-a-Ballaghs, moved past to the strains of their own march. " The British Grenadiers " is a good tune, and Fusilier regiments are not often brigaded together, so that this lack of variety is seldom noted, yet there are so many good Irish quick-steps unused that perhaps the Fusilier regiments from Ireland might be permitted to use one of them as an alternative.

After the Infantry came the Field Ambulances, and after them the squadron of the South Irish Horse. These were followed by rank after rank of guns with the Engineers and Army Service Corps bringing up the rear. The long lines of gleaming bayonets, and the horses, guns, and wagons, passing in quick succession, formed a magnificent spectacle. Not by dragon's teeth had this armed force been raised in so short a time, but by unresting and untiring work.

As a result of these inspections the following orders were issued :—

" 10*th Division Order* No. 34.   1*st June*, 1915.

" Lieutenant-General Sir B. Mahon received His Majesty's command to publish a divisional

order to say how pleased His Majesty was to
have had an opportunity of seeing the 10th
Irish Division, and how impressed he was
with the appearance and physical fitness of
the troops.

" His Majesty the King recognises that it
is due to the keenness and co-operation of
all ranks that the 10th Division has reached
such a high standard of efficiency."

" The General Officer. Commanding 10th
Irish Division has much pleasure in informing
the troops that Field-Marshal Earl Kitchener
of Khartoum, the Secretary of State for War,
expressed himself as highly satisfied with all
he saw of the 10th Division at the inspection
to-day."

After these two inspections the men began
to hope that they would soon be on the move,
but the regular routine continued, and all
ranks began to get a little stale. The period
of training had been filled with hard and strenuous work, and as the days of laborious and
monotonous toil crept on, one felt that little
was being gained by it. It is not an exaggeration to say that so far as physical fitness was
concerned, the whole of the Division which
went as an organised whole to Gallipoli was
in better condition at the end of April than
when they left England. Infantry, engineers,
and the Royal Army Medical Corps were all
fully trained and qualified for the work they

were called on to do. The transport were not, but then the transport were left behind in England. It is possible, too, that the artillery gained by the delay, but they did not accompany the Division, and the two brigades that eventually landed in the Peninsula were competely detached from it. The staff certainly gained much experience from their stay at Basingstoke, but on reaching Gallipoli the Division was split up in such a manner that the experience they had acquired became of little value.

Just as we were beginning to despair of ever moving, on the 27th of June the long-expected order arrived, and the Division was warned to hold itself in readiness for service at the Dardanelles.

CHAPTER II

MUDROS AND MITYLENE

*" When in Lemnos we ate our fill of flesh of tall-horned
oxen."—Homer.*

IT will now be proper to describe the doings
of the Division in somewhat fuller detail.
The immediate result of the warning received on June 27th, which was officially
confirmed on July 1st, was to throw an enormous amount of work upon officers and N.C.O.'s.
Already the gaps in our strength had been filled
up by drafts drawn from the 16th (Irish)
Division, and now it was necessary for the whole
of the men to be re-equipped. Helmets and
khaki drill clothing had to be fitted, much of
the latter requiring alteration, while the adjust-
ing of *pagris* to helmets occupied much attention,
and caused the advice and assistance of men
who had served in India to be greatly in demand.
At the same time new English-made belts and
accoutrements were issued, the American leather
equipment, which had been given out in March
and had worn very badly, being withdrawn.
We had gained one advantage from the numer-

ous false alarms that rumour had sprung upon us, the men's field pay-books and field conduct-sheets were completely filled in and ready. This turned out to be extremely fortunate, as the company officers, sergeant-majors, and platoon sergeants found that the time at their disposal was so fully occupied that they would have had little leisure left for office work. The pay lists were closed and balanced, and sent with the cash-books to the Regimental Paymaster ; any other documents which had not already been sent to the officer in charge of records were consigned to him, and at last we felt we were ready.

One symptom of the conditions under which we were going to fight was to be found in the fact that we lost some of our comrades. The Heavy Battery and the squadron of the South Irish Horse were transferred to other divisions destined for France, while the transport, both Divisional and Regimental, was ordered to stand fast at Basingstoke. Worse than this, all regimental officers' chargers were to be handed over to the Remount Department. This indication that we were intended for a walking campaign caused considerable dismay to some machine-gun officers, who had invested in imposing and tight-fitting field boots, and were not certain whether they would be pleasant to march in. As for the men of the machine-gun detachments, their feelings were beyond ex-

D

pression. The knowledge that gun, tripod, and belts would have to be carried everywhere by them in a tropical climate deprived them of words. However, they were too delighted to be on the move at last to grumble for long.

In the week beginning July 5th the departure began. The trains left at night, and battalions would awake in the morning to find tents previously occupied by their neighbours empty. The weather had changed to cold showers, and the men marching through the night to the station had reason to be thankful that their drill clothing was packed away in their kit-bags, and that they were wearing ordinary khaki serge. The helmets, however, were found to keep off rain well. Units were so subdivided for entraining purposes that there was little ceremony and less music at the departure. The men paraded in the dark, marched through the empty echoing streets of the silent town, sometimes singing, but more often thoughtful. The memory of recent farewells, the complete uncertainty of the future, the risks that lay before us, alike induced a mood that if not gloomy was certainly not hilarious. The cheerful songs of the early training period were silent, and when a few voices broke the silence, the tune that they chose was " God Save Ireland." We were resolved that Ireland should not be ashamed of us, but we were beginning to realise that our task would be a stiff one.

The composition of the Division was as follows :—

DIVISIONAL STAFF.

G.O.C. : Lieut.-General Sir B. T. Mahon, K.C.V.O., C.B., D.S.O.

Aide-de-Camp : Capt. the Marquis of Headfort (late 1st Life Guards).

General Staff Officer, 1st Grade : Lieut.-Col. J. G. King-King, D.S.O., Reserve of Officers (late the Queen's).

General Staff Officer, 2nd Grade : Major G. E. Leman, North Staffordshire Regiment.

General Staff Officer, 3rd Grade : Captain D. J. C. K. Bernard, The Rifle Brigade.

A.A. and Q.M.G. : Col. D. Sapte, Reserve of Officers (late Northumberland Fusiliers).

D.A.A. and Q.M.G. : Major C. E. Hollins, Lincolnshire Regiment.

D.A.Q.M.G.1 : Major W. M. Royston-Piggott, Army Service Corps.

D.A.D.O.S. : Major S. R. King, A.O.D.

A.P.M. : Lieutenant Viscount Powerscourt, M.V.O., Irish Guards, S.R.

A.D.M.S. : Lieut.-Col. H. D. Rowan, Royal Army Medical Corps.

D.A.D.M.S. : Major C. W. Holden, Royal Army Medical Corps.

29TH BRIGADE.

G.O.C. : Brigadier-General R. J. Cooper, C.V.O.

Brigade Major : Capt. A. H. McCleverty, 2nd Rajput Light Infantry.

Staff Captain: Capt. G. Nugent, Royal Irish Rifles.

Consisting of :—

10th Hampshire Regiment, commanded by Lieut.-Col. W. D. Bewsher.

6th Royal Irish Rifles, commanded by Lieut.-Col. E. C. Bradford.

5th Connaught Rangers, commanded by Lieut.-Col. H. F. N. Jourdain.

6th Leinster Regiment, commanded by Lieut.-Col. J. Craske, D.S.O.

30TH BRIGADE.

G.O.C. : Brigadier-General L. L. Nicol.

Brigade Major : Major E. C. Alexander, D.S.O., 55th Rifles, Indian Army.

Staff Captain : Capt. H. T. Goodland, Royal Munster Fusiliers.

Consisting of :—

6th Royal Munster Fusiliers, commanded by Lieut.-Col. V. T. Worship, D.S.O.

7th Royal Munster Fusiliers, commanded by Lieut.-Col. H. Gore.

6th Royal Dublin Fusiliers, commanded by Lieut.-Col. P. G. A. Cox.

7th Royal Dublin Fusiliers, commanded by Lieut.-Col. G. Downing.

31ST BRIGADE.

G.O.C.: Brigadier-General F. F. Hill, C.B., D.S.O.

Brigade Major : Capt. W. J. N. Cooke-Collis, Royal Irish Rifles.

Staff Captain : Capt. T. J. D. Atkinson, Royal Irish Fusiliers.

Consisting of :—

5th Royal Inniskilling Fusiliers, commanded by Lieut.-Col. A. S. Vanrenen.

6th Royal Inniskilling Fusiliers, commanded by Lieut.-Col. H. M. Cliffe.

5th Royal Irish Fusiliers, commanded by Lieut.-Col. M. J. W. Pike.

6th Royal Irish Fusiliers, commanded by Lieut.-Col. F. A. Greer.

DIVISIONAL TROOPS.

5th Royal Irish Regiment (Pioneers) commanded by Lieut.-Col. The Earl of Granard, K.P.

DIVISIONAL ARTILLERY.

Brigadier-General, R.A. : Brigadier-General G. S. Duffus.

Brigade Major : Capt. F. W. Barron, R.A.

Staff Captain : Captain Sir G. Beaumont.

Consisting of :—

54th Brigade Royal Field Artillery, commanded by Lieut.-Col. J. F. Cadell.

55th Royal Field Artillery, commanded by Lieut.-Col. H. R. Peck.

56th Brigade Royal Field Artillery, commanded by Brevet-Col. J. H. Jellett.

The 57th (Howitzer) Brigade, R.F.A., remained in England.

ROYAL ENGINEERS.

Commanding Officer, Royal Engineers : Lieut.-Col. F. K. Fair.

Consisting of :—

65th Field Company, R.E.
66th   ditto
85th   ditto
10th Signal Company, commanded by Capt. L. H. Smithers.

ROYAL ARMY MEDICAL CORPS.

30th Field Ambulance, commanded by Lieut.-Col. P. MacKessack.

31st Field Ambulance, commanded by Lieut.-Col. D. D. Shanahan.

32nd Field Ambulance, commanded by Lieut.-Col. T. C. Lauder.

10th Divisional Cyclist Corps, commanded by Capt. B. S. James.

There is one particular in which the British Army may fairly claim to be superior to any force in the world, and that is in embarkation. Years of oversea expeditions, culminating in the South African War, have given us abundant experience in this class of work, and the fact that even in a newly formed unit like the 10th Division every battalion contained at least one officer who had taken a draft to India, helped to make things run smoothly. The voyage itself was uneventful. For the most part the troopships employed were Atlantic liners, and the accommodation and food provided for officers might be called luxurious. There were, however, two flies in the ointment. The architect of the boats had designed them rather for a North Atlantic winter than for summer in the Mediterranean, and the fact that at night every aperture had to be tightly closed for fear lest a gleam of light might attract an enemy submarine, made sleep difficult. The men, who were closely packed, found it impossible in their berths down below, and the officer of the watch was obliged to pick his way among hundreds of prostrate forms as he went from one end of the deck to the other.

The second grievance was lack of deck space, which precluded anything in the shape of violent exercise. Attempts at physical drill were made wherever there was an inch of spare room, and for the rest lectures and boat drill whiled away the tedium of the day. Almost the only soldiers on board with a definite occupation were the machine gunners perched with their guns on the highest available points, and keeping a keen look-out for periscopes. Responsibility also fell upon the officer of the watch, who was obliged to make a tour of the ship, looking out for unauthorised smoking and unscreened lights every hour, and reporting "All correct" to the ship's officer on the bridge. For the rest, the foreseeing ones who had provided themselves with literature read ; officers smoked and played bridge ; men smoked, played "House" and dozed ; but through all the lethargy and laziness there ran a suppressed undercurrent of suspense and excitement.

The bulk of the transports conveying the Division called at Malta and Alexandria, on their way from Devonport to Mudros, but one gigantic Cunarder, having on board Divisional Headquarters, 30th Brigade Headquarters, the 6th Leinster Regiment, 6th and 7th Royal Munster Fusiliers, and detachments of the 5th Royal Irish Regiment (Pioneers), and 5th The Connaught Rangers, sailed direct from Liverpool to Mudros, and cast anchor there on July 16th. These troops were the first of the Division to reach the advanced base of the Dardanelles operations, and it was with eager curiosity that they looked at the novel scene. They were in a land-locked harbour, which from the contour of the hills surrounding it might have been a bay on the Connemara coast had not land and sea been so very different in colour. Soft and brilliant as the lights and tints of an Irish landscape are, nothing in Ireland ever resembled the deep but sparkling blue of the water, and the tawny slopes of the hills of Lemnos. Northward, at the end of the harbour, the store-ships and water-boats lay at anchor ; midway were the transports, and near the entrance the French and British warships.

On the eastern shore dust-coloured tents told of the presence of hospitals ; and to the west, lines of huddled bivouacs indicated some concentration of newly-arrived troops. The heart of the place, from which every nerve and pulse throbbed, was a big, grey, single-funnelled liner, anchored near the eastern shore. Here were the headquarters of the Inspector-General of Communications, and the Principal Naval Transport Officer ; here the impecunious sought the Field Cashier ; and the greedy endeavoured (unsuccessfully, unless they had friends aboard) to obtain a civilised meal. Next to her a big transport acted as Ordnance Store, and issued indiscriminately grenades and gum-boots, socks and shrapnel. At this time, no ferries had been instituted, and communication with these ships, though essential, was not easy. If you were a person of importance, a launch was sent for you ; if, as was more likely, you were not, you chartered a Greek boat, and did your best to persuade the pirate in charge of it to wait while you transacted your business on board.

We had ample time to appreciate this factor

in the situation as it was three days before we disembarked. During that time we succeeded in learning a little about the conditions of warfare in what we began to call " the Peninsula." Part of the 29th Division, which by its conduct in the first landing had won itself the title of " Incomparable," was back at Mudros resting, and many of its officers came on board to look for friends. Thus we learned from men who had been in Gallipoli since they had struggled through the surf and the wire on April 24th the truth as to the nature of the fighting there. They taught us much by their words, but even more by their appearance ; for though fit, they were thin and worn, and their eyes carried a weary look that told of the strain that they had been through. For the first time we began to realise that strong nerves were a great asset in war.

At last the order for disembarkation came, and a string of pinnaces, towed by steam launches from the battleships, conveyed the men ashore. Kits followed in lighters, and wise officers seized the opportunity to add to their mess stores as much stuff as the purser of the transport would let them have. It was our last contact with civilisation.

On the beach there was a considerable amount of confusion. The western side of the harbour had only recently been taken into use by troops, and though piers had been made, roads were as

yet non-existent. Lighters were discharging kit
and stores at half-a-dozen different points, and
the prudent officer took steps to mount a guard
wherever he saw any of his stuff. In war,
primitive conditions rule, and it is injudicious
to place too much confidence in the honesty of
your neighbours.

At last the over-worked staff were able to
disentangle the different units, and allot them
their respective areas, and the nucleus of the
Division found itself installed in the crest of a
ridge running northward, with the harbour on
the east, and a shallow lagoon on the west.
Across the lagoon lay a white-washed Greek
village, surrounded by shady trees, in which
Divisional Headquarters were established, and
behind this rose the steep hills that divided
Mudros from Castro, the capital of Lemnos.
Further south was another village with a
church ; otherwise the only features of the
landscape were a ruined tower and half-a-dozen
windmills. Except at Divisional Headquarters
there was not a tree to be seen. The ground
was a mass of stones. Connaught is stony,
but there the stones are of decent size. In
Mudros, they were so small and so numerous
that it took an hour to clear a space big enough
for a bed. Between the stones were thistles
and stubble, and here and there a prickly
blue flower. In the distance one or two patches
of tillage shone green, but except for these

everything was dusty, parched and barren. On the whole an unattractive prospect.

However, it was necessary to make the best of it, and soon the bivouacs were up, though their construction was made more difficult by the complete absence of wood of any kind. The men had been instructed to supplement the blanket, which they had brought from England, by another taken from the ship's stores, and the hillside soon presented to the eye an endless repetition of the word " Cunard " in red letters. Officers soon found it impossible to obtain either shelter, tables, or seats sufficient for a battalion mess, and companies began to mess by themselves. Few parades could be held, for there were very few lorries and no animals at all in Mudros West, so that practically everything required by the troops had to be carried up from the beach by hand. Most of the camps were nearly a mile from the Supply Depot, so that each fatigue entailed a two-mile march, and by the time that the men had carried out a ration fatigue, a wood fatigue, and two water fatigues, it was hard to ask them to do much more. A few short route marches were performed, but most commanding officers were reluctant to impose on the men harder tasks than those absolutely necessary before they became acclimatized.

Already we were beginning to make the acquaintance of four of the Gallipoli plagues—

SARI BAIR

MUDROS. THE AUTHOR'S BIVOUAC
(In the background is the officers' mess)

dust, flies, thirst and enteritis. Our situation on the spur was exposed to a gentle breeze from the north. At first we rejoiced at this, thinking it would keep away flies and make things cooler ; but soon we realized that what we gained in this respect we lost in dust. From the sandy beach, from the trampled tracks leading to the supply depôts, from the bivouacs to windward, it swept down on us, till eyes stung and food was masked with it. It became intensified when a fatigue party or, worst of all, a lorry, swept past, and the principal problem confronting a mess-president was to place the mess and kitchen where they got least of it.

The flies were indescribable. For a day or two they seemed comparatively rare, and we hoped that we were going to escape from them ; but some instinct drew them to us, and at the end of a week they swarmed. All food was instantly covered with them, and sleep between sunrise and sunset was impossible except for a few who had provided themselves with mosquito nets. Not only did they cause irritation, but infection. There appeared to be a shortage of disinfectants, and it was impossible either to check their multiplication, or to prevent them from transmitting disease. They had, however, one negative merit : they neither bit nor stung. If instead of the common housefly we had been afflicted with midges or mosquitoes, our lot would have been infinitely worse.

The third plague was thirst. In July, in the Eastern Mediterranean, the sun is almost vertical ; and to men in bivouac whose only shelter is a thin waterproof sheet or blanket rigged up on a couple of sticks, it causes tortures of thirst. All day long one sweats, and one's system yearns for drink to take the place of the moisture one is losing. Unfortunately, Lemnos is a badly-watered island, and July was the driest season of the year. All the wells in the villages were needed by the Greek inhabitants : and though more were dug, many of them ran dry, and the water in those that held it was brackish and unsuitable for drinking. The bulk of the drinking-water used by the troops was brought by boat from Port Said and Alexandria, and not only was it lukewarm and tasteless, but the supply was strictly limited. The allowance per man was one gallon per day ; and though on the surface this appears liberal, yet when it is reflected that in 1876 the consumption of water per head in London was 29 gallons,* it will be seen that great care had to be exercised. Even this scanty allowance did not always reach the men intact, for the water carts of some units had not arrived, and so the whole of it had to be carried and stored in camp-kettles. In order to spare the men labour,

---

* Table in Humber's *Water Supply of Cities and Towns* (London, 1876), p. 86.—Quoted by Hodgkin in " Italy and her Invaders," Vol. 4, p. 172.

arrangements were made by which these camp-kettles were to be carried in a motor-lorry ; but on the primitive roads so much was spilt as to render the experiment futile. Even in carrying by hand, a certain amount of leakage took place. In order to control the issue of water, most of it, after the men had filled their water-bottles, was used for tea, which though re-freshing, can hardly be called a cooling drink. However, Greek hawkers brought baskets of eggs, lemons, tomatoes and water melons. The last, though tasteless, were juicy and cool, and the men purchased and ate large quantities of them.

Possibly they were in part to blame for the fourth affliction that befell us in the shape of enteritis. Though not very severe, this afflic-tion was widespread, hardly anyone being free from it. A few went sick, but for every man who reported himself to the doctor, there were ten who were doing their duty without complain-ing that they were indisposed. Naturally, men were reluctant to report sick just before going into action for the first time ; but though they were able to carry on, yet there was a general lowering of vitality and loss of energy due to this cause, which acted as a serious handicap in the difficult days to come.

Some thought that this epidemic was caused by the food issued to the men, and it was certainly possible to imagine a diet more suited to a tropical climate than salt bully beef and hard dry biscuits. An issue of rice was, however, sanctioned, and this boiled with currants formed the men's usual midday meal—the inevitable stew of bully, cooked in a dixie with dessicated vegetables, being reserved till the evening. The rice would have been nicer had it been cooked with milk, but the small allowance of condensed milk available was needed for tea. The bully, too, could have been made more palatable had curry-powder been forthcoming, as the officers' messes which possessed this condiment found it invaluable in disguising the peculiar flavour. Tinned meat is not suited to tropical climates. However, very few officers' messes had brought much in the way of stores, as they were uncertain whether they would be able to carry them, and all officers soon found themselves reduced to the same rations as the men, supplemented by the few eggs and tomatoes obtainable from Greek hawkers. Except for these hawkers, Mudros West had no resources for shopping at this time. All villages were out of bounds, and there was at this period no canteen—even a Greek one.

One advantage, however, the place possessed : the bathing was magnificent. From 8 a.m. to 6 p.m. (or, as we were learning to call it, from 8 to 18 o'clock), it was forbidden, as the doctors feared sunstroke ; but at six in the evening the bulk of the day's work over, everyone who could

leave camp trooped down to a little bay. The
men undressed on the shore, the officers on a
small pier which ran out far enough to make a
dive possible. The water was perfect—warm
enough to make it possible to stay in for an hour,
and yet cool and refreshing after the heat and
dust of the day. The western sun, no longer
blazing fiercely overhead, made dressing and
drying a pleasure ; and the walk up the hill to
the evening meal in the twilight made one feel
that the world was not such a bad place after all.
There was more cheerfulness and laughter at the
bathing place than anywhere else in Mudros.
Many friendships were made there, some soon
to be severed by Death, and men who had
begun to harp on the truth of Kipling's words :

> " Comfort, content, delight,
> The ages slow brought gain.
> They vanished in a night :
> Ourselves alone remain."

were forced to admit that pleasure and happiness
had not completely vanished from the world.

While the first comers were becoming hardened
to the discomforts of the Island, the remainder
of the Division began to arrive. They had
called at Alexandria, the base of the Mediterranean Expeditionary Force, and had left there
the details allotted to the base and the bulk of
their kit, wagons and water-carts. The
artillery had also been ordered to remain in

E

Egypt till further orders. The rest of the 29th
Brigade, with their Brigade Headquarters,
arrived between the 23rd and 29th of July, and
they were followed by the rest of the Pioneer
Battalion, the Field Companies of the Royal
Engineers, the Signal Company, who found
their motor-cycles more hindrance than help
on the roadless Island, the Cyclists, and the
Field Ambulances. These last no sooner
arrived than they were called on to receive
patients, for the prevalent malady had already
knocked some men out. It was a severe test,
but the doctors and orderlies rose to it splendidly,
providing for their patients from their own
private stores when Government supplies were
not available.

The newly-arrived units were for the most
part employed on fatigues. Everything needed
on the Peninsula had to be carried up to camp :
everything else, including the base kits of the
units who had not called at Alexandria, had to
be carried back again to the beach, where a
dump was being formed inside a barbed wire
fence. Officers were ordered to lighten their
valises, so that they could be carried with ease
by one man, and there was much cogitation as to
what should be taken and what left behind. As
a matter of fact, we saw so little of our valises
after landing in the Peninsula that the careful
distinction established between essentials (bedding, spare socks and shirt) and non-essentials

(spare coat and breeches and boots,) was wasted. Most of us determined to rely on our packs, which we stuffed with a mackintosh, razor, soap, sponge, and (in my own case) a couple of books. From this packing, however, the 29th Brigade were distracted by Brigade night operations, which took the form of an attack on a hill five miles away. The march in the dark over broken and stony ground proved very trying to the men, who had not recovered the condition which they had lost on the voyage, and many of them dropped off to sleep as soon as they halted. It became clear to us that our task was likely to be an arduous one.

Meanwhile, we began to wonder as to the whereabouts of the remainder of the Division, since half of the 30th Brigade and the entire 31st had not landed. The transports conveying them had reached Mudros, but owing to the shortage of water it had been decided not to land them there, but to send them to Mitylene. The fact that it was found impossible to concentrate three divisions at Mudros simultaneously, illustrates the enormous increase that has taken place in the numbers employed in modern war. The most famous military expedition of ancient history had its rendezvous and base at Lemnos before it proceeded to attack Troy, and it would appear probable that Mudros Bay, the largest and best harbour on the Island, was the one used by the fleet of Agamemnon. There seems no reason to suppose that the water supply there has diminished, and it is certain that as the time needed for the voyage was longer, the sailing ships and oared galleys in which the Greek host made their way to the Trojan plain, must have been furnished with a copious supply of drinking water before they set sail. Homer does not record the fact that they suffered from thirst, and so it is clear that the whole army was able to subsist on what proved insufficient for less than 50,000 British soldiers. The theory of Professor Delbrück* that the numbers taking part in ancient battles were grossly exaggerated, seems to rest on some foundation.

In some respects the units that went to Mitylene were more fortunate than the rest of the Division. They did not disembark, but remained on board the liners which had brought them out from England, thus securing good food and immunity from dust and flies. Mitylene, moreover, is far more beautiful than Mudros, and its smiling farms set in the midst of fruit trees and olive groves,were more welcome to the eye than the bare stony hills of Lemnos. There was, too, a larger and more friendly Greek population. Boats from the shore came out loaded with melons, grapes, and other varieties of fruit, so that those men who were possessed

* *Numbers in History*, by Dr. Hans Delbrück, London University Press, 1914.

of money could get a change of diet. The worst
that the 31st Brigade and 6th and 7th Dublin
Fusiliers had to complain of, was dullness.
Except for bathing and an occasional route
march on shore, there was but little to break the
monotony of shipboard life ; and after a week
or so in harbour, everyone was beginning to be a
little " fed-up."

They disliked, too, the fact that they appeared
to have lost the rest of the Division, and had no
information about their future movements ;
but they were no worse off in that respect than
the rest of us. All that we knew was, that we
were part of the 9th Corps, commanded by
Lieut.-General Sir F. Stopford. We knew little
of him, but we knew that he was an Irishman
and were prepared to take him on trust.
Battalion commanders had been issued with
sets of maps which, when put together, covered
the whole of the Gallipoli Peninsula and part of
the Asiatic coast ; but possibly this was only a
" blind." Rumours, of course, were plentiful
and very varied : a strong favourite was one
which may conceivably have been encouraged
by those in authority, and which suggested that
we were intended to make a descent on Smyrna.
The fact that the remainder of the Division were
known to be at Mitylene tended to confirm this,
though there were sceptics who flouted this view
and declared that we were to land near Enos in
order to co-operate with the Bulgarian Army.

We had already been informed by irrespon-
sible individuals that Bulgaria had declared war
on Turkey. All these rumours undoubtedly tried
the nerves of the troops, but secrecy was absolutely essential. The Island was not entirely
under Allied control, a considerable part of the
population were Turks, and any leakage of
information would have proved fatal to the
General's plans. As it was, we could see in
the evening, as the ferry boats sailed out with
their loads of reinforcements past the cheering
battleships, bonfires kindled on the heights in
order to inform the enemy on the mainland of
the numbers and strength of the troops being
moved. Some of us, as we watched them,
recalled the beacons which signalled to Argos
from the same peaks the news that Troy had
fallen, and wondered if the day was soon to come
when they would announce the capture of
Constantinople.

In order that the movements of the Division
may be understood, it is now necessary to give a
short summary of the plan of campaign adopted
by General Ian Hamilton ; but it must be borne
in mind that at the time regimental officers and
men knew nothing of what was intended.

The objective of the Mediterranean Expeditionary Force was to secure the high ground
commanding the Narrows of the Dardanelles,
and to silence or capture the Turkish batteries
which barred its passage to the Fleet. In

order to achieve this object, Sir Ian Hamilton
had at the end of April landed the bulk of his
forces at the Southern extremity of the Gallipoli
Peninsula. The landing was achieved by the
29th Division, much assisted by a subsidiary
landing on the Asiatic coast executed by a
French Division. On the following day the
French re-embarked and joined the British in
Gallipoli.

At this period Sir Ian Hamilton had at
his disposal at Cape Helles the 29th Division,
the 43rd (East Lancashire) Territorial Division,
the Royal Naval Division, and two French
Divisions. With these troops, he made repeated
assaults on the Turkish positions, on Achi Baba,
but although he succeeded in considerably
enlarging the area held by him, the main Turkish
defences remained intact. Reinforcements in
the shape of the 52nd (Lowland) Territorial
Division and the 29th Indian Brigade hardly
did more than compensate for wastage due to
wounds and disease ; and by the beginning of
July it was clear to the Commander-in-Chief
that, in spite of the desperate courage displayed
by his troops, little was to be gained by keeping
on hammering at Achi Baba. If it were won it
would only be at a terrific cost, and its capture
would not mean decisive victory, as behind lay
another and taller mountain, Kilid Bahr, which
barred the way to Maidos and the Narrows.

Fortunately, Cape Helles was not the only

foothold that we had gained in the Peninsula.
While the landing there was taking place on
April 25th the Australian and New Zealand
Army Corps, under General Sir William Birdwood, had succeeded in establishing itself on
shore about a mile north of Gaba Tepe, about
halfway up the western coast of Gallipoli.
It was a marvellous achievement for troops who
had had little more than six months' training,
but in physique and courage Australians and
New Zealanders are unsurpassed by any soldiers
in the world, and the conditions under which
they were called on to fight made initiative and
endurance of greater value than rigid discipline.
In their first success they pressed on half-way
across the Peninsula ; but the ground that they
occupied was too great in extent to be held by
two Divisions, and they were forced to fall back
to the coast.   There they held an irregular semicircle drawn at a radius of about a mile from the
little cove, christened in their honour *Anzac*.
In parts, the Turkish lines were close to the
beach, and the Australians clung to the crest
with nothing but a precipice between them and
the sea : elsewhere a narrow salient pointed
inland into a tangle of hills and gullies, meeting
with the usual fate of salients in being bombarded from both flanks.   As a matter of fact,
the whole Anzac position was a salient, and even
the beach was regularly swept by the enemy's
artillery and pestered by snipers posted on the

SARI BAIR FROM SUVLA.
(From a water colour by Captain Drummond Frish, Royal Irish Rifles)

hills to the northward. However, small as the area gained was, it provided a foothold from which Sir Ian Hamilton could launch his next attack.

The plan adopted for this was as follows :—

He proposed to send to Anzac as many reinforcements as space and water would permit, smuggling them in under cover of darkness. This done, he would take advantage of the absence of moonlight on the night of the 7th of August to break out northward from Anzac and seize the backbone of the Peninsula—the high ridge of Sari Bair. This hill ran north-east from Anzac for about four miles, and from its highest point commanded Maidos, the Narrows, and the whole of the lines of communication by which the Turks on Achi Baba were supplied. At the same time, the remainder of the re-inforcements for whom there was not room at Anzac, were to effect a landing at Suvla Bay about six miles up the coast, advance in a south-easterly direction across the plain, and establish themselves on the northern end of the Sari Bair ridge, thus protecting the flank of the Anzac force. While the Turks were known to be in strength opposite Anzac, and to have reserves at Maidos, it was believed that Suvla Bay was weakly guarded.

Sir Ian Hamilton was able to dispose of the following troops to execute this operation. He had at Anzac the two Divisions of the

Australian and New Zealand Army Corps, and reinforced them by the 29th Indian Infantry Brigade from Cape Helles. The reinforcements he received, and was still receiving, from England, consisted of the 10th, 11th and 13th New Army Divisions, together with the infantry of the 53rd (Welsh) and 54th (East Anglian) Territorial Divisions. The last of these Territorials were not due to reach Mudros till August 10th—three days after the commencement of operations. The whole of these reinforcements on August 1st were either still at sea, or divided between the islands of Imbros (16 miles from Gallipoli), Lemnos (60 miles) and Mitylene (120 miles away).

The Commander-in-Chief decided to reinforce the two divisions already serving at Anzac under Sir William Birdwood, by the Indian Brigade, the 13th Division and the 29th Brigade of the 10th Division. All these troops had to be conveyed to Anzac, and hidden there before the commencement of operations. To the landing at Suvla Bay he allotted the 11th Division supported by the 10th Division (less one brigade). The 53rd and 54th (Territorial) Divisions were retained as general reserve. The control of the operations at Anzac was entrusted to Sir W. Birdwood, who placed Major-General Sir A. Godley in charge of the attack on Sari Bair. The troops allocated to this operation were the Australian and New

Zealand Division, two Brigades of the 13th Division, and the Indian Brigade. The Anzac position was to be held, and the feint attack on the Lone Pine position executed by the 1st Australian Division. The 29th Brigade (10th Division) and 38th Brigade (13th Division) were held in reserve. At Suvla, Sir F. Stopford was in command, and it was decided that the 11th Division which was concentrated at Imbros should execute the first landing, and that the 30th and 31st Brigades of the 10th Division should arrive from Mudros and Mitylene at dawn in support.

It will be seen how great a part in these operations was to be played by newly-formed units which had had no experience of war. The Australians, New Zealanders, and Indians had been in the Peninsula for three months, and though their ranks had been thinned yet those who remained were hardened and acclimatized. The New Army and Territorial Divisions had come straight from England, and though the 13th Division had spent ten days in the trenches at Helles, the remainder as units had never heard a shot fired in anger. It is true that they had many experienced soldiers in their ranks. The General Commanding the 10th Division had seen the last warriors of Mahdism lying dead on their sheepskins around the corpse of their Khalifa. One of the Brigadiers had witnessed the downfall of Cetewayo's power at Ulundi ;

another had marched with the Guards Brigade
across the desert to Tel-el-Kebir ; while the
third had played his part in the desperate
fighting outside Suakim in 1884. Nearly all the
Colonels and many of the Company Commanders
had served in the South African War, and so had
a number of the senior N.C.O.'s. Nevertheless,
the men, as a whole, were inexperienced, and the
organization of the units had not been tested
under the stern conditions which prevailed in the
Peninsula. To attempt the landing at Suvla
with untried troops, and staffs which had not
been tested on service and were not in the habit
of working together, was a great adventure ; but
the prizes of victory were great.

One thing was certain : never did soldiers go
forth to battle with sterner and more resolved
determination to maintain the honour of their
country and their regiment unsullied than the
men of the 10th Division. It was the first trial
of the New Army in a great battle. We
remembered the traditions of our regiments—
traditions dearly gained and dearly cherished
by generations of Irish soldiers. On the colours
of the Royal Irish Fusiliers blazed the glorious
name of Barrossa, and the Connaught Rangers
cherished the memory of Salamanca and the
storming of Ciudad Rodrigo and Badajos.
The Royal Irish, the oldest Irish regiment of
the line, had fought at Namur and Blenheim,
and there was no lack of glory won in more

recent fighting for the Dublins round Ladysmith and the Inniskillings at Pieter's Hill had performed deeds never to be forgotten. Each and every regiment had had its name inscribed on the scroll of fame by the men of the past : the 10th Division were resolute that their Service battalions should be worthy of those imperishable traditions.

CHAPTER III

THE 29TH BRIGADE AT ANZAC

" Then lift the flag of the Last Crusade
And fill the ranks of the Last Brigade ;
March on to the fields where the world's remade
And the Ancient Dreams come true."—*T. M. Kettle.*

ON August the 4th, as the Division were bemoaning the fact that the first anniversary of the war had arrived without their having heard a shot fired in action, the 29th Brigade received orders to send three officers and approximately 180 men from each battalion to the newly formed Divisional Base Depôt. These were intended to remain at Mudros and to act as a first reinforcement when needed. As a rule, the officers and men selected for this duty were those who were in bad health, as it was hoped that a few days' rest might make them better acclimatized. They were, however, highly disgusted at being left behind, not knowing that they would rejoin in less than a week. They marched over to their new camp on the afternoon of the 4th, and those who were left packed up in earnest. That evening, definite orders were received : battalions were to hold themselves in readiness to embark for the Peninsula at 9 a.m. next day, and C.O.'s were permitted to inform Company Commanders in confidence that the destination was Anzac. At that time, no one had ever heard of the place, but diligent search on the numerous maps, with which units had been supplied, at last revealed Anzac Cove marked a mile north of Gaba Tepe. " The Australian place," the best informed called it. So the Brigade were not destined to make a new landing. That, at any rate, was something to know, and we had to content ourselves with it, for nothing further was divulged. Subalterns and the rank-and-file did not even know what the destination was : all that they were told was that we were to embark.

Before dawn, each of the two chaplains attached to the Brigade held a service. The Church of England Chaplain, the Rev. J. W. Crozier, celebrated Holy Communion in the operating tent of the 30th Field Ambulance, while Father O'Connor said Mass in the open air just outside the camp. It had been decided that the Chaplains were not to come with the Brigade, but were to remain with the Field Ambulance. This decision caused much regret, not only to the Chaplains themselves, but to all ranks in the Brigade. The Roman Catholics in particular disliked losing Father O'Connor even temporarily, for he was personally loved by the men, and in addition the Irish soldier faces death twice as cheerfully when fortified by the ministrations of his Church. Never were more reverent and solemn worshippers seen than at those two short services at Mudros, as the well remembered words were murmured, and the grey twilight shone faintly on the faces of many who were soon to die.

As the last prayers were uttered, the dawn was breaking, a grey dawn fretted with many clouds. The congregations dispersed and took up the burden of work and war again. A hasty breakfast was swallowed, valises were strapped up and carried by fatigue parties down to the pier, while the men rolled up their blankets and ground sheets and fastened them to their packs. In the deserted lines, officers were endeavouring to prevent improvident soldiers from eating or leaving behind them part of the three days' rations with which they had just been issued, while bands of predatory Greek children, who were on the look-out for anything that they could pick up, were driven away with threats and sometimes with blows. Then between eight and nine o'clock the battalions fell in, ready at last for the great adventure.

It is often difficult for the historian, writing years after the event, to ascertain the exact dress worn by those who took part in the events portrayed in his page, and so it may be well to put on record the outward aspect of the Irish Division when it left for Gallipoli. Officers and men were dressed alike in thin, sand-coloured khaki drill. Shorts were forbidden, and the men wore their trousers tucked into putties of the darker khaki shade that is worn in England. Except for the metal shoulder titles, there were not many marks to distinguish the different units, since England had been left at such short notice that there had been little time to procure badges of coloured cloth to sew on the big mushroom-shaped helmets. The Royal Irish Rifles had improvised a green and black patch, however, and the officers of the Hampshires had mounted a claret and yellow one. The Colonel of the Leinsters had with infinite ingenuity procured ink, and stencilled an enormous black " L " on the side of each helmet. The Connaught Rangers had ordered shamrock badges with the device " 5 C.R.," but their ambition was their undoing, since these elaborate decorations took so long to make that they did not reach the Peninsula until most of those who were to wear them had been killed or invalided. The 7th Munsters were more fortunate, and went into action with a green shamrock on each arm just below the shoulder. A few Fusilier officers sported a hackle of the regimental colour, but this conspicuous ornament drew too much attention to the wearer to make it safe in Gallipoli. It

F

mattered less what the men wore on their bodies, since it was almost impossible to see it, so heavily were they laden.

They hardly looked like fighting, and would have run a poor chance if they had had to swim. On their backs they had their great-coats, rolled in their packs, on top of which they carried two blankets and a waterproof sheet. Their haversacks contained three days' rations ; in their pouches, and festooned round their necks, were two hundred rounds of ammunition, and in addition to rifle, bayonet, entrenching implement and water-bottle, every man carried either a pick, shovel, or camp-kettle. The signallers and machine-gunners were loaded up with their technical equipment, and the effect of the whole parade, topped as it was by broad-brimmed sun-helmets, suggested strength rather than mobility. Heavily the columns swung down to the beach, and there waited, for embarkation proved a slow process. The sun was hot, and there was no shade, so that many of the men emptied their water-bottles before they had been there long, though fortunately it was possible to refill them at a neighbouring well. Many more bought water-melons, and the far-seeing laid in a stock of as many eggs and lemons as they could carry, to take to the Peninsula. The loads that the naval pinnaces could carry were small, and it was only after repeated journeys that at 3.30 p.m.

the whole Brigade embarked. The infantry were not accompanied by either the Field Company Royal Engineers, or the Field Ambulance, which were usually attached to the Brigade. They were to accompany the remainder of the Division.

The ships used as ferries between Mudros and the Peninsula were not large, and the men found themselves tightly packed fore and aft, with only just enough room to squat or lie on the decks. The boats had, however, seen plenty of service, and their officers and men were able to supply abundance of good advice. As soon as night fell, no lights of any kind were permitted, and consequently it was necessary for every man to remain close to his kit, or fearful confusion would follow at disembarkation. It was evident that landing was likely to be somewhat of a trial, as even the numbers of changes of station that the Brigade had had at home had given them no practice in disembarking in pitch darkness. No food was obtainable on board, but there was plenty of hot water, so that the men were able to make tea in their mess-tins to wash down the bully and biscuit taken from their iron ration.

All ranks had settled down pretty comfortably by the time the boats approached Imbros, and the sun sank in a dark bank of clouds behind the Lemnos hills. A few slept, but most were too excited to do so ; for as the ship approached

the invisible coast the flashes of the guns
became visible, and a broad searchlight beam
stabbed the sky from the summit of Achi Baba.
A little further up the coast a destroyer had
focussed her searchlight on a path down the
face of a cliff, and the round circle of light
looked for all the world like a magic lantern
in a village entertainment at home. On they
steamed, leaving all this behind, and most
dozed off, only to be awakened by the stoppage
of the boat. By straining one's eyes one could
see a few more ships anchored close by, but the
only other sign of life was a couple of dim
lights, which seemed to be high overhead.
This was Anzac.

The Brigade was soon, however, to discover
that the Turks were vigilant, for a sniper,
hearing the rattle of the anchor-chain of one
of the boats, fired at a venture and wounded a
man of the Leinster Regiment in the chest.
A Connaught Ranger was also wounded in
the hand. Clearly the warnings against lights
and noise were justified. However, nothing
could be done but to get the men into their
equipment and wait. At last the lighters
grunted up alongside and disembarkation began.
The darkness was intense, and it was impossible
to speak above a whisper. Men of all companies
were crowded together ; N.C.O.'s were quite
unrecognisable, and no previous rehearsal had
been possible. However, good will triumphed

over these obstacles. One by one the men and their burdens were hurried into the lighters, the specialists unloaded their technical equipment, and disembarkation proceeded smoothly, if not quickly.

By the time the last ship began to unload her troops the first traces of the dawn were appearing in the sky, and the sailors on the lighters became very anxious. Not only was it undesirable that the Turks should learn that large reinforcements were being sent to Anzac, but the whole of the harbour was exposed to the fire of the enemy's guns, and if the slow-moving lighters were detected by daylight, they would have to pass through a storm of shrapnel, and would have suffered many casualties. Most of the men did not realise this, and were inclined to be deliberate in their movements, but, bustled by sailors and officers, they got ashore safely. They found themselves in the grey dawn standing on the shores of a little bay. Above them towered broken sandy slopes, at the foot of which stood a narrow strip of beach, covered with sand-bagged dug-outs and piles of forage and rations. They massed under cover of these ; officers and company-sergeant-majors hurriedly checked their numbers as far as it was possible to do so, and then they were led away by New Zealand guides to a dangerous position.

A certain amount of cover had already

been prepared by Australian and New Zealand digging parties, in what was very rightly known as Shrapnel Gully. Battalions followed the guides up a low ridge of sandhills, through a short sap, and past a row of water-tanks, on to a path which wound up between two high hills. It was, as we discovered later, wider than most gullies in Gallipoli, and if anything the slopes were gentler ; but it was a fair specimen of its kind. On the southern side the formation was regular ; to the north a smaller gully running into it formed a sort of bay about two hundred yards in circumference. Both slopes were covered with low prickly scrub, rising at its highest to about four feet ; in between were patches of sand and the dug-outs prepared for the brigade. To the south these were arranged regularly in rows, something like the galleries of the model coal-mine in the South Kensington Museum, and these were allotted to the Hampshires, Rifles, and Leinsters. On the northern slope they were arranged irregularly on the side of the small bay, and were occupied by the Connaught Rangers. Brigade Headquarters were established in a sand-bagged dug-out close to the road that ran down the bottom of the gully.

The men were distributed among their dugouts, and the officers sat down to take stock of the situation. We had arrived, but that was all that we knew. There was any amount of noise, but nothing to look at, and as the noise of firing seemed to come from every point of the compass, including the sea, it hardly enlightened us as to where in particular the fighting was going on. It was impossible to try and see anything, as all ranks had been warned that to go up to the top of any of the hills would probably be fatal. Standing orders, however, had been issued to company commanders, who sat down in their dug-outs to study them. No fires or lights of any kind were allowed after dark, and green wood was never to be used for fires. These were obvious precautions, as light or smoke would be certain to cause heavy shelling.

An order was also issued that every man was to wear a white band six inches wide, on each arm, and a white patch eight inches square, in the middle of his back. The materials for these had been brought with battalions from Mudros, and all ranks set to work at tailoring. It was clear from this that we were likely to take part in a night attack, and this impression was confirmed by the warning soon passed round that men were to rest as much as possible during the day. Absolutely nothing more was known, not even where the remainder of the Division were. It was not until a conference of Commanding Officers was held at Brigade Headquarters at

4.30 p.m. that it was discovered that the brigade was on its own! We also received orders that the men's packs, great-coats, blankets, and waterproof sheets, together with all the officers' valises, were to be left in our present position, one N.C.O. and eight men per battalion remaining in charge of them. Units were instructed to hold themselves in readiness to move off at 1 a.m. the following morning.

Though we had been told to rest, the heat and the flies made sleep impossible. Just before leaving Mudros, a mail from home had arrived, so there were a few three-week old English papers to look at, and the rest of the time was spent in watching the Australians passing up and down the road at the bottom of the gully. They were the first Australians that we had seen, and one could not help admiring their splendid physique and the practical way in which they had adapted their costume to the conditions prevailing on the Peninsula. Some were stripped to the waist, and few wore more clothing than boots, a slouch hat, a sleeveless shirt, open at the breast, and a pair of the shortest shorts that ever occurred to the imagination of a tailor. As a result of this primitive costume, they were burnt to a rich brown by the Gallipoli sun. They were splendid men, but quite different in physique from the European, for their sloping shoulders, loose-knit limbs, and long thin legs suggested an apparent reversion to the kangaroo type as the result of climatic conditions. Above all, they seemed absolutely devoid of nerves; three months of constant shelling, which had left its mark even on the veterans of the 29th Division, appeared to have no effect of any kind on the Australians. Clearly, they were very good men to fight side by side with.

About eleven a.m. the Turks began to shell the gully with shrapnel. Most of their shells were badly fused, and burst too high, but one " blind " shell knocked off the head of a Connaught Ranger. A man in the Rifles was also killed, and these catastrophes had the effect of inducing the men who had been watching the bursting shells with great curiosity, to take cover in their dug-outs. In spite of this precaution, each unit had several men wounded, Lieutenant Mayne of the Rifles also being hit. About noon the bombardment slackened for a time, only to be renewed about three in the afternoon and continued till dusk with redoubled intensity. Many men were grazed or bruised by spent bullets or fragments of shell, but refused to report themselves to the Doctor. Though we were unaware of it at the time, we were suffering from Turkish retaliation for the attack on Lone Pine, which was going on half-a-mile away, for the Turks knowing that Shrapnel Gully was about the only spot in the Anzac area where reserves could be sheltered from their view, were systematically searching it with their fire. Had their fusing been more accurate, and had dug-outs not been prepared in readiness for the brigade, its losses would have been heavy. As it was, the Turks hardly got value for the shells they expended, and the men were encouraged by the result of their baptism of fire.

It was impossible to cook the men any dinner, and after a few mouthfuls of cold bully and lukewarm water they fell asleep in their dug-outs as soon as it became dark. At 12.30 a.m., on Saturday, the 7th, orders were received to fall in, but the order was easier to give than to execute. " Falling in " presupposes a parade ground of some sort, and on a steep slope covered with bushes and dug-outs it was not easy to discover an assembly post. Even when it had been chosen by daylight, it was hard to find it in the pitch darkness, and the men scattered in many little dug-outs were slow in coming together. In some cases a company commander thought that he had been left behind by his company, only to discover that it had not yet been awakened. The innate perversity of inanimate objects, too, had full play ; watches stopped, electric flashlights refused to flash, and lanyards attached themselves to every bush in the neighbourhood.

Eventually, however, the men were collected, their numbers checked, and the brigade moved

off in single file down the road at the bottom
of the gully in the direction of the sea.   The
Leinsters led, followed by the Irish Rifles,
Connaught Rangers and Hampshires in the
order named.   Progress was slow, which was
fortunate, as the numerous halts made it
possible for men who had been late in waking
to join their units.   At last, however, the head
of the long column reached the bottom of
Shrapnel Gully and turned northward, moving
up a subsidiary gully in the direction of Russell's
Top.   At that time, however, we knew nothing
of where we were going or what we were to do,
though we could see the Great Bear hanging
low over the hill tops, and knew that we were
going north.   The night was very dark, and
only the ôutline of the hills against the star-lit
sky, and the faint white line of the path were
visible.   Here and there an officer came hurrying
up.   " Are you the South Lancashires ?   Where
are the 13th Division ? "   It was impossible
to answer these queries, for we knew nothing
of anybody's whereabouts, and the noise was
so terrific that the words would have been
inaudible.

From every hill-top came the rattle of
musketry, but the dominant note in the
symphony came from the guns of the monitors
drawn in close to the beach at Anzac.   They
sounded as if they were only ten yards away,
although it must have been a full mile.   To

this accompaniment the long line traced its way up the gully for about an hour, halting every five minutes. While doing this, three miles to the northward, the assaulting columns were working up the Aghyl and Chailak Deres to the assault of Sari Bair, but we knew nothing of this at the time. At last the order came to turn about and retrace our steps, leaving the 6th Leinster Regiment to act as support to the Australians. The remainder of the Brigade slowly returned to Shrapnel Gully.

There throughout the day they waited at the side of the road, never knowing when they might be called on to move. Every staff officer who came near was cross-questioned, but they knew little more than ourselves. Rumours, of course, were manifold, and for some curious reason they all centred round a position known as Prussian Officers' Trench. Twice we heard that it had been taken, and twice that the attack on it had failed. To us it seemed as if the capture of this position was vital to our success, although as a matter of fact, it was purely a subsidiary operation. We knew nothing of the fighting at Lone Pine, we had then never heard the name of Sari Bair, we were completely ignorant that our comrades were at that moment landing at Suvla ; all our interest was centred on this one name caught from a passing Australian. They were passing pretty frequently now, some on stretchers, and others limping down unattended from the fight at the head of the gully, but they were not communicative. " Pretty tough up there," was as a rule their only response to the volley of queries that came whenever a man looked strong enough to answer.

The wait lasted all day, varied by shrapnel fire. No doubt the three battalions were retained there, as the position was central and covered from view, while if the Turkish counter-attacks on the recently captured Lone Pine position should be successful, their services would be badly needed. At 7 p.m., however, General Cooper was instructed to send a battalion into the Southern section of the Anzac area, to act as Reserve to the first Australian Brigade. No attack had been launched from this part of the defences, and it was feared that the Turks might retaliate for the attack on Sari Bair by attempting to crush Anzac from the South.

The Connaught Rangers, who were selected for this duty, reached the position allotted to them at 8.10 p.m. They detached one company to Brown's Dip, where they were employed in burying the Turks and Australians who were killed in the Lone Pine fighting. The unpleasantness of the task was increased by the fact that the position was being heavily shelled, and several men were wounded. On the following day (August 8th) the Connaught Rangers were again moved, this time to Victoria Gully, about three - quarters of a mile nearer Anzac Cove. The detached company at Brown's Dip was relieved by another from the same battalion, which carried on the duty of burial party, and also sustained a number of casualties. The rest of the battalion remained in reserve at Victoria Gully throughout the 9th of August in dug-outs, which had been hastily constructed, and which they did much to improve.

By this time the Battalion were becoming something of connoisseurs in the qualities of dug-outs. Dug-outs are of two kinds, those you dig for yourself and those you dig for somebody else. In the former case, you collect as many sand bags, pieces of corrugated iron, pit props, and other miscellaneous building materials as your ingenuity or your dishonesty can achieve, and then proceed to dig yourself an eligible residence. The depth dug is usually in inverse proportion to rank : the higher, the deeper, though to go too deep was considered to exhibit a somewhat excessive desire to be safe at all costs. The Australians had a story of an officer whom they did not like, and on whose courage they (probably unjustly) reflected. They declare that he was severely wounded, as the rope broke while he was being lowered into the dug-out, and he fell the remaining eighteen feet.

The dug-out that is dug for another is not

so elaborate. You burrow into the vertical face of the hill until a cavity large enough to contain a man is created, and leave it for the occupant to make the best of. Before he has learnt to do this, he has probably bumped his head several times and filled his hair with earth. At the same time, however small it may be, it is unwise to forsake the burrow constructed for you by the experienced inhabitant and strike out a line for yourself. Two officers who attempted to do this were quickly disillusioned. Their first effort installed them in a cemetery, where a corpse was awaiting burial. Their second reopened a recently filled in latrine, while the third found them in the midst of buried Turks. Then they gave it up.

It is now necessary to return to the doings of the 6th Leinster Regiment, and since this battalion was detached from the 29th Brigade throughout the battle of Sari Bair, it will be simpler to give an account of all its actions in this chapter. Though it played a distinguished part in the fight, yet its deeds were performed in a separate theatre and can be understood without a detailed description of the operations elsewhere. At about 3 a.m. on August 7th, the Leinsters were detached from the 29th Brigade and allotted to the 1st Australian Division in order to act as General Reserve for the Northern sector of the old Anzac Defences.

In framing his plans, Lieut.-General Sir William Birdwood was compelled to take into account the possibility that instead of concentrating their forces at Suvla or on Sari Bair, the enemy might decide to make a desperate attack on Anzac, in the hope of breaking through there and cutting the columns operating on Sari Bair off from the sea. It would, no doubt, have been possible for us to obtain supplies and ammunition from Suvla once the landing there had been effected, but the organisation of new lines of communication must inevitably have taken time, and the position of the force would have been a critical one. Two battalions from the General Reserve were, therefore, placed at the disposal of the 1st Australian Division, and of these the 6th Leinsters was one.

The dispositions adopted were as follows : "B" Company, under Major Stannus, went to Courtney's Ridge, and "C" Company, under Major Colquhoun, to Quinn's Post. The other two companies and Battalion Headquarters remained at the end of Shrapnel Gully. This disposition was adhered to throughout the 7th and 8th, the detached companies earning the praise of the Australians to whom they were attached by the keenness and alacrity with which they carried out the duties that fell to their lot. Naturally, like everyone else in the Anzac area, they suffered from shrapnel and snipers, but the casualties during this period were not heavy.

At sunset on the 8th, the detached companies were withdrawn to Battalion Headquarters, and the whole unit was warned to hold itself in readiness to move at five minutes' notice. By this time it was clear to the Higher Command that little danger was to be apprehended from Turkish attacks on Anzac, while the struggle for the Sari Bair ridge was still in a doubtful state, and the presence of a fresh battalion might make the difference between victory and defeat. Accordingly the men of the Leinsters lay down formed in close column of platoons, girt with all their accoutrements and tried to slumber.

Sleep does not come easily when one is wearing full equipment and another man's boots are within an inch of one's face, while an increasing bombardment rages all round ; but at Anzac men were tired enough to welcome any possibility of rest. During the night they were not disturbed by fresh orders, and at dawn there was sufficient time to cook tea and refill water-bottles. At 8 a.m. on the 9th, the battalion marched off making its way northward in single file until Number 1 Post was reached. Here there was a halt and a long wait, during which the battalion crowded up behind such shelter as was afforded by a small knoll. Water-bottles were again replenished, and the provident forethought of Colonel Craske procured a number of petrol tins filled with

G

water, which were carried by the battalion as a reserve. After a midday meal of bully and biscuit had been eaten, the battalion received orders to proceed to the relief of the New Zealand battalions holding Rhododendron Spur. This ridge, which was an outcrop of the main Sari Bair range, had been seized by the New Zealanders at dawn on the 7th, and was still held by them.

On the way there, the Leinsters met with an experience similar to that endured by the 31st Brigade at Suvla on the morning of the 7th, for in order to reach the gully leading where they wanted to go, they were compelled to traverse 400 yards of open country, which was exposed to heavy hostile fire. Not only were snipers hidden in the scrub on the hillsides doing their worst, but the space was also covered by a machine-gun high on the slopes of the Chunuk Bair, and shrapnel was continually bursting over it.

Little spurts of dust continually rising where the bullets had struck made the prospect of crossing this area an unattractive one, but the Leinsters doubled briskly across, half a platoon at a time, and luckily did not incur severe losses. They then entered a gully which was not much safer than the open space, as every corner was under machine-gun fire, and during half the time the men were bending double to avoid observation, and during the other half racing forward to avoid its consequences. Somewhat exhausted by this, and by the great heat, the Leinsters reached the foot of Rhododendron Ridge at three in the afternoon.

Here they remained till dusk in order to carry out the relief after dark ; but while they waited the enemy's shrapnel again found them out and one officer and several men were killed. At nightfall, " A " and " D " Companies relieved the New Zealanders, the two others remaining behind the crest in support. The ridge was joined to the main chain of the Chunuk Bair ridge by a col, and in front of this the shallow trenches, which marked the furthest point gained by our advance, had been dug. They were not deep and had not been well sited, but at any rate they served to indicate the line to be held.   On the right of the Leinsters the 8th Royal Welsh Fusiliers held a line extending back to the old Anzac position ; while on the left, the 6th Loyal North Lancashire Regiment were in possession of the crest of the Chunuk itself.

Throughout the night the Turkish artillery kept up a continual fire, and at daybreak their counter-attack was launched. The general course of these operations will be described in greater detail in the following chapter. For the present, it suffices to say that a Turkish force, estimated at more than a division, came rolling over the crest of the Chunuk Bair against the three battalions holding it. The main force of the attack fell on the Loyal North Lancashires, and to use Sir Ian Hamilton's words, "overwhelmed them by sheer force of numbers." On their left, three companies of the Wiltshires who had only just arrived on the hill were caught in the open and annihilated. But on the right the Leinsters stood their ground. At last the moment had arrived to which they had so anxiously looked forward. Turk and Irishman, face to face, and hand to hand, could try which was the better man. Modern warfare is so much a struggle of moles, of burrowing and creeping and hiding that it is with a thrill of joy that the soldier looks on the face of his enemy at close quarters. In spite of the odds, the two companies in the front line succeeded in checking the attack, and at the crucial moment they were reinforced by " B " and " C " Companies from the support line. It is said that the alarm was given to the latter by a New Zealander, who ran down the hill shouting, " Fix your bayonets, boys, they're coming ! " and that on hearing this the men seized their weapons and rushed up the hill without waiting to put on their putties or jackets. It is certain that Colonel Craske led them into action with a cheer, and that their arrival was most timely. Shouting, they flung themselves into the fray, and drove the Turks back after a desperate struggle at close quarters.

It was impossible that such success could be gained without loss, but the Leinsters were fortunate in escaping more lightly than the English regiments on their left. They had, however, three subalterns killed and several officers wounded in this fight, among them Colonel Craske himself, who received a bullet wound in the arm. He was a gallant soldier, who had won the D.S.O. in South Africa, and his men long remembered the way in which he had led his battalion into action. He carried on for a time, but the wound proved serious, and he was obliged to hand over his command to Major R. G. T. Currey. Another officer of the Leinsters who was wounded in this action was Captain J. C. Parke, who was also hit in the arm. Before the War he was one of the greatest, if not the greatest, lawn tennis players in the British Isles, and had represented the United Kingdom in the Davis Cup. Now, though the injury he had received threatened to incapacitate him for his favourite game, he took misfortune with the same smiling composure with which he had been wont to confront all the chances of life.

But while the Leinsters were collecting and bandaging their wounds, on their left the soil was carpeted with dead. The main Turkish attack, after overwhelming the Wiltshires and Loyal North Lancashires, had pressed onward to try and drive the British off Rhododendron

Ridge.   As they came over the ridge they were full in view of our fleet, and every gun in the ships as well as the bulk of the artillery at Anzac was turned on to them.   They fell by thousands, and as the few survivors struggled on, they were met with the fire of a concentrated battery of New Zealand machine-guns.   Line after line fell, and those who had the good fortune to escape hastened to place themselves in safety on the further side of the ridge.

The western slope of the Chunuk became No Man's Land, and Rhododendron Ridge remained in our hands, but the price that both sides had paid was terrible.   In a land of dry bushes and stunted oak and holly like Gallipoli, the great shrubs that give the ridge its name must in Spring present a feast of beauty to the eye, but they stand in the midst of a cemetery, and are but the adornments of the grave.   Around them Turk and Briton and Anzac lie side by side in glorious fellowship, in a graveyard bought at a great price and made lovely to the eye by the bounty of Nature.   To the soul, the spot is made holy by the memory of what passed there and of the courage and self-sacrifice of those who lie under its sod.

The fact that we had been driven off the Chunuk made a modification of the line necessary in order to join up with the position on Rhododendron Ridge, which now marked the boundary of our gains.   The Leinsters rested for a little and began to dig in on the new line in the afternoon. The work proved difficult, since whenever the working parties showed themselves the enemy opened with shrapnel, and in consequence as long as daylight lasted very little headway was made.

After dark, however, a fresh attempt was begun and " B " and " C " Companies of the Leinsters were sent out to dig themselves in. The men had had practically no sleep since the uneasy slumber snatched on the night of the 8th, and had fought a stiff action in the morning, but they worked with a will. Progress was, however, slow, as under cover of darkness the Turks were creeping forward, and soon every bush contained a sniper. For a while work went on by fits and starts, advantage being taken of every lull to make headway with the trench until heavier firing compelled the working parties to take cover. At the end of two hours the hindrance to the work was found to be greater than could be borne. It seemed not unlikely that the annoyance was caused by a comparatively small number of snipers, so No. 9 Platoon was sent out in front of the line to drive them away, and then act as a covering party. The officer commanding this platoon (Lieutenant Barnwell) soon discovered, however, that the Turks had advanced in considerable force, and that his men were outnumbered. A grim struggle was waged in the darkness, and when the platoon at last extricated itself it left nearly half its strength killed and wounded behind it.

Work on the trench now became quite out of the question, and the Leinsters had to fight hard to hold their ground against the repeated attacks of the enemy. At last matters looked menacing and " A " and " D " Companies who had been in support were called up into the firing line. In this fighting Major Stannus who commanded " B " Company, was wounded. It was stern work, for the night was pitch dark and the tired men could see but little except the flash of the hostile rifles. Again and again a wave of shadowy figures pressed forward in close ranks only to be driven back by rifle-fire at close range and bayonet charges.

At last, as the sky grew pale with the dawn, the Turks massed for a final effort. They came on with determination, and the Leinsters, knowing that there was hardly another formed unit available as reserve in the Anzac area, resolved to meet the attack with a counter-charge. With a ringing yell the line of grey bayonets surged forward against the foe, to prove once again that to attack is not only the best defensive policy but is that best suited to the Irish temperament. The Turks faltered as the charge swept against them, and the Leinsters were at last able to take their revenge for the losses of the night. Fatigue and thirst were forgotten and men after much suffering exulted in the taste of victory at last. The pursuit became almost too eager. At one point Captain D'Arcy Irvine and Lieutenant Willington at the head of " D " Company pressed after the enemy so hotly that they were cut off and have never been heard of again. Probably they were surrounded and killed, and their bones still lie with those of many another brave fellow on the slopes of the Chunuk Bair.

All ranks acquitted themselves well in this charge, but the courage displayed by Captain Lyster who commanded " A " Company was so conspicuous as to earn for him the Military Cross. Rewards of this kind were not very freely bestowed in Gallipoli, and to have gained one in a battalion like the Leinsters, which never failed to hold the position allotted to it, was an indication that the officer who won it was a man of exceptional distinction. In addition to this honour, Colonel Craske received a C.M.G., while the whole battalion were thanked by General Godley for the good service done on this occasion.

The charge achieved its object, since the spirit of the Turks was temporarily broken and their snipers were driven back. As a result the battalion spent a quiet day on the 11th. The arrangements for supplying water initiated by Colonel Craske had worked well on the whole, and though the men were often thirsty like everyone else in the Peninsula, they did not suffer so much from thirst as some other units. The petrol tins proved of great assistance, as they enabled a reservoir to be formed for each company or platoon which could be easily controlled. When the whole water supply of the unit is contained in the water-bottles of individual soldiers it becomes impossible for officers and N.C.O.'s to check the improvident use of it, and so in times of dearth a central reservoir becomes a necessity.

On the evening of the 11th, the Leinsters were relieved and marched back in the direction of the beach. They had well earned a rest, since they had been fighting hard for thirty-six hours and had been going for two days without sleep. They had, however, acquitted themselves well and were in good spirits.

CHAPTER IV

SARI BAIR

" So desperate a battle cannot be described. The Turks
came on again and again, fighting magnificently, calling
upon the name of God. Our men stood to it, and maintained, by many a deed of daring, the old traditions of their
race. There was no flinching. They died in the ranks
where they stood."—*General Sir Ian Hamilton.*

I N order to follow the details of the battle of
Sari Bair, it is necessary to understand
something of the configuration of the
country north-east of Anzac. At Lone Pine and
Quinn's Post the Australians had gained a
footing on the southern extremity of the Sari
Bair range. Thence it ran, increasing in height
as it got further from the sea, for about five
miles to the north-east, forming the main
watershed of the Gallipoli Peninsula. From its
sides started the gullies known as Deres, which
were of paramount importance in the course of
the fighting. In Spring they were foaming
torrents, but in August they were bone-dry and
formed the only paths in the wilderness by which
it was possible to gain the foot of Sari Bair.
The country on each side of them was covered by

impassable scrub intersected by invisible preci-
pices, but the sandy beds of the Deres afforded
smooth, if not easy going.   In places they ran
through deep ravines but, for the most part,
their banks were from four to six feet high and
lined with prickly scrub and an occasional
barren olive tree. They would have been
invaluable as roads, had it not been for the fact
that long stretches of them were under constant
fire from the Turkish machine guns on Sari Bair,
and could therefore only be safely used at night.

The principal gullies beginning from the North
were Asmak Dere, Aghyl Dere, Chailak Dere
and Sazli Beit Dere.   The last of these ran
down to what, on the 6th of August, was the
Northern extremity of the Anzac position.
Between it and Chailak Dere, a spur left the
main ridge of Sari Bair and ran down towards
the sea : after it came into Christian hands,
this spur was christened Rhododendron Ridge
and played an important part in the August
fighting. The portion of the Sari Bair range,
which was joined by Rhododendron Ridge, was
known as the Chunuk Bair and here the battle
was to rage most fiercely.   It culminated to the
northward in a summit called Hill Q., and thence
the range trended eastward to Koja Chemen
Tepe, the culminating height of the position and
the objective of the Suvla force.   Half-way
down the slope of the Chunuk Bair facing the
Gulf of Saros, was a patch of cultivation known

as The Farm. The whole of the seaward face of the Chunuk Bair was covered with prickly scrub about four feet high and cut by narrow ravines running down to the Aghyl Dere which starts just below The Farm.

On the night of August 6th General Godley had launched his attack northward from Anzac. By 1.30 a.m. on the 7th the mouths of the Chailak Dere and Aghyl Dere had been seized and a strong lodgment made on Damakjelik Bair, a detached hill between the Asmah and Aghyl Deres. This lodgment protected the left flank of the assault on the Chunuk Bair which was then launched.

By dawn the left assaulting column had forced its way up the Aghyl Dere, and the Indian Infantry Brigade had occupied The Farm, while on the extreme left the 4th Australian Brigade had reached the Asmak Dere, and were advancing towards Koja Chemen Tepe. The advance of the New Zealanders up the Chailak Dere had been slower, but soon after 6 a.m. they had stormed the Turkish trenches on Rhododendron Ridge, and established themselves at the point where that ridge joins the Chunuk Bair. At the same time they got into touch with the Indian Brigade on their left. Preparations were made for an assault on the main Chunuk Ridge, but the troops were terribly exhausted by their night marches in an impossible country, and the arrival of Turkish reinforcements made further advance by daylight impossible. It was decided to allow the troops to rest, and attack again just before dawn on the 8th.

For this attack the New Zealanders, Australians and Indians who had taken part in the first day's fighting were reinforced by six battalions of the 13th Division. On the right the assault from Rhododendron Ridge on the Chunuk Bair was successful, and a firm footing on the crest was gained ; but the centre attack was unable to advance much further than The Farm, and the attempt on Koja Chemen Tepe was unsuccessful. The General resolved to attack again under cover of darkness, and called up the two battalions of the 29th Brigade, which had not already been allotted any duty, to take part in it.

The Hampshires and Royal Irish Rifles had moved at 1 a.m. on the 8th from their bivouacs in Shrapnel Gully, to Rest Gully. This gully was situated near the southern end of the great sap which ran northward from Anzac Beach towards what was known as No. 2 Post. The cove of Anzac itself, between the headlands of Hell Spit and Ari Burnu, though often swept by Turkish fire, was concealed from the enemy's view by overhanging cliffs. To the northward, however, the beach was commanded throughout its length by the heights of the Chunuk Bair, and men moved on it by daylight at their peril. In order to facilitate movement by day, Australians and New Zealanders working by night had dug a sap wide and deep enough to hold a mule, which ran northward parallel with the sea for nearly a mile. This had acquired the name of "*The Anzac Sap.*"

About 10 a.m. on the 8th, the Hampshires and Rifles fell in, and followed Brigade Headquarters along this sap in single file, until they reached its northern end at No. 2 Post. At this point General Godley had established his headquarters, and here the two battalions collected and waited for the greater part of the day. Late in the afternoon they again moved northwards, and entered the area which had just been won from the enemy. Here they came under fire from hostile snipers, but worse was to come. They had been ordered to move up the Chailak Dere, but the Turks were well aware that this was one of the few paths by which reinforcements could approach the Chunuk Bair, and were shelling its entrance persistently.

In small parties the men dashed through the barrage, and in most cases got off without heavy losses. Lieutenant Graham Martyr's platoon of the Irish Rifles, however, was unlucky, and was almost annihilated. Having passed this dangerous spot, the whole long procession moved on in Indian file up the deep bed of the Dere. Progress was slow, since the gully was half choked already with supplies and reinforcements going up to the hills, as well as

with the wounded coming down. As dusk fell
the two battalions bivouacked on the slopes
leading down to the Gully. They did not
however have much time for rest, since at 9.15
p.m. they were aroused to take part in the
assault on the Chunuk Bair. For this, three
columns were being organized, the Rifles and
Hampshires being allotted to the centre column,
which was under the command of Brigadier-
General A. H. Baldwin, who had previously
commanded the 38th Brigade. Besides the two
10th Division battalions, General Baldwin had
also the 6th East Lancashires and 5th Wiltshires,
which belonged to the 13th Division. The
column which was to move on the right of the
centre column was commanded by Major-
General F. E. Johnston, and consisted for the
most part of New Zealanders. It was intended
to operate from and extend the territory already
gained on the Chunuk Bair. To the left a column
under Major-General H. V. Cox, consisting
of the 4th Australian Brigade, the Indian
Brigade, and four battalions of the 13th Division,
was to attack Hill Q. at the northern end of the
Chunuk Bair.

General Baldwin's column was entrusted with
the task of moving up the Chailak Dere and
attacking Hill Q. from the south-west, with its
flanks protected by the columns on the right and
left. The intention of the Commander-in-Chief
had been that this centre column should start

from the Chailak Dere and deploy behind the line already occupied by the New Zealanders, moving thence at dawn along the crest of the Chunuk Bair to assault Hill Q. Unfortunately, however, this complicated manœuvre miscarried, as the guides allotted to the column missed their way, with the result that the troops, after alternately marching and halting all through the night, found themselves at dawn on the 9th in the Aghyl Dere at the foot of the Chunuk. The column on the left had been more fortunate, and its head succeeded in reaching its objective, occupying the col which connects Hill Q. with the Chunuk Bair. Hardly however had the Gurkhas and South Lancashires gazed on the town of Maidos and the Dardanelles crowded with transports bringing up reinforcements for the enemy, when they were shelled off the position, which was promptly re-occupied by the Turks.

Meanwhile General Baldwin's column was closing up and getting into formation for the attack. The men went forward with splendid spirit, but the task they were called on to perform was beyond human power. Not only did the enemy's shrapnel fire redouble its force, but the whole of the left flank was enfiladed by hostile machine-guns, which almost wiped out the East Lancashires. In this advance many of the officers of the Rifles were wounded. To climb the Chunuk in broad daylight in the face of an enemy well supplied with machine-guns and possessing observation posts from which he could direct the fire of his still unsubdued artillery, was a harder feat than the storming of the breach of a hostile fortress in the Napoleonic wars, since the distance to be covered was so long and so rugged, that it was impossible to maintain the impetus of the charge. An attempt to find easier ground to the left failed, and so the Rifles and Hampshires took up their position behind the crest of a small under-feature which jutted out some three hundred yards from The Farm.

General Baldwin was accompanied to this position by General Cooper and the staff of the 29th Brigade, who, since the whole Brigade had been allotted piecemeal to different Commanders, came up to assist in passing orders. At 9 a.m. a company and a half of the Hampshires under Major Pilleau were ordered to move up the slope to the right and try to get in touch with the New Zealanders of General Johnston's column. While doing so they came under heavy shrapnel fire, but succeeded in working their way up to that part of the ridge which was in the hands of the New Zealanders.

The position thus gained was maintained throughout the 9th, the Hampshires holding a line down the seaward slopes of the Chunuk Bair, and then turning almost at right angles towards the north-east along the crest of the under-feature above The Farm. The Rifles

BRIGADIER-GENERAL R. J. COOPER, C.V.O., C.B.
COMMANDING 29TH BRIGADE

prolonged this line on the left to a point where it was taken over by the two battalions of the 38th Brigade. This left flank was somewhat in the air, as the flank-guard on the Damakjelik Bair was more than a mile in rear of the line. The only protection to this flank was that afforded by the Left Column under General Cox, which had succeeded in occupying Hill Q. at dawn and had been driven off it. These had now withdrawn to the line of the Asmak Dere, but they were terribly exhausted. The Australians and Indians had been marching and fighting in a tropical climate for forty-eight hours without relief, while the New Army battalions had lost heavily, especially in officers.

Throughout that day Baldwin's column lay out on the face of the Chunuk Bair. Pinned to their positions by the Turkish shrapnel which hailed on them without respite, they suffered terribly from the scorching rays of the sun. Shade there was none, for the scrub was so prickly that it was impossible to crawl underneath it, while nothing short of direct cover afforded any protection from the sun vertically overhead. Water was terribly scarce ; although wells had been discovered in the bed of the Aghyl Dere, it was a task of great difficulty to convey the water up to the troops, since part of the Aghyl Dere was swept by the enemy's fire. The torments of thirst were increased by the fact that the only food available for the men was salt bully beef and hard dry biscuit. It was an effort to swallow more than a few mouthfuls, and to the weakness caused by enteritis was added the weakness of inanition.

The casualties did not appear heavy, but they steadily mounted up, and in the course of the day each of the 29th Brigade battalions lost about a fifth of its strength. Night brought relief from the sun, but no rest, for the battalions were ordered to entrench themselves where they stood. The exhausted men were incapable of heavy labour, but a narrow shallow trench was gradually excavated. Night too gave an opportunity to send the wounded away, for after hasty dressing had been applied by battalion medical officers they had, of necessity, been obliged to await a convenient occasion for their removal. The nearest hospital was four miles away on the shore at Anzac, and a terrible burden thus fell on the stretcher-bearers, who had to carry their comrades all this distance. Every man who could limp or hobble down to the beach, walked, but the serious cases were numerous, and the battalion establishment of stretcher-bearers (which had not been fixed with such an abnormal campaign in view) found itself severely taxed. During the night the New Zealand Brigade on the right of the Hampshires, was withdrawn and relieved by part of the Wiltshires and Loyal North Lancashires, and also by the 6th Leinsters.

Dawn came, and with it the Turkish counter-attack. Throughout the night their artillery had thundered unceasingly, but before daybreak it redoubled in violence. As the light grew, an enormous mass of the enemy threw itself against the battalions holding the lodgment effected by the New Zealanders on the crest of the Chunuk Bair, while further hordes moving down from the north and Hill Q. attacked Baldwin's column at The Farm. The two battalions on the crest were almost annihilated, and the ground they held was lost. Fortunately, however, as was described in the last chapter, the momentum of the attack was checked by our artillery.

The Turks moving down the crest of the Chunuk were in full view of the fleet, and the fire brought to bear on them was so terrific that their reinforcements were unable to penetrate the barrage. They pressed on against Rhododendron Ridge, but were stopped by the concentrated fire of ten New Zealand machine-guns which were placed in position by a famous Hythe musketry expert. But although for the time the danger was lessened and the Turkish losses were enormous, yet the fact that the two battalions holding the Ridge of the Chunuk had been driven back, left the right flank of the Hampshires dangerously exposed. Although its losses were very heavy, this company and a half which had been sent out to maintain connection with the ridge succeeded in holding its ground.

The remainder of the Hampshires were now up in the firing line on the right of The Farm position, but were losing very heavily. Colonel Bewsher who commanded them had been seriously wounded in the head about 6 a.m., and was resting before making his way down to the beach when a wounded sergeant-major informed him that there appeared to be no officers left unhurt. He, therefore, wounded as he was, returned to the firing line, and discovered that although there were still two captains with the detached company and a half, the remainder of the battalion had not only lost all its officers but all its company sergeant-majors and quartermaster-sergeants as well. One machine-gun had been put out of action by a shell, but the men were holding their ground manfully.

Meanwhile, on the left, the hostile attack developed with even greater force. Orders had been received to send the 5th Wiltshires to relieve the New Zealanders on the crest of the Chunuk, but one company had been retained as its withdrawal would have left part of the line completely unmanned. A company of the 9th Warwicks had come up to relieve the Wiltshires, but were found to be very weak. There were also on the left in addition to the Royal Irish Rifles, about 50 men, all that remained of the

East Lancashires, and a few Ghurkas and Maoris belonging to the left column who had retired down the hill and joined General Baldwin.

Against these few exhausted men, less than a thousand in all, the Turks were free to throw the whole of their reserves, since by this time (dawn, Tuesday) it was clear that the advance from Suvla was not likely to get much further. They came on again and again, covered by a very heavy shrapnel fire, and again and again they were driven back. Our losses, however, were terribly heavy and they could afford to lose ten men to our one, for our last reserves (except for one battalion five miles away) were already up in the firing line. Worst of all were the casualties in officers. The dawn was misty and just as it began to grow light General Baldwin was killed. Almost at the same instant General Cooper fell, severely wounded in the lungs. Colonel Bradford of the Rifles was then the senior officer with the column, but just as he was informed that the command devolved upon him, he, too, fell seriously wounded.

In quick succession, Major Morphy, the second-in-command of the Rifles, received a bad wound in the thigh, and Major Eastwood, their Adjutant, was killed. Very shortly afterwards Captain McCleverty, the Brigade Major, was hit by a bullet which passed through both cheeks and broke his jaw, while Major Wilford of the Rifles, on whom the command of his battalion had devolved and who had exhibited great courage and resource, sustained a severe wound in the head. Colonel Bewsher of the Hampshires, who had been wounded twice but was able to stand, then took over the command of all that was left of General Baldwin's force. The oft-repeated attacks continued, nearly all the junior officers were down, and though our thin line was never actually pierced yet in many places the enemy came so near that they fought with our men at close quarters. In an effort to repulse a rush of this kind on the left about 9 a.m. Captain Gerald Nugent, Staff Captain of the 29th Brigade, fell, revolver in hand, leading his men forward. His death was a sorrow to the whole brigade, for he was a man in a thousand. The surliest cynic who cultivated a grievance against all Staff Officers found himself quite unable to resist Nugent's kindness of heart and wonderful charm of manner. The manner of his death was suited to his bright and unselfish life.

About this time Colonel Bewsher came to the conclusion that the position was untenable. On the right the enemy had reoccupied the crest of the Chunuk Bair and were pressing the Hampshires hard, while on the left General Cox's column had retired to the Damakjelik Bair in rear, leaving the Chunuk completely exposed on that flank. There appeared nothing to prevent the Turks from establishing themselves in the Aghyl Dere and so cutting the only line of communication. The casualties, too, had been terrible. Every staff officer on the hill was either killed or wounded. The Hampshires and Rifles had only four officers left between them and the English companies were in just as bad case. The fight had been raging for over four hours, the men were utterly exhausted, and there was no sign of reinforcements. Colonel Bewsher, therefore, ordered a retirement which was carried out in a regular and orderly manner. This little mixed force, drawn from seven different units, comprising in its number men from Winchester and Salisbury, Birmingham, Burnley and Otago, Belfast and Khatmandu, had held a weak position against enormous odds, with little food and less water, for over 24 hours, and when they retired had hit the enemy so hard that they were not pursued.

Even then they were not disposed of, for at the bottom of the hill a staff officer (Captain Street) who was arranging to send up water and ammunition, called to them to come on again and they responded. The Hampshires on the right under their last officer, the Rifles in the centre, and the Wilts and Warwicks on the left, turned their faces again to the Hill of Death and advanced once more. The effort was futile for by this time the Turkish line was strengthened by machine-guns, but it was heroic, a vindication of the power of the spirit of man to soar above hunger and thirst and the imminent fear of death, and place itself on a level with that of the heroes.

Both battalions had suffered terribly. The Hampshires, who had gone into action on the morning of the 9th, with a strength of approximately twenty officers and over 700 men, had at noon on the 10th one combatant officer (Captain Hellyer) and not more than 200 men fit for duty. A few more who had lost their direction in the retirement rejoined in the course of the following day. The Rifles were in nearly as bad a condition. They were commanded by their junior captain, who had only been promoted to that rank at Mudros, and two subalterns were all the combatant officers that he had under him. The men, too, had been driven back in small parties and had been scattered, and it was clear that neither of the battalions was in a position to fight again for some days. Fortunately for their personal well-being, both of their quartermasters had survived the fight. Lieutenant Dowling of the Rifles had toiled unceasingly in drawing and attempting to send up rations, water, and above all, ammunition. The Rifles, too, had obtained devoted service from their doctor, Lieutenant Adam, R.A.M.C., who had worked like a hero in dealing with the hundreds of cases that had passed through his hands.

The Hampshires had found their quartermaster a tower of strength. Not only had Lieutenant Saunders worked magnificently throughout the fight, but in the difficult days of reorganization, he turned his hand to anything and acted as Adjutant and Company Commander and in any other capacity in which he could be of use. In spite of the misfortunes of his battalion he remained cheerful and imperturbable, and it was refreshing to look at his beaming, bearded face. In recognition for the good work he had done he was awarded the Military Cross. A quartermaster is described as a non-combatant officer, and his services are not always fully recognized, but in Gallipoli he was exposed to fully as much danger as anyone else, while the load of responsibility on his shoulders was far greater. Any negligence on his part meant that his battalion would go hungry and thirsty and lack ammunition at a pinch. Soldiers will agree that no man does more important work and better deserves recognition than a good quartermaster.

Meanwhile, the last battalion of the brigade was hurrying towards the scene of action. At 7 a.m. on the morning of the 10th the Connaught Rangers received orders to prepare to move at once. The detached company, which had been doing fatigue work at Brown's Dip all night, was hastily recalled, and in less than an hour the battalion moved off. It was necessary for them to take a circuitous route to the beach for fear that the Turkish observers on Gaba Tepe should notice that the right of the Anzac position was being weakened. At 9 a.m. Anzac Cove was reached, and the battalion hurried on northwards. As it entered the long sap leading to No. 2 Post, it began to realise the severity of the fighting for the first time, for the sap was full of wounded.

Most of these wounded, too, belonged to the Leinsters, Hampshires, and Irish Rifles, and their number made it clear that the brigade had suffered heavy losses. It was only, however, when checks in the march allowed an opportunity of speaking to the less seriously injured that the full extent of the casualties became clear. The officers of the Rangers heard with growing sorrow that the whole Brigade Staff were either killed or seriously wounded, and that the Rifles and Hampshires had practically ceased to exist. They saw carried past them, with drawn set faces, half masked by dry and clotted blood, men who had worked and played with them at the Curragh and Basingstoke, whose wives and children were their friends. Even in the pale, unwashed, unshaven faces and strained and suffering eyes of the less seriously wounded who paused to speak to them, they read the realization of the ordeal that lay before them. Behind all was the thought of the friends lying up on the slope of the Chunuk Bair, whose families would never look on them again.

It was an unnerving ordeal for a young regiment, but, fortunately, there was little time for reflection, and the Rangers hurried on. At No. 2 Post there was a short halt, while Colonel Jourdain interviewed General Birdwood and General Godley, who informed him that the Turks had broken through a section of the line, and that his battalion was placed under the command of General Cox to help him to retrieve matters. He was exhorted to move forward as quickly as possible, as the need for reinforcements was urgent. Accordingly, before the rear of the battalion had extricated itself from the sap, the head was in motion again. It must be borne in mind that except for the brief information which the Colonel had received from General Birdwood, officers and men alike were completely ignorant of the previous operations. They knew nothing of the extension of the Anzac position northward on the night of the 6th, nor of the repeated attacks on the Chunuk Bair ; above all, they were unaware that a landing had taken place at Suvla. It was, however, clear to them that they were in new country, for up to No. 2 Post they had moved by well-trodden paths protected at any point of danger by saps and sandbags. Now they were in open country, with the sea on their left, and on the right a range of low foothills, which in places sank sufficiently to enable them to see the ridge of the Chunuk high above them.

Here and there accoutrements hurriedly cut off a wounded man showed that Turkish shrapnel and snipers had to be reckoned with, but there appeared to be a momentary lull in the fighting. Past the mouth of the Chailak Dere the Rangers hurried in single file sweating under the pitiless sun past Bauchop's Hill, and over a low *nek* into the Aghyl Dere. Here, again, their progress grew slower, for the gully was narrow and filled with wounded and mules and resting Ghurkas. It was stiflingly hot, and the smell of the mules and the dust, shut in tightly between the high scrub-fringed banks of the gully, were almost unendurable. The Rangers moved forward for a hundred yards at a time, until at 11.15 a.m. General Cox's headquarters were reached.

The halt there was a brief one for the Rangers were at once directed to place themselves under the orders of Brigadier-General W. de S. Cayley commanding the 39th Brigade, for the purpose of reinforcing his line. Below General Cox's headquarters, the Aghyl Dere forked into two branches, one coming from the Damakjelik Bair, the other, the southern branch, from the foot of the Chunuk. Along this southern branch the Rangers went in single file for about four hundred yards, passing an extemporized dressing station crowded with Ghurkas in slouch hats, and broad, baggy shorts, until they reached a point where a spur ran down from the Damakjelik Bair and gave a certain amount of protection against rifle fire from the Chunuk. Here, General Cayley had established his headquarters in the narrow protected area ; in rear of it were crowded all that remained of three or four English battalions. Above, the crest was lined by Sikhs. Into this zone of safety the Rangers hurried, and after forming up, lay down to rest while their Colonel went to General Cayley for orders. The General was established in an observatory of boughs, which gave some shelter from the view of snipers on the Chunuk, and after giving Colonel Jourdain and the officers who accompanied him a very welcome cup of tea, he proceeded to explain the situation.

Although General Baldwin's column had been driven from The Farm position, yet, apparently, it had not yet been occupied by the Turks. It was believed that they were greatly exhausted and had been much discouraged by the heavy losses inflicted on them by our artillery, and it was considered that it might be possible to re-occupy The Farm position. Accordingly " A " and " B " Companies of the Connaught Rangers were ordered to advance up the Aghyl Dere, climb the slopes of the Chunuk Bair as far as The Farm, and occupy the position which was reported to have been partly entrenched. The men were much exhausted, since they had marched about seven miles in the noonday heat without regular halts. They were allowed an hour's rest, and endeavours were made to fill their water-bottles, but very little water was obtainable, as the allowance at Anzac had been reduced to a pint a day per man. Extra ammunition was given out, and sandbags and entrenching tools were carried by the men. About two in the afternoon, " B " Company, who were to keep The Farm on their right hand, led off into the scrub on the left of the gully. " A " Company followed them, and for about two hundred yards were able to work along the bed of the Dere itself, crouching under the high bank to avoid the bullets which whistled overhead.

Although the main body of the enemy had retired behind the main crest of the Chunuk Bair, yet they had pushed forward snipers and machine-guns in sufficient numbers to render the advance of the two companies a decidedly unpleasant proceeding. A sudden turn in the direction of the gully brought the commander of " A " Company, who was at the head of his column, face to face with a long bare stretch of sand running for three hundred yards straight in the direction of the Chunuk Bair, which was filled with corpses and with the equipment that showed where a wounded man had fallen. Instinctively, he ran forward as the bullets began to throw up the sand all round him, and was followed by his signallers and observers and the men of the leading section. For about fifty yards they ran on until they reached a spot where a cross gully, running down from Rhododendron Ridge, afforded some protection from the pitiless machine-gun fire, but in that fifty yards half of the dozen men had fallen. Accordingly, the subaltern of the leading platoon was sent back to warn the remainder of the company, not to attempt to use the Dere, but to work their way through the scrub on its right. He ran the gauntlet successfully and the advance continued slowly.

Unfortunately, it had been impossible to give the men any definite objective, as from below The Farm was invisible, and many of them lost their way in the thick undergrowth, but about a platoon and a half of each company found its way through the bushes fringing the Aghyl Dere and commenced the ascent of the Chunuk Bair. Once they began to climb they were comparatively free from the attentions of the snipers and machine-guns, since the lower slopes of the hill were dead ground, but the climb itself was almost intolerable. The ascent was extremely steep, and covered in scrub, in which lurked enormous boulders. The sun was still tropical, and the men, most

I

of whom carried picks or shovels, as well as their weapons, were heavily laden. Often a man was obliged to lay down his rifle to haul himself up a rock, and found it an almost intolerable burden to have to take it up again. It was only by halting and resting every ten minutes that it was possible to make any progress. The officers, who did not know that they might not find the whole position in the hands of the Turks, did their utmost to retain in the men a sufficient reserve of energy to enable them to charge if it proved necessary. As The Farm came in sight three hundred yards ahead, an irregular extension was formed on the hillside, and the two companies got into touch again. " B " on the left, " A " on the right, pressed forward to reach their objective. It was unoccupied.

Unoccupied by the Turks, indeed, yet there were many relics of the struggle that had been waged there at dawn. A narrow ditch hardly a foot deep showed where an attempt had been made to entrench the position, while scattered round it were sandbags and entrenching tools, rifles and bandoliers of ammunition in a confusion so unnatural that it seemed horrible. Normally, such things are carefully stored and arranged, and even more carefully accounted for, and to see them thrown broadcast about a bare hillside was desolate indeed. Among them lay the men who had used them ;

some groaning for water, while others, under the influence of the scorching sunshine, had already begun to give forth the unspeakably foul sweet odour of corruption that in those August days tainted half the hills and valleys of Gallipoli. The sight was depressing enough, but at least the enemy were not there, and the men would be able to rest before they had to fight.

As the senior officer on the position was congratulating himself on this, a concealed machine-gun opened on the right about two hundred yards away. The right flank of " A " Company was in full view of it, and both Captain Massy, who commanded there, and a subaltern with him were wounded. Captain Massy, however, remained calm, and after binding up his comrade's wounds as neatly as a man with a bullet-hole through his right arm was able to, he withdrew his men to join the remainder of the company on the left. These were screened from the direct view of the hostile machine-gunners by bushes, but the gun was firing at every sound, which made movement, and still more digging, impossible. Gradually, however, sandbags were filled, and a traverse made of them, which protected the men as long as they lay still. A few picked shots were detailed to fire at intervals into the bushes where the invisible machine-gun appeared to be, and the knowledge that they were retaliating encouraged them greatly. Further comfort was given by the capture of a Turkish sniper, who had been found lurking in the bushes behind us. None of the men had ever seen a Turk before, and the general curiosity as to his appearance served to distract the men's minds from their immediate prospects.

These, as they presented themselves to the officer who found himself temporarily in command, were by no means cheerful. The trench which the men were supposed to hold would require at least six hours' work before it would give decent protection from shrapnel. It was also badly sited and only gave a field of fire of a few yards. The men available for work on it were few in number and very weary. There was sufficient food and plenty of ammunition, but water was very scarce, for those who possessed sufficient self-control to refrain from drinking during the weary climb, had been unable to resist the entreaties of the wounded, and had allowed them to empty their water-bottles.

The only road by which supplies of any kind could be obtained was the Aghyl Dere, which was swept by the enemy's fire. In addition, it was also known that very few reinforcements were obtainable. Finally, both flanks of the position were " in the air," the right being already dominated by a hostile machine-gun, which was placed so as to enfilade the line. It was clear that if, after dark, the Turks were to attack, the detachment would be in a hopeless position, and were bound to be either captured or destroyed. However, orders had been given that the line was to be held, and there was nothing to be done but obey them. The men were, therefore, instructed to rest until darkness made it possible for them to improve their position, and all ranks lay down and awaited the enemy's attack.

Before it developed, however, General Cayley sent orders that the detachment was to withdraw at dusk, bringing with it all the wounded who were lying on the face of the hill. Major Money, of " B " Company, who had now taken over the command, at once detailed a party under Lieutenant Blake to cover the withdrawal, and as it was within an hour of sunset, began to collect the wounded at once. These for the most part belonged to the East Lancashire and Wiltshire Regiments, with a few of the Royal Irish Rifles. They had lain out from dawn to dusk under the burning rays of the Mediterranean sun without food, water, or attention, and suffering agonies.

By the time they had been collected, the sun was setting, and the pilgrimage of pain began. There were no stretchers, nor were even waterproof sheets available, so that each wounded man had to be carried by his shoulders and legs. The mountain was pathless, and in the growing darkness the bearers made many a false step, which must have caused torture to the sufferers. Some shrieked with pain, others showered blessings on the heads of the men who were saving them from an agonizing death by thirst, and in the growing dusk, the load of misery was slowly carried to the foot of the hill. To the credit of the Turkish machine-gunners it must be said that they made no attempt to fire as soon as they perceived that wounded were being removed.

On this, as on other occasions in Gallipoli, we were glad to be able to respect the chivalry of our foes. An attempt was made to bring down some of the rifles and equipment that were scattered over the face of the Chunuk Bair, but there were hardly enough men to carry them, and some had to be abandoned. It was after 7 p.m. before the covering party withdrew, being the last British troops to occupy the Chunuk Bair. Among them was Captain Massy, who, ignoring his wound, had insisted on remaining till all the wounded had been removed. For his gallantry on this occasion he was awarded the Military Cross.

It was dark before the Aghyl Dere was reached, and the Rangers were glad to find that the two remaining companies of their battalion had been employed in entrenching a line on each side of the gully and making sand-bag traverses on each side of it. All the wounded who had fallen in the earlier fighting had been dressed and removed. This was a feat requiring extraordinary courage and endurance on the part of the battalion stretcher-bearers. They had been obliged to go into the exposed section of the Agyhl Dere under a storm of bullets, in order to bring out the wounded, and yet they not only did so, but often dressed the man's wounds under fire before they removed him. Then after the Medical Officer had treated him they had to bear their heavy burden all the way to the beach, returning only to plunge into the fire-swept zone again and rescue another comrade.

There were no men in the force who did their duty more strenuously and fearlessly than the stretcher-bearers of the 5th Connaught Rangers on the 10th of August, 1915, and officers who had grumbled at having to allot some of their best and strongest men for non-combatant duties realized how well it was that they had done so. Nor must the part played by the medical officer be forgotten. Lieutenant J. I. O'Sullivan, Royal Army Medical Corps, found himself confronted by the débris of two brigades, but he rose to the occasion magnificently. Unpacking his paniers under a bush just behind the line, he not only worked on till long after dark without a rest, but remained cheerful and encouraging through it all. Only those who passed through his hands know what they owe to him.

So at sunset on August 10th ended the Battle of Sari Bair, which had begun on the night of the 6th. It had been hard fighting, and Mr. Ashmead Bartlett, the newspaper correspondent, has described it as the hardest battle in which British soldiers have been engaged since Inkerman. Those who took part in it, however, prefer to think of General Godley's restrained but deeply significant testimony :—

" I do not believe that any troops in the world could have accomplished more. All ranks vied with one another in the performance of gallant deeds, and more than worthily upheld the best traditions of the British Army."

NOTE.—Since this chapter was written, Brigadier-General Cooper has been awarded a C.B., and Colonel Bewsher of the Hampshires, and Major Wilford, Indian Army (attached Royal Irish Rifles) have received the D.S.O. for their services in this action.

CHAPTER V

SUVLA BAY AND CHOCOLATE HILL

" Death is nothing ; but to live vanquished and without
glory is to die every day."—Napoleon.

I F you sail up the western coast of the Gallipoli
Peninsula, soon after passing Anzac Cove, you
will notice that the hills which have fringed
the shore all the way from Cape Helles begin to
run further inland, and that a gradually widening
strip of level ground becomes visible between
the cliffs and the sea. The coast line, too,
which has hitherto pointed north and south,
turns in a north-westerly direction, and thus
increases the extent of plain until it culminates
at the end of four miles in a cape known as
Nibrunesi Point. Two miles north of Nibrunesi
is another promontory called Suvla Point, and
these are the two extremities of a semi-circular
bay, which had no name on the original maps
issued to the army, but which was soon to be
well known as Suvla Bay. It is a name which
has brought sorrow to many homes, and which
will be perpetually associated with failure,
but there are many glorious memories associated
with it.

There are old and historic regiments that think more proudly of Maiwand and Chillian-wallah than of victories gained with less stern fighting; and it may well be, that in the future the four Fusilier regiments from Ireland and the Royal Irish Regiment will be glad to remember that their service battalions fought at Suvla. A year later, at Salonica, when the gates of the Supply Depôt were christened after great battles of the war, the name of Suvla was thought not unworthy to be associated with those of Ypres and Verdun. Greater glory no man could ask for, and none of the few survivors of the 10th Division could pass that gate without a throb of pride.

Suvla was well suited to a landing, since the beach shelved gently and offered a long slope of sand on which lighters could run ashore. West of Nibrunesi Point an isolated hill, known as Lala Baba, rose to a height of a hundred and fifty feet close to the shore, while behind this was the curious feature known as the Salt Lake. In August, this was dry and presented a surface of white sticky mud nearly a mile across gleaming brightly in the sun. North-east of the Salt Lake the ground rose gently till it culminated in Tekke Tepe, nine hundred feet high and four miles inland. South of Tekke Tepe and about three miles east of the Salt Lake, was the village of Anafarta Sagir in a cultivated valley. South of this again was a lower ridge known as Scimitar Hill, and then another valley containing the village of Biyuk Anafarta. South of Biyuk Anafarta the ground rose steeply to form the main chain of the Sari Bair. Between the two Anafartas and the Salt Lake was a cultivated plain, studded with

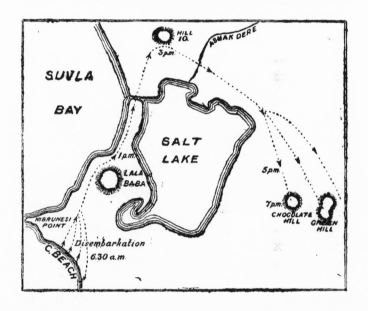

little cornfields and isolated olive trees, but from this plain, nearly two miles inland, rose two isolated hills, about two hundred feet high, known as Yilghin Burnu (or Green Hill) and Chocolate Hill.

The landscape was finally framed by a high crest running inland in a north-easterly direction from Suvla Point, falling steeply in cliffs to the Gulf of Saros on the north, but presenting a gentler slope to the southern plain. This ridge reached a height of 400 feet near the sea and was there called the Karakol Dagh, while further inland, where it maintained an average height of 600 feet, it was known as the Kiretch Tepe Sirt. From its crest could be seen the whole of the plain enclosed by Tekke Tepe, Sari Bair and Damak-jelik Bair, on which the battle was destined to be fought.

The Commander-in-Chief had planned that the transports conveying the 11th Division from Imbros were to leave as soon as night fell on the 6th, and effect their landing under cover of darkness. The 10th Division, having a longer voyage (Mudros being 60 and Mitylene 120 miles away) were intended to reinforce them on the following day. It was believed that the Turks would be taken by surprise, and that little or no resistance was to be anticipated. Three landing places had been arranged for ; one known as Beach A in Suvla Bay itself, the others, Beach B and Beach C, on the shore south of Nibrunesi Point. The three Brigades of the 11th Division landed simultaneously, and met with slight resistance from a Turkish picket entrenched on Lala Baba. The hill was, however, taken with the bayonet, and the whole of the beaches made good, while the 11th Manchester Regiment drove the enemy's out-

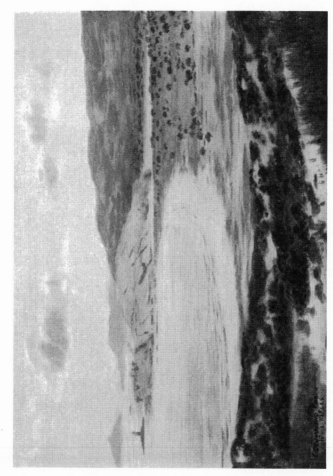

SUVLA, SHOWING LALA BABA AND THE SALT LAKE

(From a water-colour by Captain Drummond Fish, Royal Irish Rifles)

posts on the Karakol Dagh back on to the Kiretch Tepe Sirt. By the time this much had been gained, day dawned and the first portion of the 10th Division began to appear on the scene.

This consisted of the 31st Brigade and the two battalions of Royal Dublin Fusiliers, which had been waiting at Mitylene, the whole force being under the command of Brigadier-General F. F. Hill. Early in the afternoon of the 6th, the battalions had left the transports, on which they had spent nearly a month, and transferred themselves to trawlers and channel steamers. At sunset they weighed anchor and steamed northward, all, except a few on board, being completely ignorant of their destination. The lights on the shore told them that they had passed Achi Baba, and as they steamed by Anzac, the noise of battle at Lone Pine and on Sari Bair reached them from afar. Just as the pale morning light began to make it possible to distinguish the difference between sea and land, the ships anchored off Nibrunesi Point.

In the original plan of operations it was designed that the 11th Division should form the right wing and the 10th the left of the advance, and with this scheme in view it had been arranged to land the 10th on Beach A, inside Suvla Bay. The landing at Beach A during the night had, however, been considerably delayed owing to the fact that many of the lighters had run aground in the shallow waters of the bay, and the Naval Authorities had, therefore, decided to land General Hill's force on Beach C below Nibrunesi Point. At the same time, General Hill was directed to reinforce the 11th Division, placing himself under the orders of Major-General Hammersley, who commanded that unit.

The process of disembarkation began about 5.30 a.m., the first two lighters taking to the shore a company of the 6th Inniskillings and a company of the 5th Royal Irish Fusiliers, as well as General Hill and his staff.

It was at once clear to all that the Turks had not been completely taken by surprise. The scrub which covered the slopes of all the surrounding hills, combined with the scattered olive groves to make it impossible to detect the numbers of the enemy, but it was obvious that they were well supplied with artillery. Their shrapnel was bursting fiercely over the men of the 11th Division as they moved forward, and as soon as the lighters reached the beaches, an effective barrage was at once established there. Even the troops awaiting disembarkation were under fire, and suffered the painful experience of having to lie down, closely packed together, and unable to retaliate. The lighters were obvious and easy targets, and in one boat alone the 7th Dublins lost an officer and seventeen men. On the whole, however, the force was lucky, and the casualties on landing were not heavy. Little could be done to keep down the hostile artillery fire, since the enemy's guns were well concealed, and but few of our batteries had landed. Two mountain guns on Lala Baba kept up a constant fire, and the warships co-operated, though lack of facilities for observation rendered their fire comparatively ineffective.

General Hill reached the landing place two hundred yards south of Nibrunesi Point about 6.30 a.m. Leaving orders for units as they landed to rendezvous on the seaward side of Lala Baba, he went in search of General Hammersley in order to ascertain his wishes. At this time the Turkish detachments, which had been watching the beaches, were retiring slowly across the wooded plain which stretches between the Salt Lake and Anafarta Saghir, pursued by the 11th Division. This pursuit, however, was considerably impeded by the fact that two small eminences, each about a hundred-and-sixty feet high, about half-a-mile from the south-eastern corner of the Salt Lake, were still in the enemy's hands. These positions were afterwards known as Chocolate Hill and Green Hill respectively, the Turkish name for the range being Yilghin Burnu. As long as the Turks held these knolls, they were in a position to bring enfilade artillery fire to bear on the advance across the Anafarta plain ; and accordingly General Hill was directed to co-

operate with two battalions of the 11th Division
in their capture. This order had unfortunately
the result of making any future junction with
the portion of the Division under Sir Bryan
Mahon's command impossible, since that was
directed to guard the left flank of the advance,
while General Hill's force was to move to the
extreme right. Owing to this detachment of a
Brigade and a half, the work of the Staff tended
to become more difficult.

By the time that General Hill rejoined his
force with these orders, he found that the 6th
Inniskillings and 5th Royal Irish Fusiliers had
reached the rendezvous under Lala Baba.
Two companies of the 7th Dublins under Major
Lonsdale, the second-in-command, had also
arrived there, and the remainder of the battalion,
followed by the 6th Dublins and 6th Royal
Irish Fusiliers, were coming up. The latter
unit had been put ashore some way down the
beach, and had had to march a considerable
distance in order to reach Lala Baba.

The process of disembarkation and assembly
had naturally taken a considerable time, and it
was not till close on noon that the advance
began. In order to reach the northern shores
of the Salt Lake, and get in touch with the 11th
Division, the units of General Hill's force had
to pass over a narrow neck of land between the
Salt Lake and the sea, on which the hostile
artillery had carefully registered. Every minute

it was swept by bursts of shrapnel, and the only way in which it crossed was by a section at a time rushing over it and trusting to luck. It was a trying ordeal for young troops engaged in their first action, but they faced it cheerfully. The 7th Dublins in particular were much encouraged by the example of their Colonel. As an old soldier, he knew that there were times when an officer must be prepared to run what would otherwise appear unnecessary risks ; so while everyone else was dashing swiftly across the neck, or keeping close under cover, it is recorded that Colonel Downing—a man of unusual height and girth—stood in the centre of the bullet-swept zone, quietly twirling his stick. The sight of his fearlessness must have been an inspiration to his men.

As soon as each battalion had crossed the neck, it formed up on the low ground north of the Salt Lake, under the slight amount of cover afforded by a low eminence known as Hill 10. When all had got across, the advance eastward began. The crossing of the neck had occupied a good deal of time, and it was close on 3 p.m. For more than four hours the sun had been directly overhead, a blinding glare was reflected from the shining surface of the Salt Lake, and the heat was almost overpowering. Few of the men had slept during the night, since excitement and the discomfort caused by their closely - packed quarters on board the fleet

K

sweepers had combined to keep them awake.
Except for a cup of tea about 3 a.m., and a
mouthful hastily swallowed before moving off,
they were fasting, and already many of the more
improvident had emptied their water-bottles.
In addition, these young soldiers who had never
seen war before, had been since four in the
morning exposed to shrapnel fire, with but little
chance either of taking cover or of retaliating.
They had seen their comrades fall stricken at
their sides without the consolation of knowing
that the enemy was suffering to an equal extent.
However, the prospect of action was encouraging, and it was with confident faces that they
turned towards the foe. Their one desire was
to come to close quarters with the enemy on
their immediate front, but he was invisible.

From the low ground across which they were
moving little could be seen but the masses of
scrub backed by the semicircle of hills, and only
broken by the minarets of Anafarta. The three
leading battalions (6th Inniskilling Fusiliers,
5th Royal Irish Fusiliers and 7th Dublins)
crossed the dry bed of the Azmak Dere, and
began to turn southward towards Chocolate
Hill. Up to this point the left flank of the
movement had been protected by the troops
of the 11th Division, who were advancing
in the direction of Anafarta, but every
yard gained to the southward tended to throw
this flank more and more into the air.

Though invisible, the enemy was making his presence felt. Round white balls of shrapnel were continually forming overhead, and out of the dense bushes rifle bullets came whizzing past the men's heads. Now and then a Turkish sniper was caught, sometimes festooned in boughs to enable him to escape notice ; but the casualties caused by snipers were not so serious on the first day as they became later. The heaviest losses were caused by the artillery, for near the sea the scrub was thinner, and the long lines of men slowly advancing were plainly visible to the enemy's observers on the surrounding hills. Occasionally too, a Taube buzzed overhead, making its observations with comparative impunity, since except on the ships, there were no anti-aircraft guns.

Still the men pressed on, driving the Turks through the scrub before them. It was unpleasant work, particularly for officers, since little or nothing was known, either of the country or of the strength of dispositions of the enemy, and at any moment a platoon might have found itself confronted by a heavy counter-attack launched from the depths of the scrub, or enfiladed by hidden machine guns. Also, it proved a good deal harder to keep in touch with other units than it had in training days at the Curragh or in the Phœnix Park. The danger of pushing on too fast and finding oneself isolated was no imaginary one, but was alarmingly illustrated by the disaster which befell the 1st /5th Norfolks four days later. Nor did the tropical heat, which wore out and exhausted the men, help to quicken the movement. All these considerations combined with the pressure exercised by the enemy on the left flank of the Royal Irish Fusiliers tended to make the advance slow.

The dispositions of the force for the attack were as follows :—

On the right " A " and " B " Companies of the 6th Royal Inniskilling Fusiliers were in the firing line, supported by " C " and " D " Companies of the same unit ; and by the 6th Royal Irish Fusiliers who had been brought up from the reserve. The 5th Royal Irish Fusiliers were on the left, having " A " and " B " Companies in the firing line and " C " and " D " in support. Owing to the fact that the left flank was exposed, this battalion was gradually being compelled to face in a south-easterly direction, with the result that a gap began to appear between it and the 6th Inniskillings. This gap was filled by " A " Company of the 7th Royal Dublin Fusiliers, closely supported by " D " Company (" The Pals ") of the same unit. The 6th Royal Dublin Fusiliers, who had been the last to come ashore, were still in reserve, and the 5th Inniskillings had not yet landed.

Steadfastly the Fusiliers went forward, moving on a line parallel to that which they had taken

BRIGADIER-GENERAL F. F. HILL, C.B., C.M.G., D.S.O.
COMMANDING 31ST BRIGADE

in the morning, but in the opposite direction.
As they passed the Salt Lake, the Inniskillings,
who were on exposed ground, suffered severely,
as many of the men stuck in the swamp. Land-
mines, too, which exploded on contact, were
encountered and caused losses, while the shrapnel
burst overhead unceasingly. Nothing, however,
could have been more encouraging to the men
than the demeanour of their leader. Wherever
the danger was greatest General Hill was to be
found, calm and collected, trying to save the
men as much as possible. His fearlessness, his
complete disregard of personal danger, set an
inspiring example, and officers and men alike
went forward more cheerfully, thanks to the
lead given them by their General.

As the advance continued high explosive shells
were mingled with the shrapnel, and though
they did not claim so many victims, they were
infinitely more trying to the strained nerves
of the weary men in the ranks.   By 5 p.m. they
had come within 300 yards of the hill, and were
under a heavy rifle fire.   By this time the men
were very weary.   They had had a long voyage
of 120 miles under most uncomfortable conditions, they had been under unceasing artillery
fire for more than twelve hours, they had
marched more than five miles burdened by rifle
and ammunition through the noon of a tropical
day, and it was no wonder that they were exhausted.   Chocolate Hill, too, was a formidable

proposition : though only a hundred and sixty feet high, it rose steeply from the plain, and it was now obvious that it had been carefully prepared as a defensive position, for its sides were seamed by trenches. Though it was impossible to ascertain how strongly those trenches were held, yet it was clearly imperative that the men should have a rest before making the assault.

While the fleet and the batteries that had now been landed bombarded the position, the men of General Hill's force lay down in their ranks on the sun-baked ground, firing a shot from time to time, but with abundant leisure to look about them. On their right they could see the white houses and tiled roofs of Anafarta Saghir, while to the left they gazed across the shining white surface of the Salt Lake, past Lala Baba, to the bay crowded with warships and transports and hurrying launches, and to the calm and splendid peak of Samothrace. Many of " D " Company (" The Pals ") of the 7th Dublins were men who had taken degrees at Trinity or the National University, and they may well have recalled past studies and thrilled to remember that the word " Samothrace " had always been associated with Victory. Most of all, however, they watched the hill in front of them and wondered what fate might have in store for them there.

At last the bombardment ceased and the lines rose. General Hill had ordered that at all costs the position was to be taken before dark, and reinforced by two battalions of the 11th Division at 7 p.m. the charge began. On one flank the Inniskillings and on the other the Irish Fusiliers pressed forward. " A " Company of the 7th Dublins, led by Major Harrison, a splendid soldier, closely supported by " The Pals " under Captain Poole Hickman (a barrister who had served in the ranks of the Company which he now commanded) made for the centre of the hill. The gleaming line of bayonets recked little of the Turkish fire, but rushed onward up the slopes. The Turk, on the defensive always, stands his ground well, and in more than one place the bayonets crossed ; but the rush of the Irish charge was not to be denied. Fatigue and thirst were forgotten as the Fusiliers, exulting in the force of their attack, dashed over trench and communication trench until the crest of the hill was gained.

As they reached it, the sun sank behind Samothrace, and the impending darkness made further pursuit fruitless. There was much work to be done in the short Southern twilight, for the hill was a maze of trenches and dug-outs, with paths leading everywhere and nowhere, so that it was hard to find one's way. Outposts were hastily detailed and pushed forward over the crest, and the battalions which were much mixed, after a hurried reorganization, bivou-acked on and around the hill that they had taken. Their work, however, was by no means at an end, for it was necessary to make arrangements for bringing up food and water, to replenish ammunition, to bury the dead, and to collect the wounded. This last was by no means a pleasant task, since they were scattered all over the area across which the attack had taken place, and in the darkness it was easy for an unconscious man lying under a bush to escape notice. Here, as everywhere, however, the stretcher-bearers worked magnificently, and the doctors who had marched with their units all day, settled down to a night of strenuous labour. It is impossible to exaggerate the devotion to duty displayed by the regimental Medical Officers : they utterly ignored their own fatigue in order to ease the sufferings of their comrades.

While they were working, the task of replenishing supplies was going forward, though it proved to be one of considerable difficulty. The heaviest share of the burden fell on quartermasters of units and on the staff at the beach, who were left to regulate this matter. The night was pitch dark, and lighters were discharging their loads at various points along two miles of beach, so that it was by no means easy to find the stores required, or when they were found to entrust them to the representative of the unit that required them. Fortunately, however, a considerable surplus of rations and ammunition had been brought on the fleet sweepers from Mitylene, and this was divided among quartermasters. It was then necessary to have it sent up to Chocolate Hill, and since no animals or transport of any kind were available, this task became one of considerable difficulty. However, the men of the 6th Dublins, who had been in reserve during the day, were employed on this service, and their fatigue parties toiled throughout the night transporting the heavy boxes over the two-and-a-half miles of broken ground that intervened between the beach and the hill.

The crux of the whole situation was water. The single water-bottle that each man had brought ashore had long been empty, and all were parched with thirst. Though some water lighters had run aground in the bay, others had reached the shore, but there were no vessels of any kind in which the priceless fluid could be carried up to the firing line. In view of the facts that the position had only been captured at dusk, and had barely been consolidated, and that it was reasonable to expect that the enemy would counter-attack, it was felt that it was impossible to send men down to the beach to fill their water-bottles, and yet there appeared no method by which the water could be conveyed to the position. Petrol cans and biscuit-tins were not forthcoming, and though Lieutenant Byrne, the Quartermaster of the 6th Dublins, tried the experiment of sending up water in empty small-arm ammunition boxes, it was not wholly successful. At last the camp-kettles belonging to units came ashore, and by utilizing these, a scanty supply of water was sent up into the firing line. This work of organizing the supply of water, food and ammunition occupied the whole of the night of the 7th, and it was not till late on the 8th that it was complete. The main responsibility for it so far as General Hill's force was concerned, rested on Capt. T. J. D. Atkinson, the Staff Captain of the 31st Brigade. He received invaluable assistance from Lieutenant and Quartermaster R. Byrne of the 6th Dublins, who on this, as on many other occasions, displayed such conspicuous ability and energy as to gain him the Military Cross.

Meanwhile, units began to take stock of their losses. Judged by the scale of later fighting in the Peninsula the casualties were not very heavy, though at first sight they appeared formidable enough. However, having regard to the fact that the troops had been under constant shell fire for twelve hours and at the end of it had taken an entrenched position by assault, the force could consider itself fortunate in not having suffered more severely. The bulk of the wounds were caused by shrapnel, which tended to confirm the impression that the hostile infantry who held Chocolate Hill were not very numerous. Had they been in equal strength to our men and been well supplied with machine guns, the losses sustained in the attack must inevitably have been far greater. Nevertheless, the capture of the Chocolate Hill-Green Hill position was a highly creditable performance for young troops who were receiving their baptism of fire. When it is remembered that they had been on the move throughout the greater part of the day in a temperature of well over 100°, the dash and determination exhibited by all the Irish regiments engaged augured well for their future.

Unfortunately, several senior officers had fallen. The 7th Dublins lost Major Tippett, who had served for years in the old Dublin City Militia, and had left the security of a political agent's post in an English country constituency to die in his old regiment. Lieutenant Julian of the same battalion, who died of his wounds, was a young officer of great promise, whose death was deeply mourned. The 5th Royal Irish Fusiliers, who had suffered severely from the enemy on their left flank, lost Major Garstin killed ; and their Adjutant and nearly a dozen more officers wounded. In traversing the open ground by the Salt Lake and in the assault on the hill, the 6th Inniskillings had also sustained many casualties. Colonel Cliffe (destined to die later in France) was wounded, and so was Major Musgrave, his second-in-command ; while half-a-dozen more officers were *hors de combat.* One of these was the Quartermaster, Lieutenant

Dooley, who was struck by shrapnel while superintending the unloading of ammunition from a lighter on the beach.

While Chocolate Hill was being attacked, the remainder of the Division was hotly engaged to the northward.

When Sir Bryan Mahon arrived from Mudros with the 6th and 7th Royal Munster Fusiliers and the 5th Royal Irish Regiment, he found that the force under General Hill had already landed, and was in action. Nothing remained of the Division which he had raised and trained for nearly a year, but the three battalions which he had brought with him and the 5th Royal Inniskilling Fusiliers, which had not begun to disembark. It was an extraordinary position for an officer who was a Lieutenant-General of three years' standing, and had commanded a division for more than six years, to find himself entering into an action with only four battalions under his command, the whole of the rest of his command having been diverted elsewhere. However, he made the best of the situation and proceeded so far as the force at his disposal would permit, to carry out the task which had been allotted to the Division, namely advancing on the left of the 11th Division and securing the Kiretch Tepe Sirt.

Beach " A " had been found unsuitable for use, as the water near it was so shallow that the lighters ran aground at a considerable distance

BRIGADIER-GENERAL L. L. NICOL, C.B., COMMANDING 30TH BRIGADE

from the shore. The Navy had by this time
found a better landing place on the north shore
of Suvla Bay, slightly to the east of an isolated
peak called Ghazi Baba, which rises from the
shore. To this new landing place the two
Munster battalions of the 30th Brigade with
Brigadier-General L. L. Nicol and their Brigade
Headquarters and the Divisional Pioneer
Battalion were directed. It proved by no means
ideal, since many of the lighters ran aground a
considerable distance from the shore, and
officers and men had to plunge into the water,
which was waist deep, and wade to the land.
Fortunately, wet clothes were soon dried by the
Gallipoli sun, but the stranded boats afforded
excellent targets to the Turkish artillery. On
reaching the shore a little before noon, the 6th
Munsters who landed first found that the enemy
had sown the beach with land mines which
exploded on contact. Sveral men were injured
by these, while the Adjutant of the 6th Munsters
was knocked down, but not hurt.

The orders given to the two battalions of
Munsters and the Royal Irish who acted as
support, were to climb the Kiretch Tepe Sirt
Ridge at its western end and push forward
along the crest as fast as possible. A certain
amount of ground had been made good in the
course of the night by the 11th Manchester
Regiment, but it was desirable that the whole
ridge should be secured as quickly as possible

in order to safeguard the left flank of the advance across the Anafarta plain. The Munsters accordingly struggled up the steep bushy slope under the burning rays of the midday sun, and deployed for advance about 1.30 p.m. The 6th Munsters were on the left and the 7th on the right. They then pushed forward, but it was at once obvious that the country was one which offered many advantages to an enemy who wished to fight a delaying action.

Although from a distance the Kiretch Tepe Sirt appeared to be a long whale-backed hill six hundred feet high, yet its sides were seamed with gullies and tiny peaks almost invisible from below, which detached themselves from the main contour of the crest line. Moreover, it was covered with dense oak and holly scrub, which entirely concealed the numbers of the enemy and made it impossible to ascertain whether a unit was being opposed by a handful of snipers or a battalion. As they pushed through this dense thicket, the Munsters passed many indications of this fight waged by the 11th Manchesters, and soon the sight of fly-infested corpses ceased to cause a shudder. Soon they came in contact with the battalion itself, or rather what was left of it, since it had suffered heavily. Its Colonel was wounded, his second-in-command killed, and nearly half its strength were out of action. Those who remained were exhausted and very thirsty, and were unable to advance further. The Turks were holding a rocky mound which commanded the crest of the ridge for about six hundred yards to the west of it. From this point of vantage they were pouring a considerable volume of rifle fire on any troops who attempted to advance. Having taken in the situation, the Munsters went forward to attack the position, and had succeeded in getting within about a hundred yards of it when darkness fell.

In this engagement, fought in an unknown country against an enemy who knew every track and gully, and was able to leave snipers in the bushes behind him as he retired, the Munsters suffered severely, but were ready to advance again at dawn. A night attack was considered impracticable, since the country was absolutely unknown to the troops and very intricate. On the following day (the 8th) the Turkish position was attacked and finally stormed. The party of the 6th Munsters who took the culminating point, were led by the second-in-command of their battalion, Major Jephson, and the knoll was christened after him, Jephson's Post. Further advance proved impossible, the enemy being in possession of a strongly entrenched position, extending right across the ridge, and steps were taken to dig in on the line held.

In this brisk engagement the two battalions of Munsters, supported by the Royal Irish

Regiment, and on the 8th by the 5th Royal Inniskilling Fusiliers, had had to contend with an enemy possibly weaker in numbers, but possessing an intimate knowledge of the country and favoured by the lie of the ground. It was believed at Headquarters that the Turkish force on the Kiretch Tepe Sirt consisted of close on 700 Gendarmeries, who had been for months patrolling the Suvla district, and had the advantage of having already prepared entrenchments on the ridge. Against such a foe it was no mean achievement for a newly landed force to have advanced over two miles in a puzzling and intricate country and to have expelled the enemy from a well-fortified position, the whole being accomplished within twenty-four hours of landing.

Naturally, there were numerous casualties. The 7th Munsters suffered most severely, having Captain Cullinan, Lieutenant Harper, Lieutenant Travers and 2nd-Lieutenant Bennett killed, and Major Hendricks, Captain Cooper-Key, Captain Henn and half-a-dozen subalterns wounded. In the 6th Munsters, Lieutenant J. B. Lee, a Dublin barrister, was killed on the 7th, and Major Conway, a Regular officer of the Munster Fusiliers, fell in the assault on Jephson's Post on the 6th. Several subalterns were wounded, and there were numerous casualties among the rank and file. It was, however, fortunate that the enemy had no machine guns, and that the thick scrub made it hard to direct their artillery fire with accuracy, or the losses would have been far heavier.

For a week the battalions held the line that they had captured, being reinforced by the 5th Inniskillings, who took over the trenches on the northern slope of the ridge looking down on to the Gulf of Saros. This flank was guarded by a destroyer, which did invaluable service by giving notice of enemy movements, by searchlight work at night, and by rendering artillery support when necessary.

The period spent in these trenches was by no means an enjoyable one, for water was very short and had to be fetched from a considerable distance away. Shade there was none, since the sun pierced vertically downwards, and the prickly scrub gave but little cover from above. The trenches had been hastily constructed in a sandy soil that crumbled and fell in at the first opportunity and required constant work at them. By day the Turkish snipers made this impossible, so the men lay, too hot and thirsty and tormented by flies to sleep, and by night they were stirred up to work again. To add to the horror of the position, the unburied bodies of those who had fallen in the previous fighting, lying in inaccessible gullies or in the midst of the scrub, began to spread around the foul, sweet, sickly odour of

L

decay. Once smelt, this cannot be forgotten, for it clings to the nostrils, and many a man recalled how true an insight Shakespeare had into the soldier's mind when he made Coriolanus use as his expression of supreme contempt the words :

"Whose love I prize
As the dead carcases of unburied men
That do corrupt the air."

This, however, was only an aggravation of the situation ; the real trouble was thirst. Men lied to get water, honest men stole it, some even went mad for want of it ; but it was cruelly hard to obtain. Owing to some error, an insufficient supply of vessels for carrying it had arrived from Mudros, and it became necessary to send down a platoon from each company with the company's water-bottles to the beach to fill them. It was a long and trying walk in the dark, and even when the beach was reached, water was by no means easy to obtain, since thirsty soldiers had cut holes in the hoses that filled the tanks on shore from the water-boats, and consequently much was wasted.

It had been hoped to utilise the resources of the country, but the Turks had foreseen our difficulties, and when the Engineers examined a well near Ghazi Baba, they found it surrounded by a circle of land-mines. Other wells further inland were well watched by snipers. Nor even when sufficient water was obtainable, was it easy to convey it back to the battalion. Some water-bottles leaked ; others had been only half filled, or carelessly corked, while occasionally a thirsty soldier took advantage of the darkness to refresh himself from one of the bottles which he was carrying. As a result, when the bottles were distributed, there were bitter complaints from the men who found themselves presented with only a few spoonfuls of water as a supply for twenty-four hours. Tea-making, too, became difficult, since it was almost out of the question to obtain the water required in equal quantities from each man.

It soon became clear that the system of regulating the whole water supply of the unit by the water-bottle of the individual soldier was not a sound one, since the improvident consumed their day's supply at once, and the fool who lost his water-bottle was in a hopeless position. Commanding officers and company commanders first began by pooling all water-bottles, and issuing their contents in mess-tins from time to time ; while gradually they collected petrol and biscuit tins in which to store a reserve fund. Thanks to these measures, and to the experience gained by the men, matters gradually improved.

Two events that occurred during this period gave some fillip to the spirits of the men on the ridge. The first of these was the arrival of a mail which brought not only letters and papers, but also parcels, and some of these parcels contained cake. Cake was a priceless boon in Gallipoli. Home-made and home-packed ones sometimes met with disaster and arrived in the form of crumbs, but those made by an expert, and sealed in an air-tight tin arrived safely, and were more welcome than anyone unacquainted with the ration biscuit can imagine. The ration biscuit takes various forms, some of which are small and palatable, but the type most frequently met with in Gallipoli was large and square, possessing the appearance of a dog biscuit and the consistency of a rock. It was no doubt of excellent nutritive quality, but, unfortunately, no ordinary pair of teeth was able to cope with it. Some spread jam upon it, and then licked the surface, thereby absorbing a few crumbs ; others soaked it in tea (when there was any) ; while a few pounded it between two stones, and found that the result did not make bad porridge. After a week of this regimen, it is easily imagined how glad men were to put their teeth into something soft again.

The second encouragement was the arrival of the first reinforcements from Mudros. The worn and jaded men who had spent a week on the ridge, and had lost the glamour and excitement caused by the first experience of action, were surprised to find how glad their comrades were to rejoin them. The tawny scrub and fresher air of Gallipoli seemed delightful to them after Mudros, and their pleasure was so infectious that many of the older hands came to the conclusion that the Peninsula was not such a bad place after all.

During the first two or three days spent in holding the ridge position, the attention of officers was given more to the details of water supply than to the movements of the enemy. The latter had, however, been reinforced, and were becoming more aggressive. The Kiretch Tepe Sirt was of considerable tactical value to them, as if they were able to regain their ground, they would be able to enfilade our troops on the Anafarta plain, as well as being able to watch all movements on the beaches. Not only therefore did they push forward snipers, who picked off individual officers and men—among them Lieutenant Burrows, Machine-gun Officer of the 6th Munsters ; but more organised attempts at lodgments were made, and patrol fights were not uncommon. One of these may be described as typical. The 6th Munsters, who were holding Jephson's Post, discovered that the Turks were digging in close to their immediate front, and Colonel Worship gave orders that a party under Captain Oldnall were to attack them at dawn and drive them out. Lieutenant Waller, R.E., accompanied the party in charge of the bombers.

Just before daylight the attack was made, and after a strenuous struggle, in which Captain Oldnall was seriously and Lieutenant Gaffney mortally, wounded, the post was seized. Lieutenant Waller displayed the most conspicuous courage in going out three times under very heavy fire to rescue Lieutenant Gaffney and two other wounded men. It is the custom of the corps of Royal Engineers to disregard all danger in the performance of their duty, and Sapper Officers have many splendid achievements to their credit. But no sapper officer can ever have shown greater courage and self-sacrifice than Lieutenant Waller did on this occasion. His action was worthy of the best traditions of his Corps.

The post captured turned out to be the end of a Turkish communication trench leading down to the south-east end of the ridge. It was blocked with sand-bags, and the portion nearest the Munsters' trench retained as an advanced post. The garrison holding this were somewhat surprised when later in the afternoon an enormous Turk came wandering up the trench alone with an armful of bombs, but he was promptly made prisoner by Lieutenant J. L. Fashom, of the Munsters, who disputed with Lieutenant Burke, of the Connaught Rangers, the claim to be the smallest officer in the 10th Division.

Incidents like this enlivened the general monotony, but on the whole the time spent in these trenches was a dreary, thirsty one, and all ranks were pleased when it became evident that the remainder of the Division was beginning to rejoin them, and that there was some prospect of an advance.

CHAPTER VI

" If you can force your heart and nerve and sinew
To serve your turn long after they are gone,
And so hold on when there is nothing in you,
Except the will that says to them ' Hold on.' "
—*Kipling.*

BEFORE dealing with the battle of Kiretch Tepe Sirt, it is necessary to give some account of the doings of General Hill's force after the capture of Chocolate Hill on the 7th. Dawn on the 8th found them bivouacking on the position they had taken on the previous evening and during the day, a defensive trench system, including both Chocolate Hill and Green Hill (Hill 50), 500 yards to the eastward of it. By this time the line taken up by our troops ran from the sea at Beach " B " to the two hills held by the 31st Brigade and thence northward across the Anafarta Plain at an average distance of three miles from the sea.

Throughout the 8th no advance was made from this line, since the Corps Commander was of opinion that the troops were very exhausted, and that there was insufficient artillery support at his disposal to justify him in making an attack on an enemy of unknown strength possessing the advantages of a superior position and knowledge of the ground. Unquestionably there was a considerable amount to be said in favour of this contention. On the previous day the enemy's barrage fire had taken a heavy toll of casualties, and but little effective reply had been made to it. This was in part due to difficulties of observation, but also to the fact that up to the 8th, only three batteries had been landed, two of which, being mountain batteries, possessed only guns of small calibre. There were also the guns of the ships, but it was not always easy to communicate with the fleet in time to achieve the desired object, and it must also be borne in mind that space in a warship is limited, and that once its magazine is empty it cannot quickly be replenished. Added to these considerations the fact that the men were suffering terribly from want of water, that no transport of any kind was available, and that in consequence every unit found itself compelled to detach about a quarter of its men for the purpose of carrying up rations and ammunition, made it not unnatural for a commander to exercise caution.

On the whole, the 8th was a quiet day for the troops, though the sun shone as fiercely as ever and there was plenty of work to be done in burying the dead and getting up supplies. There was not much shelling, but hostile snipers were ubiquitous and much in evidence. These crawled up through the scrub or climbed trees in such manner that they commanded the greater part of our line, and made it dangerous to move about.

On Monday, the 9th, the Corps Commander had decided to attack the high ground behind Anafarta Saghir with the 11th Division and part of the newly-landed 53rd (Territorial) Division. For the purpose of this attack, General Hill was ordered to place two battalions under the orders of the General Officer Commanding the 32nd Brigade (11th Division). The 6th Royal Irish Fusiliers and the 6th Royal Dublin Fusiliers, neither of which had sustained very heavy losses in the previous fighting, were detailed for this duty and co-operated in the attack. The objective allotted to them was a height known as Hill 70, the culminating ridge of a spur which ran out to the north-east of Chocolate Hill between the hill and Anafarta Saghir about a mile and a half south-west of that village.

As soon as the advance began, it became evident, both from the increase in the volume of musketry and from the growing intensity of the hostile artillery fire, that the Turks had been heavily reinforced, but in spite of their losses, the Fusiliers effected a lodgment on the ridge. For a time they clung to it though the enemy were delivering repeated counter-attacks, and a series of bush fires caused by their shells made the position almost untenable. and threatened the wounded with the most terrible of deaths. Further to the left, however, the 32nd Brigade found that they were unable to hold the ground that they had won in their first advance, and were compelled by attacks on their flanks to withdraw to their original alignment.

The Fusiliers, who had suffered heavily under the violent Turkish attacks, conformed to their movements and returned to their first position. Captain Johnston, the Adjutant of the 6th Royal Irish Fusiliers, was killed and so was Lieutenant MacDermot of the same regiment, which also lost eight officers wounded: the Dublins also lost heavily. In the course of this action, a curious incident is said to have occurred. The Medical Officer of the 6th Dublins had followed his battalion in its forward movement, and had established his advanced dressing station under a tree in the newly-captured territory. After a time he noticed that several of the wounded, who were brought back by the stretcher bearers, were hit a second time as they lay waiting to have their wounds attended to. A search was made for snipers in the surrounding bushes without result, but eventually a Turk was discovered perched in the tree itself.

While these operations were in progress, the remainder of General Hill's force had been employed in support. While fulfilling this rôle, they suffered both from the ubiquitous snipers and from the enemy's shrapnel fire, which had become far heavier than it was two days earlier. The casualties, however, were not very heavy, except in the two attacking battalions. Another sphere of usefulness was also found for portions of the supporting units.

The prolonged fire fight waged by the 11th Division had exhausted their ammunition, and officers and men from General Hill's force were detailed to carry up fresh supplies. It is not particularly pleasant work, carrying up thousands of rounds of ball cartridge in a tropical country through bushes infested with snipers, but the men did it splendidly. Lieutenant J. F. Hunter, of the 6th Inniskilling Fusiliers, was afterwards awarded the Military Cross for the courage and disregard of danger exhibited by him on this occasion. Often, too, the ammunition carriers when they had delivered their loads attached themselves to the nearest unit and joined the firing line. Captain Tobin and a party of the 7th Dublins fought side by side with an English regiment in this manner throughout the day. There was little wrong with the *morale* of the troops when men voluntarily thrust themselves into the positions of greatest danger.

On the following day, August 10th, the day on which the struggle on Sari Bair reached its height, another unsuccessful attack was made on the Anafarta ridge, but in this General Hill's force took no part. They were now, and for the rest of the week occupied in holding the line that they had captured on the 7th through Green Hill. This position was heavily shelled by the enemy and some units lost heavily.

Throughout this period, however, the troops suffered most for want of water. Though by this time a certain number of petrol cans and other receptacles for carrying water had been obtained yet these were quite insufficient to satisfy the men's consuming thirst. It is hard to find words to convey the true state of affairs. No doubt it would be too much to say that at home thirst is unknown, but at any rate the passionate craving for water felt in Gallipoli is seldom experienced. When the water came up, the most careful supervision was needed in order to see that the much-needed liquid was used to fill the water-bottles and not consumed at once. When the bottles were filled, or rather had received their share, since there was not water enough to fill them, it was necessary to watch them vigilantly in order to make the supply last as long as possible.

Some men became hardly responsible for their actions ; the heat was intense, the biscuit was dry and the bully beef very salt, while many men were suffering from dysentery or enteritis and were parched with fever though they were unwilling to report sick in the face of the enemy. In such times surface civilization vanishes, and man becomes a primitive savage. A few men crept away to look for water by themselves, others stole bottles from their neighbours and emptied them, but on the whole the discipline of the force stood the strain remarkably well. It was a severe trial for young unacclimatized soldiers who had less than a year's service, but the months of training had not been in vain. The men knew and trusted their officers, and felt that they would do their best for them. Perhaps the officer's position was hardest of all. Thirsty himself, rationing himself by spoonfuls in order to make the contents of his water-bottle last longer, he was compelled to watch his men suffering from pangs which he could not relieve, and at the same time to try and keep their spirits up by laughing and joking with them. There had always been friendship between the officers and men of the 10th Division, but a bond not easily to be broken was cemented in those scorching suffering days.

By this time it had become evident to the Higher Command that no further progress could be made at Suvla without reinforcements, and steps were taken to obtain them from Egypt and from the Cape Helles area. In the

THE 7TH DUBLINS IN THE TRENCHES AT CHOCOLATE HILL.
(From a water colour by Captain Drummond Fish, Royal Irish Rifles)

meanwhile it was decided that the 10th Division should be reunited, and accordingly, one by one, the battalions of General Hill's force were relieved from their posts on Chocolate Hill and Green Hill and marched down to the beach to rest.

The battalions as they tramped back to the shore again were very different in appearance from those that had marched up from it less than a week before. Officers and men alike were dirty and unshaven, for water had been precious, and the sweat dried on the face, and the five days' growth of stubble told plainly of the hardships they had been through. Even more clearly did the eyes tell it, and the worn cheeks and leanness of limb. Clothes and boots had not been taken off since landing, and both were soiled with sweat and blood. There were many gaps in the ranks : death, wounds and sickness had taken their toll, and nearly every man had to mourn for a lost comrade, yet for all the sorrow and the weariness there was something in the men's bearing that was not there before. When they landed they were full of high hopes and eager to justify splendid traditions, but they were untried. Now they had proved themselves, and faced the future filled with confidence gained from their own deeds. The move began on the 10th and was completed when the 7th Dublins marched down on the 13th.

On the beach, though the comfort of the rest-camp was nothing to boast of, men were at least able to wash and shave, though the amount of fresh water available for this purpose was limited, and the man who got a mugful was lucky. Even so, most hurried to remove the long stubble that covered their chins, for a five days' old beard is not only unsightly, but uncomfortable, pricking and tickling the skin at every movement, and harbouring any quantity of dust and sand. Fortunately too, though fresh water was scarce, the sea was at hand, and it was possible to bathe. Some poet should sing of the delight of bathing in Gallipoli. Not even Mr. Masefield has done it justice. In the water one could for the first time be cool and free from care, though not from danger. By day the water sparkled in the sunshine: at night the form of the swimmer was outlined in phosphorescence and great bubbles of glowing light broke round him as he moved, and by day and night alike the bather could free himself from the burden of responsibility which weighed him down on shore. As Antaeus renewed his strength whenever he touched the earth, so the Island people gained fresh stores of endurance from a dip in the sea. In the water, too, all men were equal, and rank could be laid aside.

After resting for a day or so on the beach, and receiving the first reinforcement which had just arrived from Mudros, the 10th Division (less

29th Brigade) concentrated on the Kiretch Tepe Sirt, General Hill's force once more coming under the command of Divisional Headquarters. As General Birdwood had reported that Anzac was not yet in a position to co-operate in an attack on Ismail Oglu Tepe, it was decided to occupy the Turks by attacking along the crest of the Kiretch Tepe Sirt, and thus rendering it impossible for them to bring an enfilade fire to bear against our operations on the Anafarta plain. This attack was to be made on August 15th, and the 10th Division was ordered to undertake it. They were to be assisted on their left by the guns of two destroyers in the Gulf of Saros, and on their right by the 162nd Brigade of the 54th Territorial Division. Artillery support was also, of course, arranged for. The task before the Division was one of considerable difficulty since the enemy occupied a strongly entrenched position, and was known to have received large reinforcements. However, waiting would only make him stronger, and everyone was pleased at the prospect of action.

The 15th of August was not only a Sunday, but also the day known in Ireland as " Lady Day in Harvest," a great Church festival, and the chaplains had endeavoured to arrange services for their battalions. These had to be hurried through or attended only by the few who could be spared, but nevertheless Canon McLean was able to adminster Holy Communion

M

to some of the officers and men of the Dublins, and Father Murphy visited each battalion of the 30th Brigade and gave the men absolution. Then at peace with God they turned their faces again towards the enemy.

The dispositions adopted for the attack were as follows : The 30th Brigade (Dublins and Munsters) were to form the left wing of the advance, with the extreme left of the 7th Munsters resting on the Gulf of Saros. They thus covered the whole of the northern and part of the southern slope of the Kiretch Tepe Sirt. To their right two battalions of the 31st Brigade were to advance through the southern foothills of the Kiretch Tepe Sirt and across the open plain to attack a spur known as Kidney Hill, which jutted out southward from the main chain of the ridge. The 5th and 6th Royal Irish Fusiliers and the 7th Royal Dublin Fusiliers were in reserve.

Soon after noon the attack commenced, and it was at once evident that the Turks were holding their position in strength, the volume of fire which they were bringing to bear on our men being infinitely greater than that which had greeted us at the first landing. A captured Turkish officer afterwards declared that they had in their firing line six fresh battalions, each possessing twelve machine-guns. The rattle of these seventy-two guns was painfully prominent, and made it clear that the advance would be a costly one. The actual crest of the hill was a bare rocky ridge covered with great scattered boulders running for about a mile-and-a-half at a height of six hundred feet above sea level. Part of the ridge rose about fifty feet higher than this, and from this central portion three small eminences stood out. The central one of these was known as the " Pimple," and was marked by a cairn of stones.

The Division had gained a footing on the western end of the ridge on August 8th by capturing the position afterwards known as Jephson's Post, and now the Turkish trenches ran across the hill between that point and the " Pimple." On the northern face the slope fell steeply away from the crest, so steeply as to be almost precipitous until it reached a height of three hundred feet above sea-level. from which contour the descent to the sea was more gradual though the ground was intersected by numerous gullies. On the southern face the hill also fell away rapidly for about three hundred feet, after which the descent became more easy, and various knolls and foot-hills detached themselves from the main range. Both slopes of the hill were covered with thick dry scrub, which had in a few places been set on fire either by matches or shells, and consequently had become blackened. This prickly scrub was a great impediment to movement of any kind and rendered all operations painfully slow.

For more than two hours after the commencement of the action, but little ground was gained. The enemy's rifle and machine-gun fire was well sustained, and efficiently supported by artillery, and it was considered rash to advance until a fire fight had done somewhat to silence the Turks. During this stage of the action, Major Jephson, of the 6th Munsters, was mortally wounded on the peak that, a week earlier, had received his name, and several other casualties occurred among officers and men. At last, General Nicol, seeing that the Turkish fire showed no signs of slackening, and that darkness would soon make further operations impossible, directed that an attempt to advance should be made along the northern slope of the ridge. The order was at once complied with. Two companies of the 6th Munsters and two of the 6th Dublins pressed forward accordingly, and succeeded, thanks to a piece of dead ground, in traversing about half of the five hundred yards that lay between Jephson's Post and the Turkish line of defence.

There for a while they rested, and then about 6 p.m. with the setting sun at their backs they charged the Turkish positions. Crags and scrub and cliff were as nothing to them, nor did they regard the hostile fire but rushed on with gleaming bayonets in the force of an irresistible attack. Few of the Turks stayed to meet them, and those that did were in no mood to receive the charge, but held up their hands and surrendered. Then as the Dublins and Munsters, Major Tynte of the 6th Munsters at their head, gained the enemy's position, they gave a rousing cheer. It was taken up by the troops in support and by all who watched the magnificent charge until from the Gulf of Saros to the Salt Lake the air resounded with the shouts of victory. There had not been much cause for cheering at Suvla, and the sight of the dashing attack and the sound of the Irish triumph cry, thrilled the hearts of many who had previously been despondent, and awakened hope once more in their breasts. Most surprising of all was its effect on the Turks. They had been heavily bombarded by the destroyers, they had seen a position that they believed impregnable taken with the bayonet, and now with the magic of the cries of the infidels ringing in their ears, they abandoned their trenches and retired in haste.

The Dublins and Munsters pursued and drove them before them until the whole of the northern slope of the Kiretch Tepe Sirt as far as and even beyond the " Pimple " was cleared. The men were disappointed that more of the enemy did not stay to face them. One soldier was heard to cry to a stout Turk who fled before him : " I don't want to stick ye behind. Turn round now and I'll stick ye in the belly dacent." Then, as night was falling and nearly a mile of ground had been gained, a halt was called so that the captured position might be consolidated.

On the right, meanwhile, the attack had unfortunately been less successful. The main attack on Kidney Hill had been entrusted to the 5th Inniskilling Fusiliers, who, owing to the fact that they had not disembarked till evening of the 7th, had sustained fewer casualties than the rest of the Division ; it was to be supported by the 6th Battalion of the same regiment. The Inniskillings had probably the most difficult task of any unit before them.

On the seaward side of the Kiretch Tepe Sirt the guns of the destroyers were of tremendous assistance to the attack, but they were unable to fire over the ridge. The remainder of our artillery, especially the mountain batteries, did their best to keep down the enemy's fire, but they were shooting at a venture since the exact position of the enemy's trenches was not accurately known. In consequence of this comparatively little had been done to prevent the Turks on Kidney Hill from bringing their full rifle and machine-gun fire to bear on our advance. The nature of the ground, too, lent little help to the attackers. Though the scrub was thick and prickly enough to break up the advancing lines into small groups, and to render it impossible for an officer to influence any more than the four or five men who happened to be in sight of him, yet on the plain it grew in scattered clumps. Between these clumps were patches of sand or withered grass, on which the enemy were able to concentrate their rifle and machine-gun fire. Added to this, the fact that from the surrounding hills the Turkish gunners could see every detail of the advance over the plain (khaki drill shows up clearly in the Gallipoli scrub) and could spray it with shrapnel and high explosive, made the operation three times as difficult. Nor was there any distraction elsewhere in the Suvla area. The hostile artillery was able to concentrate its whole force on the Inniskillings.

At noon the battalion began its advance, " A " and " D " Companies leading. There lay before them a gradual ascent dotted with scrub for about two hundred yards, and then half-a-mile of flat ground, from which Kidney Hill rose abruptly.

The Turkish trenches were invisible and consequently there was little attempt to subdue the enemy by a fire fight. The platoons went straight forward, racing over the exposed patches, losing officers and men at every step. The fire grew hotter and hotter and men fell more and more quickly, but still the front line pressed only to be swept out of existence. The distance was too far to cover in a single rush, and no troops in the world could cross the five hundred yards in front of the enemy's trenches at a walk and live. The supports came up and another attempt was made, but again the lines melted away. The task was one impossible of achievement, for it is now known that against modern weapons in the hands of an undemoralised enemy, a frontal attack by daylight on an entrenched position a thousand yards away is certain to fail. Yet even when they had failed, the 5th Inniskillings did not fall back. Nearly all the officers were down, but little groups of men still clustered in the bushes waiting for orders. They could not advance ; they would not retire until they were told to. Lieutenant G. B. Lyndon, of the 6th Inniskillings, went out after sunset and collected many of these little parties and brought them in. For this he received the Military Cross. Invaluable service, too, was done by the stretcher-bearers of the battalions and field ambulances, who here, as everywhere, showed themselves fearless and tireless in the performance of their duties.

The casualty list was a terribly heavy one. Colonel Vanrenen, of the 5th Inniskillings, was killed, and so were Captain Robinson, Captain Vernon, Lieutenant McCormack, Lieutenant Nelis, and Lieutenant Grubb of the same unit. Both its Majors were wounded, together with two captains and nearly a dozen subalterns. The losses among the rank and file were in

THE ANAVARTA PLAIN

(From a water colour by Captain Drummond Fish, Royal Irish Rifles)

proportion, and the whole organisation of the regiment was temporarily shattered. The 6th Inniskillings, who were in support, had been heavily shelled, but had been lucky in escaping severe loss.

The result of the failure of the right attack was that while we held the northern slope of the Kiretch Tepe Sirt up to and even beyond the Pimple, yet on the Southern face of the hill we had been unable to advance our line much beyond the trenches which we held when operations on the 15th began. As a consequence, the line held by the Division somewhat resembled a Z. The upper horizontal was represented by a line of trench running from the Gulf of Saros to the most advanced point on the crest of the ridge that was reached by the charge of the 6th Munsters and 6th Dublins. This trench was exposed to fire not only from the hills which continued the line of the Kiretch Tepe Sirt eastward, but also from a spur known as 103, which ran northwards into the sea. The diagonal joining the two horizontals of the Z was represented by a line running along the northern or seaward slope of Kiretch Tepe Sirt just below the crest. The crest itself, since it was liable to be swept by shrapnel and machine-gun fire, and since its rocky nature made it difficult to entrench, was not held except at the lower horizontal, which represented the trench running past Jephson's

Post, from which the attack had begun. The position thus created was clearly far harder to hold than if it had been merely a trench running across the ridge from North to South, and would obviously require far more men. The two battalions from the Reserve were, therefore, called up without delay.

The 7th Dublins had begun to move forward already, and were advancing under circumstances of some difficulty. The enemy's artillery were shelling the line behind our position with considerable vigour, and in addition snipers were more than usually active. One of these pests, who was ensconced in a bush, succeeded in shooting Colonel Downing in the foot, and though the Colonel promptly retaliated with his revolver, and insisted that the wound was trivial, he found himself unable to walk and was compelled to leave his beloved battalion. Major Harrison took over command of the Unit.

After the reserves came up, the dispositions made for the defence of the line running just below the crest of the Kiretch Tepe Sirt were as follows :—The extreme end to the eastward was held by the 6th Royal Irish Fusiliers ; next to them came the 6th Munsters, and beyond them " D," " A " and " C " Companies of the 7th Dublins. " B " Company of the last-named regiment had been sent down the hill on the seaward side to dig a trench covering

Hill 103. The 6th Dublins, who had sustained heavy losses in the charge, were withdrawn to rest. These dispositions were adopted just before nightfall. The soil of the ridge was too stony to admit of much entrenching, and in most cases the men lay down on their arms just behind the crest on the seaward side, though in one or two spots stone *sangars* were constructed. They were given but little time to work before they were attacked. The knowledge that no advance had been made on any part of the plain below made it possible for the enemy to employ a large proportion of his reserves in the recovery of the ground lost on the Kiretch Tepe Sirt, while the fact that the Southern slope of the hill was still in his possession enabled him to push men along it to attack any portion of our long, thinly-held line at close quarters.

The first of the hostile counter-attacks began about 10 p.m., when a wave of Turks who had crept along the landward slope and up to the crest in silence, burst over it with a yell and fell upon the British line. Fortunately, our men were not taken by surprise ; a roar of musketry at close range received the enemy, and when it came to bayonet work our *morale* proved more than sufficient to dispose of the foe. After a stiff fight, the attackers disappeared over the crest leaving a good proportion of their numbers behind them on the

ground. Listening posts were then sent out
to the further side of the ridge in order to
preclude the possibility of a surprise attack
succeeding, and the remainder of the tired men
lay down again, rifle in hand to secure as much
rest as possible.

Little sleep was allowed them. Before the
first light of the early summer dawn began to
appear in the sky, the listening posts were
driven in, and a fresh Turkish attack was made.
On this occasion the assault was led by bomb-
throwers, and although those who crossed the
crest and came to close quarters were disposed
of by the Irish with rifle and bayonet, yet a
considerable force of the enemy, well-furnished
with grenades, succeeded in establishing themselves on the southern slope of the Kiretch
Tepe Sirt. From this position they proceeded
to bomb the whole length of our line incessantly,
throwing the grenades over the crest of the
ridge so that they burst in the midst of our
ranks with deadly effect. Had the Fusiliers
been in possession of enough bombs they could
have retaliated in kind, but the few that they
had were quickly used, and no more were
forthcoming. Even if they had been, the con-
test would scarcely have been a fair one, since
the grenade employed by the Turks in Gallipoli
was infinitely superior to that issued to the
British. The latter was an extemporised production, consisting of a detonator inserted

in a jam tin and furnished with a fuse, which had to be lighted with a match.

The Turkish bomb, which was shaped like a cricket-ball, was both more accurately fused and easier to throw. However, could they have been obtained, the Dublins and Munsters and Irish Fusiliers would have been glad even of jam-tins, since they would have enabled them to make some reply to the enemy. Rifles and bayonets were useless against an invisible foe, on the other side of a rocky ridge. The two forces were, to use a homely comparison, in the position of men sitting in the gutters of a house and fighting across the roof. Under these circumstances grenades were obviously the most effective weapon, and the side that lacked them suffered from an appalling handicap.

As day broke, officers were able to take stock of the situation, though the sight that met their eyes was not encouraging. On every side men had fallen, and the strain on the survivors was appalling, for the rain of bombs still continued. Here and there individual officers organised attempts to drive the enemy back at the point of the bayonet, but without success. A description of one of these efforts will serve to make clear the fate with which they met. Major Harrison, of the 7th Dublins, finding that his line was becoming dangerously thin, determined to try the effect of a charge. He selected for this purpose a party of "D" Company,

"The Pals," under the command of Captain Poole Hickman.

The men were only too delighted at the prospect of action, and charged fearlessly up the hill. As they appeared on the crest, however, they were met by a storm of concentrated rifle and machine-gun fire. Captain Poole Hickman fell mortally wounded, but Major Harrison rushed forward bareheaded and took his place, leading his men on till they reached the Turkish line. There he was struck by a grenade thrown at close quarters, and of all the gallant spirits who had followed him so pluckily only four made their way back over the crest to their battalions. Similar charges made elsewhere met with similar results; in some cases a whole platoon disappeared and was never seen again. Among the officers who were lost in this way were Captain Grant, 6th Munsters, and Lieutenant Crichton, 7th Dublins. It was obvious that to cross the crest by daylight meant death, since the Turks had been able to instal machine-guns in positions that enfiladed it.

Since advance was impossible, the troops were compelled to remain on their position, exposed to a perpetual fire of grenades, to which they had no means of replying. The sun rose higher in the sky and reached the zenith and still the bombing went on without intermission, and the men of the 10th Division continued to suffer and endure. The faces of dead comrades, lying at their sides, stiffened and grew rigid, and the flies gathered in clouds to feast on their blood, while from the ridge in front came the groans of the wounded, whom it was impossible to succour. The men lying behind the crest knew that at any moment a similar fate might come to any of them, and they might fall a shattered corpse, or be carried back moaning, but still they held on. The unceasing noise of the bursting grenades, the smell of death, the sight of suffering, wore their nerves to tatters, but worst of all was the feeling that they were helpless, unable to strike a blow to ward off death and revenge their comrades.

It is by no means easy to realise what the men felt during this ordeal. Perhaps the strongest emotion was not the sense of duty, the prompting of pride, or even the fear of imminent death, but blind, helpless rage. In a charge or an advance a soldier rarely feels anger. His whole soul is concentrated on reaching a definite objective, and though he is prepared to kill anyone who stands in his way, he does so without passion. The exultation born from rapid movement, the thrill produced by the sense of achievement, banish all personal feelings. But lying on the ridge under the pitiless bombing, watching the mangled bodies of the dead, men had time to think, and the fruit of their thoughts and of their impotence was black and bitter hatred of the enemy. They were ready to run any risk in order to do something to hurt him.

Some tried to catch the Turkish bombs as they were falling and throw them back into the enemy's lines before they exploded. Five times Private Wilkin, of the 7th Dublins, performed this feat, but at the sixth attempt he was blown to pieces. Elsewhere men, sooner than lie impotent, took up stones and hurled them at the foe. Everywhere the few remaining officers moved about among their men, calming the over-eager, encouraging the weary, giving an example of calmness and leadership, of which the land that bore them may well be proud. In doing this they made themselves a mark for the inevitable snipers, who by now had ensconced themselves in coigns of vantage on the crest of the ridge, and many died there. Thus fell Capt. Tobin, of the 7th Dublins, a man greatly beloved. Here, too, fell Lieut. Fitzgibbon and Lieut. Weatherill, of the same regiment. Fitzgibbon, a son of the Nationalist M.P. for South Mayo, who, in the black days of Ireland's past had had many a dispute with the forces of the law, and had now sent his son to die gloriously in the King's uniform ; Weatherill, a boy who had made himself conspicuous in a very gallant battalion for courage. Here, too, many other heroic souls laid down their lives, but still the line held on.

The sun reached the west and began to sink ; the ranks were thin, the men were weary, and many mangled bodies lay along the fatal ridge. The 6th Royal Irish Fusiliers, exposed both in front and in flank, had been practically annihilated. Their 5th Battalion came up to reinforce them and shared their fate. Three officers of this regiment, Captains Panton and Kidd, and 2nd-Lieut. Heuston, earned the Military Cross by the inspiring example they gave on this occasion. The last-named was reported as " wounded and missing," and was probably killed in this fight. Nearly all the officers of the Irish Fusiliers had fallen, and the other regiments were in nearly as bad a case ; but still the line held on. Tired and hungry and thirsty as they were, unable to strike a blow in their own defence, yet still the men of the 10th Division were resolved not to retire a step until the order to do so came. They were but young soldiers, who had had less than a year's training, and had received their baptism of fire only a week earlier ; but they were determined that however stern the ordeal they would not disgrace their regiments.

In old days, in the thick of a hard-contested struggle, men rallied round the colours—the visible symbol of the regimental honour. There were no colours to rally round on the slope of

N

the Kiretch Tepe Sirt, but the regimental name
was a talisman that held the battered ranks
to their ground.   Their regiments had in the
past won great glory, but neither the men of
the 87th who cleared the pine woods of Barrosa
with the cry of " Faugh a Ballagh ! " nor the
Dublins and Munsters who leapt from the bows
of the " River Clyde " into certain death, need
blush to own comradeship with their newly-
raised Service Battalions, who died on the
Kiretch Tepe Sirt.

Darkness at last fell, and the sorely-tried
men hoped for relief.   This was indeed at hand,
though it did not take the form of fresh troops.
None were available, so the units of the division
who had suffered heavily in the charge of the
previous day, and who had had less than
twenty-four hours' rest, were called up again.
The 6th Dublins, and with them the 5th Royal
Irish (Pioneers), took over the line of the ridge
from the battalions who had held it so stoutly.
Nor were their sufferings less, for throughout
the night the bombing continued, and our men
were still unable to make any effective retaliation.   Many officers and men fell, but the remainder set their teeth and held their ground,
until at last they received the order to withdraw
from the untenable position. Not a man
moved until he received the order, and then
slowly, deliberately, almost reluctantly, they
retired. Bullets fell thickly among them, and

took a heavy toll, one of those killed being 2nd-Lieut. W. Nesbitt, a young officer of the 6th Dublins, who, though junior in rank, had made a tremendous impression by his character, and had earned the name of "the Soul of the Battalion." Before he was hit, the 6th Dublins had had Major Preston and their Adjutant, Capt. Richards, killed, and in the course of these operations three subalterns, 2nd-Lieut. Clery, 2nd-Lieut. Stanton, and 2nd-Lieut. McGarry, were reported missing. Probably they died in some unseen struggle, and their bones now lie in a nameless, but honoured grave on the field where their regiment won such fame.

Gradually the shattered units withdrew to their original line, but when the roll was called there were many names unanswered. The charge on the 15th had cost many lives, the holding of the captured position very many more, and yet all the effort and all the suffering seemed to have been futile. The 10th Division had been shattered, the work of a year had been destroyed in a week, and nothing material had been gained. Yet all was not in vain. It is no new thing for the sons of Ireland to perish in a forlorn hope and a fruitless struggle ; they go forth to battle only to fall, yet there springs from their graves a glorious memory for the example of future generations. Kiretch Tepe Sirt was a little-known fight in an unlucky campaign, but if the young soldiers of the 10th Division who died there added a single leaf to Ireland's crown of cypress and laurel, their death was not in vain.

CHAPTER VII

KABA KUYU AND HILL 60

" Oh, bad the march, the weary march, beneath these alien skies,
But good the night, the friendly night, that soothes our tired eyes ;
And bad the war, the weary war, that keeps us waiting here,
But good the hour, the friendly hour, that brings the battle near."
—*Emily Lawless.*

AFTER the close of the battle of Sari Bair, the 29th Brigade of the 10th Division was in urgent need of re-organisation. The Brigade Staff had ceased to exist, and the Hampshires and Rifles were in almost as bad a case, since almost every officer was killed or wounded. The Leinsters, though they had sustained serious losses, had still a fair number of senior officers left, and the Connaught Rangers had suffered less severely, having up to the 11th only lost five officers. The latter unit was therefore retained in the front line, while the other battalions were withdrawn to refit.

Throughout the 11th the Rangers held the line, which had been entrenched by two of their companies on the 10th, between the foot of Rhododendron Ridge and the north-eastern extremity of the Damakjelik Bair. This line, based on two natural ravines, was a strong one, but General Cayley considered that it was too far in rear, and accordingly after sunset on the 11th the Battalion advanced to an underfeature at the foot of the Chunuk Bair, and commenced to dig in there.   The advance was by no means an easy one, since it had been impossible to make a detailed reconnaissance of the ground over which it had to take place, as by day it was exposed to the enemy's fire from the Chunuk. In consequence of this the left flank unexpectedly found themselves descending a slope so steep that it was almost a precipice.   Fortunately, there were bushes at the bottom to break the fall of those whose feet slipped, and if the bushes happened to be prickly ones, well, it was no good complaining about trifles in Gallipoli.

The position when reached was not an ideal one.   Though protected to a certain extent from bullets from the Chunuk, it did not afford a very good field of fire, and lack of shelter from the sun, shortage of water, and the smell proceeding from a gully full of corpses, combined to make the position of those holding it unpleasant.   The greatest disadvantage, however, was the fact that the only avenue of approach to the trench line was the Aghyl Dere, which was swept by a hostile machine-gun.   Supplies and ammunition had to be carried up under cover of darkness, and everyone who went up or down by daylight was obliged to run the gauntlet for about three hundred yards. Several casualties were caused while doing this, among the sufferers being the senior Captain of the Rangers, Captain Hog, who received the wound from which he died in this manner. He was a man of forty-five years of age, who had served in the 1st Battalion of the Rangers in South Africa, and had rejoined from the Reserve of Officers at the beginning of the war. Though double the age of some of his comrades, he had set them a magnificent example by the way in which he accepted hardships, and the loyalty with which he submitted to the commands of men younger than himself.

The hardships were by this time considerable, since officers and men alike were reduced to bully beef and biscuits. It had been impossible to bring any mess stores to the Peninsula, and though each officer had stuffed a tin of sardines, or some potted meat into his haversack, these did not last long, and the rather reduced ration of a tin of bully beef and four biscuits *per diem* was all that was obtainable by anyone. Cooking was practically impossible, though occasionally one got a cup of tea, and men ate at odd moments, seldom sitting down to a regular meal. It was noticeable that on the whole the single men stood this discomfort better than those who were married. In part, no doubt, this was due to the fact that they were younger, but some of the oldest men proved to be the toughest. One old sergeant, who had marched to Kandahar with Lord Roberts in 1879, went through the whole Gallipoli campaign with the Division, and also through the operations in Serbia in December without once going sick. The married men were more used to being looked after, to having their comfort considered, and to decent cooking, and to regular meals, and the semi-barbaric existence upset them. Those who stood it best were the tinkers, members of that strange nomad tribe who in Ireland take the place of the English gipsies. It was no new thing for them to eat sparingly, and sleep under the stars, and their previous life made it easy for them to adapt themselves to circumstances.

For three days the Rangers held this position, and during this period the re-organisation of the Brigade proceeded. The only Battalion Commander left unhurt was Lieutenant-Colonel Jourdain, of the Connaught Rangers, who took over command as a temporary measure, but on the 13th he was succeeded by Lieutenant-Colonel G. K. Agnew, M.V.O., D.S.O., Royal Scots Fusiliers. Captain R. V. Pollok, 15th Hussars, was appointed Brigade Major, and on August 20th, Captain R. J. H. Shaw, 5th Connaught Rangers, took up the post of Staff Captain. The officers and men of the first reinforcement who had been left at Mudros rejoined their units on the 11th, and were very welcome. In two cases officers arriving with this draft found themselves in command of their battalions, since Major Morley, of the Hampshires, and Captain R. de R. Rose, of the Rifles, were senior to any of the few surviving officers of their units. The task before them was by no means a light one, for the whole company organisation had been destroyed, and nearly all the officers and senior N.C.O.'s were *hors de combat.* However, they buckled to it with a will, and every suitable man received temporary promotion.

On August 13th, the Connaught Rangers were withdrawn from the line they were holding and given four days' rest, which was, of course, broken by numerous demands for fatigues. It is the universal experience of soldiers that in this war one never works so hard as when one is supposed to be resting. On the 17th they relieved the 6th South Lancashire and 6th East Lancashire Regiments in trenches, which they held for three days, and considerably strengthened. On the 20th they were withdrawn from these trenches, and ordered to hold themselves in readiness to join General Cox's Brigade and take part in an attack on the following day.

This attack had been planned in order to co-operate with the movements at Suvla. Reinforcements in the shape of the 29th Division from Cape Helles, and the 2nd Mounted Division (without their horses) from Egypt, had arrived there, and an attack on Ismail Oglu Tepe had been planned. This steep, thickly-wooded hill acted as buttress to Koja Chemen Tepe, and as it overlooked the whole of the Suvla Plain, afforded a valuable observation post to the enemy's artillery. With it in our hands we should not only be able to interrupt communication between the two Anafartas, but would have gained a valuable *point d'appui* for any further attack.

Communication between the Anzac and Suvla forces had been obtained on the 13th at Susuk Kuyu, north of the Asmak Dere, but it hung by a narrow thread. It was therefore decided that simultaneously with the attack on Ismail Oglu Tepe, General Birdwood should attack the Turkish trenches north of him, and endeavour to win enough ground to safeguard inter-communication. The execution of this operation was entrusted to Major-General Cox, who was allotted the whole of his own Indian Brigade, two battalions of New Zealand Mounted Rifles, the 4th South Wales Borderers from the 11th Division, and the 5th Connaught Rangers and 10th Hampshires from the 29th Brigade. All these units had suffered heavily in the fighting a fortnight before, and the Indian Brigade in particular was terribly handicapped by the fact that it had lost almost all its British officers.

THE ANAFARTA PLAIN FROM THE SOUTH
(From a water-colour by Captain Drummond Fish, Royal Irish Rifles)

The objective of this attack was contained in the salient enclosed by the sea on the west, and the Damakjelik Bair on the south. A thin line of outposts close to the sea connected Anzac and Suvla, but the low ground which they held was commanded by a hill known as Kaiajik Aghala, or Hill 60. At the point where this eminence began to rise in a gentle slope from the plain, about four hundred yards north of the Damakjelik, stood two wells called Kaba Kuyu. These wells were extremely valuable to the Turks, since they, too, were short of water, and it was against them that the first stages of the attack were to be directed. There was, indeed, no object for which any man in the rank and file would more willingly fight in Gallipoli in August than a well. At the same time the wells, which the Turks were known to have entrenched, were not the sole objective. The capture of Hill 60 was extremely desirable, since not only did it menace inter-communication between Suvla and Anzac, but with it in our hands we should be in a position to enfilade a considerable portion of the Turkish forces, which were opposing the attack from Suvla. General Cox disposed of his forces as follows. On the extreme left the 5th Ghurkas were to sweep across the low ground near the sea and get in touch with the right flank of the Suvla force. In the centre, the 5th Connaught Rangers were to deploy in a gully of the Damakjelik Bair, known as South Wales Borderers' Gully, and charge across three hundred yards of open ground to capture the wells. On the right, the two battalions of New Zealanders, under Brigadier-General Russell, forming up behind the trenches on Damakjelik Bair were to make an attack on Hill 60 direct. Still further to the right a feint attack, intended to draw off the Turkish reserves, was to be executed by the 10th Hampshire Regiment. The remainder of the force was in reserve.

The Connaught Rangers reached South Wales Borderers' Gully after dark on the 20th and bivouacked there for the night. As the attack was not to be launched till 3 p.m. on the 21st, they had a long wait before them, but there was plenty to be done. Officers spent the morning in visiting the trenches held by the South Wales Borderers on Damakjelik Bair and inspecting their objective through a periscope, for the enemy snipers were too active to permit of any direct observation. The Turks had constructed a trench in front of the wells to guard them, which was connected with their main position by a communication trench improvised from a deep water course which ran eastward. To the northward a sunken road led from the wells in the direction of Anafarta. No barbed wire appeared to have been erected, but it was obvious that the crest of Hill 60 was strongly entrenched and held.

After this reconnaissance, orders were issued for the attack, and while they were being prepared, officers and men alike were receiving the consolations of religion. For the Church of England men, the Rev. J. W. Crozier celebrated Holy Communion ; and Father O'Connor gave absolution to his flock. The bullets of snipers were whistling overhead, and ploughed furrows through the ground as the men knelt in prayer and listened to the message of peace and comfort delivered by the tall khaki-clad figure. In a few hours they were to plunge into a hand-to-hand struggle with the old enemy of Christendom, and their pulses throbbed with the spirit of Tancred and Godfrey de Bouillon, as they fitted themselves to take their places in the last of the Crusades.

Nor was encouragement from their Generals lacking. Two hours before the advance was due to begin, Major-General Godley visited the gully and addressed as many of the men as could be collected. His speech was not a long one, but he told them what he expected them to do. One regiment had already failed to capture the wells ; now the Rangers were to do it with the cold steel. The men were not permitted to cheer, but their faces showed their feelings. General Godley, himself an Irishman, showed an intimate knowledge of the Irish character by delivering this address. The knowledge that the credit of their regiment was at stake and that the eyes of their leaders were on them, was sufficient to nerve every man to do his utmost. As a matter of fact, the spirit of the men was excellent ; though dysentery and enteric were raging not a man reported sick that morning for fear of missing the fight.

At 2 p.m. the men paraded and worked slowly forward to the old Turkish trench running across the mouth of the gully from which the attack was to be launched. There was only sufficient frontage for a platoon at a time to extend, so the advance was to be made by successive waves of platoons, " C " Company leading, followed by " D," whilst " A " and " B " Companies were kept in support. Though every precaution was taken to avoid making dust and so attracting the attention of the Turks, yet bullets were continually falling among the men, and two officers were wounded before the hour to advance arrived. This was prefaced by a violent bombardment of the enemy's position, conducted not only by the batteries at Anzac, but also by the monitors in the Gulf of Saros, which were in a position that enabled them to enfilade the enemy's line. The noise and dust were terrific, but most of the Turks were well under cover and did not suffer seriously.

Meanwhile, the men waited. A hundred years earlier an officer of the Connaught

Rangers had described the appearance and feeling of his battalion as they stood awaiting the signal that was to call them to the assault of the great breach of Ciudad Rodrigo, and his description might have been fitted to their descendants in Gallipoli. Here and there a man murmured a prayer or put up a hand to grasp his rosary, but for the most part they waited silent and motionless till the order to advance was given. At last, at 3.40, the bombardment ceased, the word came, and the leading platoon dashed forward with a yell like hounds breaking covert. They were met with a roar of rifle fire, coming not only from the trench attacked, but also from Hill 60, and from snipers concealed in the scattered bushes. Not a man stopped to return it ; all dashed on with levelled bayonets across the four hundred yards of open country, each man striving to be the first into the enemy's trench. That honour fell to the platoon commander, Second-Lieutenant T. W. G. Johnson, who had gained Amateur International Colours for Ireland at Association Football, and was a bad man to beat across country. Rifle and bayonet in hand, he made such good use of his lead that before his platoon caught him up he had bayoneted six Turks and shot two more. For these and other gallant deeds he was awarded the Military Cross.

The Turks stood their ground well, but succumbed to superior numbers, for soon the supporting platoons came up, while "D" Company moving more to the left was prolonging the line in that direction. The whole of the trenches guarding the wells, together with the wells themselves, were now in the hands of the Rangers, while the communication trench leading to Hill 60 was cleared and blocked, and the two companies in support were moved forward.

Meanwhile the New Zealanders' attack on Hill 60 was not making quite such satisfactory progress. The hill was both fortified with care and held in strength by the enemy, and though General Russell had succeeded in making a lodgment at its foot, he was unable to get further. The Rangers had been ordered, after seizing the wells, to do their utmost to assist his attack, and accordingly "A" Company was detailed to advance and attack the western slopes of the hill. By this time companies had become very mixed, and the charge was composed of a crowd of men belonging to all the companies, mad with the lust for battle. Their officers did little to restrain them, for their Irish blood was aflame, and they were as eager as the men. The line surged up the bare exposed glacis, only to encounter tremendously heavy rifle and machine-gun fire from the crest. At the same moment the enemy's guns opened, displaying marvellous accuracy in ranging, and the attack was annihilated.

In spite of this the men went on as long as they were able to stand, and fell still facing the foe. From the wells below their bodies could be seen, lying in ordered ranks on the hillside, with their bayonets pointing to the front.

It was clear that further advance was impossible, and it only remained for the survivors to consolidate the captured position, which was now being heavily shelled. At 5.15 p.m. the 5th Ghurkas, who had been unable to advance earlier in the afternoon, came up and took over the left flank, including the sunken road running towards Anafarta. The Rangers were then concentrated near the wells, which they protected by a sandbag barricade, while steps were taken to get in touch with General Russell's New Zealanders, who were digging themselves in at the foot of Hill 60, a little further to the east. A portion of the gap between them and the Rangers was bridged by the captured Turkish communication trench, and a sap to cover the remainder was begun at once.

Contrary to anticipation, the enemy did not launch a counter-attack to endeavour to recapture the wells, but their artillery was taking a heavy toll of the conquerors, and officers and men were falling fast. The Adjutant of the Rangers, Captain Maling, an officer to whose judgment and courage the

o

battalion owed an incalculable debt, was severely wounded here, and the Sergeant-Major, who had joined in the charge, had already been carried off with a wound in his leg. " D " Company had only one officer left, and its sergeant-major and quartermaster-sergeant had fallen, while " C " Company had had all its officers hit, two of them fatally. Nevertheless, the men worked hard to put their position in a good state of defence, and before nightfall their object was achieved. At 7 p.m. communication with the New Zealanders was obtained, and two platoons under Lieutenant Blake effected a junction with them.

All through the afternoon the devoted stretcher-bearers were transporting their burdens to the dressing-station in South Wales Borderers' Gully, where the doctor and the priest waited to render devoted service. The labour imposed upon them may be imagined from the fact that over a hundred and fifty cases passed through this dressing-station alone. Now, nightfall made it possible to get up supplies and ammunition. By this time the lesson of the battle of Sari Bair had been learnt, and everything had been carefully pre-arranged. The staff of the 29th Brigade were indefatigable in getting up food and water, and though the Brigade-Major, Captain Pollok, was wounded by a stray shot, his place was well filled by the Staff-Captain. By daylight the whole position was in a thoroughly defensible state, being well-stocked with food, water and ammunition.

During the night, however, the New Zealanders had had a bad time, and in this the two platoons of Connaught Rangers which had joined them shared. Their position at the foot of Hill 60 was near enough to the Turkish trenches at the top to enable the enemy to throw down bombs, and this they did all night. At intervals, too, they charged down with the bayonet in large numbers only to be repulsed. Heavy casualties were caused in this fight, and among the killed was Lieutenant Blake. His place was taken by Sergeant Nealon, an old soldier, who had taken his discharge long before the war and started business in Ballina. When war broke out he was among the first to re-enlist, and so inspiring was his example that Ballina disputes with Belfast the credit for having the largest number of recruits in proportion to population of any town in Ireland. No man ever looked less martial, but his stout, comfortable figure concealed the spirit of a hero. When his officer fell he took over the command, led back a mixed group of Rangers and New Zealanders to a sector of trench that had been adandoned owing to the violent bombing that it was suffering, and held it until he was relieved. Another N.C.O. of the Rangers who distinguished himself here was Sergeant John O'Connell, an Irish American, who went out under heavy fire to bring in a wounded New Zealander who was endeavouring to get back under cover. For this and for unvarying courage he was awarded the D.C.M.

On the morning of the 22nd, the newly-landed 18th Australian Battalion arrived on the scene, and attacked the crest of the hill, in company with the New Zealanders. For a time one trench was captured, but the captors were unable to maintain themselves in it, and were driven out by bombing. The Rangers did not take part in this attack, and on the evening of the 22nd were relieved, and returned to their bivouac in South Wales Borderers' Gully.

This engagement has been described in greater detail than its intrinsic importance perhaps deserves, because hitherto the capture of Kaba Kuyu Wells has not been officially attributed to an Irish regiment at all.

The Rangers had not to complain of any lack of immediate recognition, since on the day following their withdrawal Lieutenant-General Sir W. Birdwood, accompanied by Sir A. Godley and General Cox, visited their bivouac. He congratulated them on their gallantry, and promised them four days' rest, after which he intended to call on them for another attack. Sir A. Godley and General Cox were also warm in their congratulations.

Nor was the applause of their comrades lacking, since the Australians and New Zealanders were loud in their praises of the dash and courage of the battalion. This memory long continued with them. More than three months later, Mr. John Redmond, M.P., was showing a party of Australian convalescents over the House of Commons, and asked them if they had seen anything of the 10th (Irish) Division. They replied that they had, and in their opinion the charge made by the Connaught Rangers at Kaba Kuyu was the finest thing they had seen in the War. This praise was worth having, since no men on earth are better able to appreciate courage and are less prone to be imposed upon than the Australians. They have no use for paper reputations ; they judge only by what they have seen with their own eyes. Tried by this exacting standard, the Rangers were none the less able to abide it.

While the attack on Kaba Kuyu and Hill 60 was being executed the 10th Hampshires were carrying out their feint. They achieved their object in distracting the enemy's attention, but, unfortunately, incurred heavy losses. Major Morley, the Commanding Officer, was wounded, and Captain Hellyer, the only officer of the battalion who had come through the stiff fighting on Sari Bair on the 10th unhurt, was killed. The casualties among the rank and file amounted to close on a hundred and fifty. Nor had the Connaught Rangers come off lightly, having lost twelve officers and over two

hundred and fifty men. It is interesting to
note how much more severely units suffer in
modern war than a hundred years ago. Under
Wellington in Spain and Portugal, the Connaught Rangers played a distinguished part
in many great battles and sieges. At Busaco,
in company with half a battalion of the 45th
Foot, they charged and routed the eleven
battalions of Merle's French Division. They
attacked the great breach at Ciudad Rodrigo,
and stormed the Castle of Badajoz. At Salamanca, in company with the other two battalions
of Wallace's Brigade, they crossed bayonets
with Thomieres' Division and drove eight
battalions off the field in disorder. All these
were famous engagements, and in them the
88th deservedly won great glory, yet in
none of them were their losses as heavy as
those incurred by their newly-formed service
battalion in the little-known engagement at
Kaba Kuyu.*

Elsewhere the issue of the fighting had not
been propitious to our arms, since in spite of

---

* The exact figures are :—

		Killed		Wounded		Missing	
		Officers.	Other ranks.	Officers.	Other ranks.	Officers.	Other ranks.
Busaco	...	1	30	8	94	—	—
Ciudad Rodrigo	...	—	7	4	23	—	—
Badajoz	...	3	28	7	106	—	—
Salamanca	...	2	11	4	110	—	8
Kaba Kuyu	...	3	43	9	159	—	47 Nearly all killed.

The Peninsular figures are taken from Oman's *Peninsular War*,
Volumes III and V.

the never-failing courage of the 29th Division and the magnificent gallantry displayed by the Yeomen, the attacks made from Suvla had failed. The losses were terribly heavy, a very brave Irish Brigadier-General, the Earl of Longford, K.P., having fallen in the forefront of the battle. In consequence of these heavy casualties it was impossible to conduct further offensive operations at Suvla until reinforcements should arrive. It was, however, eminently desirable to effect the capture of Hill 60, since it constituted a perpetual menace to the Suvla-Anzac line of communication. So long as the Turks were able to maintain their position on its crest, not only were they able to enfilade the trenches at Suvla, but also they possessed the power of massing troops behind it and launching them suddenly against our line. They were fully aware of the advantage which this gave them, and had made the defence of the hill extremely strong.

It was determined to make an assault on this position at 5 p.m. on August the 27th. Brigadier-General Russell was placed in command of the assaulting parties, which consisted of 350 Australians who formed the right attack, 300 New Zealanders and 100 Australians, who composed the attack on the centre, and 250 Connaught Rangers, who formed the left attack. By this time units at Anzac were so reduced by casualties and sickness that instead of merely detailing units the numbers required were also specified. At the time the orders were issued the Rangers could only muster seven officers, three hundred men, and of these more than half the officers, and a large proportion of the men were suffering from dysentery or enteritis.

The Australians were to attack the trenches running to the base of the hill in a south-easterly direction. The New Zealanders had as their objective the summit of Hill 60 itself, while the Rangers were given as their objective the system of trenches running from the crest northwards towards Anafarta. At 3 p.m. the assaulting parties of the Rangers filed down the sap, which had been dug to connect Kaba Kuyu with South Wales Borderers' Gully, and into the trenches round the well which they had captured a week earlier. They were narrow and were manned by the Indian Brigade so that progress was slow, but by 4 p.m. the storming party of fifty men had reached the point from which the left assault was to commence.

At four the bombardment began. Ships, howitzers, mountain-guns, all combined to create a babel which if less intense than that of the previous week, was nevertheless sufficiently formidable. The trenches were so close to one another that our troops waiting to advance were covered with dust from the high explosives, but no injury was done. At last, at five, the

bombardment ceased and the stormers, led by
Lieutenant S. H. Lewis, went over the top.
They were into the Turkish trenches almost
before the enemy were aware of their coming
and forced their way along them with bayonet
and bomb. The supporting parties, however,
were not so fortunate. The range to the
parapet from whence they started was
accurately known to the enemy, and from every
part of the trench which was not actually under
assault violent machine-gun and rifle fire opened.
Man after man as he climbed over the parapet
fell back into the trench dead, yet the next
man calmly stepped forward to take his place.
One old soldier, a company cook, Private Glavey,
of Athlone, as his turn came, said : " I have
three sons fighting in France and one of them has
got the D.C.M. Let's see if the old father
can't get it now," and advanced to meet the
common fate.

Now, too, the enemy's artillery opened, and
as, unmenaced elsewhere, they were able to
concentrate all their forces on the defence
of Hill 60, their fire was terrific. Incessant
salvoes of shrapnel burst overhead, while
the parapet of the trench from which the
advance was taking place was blown in by high
explosive. Yet, still, the men went on over the
parapet and gradually a few succeeded in
struggling through the barrage, and in reinforcing their comrades in the captured trench.

There a stern struggle was taking place, but by dint of hard hand-to-hand bayonet fighting the Turks were driven out, and at six p.m. the Rangers had carried the whole of their objective.

The Australians on the right had encountered concentrated machine-gun fire and had been unable to make any progress, but the New Zealanders had carried the trenches on the southern side of the crest and a few of them had worked along and joined up with the Rangers. When night fell the whole of the southern face of the hill was in British hands, but the Turks were not disposed to acquiesce in this decision. As there was no indication of any attack elsewhere, they were free to use the bulk of their reserves at Hill 60, and wave after wave of assailants hurled itself on the position. There was a half moon which enabled the outlines of the charges to be seen as the mass of Turks surged forward preluding their onset with a shower of bombs. The Rangers suffered particularly badly in this respect, since parallel to the trench they held ran two newly-dug Turkish communication trenches which were within bombing distance. There were not enough men available to assault these trenches or to hold them if they were taken, for the losses in the attack had been heavy. It was true that the remainder of the Connaught Rangers had been sent up as a reinforcement, but this only amounted to forty-four men, most of whom were weakened by dysentery.

Again and again, the Turks attacked, mad with fanaticism, shrieking at the top of their voices and calling on Allah. The Irish, however, were not impressed. As one Connaught Ranger put it, " they came on shouting and calling for a man named Allen, and there was no man of that name in the trench at all." Still, however, the merciless bombing continued and the trenches slowly became encumbered with dead. It was a soldiers' battle : every officer but one on the Rangers' position was wounded, and in any case the trench was so blocked with débris from the bombardment and Turkish and Irish corpses, that it became almost impossible to move from point to point. Lieutenant Lewis who had led the charge, was wounded in two places. He had himself lifted on to the parapet in the hope of being able to make his way down to the dressing-station, but was never seen again.

At last about 10.30 p.m., after the fight had lasted five hours, a crowd of Turks succeeded in entering the Rangers' trench near its northern extremity. This northern end was held by a small party of men who died where they stood. The remainder of the trench was, however, blocked and further progress by the enemy arrested. Still the fight raged and bombs and ammunition were running short, while the losses became so heavy that it was growing harder and harder to procure. Major Money, who was in command of the advanced position, sent for reinforcements, but found that they were unobtainable. Fresh Turkish attacks kept coming on, and for every assailant that was struck down, two more sprang up in his place. It was clear that soon the defenders would be swept away by force of numbers, and they were compelled at midnight to fall back to the southern end of the captured trench. This point they blocked with a sandbag barricade and held until at last they were relieved at 8.30 a.m. on the 28th. Five hours earlier the 9th Australian Light Horse had attempted to recover the trench from which the Rangers had been driven, but found that the Turks were too strong. It was not until the 29th that a combined attack launched from the position which the New Zealanders had taken and had been able to hold, finally established our line on the northern slopes of Hill 60.

The Turkish losses were enormous and were nearly all inflicted in fighting at close quarters. The captures from them included three machine-guns, three trench mortars and 60,000 rounds of small arm ammunition, while Sir Ian Hamilton estimated that 5,000 Turks had been killed and wounded. When it is remembered that the total strength of our attacking columns was under a thousand, and that the reinforcements received in the course of the fight barely reached that figure, it will be realized that each of our men must have disposed of at least two of his opponents. Unfortunately, our losses were by no means small : of 250 Connaught Rangers who charged over the parapet on the 27th, less than a hundred returned unwounded.

The battalion had, however, no reason on this occasion to complain of lack of official recognition, since Sir Ian Hamilton in his official despatch paid an eloquent tribute to the deeds of the Connaught Rangers. His words may be quoted :

> " On the left the 250 men of the 5th Connaught Rangers excited the admiration of all beholders by the swiftness and cohesion of their charge. In five minutes they had carried their objective, the northern Turkish communications, when they at once set to and began a lively bomb fight along the trenches against strong parties which came hurrying up from the enemy supports and afterwards from their reserves. At midnight fresh troops were to have strengthened our grip on the hill, but before that hour the Irishmen had been out-bombed."

That the battalion acquitted itself so well was in the main due to the manner in which it had been trained by its Commanding Officer, Lieut.-Colonel Jourdain. He thoroughly understood the men with whom he had to deal, and had instilled into all ranks a rigid but sympathetic discipline which proved invaluable in time of trial. He was unwearied in working for the comfort of his men, and was repaid not only by their respect and affection, but by a well-earned C.M.G.

CHAPTER VIII

ROUTINE

" Scars given and taken without spite or shame, for
the Turk be it said is always at his best at that game."
—G. K. Chesterton.

B EFORE continuing to describe the doings
of the 30th and 31st Brigades after their
withdrawal from the Kiretch Tepe Sirt, a
word must be said about the units which were
attached to them, the Pioneer Battalion, the
Royal Engineers and the Field Ambulances.
Details of the movements of these units are
hard to obtain, but it would not be fair to over-
look them.

The Pioneer Battalion, the 5th Royal Irish
Regiment, was trained as an infantry unit but
also received instruction in engineering work,
especially in road-making. The majority of its
men were miners or artificers and its function
was to do the odd jobs of the Division and also
to provide a guard for Divisional Headquarters.
On the Peninsula, however, these duties soon
fell into abeyance, since it was called on to fill
up gaps in the line, and did so eagerly. It was
an exceptionally fine battalion, formed by

Lord Granard, whose ancestor, Sir Arthur Forbes, had first raised the 18th (Royal Irish) two hundred and thirty years before, and possessed an unusually large proportion of Regular officers. Fighting under difficult conditions, usually by detached companies, it did well wherever it was engaged, losing Lieutenants Costello and MacAndrew killed, and Major Fulda, Captain Morel, and half a dozen subalterns wounded.

The Engineers at Suvla, as everywhere, fully justified the splendid reputation of their corps. Few braver actions were noted in the Division than Lieutenant Waller's rescue of three wounded men on the Kiretch Tepe Sirt, and throughout the campaign the Sappers defied danger and did their duty.

The 30th Field Ambulance, which disembarked at Suvla without its bearer section on the afternoon of the 7th, was, for the first ten days of the campaign, working single-handed. Then the 31st and 32nd arrived and the pressure became less, but all the ambulances were working under great difficulties. There was little room for them, they had been unable to bring all their stores with them, and, as will be told later, medical comforts were conspicuous by their absence. In spite of these handicaps, they had to deal, not only with a very large number of wounded, but with a never ceasing flow of sick. The doctors, however, did admirable work and everyone was loud in praise of the Ambulance stretcher-bearers who used regularly to go out under heavy fire across the plain to bring in the wounded.

After the close of the fighting on August 17th, what was left of the 30th and 31st Brigades was withdrawn to the rest camp on the beach at Suvla. The fighting had reduced their strength terribly and nearly three-quarters of the officers and half the men who had landed ten days earlier, had fallen or been invalided. Worst of all, was the fact that, owing to so many senior N.C.O.'s having been hit, the internal organization of units had been practically destroyed. An extemporized Company Quartermaster-Sergeant, who possesses no previous knowledge of his work, will rarely be successful in promoting the comfort and efficiency of his men, however hard he may try. Matters were made even more serious by the continued sickness, which became worse and worse when units were withdrawn from the front line. Many who had been able to force their will power to keep them going on, while actually opposed to the enemy, now succumbed, and among them an officer, whose departure inflicted a serious loss on the Division as a whole and on the 31st Brigade in particular.

On August 22nd, General Hill, who had been in bad health ever since landing in Gallipoli, was invalided, suffering from acute dysentery. His departure was deeply regretted by his Brigade,

BRIGADIER-GENERAL J. G. KING-KING, D.S.O.

who had learnt to admire his coolness and courage, and to appreciate his constant attention to their comfort. Though the Staff Captain of the Brigade, Captain T. J. D. Atkinson, had been wounded on the 16th, fortunately the Brigade-Major, Captain Cooke Collis, still remained, and as the command was taken over by Colonel King-King the General Staff Officer (1) of the Division, officers and men did not feel that they had to deal with a stranger.

It was marvellous how many men who were in bad health, resisted the temptation to go sick and be sent on board the white hospital ships, where there was shade and ice and plenty to drink. No man was invalided who was not sick, but there were very few people doing duty in Gallipoli who did not from time to time possess a temperature, and none whose stomachs were not periodically out of order. The doctors did their utmost to retain men with thier units, but all medical comforts were difficult to obtain, even condensed milk being precious, and to feed men sickening for dysentery on tinned meat, is to ask for trouble. Rice was a great stand-by, though the men did not much appreciate it unless it was boiled in milk. It was therefore inevitable that men reporting sick should be sent to the field ambulances, and since these were little better off than the regimental M.O.'s so far as provision for special diet was concerned, and since their resources were over-

P

taxed, it followed that it was almost invariably necessary to send invalids away overseas. Though all ranks belonging to them showed the utmost devotion to duty, and worked till they were worn out, a field ambulance at Suvla was not a place in which a quick recovery could be made. True, it had tents, and it is hard to appreciate the amount of solid comfort offered by a tent to one who has spent weeks in the open under a tropical sun. There were also a certain number of beds, and it was very pleasant to find doctors and orderlies taking an interest in you, and doing their best to make you comfortable.

There were, however, discomforts which they were powerless to remove. One was the swarm of flies which made sleep by day impossible, and another was the shortage of water. The worst, however, was the enemy fire : for although the Turk respected the Red Cross flag, yet the hospitals were close to the beach, and not far from some of our batteries, which naturally drew the enemy's artillery. The sound of the shells rushing through the air, and the shock of their explosion were plainly heard and felt by the patients in hospital, and threw an additional strain on nerves that were already worn out. It could not be helped ; there was no room on the peninsula to put hospitals at a distance from fighting troops, but it was very hard on the sick and wounded.

Gradually, however, things grew better. Medical comforts began to be forthcoming ; fresh bread was baked at Imbros and sent across, milk was less scarce, and a few eggs were issued not only to hospitals, but in some cases to medical officers of battalions. They also obtained a compound known as tinned fowl, which appeared to consist entirely of bones. Fly whisks and veils were provided by the British Red Cross, an organization to which the soldier owes more than he will ever be able to say. By the flexibility of its management, and its freedom from red tape, it has done wonders to secure the speedier recovery of our wounded.

The rest-camp to which the residue of the nine battalions came, was somewhat of a jest. It was situated on the beach, and consisted of a collection of shallow dug-outs burrowed into the yielding sand. As it was close to some of the extemporized piers at which the lighters bearing the rations and ammunition were unloaded, and was in the neighbourhood of the A.S.C. and Ordnance Depôts, it naturally attracted a good share of the shells which the Turks directed at those points, and casualties were by no means infrequent. However, the men were able to take off the clothes which they had worn for nearly a fortnight, and wash. Some shaved, but others thought it waste of time and also of the more precious water. Bathing was possible, for the sea was close by, and the delight of plunging into the warm sparkling sea was hardly diminished by the thought that a Turkish shell might possibly find you out as you did so.

The period in the rest-camp gave an opportunity of writing home, and describing, as far as the censorship permitted, the events of the previous week. It was clear that the first attempt at Suvla had not been successful, but reinforcements were arriving nightly, a new General (Major-General H. B. de Lisle) had taken over command of the 9th Corps, and everyone was hoping for eventual success. In this they were much assisted by rumour, which produced scores of encouraging "shaves." Occasionally one heard that General Botha with a large force of Boers, had landed at Helles, but the favourite and apparently best-authenticated report, was that an army of 150,000 Italians had landed at Bulair and were taking the Turks in reverse. It did not seem to occur to any of those who circulated this report that their guns must have been heard at Suvla if they were really doing so. By this time, however, most sensible people had discovered that nothing is ever so thoroughly well-authenticated as a thoroughly baseless rumour, and believed nothing that they were told. At any rate the "canards" gave a subject for conversation, and helped to pass the time.

On August 21st, General de Lisle proposed

to take the offensive again, having been reinforced from Egypt and Helles. Although the
Turks had by now brought up ample reinforcements, and carefully entrenched their whole
line, it was thought that it might be possible
to capture Ismail Oglu Tepe, a wooded hill,
which buttressed the Khoja Chemen Tepe.
This attack General de Lisle entrusted to the
11th and 29th Divisions, the latter being on
the left. The 53rd and 54th Territorial Divisions were to hold the remainder of the line
northwards to the Gulf of Saros, including the
trenches on the Kiretch Tepe Sirt. The newly-
landed 2nd Mounted Division (Yeomanry) and
the two brigades of the 10th Division, which
had suffered so heavily in the previous fighting
as to be almost unfit for further aggressive
action, were placed in Corps Reserve. At the
same time the co-operation of the Anzac troops,
which took the form of the attack on Kaba Kuyu
and Hill 60, and was described in the previous
chapter, was arranged for.

The 10th Division was disposed as follows :—

The 31st Brigade, which was allotted as
reserve to the 29th Division, formed up behind
Hill 10 on the northern shores of the Salt Lake.
There was very little cover, and the 6th Inniskilling Fusiliers, who found themselves in rear
of one of our batteries, suffered severely from
the shell fire with which the Turks retaliated on
it. The 30th Brigade were at Lala Baba at

the south-western angle of the Lake. At
3 p.m. the attack was launched, and the front
line of Turkish trenches were occupied. Atmos-
pheric conditions, however, were unfavourable,
and further progress was only made with great
difficulty, the 11th Division, which had been
much weakened by previous fighting, finding
it almost impossible to get on. The reserves
were then called up, and the Yeomen went
forward across the bare shell-swept plain.

The long extended lines suffered heavily
as they moved forward to a position in rear of
Chocolate Hill, but though they were young
troops who had never been in action before,
there was no wavering, and the formation was
preserved throughout. About the same time
the 30th Brigade received orders to advance
and occupy the Turkish trenches, which had
been captured at the commencement of operations. As they moved forward to do this
they, too, came under a heavy fire of shrapnel
and sustained numerous casualties, among
them being Lieut.-Col. Worship, of the 6th
Munster Fusiliers, who was wounded in the
foot. The most active part in these operations,
however, so far as the 10th Division was concerned, was taken by the stretcher-bearers of
the three Field Ambulances, who had just
arrived. Again and again they went out over
the shell-swept plain, picking up the wounded
of the 11th and 29th Divisions, and bringing

5TH ROYAL IRISH FUSILIERS IN THE TRENCHES

Official photograph issued on behalf of the Press Bureau, Crown copyright reserved

them back to the hospitals on the beach. The work was not only hot and heavy, but dangerous, since although the Turk proved a fair fighter on the whole and respected the Red Cross, yet his shrapnel could not discriminate between fighters and non-combatants. Good and plucky work done on this occasion earned the D.C.M. for Staff-Sergeant Hughes and Corporal Fitch, of the 30th Field Ambulance.

On the following day, the two brigades moved southward, and took over the front line trenches, the two Inniskilling battalions being just north of Chocolate Hill, with the Royal Irish Fusiliers on their right, and the 30th Brigade prolonging the line to the southward. At the same time, Divisional Headquarters were transferred from the Kiretch Tepe Sirt to Lala Baba. While the Division was holding this southern sector, it very nearly came in touch with part of its detached Brigade operating to the north of Anzac ; and the 6th Dublin Fusiliers from their trenches were able to watch the charge of the 5th Connaught Rangers on August 27th. The 29th Brigade, however, remained under the orders of the Anzac Command.

After the fight of the 27th-28th of August, described in the last chapter, this Brigade also became incapable of further aggressive action. Every battalion had lost about three-quarters of its strength, while the casualties in the commissioned ranks had been exceptionally heavy. Sickness was bad here, as elsewhere, and early in September three out of the four units composing the Brigade had only two officers apiece left. The 6th Leinsters were in better case ; but even with them, sickness was taking its toll—Major Currey, the C.O., being one of the victims. He was succeeded by Major Colquhoun. The battalion remained with the New Zealand and Australian Division, doing duty in the trenches at " Russell's Top " until August 26th, when it withdrew to Anzac and joined the Royal Irish Rifles in " Reserve Gully."

The Rifles and Hampshires, which suffered terribly in the Sari Bair fighting, were retained behind the Aghyl Dere line for about a week after the 10th August. Then the Rifles returned to Anzac, where it took up its quarters in Reserve Gully. After the feint attack on August 21st, in which they suffered so heavily, the 10th Hampshires were also withdrawn to the beach, bivouacking near No. 2 Post. The Brigade was completed by the arrival of the 5th Connaught Rangers, who, after the assault on Hill 60 on the 27th August, remained in reserve for a week and then moved back to a bivouac on Bauchop's Hill.

Though two companies of the Royal Irish Rifles were lent to General Walker, of the Australians, and did duty for him for three weeks, the bulk of the Brigade were employed on fatigue duties. These included road-making, unloading ration boats, and guarding Turkish prisoners. The work was hard, the sun still hot, and the enemy's shells did not spare the fatigue parties, but casualties were not heavy.

During this period the 29th Brigade received a new commander. Colonel Agnew returned to Mudros on September 9th, and on the 22nd September Brigadier-General R. S. Vandeleur, C.M.G., who had come from the Seaforth Highlanders in France, took over command. Major T. G. Anderson, R.F.A., had previously been appointed Brigade-Major.

While in many respects fighting in Gallipoli was more unpleasant than in France or Flanders, yet its trench warfare had certain advantages over that engaged in there. Though the heat by day and the cold by night were trying, yet there was but little rain, and it was easy to keep the trenches dry. Except on the Kiretch Tepe Sirt and close to the sea, the soil was firm, so that the sides of trenches did not require much revetment, and repairs were not constantly called for. Above all, the character of the enemy gave the defender an easier time.

The Turk is inflexibly stubborn in defence, and when stirred up to make a mass attack, he appears fearless of death : but he is not an enterprising foe. Except at one or two points— notably at Apex and at Quinn's Post in the

Anzac area, where the opposing trench lines were close together, and trench mortars and bomb-throwers raged perpetually—he was content to leave the enemy to the attention of his snipers. These, of course, were persistent and ingenious, and any point in a trench which could be overlooked, either from a tree or from high ground in the enemy's lines, required to be specially defended. Otherwise, however, the Turk was not much disposed to institute aggressive enterprises, and his bombardments, though intensely annoying, and causing a good many casualties, were not to be compared in intensity with those employed by the Germans in Flanders.

Trench-life, however much its details may be mitigated, is none the less painfully monotonous, and in the Peninsula there were none of the distractions sometimes experienced on the Western Front. There were only two breaks in the tedium : the arrival of the mail and a visit from a chaplain. The latter should perhaps have precedence, both out of respect for his cloth and because it happened more frequently. Walking about at Anzac and Suvla was neither pleasant nor safe ; but the chaplains were quite indefatigable, and would walk any distance and brave any danger in order to visit the units to which they were attached. By dint of untiring endeavour, the Church of England and Roman Catholic chaplains used, as a rule, to hold a service for each of the battalions in their charge on Sunday, and one during the week as well. Sometimes these services took place right up in the firing line, the celebrant moving along the trench to each communicant in turn. It was in this manner Canon McLean celebrated Holy Communion for the 6th and 7th Dublins an hour before the advance on the 15th of August. Often, too, the priests were able to give absolution to their flock before they went into action. Besides doing this, the Roman Catholic chaplains heard confessions regularly, and all denominations were indefatigable in ministering to the sick.

Apart, however, from the spiritual side of the question, the mere presence of the " Padre " himself was stimulating. The Division had been exceptionally fortunate in its chaplains. The robust cheerfulness of Father Murphy, the recondite knowledge of Father Stafford, Father O'Farrell's boyish keenness, and the straightforward charm that made Father O'Connor such a good sportsman and such a good friend, were coupled with a fearlessness and devotion to duty common to all, that made them beloved by their own flock and liked and respected by those of other creeds. There was but little colour in Gallipoli ; grey olives, bleached scrub and parched sand combined to make a picture in monotone, and, even to the Protestant eye it was grateful to see, as the one gleam of colour in a dreary landscape, the shining golden chasuble of the priest as he celebrated Mass. Few who beheld those services will ever forget them ; the circle of kneeling worshippers, the robed figure in the centre, the long shadows cast by the newly-risen sun, and the drone of the shells passing through the air overhead, made an ineffaceable impression on the mind.

Nor were the Protestant chaplains behind their Roman Catholic colleagues in zeal and cheerfulness. The Reverend S. Hutchinson in the 31st Brigade, and the Reverend J. W. Crozier (a son of the Primate of All Ireland) in the 29th, worked untiringly and devotedly for the good of the men who belonged to the Church of England. Nor should the Reverend F. J. Roche, who was Church of England Chaplain to the Divisional Troops, be forgotten. Originally, he was sent to Cairo with the Artillery of the Division ; but he had seen service in South Africa in the Imperial Yeomanry, and was mad to get into the firing line once more. By dint of many entreaties and much ingenuity, he finally succeeded in reaching Suvla on August 29th, and laboured unceasingly with the Pioneers and Royal Engineers. He was a man of exceptionally high character, and all who knew him were grieved when two days before the Division left the Peninsula he was invalided with dysentery. Unfortunately, the attack was a severe one, and after rallying slightly he died in hospital at Alexandria. The Presbyterian and Methodist chaplains, too, did excellent work, though since their flock was so widely scattered they had less opportunity of becoming personally known to those outside it.

The jewel of the Protestant chaplains, however, was Canon McLean. Although he must have been nearly sixty years of age, and was probably the oldest man in the Division, he had the heart of a boy and the courage of a lion. No dangers or hardships were too great for him to endure, and his one regret was that his cloth did not permit him to lead his Brigade in a charge. He had, too, the more valuable form of courage—the power of patient endurance, for though seriously ill with dysentery, he absolutely refused to go sick and leave his men. There were many brave fellows in the Division, but none gained a greater reputation for courage than Canon McLean.

The second great alleviation of the monotony of trench life was the arrival of the mail. In France, this happens daily, and is taken as a matter of course ; but in Gallipoli it rarely arrived more often than once a week, and great joy was felt in the battalions when Brigade headquarters telephoned that a mail was coming up. Expectation grew, until at last the Indian *drabis* led up their grunting mules, and deposited the mail-bags at the door of the Headquarters dug-out. Orderly sergeants of the companies were at once summoned, and the slow process of sorting began—a process made even slower by the fact that in many cases the writers had not indicated anything more than the name of the addressee, and that it took a considerable time in an Irish regiment to ascertain which Private Kelly was meant.

"The postmark's Glasgow. Is either of your Kelly's a Scotsman, Sergeant McGrath?" the Adjutant would say.

"They are not, sorr. One's a Mayo man and the other's from Dublin. Try 'B' Company, sorr."

The Orderly Sergeant of "B" also disclaims any Scotch Kelly, but is reminded by the signalling sergeant of a Glasgow man of that name who went sick from Mudros. Repeated *ad infinitum* this process takes time, and it was long before the officer who had undertaken the sorting could turn to his own correspondence. Then followed the painful task of returning the letters that could not be delivered. These were sent back from companies to the orderly-room and were there sorted into three piles :—

    Dead,

        Missing, and

            Hospital.

The officer then endorsed each, writing the word in an indelible pencil, always dreading that by some accident this might be the first intimation of the casualty that the sender of the letter had received. The "Hospital" letters, of course, were not returned to the writer, but were sent in pursuit of the addressee round Mudros, Malta, and Alexandria, usually returning to the Battalion after he had rejoined it.

Nor did one's own mail consist entirely of personal letters, for the officers who survived found themselves in September receiving many letters from the relatives of their comrades who had fallen begging for details of how they died. These letters were not easy to answer, since details were often lacking, and the writer was always afraid of inadvertently opening the wound again; but it was a labour of love to reply to them. More amusing semi-official letters were also received, such as the demands of railway companies for sums of three-and-sixpence due by men who had travelled without tickets four months earlier. As even supposing the men in question had not been killed or wounded, they had certainly received no pay for more than a month, and were unlikely to receive any for an indefinite period, so the prospect that the Company Officer would be able to recover the debts before being killed or wounded himself did not seem large.

With the mail came newspapers and sometimes parcels. The latter were specially welcome, since they served to fill up the nakedness of the officers' mess, and as a rule they arrived safely when sent by parcels post. Complaints of non-arrival of parcels were indeed frequent, but in most cases this was caused either by inaccurate addressing, or by careless packing. Very seldom was a parcels mail-bag opened for sorting at the battalion without the bottom being found to be filled with broken cigarettes, crumbs of crushed cake, and a mass of cardboard, brown paper and string. It must be remembered that the mails had to stand a good deal of rough handling. The bags were sent by ship to Alexandria, then thrown on to a lorry and jolted over the stony streets to the Base Post Office, there sorted, sent on shipboard again, conveyed to Mudros, transhipped to Suvla, Anzac, or Helles, thrown overboard on to a lighter, dumped on the beach, and finally carried up to their destination on the back of a pack mule. It was not astonishing that a parcel was occasionally crushed, or even that a bag sometimes fell into the sea. Under normal conditions, however, parcels usually arrived safely.

The arrival of parcels meant a welcome addition to mess stores, for although the A.S.C. had recovered from the natural confusion caused by the operations at the beginning of August, and rations were regular and plentiful, yet the diet became painfully dull. It must be remembered that in Gallipoli, unlike the

Western Front, there was absolutely no possibility of using the resources of the country. In France, it is often possible to buy eggs, butter, and perhaps a chicken, not to speak of wine or beer ; but on the Peninsula there was literally nothing obtainable. From Suvla the distant houses of the Anafarta's mocked the eye with the sight of human habitations ; but Anzac was literally a desert. The map, it is true, marked a spot as " Fisherman's Hut," but both fishermen and their nets had departed, and the huts had fallen into ruin. Nor did Nature supply anything—except where the trampled stubble told of a ruined cornfield, all was barren, dry scrub, and prickly holly and bare, thankless sand. With such destitution all round, it was no wonder that the post was eagerly looked for.

The most welcome gift of all was tinned fruit, since these and the syrup that came with them quenched thirst. Lemonade tablets, too, were welcome, and sauces and curry-powders to disguise the taste of the eternal bully-beef, were much appreciated. Some things failed to stand the climate ; chocolate usually arrived in a liquid condition, while a parcel of butter became a greasy rag. (It must be borne in mind while reading this description of life in Gallipoli that the Expeditionary Force Canteens were not established there till after the 10th Division had left the Peninsula. They did

Q

a great deal to fill the want, though it was almost impossible to keep them properly stocked.)

Although life in September was distinctly less trying than it was in August, yet it had its disadvantages. Among them was the fact that wherever a battalion occupied an old Turkish bivouac, it found that the enemy had left behind a peculiarly ferocious breed of flea. There were other minor annoyances in washing ; but the main disadvantage of Gallipoli unquestionably was the uncertainty of life. The whole Peninsula was exposed to shell fire, and much of it to snipers as well, and though some places were less dangerous than others, it was impossible ever to feel that one was safe. Every day almost one heard of a fresh casualty. Now an orderly was hit as he brought a message ; now a cook fell as he bent over his fire ; another day the storeman looking after kits on the beach was killed ; or a shell made havoc among a party drawing rations or water.

Drawing rations was one of the most dangerous occupations on the Peninsula, especially at Anzac, and was usually performed at the double. The beaches, where the supply depôts were situated, were among the enemy's favourite targets, as they knew that there were always people moving there, and they shelled them persistently. In France, the A.S.C. are said to have safe and " cushy " jobs ; but this was certainly not the case in Gallipoli. Their work, in addition to being dangerous, was not exciting, which made things worse ; for though Death is the same wherever he comes, it is easier to encounter him in a charge than when cutting up bacon. The memory of the courage of their representatives at Suvla and Anzac should always be a proud one with the A.S.C.

But though the beaches were particularly nasty spots, there was no escaping from Death anywhere. If one took a walk one was almost certain to pass a festering and fly-blown mule, or a heap of equipment that showed where a man had been wounded. At one point a barricade of sandbags suggested that it was wise to keep in close to them, at another a deep sap had been dug to allow secure passage through an area commanded by the Chunuk Bair. The blind impartiality of shrapnel spared no one : the doctor of one battalion sent a man to hospital who was suffering from bronchitis, and was surprised to discover afterwards that when admitted he was suffering from a wound in the right arm which he had acquired on the way down. Even if one remained in one's own bivouac or trench, there was no assurance of safety. It was always possible that a sudden shell might catch one outside one's dug-out and finish one. Several fell in this way, among them one of the finest officers in the Division, Major N. C. K. Money of the Connaught Rangers. He was a magnificent soldier, always cool and resourceful, and had made his mark on every occasion on which his battalion was engaged. After coming untouched through three stiff fights, and being awarded the D.S.O. for his courage and capacity, he was mortally wounded in bivouac by an unexpected burst of shrapnel. It was a miserable end for one who had done so much, and was destined, had he lived, to do so much more.

After a few weeks on the Peninsula one grew into a fatalistic mood. Most of one's friends had already been knocked out, and it seemed impossible that in the long run anyone could escape. Sooner or later the shrapnel was bound to get you, unless dysentery or enteric got you first. If you were unlucky, you would be killed ; if lucky, you would get a wound that would send you either home, or at any rate to Malta or Alexandria, or some other civilized place. Only one thing seemed out of the question, and that was that one should see the end of the campaign. Certainly very few of us did.

CHAPTER IX

LAST DAYS

" It is better not to begin than never to finish.'
—Serbian Proverb.

AT the beginning of September a portion of the Divisional Artillery arrived in the Peninsula. The three brigades (54th, 55th and 56th) which sailed from England with the Division, had been landed at Alexandria and sent into camp near Cairo. Rumour had assured the remainder of the Division that they were ultimately destined for Aden, but in this as in almost every other instance, rumour lied. After about three weeks in Egypt, where a certain number of horses died as the result of eating sand which caused colic, the 55th and 56th Brigades were transferred to Mudros and thence without their horses to the Peninsula. The 55th Brigade went to Cape Helles, where it took up a position near the Great Gully with its sixteen guns crowded closely together, and suffered a good deal in that congested area from the enemy's shell-fire. This brigade was definitely removed from the Division and had no further, dealings with it. The 56th Brigade, on the other hand, came to the Suvla area, though it did not actually rejoin the Division. Gun positions were not very easy to discover, but the " A " and " B " Batteries of the Brigade came into action below Lala Baba. " C " Battery was out on the plain in a low-lying spot, which was flooded out by the November blizzard, while " D " Battery moved southward into the Anzac area. Here they took up a position on the Damakjelik Bair near the South Wales Borderers' Gully facing northward, which enabled them to enfilade the Turkish trenches on Scimitar Hill, and did excellent work. The whole Brigade remained in its positions when the rest of the Division left the Peninsula, and did not depart till the final evacuation of Suvla and Anzac. They consequently definitely severed their connection with the 10th Division.

Throughout September the days passed with monotonous regularity. The routine of trench work, and the telling off and supervision of fatigue parties did not do much to occupy the imagination, and plenty of time was spent gazing out over the sea to Imbros and Samothrace and wondering what was going to happen next. There did not seem much prospect of an advance but it was never easy for junior officers and men to tell what was brewing.

It was somewhat trying to the nerves to know that one was never certain that one would not be required at a moment's notice. Even when

IMBROS FROM ANZAC

(From a water colour by Captain Drummond Fish, Royal Irish Rifles)

nominally resting behind the line units were frequently obliged to stand to in consequence of an alarm of some kind. By this time, blankets and officers' valises had been retrieved, but one felt that one was tempting Providence if one undressed or even took off one's boots at night, for one was always liable to be roused suddenly. The Turks, during this period, were not in at all an aggressive mood, but they too, were subject to nerves, and used occasionally to open fire all along the line for no particular reason. Except for these spasms of nervousness, however, they confined their attention to sniping, intermittent shelling, and where the trenches were very close together, to trench mortar work and bombing.

Two minor distractions were the swallows and the " Peninsula Press." In August Anzac was a singularly birdless place ; in fact except for one cornfield the area had no sign of life of any kind. About the middle of September, however, it was invaded by troops of swallows on their way southward, and every gully was full of diving, swooping birds. They brought back many memories of home and of warm Spring evenings and long twilights, and it was a pleasure to watch them circling past the dug-outs. They did not seem to mind the shell-fire, and there was much discussion as to whether they would winter in Gallipoli, but we did not remain in the Peninsula long enough to make sure.

The other alleviation of the dulness was a half-sheet of news issued by the Authority and entitled " The Peninsula Press." The perusal of this piece of foolscap, which was printed at Army Headquarters and sent to units with more or less regularity, was sufficient to fill one with admiration for the art and mystery of journalism. It was surprising how different the string of communiqués and bulletins served up raw without amplification or comment was from the newspaper that one had been accustomed to. For the first time one realized the enormous importance of sub-editing. Nor were the communiqués very informing, since for the most part they dealt with Polish towns whose names had never been heard of before by any of us. An atlas was a possession extremely rare in Gallipoli, so we were compelled to take the bulk of the news on trust and hope for the best.

Another minor inconvenience was lack of exercise. In the early days of August there had been no reason to complain on this score, but by the time that we had settled down to routine work in September, many found it hard to keep in condition. Unless you went out with a fatigue party ration-carrying or road-making, your work was confined to a comparatively small area. Walks for the sake of exercise only were discouraged by those in authority, partly because officers were few and could not easily be spared from the possible call of duty that might come at any time, and partly because walking, unless you confined your movements to saps, was not a particularly safe amusement. It was extremely easy to go out for a stroll and come home on a stretcher. Added to this was the possibility, that if you went outside the area in which you were known that you might be taken for a spy. Lurid stories were told of unknown officers who had walked the whole length of Anzac Beach asking questions and then disappeared, and though like most rumours these were probably quite unfounded, yet there was always a chance that some over-zealous and suspicious individual might give you an unpleasant half-hour. All these considerations tended to make walking for pleasure an amusement to be indulged in with moderation.

Fairly soon, however, officers began to work at training again, for early in September steps were taken to fill up the depleted ranks of the Division. The first reinforcements had been quickly absorbed on their arrival from Mudros, and by the end of August every unit was much below strength. Since under normal conditions the voyage from England to Mudros usually occupied from ten days to a fortnight it naturally took some time before the gaps in the units were filled. At the end of the first week in September, however, news was received that the first drafts from home had arrived. The men who composed these drafts were for the most part drawn from the reserve battalions of Irish regiments and were excellent material, many of them being men of the old Regular Army who had been wounded in France.

The summer of 1915 in Flanders had been a comparatively quiet one, since there had been a lull in the fighting after the second battle of Ypres. The Regular Battalions of the Irish Regiments serving there had made comparatively small demands on their Reserve Battalions for reinforcements, and consequently large and good drafts were sent out to the 10th Division. This consideration, however, did not apply to the Inniskilling, Munster and Dublin Fusiliers, whose 1st Battalions were serving in Gallipoli with the 29th Division and had sustained terrible losses. Unfortunately, the officers who accompanied the first drafts were not those who had been trained with the units of the division, and had been left behind as surplus to establishment, but were drawn, as a general rule, from Scotch regiments. They were excellent fellows and showed no lack of keenness or courage, but officers who had had some previous knowledge of the units in which they were serving would have been more useful, and in addition, from the sentimental point of view, it was felt that an influx of trews and glengarries tended to remove the Irish character of the Division. However, with the later drafts received, a number of Irish officers did arrive.

It was not entirely an easy matter to assimilate these reinforcements. As a rule, a draft is a comparatively small body of men which easily adopts the character of the unit in which it is merged. In Gallipoli, however, units had been so much reduced in strength that in some cases the draft was stronger than the battalion that it joined, while it almost invariably increased the strength of what was left of the original unit by half as much again. As a result after two or three drafts had arrived, the old battalion had been swamped. For many reasons this was unfortunate. It took a considerable time for the officers and N.C.O.'s even to learn the names of the newcomers, still more to acquire that insight into their characters necessary for the smooth working of a company or platoon. The shortage of good and experienced N.C.O.'s, too, had the result of throwing rather too much influence into the hands of bad characters. In every large body of soldiers there are bound to be men who dislike danger and do their best to avoid it. As a rule these undesirables are known and are unable to do much harm ; but among an influx of young soldiers a few men of this stamp, posing as experienced veterans, may do a considerable amount of mischief, till they are discovered and dealt with.

It was unfortunately impossible to adopt the most favourable method of assimilating the new men. To teach men to act together, to recognise and obey the voice of their officer or sergeant there is nothing like drill, and particularly drill in close order. Only from drill can be obtained the surrender of individuality in order to achieve a common purpose which is the foundation of military discipline. It is on the barrack square that a platoon or company first " gets together " and realises its corporate entity ; it is " on the square " that an officer first begins to distinguish his men and to discriminate between their characters, and it is " on the square " that men first begin to know their officer. Barrack square drill is not, as it was in the Eighteenth Century, the end-all and be-all of military training, but it is an indispensable foundation for it, and no effective substitute has ever yet been found to take its place.

Unfortunately, in Gallipoli, drill was out of the question. When on the move, men straggled along in single file without thought of step, while the duties of trench-manning, road making, or onion carrying, did not encourage smartness. While off duty the men were scattered round a rabbit warren of dugouts, and any gathering for parade purposes was at once dispersed by hostile shrapnel. All that could be done was to practise bombing in disused Turkish trenches and carry out the usual inspections of rifles, ammunition and iron rations. The severity of the handicap thus imposed upon battalions will be best appreciated by those who have served in France. There units periodically go behind the line to rest, and during the rest-period are able by drill and discipline to learn to know and assimilate their new men.

Among other matters that had to be faced was the training of specialists. Most battalions had lost the bulk of their machine-gunners and signallers and it was extraordinarily rare to find a unit in which both the signalling and machine-gun officer survived. If they did the Adjutant probably did not, and one of them had been promoted to fill his place. In any case, fresh officers and men had to be trained for the duty. It proved to be unfortunate that very few of the officers who joined with drafts had had any training in either of these branches. A reserve battalion, if well-organized, should be a kind of military university in which an energetic officer can pick up some knowledge of every branch of infantry work since he can never tell what he may not be required to do when posted to a battalion on active service. The power to command a platoon is only the foundation, not the climax, of a subaltern's training. Fortunately, in addition to the second-lieutenants who accompanied drafts, a certain number of officers and men rejoined from hospital. These had mostly been wounded or gone sick during the fighting at the beginning of August, and they formed a very welcome reinforcement, since they were both experienced and seasoned to the climate.

Unfortunately, as much could not be said for the new drafts, who suffered very badly from dysentery. It was a common experience for a company commander to congratulate himself on having discovered a good sergeant-major or platoon-sergeant only to hear on the following day that he had been invalided. The men who had been wounded in France seemed to be peculiarly liable to dysentery.

While steps were being taken to reorganize the shattered units, rumours began to spread that the Division was to leave the Peninsula to rest. By this time most people had begun to discredit all rumours, but it appeared possible that there might be something in this. It was known that both the 29th Division and what was left of the original Australians had been removed to Mudros for a change of ten days or so, and from a military point of view it was eminently desirable to give the Division a chance of training its new drafts in a spot free from shell-fire.

It was, however, very uncertain when and where we were to go. The place varied between Mudros and Imbros, while the time suggested was always " next week." Finally, the 29th Brigade received orders on September 28th to prepare to move on the following evening, not to

either of the places anticipated but to Suvla.
For a moment people thought that an attack
was in prospect since a day or two earlier " The
Peninsula Press " had announced great victories
in France. Since units of the Division had been
paraded at Mudros in July and ordered to cheer
for the impending fall of Bagdad, most people
were a little distrustful of official bulletins, but
if it really was true, and the German line was
broken both at Loos and in Champagne, then,
of course, we should push the enemy as hard as
possible wherever we could. All these specula-
tions were shattered, however, early on the 29th,
by the cancellation of the orders to proceed to
Suvla, and the receipt of instructions to embark
at Anzac for Mudros on the same evening.

Somehow one was not as glad to be leaving
Gallipoli as one had anticipated. To be sure
it was all to the good to be out of the shelling
for a time and the Turks took steps to intensify
the pleasure caused by this prospect by firing
on the bivouacs of the 29th Brigade on their
last day with unusual vigour. One shell fell
immediately outside the guard room of the
Connaught Rangers, but fortunately failed to
explode. Another burst in the camp of the
Royal Irish Rifles and wounded Lieutenant
Elliot. This officer was the last survivor except
for the Quartermaster and Doctor, of the
officers of the battalion who had landed at
Anzac on August 6th, and was unlucky in being

hit on the last day. Even the prospect of
immunity from bombardment could not however disguise the fact that one was sorry to leave.

As the 29th Brigade filed down the long
sap to Anzac in the darkness, as the 30th and
31st Brigades retraced their steps past Lala
Baba and over the beaches at Suvla, it was
impossible to avoid retrospect. We had passed
that way less than two months before, but going
in the opposite direction full of high hopes. Now
we were leaving the Peninsula again, our work
unfinished and the Turks still in possession of
the Narrows. Nor was it possible to help
thinking of the friends lying in narrow graves
on the scrub-covered hillside or covered by the
débris of filled-in trenches, whom we seemed to
be abandoning. Yet though there was sorrow
at departing there was no despondency. We
had the memory of strenuous effort and achievement to inspire us, and the bond of friendship
among the few officers who survived had been
knit closer than it had ever been before. The
men, too, felt a new spirit towards their officers,
and the hard times they had shared together had
cemented the feeling of comradeship which had
always existed. They knew now that whatever
the danger might be their officers would be the
first to face it, and the officers had proved that
their men would follow them anywhere. Once
that sentiment exists in a battalion it is impossible to break its spirit.

The 29th Brigade reached Mudros at dawn on September 30th and went under canvas in the Mudros East area, which was on the opposite side of the harbour to the bivouac they had previously occupied. The remainder of the Division followed them thither in the course of the week. There was unfortunately not many of the original Division left.

Though the Divisional Staff had not greatly changed, only one brigadier still held his original command. This was Brigadier-General Nicol, who had won the admiration and affection of the 30th Brigade by his unfailing courage and tenacity. He was not a young man, but in spite of the sickness which afflicted everyone in Gallipoli he resolutely refused to go to hospital, and by his example encouraged many younger officers to " stick it out." Of the original Brigade Staffs only one Brigade-Major, Captain Cooke Collis, and one Staff Captain, Captain Goodland, survived, and sickness and wounds had so thinned the ranks of the commanding officers that only Lieutenant-Colonel Jourdain of the Connaught Rangers, Lieutenant-Colonel Cox of the 6th Royal Dublin Fusiliers, Lieutenant-Colonel Pike of the 5th Royal Irish Fusiliers, and Lieutenant-Colonel Lord Granard of the Royal Irish Regiment, were still with their units. One Lieutenant-Colonel, Vanrenen, of the 5th Inniskillings, had fallen, and the other eight were wounded or sick. The battalions,

R

too, had suffered terribly, and it was an exceptional unit that possessed more than half-a-dozen
of its original officers and 200 of the men who had
gone with it to the Peninsula at the beginning
of August. Even of these a fair proportion had
spent part of the time in hospital and rejoined ;
those who had seen the campaign through from
start to finish were rare.

There was, however, little time to think of
these matters. The concentration of the
Division was not completed till October 3rd
and on October 4th its first two battalions sailed
for another theatre of war.

CHAPTER X

RETROSPECT

" So awakened in their hearts the strongest of all fellow-ships, the fellowship of the sword."—W. B. Yeats.

WHAT does one recollect most clearly when one looks back at Gallipoli ?

A multitude of memories cluster together : dry, sand-floored gullies, thirsty men crowded round a well, Indians grooming their mules, lithe, half-naked Australians, parched, sun-dried scrub, but above and beyond all these one remembers the graves. Not a man came back from the Peninsula without leaving some friend behind there, and it is bitter to think that the last resting-place of those we loved is in the hands of our enemy. Not all the dead of Gallipoli lie in the Peninsula itself. There are crowded cemeteries at Malta and Alexandria, and many a brave body has been lowered over the side of a hospital ship into the Aegean to mingle his bones with those of Argonauts and Crusaders and all the heroes of a bygone age. Nevertheless, when one thinks of Gallipoli one thinks first of graves.

You could not walk far in the Peninsula

without seeing them, sometimes thickly crowded together outside a field-ambulance, sometimes a solitary cross marking the spot where a sniper's victim had been buried. Each of these tombs had at its head a little wooden cross bearing the man's name, regiment, and rank, and the date of his death, and in some cases his comrades had done a little more. Here Australian gunners had made a pattern with fuse caps on the earth that covered their friend, and there a lid of a biscuit-tin had been beaten into a plaque, bearing a crucifix. Death had made strange bedfellows : in one little cemetery high up at the Chailak Dere behind Rhododendron Ridge there lay side by side Private John Jones, Royal Welsh Fusiliers and Sergeant Rotahiru of the Maoris. From the two ends of the earth Christian and Buddhist and Sikh had come to fight in the same cause, and in death they lay together. It was my lot in the last days of September to endeavour to compile a register of where the men of my Battalion had been interred, and as I went from grave to grave writing down the name of one Irishman after another I was irresistibly reminded of Davis's lines :

> " But on far foreign fields from Dunkirk to Belgrade
> Lie the heroes and chiefs of the Irish Brigade."

Now the age-long quarrel with the Turk had carried Irishmen even further afield and the " Wild Geese " who fought on the Danube under

Prince Eugene found their successors in those of the 10th Division who lay under the Cross of Christ in the barren waste of Gallipoli.

Not indeed that every grave was marked with a cross. Some had fallen within the enemy's lines and others were hastily buried under the parados of a captured trench without even a stone to mark where they lay. In the heat of battle, it was impossible to delay for forms and ceremonies, and often even the names of the fallen were not noted. Only those who died in hospital were buried with proper rites, but it mattered little where the bodies of the heroes rested. The whole land is one shrine, made sacred by the memory of devotion to duty and self-sacrifice, and no man could wish to lie elsewhere than in the ground he had won from the enemy.

Yet it seemed a pity that it should be knocked to pieces so soon. Much labour spread over many weary months had gone to form it and to make it worthy of the name of Irish, and it was tragic that it should practically be annihilated with so little tangible result achieved. It is not perhaps altogether easy for the civilian to understand how sorrowful it seems unless he realises that a unit trained to arms has a spiritual as well as a material being. A battalion of infantry is not merely a collection of a thousand men armed with rifles ; it is, or at any rate, it should be, a community, possessing mutual hopes, mutual fears, and mutual affection.   Officers and men have learnt to know one another and to rely on one another, and if they are worth their salt, the spiritual bond uniting them is far stronger and more effectual for good than the power conferred by rank and authority.   In the 10th Division the bonds uniting all ranks were unusually strong.   In the first place came love of Ireland shared in equal degree by officers and men. Second to this, and only second, was pride of regiment, happiness at forming part of a unit which had had so many glorious deeds recorded of it and resolution to be worthy of its fame.   The names of the battalion, Dublins, Munsters, Inniskillings, Connaught Rangers, spoke not only of home, but also of splendid achievements performed in the past, and nerved us to courage and endurance in the future.   ,

Above and beyond these feelings, common to all Irish soldiers, the 10th Division had a peculiar intimacy gained from the circumstances of its formation.   It was the first Irish Division to take the field in war.   Irish Brigades there had often been ; they had fought under the fleur-de-lys and the tricolour of France and under the Stars and Stripes as well as they had done under the Union Jack. But never before in Ireland's history had she sent forth a whole division (but for one battalion) of her sons to the battle-field.

The old battalions of the Regular Army had done magnificently, but they had necessarily been brigaded with English, Scotch and Welsh units. The 10th Division was the first Division almost entirely composed of Irish battalions to face the enemy. Officers and men alike knew this and were proud of their destiny. As the battalions marched through the quiet English countryside, the drums and fifes shrilled out "St. Patrick's Day" or "Brian Boru's March," and the dark streets of Basingstoke echoed the voices that chanted "God Save Ireland" as the units marched down to entrain. Nor did we lack "the green." One unit sewed shamrocks on to its sleeves, another wore them as helmet badges. Almost every company cherished somewhere an entirely unofficial green flag, as dear to the men as if they were the regimental colours themselves. These constituted an outward and visible sign that the honour of Ireland was in the Division's keeping, and the men did not forget it.

There was singularly little jealousy in the Division. Naturally, where there were two battalions of one regiment in the same brigade, each one of them cherished the belief that they and they alone were the true representatives of the old regiment, but this was only wholesome emulation. Where this cause for rivalry did not exist units were on very good terms, and at Basingstoke, where the different messes

first really got to know one another, there was
any amount of friendship and good fellowship.
Every battalion, of course, believed that it was
the finest Service Battalion in the Army, but
it was also convinced that the remainder of
the Division, though inferior to itself, reached
a very much higher standard than any other
unit in K.1.

Having regard to this sentiment it was with
great regret that officers and men found that
the Division was not destined to take the field
as a whole.   The first shock was the loss of
the artillery, and the realisation that we should
be compelled to rely on the support of strange
gunners when we took the field.   Next came the
fact that the 29th Brigade was detached and
sent to Anzac, where in turn it met with yet
further sub-division, its battalions going into
action as isolated units.

Finally, the mischance that sent the 5th
Inniskillings, the two battalions of Munster
Fusiliers, and the Pioneer battalion into action
on the Kiretch Tepe, while the remainder of
the 30th and 31st Brigades were fighting under
General Hill at the other end of the Suvla
area, destroyed the last chance that the Division
as a whole might place some distinct achievement
to its credit.

Of the dash and eagerness of the men there
was no doubt.   All they needed was to be told
what they were to do, and they would carry it

out whatever the cost. They showed, too, on the 16th August, that in addition to eagerness in the charge, a quality never lacking in Irish soldiers, they possessed the rarer and finer military quality of dogged tenacity. Whoever may be blamed for the small success achieved in Gallipoli, no discredit rests on the rank and file of the 10th Division.

The circumstances attending the formation of absolutely new units had brought officers and men into a somewhat unusual relationship. In the old Regular Army, except for a few N.C.O.'s and old soldiers who have wives and families in married quarters, and an occasional indiscreet youth who marries off the strength, the family life of the soldier never comes under the officers' notice at all. In the New Army things were very different. The rapid expansion of our military forces that took place in August and September, 1914, had placed a tremendous strain on the resources of Paymasters and Record Officers. The confusion and delay inevitably caused by this often meant considerable hardship to the soldier's family, and he had no one to turn to for help but his officer.

First came the question of men whose employers were prepared to increase their pay to the level of their previous wages provided they could prove that they had enlisted. As a rule, the official papers were long in coming, and in consequence company-commanders made out certificates that the men were serving, which, though unofficial, proved effective. Next came the question of allowance ; separation allowance and allowance to dependants, which involved an enormous amount of work and entailed a close acquaintanceship with the details of each man's family history. Finally came the work of stamping and keeping up-to-date the National Insurance cards, which formed the last remaining bond that linked the soldier to his civilian life.

Meanwhile, officer and man had been gaining insight into each other's character. The Company Commander had watched his men change from a mob in civilian clothes to a disciplined body in khaki. He had been busy picking out the intelligent, encouraging the backward, stimulating the lazy, and checking the first steps of a few towards drunkenness and vice. In all this he had had the invaluable assistance of his company sergeant-major, and an intimacy had grown up between them of no ordinary kind. When it was severed, as it too often was, on the field of battle, the survivor felt that he had been maimed and deprived of an invaluable support.

On a smaller scale a similar relationship arose between the subaltern and his platoon-sergeant, while among the specialists, signallers and machine-gunners, the bond between officer and men was even closer as became those who shared a common mystery. The whole unit had grown up together ; the men in the ranks had watched the subaltern who had joined ignorant of the rudiments of drill acquire knowledge and self-confidence, and in the process had learned to trust him themselves. The officers had seen with pleasure a boy selected for a lance-corporal's stripe because he showed signs of intelligence, gradually gaining experience and the power to command men, until sometimes he graduated into an excellent sergeant. There were many common memories ; wet days on the Curragh, long treks in the Hampshire dust, scuffles in the hedgerows during a field-day, bivouacs in a twilight meadow, all combined to cement the feeling of friendship between officer and men. Sometimes these memories went back to a period before the War. Nearly all the officers were Irish, and most of them were serving in their Territorial units, with the result that they often found privates who were their near neighbours and knew the woods, and the bogs, and the wet winding roads of home. All this was good ; it gave the Division a char-acter that it could not otherwise have obtained, but it had its black side when men began to fall. It was not merely Number So-and-so Private Kelly who was killed, it was little Kelly, who had cooked (very badly) for the mess at Basingstoke, or Kelly who had begged so eagerly not to be left behind with the first reinforcements, or Kelly, the only son of a widowed mother, who lived on the Churchtown Road, three miles from home.

To the staff and the High Command, men must necessarily be no more than cyphers on a casualty list, but to the regimental officer it is very much otherwise, and every man who falls causes a fresh pang to his commander's heart. Few things are more distressing to an officer than to hear the roll of his unit called after an engagement, to look in vain among the thinned ranks for many familiar faces, to hear no answer given to name after name of the men with whom his life has been bound up for months. This and not any extreme of physical suffering is the hardest ordeal that a soldier has to face.

Nor was this loss of friends and comrades the only cause of sorrow. The same feelings have been felt in every unit of the New Army after a strenuous engagement, but the 10th Division had a special reason for regret since the 10th Division was a thing unique in itself. Ireland is a land of long and bitter memories, and those memories make it extremely difficult for Irishmen to unite for any common purpose. Many have believed it impossible, and would have prophesied that the attempt to create an Irish Division composed of men of every class, creed and political opinion would be foredoomed to failure. And yet it succeeded.

The old quarrels, the inherited animosities were forgotten, and men who would have scowled at one another without speaking became comrades and friends. Only those who know Ireland can realise how difficult this was.

The Division was not composed of professional soldiers ; many of the officers and men had played, or, at least, had relatives who had played, an active part in the agrarian and political struggles that have raged in Ireland for the last forty years. Yet all this went for nothing ; the bond of common service and common sacrifice proved so strong and enduring that Catholic and Protestant, Unionist and Nationalist, lived and fought and died side by side like brothers. Little was spoken concerning the points on which we differed, and once we had tacitly agreed to let the past be buried we found thousands of points on which we agreed. To an Englishman this no doubt appears natural, for beneath all superficial disagreements the English do possess a nature in common and look on things from the same point of view, but in Ireland up to the present things have been very different. It is only to be hoped that the willingness to forget old wrongs and injustices, and to combine for a common purpose, that existed in the 10th Division, may be a good augury for the future.

No doubt the experience of the two other Irish Divisions of the New Army has been the same. Both of them have since won abundant glory in France. When the War is over, all these combats shared together, and dangers faced side-by-side, should count for something in the making of the new Ireland.

No doubt it may seem to the outsider that all this is founded on an unstable foundation, and that the 10th Division did not do so much after all. Measured by the scale of material results he may seem correct. At Suvla, indeed, they claim to have taken Chocolate Hill and to have gained ground along the Kiretch Tepe Sirt, part of which they were unable to hold. At Anzac two battalions seized part of the Chunuk Bair and held it until they were driven off, a third succeeded in maintaining its position on Rhododendron Ridge, while the fourth captured the wells of Kabak Kuyu and gained a footing for a time on Hill 60. All these were but incidents in what was itself an unsuccessful campaign, yet officers and men did all that was required of them. They died. There was no fear or faltering, there was no retirement without orders.

The 10th Division, young soldiers without knowledge or experience of war, were plunged into one of the hardest and fiercest campaigns ever waged by the British Army, and acquitted themselves with credit. They make no claim to exclusive glory, to have done more than it was their duty to do, but they have no cause to be ashamed. Their shattered ranks, their enormous list of casualties, show clearly enough what they endured, and the words used by Sir Ian Hamilton of one brigade are true of the whole Division. He wrote :—

> " The old German notion that no unit would stand a loss of more than 25 per cent. had been completely falsified. The 13th Division and the 29th Brigade of the 10th (Irish) Division had lost more than twice that proportion, and in spirit were game for as much more fighting as might be required."

This may reasonably be applied to the 30th and 31st Brigades as well as to the 29th, for the best proof of the enduring spirit of the Division may be found in the fact that when after having lost nearly 75 per cent. of its original strength, it was hastily filled up with drafts and sent under-officered and barely rested to fight a new and arduous campaign single-handed, it did creditably.

In some quarters, particularly in Ireland, which is a sensitive and suspicious country, it has been suggested that the services of the Division have not been adequately recognized. Little is to be gained by engaging in a controversy on this point. No doubt if on the grounds that the Gallipoli campaign was unsuccessful, the men who fought there are refused a clasp to their medals, and the regiments who took part in it are not permitted to add its name to the battle honours on their colours, much resentment will be aroused, but it is hardly likely that this will occur. If precedents are needed,

Talavera and Busaco, both of which figure as British victories, were followed by retirements and by no definite result other than the exhaustion of the enemy's forces. Corunna, too, which was merely a repulse of a pursuing enemy, followed by embarkation and evacuation, is considered a victory, and while these names are emblazoned among the battle-honours of regiments there is little reason for excluding Gallipoli, where men suffered as much and fought as bravely.

But, after all, these considerations, though sentiment endears them to the soldier, are minor matters. The soldier's true reward is the gratitude of his fellow-countrymen, and that we have in full measure obtained. Ireland will not easily forget the deeds of the 10th Division.

APPENDIX A

ON AUTHORITIES

IN writing this Book I have in the main been guided by my own memory and by information obtained from other officers, but I have also read almost every book dealing with Gallipoli that has been published up to the present (February, 1917). Three of these have been of great value to me, since their authors served with the Division. The first (*At Suvla Bay by John Hargrave. Constable*) was written by a sergeant in the 32nd Field Ambulance and describes in graphic language the experiences of a stretcher-bearer. It is illustrated by a number of sketches from the author's hand. The second book (*Suvla Bay and After, by Juvenis. Hodder and Stoughton*) is also a record of individual experiences. Though the author is anonymous and is very reticent in giving detailed information of any kind, yet he appears from internal evidence to have been an officer in the 5th Royal Inniskilling Fusiliers. His narrative describes life on the Peninsula from the 8th to the 15th, on which date he was wounded.

It also gives a vivid account of hospital life at Mudros.

Both these works are first-hand evidence of the doings of individuals, but the third is of greater value to the historian.   It is a record of the services of the 5th (Service) Battalion of the Connaught Rangers between the 19th of August, 1914, and the 17th of January, 1917, compiled by its commanding officer and printed for private circulation by Frederick Hall at the Oxford University Press.   This work not only provides a clear and vivid narrative of the movements of the battalion, but also gives invaluable information as to orders, strength and casualties.   If a similar work were compiled for each unit, the task of the historian would be easy.

I regret that the book dealing with the history of D Company of the 7th Royal Dublin Fusiliers, which has been written by Mr. H. Hanna, K.C., was not published in time to allow me to read it before writing this work. Mr. Hanna has, however, been kind enough to allow me to read part of his proof-sheets, and the information which I obtained from him has been of great assistance to me.

I have also studied the letters from officers and men which appeared in the Irish Press in the Autumn of 1915, but I have not as a rule considered their statements as unimpeachable unless they were confirmed by some independent authority.

APPENDIX B

CASUALTIES TO OFFICERS
(STAFF AND INFANTRY ONLY)

STAFF :

Killed :

Capt. G. W. Nugent, Staff Capt., 29th Brigade.

Wounded :

Brig.-Gen. R. J. Cooper, G.V.O., 29th Brigade.
Major D. J. C. K. Bernard, G.S.O. III.
Capt. A. H. McCleverty, Brigade-Major, 29th Brigade.
Capt. T. J. D. Atkinson, Staff Capt., 31st Brigade.

5TH ROYAL IRISH REGIMENT (PIONEERS).

Killed :

Lieut. R. MacAndrew.
2nd Lieut. J. P. Costello.

Wounded :

Major J. L. Fulda.
Capt. E. C. Morel.
Capt. J. R. Penrose Welsted.
Lieut. E. C. Beard.
Lieut. J. N. More.
2nd Lieut. C. Bewicke.
2nd Lieut. L. M. Lefroy.

Missing :

Lieut. J. R. Duggan.

5TH ROYAL INNISKILLING FUSILIERS.

Killed :

Lieut.-Col. A. S. Vanrenen.
Capt. R. W. Robinson.
Capt. C. E. G Vernon.
Lieut. H. H. McCormack.
Lieut. J. E. T. Nelis.
2nd Lieut. D. J. Grubb.

Died of Wounds :

Lieut. J. R. Whitsitt.

Wounded :

Major T. A. D. Best.
Major C. S. Owen.
Capt. W. C. G. Bolitho.
Capt. V. H. Scott.
Lieut. F. C. Stigant.
Lieut. T. T. H. Verschoyle.
Lieut. T. E. Hastings.
Lieut. F. M. McCormac.
Lieut. O. G. E. MacWilliam.
2nd Lieut. G. C. Ballentine.
2nd Lieut. R. R. A. Darling.
2nd Lieut. L. F. Falls.
2nd Lieut. M. W. F. Hall.
2nd Lieut. I. A. Kirkpatrick.

6TH ROYAL INNISKILLING FUSILIERS.

Killed :

2nd Lieut. W. S. Collen.
2nd Lieut. I. J. Smyth.

Wounded :

Lieut.-Col. H. M. Cliffe.
Major G. C. B. Musgrave.
Lieut. and Qrmr. J. J. Dooley.
Lieut. S. T. Martin.
Lieut. A. B. Douglas.
2nd Lieut. J. F. Hunter.
2nd Lieut. W. Porter.

10TH HAMPSHIRE REGIMENT.

Killed :

Capt. C. C. R. Black Hawkins.
Capt. W. H. Savage.
Lieut. G. L. Cheeseman.
Lieut. P. C. Williams.
2nd Lieut. S. A. Smith.
2nd Lieut. O. S. Whaley.

Died of Wounds :
Capt. G. E. Hellyer.

Wounded :
Lieut.-Col. W. D. Bewsher.
Major L. C. Morley.
Capt. T. A. Shone.
Capt. C. C. Waddington.
Capt. F. M. Hicks.
Lieut. L. Whittome.
Lieut. J. H. Tanner.
Lieut. C. C. Griffith.
Lieut. J. Clement.
2nd Lieut. I. H. German.
2nd Lieut. J. Morse.
2nd Lieut. C. Grellier.
2nd Lieut. G. S. H. De Gaury.

Wounded and Missing :
Major A. L. Pilleau.
Capt. C. B. Hayes.
Lieut. P. L. Bell.

6TH ROYAL IRISH RIFLES.

Killed :
Major and Adjt. W. Eastwood.
2nd Lieut. J. H. B. Lewis.
2nd Lieut. A. W. Richardson.

Died of Wounds :
Capt. J. F. Martyr.

Wounded :
Lieut.-Col. E. C. Bradford.
Major A. L. Wilford.
Major H. J. Morphy.
Capt. P. D. Green Armytage.
Capt. F. E. Eastwood.
Capt. R. H. Lorie.
Capt. R. O. Mansergh.
Lieut. N. McGavin.
Lieut. T. W. E. Brogden.
Lieut. D. Campbell.
Lieut. J. H. Pollock.
2nd Lieut. A. F. Harvey.
2nd Lieut. G. B. J. Smyth.
2nd Lieut. J. Murphy.
2nd Lieut. J. G. Martry.
2nd Lieut. W. G. Ryan.

5TH ROYAL IRISH FUSILIERS.

Killed :
Major W. F. C. Garstin.
Capt. W. J. Hartley.
2nd Lieut. C. Crossly.

Died of Wounds :
Capt. G. G. Duggan.
Capt. A. W. Scott-Skirving.

Wounded :
Major F. W. E. Johnson.
Capt. E. M. McIlwain.
Capt. and Adjt. P. E Kelly
Capt J. A. D. Dempsey.
Capt. H. G. Whyte.
Lieut. J. B. Atkinson.
Lieut. W. A. Beattie.
Lieut. C. F. N. Harris.
Lieut. C. A. Murray.
Lieut. R. V. Murray.
Lieut. J. A. Blood.
2nd Lieut. J. L. Chalmers.
2nd Lieut. P. H. D. Dempsey.
2nd Lieut. E. A. Evanson.
2nd Lieut. F. A. Nowell.
2nd Lieut. L. C. Fitzgerald.
2nd Lieut. J. L. Bennett.

6TH ROYAL IRISH FUSILIERS.

Killed :
Major H. M. Taylor.
Capt. and Adjt. J. C. Johnston.
Capt. B. V. Falle.
Lieut. L. Tolerton.
Lieut. J. S. Schute.
2nd Lieut. H. M. MacDermot.
2nd Lieut. G. F. Dobbin.
2nd Lieut. P. S. Snell.
2nd Lieut. W. A. Birmingham.

Wounded :
Lieut.-Colonel F. A Greer.
Capt. W. A. Woods.
Capt. F. G. M. Wigley.
Capt. H. F. Belli Biver.
Capt. F. R. M. Crozier.
Capt. F. Jackson.
Lieut. G. H. Gallogly.
Lieut. F. H. Ledgerwood.
Lieut. A. L. Gregg.
Lieut. P. C. Tudor Craig.
2nd Lieut. J. C. McCutcheon.
2nd Lieut. C. F. Kennedy.
2nd Lieut. R. S. Trimble.
2nd Lieut. W. R. Egar.
2nd Lieut. C. E. T. Lewis.

Missing (believed killed) :
2nd Lieut. C. M. A. Barker.
2nd Lieut. J. J. Beasley.
2nd Lieut. F. G. Heuston.

5TH CONNAUGHT RANGERS.

Killed :

Lieut. A. J. W. Blake.
2nd Lieut. J. E. Burke.
2nd Lieut. G. R. Bennett.

Died of Wounds :

Major N. C. K. Money.
Capt. A. S. Hog.

Wounded :

Major H. J. Nolan Ferrall.
Capt. and Adjt. H. W. B. Maling.
Capt. A. Webber.
Capt. F. C. Burke.
Capt. G. J. B. E. Massy.
Capt. B. W. Bond.
Lieut. J. W. Cartmell Robinson.
Lieut. T. S. P. Martin.
Lieut. F. J. Charlton.
Lieut. O. M. Tweedy.
2nd Lieut. A. D. Mulligan.
2nd Lieut. J. Wallace.
2nd Lieut. T. W. G. Johnson.
2nd Lieut. E. J. G. Kelly.
2nd Lieut. A. St. J. Mahony.

Wounded and Missing :

Lieut. S. T. H. Lewis.

6TH LEINSTER REGIMENT.

Killed :

Lieut. N. J. Figgis.
Lieut. G. W. B. Gough.
2nd Lieut. A. R. Toomey.
2nd Lieut. W. S. C. Griffith.
2nd Lieut. H. G. Hickson.
2nd Lieut. J. V. Y. Willington.

Wounded :

Lieut.-Col. J. C. Craske, D.S.O.
Major T. R. Stannus.
Lieut. A. J. Jennings.
2nd Lieut. H. D. Little.

Missing (believed killed) :

Capt. C. C. D'Arcy Irvine.

6TH ROYAL MUNSTER FUSILIERS.

Killed :

Major E. P. Conway.
Lieut. J. B. Lee.
Lieut. G. W. Burrowes.

Died of Wounds :

Major J. N. Jephson.
2nd Lieut. L. A. Gaffney.

Wounded :

Lieut.-Col. V. T. Worship,D.S.O.
Capt. H. G. Oldnall.
Capt. H. G. Livingston.
Capt. C. Y. Baldwin.
Lieut. G. W. N. N. Haynes.
Lieut. A. T. Lee.
Lieut. E. A. Thornton.
2nd Lieut. H. M. Chambers.
2nd Lieut. T. E. Hearn.
2nd Lieut. J. I. Comerford.
2nd Lieut. J. W. L. Rathbone.
2nd Lieut. S. C. Webb.

Missing :

Capt. J. B. T. Grant.

7TH ROYAL MUNSTER FUSILIERS.

Killed :

Capt. R. H. Cullinan.
Capt. J. V. Dunn.
Lieut. K. E. O'Duffy.
Lieut. S. R. V. Travers.
2nd Lieut. E. M. Harper.
2nd Lieut. F. E. Bennett.
2nd Lieut. W. H. Good.

Wounded :

Major C. L. Hendricks.
Capt. A. L. Cooper Key.
Capt. W. F. Henn.
Capt. M. Wace.
Capt. H. Aplin.
Lieut. W. E. McClelland.
Lieut. H. G. Montagu.
Lieut. T. D. Hallinan.
Lieut. C. E. Longfield.
Lieut. R. E. Lawler.
2nd Lieut. V. J. Magnier.
2nd Lieut. F. S. L. Stokes.
2nd Lieut. J. L. Fitzmaurice.

6TH ROYAL DUBLIN FUSILIERS.

Killed :

Capt. A. J. D. Preston.
Capt. and Adjt. W. R. Richards.
Lieut. J. J. Doyle.
2nd Lieut. W. C. Nesbitt.
2nd Lieut. F. B. O'Carroll.
2nd Lieut. W. F. C. McGarry.

Died of Wounds :
2nd Lieut. W. L. G. Mortimer.

Wounded :
Capt. W. H. Whyte
Capt P. T. L. Thompson.
Capt. R. B. C. Kennedy.
Capt. J. Luke.
Capt. J. J. T. Carroll.
Capt. W. S. Lennon.
Lieut. C. A. Martin.
2nd Lieut. R. W. Carter.
2nd Lieut. C. F. Healy.
2nd Lieut. M. Moloney.

Wounded and Missing :
Major J. G. Jennings.
Lieut. D. R. Clery.
2nd Lieut. R. Stanton.

[All these are believed to have been killed.]

7TH ROYAL DUBLIN FUSILIERS.

Killed :
Major C. H. Tippet.
Major R. S. M. Harrison.
Capt. P. H. Hickman.
Capt. G. Pige Leschallas.
Capt. R. P. Tobin.
Lieut. M. J. Fitzgibbon.
Lieut. A. J. Russell.
2nd Lieut. E. T. Weatherill.

Died of Wounds :
Lieut. E. L. Julian.

Wounded :
Lieut.-Col. G. Downing.
Capt. L. S. N. Palmer.
Lieut. C. B. Girvin.
Lieut. A. W. MacDermott.
2nd Lieut. C. D. Harvey.
2nd Lieut. H. L. Clover.
2nd Lieut. G. Hicks.
Lieut. A. M. Eynaud (Royal Malta Regiment of Militia attached.)

Missing :
2nd Lieut. A. G. Crichton.

I regret that I have been unable to compile a full list of casualties in the Royal Artillery, Royal Engineers, Army Service Corps and Royal Army Medical Corps. Among those who were killed and wounded were :—

Killed :
Capt. H. J. Sudell, Army Service Corps.

Wounded and Missing (probably killed) :
2nd Lieut. M. W. Prettyman Royal Engineers.

Wounded :
Capt. C. R. Satterthwaite, Royal Engineers.
Lieut. C. Patteson, Royal Engineers.
Lieut. L. Cassidy, Royal Army Medical Corps.

APPENDIX C

NAMES OF OFFICERS, NON-COMMISSIONED OFFICERS, AND MEN MENTIONED IN GENERAL SIR IAN HAMILTON'S DESPATCHES

JANUARY AND MARCH, 1916

STAFF :

Lieut.-General Sir B. T. Mahon, K.C.V.O., C.B., D.S.O.
Colonel (temporary Brigadier-General) F. F. Hill, C.B., D.S.O.
Lieut.-Col. (temporary Brigadier-General) J. G. King King, D.S.O., Res. of Officers.
Major M. J. N. Cooke Collis, Royal Irish Rifles.
Capt. A. H. McCleverty, 2nd Rajput Light Infantry.

ROYAL ENGINEERS.

Lieut.-Col. F. K. Fair.
Temporary Lieut. C. Patteson.
Temporary Lieut. J. H. de W. Waller.

ROYAL IRISH REGIMENT.

Temporary Lieut.-Col. Rt. Hon. B. A. W. P., Earl of Granard, K.P., G.C.V.O.
Temporary Major V. M. B. Scully.
No. 5,615, C.S.M. R. Gallagher.
No. 223, C.S.M. M. McGrath.
No. 2,797, Lance-Corporal A. Laughlin.
No. 2,821, Lance-Corporal W. Grant.
No. 1,251, Private J. C. Keefe.

ROYAL INNISKILLING FUSILIERS

No. 12,519, Corporal J. Matchett.
No. 12,515, Private A. Mason.
No. 13,272, Private R. Bannon.
No. 13,981, Private J. Cox.
Temporary Lieut.-Colonel H. M. Cliff.
Temporary Lieut.-Col. M. P. B. Frazer.
Temporary Major G. C. B. Musgrave.
Temporary Capt. R. H. Scott.
Temporary Lieut. C. G. Barton.
Temporary Second-Lieut. G. B. Lyndon.
No. 7,817, Sgt. M. Garrett.
No. 17,986, Lance-Corporal W. Wynne.
No. 11,792, Lance-Corporal J. Maple.
No. 19,955, Private P. O'Kane.
No. 11,832, Private J. Lamont.
No. 12,720, Private T. Millar.

HAMPSHIRE REGIMENT.

Temporary Lieut.-Col. W. D. Bewsher.
Temporary Capt. F. M. Hicks.
Temporary Capt. P. H. Hudson.
Quartermaster and Hon. Lieut. W. J. Saunders.
No. 4,410, Temporary Sergeant-Major J. Smith.
No. 42,196, Company Sergt.-Major W. T. Groves.

No. 4,545, Sergeant T. Sturges.
No. 10,205, Private F. Biddi-
combe.
No. 9,871, Private J. C. R.
Moxham.
No. 14,938, Private F. Dyer.
No. 14,295, Private E. P. Shawe.

ROYAL IRISH RIFLES.

Lieut.-Colonel E. C. Bradford.
Temporary Major W. Eastwood.
Temporary Major H. L. Wilford.
Regimental Sergeant-Major P.
Mulholland.

ROYAL IRISH FUSILIERS.

Temporary Lieut.-Col. M. J. W.
Pike.
Major F. W. E. Johnson.
Capt. P. E. Kelly.
Temporary Capt. H. S. C. Panton
2nd Lieut. C. Crossley.
Temporary Capt. G. M. Kidd.
Temporary Lieut.-Col. F. A.
Greer.
Temporary Major M. J. Thomp-
son.
Temporary Capt. P. C. Tudor
Craig.
Temporary Lieut. A. L. Gregg.
Quartermaster and Hon. Lieut.
S. L. Cleall.
Temporary 2nd Lieut. F. G.
Heuston.
No. 12,169, Sergeant J. Donohoe.
No. 12,166, Sergeant G. O'Neill.
No. 11,892, Sergeant G. Thir-
kettle.
No. 1,991, Lance-Corporal G.
Cassells.
No. 15,641, Private C. Kipps.
No. 13,703, Private C. Lees.

CONNAUGHT RANGERS.

Temporary Lieut.-Col. H. F. N.
Jourdain.
Temporary Major N. C. K.
Money.
Temporary Major B. R. Cooper.
Capt. H. B. W. Maling (Adjt.)
Capt. G. J. B. E. Massy.
Temporary Lieut. A. J. W.
Blake.
Lieut. S. H. Lewis.

No. 3,010, Temporary Sergeant-
Major J. Hudson.
No. 319, Acting C.Q.M. Sergeant
M. Nealon.
No. 652, Sergeant J. O'Connell.
No. 6,757, Sergeant J. McIlwaine.
No. 824, Acting Corporal J.
Doyle.
No. 83, Private J. Geehan.
No. 3,831, Private J. Sweeney.
No. 529, Private M. Kilroy.

LEINSTER REGIMENT.

Lieut.-Col. J. Craske, D.S.O.
Temporary Capt. C. Lyster.
Temporary Capt. C. W. D'Arcy
Irvine.
Capt. H. W. Andrews (Adjt.)
Temporary 2nd Lieut. H. G.
Hickson.
No. 8,120, Company Sergeant-
Major H. H. Anderson.
No. 833, Sergeant J. Henry.
No. 1,201, Sergeant E. W. Bruce.
No. 3,134, Private J. Carolan.

ROYAL MUNSTER FUSILIERS.

Temporary Lieut.-Col. M. A.
Tynte.
Major J. N. Jephson.
Temporary Capt. B. R. French.
No. 250, Company Sergeant-
Major J. Murphy.
No. 26, Sergeant J. Ring.
No. 176, Sergeant W. Connors.
No. 545, Corporal R. Saunders.
Temporary Major G. Drage.
Temporary Major H. Aplin.
Temporary Lieut. H. Fitz-
maurice.
Temporary Lieut. E. M. Harper.
Temporary Capt. G. H. Davis.
Temporary Lieut. S. R. V.
Travers.
Temporary 2nd Lieut. F. T. S.
Powell.
Qr. Master and Hon. Lieut. C.
Lindsay.
No. 10,397, Sergeant-Major M.
Stacey.
No. 2,364, Company Sergeant-
Major R. Mason.
No. 2,501, Private W. Bellamy.
No. 2,521, Private H. Carbult.

ROYAL DUBLIN FUSILIERS.

Temporary Lieut.-Col. P. G. A. Cox.
Temporary Major W. H. Whyte.
Capt. A. J. D. Preston.
Capt. P. T. L. Thompson.
Capt. W. R. Richards.
Qr. Master and Hon. Lieut. R. Byrne.
No. 13,507, Temporary Sergeant-Major J. Campbell.
No. 17,141, Sergeant J. West.
No. 13,197, Corporal E. Bryan.
Lieut.-Col. G. Downing.
Major R. S. M. Harrison.
Major M. P. L. Lonsdale.
Temporary Major C. B. R. Hoey.
Temporary Capt. R. P. Tobin.
Temporary Capt. L. S. N. Palmer.

Temporary Capt. G. N. Williamson.
No. 14,153, Regimental Sergeant-Major A. Guest.
No. 14,133, Company Sergeant-Major W. Kee.
No. 14,972, Company Sergeant-Major T. Haig.
No. 14,275, Company Sergeant-Major H. Robinson.
No. 14,150, Sergeant A. E. Burrowes.
No. 14,645, Sergeant E. C. Millar.
No. 13,852, Private A. E. Wilkin.
No. 25,563, Company Sergeant-Major C. Lynch.

CHAPLAIN'S DEPARTMENT.

Rev. R. A. McClean.

APPENDIX D

HONOURS AWARDED TO OFFICERS NON-COMMISSIONED OFFICERS AND MEN OF THE TENTH DIVISION

C.B.

Col. (temp. Brig.-Gen.) R. J. Cooper, C.V.O., Res. of Off.

C.M.G.

Col. (temp. Brig.-Gen.) F. F. Hill, C.B., D.S.O.

Lt. Col. J. Craske, D.S.O., Leinster Regt.

Major (temp. Lt.-Col.) H. F. N. Jourdain, The Connaught Rangers.

D.S.O.

Major (temp. Lt.-Col.) W. D. Bewsher, Res. of Off.

Capt. (temp. Major) N. C. K. Money, Indian Army (att. Connaught Rangers).

Capt. (temp. Major) A. L. Wilford, Indian Army (att. Royal Irish Rifles).

To be Brevet Colonel in the Reserve of Officers.

Lt.-Col. (temp. Brig.-Gen.) J. G. King-King, Res. of Off.

MILITARY CROSS.

Temp. Capt. G. M. Kidd, Royal Irish Fusiliers.

Temp. Capt. C. C. J. Lyster, Leinster Regt.

Capt. G. J. B. E. Massy, The Connaught Rangers.

Temp. Capt. H. S. Panton, Royal Irish Fusiliers.

Temp. Lt. J. F. Hunter, Royal Inniskilling Fusiliers.

Temp. Lt. C. Patteson, Royal Engineers.

Qr.-Master and Hon. Lt. W. J. Saunders, Hampshire Regt.

Qr.-Master and Hon. Lt. R. Byrne, Royal Dublin Fusiliers.

Temp. Sec. Lt. F. G. Henston, Royal Irish Fusiliers.

Temp. Sec. Lt. G. B. Lyndon, Royal Inniskilling Fusiliers.

D.C.M.

No. 8120 Sergt. H. Anderson, 6th Leinster Regt.

No. 2501, Pte. W. Bellamy, 6th Royal Munster Fusiliers.

No. 1470, Pte. F. Biddlecombe, 10th Hampshire Regiment.

No. 10205, L.-Sgt. S. Bowers, 10th Hampshire Regt.

No. 41627, Pioneer T. L. Campbell, Royal Engineers.

No. 3134, Pte. J. Carolan, 6th Leinster Regt.

No. 177, Sergt. W. Connors, 6th Royal Munster Fusiliers.

No. 12169, Sergt. J. Donohoe, 6th Royal Irish Fusiliers.

No. 33452, Corpl. S. A. Fitch, 30th Field Ambulance.

No. 83, Pte. J. Geehan, 5th Connaught Rangers.

No. 14153, Acting Sergt.-Major A. Guest, 7th Royal Dublin Fusiliers.

No. 32611, Sergt. G. Hughes, 30th Field Ambulance.

No. 15641, Pte. C. Kipps, 6th Royal Irish Fusiliers.

No. 11832, Pte. J. Lamont, 6th Royal Inniskilling Fusiliers.

No. 11782, C. - Sergt.-Major C. Lynch, 5th Royal Inniskilling Fusiliers.

No. 12515, Pte. A. Mason, 5th Royal Inniskilling Fusiliers.

No. 2464, Acting C. - Sergt. - Major R. Mason, 7th Royal Munster Fusiliers.

No. 17792, Lance - Corpl. J. Meckle, 6th Royal Inniskilling. Fusiliers.

No. 250, C. - Sergt. - Major J Murphy, 6th Royal Munster Fusiliers.

No. 642, Sergt J O'Connell, 5th Connaught Rangers

No 1251, Pte J O'Keefe, 5th Royal Irish Regiment.

No. 4545, Acting C.-Sergt -Major T. Sturges, 10th Hampshire Regiment.

No 17986, L.-Corpl. St. C. P. Wynne, 6th Royal Inniskilling Fusiliers.

Clasp to D.C.M.

No. 3010, Sergt.-Major J. Hudson, 5th Connaught Rangers, was awarded a clasp to the D.C.M. won by him in South Africa when serving with the Irish Guards.

INDEX

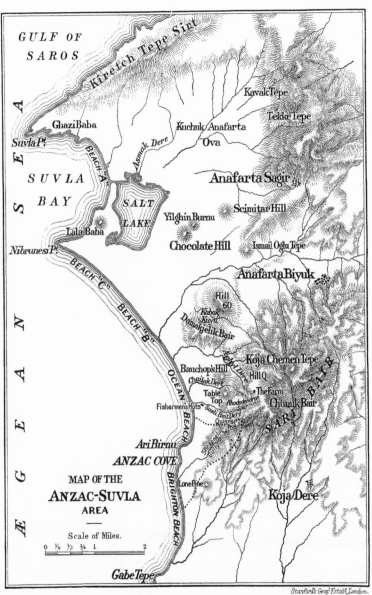

GULF OF
SAROS

Kiretch Tepe Sirt

Kavak Tepe

Tekke Tepé

Ghazi Baba

Suvla Pt.

Asmak Dere

Kuchuk Anafarta
Ova

BEACH "A"

Anafarta Sagir

SUVLA

BAY

SALT
LAKE

Yilghin Burnu

Scimitar Hill

Lala Baba

Chocolate Hill

Ismail Oglu Tepe

Nibrunesi Pt.

BEACH "C"

BEACH "B"

Anafarta Biyuk

Hill
60

Kabak
Kuyu

Damakjelik Bair

OCEAN BEACH

Bauchop's Hill

Koja Chemen Tepe

Chailak Dere

Hill Q

Table
Top

Rhododendron
Spur

The Farm

Chunuk Bair

Fishermens Huts

Sazli Beit Dere

Quinn's

SARI BAIR

Ari Birnu

ANZAC COVE

Shrapnel Gully

MAP OF THE
ANZAC-SUVLA
AREA
—
Scale of Miles.

0   ¼ ½ ¾ 1   2

Lone Pine

BRIGHTON BEACH

Koja Dere

Gabe Tepe

Stanford's Geog.l Estab.t, London.

S   E   A

A   E   G   E   A   N

Dotted Line·········· represents roughly the boundary of Anzac Area
on Aug. 4, 1915.

Errata

p. 23	11th line from bottom	read 74 feet instead of 73
p. 28	20th line from bottom	. . . that year <u>Gardners</u> . . .
p. 35	top caption, line 2	. . . at <u>Red House</u> Bridge . . .
p. 55	line 14	. . . the <u>navigable</u> underground . . .
p. 80	first caption, line 14	. . . now <u>partly</u> filled in . . .
p. 100	caption	No. 8 is River Brun; River Calder is at the south of the embankment.
p. 104	2nd line after quote	. . . Henfield (<u>now called Enfield</u>) . . .
p. 105	caption, 2nd line	. . . engine <u>house</u> . . .
p. 106	caption, 10th line from bottom	. . . about <u>eighty</u> years ago.
p. 110	caption, line 10	omit <u>tidily</u>
p. 124	2nd caption, line 4	. . . dredger <u>No. 11</u>, together . . .
p. 143	3rd line from bottom	. . . Hargreaves (<u>Lancashire</u>) Ltd . . .
p. 149	7th line from bottom	. . . and <u>Jesse</u> Hartley . . .
p. 163	caption, line 10	. . . Barnsley Canal <u>or</u> from . . .
p. 173	line 1	replace sentence with
		'The Constables were paid 18*s*. per week. They were instructed, together with all the company's agents, lock-keepers and ban rangers, to report any pilfering to the superintendent.'
p. 205	top caption, line 2	. . . at <u>Sandhills</u> warehouse . . .

A History and Guide by Mike Clarke

with ten circular walks by John Dixon

Carnegie Publishing, 1994

The Leeds and Liverpool Canal: A History and Guide
by Mike Clarke, with ten circular walks from the canal by John Dixon

Text copyright © Mike Clarke 1990, 1994 and 2003
Walks copyright © John Dixon 1990, 1994 and 2003

First published in hard cover in 1990 by Carnegie Press, Preston

This edition published in 1994 by Carnegie Publishing Ltd
Carnegie House
Chatsworth Road
Lancaster LA1 4SL
Tel: 01524-840111
www.carnegiepublishing.com

Reprinted 2003

British Library Cataloguing-in-Publication data
A catalogue record for this book is available from the British Library

ISBN 1-85936-013-0

Original cover painting by Ivan Frontani

Typeset by Carnegie Publishing Ltd
Printed and bound in the UK by the Alden Press, Oxford

Contents

Acknowledgements

IT was when I was living on my boat *Pluto* that I resolved to write a history of the Leeds and Liverpool Canal. At this time I was able to obtain much background material which has facilitated my more recent researches. I would like to thank the many boatmen and others who helped me at this time, particularly the Carter family of Burscough, who often ensured that my boat did not sink when I was away!

More recently, I would like to thank the staff of the various record offices at Northallerton, Bradford, Leeds, Wakefield, Doncaster, Liverpool and at the Public Record Office at both Chancery Lane and Kew. The staff at the Lancashire Record Office and at the Wigan Record Office were especially helpful, as were those at the Craven Museum in Skipton. I would also like to thank those who helped me at the various libraries along the line of the canal, in particular the staff at Blackburn Reference Library, Skipton Library and John Goodchild at Wakefield Library, not forgetting my colleagues at Accrington, particularly Alan Duckworth. Many British Waterways staff have helped with information, particularly Mrs Robinson at Dock Street, Leeds, Mr Hayes at Northwich, the staff at their archives at Gloucester, and John Gibbons of Burscough. The following people were among the many who gave me additional information: Frank Smith, Harry Major, Sam Yates, Gordon Biddle, Mrs and Mrs Oldfield, Alan Holden, Geoff Wheat and Philip Watkinson. My apologies to anyone I have omitted.

Tony Lewery and Edward Paget-Tomlinson provided the excellent line drawings for which I am most grateful, while Marilyn Frear of Wigan Education Dept., Jack Aldritt, Philip Watkinson and Jack Parkinson lent some of the photographs used. Other photographs came from Lancashire Libraries, Leeds City Libraries and Museums, Wigan Record Office, Liverpool City Engineer's Department, W. F. King of Shipley, Ben Shaw (Photo Craft), Mrs Clarkson of Silsden, the Lancashire Record Office at Preston, the Harris Museum at Preston, Mrs Gavin of Keighley, the Railway and Canal Historical Society, and William Oldfield of Riddlesden. The British Waterways Board were also most helpful in providing access to their excellent collection of illustrations. The maps, longitudinal section and graphs were drawn by Alistair Hodge and Anna Goddard of Carnegie Press. Thanks also to Dr Alan Crosby of Preston for compiling the index.

Particular thanks go to John Dixon, author of an excellent series of walking books, for the marvellous set of ten circular walks which he devised using the canal towpath; I am sure that people using the canal will find them a wonderful way of spending many happy hours.

The useful advice and guide section was compiled with the help and assistance of the British Waterways Board.

Finally, I would also like to thank Alistair Hodge for his work in editing my manuscript and for producing the maps, and his staff at Carnegie Press for providing all those cups of coffee.

Introduction

HE Leeds and Liverpool Canal was the most successful long-distance canal in Britain. In 1906 it carried 2,337,401 tons of cargo an average distance of 21.12 miles, producing around £180,000 in revenue. In overall terms of quantity of goods and distance carried, no other British canal could compare with this. The Birmingham Canal Navigation did carry more, at over seven million tons, but it did so only over short distances, the average being just eight miles. The Aire and Calder Navigation also carried slightly more, at 2.8 million tons, but here the larger size of the river locks meant that far larger boats could use the navigation.

One factor in the success of the Leeds and Liverpool was its sheer size. With a main line of 127¼ miles, it is the longest single canal in Britain. Just as important, the area through which it passes was – and is – one of the most heavily populated in the land. The canal linked Liverpool, Wigan, Blackburn, Burnley, Skipton, Keighley, Shipley, Bingley, Bradford (via the Bradford Canal) and Leeds. These towns, and others in the area, were the cradle of the revolution in textile manufacture and the Leeds and Liverpool Canal, as probably the region's single most important transport facility, thus holds a particularly important place in English, and indeed world, history.

Unlike many canals, the Leeds and Liverpool was never tied to any one particular trade or traffic. Coal, wool, cotton, limestone, grain and general cargo were all carried in huge quantities by a wide range of carriers. Partly because of this and partly because of the sheer length of the canal, the Leeds and Liverpool boasted an immense diversity of traffic. Carriers developed for particular trades and several general services were operated so successfully for so long that in negotiations with the competing railway companies the canal company usually came out on top. For many years the canal beat off the railways' competition by being more competitive, more efficient and even, it was claimed, considerably quicker on some routes than the railways.

Why, then, has the longest and arguably most important canal in Britain been so very poorly served by historians? No single book tells its story beyond the most cursory narrative. The only substantial commentary comes in Charles Hadfield and Gordon Biddle's *The Canals of North-West England*. The Leeds and Liverpool is indeed mentioned in many other books and articles, many of them listed in the bibliography, but this work has never been pulled together and properly explained. I hope that this book serves the purpose.

Yet, there are plenty of records and archives for such a study. The most important collection is in the Public Record Office at Kew in London. Among these are a statistical history, compiled at the end of the last century, giving the canal's income and expenditure, and a full set of the company minutes. These provide an excellent insight into the running of the canal, though the minutes for the latter part of the nineteenth century can be further explained by using the notes made during the meetings by Warde-Aldam, one of the company's directors, which are held in Doncaster Library Archive. The papers of two more directors remain: those of the Rev. Glover Moore in Lancashire Record Office and of Mr Darcy Wyvill in North Yorkshire Record Office. The information on the River Douglas Navigation was mainly gleaned from papers in the Wigan Record Office and from the Public Record Office at Chancery Lane. Many other records are preserved around the country and a list of sources can be found at the back of the book.

Chapter One

'Wooden boats, iron men'

Boats and boatmen on the Leeds and Liverpool

 T was 1976 and I was standing in the bar of the Farmers Arms at New Lane, near Burscough. I was waiting for Nellie, the landlady, to finish feeding my dog Pluto before pulling me a pint. Tom Draper was on the way to the dartboard and, as he passed me, he said, 'You've got working through them swing bridges single-handed well sorted out.' It wasn't really praise, just an observation, but it made me feel that I was at least some way towards knowing how to handle a barge. New Lane was one of several communities around Burscough that were built in the nineteenth century to house boatmen and their families. Although twelve years had gone by since the last loaded coal boat had passed here on its way to Liverpool, there were still many ex-boatmen living at New Lane, and little happened on the canal that they missed.

The families of many of them had lived by and worked on the canal for generations, with names such as Cheetham, Gibbons and Forshaw being recorded as boatmen or flatmen as early as the 1841 census. They were proud of this long association with the canal but not of the state into which it had fallen, particularly as so-called improvements had made it much more difficult to navigate with a traditional full-width barge, as I was finding out for myself.

Many of them gave me advice and would talk of all the boats and boatmen they had known, or their fathers had told them about. I wish I could remember a quarter of what George and John Cheetham related to me when I was with them. Now, sadly, both of them have died.

Bits of useful information were always forthcoming. I had always found it difficult to line my boat *Pluto* for the second lock at Johnsons Hillock when heading downhill. When I mentioned this casually one day, the reason was soon provided. From the third lock there was a 90° bend to the left to the second lock. When I was working the locks single-handed I always opened the left-hand ground paddle, letting the boat drop slowly in the lock by itself, while I ran on ahead to set the second lock. By opening one paddle I had unwittingly started the water in the pool between the locks turning anticlockwise. This made the boat drift markedly away from the mouth of the second lock. It all seems so easy when put down on paper, and the solution was even easier – just open the right-hand paddle instead and the motion of the water would be clockwise, which would almost line the boat up for the lock by itself.

I asked about canal songs, but no one could remember any, though melodians were often played by boatmen. There were, however, several short rhymes and sayings, such as, 'Black diamond, white diamond, all in a row, come on you fancy boatman, and I'll show you the way to go.' Another was, 'Wooden boats, iron men'. I soon came to understand the second saying from my own experience. The cabins of wooden boats were much cosier than those on the later iron and steel boats but they had one decided disadvantage. During dry weather the timber decks above the cabin would shrink, no matter how many buckets of water you poured over them during the day. The caulking would come apart and several times I awoke at night with my bedding soaked when it rained after a period of dry weather. All you could do was turn over and go back to sleep. I only got out of bed on one occasion but quickly realised the misery of getting back into a cold, wet bed.

In the early-1970s, there were few wooden boats left on the canal and

The traditional Leeds and Liverpool barge, Pluto, *seen here in 1976 at Runcorn on the Bridgewater Canal.* Pluto *was built in 1939 for Canal Transport Ltd and carried general cargo. The author lived on board for five years and is here seen at the tiller.* (Photo, British Waterways Board.)

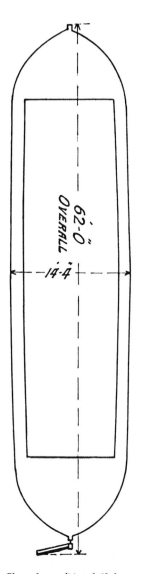

Plan of a traditional 62-feet Leeds and Liverpool 'short' boat. Although the Liverpool to Wigan section of the canal could accommodate longer boats, this was the standard length of boat for the canal.
(Drawn from a plan held by the B.W.B.)

those there were would hardly have been able to carry a cargo. However, I thought some effort should be made to preserve a motor boat, so I bought the *Pluto* from Albert Blundell in 1972. He had called her the *Denise* during his ownership but I re-instated the name used by Canal Transport Limited, the original owners. I was soon confronted by the problems of maintenance, never properly overcome with the limited income available to me. When new, the price of a Leeds and Liverpool boat was about three times that for a narrow boat. Subsequent repair costs were in a similar ratio, so to make the best use of my money I had to undertake all the repair work myself. There is nothing like practical experience for learning, and I quickly developed an intimate knowledge of boat construction on the Leeds and Liverpool.

During my work on *Pluto*, I was able to find out for myself much about how the canal was worked and boats built, but there were still many unanswered questions. I embarked upon research to find out more about the early history of the canal, to try and find out why traditional methods had evolved in a particular way.

Traditional boats in Lancashire and Yorkshire

IN 1770, when building of the canal was begun, the size of the locks was based upon the vessels then in use on either side of the Pennines. In Yorkshire, boats sixty feet long by fourteen feet beam already operated on the Aire and Calder, often working down the tidal Humber as far as Hull. In Lancashire, the boats used on the Weaver, and Mersey and Irwell Navigations were often slightly larger, but there were still many with similar dimensions. Others were smaller, enabling them to work into shallow rivers and estuaries, and up lesser navigations, such as the Douglas. It seems plausible, therefore, that the lock size adopted by the canal was based on the vessels used in Yorkshire, and the fact that the canal was initially planned and organised from Yorkshire tends to confirm this.

Although partially opened in 1773, the two ends of the canal were not connected for some forty years, with the sections each side of the Pennines operating separately. Consequently, there were differences in the types of boat used on either side of the Pennines. In Yorkshire, the canal barges developed from the 'keel', the coastal trading vessel of the Humber estuary. They were originally of clinker construction, each plank overlapped and was riveted to its neighbour, the two planks being clenched together sufficiently to form a watertight seal. Over the years, the shape of the hull had evolved such that the bow had become full and bluff, resulting in a boat which could carry a large tonnage, but which was slow through the water.

In Lancashire, the canal barge was similar in construction to the 'flat', the coastal sailing vessel of the Irish Sea. These were of carvel construction, where adjacent planks butted up to each other, the joint between being caulked with oakum to make it watertight. The method used for framing carvel boats tended to make them stronger than clinker boats. The bows of Lancashire-built boats were much finer than those in Yorkshire, resulting in a boat which, although not capable of carrying such a large cargo, was easy to draw through the water. To increase the carrying capacity of boats in Lancashire, the square stern was adopted and was often used on the canal.

In 1816, following the completion of the canal, these different methods slowly merged, though it still remained possible to tell where a boat had been built from its shape. Clinker construction died out during the mid-nineteenth century, as the riveted wooden joint, fine for sea-going boats, suffered from abrasion when boats worked regularly through locks. The square stern also began to be built at boatyards in Yorkshire, and was probably introduced to other Yorkshire canals via the Leeds and Liverpool. The framing in the bow and stern was one area where differences remained. In Lancashire, the frames radiated from the end of the keelson (a large piece of wood placed centrally above the frames and over the keel to form a backbone to the vessel) while in Yorkshire they were virtually at right angles to the transverse frames in the centre of the boat. The bluff bows of Yorkshire boats were a consequence of this variation in framing.

Besides these regional variations, there were also differences between boats used for merchandise and those for mineral traffics. With the former, cargoes needed to be protected from the weather and, if possible, theft. This was accomplished by covering the hold with tarpaulin sheets, stretched over three lines of supports. To fix these sheets to the boat it was necessary to provide coamings around the hold, with fourteen-inch wide gunwhales on either side, allowing access for the crew to wedge the sheets against the coamings, and make the hold waterproof. For mineral traffic, no protection was required for the cargo, and the boats were only fitted with narrow gunwhales, nine inches wide, to allow the crew to pass from bow to stern. When loaded, planks were sometimes placed over the cargo for this purpose. A raised headledge was sometimes provided at either end of the hold to enable bulky cargoes to be piled up without spilling onto the deck. These were most noticeable on Yorkshire boats.

Square- and round-stern boats often had different uses. A square stern increased carrying capacity and was often used on coal boats where it was important to carry the maximum tonnage. But there were disadvantages: steering was more difficult because the transom restricted the flow of water to the rudder and they were slower through locks as the boat had to be right into the lock chamber before the gates could be shut. Round sterns were common on merchandise boats,

A typical coastal and estuarial flat. Many of the early flats had lowering masts so that they could work up into river navigations like the Douglas, enabling them to negotiate most bridges on the way. Flats on the west coast of England generally had a square stern like this one, and this design became common on barges on the Lancashire side of the Leeds and Liverpool Canal, whence it spread not only to the Yorkshire side of the canal but to other canals as well. A traditional square-sterned Leeds and Liverpool barge can be seen at Ellesmere Port Boat Museum.
(Drawing, A. J. Lewery.)

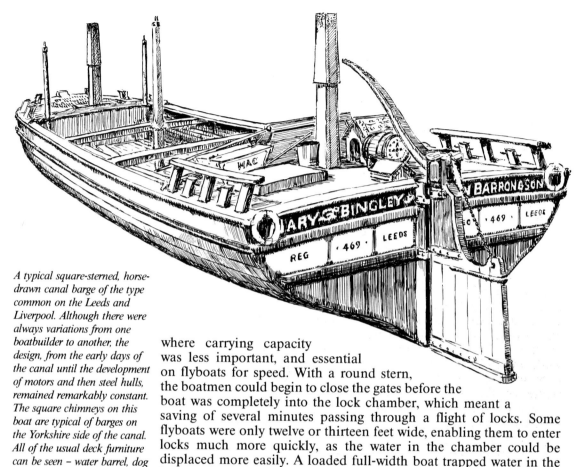

A typical square-sterned, horse-drawn canal barge of the type common on the Leeds and Liverpool. Although there were always variations from one boatbuilder to another, the design, from the early days of the canal until the development of motors and then steel hulls, remained remarkably constant. The square chimneys on this boat are typical of barges on the Yorkshire side of the canal. All of the usual deck furniture can be seen – water barrel, dog kennel and cabin vent. Note also the box where the horse's proven – a mixture of chopped hay, oats and beans – was kept. The stern rails were still common on wooden boats, though they were really just a throw-back to the boat's origins as a sea-going flat. Either side of the hold are the two towing masts, with the lutchet, used particularly in locks, fixed to the forward cross beam. They are seen here in upright position, although they would often be removed when the boat was moored up or otherwise not in use. This drawing is of the Mary of Bingley, a photograph of which can be seen on page 163.
(Drawing, E. Paget-Tomlinson.)

where carrying capacity was less important, and essential on flyboats for speed. With a round stern, the boatmen could begin to close the gates before the boat was completely into the lock chamber, which meant a saving of several minutes passing through a flight of locks. Some flyboats were only twelve or thirteen feet wide, enabling them to enter locks much more quickly, as the water in the chamber could be displaced more easily. A loaded full-width boat trapped water in the lock and, with little clearance between the boat and the lock sides, slowed the boat's entry into the chamber.

With so many variations, there were never hard and fast rules governing the type of boat involved in a particular trade. The availability of cargoes and boats was the overriding concern. For example, coal boats were used for the carriage of grain during the time in the mid-nineteenth century when the merchandise carrying trade was leased to railway companies, and when there was a shortage of boats afterwards. Boatmen had their own preferences, and when the company was rebuilding its fleet of merchandise boats at the end of the railway lease, Warde-Aldam noted:

> The Shipley boats are not satisfactory, they are rather bluff and dreary, and perhaps built too cheaply. The Lancashire men seem to have a prejudice against Yorkshire boats. The boats built at Riley Green are also not very well liked.[1]

Riley Green boats were lightly built and consequently not really suitable for use in the docks where boats had to withstand being crushed by larger vessels. However, they were liked in the coal trade, where their fine lines and construction made them speedy without reducing their carrying capacity. Other variations occurred with the

Above: *A horse-drawn merchandise boat (left) passes a motor coal boat. The square stern provided the boat painter with the greatest surface area on which to practise his art.* (Drawing, A. J. Lewery.)

Left: *A Leeds Co-operative coal boat in Rider's Dock at Leeds in around 1950. The Co-op had a major coal wharf directly opposite the river lock on the Aire at Leeds. The head ledges, used to increase the carrying capacity of lighter bulk cargoes, such as household coal, can be seen at either end of the hold.* (Photo, Leeds City Libraries.)

introduction of steam- and diesel-powered boats. Most of these had round sterns, though occasionally a square-sterned boat had a motor fitted to it. More significant for the boatmen was the reduction in living accommodation caused by the installation of an engine.

On horse boats there were cabins at both bow and stern. That at the stern provided the main living accommodation and was entered through a hatch, or scuttle hole, on the left hand side of the deck near to the hold. On all merchandise, and some coal, boats there was also a door in the rear bulkhead, below the scuttle, giving access to the hold. The headroom inside the cabin was only about four feet, and though some boats had raised decks which increased the internal height, they were the exception. All furniture was built in, the central feature being a stove fixed in the middle of the bulkhead. These cast iron stoves were about twelve inches square by three feet high and were open fronted. A hob clipped on to the top of the firebars so that a kettle could be boiled, or food cooked. Some Yorkshire boats had an oven fitted to the side of the stove, but these were considered unusual. Yorkshire stoves were also more ornate, with flowers and other decorations cast into the front plate. They were of tapering section and can be recognised by their

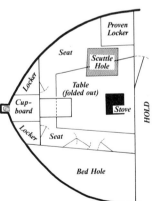

Typical layout of a bow cabin on a motor boat.

A typical bow cabin aboard a Lancashire motor boat. On horse-boats the main accommodation was in the stern, but the introduction of engines meant that the bow cabin had to be used. In what was a fairly constant and standard layout, a bed-hole was provided on either side of the cabin for each of the two-man crew. Here we see the boatman sitting in his bed-hole, supping an early morning cuppa. The fold-down table can be seen, as can the stove on the left, complete with a kettle that would be kept boiling or warm all the time. The cabin would allow only about four feet of headroom.

(Drawing, A. J. Lewery.)

distinctive square chimneys made of wood and lined with sheet steel. Lancashire stoves finished with a flat top, curving up in the middle to a circular chimney. Brass ornaments decorated this flat top, and few boats would be without their miniature brass fender (fire guard). Round the edge of the top, overlapping the stove by a couple of inches, would be a lace trimming. Chimneys were usually in two sections, those in Lancashire being linked by chain to prevent them being lost if they were knocked down. The number of sections used depended on the load being carried: the less the weight, the lower the clearance under bridges, with the height of the chimney being adjusted accordingly.

On the right-hand side of the cabin was the double bed, used by the captain and his wife, should she be accompanying him. It was separated from the rest of the cabin by a wall of six panels, three of which were hinged for access to the bed, though on some boats opening panels were not provided, and a curtain sufficed. At the rear of the cabin were three cupboards; the centre one was the largest and it folded down to form a table. Two drawers were provided under the cupboards. There was a small shelf above the cupboards and bed panelling for ornaments. In the right-hand corner, against the bulkhead, was a locker, about eighteen inches square and the full height of the cabin, which held the horse's proven. Finally, a bench was fitted against the bed panelling, under the table cupboard and along the right hand side of the cabin, underneath which was stored coal, washing utensils and other items. On some boats there was another small bed compartment on the right-hand side of the cabin. Footwear was stored under the bed, reached through a gap in the panelling under the bench. This space could also be used for the chamber pot.

The bow cabin was similar, the main difference being that a single bed was provided on each side of the cabin. As the cabin was symmetrical, access was through a scuttle hole in the centre of the deck. Sometimes the stove at the bow was smaller, as all cooking was done in the stern cabin. With the introduction of engines, the stern cabin became the engine room and the bow cabin the main living accommodation. The layout was unchanged, as few motor boats were used regularly by families, so accommodation was only required for the captain and mate.

On deck, water was carried in a five-gallon barrel which rested on its side in a cradle. A dipper, like the a measure, was used, access being through a hole cut in the top of the barrel. The inside of the barrel was well covered with pitch to stop the water from becoming tainted. Every boatman had his favourite place for filling up with water, the barrel being refilled when they passed. Water from the top of the five-rise locks at Bingley was particularly well liked. Coal boats would often carry a dog kennel, even if the boatman did not own a dog. A proven tub was provided for the horse and this was filled each day from the store in the cabin. Merchandise boats were less likely to have a kennel and their proven supply was carried in sacks, often draped over the sheets covering the rear of the hold. Ventilation of stern cabins was augmented by a hole, about nine inches by six inches, cut in the centre of the deck, which was covered by a small kennel shaped box. A bucket

The motor barge, Mu, which was built in 1926 for B. C. Wall's of Bradford, one of the three main canal carriers before amalgamation into Canal Transport Ltd., seen here passing Buck Woods, Shipley, in 1937, by which time she was being operated by Canal Transport Ltd. When bicycles became relatively inexpensive, they were a very common and useful way for the mate to go ahead of the boat in order to set locks and swing bridges. (Photo, W. F. King, Shipley.)

Scrollwork drawn from the wooden chimney of a Leeds and Liverpool Canal barge. (Drawing, A. J. Lewery.)

of water was often kept on deck, for boatmen to wash their clogs before entering the cabin, though many simply preferred to remove them.

The panelling inside the cabin was invariably grained, with a choice of light oak, dark oak, or mahogany. Two shades were generally used. For example, the panel surrounds could be mahogany with the centre light oak. The moulding strip between the panel and surround would then be painted green or red, to match the bench around the cabin. The floor was scrubbed white, but there would be a red lead band, about one and a half inches wide, around the bench supports and the floor edge. Where these formed a sharp angle, the painted edge would be scalloped. Inside the bed hole, the lining would be grained, with the top of the bed and the panel sides white. The underside of the deck was also white, with the beams mahogany. The bulkhead was usually blue, though the door into the hold was grained. It is worth remembering that the paints used would have been oil based, which meant that they would have to be varnished after application. This led to the colours changing as the varnish darkened; white, for example, soon becoming cream in colour.

Boat decoration

PAINTING was always carried out at a boatyard. All of the skilled men could paint, though the signwriting and scroll work was usually the job of one man, who, although not necessarily trained, would usually have many years' experience. Often the painter was also the yard foreman or one of the longer serving tradesmen. These men became highly proficient and some painted for a hobby as well. This led to an extremely high standard of decoration, of which both the painter and boatman were justifiably proud.

The style of boat painting on the Leeds and Liverpool is unique, though it does contain many features found elsewhere. Originally, it was probably based upon the decoration used on coastal sailing craft, from which Leeds and Liverpool boats are descended. The standard of decoration declined during the 1930s with the introduction of steel boats, although the wooden boats that were built at the time did maintain the old traditions. The steel boats represented an attempt at austerity, as they needed less docking, and the simpler painting style reflected this. Wooden boats required more care on the part of the boatmen, who were encouraged to look after them by the high quality of the paintwork. Boatmen preferred wooden boats, which handled better and whose cabins were more comfortable to live in (provided the deck did not leak!). Wooden boats would also be repaired by the old craftsmen working to standards established for generations, of which the paintwork was just one part.

The decoration of the bow was common to all wooden boats, with the top plank, above the main guard being painted. Panels, about three feet long on either side of the stem post, contained the boat's name, followed by two or three smaller panels decorated with scrolls,

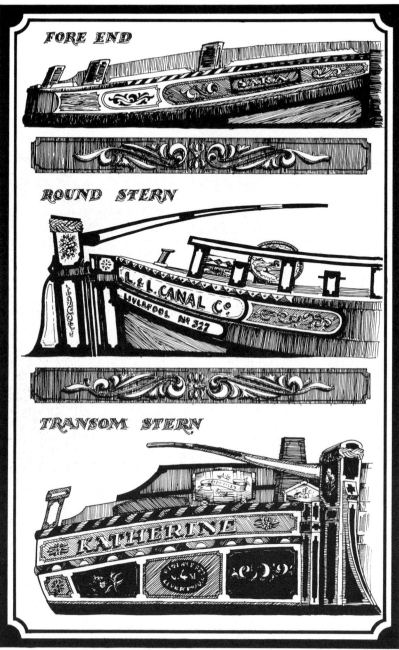

FORE END

ROUND STERN

TRANSOM STERN

Left: *Typical designs commonly seen on Leeds and Liverpool barges. The scrollwork would be used to fill in blank areas and did not conform to any standard pattern, the precise design being left up to the individual painter. The designs were not usually symmetrical, as it was important for the whole panel to be covered, irrespective of its shape.* (Drawing, A. J. Lewery.)

Top, right: *A Bradford flyboat (No. 253) with the captain, Mr Alty, probably photographed at the top of Bingley Five-Rise. It is doubtful if all four men were part of the crew. Usually, fly-boats had three men at most – one went ahead to set the locks, one looked after the horse, opening the paddles and gates at the bow, while the steerer shut the gates and paddles at the stern. The melodian seen here was the usual boatman's instrument.* (Photo, John Vickers.)

Bottom, right: *John Parke's boat* Plato, *built in 1916 for the Liverpool coal trade. This boat was based at Burscough, where many boatmen's families lived. If at all possible, men would try to arrange things so that they could tie up at Burscough as often as possible. The boat is shown here at Burscough with all the boatman's family on board. Plato's decoration is fairly typical of Liverpool coal boats, with intricate scenes painted on panels on the stern. The paintwork would require frequent washing down when the boat was engaged in this trade.* (Photo, Philip Watkinson.)

bunches of fruit, or other devices. These panels were in bold colours, sometimes grained and surrounded by a contrasting border with scalloped corners. The D iron protecting the edge of the deck would be picked out with a variety of geometric designs, such as triangles or stripes, and these would have scroll work added to them. The decoration ended as the boat approached its full width because of inevitable damage in locks and bridge holes. The top of the stem post,

next to the top plank, had a single panel painted on each side, which contained the mark of the town where the boat was registered; for example, a liver bird represented Liverpool. Underneath the main guard a triangular area of the hull would be varnished, possibly a legacy of the Yorkshire keel tradition. Sometimes this was replaced by a white triangle, which made the boats easier to see when working at night. On some boats the varnishing would include the plank underneath the rubbing strake and extended over the full length of the hull.

On a round stern the decoration was similar to the bow, though the main guard, which did not reach to the stern, was replaced by a panel giving the registration number on the left-hand side, with the town of registration on the right. The boat's name appeared only on the left-hand side of the stern post, with the panel on the right hand bearing the name of the boat's owner. The stern post and the top of the rudder were more profusely decorated than the stem post, with panels containing scroll work and the like.

The square transom provided the largest area for the boat painter's art, which reached its peak of development on coal boats working to Liverpool. The boat's name and owner were painted in deeply shadowed lettering across the top panel of the transom. The area beneath this, above the lower iron guard, was divided into three or four panels, sometimes oval in shape. One of these would contain the registration details, again including the registration authority's emblem. The other panels contained the usual scrolled patterns with the iron guards painted in repeating geometric designs. On some boats there would be a picture in one of the panels. Besides roses and bunches of flowers, there could be still life portraits, animals, or landscapes; as one retired painter said, 'You'd a job to think of something new'.[2] Somewhere, usually at the top of the stern post, the date when the boat was painted would be included, as health inspectors could be quite strict in following the regulations governing the regular painting of cabins.

The decks, fore and aft, were painted with red lead, while the covering boards, around the edge of the deck, and the cabin hatch covers were green or blue. The side decks were always white, as this increased their visibility at night, though the toe boards, at the edge, were often red. The bollards were often red, with white panels to make them stand out at night. The decoration would be completed by a curved design, often in blue, on the deck behind the stem post. Coamings, where fitted, would be painted in a strong, contrasting colour. On motor boats, the cabin sides usually contained the owner's name, but they were never decorated to the same extent as the transom. Even less decoration appeared on the iron and steel motor boats, possibly because their paintwork was far more vulnerable, as their smaller iron guards did not protect the paintwork as much as those on wooden boats.

Besides the iron guards, rope and wooden fenders were used to protect paintwork. Often two sets were available, a working set made from old rope, which inevitably became worn, and a set used for show, made from cotton and scrubbed white. The latter would not be used when the boat was moving because of the risk of them becoming blemished. Some boatmen did not like to use fenders, maintaining that they were the sign of a man who could not control his boat properly. They were certainly not used early in the canal's history, as the committee complained in 1815 about the damage caused to locks by iron work fitted as protection at bow and stern. Such ironwork was ordered to be removed and boatmen told to use rope straps to stop their boat from touching the gates while passing through locks.

Finally, the items on deck, such as the water barrel, dog kennel and proven box, would be painted. These were usually the property of the boatman who had them decorated at the boatyard. Similar designs to those on the transom were used, with the addition of the boatman's initials in the centre of a panel. Much was made of the decoration of the water barrel, with the two ends receiving some of the painter's best work.

Boatyards on the canal

THERE were numerous boatyards situated along the canal; in fact, over thirty sites have been identified. They varied from the small yard, where the men also served as carpenters and blacksmiths to the local community, to the large ones that were owned by companies involved in carrying. They can be roughly divided into three groups; those owned and operated by the canal company; those which only repaired the boats of their owners; and those which would repair boats for anyone.

The canal company's main yard was at Burnley, where their maintenance boats were repaired. This yard also contained the company's sawmill, providing timber for the other maintenance yards. Boats for repair were pulled out sideways, on a slipway, and new boats were built on a wharf next to the canal and were launched sideways down temporary guides. The company also had a slipway at Briars Mill yard, near Burscough, but this closed in the 1880s and work was transferred to the new yard at Wigan. This yard was mainly concerned with maintenance of the carrying fleet. Two covered slipways were constructed below the twenty-third lock, and in 1888 a repair shop was built for work on the steam engines and boilers in the company's boats. Quite major repairs could be carried out, and facilities included a large blacksmith's shop with a pneumatic hammer. A covered dry dock was also provided, above the lock, where water could be drained off easily. Maintenance boats may also have been built at the company's other yards, at Bank Newton and Apperley.

One of the largest boatyards on the canal was owned by Wigan Coal and Iron Company, and was situated at the old Haigh Ironworks, near the top of Wigan locks. At one time, this company had a fleet of more than seventy boats, though not all of these could reach the yard itself, as some were seventy feet in length. The Haigh yard had three side slips, only Hodsons having a similar number. Other firms to have their own yards were John Parkes & Son at Bank Hall in Liverpool and the Ince Hall Coal & Cannel Company at Wigan. There was also a dry dock at Bank Hall Colliery in Burnley for the use of coal boats working from there.

The canal company used many of the smaller dockyards for the

construction and repair of its carrying fleet.
Four in particular had been established for
many years and were used regularly. These
were: G. E. Ramsey of Shipley, T. & J.
Hodson of Whitebirk, J. & J. Crook of Riley
Green, and James Mayor of Tarleton. The
Riley Green business had been set up in
about 1800 by Thomas Crook, a boat owner
who decided he could carry out repairs for
less than he was being charged. Hodsons
were Burnley boatbuilders who moved to
Whitebirk in about 1875 when the canal
company provided them with a yard to build
and repair the Company's carrying boats.

Mayor's have not been in business for
quite so long, although the family have been
boatbuilders at Tarleton and Hesketh Bank
for generations. They originally operated
from a site on the tidal Douglas, where they
repaired coastal sailing vessels as well as
canal barges. In 1926 they moved to their
present location on the site of the old railway
yard at Tarleton. Prior to this move it had
been a family concern, but in 1927 a limited
company was set up. Shareholders included
Lancashire Canal Transport and Dean
Waddington, both canal carriers. Later, John
Hunt's of Leeds also became shareholders,
and all three firms sent their boats for repair.
In 1932, the firm took over the canal
company's boatyard at Wigan, the canal
company also becoming a shareholder. They
continued to operate both yards until 1959
when they dispensed with the Wigan site.
During the 1930s, their technical advisor, Mr
Lepine, had suggested the firm construct
electric vans and seaplanes. The directors
rejected the suggestions, considering that
they had enough problems with canal
boats.[3]

Many boatyards did expand into other
fields, as income from the repair of boats
varied with the economy. The yard at
Salterforth undertook a variety of work,
including agricultural machinery repairs
and blacksmithing, while William Rider &
Co. of the canal basin at Leeds, established
in 1863, undertook wheelwrights' work and
were timber stockists. Although based on the
Leeds and Liverpool, much of their work
was with boats operating on the Aire and
Calder, such as the Co-op coal barges, and

also those working to the power station at Armley.

Boatbuilding on the Leeds and Liverpool

Top left: Caulking a carvel-built boat was a major and time-consuming exercise. There would be about half a mile of joints to be sealed in this way, and each joint would require three strands of oakum to make it properly watertight. All other work stopped at the yard when the caulking had to be done. The oakum was often made by inmates at local gaols, from old rope or sacking teased out into yarn (the origin of the phrase 'spinning a yarn') and moistened with oil. The oakum would be hammered into place with a caulking mallet and iron. After caulking the seams would be sealed with pitch to hold the oakum in place and the whole of the hull would be painted with tar.
(Drawing, A. J. Lewery.)

Bottom, left: Men at Riley Green Boatyard caulking a new boat on the slipway.
(Photo, Wigan Education Dept.)

IT is difficult to say how long it took to build a barge, since the time obviously varied with the number of men employed and building could also be interrupted by urgent repair work. Two to three months seems to have been usual, with two craftsmen, two labourers and an apprentice employed full time. When the hull needed caulking most other work at the yard would stop for a few days and all available men would help. This was an important job. Mayor's reputation was tarnished in 1928 when two boats which they had repaired started to leak. The caulking of one of their staff was not up to standard and he was sacked after his work had been inspected.

The dimensions of the locks, to which the short boats working above Wigan were built, allowed an overall length of sixty-two feet, and a beam of fourteen feet four inches. The long boats, which worked between Liverpool and Leigh, were seventy-three feet overall, with a beam of fourteen feet six inches. A depth of four feet was guaranteed by the company, though the canal was deeper in Liverpool and at Leeds. The boats were built with a depth of four feet eight inches, measured from gunwhale to keel, though the stem and stern posts were six feet high, resulting in a shear of one foot four inches, which improved the look of the boats.

The original boats had fine lines, and it was estimated in 1850 that the average load carried was thirty-two tons. By 1874 the canal had been deepened, and the displacement of the boats improved to increase carrying capacity.[4] This resulted in an increase in their loads

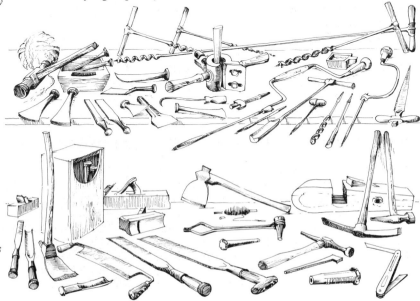

Right: A collection of boat-builder's tools, including the all-important adze and draw-knife, as well as various augers and different sizes and shapes of caulking irons.
(Drawing, A. J. Lewery.)

to around forty tons. By the 1930s, the introduction of engines had made it less important to have a boat that could be pulled easily, as had been necessary with horse boats. The shape could therefore be altered, enabling weights of more than fifty tons to be carried by a single boat. The long boats, working on the Liverpool section, could carry about twenty tons more than that taken by a short boat.

Oak and pitch pine were used in the construction of barges. First the keel of ten by three-inch oak was laid, and stem and stern posts erected. Next the frames were placed on top of the keel. These were of oak and, where the frames were curved, would be cut from timber grown specially to shape. Each boatyard had their own set of patterns from which the shape of the frames was taken. These dictated the final shape of the boat, which thus varied from yard to yard. The frames were spaced eighteen inches apart and were usually about five by three inches in section. A keelson, originally of ten-inch square pitch pine, was fitted over the keel and above the frames. Later, eight-inch by six-inch steel joists were used. The bow and stern were strengthened by twelve by four-inch oak 'hooks', fitted just below deck level from the stem post to the first cross beam, which also marked the start of the hold. The hull was now ready for planking.

Three thirteen-inch pitch-pine planks were fitted either side of the keel, the rest of the planking being of oak, normally two-inches thick, but increased to three inches for the rubbing strake, which protected the rest of the hull from abrasion. The decks could now be laid, with four by two-inch pitch pine. Two-inch pitch-pine boards were also used to line the hold. On coal boats, two beams were fixed across the hold, and eight-inch wide side decks fitted. For a merchandise boat, the stern beam was made removable so that long cargoes could be loaded easily. The beams held the sides of the boat out, against the water pressure. The wide side decks and coamings would then be fitted. The hull, after caulking, was pitched and tarred. It was then ready for launching – cabins were usually fitted after the launch.

Boats were launched sideways into the canal and the banking opposite the yard was often covered by the wash as the boat hit the water. After being launched the boat would surge across the canal, almost hitting the far bank, returning afterwards to the boatyard side. The event was usually attended by some ceremony, as this description of a launch at Tyrer's yard, near Burscough, in the 1920s shows:

> On the day of the launch a flag was hoisted which was an indication to the people in the neighbourhood that Tyrer's were about to launch a boat. On several occasions the minister of St. John's C. of E. church was present, who blessed the boat after which in the usual manner a bottle of port was broken as the boat was named.[5]

Following the launch, there was usually food provided, such as a hot pot, and the boatbuilders were often taken to the local pub.

Iron boats were introduced in the 1870s during the shortage of craft following the termination of the railway lease. A specification was drawn up by Mr Bartholomew, of the Aire and Calder, and six iron boats ordered from William Alsop of Preston in 1875, at a cost of £360. This was about £100 more than the equivalent wooden boat.[6] Later, in 1891, two steel boats were purchased for the Leeds and Wigan traffics from Liverpool. Although iron was used for dredging equipment and

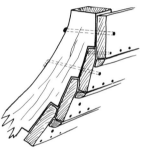

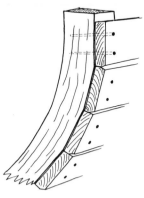

Clinker (top) and carvel construction, as used on canal barges. On the clinker-built boats, the frame were cut away to receive planks, which were placed to overlap each other slightly, as shown. Rivets or spikes were driven through smaller pilot holes to bind the two overlapping ends together and long spikes were driven through the centre of each plank, right through the frame, where it was either riveted or just bent over. The ends of the planks were protected with wooden beading but, despite this, they were still damaged regularly in locks and bridges. Largely for this reason, carvel boats became more or less universal. Here the planks are simply placed next to each other and fastened directly to the frame. A notch either in a full- or a half-'V' shape was left near the outside edge of the planks, into which the caulking was then hammered to make the joints watertight.

Darlington was the last wooden boat built by Mayor's at Wigan. This was in 1951, when this dramatic photograph showing the launch was taken. The boats were launched sideways down a temporary slipway, showering the opposite bank in spray. When the weight of the boat passed a certain point, the slipway beams would shoot dangerously upwards, as seen here. New boats were generally built in the open air, the covered slipways, from which launches were less spectacular, being reserved for the usually more urgent work of repairs. This yard was built in 1880s for the maintenance of the canal company's fleet, the workshops beyond the slips being used for repairing steam engines and later diesel engines. Mayors operated here from 1932 until 1959.

(Photo, author's collection.)

tugs, no more steel or iron barges were ordered by the company until the motor boats, built for Canal Transport Limited, were delivered in the 1930s. The Wigan Coal and Iron Company, however, may have had some built in the 1890s.

Besides their higher initial cost, there were other reasons why iron boats did not become more widely used. None of the boatyards on the canal, with the possible exception of Haigh, were equipped to repair them, and the necessary expertise had to be brought in from outside. They were disliked by the boatmen, as their weight and poor shape made them tiring for horses to tow, and the cabins were less comfortable than those on wooden boats.

In 1843, John Tayleure, of Liverpool, was given permission by the company to experiment with boats propelled by an 'archimedian screw'. Two years later, he was granted £25 to try steam power.[7] In 1852, possibly as a result of these experiments, the Ince Hall Coal and Cannel Company suggested that steam tugs be introduced on the Liverpool coal traffic. The following year, a steam boat, built by Mr Forshaw, and previously tried as a passenger boat on the Birmingham Canal, was tested. It had an eleven-horsepower, twin-cylinder engine, operating at forty pounds per square inch which drove a twenty-three inch, four foot pitch propellor. The tug was first tried with five loaded boats, the load then being reduced to three boats, and finally a single boat. Speeds varied from one and a half to two miles an hour, though in the last test, the coal boat dragged along the bottom, which reduced the speed considerably. Four empty boats were then attached, and a speed of three and a half miles an hour reached. On its own, the tug went at five miles an hour. The main problem was steering the boats being towed, though difficulties were also envisaged when trains of boats passed through locks, causing excessive use of water. A hinged outrigger was suggested, enabling the spare man to leave the tug easily to open the swing bridges.[8]

Further experiments were sanctioned and the possibility of steam powered carrying boats was explored. Even if tugs had been

Left: The motor boat Margaret *at Burscough in 1958. These heightened bow cabins were not very common, but they did provide considerably more headroom for the crew.*
(Photo, E. Paget-Tomlinson.)

Below: H. & R. Ainscough's Viktoria, *which was one of seven boats built for the firm in the 1930s, each named after one of their horses.* Viktoria, *which is still afloat today, was built in 1934 and carried grain from Liverpool docks to Ainscough's mill at Burscough (where this photograph was taken). The later grain boats had hatch covers like this to help keep the grain drier than the old-fashioned covers.*
(Photo, Philip Watkinson.)

introduced, horses were not to have been displaced until a comparison of costs was made. Because of problems with the tugs' wash, the speed was restricted to two miles per hour. A proposal by Mr Forshaw for an improved tug, capable of towing ten or twelve boats, was not taken up.

The next trial of steam power occurred in 1857, when the company allowed Burch's patent screw propellor to be tested. As a result, in 1858, the Leeds and Liverpool Canal Steam Tug Company Limited was set up, the majority of the shareholders being coal owners or merchants involved in the Liverpool coal trade.[9] The four tugs built were sixty feet long by eight feet beam and five feet deep, powered by horizontal geared engines. They could tow up to six boats along the canal at two miles per hour, increasing to five miles per hour in the river. The tugs operated between Liverpool and Appley lock and charged fifteen shillings for the return trip.

Originally, it had been intended to build twenty tugs, and the company was authorised to raise £12,000. However, after operating for about eighteen months, the service was seen to be unprofitable and the company failed. It is possible that the canal company continued to operate the tugs. Tatham certainly wanted to maintain them as they regulated the cost of horse haulage and reduced the need for dredging by keeping the mud banks moving. In 1862 there were complaints that the railways were not repairing the tugs and boats, prior to the Midland Railway withdrawing from the lease (see chapter 7).

Steam power was introduced in Yorkshire in 1866, when the Airedale Tug Company commenced towage on the river between Leeds Bridge and the first canal lock. The following year the river was dredged, presumably to give increased depth for the tugs, which also worked on the Aire and Calder.

In 1870, following a trial of a boat powered by a new type of steam engine, patented by Richard Tennant and Robert Thomas, a report was produced on the use of steam tugs. This recommended their introduction on the Wigan coal trade between Appley lock and Liverpool, with horses to be provided above Appley. Four tugs were to be purchased, similar to those on the Grand Junction or Chester Canal. They had twin eight-horsepower engines, and were capable of pulling three hundred tons at three miles per hour. They were to be built of iron, at an estimated cost of £500, though the two built by Sampson Moore and Co., and Potter and Hodgkinson, both of Liverpool, cost £760 and £740 respectively. These tugs consisted of two narrow boats, about five feet beam, with a three feet wide paddle wheel between the hulls, the engines driving each end of the paddle wheel shaft. A locomotive boiler, carried transversely, provided the steam. It was estimated that twelve horses would be needed for haulage above Appley lock. It was hoped that the system would reduce pilferage, always a problem with the coal trade, and make the supply more regular. Unfortunately, the tugs were a failure. They had been built too deep at three feet ten inches, and were consequently slow, reaching less than two miles an hour towing six boats, instead of the expected three miles per hour. They were also difficult to steer, and caused considerable damage to the banks. They had been sold by 1873, the company making a profit of £100.[10]

Steam power was finally introduced successfully in 1878, when Mr

W. Wilkinson of Wigan, in conjunction with the canal engineer, converted a barge into a tug by installing a steam driven propellor of about three feet diameter.[11] Under test, two loaded boats were towed at over two and one half miles per hour, with little damage to the banks. In 1880, following the successful conclusion to these tests, a tug was ordered for Foulridge Tunnel at a cost of £600. This tug had a rudder and propellor at each end, which eliminated the need to turn round after passing through the tunnel. The passage of the tunnel was reduced from two hours by legging to about twenty-five minutes. In the same year, four steam flyboats were ordered, enabling cargoes to be carried more quickly, with journey times being reduced by forty per cent compared to horse haulage.

The engines used were often 'diagonal compound double tandem', which means that they were of 'V' layout, with a high- and low-pressure cylinder on each side. All of the canal company engines were built by Messrs W. Wilkinson & Co. of Wigan, who produced a simple yet robust engine which could withstand use by 'semi-civilised men for drivers, i.e. ordinary barge men', as the firm described them. Field type boilers were used for their rapid steaming qualities and were usually supplied by Hough and Son, another Wigan firm. At this time Wilkinson's had patented a gear-driven steam tram and the engines used in both boats and trams were very similar. To look after their fleet of steam boats, in 1884 the company appointed John Gibson, of Glasgow, as superintendent. He was sacked three years later, and John Ross, who had formerly worked for the Shropshire Union Canal, was appointed in his place. Eventually, the company owned forty-six steam barges and ten tugs. Steam continued to be used into the 1950s, with many bye-traders operating boats that had been purchased from the company in 1921.

Diesel power was first tried in 1903, when a carrying boat was fitted with an engine supplied by the Diesel Co. for £400.[12] The trial continued until 1906, when the engine was sent to Burnley yard to drive the sawmill. In that year, Gardener's, the Manchester engine manufacturers, also suggested a trial, with fifteen- and thirty-horsepower twin-cylinder engines, fitted with reversing gear. A thirty-horsepower engine was purchased for £290, and tried for three months. These experiments were not particularly successful, and diesel engines were not used commercially until 1921, when the Clayton Carrying Co. of Morley, near Leeds, fitted a thirteen-horsepower Kelvin engine to their boat *Ina*. Three years later, Benjamin Walls had his boats *Psi* and *Theta* fitted with, respectively, an eighteen-horsepower single and a twenty-five horsepower twin-cylinder Widdop.

H. Widdop & Co. Ltd., of Keighley, were to become the main supplier of engines to carrying firms based on the Leeds and Liverpool. They were reliable engines but produced considerable vibration, which made them uncomfortable for the crews. The later engines were governed, which gave them a steady rythm. This was an advantage for those boatmen who engaged in 'step dancing' to keep warm whilst steering in winter. Widdop's only rivals were Gardener's, who supplied the engines for Ainscough's and B. & I. Transport's new boats, built in the 1930s. Not until twenty years later were Lister engines used in any numbers as replacements for old engines.

The canal horses

Horses like this one were attached to the towrope by means of a fairly simple collar harness. Chains or ropes, encased in leather (unlike the brightly painted wooden bobbins used on other canals), were attached to the swingletree behind the horse. The towrope itself was usually around eighty feet in length (to allow room for manoeuvre when boats were passing) and would wear out surprisingly quickly. It was usually attached, as here, to the nearside towing mast, but could be moved to another point if there was a strong side wind or if the boat was negotiating a tight bend. All kinds of horses would be used and blinkers would only be used if the horse was more comfortable with them. Some boatmen were adept at throwing lumps of coal at the horse to get it to work harder, while others tied a clog to the towrope, just behind the horse, which would clatter on the towpath if the horse slackened its pace too much.
(Drawing, E. Paget-Tomlinson.)

Despite the introduction of engines at various times, it is important to emphasise that horses were used for haulage throughout the working life of the canal. The last working horse boat finished only in 1960. This was the *Parbold,* operated by H. & R. Ainscough Ltd. of Burscough, which supplied coal to their mills there and at Parbold. Those who owned their own boat, or who worked for the smaller carrying companies, usually owned their own horse, though sometimes they were rented from farmers or other carriers. The larger firms, including the canal company, provided horses, and the boatman would have to take the one provided.

There was no standard type of boat horse and boatmen made the best of what was available. Medium-sized ones were preferred, as they were not inconvenienced by bridges, while mules and donkeys were used on occasion. Larger animals, such as Clydesdales, were sometimes bought by the company for use at flights of locks, where, because the boat had to be started from rest at each lock, the work was harder. The company also had many horses for the carting service which they provided from their warehouses.

Owner boatmen often had a stable attached to their house, where proven, hay and spare tackle could be kept. At other times they could use the stables at pubs and wharfs along the canal, which charged anything from sixpence to a shilling a night. If there was plenty of grass growing, and the weather reasonable, the horse could be tethered on the towpath. Horses were generally well looked after, as they could cost anything up to fifty pounds, and if it was ill you could not work. At the end of the day, the horse would always be fed and settled immediately after tying up, before the boatmen had their own meal.

Company horses used the stables provided at locks and warehouses, where they were changed, if injured or over-tired. The main injuries were sore shoulders, caused by collars which were in poor condition or badly fitted. A well-

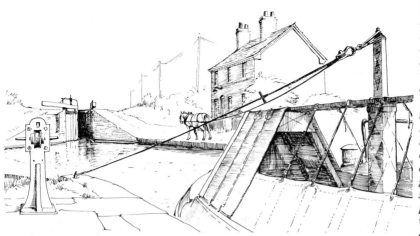

*Left: A boat is much more difficult to set in motion than it is to keep moving, so this double-purchase system was devised, whereby the horse would only require half the effort to get the boat moving. The towrope would pass through a pulley on the towing mast and, doubling back on itself, would be held on a curved hook or spike on the canal bank. After the horse had got the boat moving, a short stick attached to the rope at a pre-set distance from the end would catch on the pulley, ending the double-purchase advantage and returning the horse to straight-forward towing. When the boat had moved ahead of the hook, the end of the rope would then just slip off, the whole system thus requiring no supervision from the crew. Some of the hooks can still be seen today.
(Drawing, A. J. Lewery.)*

fitted collar was especially important for a boat horse as they had to lean into it when starting from rest. This was the hardest part of the horses' work; it was much easier keeping the boat moving afterwards. Injuries were treated by vets or horse doctors, several being employed by the company. A veterinary department was located at Liverpool and farriers shoed horses at the main canal depots.

Company horses seem to have been well looked after; for example, during eight months of 1896, only two out of the eighteen horses disposed of were worn out, one having worked for the company for twelve years. Of the others, six had suffered accidents, two were bad boaters and the rest had various illnesses. The fodder provided by the company was always of good quality, containing clover, hay, straw, corn, beans and peas. Some boatmen preferred the hay to be left long, as this made the horses stand quietly at locks.[13] The proven and hay stores were at Burscough, and a boat delivered these weekly to the stables along the canal. Because of this system, little proven needed to be carried by the company's boats as they could obtain supplies from any of the company stables.

The following description of Burscough comes from *Seets i' Yorkshire and Lancashire,* by the dialect writer, John Hartley, which was published around the turn of the century:

*Top, right: Rungs were provided on the frames of the lock gates for the captain to begin climbing even before the boat was fully in the lock, so that he could close the stern gates while the mate tied up the bow (by means of the centrally placed lutchet) and opened the paddles. To save walking all the way around, boatmen would generally open or close one gate and then leap across to the other one.
(Drawing, A. J. Lewery.)*

> Burscough is a wonderful place. This is whear th'canal horses are kept, on a big farm belangin' th'company, an' all ther provender is stored here.
>
> A chap wor hard at work mixin' bran, an' corn, an' beans, an' chop, enuff it seemed to fodder an army. When Sammy expressed his surprise at findin' sich a lot o' fine cattle [ie. horses], he laft.
>
> 'Why, sur', he said, 'wod yo' beleive 'at this compny pays forty, an' as mich as sixty guineas apiece for theas horses?'
>
> 'Well', sed Sammy, 'if awd been tell'd soa befoor awd seen what aw have, aw should ha' had mi daats abaat it, but awm foorced to believe it nah. But ha' is it 'at aw niver see onny on th' canal banks 'at luk like theas?'
>
> 'Aw cant tell you that, maister', he sed, 'for th' horses yo see here were some on 'em on th' bank to-day, an' some will goa on agean directly. Happen yo've nivver taken mich nooatice, an' yo know, fine feathers mak fine burds, an' a fine harness sets off a poor horse, an' a fine

*Bottom, right: At tight bends rollers like these were needed to stop the towrope fouling. If they jammed, they wore away quite quickly and few now survive. Those on bridges have fared rather better and some good examples can still be seen today, although deep scoring on the stonework of some bridges is evidence that they were certainly not universal.
(Drawing, A. J. Lewery.)*

harness is what we've noa use for.'

'But dooant booatmen treeat 'em badly sometimes?'

'Ther's gooid an' bad amang booatmen as amang all sooarts, but if onny one is known to ill use a horse he gets his ticket o' leave, an' that sattles him.

There were boatmen who ill-treated their horses, and many were prosecuted. For example, in 1903 the captain, his brother, and the mate of boat no. 186 were convicted of cruelly ill-treating and over-driving the company's mare no. 111, and were each fined one pound, with one pound and nine-pence costs, or one month's hard labour.[14]

The harness was fairly simple. Hames were attached to the collar, with side ropes from the hames to a swingletree behind the horse. The towrope was attached to the centre of the swingletree. There were various supports for these ropes and at the side they were protected by leather tubing. When towed by a horse, the line could be fixed to the boat at several points. Two towing masts were provided, fitted at either side of the hold at the bow. They normally projected about thirty inches above deck level, though a longer mast was available if wanted. A third mast, or lutchet, was fixed centrally to the back of the forward cross beam. This had a section which could be raised or lowered, depending upon the height of the cargo, or if the boat was loaded or unloaded. Normally the mast nearest the towpath was used, but if there was a strong side wind the position could be changed to ease steering, and for this reason too, the line could even be looped round one of the forward bollards. When working through locks, the lutchet would be used, as its position further aft made controlling the boat easier. In locks the line would often be passed through a block attached to the lutchet, the end of the line then being looped round a hook on the lock side. This double purchase system halved the effort needed by the horse to set the boat in motion when leaving the lock. The hauling line was usually about eighty feet long, and would last about six weeks. Some idea of how much rope was used can be gauged by the company's purchase, in 1919, of nine tons of cotton line in one month. Such orders were not unusual.[15]

There could be problems when two boats wanted to pass, though there were strict regulations about priority. These depended upon the cargo, flyboats having precedence, followed by those carrying merchandise, and so on down to the boats moving the lowliest of commodities – manure! Empty boats had the lowest priority of all. If the cargo was the same, boats travelling westward had to stop. The boat which stopped was supposed to pass its line under the other boat, but this was not strictly adhered to, and the line could be passed over the top of the boat if care was taken not to dislodge the chimney!

There could be difficulties if the boat ran aground, especially as this tended to pull the horse into the water. The same could happen when a boat entered a bridge, the reduction in width making it harder to pull the boat. A good horse would know this and would slow down until the boat had passed through. If a horse did fall in, it merely swam along until it reached one of the ramps set in the towpath that were thoughtfully provided so that they could get out.

The boat was steered by a tiller which was about nine feet in length. When working through locks it tended to foul the lockside, so a shorter tiller was used. Bulky loads, such as baled wool, also made steering difficult, by obscuring the view ahead, so a curved tiller was also provided. The steerer stood on a raised plank, and the tiller curved upwards so that he could reach it easily. Every boatman would have a whip, often made of leather, which was cracked to announce the boat's approach. This was done at a set distance before each lock or bridge, and priority was given to the first to crack their whip. They were also used at Hurst Wood and at Halsall cutting, where there was insufficient room for two boats to pass.

The boatmen

A normal crew comprised a captain and a mate. On family boats the captain's wife or

Right: A horse-drawn coal boat coming down Johnson's Hillock locks to join what was the southern end of the Lancaster Canal. This boat was owned by Thomas Crook (identified by the white diamond) and was used to carry coal from the Wigan area to the towns of East Lancashire. Two men formed the normal crew on these boats.
(Photo, Margaret Walton.)

Right: The Progress *and* Industry *of Silsden Co-operative Society frozen in at Bingley. The crews of these horse-drawn coal boats, including Captains Earle Dawson and Silas Clarkson, are looking glum because they were paid by the load and while the boats were frozen in they were not earning. Many boatmen allowed their horses to be used by the company for towing ice-breakers to supplement their incomes at such times.*
(Photo, Mrs Clarkson.)

Left: Boats were only slightly narrower than the bridges and when they entered them, the boat would slow down markedly. The increased tension on the towline could pull a horse into the canal, whereupon it would have to swim as far as one of the ramps set into the side of the towpath. Some of these ramps were covered with planks of wood until required.
(Drawing, top, A. J. Lewery; photo, Ben Shaw.)

children could act as mate, reducing costs, though earnings were usually sufficient to allow a mate to be employed. He would live in the bow cabin, but often ate in the stern with the captain's family. Young children were allowed on the stern deck, where they were often tethered so that they could not fall into the canal. The horse would be fed regularly every couple of hours, though the boat would not be stopped for this. The only rest the horse had was at locks, where she (they were usually mares or geldings) would be given a good feed while the lock was being worked.

Flyboats, which worked round the clock, were operated by three men, two of whom were always awake. All three would work the boat through flights of locks, but on the long pounds a set distance was

A group of boatmen photographed on the foredeck of Don, *at New Lane, Burscough.* Don *was a motor boat built for Canal Transport Ltd. in 1935.* (Photo, Philip Watkinson.)

allowed for each man to get some rest. When the boat reached its destination they could catch up on their sleep if they were not needed for unloading. The horse would be changed, when necessary, at one of the company's stables. With the introduction of steam, the crew was increased to four; again, they all helped at flights of locks, but the long pounds were divided as before, two of the men resting along each section.

It is difficult to establish where boatmen came from originally, but we know that many families worked on the canal for generations. For example, the forebears of the firm of William Oldfield, coal merchants at Riddlesden, who operated their own fleet of boats in connection with the business, were originally miners. When the canal was built, some of the family helped with the construction, becoming boatmen when it was finished. The family continued to be involved with both occupations, eventually combining them to become coal merchants, selling coal which they had carried from the Aire and Calder, and Barnsley Canal, besides that mined locally.

Trade often determined where boatmen lived, and up until the 1870s many lived in communities such as that around Hapton and Altham, carrying coal from local collieries. As these collieries became less productive the boatmen moved away, finding work elsewhere. In industrial areas, such as Hapton, it was unusual for more than two members of a family to be employed boating. The father often took his eldest son with him, while the other children worked in local textile factories. Boatmen employed carrying coal lived in small communities near to the mines, and as coal tended to be carried fairly short distances, they were able to sleep at home regularly. This was not the case for those employed in the merchandise trade.

West Lancashire had provided boatmen ever since the canal first opened. By the 1870s, Burscough had become the centre for those employed in the merchandise trade, gaining importance after the proven depot was established there in 1888. Houses, often including

Above: *The boating community at Rawlinson's Bridge, near Adlington, on the S. Lancaster. The boatmen working this length were generally known as 'Haigh cutters'. The boat here is a Wigan Coal & Iron Co. wooden horse-boat. The towing masts are lying along the gunwhales and spare tillers can be seen near the stern chimney (boatmen would keep at least one spare tiller, plus a short one for working locks).*
(Photo, Margaret Walton.)

Right: *'Bagging' time for the Lawson family on board the* Mars *at Tate & Lyle's sugar refinery near the basin in Liverpool. During the school holidays the whole family would sometimes go along for the trip. The boat is carrying coal to the refinery, while the Tate & Lyle boat in the background is loaded with ash from the boilers.*
(Photo, Philip Watkinson.)

stabling, were built for the boatmen alongside the canal from New Lane to Parbold. Shops, selling rope, proven, etc., serviced these communities and there were several bakeries next to the canal. Beer houses also opened; there were four at New Lane alone, though the number of teetotal boatmen was not insignificant. Religious guidance was not neglected and a mission was established in the hay loft of the shop at Crabtree Lane by Mr Hendricksen, of the Mersey Mission to

Seamen. This was soon found to be inadequate and a corrugated iron building, known as St. Andrew's Mission, was erected in New Lane in 1905. It is still in use today.[16] Although Burscough was the main canal town, missions were provided at several places along the canal. Burnley was an important canal centre and by 1851 it had a boatmen's lodging house, as well as the usual canalside facilities.

Boatwomen's clothes – aprons, shawls and bonnets – were fairly typical of the time, but those of the boatmen were more distinctive. Their trousers were of dark blue corduroy, held up by a leather belt, with a collarless union shirt above. Over the top of this was a 'gansey', knitted from dark blue wool, oiled to make it waterproof. Intricate patterns were knitted from halfway up the chest, below this being plain. The boatmen's wives used to knit them while their husbands were away, sitting outside their terraced houses if it was sunny, and there was much competition as to who could produce the best pattern.

The boatmen could be away from home for a week or more, and their wives would pack food for them in a woven, wicker basket. There was much skill involved in this, since those items at the bottom of the basket had to remain fresh for several days, but it meant that the boatmen only needed to stop for bread and milk once they were underway. Any cooking was done on the open stove, and the frying pan was often in use. Other meals could be prepared, though the boatmen preferred something quick which would not interrupt their work. When their men were away from home, the wives would collect their husbands' wages, and on Friday afternoons there would be a queue of women waiting to be paid at the depot at Burscough.

There was not much time for recreation, except during enforced stoppages for drought or frost. For a few years after 1897, Mr W. Reynolds, the company's horse superintendent, organised the Burscough Bridge Cattle Show and Sports. Many boats lined the canal banks, and there were competitions for the best canal horse and the best agricultural horse, with a silver Challenge Cup being presented by the company.[17] Reynolds must also have arranged for the entry of three or four of the company's horses to the Burnley May Horse Show in 1906. This is the only such occasion mentioned in the company minutes, which suggests that it must have been unusual, though bye-traders seem to have entered such events quite often.

It was the boats and boatmen that brought the canal to life. At the end of the last century, there were over a thousand boats working on the canal and when boats from other canals and those involved in maintenance are added to the figure, there must have been an average of a boat every two hundred yards. The canal was alive with activity, not just with boats passing each other, loading and unloading, but with the hum of industry along its banks. 150 years earlier the possibility of such productive factories and such a busy canal would have been simply unbelievable. Yet some adventurous Bradford merchants felt that it would be worth taking the considerable risk of promoting just such a canal. Why? In the following chapters, we will look at how the longest canal in England came to be constructed, the diverse interests that tugged the project in all sorts of different directions, and how it came to be such an immensely important means of transport for the merchants and farmers along its banks.

Chapter Two

'The conveniency of water carriage'

Eighteenth-century trade and the development of river navigations

HE Pennines have always formed a major barrier to transport, communication and trade between Lancashire and Yorkshire. Even today, with modern technology, difficulties can still be encountered in winter on the M62 motorway. How much more uncertain must transport have been in earlier centuries when packhorse or crude horse and cart were the only ways to carry goods between the two counties. The particular geography of the Pennines was therefore of great importance. Not only were the fells and moors a considerable physical barrier, but their presence influenced the very nature and type of industry and commerce which developed on their flanks. Because of the hills, Lancashire and Yorkshire developed quite distinct economies.

This is seen by the way in which Yorkshire tended to look east and south, while Lancashire had traditionally turned westwards. Yorkshire has had a long and unbroken involvement with woollen textiles, trading originally through London with the commercial centres of western Europe. Lancashire, on the other hand, had a textile industry based principally on the linen trade with Ireland, and its woollen manufacture was concerned mainly with serving local markets. In addition, there developed in the eighteenth century a considerable coastal and international shipping trade, especially with Ireland and the Americas, and it was this that provided the most important reason for the promotion of the Leeds and Liverpool Canal, since the Bradford wool merchants desperately wanted to have access to the colonial trades working out of Liverpool. This was especially marked when, during the late-eighteenth century, the manufacturers in the Bradford area gradually took over the lucrative worsted industry from its former centre in East Anglia, while those in Lancashire expanded by creating an immensely important new textile industry based on cotton which arrived from America via Liverpool – an industry which was destined, of course, to stimulate and feed a huge explosion of industrial development in Lancashire.

The Leeds and Liverpool Canal was to play an extremely important role in this industrial revolution. Long before it was ever thought of, however, entrepreneurs and merchants on both sides of the Pennines had begun to look at ways of improving inland waterways in order to move their bulky goods more quickly and cheaply. Among these were the pioneering Aire and Calder Navigation in Yorkshire and, in Lancashire, the Douglas Navigation. The importance to us of these enterprises is two-fold. First, they were significant pre-cursors of the Leeds and Liverpool and, second, both waterways were later very important to it, the Aire and Calder linking the Leeds and Liverpool to the North Sea, and the Douglas for many years joining Wigan with the Irish Sea. The Douglas Navigation was, moreover, later purchased by the Leeds and Liverpool Company.

The Aire and Calder Navigation

WOOL provided the first major spur to the improvement of water transport. As early as the seventeenth century, the woollen industry was well established in both counties. The main area for weaving stretched from Kendal in the north and Colne in the west, through Airedale to the Calder Valley in the south. Although the cloth produced was drawn from craggy Pennine sheep, and therefore rather coarse, it had the advantage of being cheap and had established for itself a large and healthy market.

London was England's principal port and the vast majority of trade was controlled from there, with its merchants purchasing the cloth and distributing it to markets overseas, especially in western Europe. The Yorkshire merchants wanted to expand, particularly into the fine wool trade, which was at this time centred in East Anglia and the West Country, but to do so they needed a supply of better quality wool than was available locally. This they obtained from the continent, Lincolnshire and East Anglia. The main problem was how to move the raw materials and finished goods between the West Riding where the work was done, and the coast at Hull or Selby. One solution which was suggested was that the River Aire should be made navigable up to Leeds and Wakefield.[1] Bills were presented to Parliament in 1621, 1625 and 1679. None of these was successful but in 1698 another Bill was introduced, a petition in its support from the clothiers of Leeds stating:

> that the towns of Leeds and Wakefield are the principal markets in the north for woollen cloth . . . that it will be a great improvement of trade to all the trading towns of the north by reason of the conveniency of water carriage, for want of which the petitioners send their goods twenty-two miles by land carriage, the expence whereof is not only very chargeable, but they are forced to stay two months sometimes while [i.e.

until]the roads are passable to market.

Despite opposition from the Corporation of York, who had been made conservators of all the tidal rivers in the area by a charter given to them by Edward IV in 1462 and who were concerned that the navigation of the River Ouse would be adversely affected, the Act was passed in May 1699 and the navigation was completed five years later. Despite the very early date of these works, some of the engineering was impressive. It has been estimated that the locks were 58-60 feet long by 14 feet 6 inches to 15 feet wide, with a depth over the cill of 3 feet 6 inches. It is possible that the depth of the river itself was less than this, however, as a boat was built for the Leeds committee in 1700 which measured 44 feet long by 13 feet wide and, drawing 2 feet 6 inches, it could only carry 15-16 tons in 17 inches of water.

During the following sixty years few improvements were made to the river but the facilities at Airmyn (near Goole) were enlarged, with staithes and warehouses being built by 1750. The town became the main port on the navigation until it was superceded by the construction of Goole itself in 1825. Another improvement undertaken was to increase the depth of the river, enabling boats of forty to fifty tons to pass. John Smeaton's report on his survey of the Aire and Calder in 1770 states:

> the original projectors . . . not having had any notion of the extensive trade that was likely to be carried on by means thereof . . . formed their plan upon too diminutive a scale, and particularly with respect to depth . . . of water.

Waterways were clearly the transport of the future, but they needed to be bigger, deeper and better.

Besides the trade in wool textiles, other major traffic on the navigation comprised corn, coal and lime. Much of the corn came from East Anglia to help feed the growing population of the area, and coal from pits near Leeds and Wakefield was delivered to the Ouse and Humber, where it was able to compete successfully with coal from Newcastle.

The importation of corn from East Anglia reflects the country's increasing need to produce its own food, partly satisfied by improvements brought about by the agricultural revolution. Farmers were realising the need for crop rotation and the advantages of fertilisation, particularly the use of lime, which thus became a commodity of rapidly growing importance. Not only used as a fertiliser, lime was needed in the building industry for mortar and decoration. The growing workforce of the West Riding textile industry needed not just food but houses to live in. This created a boom in the construction of industrial premises and housing, which prompted a search for a cheaper and more plentiful supply of lime.

A proposal for an 'Aire Navigation'

ONE of the main centres of the lime trade was at Bingley. Two of the main dealers there, a Mr Mawd and a Mr Lister, sold the impressive total of about 23,000 horse loads a year in the early-1740s. The limestone they burned was quarried locally using coal obtained from pits nearby. The supply was running out, however, and the merchants' eyes turned eagerly to the huge limestone area around Skipton.[2]

In 1744, therefore, a petition was laid before Parliament for a Bill to make the River Aire navigable from Cottingley Bridge, near Bingley, to Inghay Bridge, near Skipton, a distance of twelve miles, at an estimated cost of £8,000. As a printed paper supporting the petition stated:

> That the lime at Bingley being now so dear and scarce, the said Inhabitants cannot be supplied therewith, which is a great Discouragement and Hindrance both to Building and good Husbandry.

The merchants obviously could not rely on road transport and the inhabitants felt that the waterway would be advantageous,

> from the more easy conveyance and cheaper sale of coal, lime, wood and several other sorts of goods, merchandizes and commodities, the prices whereof, by the heavy charge of land carriage, occasioned by the badness and unevenness of the roads, are very much enhanced to the great discouragement of husbandry and other employments.

From 23,000 loads a year, Mawd and Lister expected to be able to increase traffic to 90,000, partly because they thought the navigation would allow them to reduce the cost of lime from 9d to 6d a load.

The return traffic to Skipton was coal from the collieries around Bingley. It was being carried by packhorse and sold there for household use. Not only would the navigation reduce its price from 10d to 8d per load, but the use of boats meant that the weight of each load could be increased. It was estimated that the traffic would amount to 40,000 loads per year and that four hundred tons of general cargo would also be carried.

The Bill was actively supported by Rev William Lamplough, a resident at Cottingley, who stated that he did not intend to be a shareholder. This family's long involvement with water transport was continued by his son-in-law, Col Henry Wickham, who was on the Leeds and Liverpool committee for many years, and his grandson who became an owner of the Low Moor Ironworks which relied both on the canal company's quarries at Skipton for limestone and on the canal for its delivery.

In Parliament the principal opposition to the Bill seems to have come from Lord Thanet, as a letter concerning the navigation, now in York Minster Library, written on 10 January 1743 states:

> This neighbourhood is very populous, we have the clothing trade amongst us and the cloth makers must have grass and hay for keeping horses and cows for the carrying on their trade and supporting of their family . . . We suppose Lord Thanet's opposition proceeds either from Party or picque that he is not at the head of the affair, nor has been sufficiently consulted or perhaps he may imagine that as his estates are mostly grass farms and as the cloth makers . . . send up great numbers of horses and cattle to agist [graze] upon and near his Lordships estates, and as the navigation may make grass and hay more plentiful in the places from whence those cattle are sent . . .

Whatever the reason, Lord Thanet opposed the Bill and since Mr

Simpson, agent to Lord Burlington, was induced to join the opposition, the Bill failed during the committee stage in Parliament, despite being supported by the majority of landowners along the river. If Lord Thanet's 'picque' was indeed the cause of the Bill's failure, it was to prove very expensive, for the improvement in the supply of limestone to Bradford and Bingley had to wait thirty years until the Leeds and Liverpool was built, together, ironically, with a branch canal to Lord Thanet's own quarries in Skipton.

Liverpool's trade in the eighteenth century

IF anything, Lancashire's trade was expanding even more rapidly than that of Yorkshire. In the seventeenth century, of course, most Lancastrians still worked on the land, but manufacturing and household industries were beginning to employ more and more people, albeit often still on a part-time or casual basis. In addition, the thrusting Liverpool merchants had begun to expand their contacts and trade both inland and overseas, investing and re-investing in new wharfs, warehouses and even in inland coalmines in a most enterprising fashion.

Economic change comes about in strange ways. During the later part of the seventeenth century, Parliament was concerned to regulate economic development in Ireland, and English landowners, who were well represented in Parliament, were concerned at the arrival of cheap Irish imports of live cattle which threatened to overwhelm the London meat trade. An Act was duly passed banning imports of live cattle from Ireland. The Irish farmers therefore began to move instead into the profitable and expanding colonial trade, supplying cheese, butter, meat and hides for export, often via Liverpool, to the New World.

The capacity of the wharfs at Liverpool had become overcrowded when one of the finest and most significant developments on the western seaboard, Liverpool's wet dock, was built. The Mersey estuary is exposed to the prevailing westerly winds and vessels unloading in the river were extremely vulnerable to damage from the weather, especially as the old Liver Pool was far too small to cater for the traffic. To protect shipping and to improve cargo handling by reducing the need for transhipment from boats moored in the estuary, the Corporation planned to construct a wet dock, only the second in the country. An Act of Parliament was obtained in 1710 and an engineer, Thomas Steers of Rotherhithe in Kent, was employed to construct it.

Steers soon realised that Liverpool's success as a port would depend not just upon a dock system but also upon good communications with its hinterland, and, in 1712, he surveyed the Rivers Mersey and Irwell for some Manchester gentlemen, with a view to providing an effective way of transporting goods to and from Manchester. Some idea of the type of goods to be carried can be obtained from an inscription on the survey which states:

The Inland parts of Lancashire and Yorkshire being favour'd with great

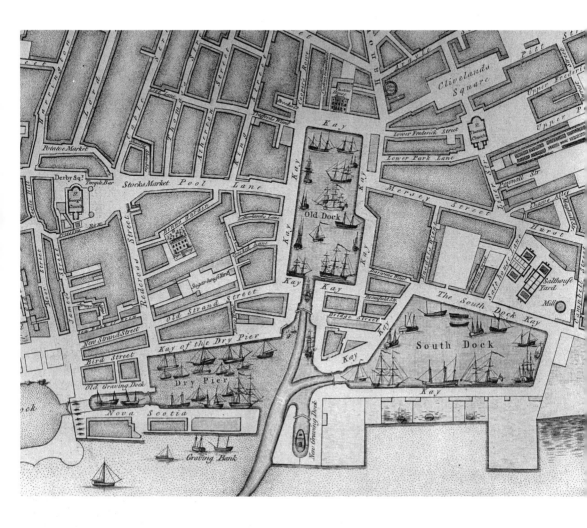

variety of valuable Manufactures in Woollen, Linnen, Cotton, etc. and that in very great quantities: has made that Neighbourhood as populous if not more so (London & Middlesex excepted) as the same extent of any part of Great Britain. The Trades of these Counties extend considerably through the whole Island, as well as abroad and the consumption of Groceries, Irish-Wool, Dying Stuff & other Imported goods consequently very great, but as yet not favour'd with the Conveniency of Water-Carriage . . . The conveniencies of the Navigation carri'd thence to Manchester might at one time or another be of the greatest Importance in time of War in Joyning a communication of the East and West Seas of Great Britain with only 28 miles of Land Carriage. The Trade made more easy . . . and Cheshire served with Coals, Flaggs & Slate far cheaper than at Present.[3]

This suggests that most of Lancashire's trade to and from the east coast was via London and was extremely vulnerable to attack, particularly in the English Channel, in the event of a war. Light, high-value merchandise, however, could stand the expense of land carriage to the North Sea coast and in 1701 Thomas Patten, who had improved

A detail of Eyes' plan of Liverpool, dating from around 1760, showing the wet docks there. Steers' old dock was built within the old Liver Pool, a small tidal inlet from the Mersey estuary. Over the next forty years, two further docks were added to seaward so that, by this date, the old dock was almost land-locked. The canal basin was built off the left of this map a decade or so later but no connection was made to the dock system itself until much later.

(L.R.O. DDX 99/6. Reproduced by kind permission of the County Archivist, Lancashire Record Office.)

the navigation of the Mersey as far as Warrington, was sending tobacco from Bank Quay in that town by cart to Stockport and then on to Doncaster by packhorse where water transport again took over for carriage to Hull.

One consequence of the developing Irish trade in agricultural provisions was a great increase in the need for a cheap and plentiful supply of salt, which was used as a preservative. Up to the end of the seventeenth century salt had been obtained either from salt marshes (in Lancashire these produced small amounts on a seasonal basis and had largely disappeared by the mid-eighteenth century) or from the brine springs or 'wiches' of Cheshire and Worcestershire. In Cheshire this brine was boiled in lead tanks until the salt crystalised. Originally the fuel used was wood, but with the progressive deforestation of the surrounding area, coal was introduced. This was brought by packhorse from the coalfield around Stoke, though transportation costs considerably increased the price of the refined salt.

The discovery of rock salt in the 1690s enabled the raw material to be moved before refining and salt works were set up on the north banks of the Mersey and in Liverpool, where coal from Prescot and St. Helens could be obtained easily and cheaply. The River Weaver was made navigable to accommodate this trade, rock salt being brought down the river to the South Lancashire saltworks and coal taken back for the refining of salt from the brine springs.

Salt refining was just one of the new industries which had sprung up in and around Liverpool to service the developing trade with the British colonies in the Americas and Africa. Iron and copper works had been set up, not just to provide anchors and other equipment for shipping and shipbuilding, but also for making articles for trade. Soap works and potteries were also built, as were refineries for sugar cane from the West Indies.

All these industries needed coal, which also had to be supplied for household use in Liverpool and for cooking and heating on board ships, where it could also be used as ballast. This demand – for a cheap, plentiful and regular supply of coal – remained one of the most important factors in future canal development in south-west Lancashire. The main supply came from Prescot, about eight miles away, but the wagons carrying the coal damaged the road so much that it was only easily passable in summer. For winter, coal was stockpiled or supplied from the coalfield on the Welsh coast of the Dee estuary. The other major sources of coal in the area, which could have supplied Liverpool, were the mines at Whitehaven, but they were too busy supplying Dublin, the fastest growing city in Europe in the eighteenth century and where there was no local supply to regulate the price.

The Douglas Navigation

IT was the rise in demand for coal which provided one of the principal reasons behind the promotion of the Douglas Navigation. It was built

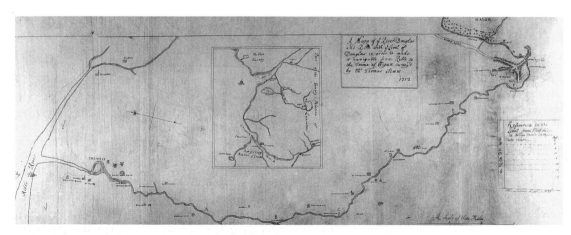

to link the Wigan coalfield, handicapped by its previous reliance on road transport, with the rapidly growing market for coal around the Irish Sea. Although many years were to pass between its inception in 1712 and its opening in 1742, it was to become an important supplier of coal. The history of the Douglas is important to us in three regards. First, it showed how successfully coal could be moved by water; second, the Douglas Navigation owned the headwaters of the river which were later needed by the Leeds and Liverpool; and third, the navigation was bought in 1772 by the Leeds and Liverpool Company.

1712 must have been a busy year for the engineer, Thomas Steers. In addition to the new wet dock at Liverpool, he was asked to survey the River Douglas from Hesketh Bank to Wild Mill, just north of Wigan. There were to be seven locks with a total rise of seventy-five feet one inch. It is not certain who he surveyed the river for, but Haigh Hall features prominently on his map and when a Bill for the navigation was presented to the House of Commons it was by Sir Roger Bradshaigh, who lived there. Bradshaigh owned much land around Wigan rich in cannel coal. Cannel burns with a bright yellow flame, like a candle, and produces little ash. It was in great demand for household use and invariably sold for a higher price than ordinary coal. By improving the transportation of coal and cannel from his estates, Bradshaigh must have hoped to establish a market in Liverpool where coal commanded a high price.

There were other reasons for the Douglas Navigation. When the Bill was presented to Parliament on 10 April 1713 there were petitions on its behalf from the Justices of the Peace, Gentlemen and Freeholders of the County Palatine of Lancaster, and from the Justices of the Peace, Gentlemen and others inhabiting the Fylde, this latter petition stating:

> that along the River Douglas and its adjacent parts, are many pits of coal, delves of stone and slate etc. the land carriage of which is not only very chargeable but dangerous; that making the said River Douglas navigable would advance the manufactures, increase trade and open a communication with several places, to the advantage thereof . . .[4]

The trade with the Fylde was important because there were no suitable ports on the south bank of the Ribble where coal and other goods could be loaded for Ireland, and most ships in this trade had to

Thomas Steers' original plan of 1712, showing the River Douglas from the Ribble (left) to Wigan. All the various houses and hamlets along the course of the river are marked, as are the corn mills on the Douglas at Wigan. Haigh Hall is prominent at the top right of the map, perhaps indicating that Sir Roger Bradshaigh was closely involved with the Bill for the navigation. Just visible crossing the River Ribble is a horse and cart, showing the location of an ancient ford across the river. The inset plan shows the river in the context of West Lancashire as a whole, with the undrained Martin Mere prominent.
(Lancs. R.O., DP 175. Reproduced by permission of the County Archivist, Lancashire Record Office.)

use either Lytham or Freckleton on the north bank. The main ports for the Irish trade at this time were the Wyre estuary to the north, or Liverpool and Chester to the south. The difficulty in navigating the shallow Ribble from Lytham to Preston reduced the number and size of ships using that port, and vessels often had to be partly unloaded before venturing so far up the estuary.

After having survived all its stages in the House of Commons the Bill was presented to the House of Lords on 8 May 1713, where it was thrown out at the committee stage on 6 June 1713, despite a petition on its behalf from the inhabitants of Manchester. Its failure was probably due to opposition from the owners of the meadow and marsh land near to the river, who had petitioned Parliament on 21 May. Riparian land-owners were always concerned about the effect a navigation would have, as it took control of the river out of their hands. They used to allow the river to flood their land occasionally, the silt deposited acting as a fertiliser and improving the quality of the soil. They were also concerned about uncontrolled flooding caused by the navigation works constricting the flow of water.

Six years passed before a second attempt was made. This time Steers was more intimately involved, being named as an undertaker for the navigation together with William Squire, a Liverpool merchant, whose brother-in-law Richard Norris also seems to have been involved. The Norrises were one of Liverpool's most influential families and we can thus see here an early example of Liverpool merchants investing money in coal and coal-related enterprises in south-west Lancashire.

It is also probable that Sir Roger Bradshaigh was involved again, though not directly. He was one of the two MPs for Wigan, and little happened there that he did not influence. His acquaintance, the tenth Earl of Derby, whose family had been prominent in Lancashire for generations, was another interested party. It is possible that he had first suggested that Thomas Steers should be appointed as dock engineer at Liverpool. His interest in the Douglas Navigation is revealed in a series of notes in the papers of his steward, George Kenyon, which questioned the details of how goods would be shipped and the cost and method of construction of the navigation. They also suggest that much of the initial cost of obtaining the Act was to be borne by Steers and that he was to be repaid out of the tolls.[5]

The 1720 petition to Parliament, from the Borough and Corporation of Wigan and the Justices of the Peace and other inhabitants and owners of land within Lancashire, stated:

> that the River Douglas . . . is capable of being made navigable for boats and lighters. That along the said River and parts adjacent are many coal-pits and delfs of stone and slate, the carriage of which is very chargeable and, to many, very dangerous; their road being across Ribble sands, two miles over, covered each tide with water, and in the passage whereof, yearly, several persons and goods are lost; that the roads being generally deep clay, are, in winter and wet seasons, troublesome and expensive; that if the said River be made navigable, it will open a way for several manufactures, advance trade and be a nursery for seamen . . .[6]

After being discussed by committee, leave was granted for the Bill to be presented and it passed its first reading on 21 January 1720. After several amendments it received its second reading just ten days later but, before the third reading, petitions were again received from the various landowners and farmers of the meadow and marsh lands bordering the river from Wigan to Hesketh Bank. This group published at least two broadsheets countering the reasons for making the river navigable, one stating:

> That making this River navigable will infallibly destroy several thousand acres of rich Meadow Lands, lying along the said River, which at present are worth from 50s to £5 an acre, but if this Bill passes into law, will not be worth 15 or 20 shillings per acre, at most.
>
> And that consequently it will lessen, if not entirely put an end to the breeding of those great Numbers of large Cattle which these parts are remarkable for, and from whence the Southern Markets are plentifully supplied, because if these Meadows are ruined there will be very little Hay in that part of the County for Winter Fodder.[7]

The market town of Ormskirk also petitioned against the Bill, the inhabitants worrying that trade would bypass the town to the detriment of their own market. After two divisions in the House which caused some delay, the Bill was finally passed to the House of Lords, with some minor amendments, on 13 February 1720, the voting being 73 for the Bill with 27 against.

In the Lords opposition was again encountered from landowners, with Thomas Hesketh of Rufford presenting their petition. Other petitions against the Bill came from Ormskirk, Preston Corporation and from some of the inhabitants of Wigan, all presumably worried about possible loss of their trade to the navigation. Those supporting the Bill came from Liverpool, Manchester, Bolton, Bury, Rochdale, the Fylde and the towns along the river.

Witnesses for and against the Bill were heard and, after discussions in committee, the Act was finally passed on 24 March 1720. It stated that William Squire and Thomas Steers, both of Liverpool, were to be the undertakers (those responsible for the construction) and listed thirty-two commissioners, whose job was to settle any difference between the undertakers and any of the landowners. The Act also stipulated a maximum tonnage rate of 2s 6d, irrespective of distance travelled, and that the whole work, from the River Ribble to Miry Lane End in Wigan, was to be completed within eleven years.

Whilst the Bill was progressing through Parliament, both Steers and Squire were in London, where they were assisted by Richard Norris. To finance the construction, the estimated profit from the navigation was divided into quarters, each of them being entitled to one share, with the remaining quarter being divided into 1,200 parts and sold at £5 each. This would have raised £6,000. Steers' estimate for the construction of the navigation was £10,000, later reduced to £8,000. It was decided that Squire should remain in London to sell shares in the navigation and that Steers would return to Lancashire to commence construction. Before he left he assigned his share in the profits to Squire in case further parts were needed for sale.

Steers started work at Rufford, where the ford was removed and a bridge was built, together with the first of the locks that would have to be built just upstream. Stone for the work was obtained from two quarries which were opened at Harrock Hill and Bartons Delf, both a little more than a mile away. The river was straightened and widened for about a mile and a half from Rufford downstream to Croston Finney, where a start was made on a second lock; below this point, the navigation would have been tidal. The only other work undertaken was the construction of a boat for trading on the river and this did carry several loads of goods – on one occasion, according to Steers, sailing five miles up the river. Steers estimated that he had expended about £700 in obtaining the Act and in construction work and that he had only received £600 from Squire.

The finances were obviously in a poor state, not unusual for businesses at that time. The navigation had obtained its Act just before the infamous South Sea Bubble and its resulting financial scandal. After soaring from £5 to £70 in a matter of weeks, the share value fell to three guineas even quicker. It is not known exactly how many of the 1,200 shares were sold, but share certificate number 942 was issued and if all the earlier ones had been sold there is a huge discrepancy between the £4,710 presumably received from the sale of these shares and the £600 that Steers claims to have received.[8]

It is interesting to note that a pack of playing cards was printed to commemorate the events surrounding the South Sea Bubble, each card representing a company, with an engraving and verse relating to that company. The River Douglas appeared on the ace of spades and the verse went as follows:

Since bubbles came in vogue, new arts are found
To cut thro' rocks and level rising ground,
That murm'ring waters may be made more deep
To drown the knave and let the fools asleep.[9]

Two shareholders took Steers, Squire and Norris to the Court of Chancery, claiming that they had created the company for their own financial gain and had no intention of making the navigation. Various depositions from those involved in the construction work or the financing were taken between 1729 and 1734 but the case was inconclusive. Possibly Squire had re-invested the money which had been raised for the navigation in other companies, hoping to make a profit for himself. We may never know. By 1730 he had left Liverpool and the last we hear of him is in a letter to customs collectors dated 21 March 1732 asking them:

. . . carefully to examine all persons that shall pass or endeavour to pass beyond the seas in order to the apprehending Wm. Burroughs, Esq. and Wm. Squire who have carryed on divers notorious fraudulent practices to the great detriment of the proprietors of the Charitable Corporation.[10]

After the initial phase at Rufford no further work was undertaken, despite the approach of the eleven-year deadline set down in the Act. The commissioners responsible for overseeing the project were then approached by Alexander Radcliffe of Ormskirk and Alexander Leigh of Wigan, who wished to take over as new undertakers. This was granted by the commissioners on 12 June 1731 and they were allowed a further eleven years to complete the navigation.

Ironically, it is possible that these gentlemen had both been opposed to the navigation originally but had changed their attitude when they realised the benefits to be gained. Leigh, through whose efforts the navigation was eventually completed, was an attorney in Wigan with a large practice, beside being steward or clerk of no fewer than seventeen manorial courts. He was also closely involved with the legal and business affairs of Sir Roger Bradshaigh and acted as advisor to him and to Earl Barrymore on matters concerning Wigan. His interests also included coal mining – hence, probably, his involvement with the navigation.[11]

The new undertakers' first action was to arrange for a new survey of the river and for this they employed William Palmer, who was the engineer engaged by the Corporation of York to improve the River Ouse navigation. He presented his report in March 1733, when he estimated the cost of completing the navigation to be £6,684-13-00. There were to be twelve locks up to Wigan with a total rise of sixty-eight feet, each to be twelve-feet wide by sixty-feet long and the river would be three-feet deep.

Interestingly, he also suggested a radical new scheme for taking the navigation from Rufford across Martin Mere to Crossens (near Southport). It would shorten the distance to the sea by six miles compared to the route by the river to Hesketh Bank, and the greater tidal range at Crossens would give more reliable access to sea-going vessels than by way of the River Douglas. Significantly, Palmer points out what was to be a constant problem – that until the navigation was extended to Tarleton the water level in the River Douglas was such that loaded vessels could only reach the tide lock for a few days at spring tides. Finally, he concluded, the provision of two routes by which the flood water of the Douglas could be channeled to the sea, either across the Mere or by the old river through Tarleton, would enable the land near the river above Rufford to be better protected from flooding. The additional work involved in crossing the Mere he estimated to cost £2,530. This adventurous proposal would have altered substantially the line of the eventual navigation and affected the subsequent development of the area around Crossens.[12] Who knows but that Southport might have become an industrialised port town, rather than the fashionable bathing resort it actually developed into.

Despite the report, however, nothing happened until November 1737 when, possibly as a result of Alexander Radcliffe having died, the undertaking was divided into six shares in trust for Alexander Leigh and Alexander Radcliffe, the shares being assigned to William Hunter and George Corbisley of Manchester, Robert Bankes of Winstanley, Humphrey Whalley, clerk curate of Billinge, Robert Whittle of Knowsley and Robert Holt of Wigan. Holt was the only one who maintained his interest in the navigation, the other shares being taken by Alexander Leigh. It was these two undertakers, Holt and Leigh, who immediately began the work of building the navigation.

Work at last began in earnest. The river was opened progressively: four locks in 1738 and a further three the following year. At the same time, land was purchased from Lord Derby for a wharf at Freckleton on the Fylde, this being to his advantage as the first traffic on the river was coal from his delf at Bispham to the Fylde.[13]

Sir Roger Bradshaigh continued to show his interest in the navigation by opposing a bid by Sir James Lowther, the owner of the largest Whitehaven collieries, to persuade Parliament to reduce the duty on coal carried around the coast in 1739. If this had passed, Lowther would have been able to monopolise the Irish Sea coal trade.

Vessels in the Whitehaven coal trade returned empty, and hence less profitably, from their main market in Dublin, whilst those from the Douglas could return from delivering coal to Lancaster and Kendal with limestone or iron, thus making it possible for the Douglas coal, which was more expensive, to compete with that from Whitehaven.

Work continued on the navigation and Thomas Steers was consulted from time to time. On 17 March 1741 he was paid three guineas for advising on the basin at Wigan and Crooke Lock, and the following year he viewed the possible site at Meols for the entrance to the navigation across Martin Mere. Leigh was still considering this scheme, but eventually dropped the idea.

The main contractor involved in the construction appears to have been Richard Fell who, although described as a carpenter from Wigan in his will (he died in 1759), was paid for all types of building work. This included the stone and brickwork at the locks and spadework in opening out the river, besides the woodwork more generally associated with his calling. Payments to him for the construction work amounted to between £5 and £10 per week on average. There were other contractors but they seem to have been employed at specific sites on the navigation whereas Fell worked all along the route. He continued to be employed after the navigation was opened, when he undertook repair work and helped with maintainance of the boats used.[14]

The navigation is completed

BY mid-1742 the navigation was ready for the commissioners to inspect, which they did on 12 June. Afterwards they declared that it complied with the Act and that the undertakers could now charge for its use. Further work was still needed, however, so perhaps the inspection had been brought forward to comply with the eleven-year clause in the Act. Unfortunately Robert Holt did not live to see the navigation open as he died on 15 September 1740, his share in the navigation being divided into six parts, two to his eldest son Edward and one each to his other children, Henry, Dorothy, Mary and Susanna. Dorothy was married to Alexander Leigh, who already owned five-sixths of the navigation, whilst Susanna was married to Jno. Chadwick of Manchester, whose family owned an iron forge near Wigan, which was supplied with pig iron from Liverpool and Furness by way of the navigation. The total cost of the construction work and the purchase of land had amounted to £9,866-8-6, very close to Steers' original estimate.[15]

Originally there were thirteen locks on the river: from the sea upstream, they were at Croston Finney, where the navigation joined the tidal river, Rufford (Holland), Wanes Blades, Bispham, Douglas Bridge (Newburgh), Chapel House, Gillibrands, Appley Bridge, Upholland (near Bank House), Gathurst, Crooke, Hell Meadow and Harrison Platt just below Wigan. The difficulties in negotiating the tidal river to Croston Finney must soon have become apparent, the lock being usable for only a few days at spring tides. To overcome this a lock and weir were constructed at Tarleton in 1747, but landowners soon complained that this weir increased the flooding in the Tarleton area by reducing the flow of the river and it seems to have been removed by the 1770s. As we shall see later, a second attempt at improving the tidal section was more successful when, in around 1800, the company canalised the River Douglas down to Tarleton, where the waterway still joins the river today.

Although there were wharfs all along the river the most important ones were around the basin at Wigan, located on the site of the present canal basin, where coal and cannel from the Haigh collieries of Sir Roger Bradshaigh were loaded, and at Gathurst, where coal from Orrell reached the navigation.

By 1747 the undertakers owned a number of 'flats', as the sailing barges of the North West were known. Seven of them were decked flats loading up to thirty or forty tons and which were suitable for carrying goods on the Irish Sea; there were five open flats loading about twenty tons, which were used only on the navigation, or on the Ribble for deliveries to Freckleton or Preston. There were several bye traders (as those owning and working their own boats are called), and colliery owners who also operated boats on the navigation.

Besides owning the port facilities at Freckleton the undertakers also rented wharfs for improved distribution of the coal and cannel by boats from the navigation.[16] These were at Milnthorpe, where J. Dowker looked after the traffic to Kendal, at Poulton, where coal could be transhipped to vessels in the Irish trade, and at Preston. In order to improve the supply of coal and cannel, the undertakers considered extending the navigation to Hindley by way of Balsden Brook, and a survey was made, but the fall of twenty-three feet four inches was considered too great and nothing more was done.[17]

1753 saw several changes, the most important being the reduction of the toll for the use of the river from 2s 6d to 1s 0d per ton in order to encourage trade.[18] The number of shareholders increased, with Lord Pollington and David Poole each purchasing a 1/36th share, probably from Alexander Leigh. They were all involved in the Parliamentary election for Wigan in that year and the navigation became a minor issue, the opposition in a partisan broadsheet stating:

> As to Mr Leigh's navigation, I would never contribute towards it, because I always thought it a wild impracticable Scheme, of certain Injury to many thro' whose Lands it was to pass, and likely to end in nothing but the Ruin of the Projector.[19]

Evidently the navigation was severely limited in its success as far as some people were concerned.

Besides the problems normally associated with a river navigation, as opposed to a still-water canal, vessels using the river had to have lowering masts in order to be able to negotiate the fixed bridges, that at Tarleton being the first encountered on the navigation. As they needed fixed masts to withstand adverse weather at sea, this effectively prohibited seagoing flats from using the navigation. To overcome this, swing bridges began to be installed in the early 1760s, when a new section of canal was built to by-pass one section of the river, from Sollom to Rufford. As we have seen, Tarleton Lock had been

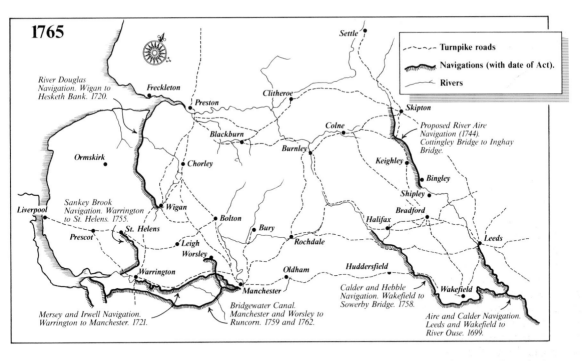

1765

Settle

- - - - - Turnpike roads

〰〰〰 Navigations (with date of Act).

⌒ Rivers

River Douglas Navigation. Wigan to Hesketh Bank. 1720.

Freckleton

Clitheroe

Preston

Skipton

Proposed River Aire Navigation (1744). Cottingley Bridge to Inghay Bridge.

Colne

Blackburn

Burnley

Keighley

Bingley

Shipley

Ormskirk

Chorley

Bradford

Halifax

Leeds

Liverpool

Sankey Brook Navigation. Warrington to St. Helens. 1755.

Wigan

Bolton

Bury

Rochdale

Prescot

St. Helens

Leigh

Worsley

Oldham

Huddersfield

Wakefield

Warrington

Manchester

Calder and Hebble Navigation. Wakefield to Sowerby Bridge. 1758.

Mersey and Irwell Navigation. Warrington to Manchester. 1721.

Bridgewater Canal. Manchester and Worsley to Runcorn. 1759 and 1762.

Aire and Calder Navigation. Leeds and Wakefield to River Ouse. 1699.

abandoned by the 1770s and may have been out of use earlier, so the new cut had the added advantage of providing access to the river further downstream than Croston Finney, thus increasing the number of days when it was possible to reach the navigation.

Towage on this new section was by man power, as on the rest of the navigation, so no towpath was built. The men pulling the boats had to clamber over stiles and along the riverbank, without the luxury of a towpath. It was not until 1800 that land for a towpath was purchased for the length from Sollom to Rufford, and this only after the local landowner complained that his fences were being destroyed by horses towing boats along that section.[20] It was also intended to improve the whole navigation so that vessels with fixed masts could use the navigation all the way upstream to Wigan, but the building of the Leeds and Liverpool and its purchase of the Douglas Navigation removed the need for these alterations.

The boats and trade on the Douglas Navigation

NO record remains of the size of the locks on the Douglas, but some idea can be obtained by consulting the Preston Register of Shipping, in which there are many locally built and owned boats. The *Speedwell*, built in 1773 at Parbold, where her owners also lived, was forty-seven feet long with a beam of 13'-8" and a depth of 4'-6", and the *William*, built at Preston in 1768 and owned at Blackburn, was 54'-9" long by

13'-9" across the beam with a depth of 4'-11". Most of the boats seem to have been between forty-five and fifty-five feet long, and either narrower than 14'-6" or more than 15'-6", which almost certainly indicates the difference between those boats capable of working up the river, and those into which cargoes were transhipped at Tarleton, Hesketh Bank, or around the Ribble estuary for delivery to ports on the Irish Sea coast.

There exist two sets of accounts for vessels which worked in the River Douglas trade, and from these some idea of the cargoes carried can be obtained, as well as a great deal of other information. The first dates from 1752-5 and relates to the flat *Expedition,* which worked only on the River Douglas itself, and to the *Liverpool, Sincerity* and *Lancaster,* which worked round the coast.[21] Outward cargoes, besides coal and cannel, comprised cinders (coke), turf and paving stones, and return cargoes included timber, hides, kelp, soap ashes, barley, beans and limestone. Limestone was by far the most important return trade and the *Expedition* was kept busy delivering loads from Tarleton and Hesketh Bank, where it was stored, to sites all along the river, returning with coal and cannel.

Coastwise, it would appear that return trips to Poulton, on the Wyre, took about three weeks while those to the Furness district could take up to six weeks. On the river the *Expedition* took about one week for the round trip to Wigan, motive power being achieved by men hauling at from 6d to 1s per day. A square sail was provided, at a cost of £2-13-3, in the event of a favourable wind. The bill for river duty, payable to Alexander Leigh, averaged about £8-0-0 per month, which at 1s per ton suggests that about 1,840 tons were carried annually by these boats.

The second set of accounts relates to the flat *Success,* which worked between Freckleton, Preston and Wigan and which covers the years 1764-8. The cargo down river was nearly all coal, with occasional loads of cinders, paving stones or slates, and upriver only limestone for delivery at wharfs along the whole length of the river. If no limestone was needed the boat returned light (empty). The weight carried on the river varied from fourteen to nineteen tons, while up to twenty tons could be delivered from Tarleton to places on the Ribble. It is difficult to estimate journey times, as the *Success* seems also to have been used for storage, particularly at the wharfs on the Ribble. One day was spent sailing from Tarleton to Freckleton, but then a fortnight might pass before she loaded again at Tarleton, or further up the river. In 1764-5 she passed along the river fourteen times, carrying a total of 225 tons, but twelve further voyages were completed that year from Tarleton to Freckleton and Preston, mainly in the summer months when shortage of water may have caused problems navigating the river.[22]

Another source of information on traffic is contained in the diaries of Holt Leigh, Alexander Leigh's son, where he notes the sums of money paid to him for river duty in the years 1771-3.[23] During 1772 he received £414 which, at 1s per ton duty, suggests that at least 8,280 tons were carried. However this must be an underestimate as gravel, for the use of the Commissioners of Preston Turnpike, was charged at the lower rate of 3d per ton, and we know that at least three hundred tons were transported. The undertakers' boats are also missing from this account, so the total carried could have been well over 10,000 tons, a not inconsiderable sum for a river navigation at that time.

Despite this apparent success, an abstract of the accounts for the construction of the navigation show that the cost of construction came to £12,385-12-0 or £15,085-6-9 if interest on the money expended was included and by 1768 this had risen to £32,226-5-1, including interest and maintainance charges.[24]

Thus, from a financial standpoint, the Douglas Navigation would appear, on paper, to have been unsuccessful. It is important to remember, however, that the figures do not allow for the increased production of coal in the Douglas Valley which it promoted. As we have seen, many shareholders were first and foremost men with coal to sell and Alexander Leigh, for one, must surely have made substantial profits from his colliery activities for him to be able to invest continually in the navigation. The financial returns obtained were typical of river navigations of the era, many of which were more concerned with improvements to the transport infrastructure in their own region, than in making money in their own right. Investors usually made more money from the increased trade rather than any huge financial return from tolls charged on their waterway.

Things changed with the advent of the canal age, when following the opening of the Bridgewater Canal, finance for canals was sought from a far wider spectrum of sources, with money coming from people all over the country. Because many proprietors no longer lived near to their canal, they did not benefit directly from local improvements and were more concerned to obtain a regular income from a profitable canal. The projected canal schemes of this time were also much larger and costlier than any previous navigation, and often sufficient money would not have been available in their locality. Many were built to serve areas of developing industry, and much of the local resources would already be invested in these. Thus the canal companies had to seek money from the established trading centres outside of their area. The Leeds and Liverpool conforms with these new circumstances, and although many of the prominent promoters had interests in local industries, an increasing number of proprietors came from beyond Lancashire and Yorkshire, notably the Quaker community of East Anglia, whose banking system, based on their established woollen industry, was closely linked to that in West Yorkshire. And it is to West Yorkshire that we must now move our attention.

Chapter Three

'A laudable and beneficial improvement'

The Leeds and Liverpool Canal is born 1764 – 1782

MONG those who have been suggested as the catalyst for the development of inland navigation, few can compare with Thomas Steers. Besides his close involvement with the Douglas Navigation, he was also named as an undertaker for the Mersey and Irwell Navigation and probably acted as their engineer. He produced plans for the Calder and Hebble Navigation and for the River Boyne in Ireland, where he was also engineer for the Newry Canal. This was constructed during the 1730s and '40s and joined the port of Newry to Lough Neagh, a distance of eighteen and a half miles. It was the first British canal to have a summit level, with all the attendant problems in water supply that this produced.

All these schemes, however, were virtual sidelines to Steers' work in Liverpool, where he created the first successful wet-dock system and was closely involved in the political and economic activity of the town. For some of his later work he was assisted by Henry Berry, who took over as dock engineer in Liverpool when Steers died and who went on to construct the Sankey Navigation, built to enable the collieries around St. Helens to compete with those of Prescot for the supply of coal to Liverpool.

The problem of the transport of coal, expensive and uncertain to move by road, was also engaging merchants in Manchester at this time. The Mersey and Irwell Navigation had been opened by 1734 and it was further proposed, three years later, to make the Worsley Brook navigable to the coal mines around Worsley. Thomas Steers was involved yet again and produced a survey; an Act was obtained the same year, but no further action was taken. Coal continued to be transported to Manchester by land and various road improvements were carried out in an attempt to improve matters. In 1753 a group of Manchester men suggested a level canal from Salford, via Worsley and Leigh, to the Wigan area; and a survey was undertaken by William Taylor, later to work with Henry Berry on the Sankey Navigation. A Bill was presented to Parliament but was lost due to the opposition of landowners and road trustees.

It was not until 1759, when the Duke of Bridgewater obtained an Act for a canal from his mines at Worsley to Patricroft, that the problem of Manchester's coal supply began to be solved. The following year a second Act was passed varying the line so that the River Irwell was crossed at Barton, and Manchester approached from the south west. John Gilbert, the Duke's agent, was initially in charge of construction, but James Brindley was taken on as a consulting engineer. The canal was open from the underground coal workings at Worsley to Castlefield in Manchester by mid-1765.

This was an immensely important canal. Until this time, inland transport by water had been looked on as a means of supplying a specific locality with the raw materials and goods needed to encourage the local economy. The real success of the Duke's canal was not only the supply of cheap coal to Manchester, but in capturing the imagination of people not just locally but all over the country and as far away as Europe. A visit to the mines at Worsley and the aqueduct at Barton became an essential part of any 'Grand Tour', and influential people flocked to the area to view these achievements. This led to a new outlook on canals and during the mid-1760s a number of schemes were proposed, both to improve transport on a local scale, and even to link one side of the country with the other.

The possibility of building such cross-country canals exercised the minds and fired the imaginations of many people. The merchants in the west-coast ports of Glasgow, Liverpool and Bristol, who traded with the American colonies, wanted to sell their colonial produce in the rich markets in the east of the country and in Europe. At the same time the manufacturers from the east wanted to enter the expanding Liverpool market. To allow this trade to develop, good cross-country links were needed. Eventually, the provision of these routes went some considerable way towards integrating the economies of east and west. Before, as we have seen, Lancashire and Yorkshire had developed along separate, distinct lines. Now they were able to advance together. Not all local variations were removed and there remained very great differences between the economies and patterns of trade on the different sides of the country, but these first significant moves towards practical cross-country routes went a long way towards opening up an interchange of opinions and opportunities between the two counties.

The idea is born

IT is with this development that the original germ of an idea for what eventually became the Leeds and Liverpool Canal was created. In all, four main canal schemes were being suggested at this time: the Forth and Clyde, which was surveyed in 1762 and 1763 and obtained its Act in 1768; the Trent and Mersey and the Staffordshire and Worcestershire, whose Acts were passed in 1766 and which were to link Liverpool, Bristol and Hull by way of the Potteries and Birmingham; and, finally, a link between the rivers Ribble and Aire, proposed in 1764, which was destined to become the Leeds and Liverpool.

The initial impetus for the Leeds and Liverpool came from east of the Pennines, from landowners and merchants around Bradford who were anxious to increase the supply of limestone to their coal mines in the Bingley and Bradford area where it could be burnt to produce lime for land improvement and building purposes. They also wanted a cheap means of delivering coal to the limestone quarries in the Craven district to reduce the price of lime for the improvement of grazing lands in the area. Lastly, and very significantly, they felt that a canal would be a reliable and speedy through route for local textile products to the developing ports of Liverpool and Lancaster and the markets beyond.

For the Liverpool promoters there were very different reasons for wanting such a canal. They required a cheap and reliable supply of coal for their manufacturing and shipping businesses, together with the opportunity to tap the growing industrial regions of Lancashire. It was this difference that was to lead to prolonged confrontation and almost to the collapse of the canal scheme. Ironically, as we shall see, it was precisely this divergence of needs which later accounted for the long and successful history of the canal.

Although we do not know the author, the *York Courant* of 7th August 1764 appears to have contained the first suggestion of a canal to link Lancashire and Yorkshire:

> As the Rivers Aire and Ribble may be so easily joined at different places and rendered navigable between Leeds and Preston at an expense which gentlemen who have estates on the banks may readily supply it is thought proper to mention it to the public at this juncture.

Perhaps we can see here the hand of one John Stanhope, a prominent Bradford landowner and attorney who was to play a large part in the canal's promotion. Although he was primarily a lawyer, he was involved with various regulations governing the sale of woollen goods and his brother, Walter, was a Leeds woollen merchant.

It seems to have been Stanhope who first engaged John Long-botham to survey a route. Certainly, one of Stanhope's servants helped Longbotham on the survey and when the first meeting was held to promote the navigation, in Bradford on 2nd July 1766, Stanhope headed the list of over a hundred subscribers to a fund for making a full plan and estimate of the scheme. Besides other members of the Stanhope family, the list includes several other people who were to have a long association with the undertaking: John Hustler, who took over the direction of the company when John Stanhope died in 1770, William Birbeck and Henry Wickham. In August Hustler wrote to Stanhope setting out the advantages of the navigation. This letter eventually became a booklet to advertise the proposed canal and was published in 1768 (see Appendix 1).

aaa Canal from Fouridge to Liverpoole. ab Canal to Lancaster.
oc Astland 8 Douglas Navigation. cd Canal to Manchester
e Canal to Blackburn
f....d°....to Clithero.
g....d°....to Burnley
h Navigable Canal supplying
i the Bason.

Part of CUMBERLAND

Broughton
Fournesfetts
Ulverstone
Kendal
Holkar hall
Part of YORKSHIRE
Lancaster
Condar
Wire
Garstang
Ribchester
Pootney
Preston
Kirkham
Ribble
Walton
Penwortham
Neals
Douglas
Wigan
Ormskirk
Atherton
Formby
Liverpoole
Prescot
Warrington
Frodsham
Mersey
Part of CHESHIRE
Weaver
Clithero
Pakiham
Whaley
Coln
Burnley
Blackburn
LANCASHIRE
Manchester
Fouridge
Miles
1   8   12   16   20

J. Longbotham 1766.

A copy of Longbotham's original survey of 1766, showing his first idea for a canal to link the Ribble and Aire rivers near Preston and at Leeds, with branches to several of the important towns near the route. At this time it should be remembered that Lancaster was still almost as important a port as Liverpool and a branch there was considered important in most of the early schemes.
(Drawn from a copy in Bradford Record Office.)

Longbotham begins work

LONGBOTHAM started work in 1765. He wrote to Stanhope about his plan to link Preston with the River Aire, with two branches leading away from the canal at Walton, near Preston. One branch was to go north to Poulton, on the Wyre, for trade to Lancaster; the other was to the south, to Liverpool. He had initially thought of continuing the second branch to link up with the Bridgewater Canal at Runcorn, a scheme which was revived later, but the channel up the Mersey from Liverpool was considered to be good enough to render this extension unnecessary.[1]

Thus, at this early stage, Preston rather than Liverpool was to be the destination on the Lancashire side. On the face of it this may appear a strange decision. Yet the Ribble-Aire gap from Preston was a natural choice. The route had been in heavy use, as one of the easiest Pennine crossings, for centuries. It had linked the Viking strongholds of York and Dublin and had been recognised, even earlier, by the Romans who had built a busy road along it. Preston was the county town, a highly important market and a developing centre of the local handloom weaving industry. Eventually the Ribble was improved to such an extent that Preston boasted the largest single wet dock in the country.

The support of the inhabitants from towns along the route was canvassed, though not always successfully. The merchants in Lancaster, for example, were not impressed and intimated that they were unlikely to support the scheme as they were:

> . . . very much strangers to the expence which may attend a canal of such great extent and seems rather fearful of its answering the intention.[2]

By August 1767, Longbotham wrote to Stanhope to say that he had completed his survey and estimate for the route from Preston to Leeds and that it was now being made ready for printing. The survey of the branches still required finishing and it was while completing this that a larger and more adventurous scheme seems to have caught his imagination. On 21 August, he wrote to Stanhope with the new idea of making Liverpool the terminus of a canal from Hull:

> . . . that it is practicable to join the two principal ports by an entire canal to carry vessels of sixty tons burthen and to deliver their respective cargoes from port to port at seven shillings and sixpence per ton and in

less time than three days.[3]

His further suggestion that branches be built to towns near the line of the canal featured in all the early Leeds and Liverpool plans. Enthusiasm for a canal to Hull, by-passing the Aire and Calder, was rekindled later, when he surveyed the Leeds and Selby Canal. His estimate for the canal from Leeds to Neas Point, which was the original Lancashire terminal, came to £101,831.

Longbotham's completed survey, from Leeds to Liverpool, was duly presented at a meeting held at the Sun Inn in Bradford on 7 January 1768. A Yorkshire committee was appointed, and John Hustler and Richard Markham were empowered to collect subscriptions to defray the cost of the plan and estimate. It was suggested that an engineer, such as Smeaton or Brindley, should check the plans and that a committee be formed in Lancashire to organise the collection of subscriptions there.

It is interesting that this committee took some time to organise as there was no one in Lancashire willing to undertake things in the way that Stanhope and Hustler had in Yorkshire, and by the time the first meeting in Lancashire had been held on 25 August 1768, at which a committee of forty gentlemen was nominated, the Yorkshire committee had already progressed the matter further and had approached Brindley to check Longbotham's survey. The two engineers may have met previously, in 1765, when Brindley took over the construction of the Calder and Hebble from Smeaton.

It took just three weeks to check the survey. This was mainly done by Brindley's assistant, Robert Whitworth, rather than by the engineer himself, though he charged one guinea per day for the work. Longbotham was allowed to accompany him, not just to provide information about his line but also

> . . . to influence Brindley as much as possible in favour of a large [i.e. broad] canal, as I have the greatest reason to suspect that he has been and will be biased as much as possible by the principal proprietors of the Staffordshire Navigation and particularly by the Duke of Bridgewater to give his report in favour of the narrow canal and narrow boats, in order that their's may communicate with it and you will find [they] have some plausible reason to offer in favour of it, which I hope much our gentlemen will not pay regard to. . . .[4]

He must have been successful, convincing Brindley of the necessity of constructing the canal to dimensions suitable for the vessels already using the Douglas and the Aire and Calder Navigations, discarding the idea of building a canal suitable only for narrow boats.

An engraving of the plan was produced to promote the scheme, and copies of the full survey, showing every field crossed and the amount of land required, were deposited in the Registry of Deeds in both counties. Those whose land was crossed by the canal had to be made aware of the scheme, and from these plans could decide if they were for or against it.

When the Bill was presented to Parliament, considerable weight was placed on landowners' opinions, and success or failure often depended upon their views. Influential members of the canal committee spent much time, prior to the application to Parliament, visiting landowners and canvassing their support. This often entailed visits to London to see men such as Lord Derby or the Earl of Thanet. John Hustler, who was a Quaker wool merchant from Bradford, was a notable promoter of the canal. Quakers were increasingly involved with the canal, with much of the canal's finances coming from the Quaker banking community in Yorkshire and East Anglia. Hustler worked tirelessly for the company, and was treasurer until his death in 1790. In common with many committee members, he became involved in coal mining in the Douglas Valley.

The 'Yorkshire and Lancashire Canal' is proposed

AN important joint meeting of the two committees, held on 19 December 1768 in Burnley, decided that application should be made to Parliament for an Act for the 'Yorkshire and Lancashire Canal'. 2,600 shares were to be issued of £100 each, with no shareholder having more than 100. This would have covered the cost of construction, estimated by Brindley to be £259,777. The tonnage to be charged for limestone, slate etc. would be ½d per mile, that for coal 1d per mile and general cargo 1½d per mile. The respective incomes from these tonnages were calculated to be £8,500, £3,500 and £8,000.[5]

It is significant that, from these estimates, five times more limestone and one and a half times more general cargo were expected to be carried than coal. They clearly thought that limestone would be by far the most important traffic. If these figures were correct the profit accruing to the canal annually would have been £21,132. They could hardly have been wider of the mark. As we shall see, coal turned out to be the main cargo, merchandise the most lucrative and limestone unimportant by comparison.

A subscription for those in Yorkshire interested in the canal was opened after a meeting at Bradford around three weeks later, on 9 January 1769. A sum of ten shillings per share was requested to cover the cost of the application to Parliament and books were opened at Leeds, Bradford, Skipton, Riddlesden, Colne, Settle, Otley and Sheffield. Unfortunately there is no similar list of locations of books for the Lancashire subscriptions. However, when many of the Liverpool subscribers withdrew their subscriptions at the end of 1769 following the argument over the route, the books were reopened, those for the west of the country being at Kendal, Lancaster, Preston, Walton, Ormskirk, Wigan, Manchester, Leyland, Newburgh and Blackburn. Liverpool was omitted, with money being sought in London instead.

It was too late to obtain the Act in the 1769 session of Parliament and the Bill was withdrawn to be presented the following year. This provided time for application to be made to all the landowners on the line of the canal to obtain their consent. It also provided the Liverpool committee with the time to challenge the route through Lancashire that had been chosen by Longbotham.

The Liverpool merchants challenge the route

THE first indication of dissension appears in the minutes of the committee held in Bradford on 14 June 1769 when Longbotham was ordered to visit Brindley with the following letter:

> Some of the Lancashire gentlemen being very warm for almost an entire alteration of the line of the proposed canal through that county (the circumstances of which the bearer Mr. John Longbottom will explain) we earnestly desire you will as expeditiously as possible settle with him the proper means of satisfying them how far it is eligible by a view of it or otherwise as you shall see necessary.[6]

What Longbotham no doubt explained to Brindley was the obsession for obtaining a cheap and plentiful supply of coal that characterised the Liverpool proprietors. To this end the Liverpool committee had themselves already had a survey made, by John Eyes and Richard Melling, and it was agreed at a meeting on 3 July that Brindley should send his assistant Robert Whitworth to view this line. Whitworth acted quickly and sent in his report just ten days later. He said he had found a discrepancy of thirty-five feet between the level at Rishton and that crossing the valley at Burnley, which although not impossible to overcome would have increased the cost greatly. He did not continue surveying any further as his time was limited and he only viewed part of the rest of the line as he rode through the country on horseback with Mr. Eyes. This was enough for the Yorkshire committee, who rejected Liverpool's revised line out of hand and tried to forestall further trouble by declaring that no one but Longbotham, Brindley or Whitworth should be employed on survey work. They were too late. On the very same day the Liverpool committee were ordering P. P. Burdett, a Liverpool surveyor, to undertake yet another survey, from the basin at Colne to Liverpool 'with accuracy and dispatch.'[7]

The line suggested by Burdett, and his assistant R. Beck, ran from Colne, through Burnley and Blackburn, to Chorley where the canal divided. One branch went direct to Newburgh, whilst the other was planned to join Alexander Leigh's Douglas Navigation at Wigan. Originally Leigh had been agitating against the canal, Hustler remarking that at the first meeting in Lancashire:

> . . . on coming to Preston we found one Lee of the Douglas Navigation who had been prejudicing the Preston gentlemen all in his power against it and prevailed so far that the Mayor and part of the Corporation came not till 4 o'clock on a second summons: which made us sick of our journey. However we found them all (except Lee) well disposed to the proposed navigation . . .[8]

Leigh seems to have wanted to save his navigation from disruption by the new canal, and he managed later in 1768 to have clauses inserted in the Bill for the canal protecting it. More important than this was the fact that a clause was also inserted allowing a connection, called Lees (Leigh's) Cut on contemporary maps, between the new canal at Newburgh and the Douglas Navigation at Dean.

Longbotham's line for the canal crossed the Douglas without any plans for either a junction to the Douglas Navigation or transhipment facilities between the two waterways. How the Liverpool merchants were expected to go along with this deliberate avoidance of the Wigan coalfields is anyone's guess. Perhaps they hoped for a change of mind on the part of the Yorkshire promoters in due course. Or perhaps they had already come to an accommodation with Alexander Leigh for a junction which would also provide a water supply for their canal.

The great objective of the merchants in Liverpool was to obtain a plentiful supply of coal at a reasonable price. It was to this end that the Sankey Navigation had been opened by 1758. The supplies of coal along this line were proving too expensive to provide Liverpool with the increasing amounts required, however, and when the Sankey's proprietors heard that the Leeds and Liverpool line promoted by the Yorkshire side would avoid the Wigan coalfield, they decided to construct a branch there themselves. This upset Alexander Leigh, who wrote to John Stanhope on 25 November 1768 suggesting a joint scheme:

> It will be in the power of the River [Douglas] to supply the town and neighbourhood of Liverpool with coal and cannel by means of your canal, whereby it will be benefited with at least eight or nine hundred pounds a year in the tonnage, besides the additional duty of back carriage of timber, merchants goods etc. to Wigan which are now carried by land. But the proprietors of the Sankey Navigation having been informed of your intentions and being apprehensive that their trade to Liverpool may suffer by your canal, have formed a scheme of proceeding towards Wigan in order to furnish themselves with our coal and cannel, and have been levelling [i.e. surveying] for some days past about this place . . .[9]

Following his initial opposition, Leigh obviously now realised that it would help his own navigation (and, perhaps more important, his coalmines) if it joined the planned canal.

The supply of coal to Liverpool continued to pre-occupy the proprietors there. It was proposed to the Liverpool committee by J. Taylor in a letter dated 31 July 1769 that it would be possible to reduce the cost of coal from the Sankey by constructing a branch from the Leeds canal near Knowsley to Runcorn where it would be joined by one built from the Sankey Navigation. This would provide a way from that navigation to Liverpool independent of the tideway, where the flats were often delayed by bad weather. Although not part of the initial proposal, an aqueduct over the Mersey to join the Bridgewater Canal was suggested. Taylor considered that:

> . . . this branch will appear to the committee to be productive of more real advantage to the public, likely to raise more money than any other part of the Leeds Canal of four times the length and very promising to pay three times the interest . . .[10]

The committee decided that a survey of the proposed line should be made for future discussion. Thus the total number of surveys under review for the route of the canal through Lancashire was no less than five. These were:

> 1) The original route, proposed by Longbotham, checked by Brindley, and promoted by the Yorkshire committee, through Whalley and Walton, and crossing the River Douglas near Tarleton. Branches were envisaged to the towns of Chorley, Blackburn, Clitheroe, Burnley and Settle, with Bradford being served by a canal from Shipley.

2) A deviation from the original line, suggested by Longbotham himself, running further to the south by way of Whalley, Leyland and Eccleston, crossing the Douglas further upstream at Parbold. This was eventually to become the original Parliamentary line.

3) A line from Colne by way of Burnley, Blackburn and Chorley to Wigan, then down the north side of the Douglas Valley to join the second line at Parbold. This was surveyed by P. P. Burdett and Richard Beck, and had the great advantage in the eyes of the Lancashire committee of giving direct access to the coalfields via a connection to the Douglas River Navigation.

4) A similar line to no. 3, as far as Wigan, then by Hindley, Newton and Huyton to Liverpool, with a branch to the Mersey opposite Runcorn. This had been surveyed at various times by John Eyes, Richard Melling and Henry Berry. The idea of a direct line from Liverpool to Wigan was resurrected in 1771 as the abortive Liverpool Canal.

5) A version of Burdett's line, but with a direct link from Chorley to Parbold. By this variation it was hoped that the increase in mileage inherent in routes 3 and 4 would be reduced, resulting in a length similar to routes 1 and 2.

Not surprisingly, because of the opposition from Yorkshire, the work of surveying these alternative lines was paid for by a ten-shilling charge per share on the Liverpool subscribers. The Liverpool committee continued to press for their revised line through East Lancashire, issuing a pamphlet against the line via Whalley. They contended that little lime, the supply of which was a major justification for the northerly route, would be used along the line as most soil there responded better to the local marls. Street sweepings and household refuse from the towns along the canal, which formed an ideal manure for the soils around Burscough, were to become an

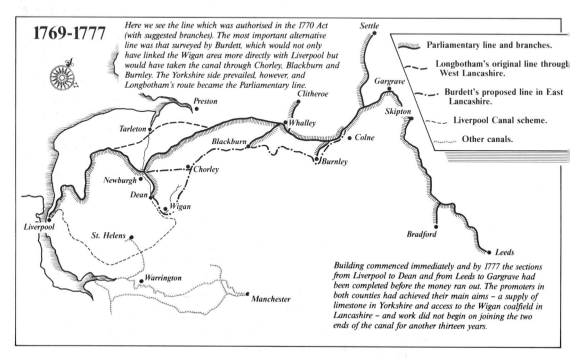

1769-1777

Here we see the line which was authorised in the 1770 Act (with suggested branches). The most important alternative line was that surveyed by Burdett, which would not only have linked the Wigan area more directly with Liverpool but would have taken the canal through Chorley, Blackburn and Burnley. The Yorkshire side prevailed, however, and Longbotham's route became the Parliamentary line.

〰〰〰〰 **Parliamentary line and branches.**

– – – **Longbotham's original line through West Lancashire.**

–·–·– **Burdett's proposed line in East Lancashire.**

– – – **Liverpool Canal scheme.**

〰〰〰 **Other canals.**

Building commenced immediately and by 1777 the sections from Liverpool to Dean and from Leeds to Gargrave had been completed before the money ran out. The promoters in both counties had achieved their main aims – a supply of limestone in Yorkshire and access to the Wigan coalfield in Lancashire – and work did not begin on joining the two ends of the canal for another thirteen years.

important traffic later.

The Lancashire committee further objected that the area served by Longbotham's route had few inhabitants and passed no market towns, which would severely restrict trade. The line by Burnley, Blackburn and Wigan, on the other hand, passed through a country rich in minerals, particularly coal, and the population was numerous, with many factories which would generate traffic along the canal. In addition lime was suitable as a fertiliser for the soil in this area.[11]

After consultation between the two committees it was decided that the surveys should be completed and that Brindley should again be called in to adjudicate. He reported back to the Yorkshire committee on 26 October 1769 that he approved of Longbotham's new line from near Leyland to Liverpool, but that his reappraisal of Burdett and Beck's line had been held up by the tardy return of Whitworth from Devonshire. In the meantime he had sent another of his assistants, John Varley, to check the level.

Yorkshire wins the day

WHEN the survey work had been completed a crucial joint meeting of both the Yorkshire and Liverpool committees was called at the Black Bull in Burnley on 11 October 1769, where Brindley reported that the cost of Longbotham's line from Colne to Liverpool, the length of which would be 66 miles, would be £174,324 whereas Burdett's line via Wigan, which was 83 miles long by Burdett's measurement, but 87 miles by Whitworth's, would amount to £240,881.

Financial prudence and perhaps the weight of the Yorkshire committee won the day. They represented a greater number of proprietors, with 930 shares having been sold in the county. Lancashire's subscriptions accounted for 740 shares, 650 of these having been purchased in Liverpool. The Yorkshire proprietors resolved that Longbotham's line should be adopted, as it would be cheaper to construct and enable easier communication with the northern parts of Lancashire and Westmorland. They still had in mind the limestone markets there, and the possibility of a link to Lancaster. It was further resolved that application be made to Parliament in the next session to obtain the necessary Act.

Not surprisingly, some of the Liverpool subscribers were disenchanted with the decision. They presented a paper, withdrawing their subscriptions and severing their connections with the navigation. The Corporation of Liverpool was among these dissenters and they withdrew their support for the inclusion in the scheme of either an option to construct a connection to the dock system there, (their consent was required as they were the owners of the docks) or for the canal to provide a supply of water for the town.

Much consultation, if not arm-twisting and cajoling, must have gone on before the next meeting of the Yorkshire committee in Leeds on 10 January 1770 at which the Liverpool subscribers agreed to support the

The Parliamentary Line of 1770

THE map reproduced on the following three pages is one of a number showing the proposed Parliamentary line that were produced by the promoters of the canal both before and after the 1770 Act was obtained. The broken line has been added to show the route which the eventual canal actually followed.

The numbers printed alongside the canal show the proposed position of the locks, and were referred to in an index giving the length of the pools and the fall of the locks. Many houses and halls are shown – their occupiers were generally those whose land was to be crossed by the canal and the map was used by the promoters' agents to show how such land was to be affected by the construction of the canal. The benefits for the region as a whole are suggested by the locations given for supplies of lime, coal and stone adjacent to the canal. At the time the canal was built, textiles were not considered to be an important traffic, Armley Mill just north of Leeds being the only textile factory shown. The other mill sites noted were generally used for grinding corn.

The Parliamentary line clings to the valley sides, close to the rivers Aire, Calder and Ribble, allowing the canal to follow the contour lines. These are also followed in crossing the West Lancashire plain, where there are long deviations to allow easier crossing of the rivers Douglas and Alt. The later deviation shows a much more confident approach to construction, as it keeps to the higher ground between Colne and Wigan.

The latest technology in use. Techniques of excavation remained remarkably constant throughout the canal and railway booms; only late in the nineteenth century were mechanical excavators used to any great extent. Here we see horse-powered barrow runs being used to excavate a cutting. Major works like these were avoided on the Leeds and Liverpool Canal wherever possible and much of the original Parliamentary line was designed as a contour canal, using the river valleys to avoid major and expensive works. (Drawing, A. J. Lewery.)

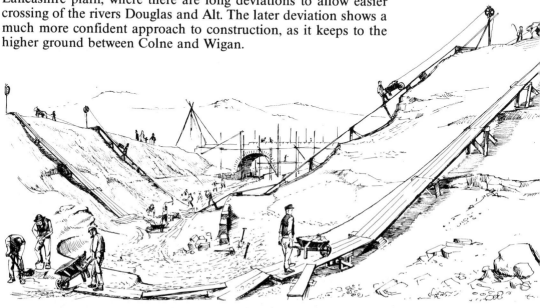

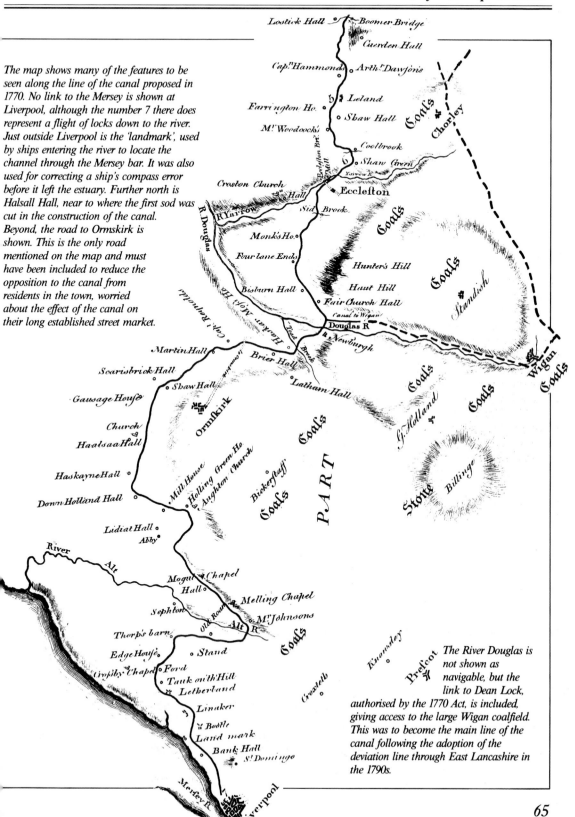

The map shows many of the features to be seen along the line of the canal proposed in 1770. No link to the Mersey is shown at Liverpool, although the number 7 there does represent a flight of locks down to the river. Just outside Liverpool is the 'landmark', used by ships entering the river to locate the channel through the Mersey bar. It was also used for correcting a ship's compass error before it left the estuary. Further north is Halsall Hall, near to where the first sod was cut in the construction of the canal. Beyond, the road to Ormskirk is shown. This is the only road mentioned on the map and must have been included to reduce the opposition to the canal from residents in the town, worried about the effect of the canal on their long established street market.

The River Douglas is not shown as navigable, but the link to Dean Lock, authorised by the 1770 Act, is included, giving access to the large Wigan coalfield. This was to become the main line of the canal following the adoption of the deviation line through East Lancashire in the 1790s.

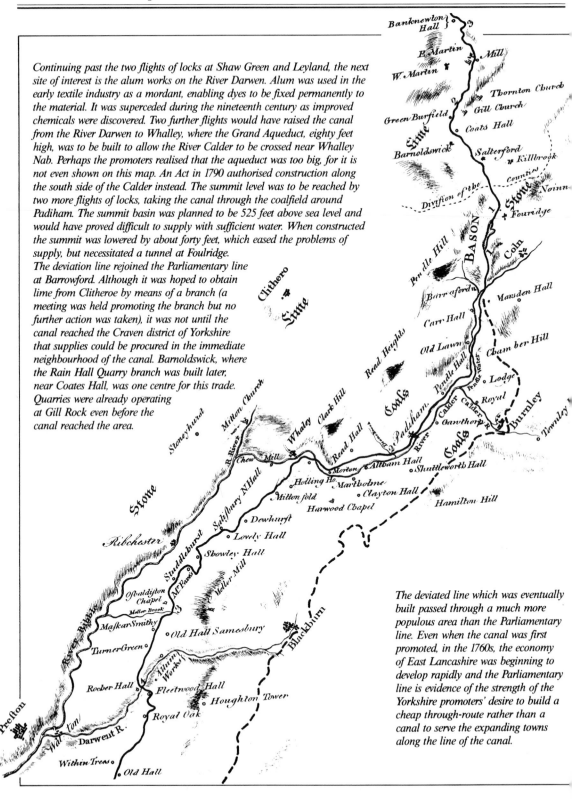

Continuing past the two flights of locks at Shaw Green and Leyland, the next site of interest is the alum works on the River Darwen. Alum was used in the early textile industry as a mordant, enabling dyes to be fixed permanently to the material. It was superceded during the nineteenth century as improved chemicals were discovered. Two further flights would have raised the canal from the River Darwen to Whalley, where the Grand Aqueduct, eighty feet high, was to be built to allow the River Calder to be crossed near Whalley Nab. Perhaps the promoters realised that the aqueduct was too big, for it is not even shown on this map. An Act in 1790 authorised construction along the south side of the Calder instead. The summit level was to be reached by two more flights of locks, taking the canal through the coalfield around Padiham. The summit basin was planned to be 525 feet above sea level and would have proved difficult to supply with sufficient water. When constructed the summit was lowered by about forty feet, which eased the problems of supply, but necessitated a tunnel at Foulridge.

The deviation line rejoined the Parliamentary line at Barrowford. Although it was hoped to obtain lime from Clitheroe by means of a branch (a meeting was held promoting the branch but no further action was taken), it was not until the canal reached the Craven district of Yorkshire that supplies could be procured in the immediate neighbourhood of the canal. Barnoldswick, where the Rain Hall Quarry branch was built later, near Coates Hall, was one centre for this trade. Quarries were already operating at Gill Rock even before the canal reached the area.

The deviated line which was eventually built passed through a much more populous area than the Parliamentary line. Even when the canal was first promoted, in the 1760s, the economy of East Lancashire was beginning to develop rapidly and the Parliamentary line is evidence of the strength of the Yorkshire promoters' desire to build a cheap through-route rather than a canal to serve the expanding towns along the line of the canal.

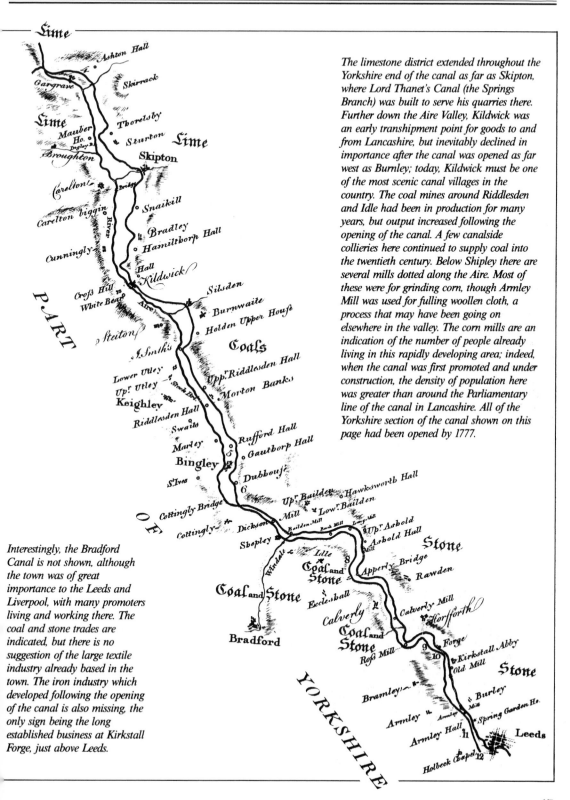

The limestone district extended throughout the Yorkshire end of the canal as far as Skipton, where Lord Thanet's Canal (the Springs Branch) was built to serve his quarries there. Further down the Aire Valley, Kildwick was an early transhipment point for goods to and from Lancashire, but inevitably declined in importance after the canal was opened as far west as Burnley; today, Kildwick must be one of the most scenic canal villages in the country. The coal mines around Riddlesden and Idle had been in production for many years, but output increased following the opening of the canal. A few canalside collieries here continued to supply coal into the twentieth century. Below Shipley there are several mills dotted along the Aire. Most of these were for grinding corn, though Armley Mill was used for fulling woollen cloth, a process that may have been going on elsewhere in the valley. The corn mills are an indication of the number of people already living in this rapidly developing area; indeed, when the canal was first promoted and under construction, the density of population here was greater than around the Parliamentary line of the canal in Lancashire. All of the Yorkshire section of the canal shown on this page had been opened by 1777.

Interestingly, the Bradford Canal is not shown, although the town was of great importance to the Leeds and Liverpool, with many promoters living and working there. The coal and stone trades are indicated, but there is no suggestion of the large textile industry already based in the town. The iron industry which developed following the opening of the canal is also missing, the only sign being the long established business at Kirkstall Forge, just above Leeds.

Bill as long as the canal was constructed from each end simultaneously. This compromise suited both committees as it solved their foremost priorities quickly. The first lengths of canal to be opened would supply Bradford with limestone from Craven, while Liverpool could obtain coal via the previously agreed connection with the Douglas Navigation at Dean. However, the petition to Parliament had already been signed and it was impossible to reinstate the agreement made previously with the Corporation of Liverpool. It was suggested that the Corporation should apply for their own Act for the supply of water and that those employed in obtaining the Canal Act would also promote this. The Act for the canal did include the link to the Mersey, so the problem, which may have been over using the canal to supply the town with water, must have been circumvented to some extent.

Discussions did begin in 1774 about a connection to the docks either by a branch canal or by a tramway. The Dock Committee seems to have wanted to control any such connection themselves and were extremely obstructive, stating on 5 October:

> . . . that this Council as Trustees for the docks at Liverpoole will not admit of the said proprietors or company of the said canal making any canal of communication into any of the said docks at Liverpoole, nor will or legally can the said Trustees make any such canal, docks or works for them upon or through any part of the North Shore lately by the Council set apart for the use of the said docks. But that the Company must make all such docks or works on the sea strand to the northwards of the said ground so laid out for the use of the docks aforesaid at their own expence . . .[12]

The cost of making, not just a canal, but also the dock work necessary where the branch met the river must have been prohibitive, and the company was unable to finance it at the time. The idea was reconsidered again towards the end of the following year but, again, nothing came of it. The expansion of the docks and of the town to the north made the planning of a link more and more difficult when buildings, such as the new barracks, were constructed upon the original line proposed for the branch canal. Improvements round the town forced up land values, and the company had already had problems with Lord Derby, a major landowner, over compensation for land taken for the main line of the canal.

Following the solution of the various disagreements between the proprietors, progress of the Bill through Parliament was swift. The Act received Royal Assent on 19 May 1770.

Before moving on to look more fully at the final planning and construction of the Leeds and Liverpool Canal, it is appropriate to mention several other projects which were planned at this time, some of which were important for the Leeds and Liverpool itself.

Only about ten yards of the Bradford Canal now survives, at its junction with the Leeds and Liverpool at Shipley, for the whole canal has been filled in over the sixty years since it closed. This photograph is looking towards and Leeds and Liverpool, which runs left to Bingley and right to Leeds.
(Photo, author's collection.)

The Liverpool Canal

DESPITE the opening of the Sankey Navigation, coal continued to rise in price in Liverpool, and, by deciding to take the shorter route by way of Ormskirk and Leyland to Colne, the Leeds and Liverpool would not serve any major coalfield which could improve the supply. At this date, the extent of the reserves of coal in the Douglas Valley was still not fully appreciated and some Liverpool proprietors were clearly not impressed by the Leeds and Liverpool's proposed connection to the Douglas Navigation.

For these reasons the idea of a canal direct from Liverpool to Wigan by way of Newton and Hindley surfaced again in 1771.[13] The scheme would affect the Sankey much more than the Leeds and Liverpool, with the coalfields to the south of Wigan being the main object of the proposed canal. Extensions were suggested, however, to Chorley and to the Douglas Navigation at Wigan.

The survey for the Liverpool Canal had been made by Richard Melling and was checked by Mr. Yeoman and Mr. Everard. The petition for the scheme was presented to Parliament early in 1772. Besides local opposition from the Sankey, the Leeds and Liverpool and many landowners, the coal owners of Cumberland and Northumberland feared that with an improved coal supply Liverpool would become a coal exporting port to the detriment of their own trade. The canal promoters countered this, circulating MPs for southern counties, suggesting that coal would be supplied to their constituencies more cheaply, and that vessels returning to Liverpool could carry their agricultural products to the expanding industrial areas of the North. Despite this, the opposition proved to be too strong, and the petition was withdrawn until the following year, so that more support from landowners on the line could be gained. Many landowners continued to oppose the scheme, this second application failing, and the plan was forgotten until 1794 when the Council at Liverpool resurrected it as a threat to the Leeds and Liverpool monopoly of the coal trade, in an attempt to obtain a reduction in the toll.

The Bradford Canal

YORKSHIRE, too, had several schemes which were to affect the Leeds and Liverpool Canal. The most important of these was undoubtedly the Bradford Canal, whose later history became more and more closely linked with the Leeds and Liverpool's. The canal was first promoted in 1770 by fourteen local merchants, including John Hustler and Abraham Balme, who were actually important members of the Leeds and Liverpool committee.

An Act was quickly obtained, being passed on 29 April 1771, for a canal about three and a half miles long, with ten locks down to the Leeds and Liverpool at Shipley. The line was probably surveyed by Longbotham, while Balme controlled the construction on the ground. The canal was built quickly and opened at about the same time as the eastern end of the Leeds and Liverpool, probably in March 1772.

The Leeds and Selby Canal

WITH the passing of the Leeds and Liverpool Act in 1770, concern began to be expressed about the condition of the Aire and Calder Navigation which had not been improved to any great extent since its construction in the early 1700s.

The undertakers of the Aire and Calder arranged in 1771 for John Smeaton to survey the whole navigation and to recommend improvements. A group, principally of Leeds wool merchants, and including several Yorkshire proprietors of the Leeds and Liverpool, suggested instead a canal from Leeds to the River Ouse at Selby.[14] They were dissatisfied with the operation of the Aire and Calder Navigation and wanted a cheaper route for the export of their goods, particularly cloth, the toll for which was extremely high by river.

A survey was undertaken by Longbotham in 1767 and a further one by Whitworth in 1769 in which they were both concerned about the lack of a reliable water supply to the summit level. A further survey was undertaken in 1772 by Longbotham, who was granted leave by the Leeds and Liverpool, though they did not actively support the scheme at this time. The line was to run from the Leeds and Liverpool terminus at Holbeck along the south side of the Aire to Methley, where the river would be crossed by an aqueduct, Selby being reached by way of a 400-yard tunnel at Fairburn. There were to be four sets of staircase locks, two two-rise and two three-rise, to take boats of fifty to sixty ton capacity. The twenty-three mile canal was to cost £59,468.

A petition was presented to Parliament for the canal in December 1772, with Longbotham's line being supported by Thomas Yeoman. At the same time the Aire and Calder was petitioning for the improvements suggested by Smeaton.

However, the Parliamentary session ended before the committee reporting on the proposals had concluded. During the winter a joint meeting between the Leeds and Liverpool and the Leeds and Selby was held, and the terms and conditions for a junction of the two canals were agreed. Subsequently the Leeds and Selby application to Parliament was supported by the Leeds and Liverpool. At the same time the Aire and Calder had been surveying its own line to Selby and, when the two schemes were brought before Parliament, the Leeds and Selby was defeated on 3 March 1774 by 105 votes to 33, while the Aire and Calder scheme passed a few months later.

The Leeds and Selby Bill was probably lost due to the difficulties in arranging a supply of water to the summit, John Hustler writing to John Stanhope about Whitworth's survey thus:

> . . . this line as is expected impracticable or too expensive. To supply water by fire engines [i.e. steam engines] would be monstrously expensive and a scant supply at least, if not a precarious one . . .[15]

The proposed tunnel and the problems of carrying the canal over coal workings would also have been detrimental to its chances of passing through Parliament.

With the loss of the Bill the Leeds and Liverpool was forced to continue its dependence on the Aire and Calder for water transport between the North Sea and Leeds. Over the years relations between the canal and the navigation became much more amicable, however, with the two companies later becoming joint owners of the Bradford Canal.

Lord Thanet's Canal (Springs Branch)

AT Skipton the agents of Lord Thanet, who owned Skipton Castle and the limestone quarries close by, decided that a branch canal to the quarries should be constructed, following the refusal of the canal company to alter their line to allow improved access to the quarries. The death of the previous Lord Thanet could have contributed to this change in attitude towards canals, as he had been the main opponent of the River Aire Navigation in 1744. The Act for the canal to the Springs near to the castle was passed in 1773, and as the length was only a quarter of a mile, it was probably opened fairly shortly afterwards. The quarries were being worked at that time by the Mercer Flatts Lime Company, but from 1785 the canal company took over the lease, which it held for the next two hundred years.

The abortive Settle Canal

IT had originally been intended to construct a branch to Settle as part of the main Leeds and Liverpool scheme.[16] However, the proprietors who lived there wrote to the committee on 20 January 1769 saying that they wished to have the power to construct the branch themselves and desired a clause to this effect be inserted in the Act. Whether this was impossible is unclear, but the final Act contained no authorisation clause for such a branch.

A petition was then presented to Parliament early in 1774 for a Bill to allow the construction of a canal fifteen miles long to Settle, but the local landowners along ten and a half miles of the line were against, with only those along two and a half miles in favour, the remaining two miles being neutral.

The canal was to have been on one level and would have left the Leeds and Liverpool at Greenberfield. After passing Horton and Newsholme, it would have reached Settle by keeping to the south side of the Ribble Valley. Coal and limestone were again to have been the main traffic, but the wool traffic to and from the Kendal district would also have been carried.

This scheme was resurrected in 1780 in an attempt to connect Lancaster to the canal system when a Settle and Ingleton Canal was proposed. The extent of the mania for canals and the optimism of some of their promoters can be seen from what the canal would have been like. The Ribble was to be crossed on an aqueduct at Settle, and after passing through a mile-long tunnel under Huntworth Hill opposite the town, the canal continued to the River Greta above Burton-in-Lonsdale. Ingleton was to be reached by a mile-long branch about one mile from Burton. The main canal was to be constructed on one level until about three miles from the Burton, where there were to be no fewer than forty-five locks down to river level. Many of these locks were to be risers, including two seven-rise sets. This canal would then join another at Burton by which the River Lune at Lancaster would be reached. The trade along the line of these canals, passing as they would through a sparsely populated district, could not have been sufficient for even the most optimistic of canal promoters, though the twenty-five mile level from Greenberfield would have provided an excellent water supply for the Leeds and Liverpool.

Work begins on the Leeds and Liverpool

FOLLOWING the passing of the Act on 19 May 1770, the committee set about construction. Some subscribers had not paid and in order to raise the £200,000 required, books were again opened, not just in Lancashire and Yorkshire, but also in London. An immediate payment of £1-10-0 was requested to cover the cost of the surveys and the application to Parliament. The Mayor of Liverpool was also approached to pay the £100 which the Corporation had promised to Longbotham on the Act being obtained.

The committee wrote to Brindley asking him to become engineer at a salary of £400 per annum with Longbotham as clerk of works at £150. James Hollingshead and John Hustler were to be treasurers in Liverpool and Bradford respectively. By the end of August Brindley had declined the invitation and Longbotham was appointed in his place.[17]

At the same meeting it is interesting to note that Mr. Varley proposed that his engines for removing earth out of the canal should be used at a cost of £7 each, reducing the cost of excavation by one third. He would have been allowed £1,000 had they worked, but a report at the November meeting notes their failure. In view of the cheapness of labour, his machine would have needed to be highly efficient to be successful. The navvy was to reign supreme in construction and excavation work around Great Britain for the next hundred years, until steam excavators were finally introduced during the building of the Great Central Railway.

At the same time four more employees were taken on: clerks for Liverpool and Leeds at £60 per annum, John Eagle as law clerk at £80 per annum and Joseph Priestley as bookkeeper at £100 per annum. Priestley was to give the company many years' loyal service. When setting out the line, he had to agree a price for the land with the owner. Normally this was arranged amicably, but if agreement could not be reached, the price was settled by commissioners. According to the Act, all persons with land in Lancashire or Yorkshire, with a yearly value of one hundred pounds, could be commissioners; a system open to

Eighteenth-century engineers surveying with the latest equipment. It is remarkable how quickly these early surveys were produced, given the nature of the equipment in use.
(A. J. Lewery.)

manipulation. In 1771, several pieces of land in Bingley were valued by this method and the owners arranged for many of their friends to be present, as commissioners. Benjamin Ferrand was sworn as a commissioner, even though his was one of the pieces of land to be valued, and in consequence, values were grossly inflated. This forced the company to take the last resort allowed in the Act. They issued a warrant, summoning a jury, whose verdict drastically reduced the price asked for the land. The company were not caught out again, and when, later that year, commissioners were summoned to value land in Lancashire, they made sure many of their supporters were present.[18]

The canal, as first set out, involved few major works, and largely followed the contours of the land. In Lancashire, the circuitous line through Burscough avoided the high ground between Liverpool and Wigan. The only excavation work of any size was at Halsall cutting, where, on 5 November 1770, the first sod was dug by the Hon. Charles Mordaunt of Halsall Hall. The first sections included several aqueducts, at Hurst Wood, near Shipley, at Newburgh and at Aintree. Following his success at Barton, Brindley loved including them in his designs, although the one he planned to build at Whalley Nab, at eighty feet in height, was excessive, even by his standards. He probably

Halsall Cutting in West Lancashire, where the first sod of the Leeds and Liverpool Canal was cut in 1770. The cutting was originally only wide enough for a single boat but was it was later widened so that two boats could pass. It is still narrower than the rest of the canal, as can be seen here, and care still had to be taken negotiating it with a 14-feet wide boat.
(Photo, author's collection.)

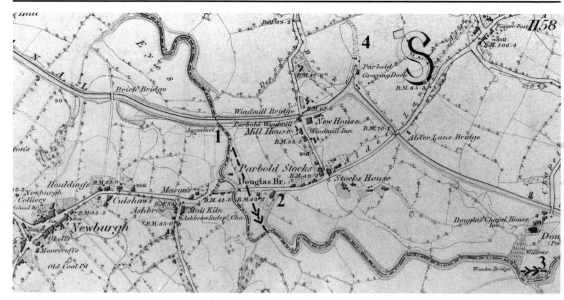

suggested the use of staircase, or riser locks, having introduced them previously on the Calder and Hebble Navigation. Their construction on a river navigation, less concerned about water supply, was reasonable, but on a still-water canal, their excessive use of water was to cause many problems. Another Brindley feature found on the first sections opened are the aqueducts carrying the canal over roads at Kildwick, Silsden and Newburgh. They were considerably more expen-sive than swing-bridges, and as a result were not used on those lengths of canal built later, though a road was built under the aqueduct at Blackburn sometime in the nineteenth century. The first agreements for construction work was soon let for the 'rampering, puddling and digging' of the Newburgh to Liverpool and the Skipton to Bingley lengths, along with agreements for the supply of timber and stone and for brickmaking.

When the first contracts for work were let they were for long sections of canal. John Tickle took the digging and puddling of the length from Bingley to Skipton (except from Kildwick to Silsden), while Samuel Weston and John Lawton undertook similar work for the whole of the Newburgh to Liverpool section. It soon became obvious that the contractors' organisational ability was not adequate for the under-taking of such long lengths, and from 20 January 1772 Longbotham ordered that every contractor had to finish and complete his own section, and that subsequently no greater length than one mile would be let to each undertaker.

Operations on this scale, over such a large area, were comparatively new and the problems of a large itinerant workforce soon made their appearance. The labourers employed on the works experienced difficulties with the local population, who seem to have wanted to make as much money as possible out of them. The committee minutes for 3 January 1771 record:

> The labourers for cutting the canal are much imposed on by extravagant charges of the innkeepers, the committee are desired to consider if any scheme can be come into for the convenience of such labourers by

A section of the 1845 Ordnance Survey map of the Newburgh and Parbold area, showing the Leeds and Liverpool and the River Douglas. By this date, of course, the Douglas Navigation had been completely by-passed and little sign of the old navigation can be seen on this map. Newburgh Aqueduct [1] was built at an angle to make access into the first lock above the aqueduct easier – the original line of the navigation is marked,[2] and the site of another lock, traces of which can still be seen today, is also marked.[3] Note how there appears to have been some work undertaken to begin extending the canal along the Parliamentary line at Parbold.[4] Part of this section was used as a graving dock at this time.

(Reproduced by permission of the County Archivist, Lancashire Record Office.)

erecting tents, booths etc. and providing them with meat and drink at a more easy expence.[19]

The committee took this seriously and by the end of the month a house had been taken for the use of the workmen. There were many other problems to be overcome in the organisation of the men employed on such a large undertaking, and it was noted that they needed constant overseeing, both to control the damages they caused and the work they undertook.

The difficulty of surveying with the rudimentary equipment available is revealed when it was discovered that a mistake had been made in the level from Shaw Green to Liverpool. Smeaton was asked to re-survey the length, but as he was not available immediately, he sent his pupil, Jessop. His report was produced in September in which he exonerates Longbotham.[20] Whilst work at Liverpool was held up for the re-survey, water was let into the canal at the Newburgh end, as boats had been launched there by 25 July 1771.

Purchase of the Douglas Navigation

WHEN the Leeds and Liverpool had presented its Bill to Parliament in 1770, the main opposition had actually come from the Douglas Navigation. They were concerned to protect their supply of water from the river's upper reaches and to avoid any damage to the navigation from the canal aqueduct at Newburgh which would restrict the height of vessels navigating the river. This opposition was purely nominal, as Holt Leigh, Alexander's son, had already approached the canal committee in October 1769 with proposals for the construction of a canal from the Leeds and Liverpool to Wigan. A pamphlet was published stating the undertakers' points of concern which, incidentally, gives much information about the condition of the navigation at that time.[21]

Open boats or barges carrying about twenty tons apparently navigated the Douglas with coal, cannel, oak bark and other merchandise. Their cargoes were transhipped at Tarleton Lock into larger sea-going vessels trading to Lancaster, Dublin, Drogheda and other places. The river was being improved so that these larger vessels, which had fixed masts enabling them to sail regularly on the Irish Sea, could load higher up the river. Five bridges on the navigation from Sollom Lock to Rufford had all been made into turn bridges, and materials had been purchased to alter six more at Tarleton, Sollom, Wains Blades, Newburgh, Appley and Gathurst.

In view of the improving nature of the river downstream, it was proposed that the Leeds and Liverpool should construct a branch canal twelve yards wide and five and a half feet deep from above Newburgh Aqueduct to join the navigation upstream, and a series of locks to connect with the navigation downstream. Not only would this connect the Leeds and Liverpool to Wigan, but also allow boats with fixed masts to by-pass the aqueduct at Newburgh and reach the upper sections of the Douglas.

Water for the Leeds and Liverpool Canal was originally to come from a large reservoir above Colne, so the decision to start construction at each end of the line must have caused some headaches. Gaining access to the waters of the Douglas was thus practically essential to overcome the company's immediate problem of supply to the Liverpool length. For this reason, it would seem inconceivable that the company began construction of the Liverpool to Newburgh length without having come to some kind of accommodation with Leigh as early as 1768 or 1769, not only on the matter of the connections between the two waterways but on the provision of water from the Douglas for the Liverpool end of the canal. Of great importance, also, was the fact that buying the Douglas Navigation allowed the company to control canal developments throughout the Douglas Valley area by transferring to themselves complete control over the water supply. A connection with the Douglas Navigation also allowed access to the coalfield around Wigan, enabling the coal companies to supply the rapidly expanding market for coal in Liverpool. A survey of the coal reserves in the Douglas Valley was requested by the committee in January 1772, shortly after the canal company had agreed to purchase the navigation from Alexander Leigh.[22]

He first proposed to sell his twenty-nine of the thirty-six shares in a letter to the committee on 21 November 1771 and at their meeting on the 25th they authorised an agreement to be drawn up. The following day Holt Leigh records in his diary that his father had sold his shares for £14,500, to be paid in four instalments at quarterly intervals.[23] They were purchased by Jonathan Blundell and William Earle, Liverpool committee members, in trust for the canal proprietors. Holt Leigh obviously played an important part in the negotiations, as he was allowed to re-purchase one share. Over the following year he purchased most of the remaining shares, though his uncle Edward Holt retained two shares. Holt Leigh had sold his shares to the company by 1785, but it was not until 1893 that the last 2/36 share was acquired by the company from Edward Leigh's descendants. Because the ownership of the Douglas Navigation remained divided, it maintained its own identity in the canal accounts. This allowed the profit from this section to be calculated and the Douglas Navigation trade was recorded separately for many years.

The old Douglas Navigation thus lasted, at least on paper, for 173 years, although the river itself had been in use for only forty-three. By 1774 Leigh's Cut had joined the navigation to the Leeds and Liverpool and when the Rufford Branch of the canal, together with a new canal alongside the river into Wigan, were built a few years later, the old river navigation was rendered redundant.

By 1782, all the lockgates on the river had been removed.[24] Little now remains of the navigation, though anyone interested can find remains of the tramway feeder system at Gathurst. There are also some river works here, including one of the weirs which can be seen from the canal towpath below the canal locks. Further down the river, at Chapel House near Parbold, a large depression in a field, visible when looking towards Wigan from the footbridge over the river, marks the site of one of the locks, and the aqueduct at Newburgh is built at an angle to the canal embankment, so as to facilitate entry to the lock which used to be just above it. Alterations to the river to improve drainage have destroyed all other signs of the navigation, particularly below Rufford, but the section of the navigation from Rufford Lock to the remains of Sollom Lock is preserved, since it later became part of the Rufford Branch of the Leeds and Liverpool.

Construction work continues

BY 19 August 1772 the junction with the Douglas had been commenced and one hundred cutters and twenty to thirty masons were employed on the Lancashire section. The work must have been progressing well as in October it was decided that twenty masons and seventy-five cutters should be sent to Whalley Nab to start work on the foundations for the grand aqueduct intended to be constructed there. Two months later Longbotham commenced laying out the line from Newburgh to Eccleston and started treating with landowners for the ground needed, before going to London to attend Parliament about the Selby Canal.

The old Douglas Navigation lock at Sollom, dating from around 1760 and preserved as part of the Rufford Branch of the Leeds and Liverpool. The early Douglas locks were probably about fourteen feet wide but this one, built about twenty years later, was over 15' 6" wide. This was one of the improvements being carried out on the navigation to allow seagoing sailing flats to reach Wigan.

(Photo, author's collection.)

The Liverpool section had been completed by January 1773, except for the embankments at Newburgh and over the River Alt near Aintree. The time necessary for earthworks of this type to stabilise always delayed the opening of lengths that included such embankments. As a result the Skipton to Bingley length was the first to be opened, on 8 April 1773, with the *Leeds Intelligencer* reporting five days later:

> On Thursday last, that part of the Grand Canal from Bingley to Skipton was opened, and two boats laden with coals arrived at the last mentioned place, which were sold at half the price they have hitherto given for that most necessary convenience of life, which is a recent instance, among others, of the great use of canals in general. On which occasion the bells were set ringing at Skipton; there were also bonfires, illuminations, and other demonstrations of joy.

Over the following months the work progressed steadily and by October thirty-one miles of canal had been completed in Lancashire and twenty-three in Yorkshire. The settlement of the embankments on the Liverpool length during the winter allowed that section to be opened officially in February 1774, though apparently improvement work still needed to be undertaken on the Douglas Navigation to allow boats to reach Wigan on the remaining river section.

The complete route from Wigan to Liverpool was opened in October. This was celebrated by a boat trip along part of the canal for the proprietors, accompanied by flags and music, cheered on by crowds along the banks, with two 21-gun salutes. The proprietors partook of cold refreshments on the quay side in Liverpool whilst the workmen, '215 in number, walked first with their tools on their shoulders and cockades in their hats, and were afterwards plentifully regaled at a dinner provided for them.' The bells were rung all day.[25]

To reach Wigan from Liverpool, boats used the new canal as far as Parbold a short distance over the Newburgh Aqueduct and where the building of the Leeds and Liverpool had been interrupted. Here they passed onto Leigh's Cut, built by the Leeds and Liverpool for the Douglas Navigation, until they reached Deans Lock (Gathurst), from where Wigan was reached by using the old navigation. A lock (the remains of which are still just visible) joined the canal to the river at Dean. At this time the whole river navigation was still used for its old purpose, with boats supplying vessels in the Irish Sea coal trade at Tarleton and at ports around the Ribble estuary.

March 1774 saw the opening of the section from Skipton down to Thackley, near Shipley, with the first boat using the five-rise locks at Bingley, passing through in a creditable twenty-nine minutes. The junction with the Bradford Canal was on this length so traffic could now start in earnest, with deliveries of coal to Skipton, and boats returning with limestone. It was reported that by June there were forty lime-kilns working between Skipton and Bradford. Gargrave had been reached by then, enabling the canal to be fed by the waters of Eshton Beck, which was to remain the main water supply for the Yorkshire side.

The extension from Thackley to Leeds was to take several more years to complete, and there were problems over deciding the exact route to be taken into the town. In mid-1775 the engineer Mr. Yeoman was asked to survey four different lines through Lord Irwin's land. However he does not seem to have been available, as the survey was

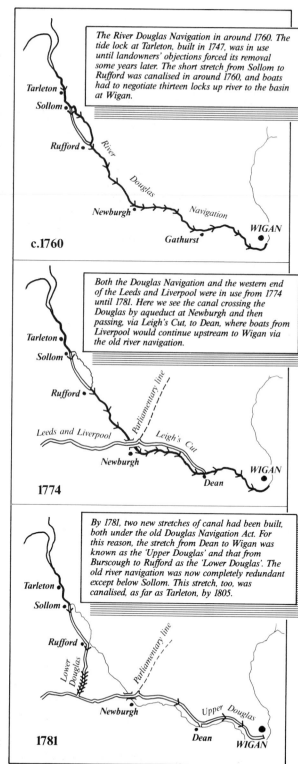

The River Douglas Navigation in around 1760. The tide lock at Tarleton, built in 1747, was in use until landowners' objections forced its removal some years later. The short stretch from Sollom to Rufford was canalised in around 1760, and boats had to negotiate thirteen locks up river to the basin at Wigan.

c.1760

Both the Douglas Navigation and the western end of the Leeds and Liverpool were in use from 1774 until 1781. Here we see the canal crossing the Douglas by aqueduct at Newburgh and then passing, via Leigh's Cut, to Dean, where boats from Liverpool would continue upstream to Wigan via the old river navigation.

1774

By 1781, two new stretches of canal had been built, both under the old Douglas Navigation Act. For this reason, the stretch from Dean to Wigan was known as the 'Upper Douglas' and that from Burscough to Rufford as the 'Lower Douglas'. The old river navigation was now completely redundant except below Sollom. This stretch, too, was canalised, as far as Tarleton, by 1805.

1781

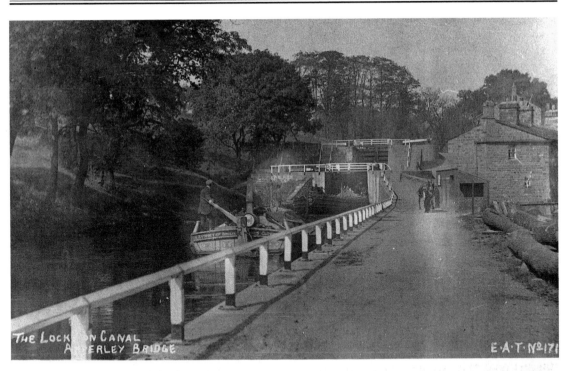

THE LOCK ON CANAL APPERLEY BRIDGE

E·A·T·Nº 171

On the section of the Leeds and Liverpool Canal in Yorkshire, all of which was built in the 1770s, riser or staircase locks were used fairly frequently. Apart from the famous Bingley-three and Bingley-five, there were several others, including the Apperley Bridge-two and the Newlay-three, both shown here. Risers used much more water than flights of single locks and they were not used for this reason on the later stretches of canal.
(Apperley Bridge, photo author's collection. Newlay photo, Ben Shaw.)

produced at the end of August by Mr. Henshall, an engineer closely involved with the Trent and Mersey Canal. The canal finally opened to Leeds in June 1777, to the usual feasting and firing of cannon.

The construction of the canal was costing much more than had been estimated and as early as October 1774 work on the aqueduct at Whalley had been stopped. In the light of subsequent developments this, and the fact that the line from Newburgh had not got beyond the marking-out stage, was a blessing in disguise for, by the time work

79

A modern photograph of the river lock at Leeds, looking into the Leeds and Liverpool Canal from the opposite side of the River Aire. The rails in the foreground are not part of a railway, but were used by a crane which unloaded coal from boats at the Co-operative Wharf. The Leeds and Liverpool warehouse seen here is now more or less derelict. It used to have an arm of the canal, now filled in, entering it from the far end. The River Aire flows from right to left.
(Photo, Ben Shaw.)

resumed on the main line, the route was very different. The materials still on hand at Whalley Nab were to be valued and the wheelbarrows already made sent to Yorkshire. This may seem pennypinching, but they represented a considerable investment, the use of wheelbarrows in civil engineering at this period being considered the latest technology.

The other important improvement suggested at this time was the complete by-passing of the Douglas Navigation. The committee decided on 27 April 1776 that the short Rufford Canal built by the Douglas Navigation in the 1760s should be repaired and connected to the main line at Moss Lane, Burscough, by a branch to be called the Lower Douglas Navigation (or Rufford Branch). A canal was also to be built from Dean, where it joined the old navigation, to Wigan and this became known as the Upper Douglas Navigation. Confusingly, these two sections maintained a separate identity, as they were actually built under the Douglas Navigation Act of 1720 and thus became part of the old navigation for accounting purposes. Only Leigh's Cut, to Dean, built for the Douglas Navigation, was allowed under the 1770 Act, which technically only authorised a canal via Whalley.

To oversee this work Richard Owen was appointed engineer for five years at 100 guineas per annum from June 1777. The line had already been decided by Messrs. Moss, Fisher, Hustler and Taylor who had obtained the consent of the landowners along the Lower Douglas. The landowners had agreed to the canal, providing Tarleton Weir was not rebuilt, unless absolutely essential, and the level of the Rufford cut was lowered to below ground level. There had already been instances of flooding here, and there were to be others over the following years. A major cause was the draining of Martin Mere and the other lands at Rufford. This resulted in the ground level subsiding, leaving the canal, which had not been designed as such, on an embankment and thereby more prone to leakage. To reduce problems here the 1783 Act required

Right: Four adjoining sections of Yates' map of Lancashire, 1786, showing the River Douglas from Tarleton, and the Leeds and Liverpool Canal from just west of Newburgh to the basin at Wigan. By 1786 the Rufford Branch from Burscough to Rufford had been completed, and can be seen running more or less parallel to Eller Brook. Just north of this can be seen the section to Sollom that was canalised in around 1760. The lock into the river at Gathurst (Dean) can also be seen (see also inset map), together with one surviving river lock just downstream and the old lock diversion at Crook, just upstream. At Wigan there is no connection to the River Douglas at this date, and the water supply for the Liverpool length still came in at Gathurst. Just visible are several watermills along the river in Wigan and on a tributary near Wrightington.
(Reproduced by permission of the County Archivist, Lancashire Record Office.)

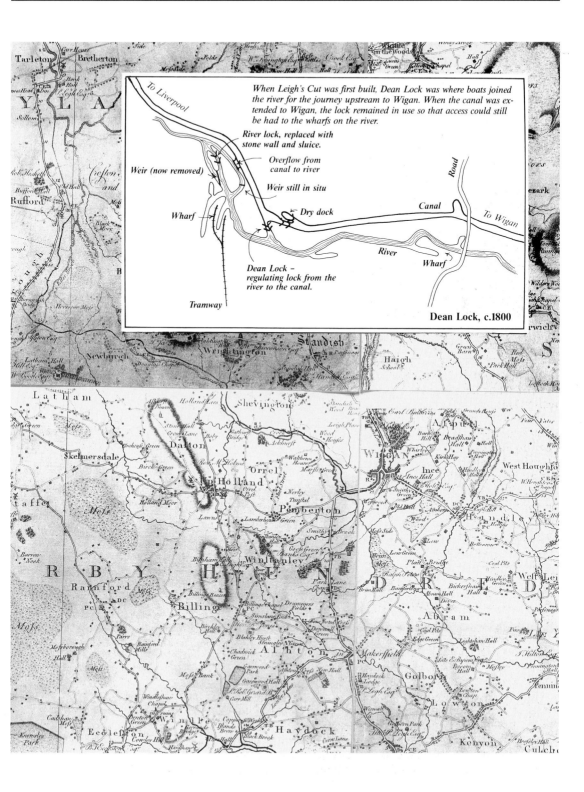

When Leigh's Cut was first built, Dean Lock was where boats joined the river for the journey upstream to Wigan. When the canal was extended to Wigan, the lock remained in use so that access could still be had to the wharfs on the river.

To Liverpool

River lock, replaced with stone wall and sluice.

Overflow from canal to river

Weir (now removed)

Weir still in situ

Road

Wharf

Dry dock

Canal

To Wigan

Dean Lock – regulating lock from the river to the canal.

River

Wharf

Tramway

Dean Lock, c.1800

the water level between Rufford and Sollom to be reduced by six inches. The modernisation of the navigation had been completed by 19 October 1781 when the committee was informed that the Lower Douglas had been opened.

The Upper Douglas, from Dean to Wigan, had probably been opened during the previous year. On 31 May 1782 the lock gates from the old Douglas river were ordered to be taken to the maintainance yard at Briers Mill near Burscough, ending the use of the old navigation. The regulating lock at Dean continued in operation, however, allowing boats to reach the coal staithes still in use on the opposite side of the river, and enabling water to be supplied to the Liverpool length of the canal.

The money runs out

THERE were now seventy-five miles of canal, but the cost had been far greater than originally estimated; £232,016 had been expended in obtaining the Act and constructing the main line of the canal, from Leeds to Gargrave, and from Liverpool to Parbold, with £53,434 spent on the purchase and improvement of the Douglas Navigation. To pay for this 2,059 shares had been issued at £100, together with an extra call of £14 per share towards the cost of the Douglas. The resulting shortfall in capital was paid off partly from the toll income and partly by borrowing money, at 5% interest, using the income from the tolls as security. This meant that the interest on the loans had to be paid off before the income from the tolls could be applied to any other purpose.

Traffic was building up steadily on both sides of the Pennines, particularly the carriage of coal to Liverpool, which must have given some satisfaction to the proprietors. However, their desire to link Lancashire and Yorkshire still had not been achieved, as the 1770 Act did not allow them to raise sufficient funds, even had the money been available. That the money ran out before any more work was done on the canal in Lancashire proved fortuitous in the end, as the 1780s, despite economic depression, saw a growth in the importance of the towns of East Lancashire. Had there been enough money to build the canal through Whalley in the 1770s, as originally planned, towns such as Burnley and Blackburn would have been served only by inconvenient branch canals. By the 1790s, when 'Canal Mania' spread through the country, allowing money for canal building to be raised easily because of the improvement in the economy, these towns had become important enough to be served by the main line of the canal, and this was to lead to a complete revision of the line of the canal between Colne and Parbold.

After the opening of the first sections, problems occurred with people living along the line refusing to accept the controls which the company introduced. Some landowners treated the canal as a stream and used it for watering their ground. Mr. Elam from near Leeds was prosecuted in 1779 for arranging for the canal bank to be cut through, where the canal passed his land. Besides the cost of the action against Mr. Elam the company placed notices in the local papers and had the canal watched overnight in order to apprehend those damaging the works. £20 was spent on these measures.[26]

Other problems arose as a result of the poor state of roads at the time. This led to the towpaths being used to evade turnpike tolls by horseriders and even by loaded carriages. The committee in 1786 resolved to prosecute such people, only those who had obtained the permission of the company being allowed to use the towpath as a road or footpath.

Income from tolls was £2,025 in 1774, and the following year there were seventy-five boats working on the canal, twenty-six in Yorkshire and forty-nine in Lancashire. The income from each side was relative to the number of boats. By 1785 income had reached £13,062 for the year, from which the company derived £8,831 profit. The main carrier on the Yorkshire side at this time was probably Messrs. Preston, Hird and Co., who became lessors of the Bradford Canal that year. They were also involved in the Bradford Limekiln Company and the Low Moor Ironworks Company and were the major user of the limestone brought down from Craven.

In Lancashire the Union Company was one of the larger carriers. They operated packet boats to Wigan in competition with Longbotham and Company, besides having general cargo boats carrying such items as sugar, corn and malt. Timber was also an important commodity, being carried in both directions: foreign imports were carried to Wigan for the Lancashire market, and locally grown wood was taken to the construction and shipbuilding industries of Liverpool.

In order to collect the tolls, offices were set up along the canal. In Lancashire these were at Tarleton and Dean House locks.[27] They sent their returns of vessels and cargoes passing to the office at Liverpool where accounts were made up and settled. These details were then sent to the head office at Bradford. In Yorkshire the main traffic office was at Leeds, also reporting to Bradford. To facilitate the collection of tonnage figures necessary for accounting, all vessels on the canal were ordered to be weighed and marked so that the load carried could be ascertained from the depth of the boat in the water.

The company provided the buildings for warehousing, but did not charge for storage, only for the use of the wharf. The carriers had their own men stationed at each depot for moving and organising the goods in storage. A result of this was that the company did not take any responsibility for goods in its warehouses. In 1782 some linen was stolen from Leeds warehouse. The company did not admit liability though they were prepared to recompense the owner for one third of the value, the remaining loss to be divided between the owner and the carrier. This was quite a generous gesture from a company hard hit by loss of trade resulting from the American War of Independence and the war with France, and struggling to repay the loans taken out to complete its construction work.

Chapter Four

'A mania for canals'

The route through East Lancashire finally resolved. 1782 – 1804

HEN the canal had first been promoted in the late-1760s Britain's economy had been moderately success-ful, the country maintaining a small surplus of income from which canal building was financed. The Ameri-can War of Independence in the late-1770s changed all this. The resulting deficit raised interest rates which in turn made the cost of canal building prohibitive. Loss of the Ameri-can market also had a particularly detrimental effect on industry in Lancashire and Yorkshire which, in turn, led to failure to raise enough money from other sources to complete the canal.

The company's finances were already stretched by the purchase of the Douglas Navigation. To regularise the situation, particularly with regard to the Douglas, an Act was obtained in 1783 giving retrospective powers for this purchase. The mortgaging of tolls was effected by allowing £20,000 to be borrowed against the lease of tolls for twenty-one years. The Act dealt with several other matters, such as the water level of the canal from Rufford to Sollom, the drainage of land there and the tolls charged on the coal traffic to Liverpool. It proposed that these should be the same as on the rest of the canal, which revived the dissension between the Lancashire and Yorkshire committees.

Building work recommences

NO work was undertaken to extend the main line of the canal between 1777, when the Shipley to Leeds section was opened, and 1790, when work restarted on constructing the canal westward from Gargrave. It was not until the improvement of the national economy in the late-1780s and the 1790s that money was again available for construction. This was to be a boom time for canals, with many schemes being proposed, several of which were to have major implications for the Leeds and Liverpool.

By the time building re-commenced there had been many changes in personnel. Longbotham, in common with many engineers at the time, did not restrict himself to his employers' work. He operated a packet boat from Liverpool, and had purchased land for coal mining in Upholland. He was in the habit of using canal company materials for these ventures, and as his book-keeping was erratic, he was continually in debt to the company. These businesses took up much time, to the detriment of his canal work and he finally resigned in 1775, though his account with the company remained outstanding, until they threatened legal action. He was clearly in financial difficulty, as his lease of the mines was terminated in 1776, following non-payment of rent. They were then leased to Hustler, Hardcastle, and Chadwick, all closely involved with the canal.[1]

Following his resignation, nothing is heard of Longbotham for some years, though he was soon involved with a plan for land drainage around the River Alt, in West Lancashire. His scheme, in 1787, for the Lancaster Canal, also included land drainage. In the early-1790s, he surveyed the Bury to Sladen extension of the Manchester, Bolton and Bury, and about that time he also produced plans for the Grand Western, and Bristol and Western Canals. His last scheme was for a new summit length for the Leeds and Liverpool, by-passing the tunnel at Foulridge, which he presented in 1792. He was an old man by then, and in 1800 he asked the committee for an annual stipend for his declining years. Less than a year later he was dead, and Priestley, who had occasionally given him money on the company's behalf, paid his funeral expenses.

From July 1775 to June 1777, Hustler took control of engineering, then Richard Owen was appointed, at one hundred guineas per annum. He had been employed by the company since 1774, having previously worked on the Bridgewater. It was he who suggested lowering the summit to the level eventually used, though his main work was the construction of the branch to Sollom, and the continuation of the canal to Wigan. When this was completed, in 1782, he was discharged, as the committee thought an engineer unnecessary. Owen then became engineer for the Lagan Navigation in Ireland, building the section from Lisburn to Lough Neagh. He was also involved with the Coalisland Canal, and other schemes in the north of Ireland. Hustler again took over responsibility for engineering on the Leeds and Liverpool, assisted by John Harrison, who looked after maintainance. This continued until 1790, when Robert Whitworth was engaged as engineer to complete the canal.

With the improved financial situation, the proprietors' thoughts turned to the completion of the canal. There had been many advances in civil engineering over the intervening years since the canal was first planned. These could allow much improvement to the line, so Hustler was requested to undertake a preliminary survey in mid-1788. It was still expected that the canal would pass down the Calder Valley, missing the growing East Lancashire towns, as the Yorkshire proprietors were still keen for the canal to become little more than a through route between Liverpool and Yorkshire, so were desirous to keep the mileage to a minimum. The promotion of trade between the ports of Liverpool and Hull, and the manufacturing districts of Lancashire and Yorkshire was advanced as a major reason for the completion of the canal in Hustler's *Explanation of the Plan of the Canal* published in 1788. At the same time Robert Whitworth was asked to review the proposed line and to make suggestions as to deviations. His choice must have been limited by the proprietors' continuing view of the canal as a through route to Liverpool.

By October the following year he presented his report in which he recommended lowering the head level by fifty-three feet, which meant carrying the canal through a tunnel 1,500 yards long. The summit was to be supplied with water from Pendle Water and Kilbrook, with reservoirs being constructed at Foulridge and above Colne, and the depth of the canal was to be increased to seven feet on the six-mile summit level, thus allowing the canal itself to act as a small reservoir.[2]

The first significant change to the route was also made at this time. It was agreed to alter the line of the canal between Colne and Whalley, keeping to the south side of the River Calder and thus eliminating the massive and expensive aqueduct at Whalley Nab. An alteration of the route to the south would open up the coalfield around Padiham, which could then communicate with the Craven district, as well as Preston. It would also improve the supply of limestone to the region south of the original canal line.

This proposed change in the line required Parliamentary approval and the company also needed permission to raise further money to

The first major change of route came in 1790, when it was realised that the proposed aqueduct at Whalley was far too grandiose. It would have been at least twenty feet higher than Rennie's spectacular Lune aqueduct on the Lancaster Canal, and at least as long. A visit to the Whalley to Accrington road near Parkhead (grid ref. 746352) confirms the magnitude of the engineering feat that this would have represented, the valley falling away steeply to the River Calder before climbing even more precipitously to the Nab. The 1790 deviation took the line of the canal south of the Calder and would have avoided crossing the river at this point. The eventual cut was further south again from this line, passing through Burnley and near to Dunkenhalgh.

(L.R.O. DDTo. Reproduced by kind permission of The Lord O'Hagan M.E.P., Exeter.)

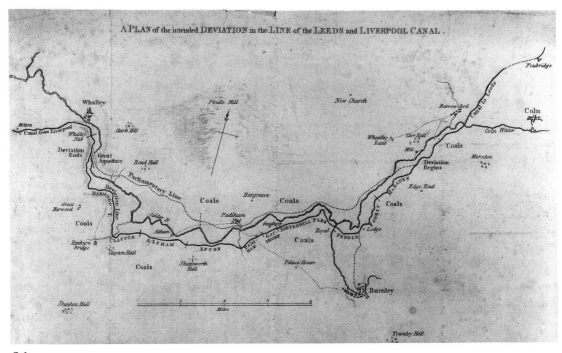

finance the renewed construction, so a Bill was presented to Parliament in 1790. The Act, for the change of route and allowing another £200,000 to be raised, was passed in June, with the only opposition coming from the trustee of the Hesketh estates in Great Harwood, through which just over two miles of the canal were to be built.

The canal committee thought that this opposition arose, not from any damage the canal would cause, but in an attempt to compel the proprietors of the canal to agree to the Croston Drainage Bill, which the Hesketh interests, based at Rufford, were pursuing in Parliament. Whitworth had examined the drainage scheme in February 1790, and his recommendations for preserving the navigation of the tidal River Douglas, which would be adversely affected, had been given to those promoting the drainage system. The Hesketh interest attempted to include consent for this drainage scheme in the Canal Bill, but were unsuccessful, though a clause regulating drainage culverts under the canal at Rufford was included.

Whitworth was asked to be the canal's engineer and he suggested a salary of 600 guineas per annum.[3] After this was agreed, he left his elder son to complete the few remaining works on the Forth and Clyde Canal, where he had been engaged previously. He brought down to Lancashire not just his younger son William, but also many of the contractors and navvies who had been working for him on the Forth and Clyde. Among these was Alexander Mackenzie, born at Muirton in 1769. He worked as a navigator or canal cutter, originally in the Colne district, and moving westward as the canal was built. In the early-1790s he married Mary Austin at Colne parish church, and eight of their eleven children were later christened there. By 1801 he had become a contractor in his own right, undertaking construction of lengths of canal, sometimes with a partner. He continued as a contractor for the company until the canal was finished, settling in Blackburn, where he died in 1836 after having been a contractor for several other canals. His eldest son, William, carried on the family tradition. He was apprenticed to Thomas Clapham, the canal company's lock carpenter at Burnley in 1811, and later worked as agent on the construction of the Union Canal, and the Gloucester and Sharpness Canal. He subsequently became the partner of Thomas Brassey, perhaps the most famous of railway contractors, dying in 1851 from overwork.[4]

In October 1790 the first contracts for work were advertised to be let, with work starting at Gargrave. From now on construction would progress westward until Wigan was finally reached in 1816, though there were to be several more interruptions to this work. By November a clerk of works and overlookers for masonry, carpentry, digging and earthworks, and for the tunnel, were taken on – Matthew Oddie, James Fletcher, John Harrison, Samuel Fletcher and William Shaw being appointed respectively. Harrison was also to continue to oversee repairs on the canal in Lancashire.[5]

At the same committee meeting it was reported that, 'Mr. Hustler the late worthy treasurer, indefatigable and disinterested promoter of this canal was dead, to the irreparable loss of this company.' His son and Mr. Peckover were to take over as treasurers. Hustler had worked hard to promote the canal and had managed to keep the scheme together in the early days when the Lancashire and Yorkshire interests had been divisive. He had also travelled constantly about the works, attended committee meetings, directed the undertaking when there had been no engineer and generally promoted the scheme.

A critical change of route is proposed

AT this point, events began to move rapidly with regard to the canal's future. No fewer than three canal projects were mooted in the early-1790s, all of which had important consequences for the Leeds and Liverpool. In addition, the Lancashire interest finally prevailed and the company decided to ask Parliament in 1793 to be allowed to complete the canal on a line through East Lancashire, similar to Burdett's suggestion in 1769.

The first of the three proposed canals was the Manchester, Bolton and Bury Canal, which had obtained its Act early in 1791. Almost immediately afterwards, Matthew Fletcher, a colliery manager from Clifton, who was much concerned with that canal, approached the Leeds and Liverpool committee and proposed a major and, eventually, a very important amendment to the proposed line of the Leeds and Liverpool. He suggested that the Leeds and Liverpool should be built from Bamber Bridge, near Preston, by way of Duxbury to join a branch of the Manchester, Bolton and Bury at Red Moss. From this

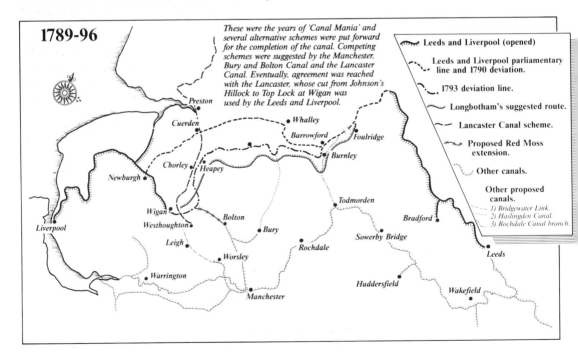

1789-96

These were the years of 'Canal Mania' and several alternative schemes were put forward for the completion of the canal. Competing schemes were suggested by the Manchester, Bury and Bolton Canal and the Lancaster Canal. Eventually, agreement was reached with the Lancaster, whose cut from Johnson's Hillock to Top Lock at Wigan was used by the Leeds and Liverpool.

Leeds and Liverpool (opened)

Leeds and Liverpool parliamentary line and 1790 deviation.

1793 deviation line.

Longbotham's suggested route.

Lancaster Canal scheme.

Proposed Red Moss extension.

Other canals.

Other proposed canals.
1) Bridgewater Link.
2) Haslingden Canal.
3) Rochdale Canal branch.

junction, it was argued, they could lock down to Wigan, passing through Westhoughton and Hindley.[6]

In September, in another significant move, Whitworth reported that he had taken levels and, in view of the lockage that would be necessary from Bamber Bridge up to the level of Red Moss, he recommended that the whole line of the Leeds and Liverpool should be altered to take it at a higher level, through Burnley, Accrington, Blackburn and Chorley to the proposed junction. He added, however, that he needed to survey the route properly to check its feasibility.[7] He had done this by the following month, when he recommended that the best level for the new line would leave the existing one above the bottom lock at Barrowford. As only the lock pit had been dug so far, this would result in little financial loss. The level of the line was critical, as the high ground at Cunliffe, between Rishton and Blackburn, needed to be passed with the minimum of excavation because of the expense.

The Leeds and Liverpool, especially, one must suppose, the Lancashire proprietors, were obviously interested in the proposal, for a joint meeting of the two canals was held on 11 February 1792 and a junction agreed, the one condition being that any extension by the Manchester, Bolton and Bury from Bury to Rochdale and Littleborough would only be undertaken with the concurrence of the Leeds and Liverpool who were worried, quite naturally, about the effect such a canal might have upon their own trade.

As with the earlier Lancashire proposal to take the canal via Wigan, this new line would increase the distance from Leeds to Liverpool, but, by taking advantage of being able to join the existing Upper Douglas Navigation at Wigan, there would be thirty feet less lockage to build, while only four miles extra cutting would be needed. As the principal works on each line were about equal, the increase in cost would only amount to between £8,000 and £10,000.[8]

More critically, it was quickly realised that the line through Burnley, Accrington and Blackburn would have far greater potential for traffic than the thinly populated Parliamentary line. This was considered to be of great importance, for, by this date, a subtle shift in emphasis was beginning to make its weight felt in the minds of the Leeds and Liverpool committee. The Rochdale Canal had already been promoted and, since its trans-Pennine line would be at least fifteen miles shorter than their own, the committee felt that they should take advantage of every opportunity to increase local trade to offset the inevitable reduction in through traffic. This shift of emphasis, whether consciously or not, was to be of great importance. Because of these advantages it was proposed to recommend that the deviation be adopted at the next General Assembly.

The Rochdale Canal

ALTHOUGH the Rochdale Canal was to be a competitor for trans-Pennine traffic, its proprietors also wanted a connecting branch to the

Leeds and Liverpool and in October 1791 they proposed that they would construct a canal from their line at Todmorden, by way of Burnley and Colne, to join the Leeds and Liverpool at Wanless Water, near the west end of Foulridge Tunnel. The motive behind this branch was once again the need for a supply of lime, this time for the country along the line of the Rochdale, though it was also hoped to obtain stone from the quarries at Worsthorne and coal from the mines at Extwistle Hall. A chance to increase limestone traffic prompted the Leeds and Liverpool proprietors to agree to the junction, provided 6d per ton was paid, as recompense for any inconvenience, on all such traffic which had not travelled more than twelve miles along their own canal.

In 1792, at one stage of the Parliamentary proceedings concerning the Rochdale Canal Bill, the Leeds and Liverpool suggested that, in return for the Rochdale dropping their plan for a canal from Todmorden to Sowerby and concentrating on the line to Wanless Water, then they would give their full support to the Bill in Parliament. George Travis replied for the Rochdale, agreeing to the terms, though how truthful he was being is open to doubt, as such a route would be considerably longer for trans-Pennine traffic.[9]

The slow progress being made in building the tunnel at Foulridge worried the Rochdale men sufficiently for them to ask, in June 1792, if it would be possible for the junction of the two canals to be to the east of the tunnel instead. They even suggested taking their branch canal through Lothersdale to reach the Leeds and Liverpool beyond Skipton, though the difficulty of building a canal over such high ground made this suggestion impractical and nothing further was heard about the scheme. The problems encountered in a branch from Todmorden would have been tremendous. One plan required over two hundred feet of lockage, with huge problems in water supply, and a second, with less lockage, involved a tunnel three miles in length. In the face of such obstacles its failure is not surprising, although for some reason the idea was resurrected in 1824. The Rochdale eventually opened throughout, from Manchester to Sowerby Bridge, in 1804.[10]

The Lancaster Canal

THE last and most important of the three canals associated with the Leeds and Liverpool at the time was the Lancaster. This canal had first been promoted in the early-1770s to run from Kendal to the Bridgewater Canal at Worsley, with the original intended line of the Leeds and Liverpool being crossed near Eccleston. Coal would have been taken from the Wigan area to the north of Lancashire, and limestone carried in return. The difficult crossings of the Lune and Ribble valleys deterred the promoters, though over the following years plans continued to be put forward.

Proposals in 1787 for land drainage around Morecambe Bay included a suggestion for a canal, but it was not until 1791 that the canal was again being actively promoted, this time with a line from Westhoughton to Kendal, crossing and probably joining the Leeds and Liverpool's Parliamentary line at Clayton Green, south of Preston. The deviation which the Leeds and Liverpool were hoping to adopt ran virtually parallel to this line from Heapey, near Chorley, to Wigan. Because of the proximity of the two routes, a deputation from each canal met at Settle on 21 February 1792, in an attempt to come to an accommodation. The Lancaster initially requested the terms upon which they could make a junction with the Leeds and Liverpool Parliamentary line. However, as the Leeds and Liverpool now intended to follow their amended line, they replied that the Lancaster should join this.

Two routes . . . or one?

THE meeting was inconclusive, with the Leeds and Liverpool resolving to oppose the Lancaster's route in Parliament, but continuing to seek a junction between the two lines. They approached the Manchester, Bolton and Bury with a request for them to join in the opposition, reminding them that the Red Moss scheme relied for its water supply upon the Leeds and Liverpool building the deviated line. The Lancaster level was sixty feet lower than the line to Bolton and

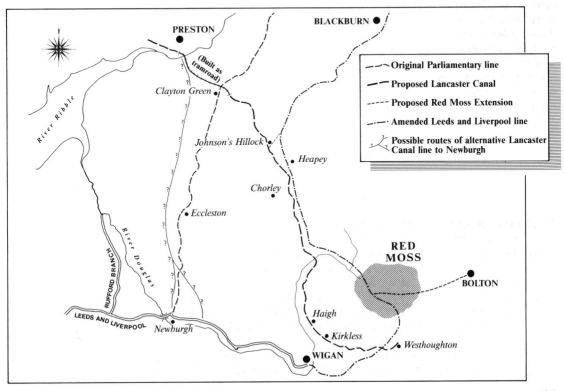

would be unable to provide it with a supply. The Lancaster was supported by the Bridgewater Canal, the two canals having a plan to provide a through route to Manchester, in direct opposition to the route of the Red Moss branch. A final approach to the Lancaster offering terms for an accommodation between the two sides was made in March with the following propositions:[11]

1) If the deviation was not made, the Lancaster should pay for the junction which would be made in the least prejudicial way for the Leeds and Liverpool.
2) If the deviation was made, the Leeds and Liverpool would pay for the junction and create the minimum inconvenience to the Lancaster.
3) No tolls were to be paid on the junctive canal.
4) All water supplied to be paid for by the user.
5) The head waters of the River Douglas to be preserved for the Douglas Navigation.
6) Satisfaction for the loss of trade to the Douglas to be settled by three independent persons five years after the completion of the Lancaster.
7) The income of the Douglas to be taken as £2,500 per annum.
8) No alteration to the line of the Lancaster between Clayton Green and Westhoughton which would affect the Leeds and Liverpool deviation.
9) The Lancaster not to oppose the Leeds and Liverpool deviation.

The majority of these terms were accepted with minor alterations by the Lancaster promoters, but no agreement could be reached on the compensation for the possible loss of trade on the Lower Douglas. The Lancaster offered a yearly dividend of 8% upon the cost of the whole Douglas Navigation, but if the income from the navigation exceeded this they were to be paid the excess. The Leeds and Liverpool were unable to agree to this and maintained their opposition to the Lancaster's Bill in Parliament.

They then proposed to the Lancaster the simple expedient that the Leeds and Liverpool would withdraw all opposition to their Bill if the Lancaster supported their deviation in Parliament. The Lancaster felt confident enough to refuse, there being no other opposition to their Bill. However, when it came before the House of Lords it transpired that there were several inconsistencies in the Bill's wording, caused, no doubt, by the speed with which it had been drawn up. This would have necessitated a new application had there been any opposition and, as the Lancaster promoters were very anxious to obtain their Act that session, an agreement was reached with the Leeds and Liverpool to withdraw their opposition, enabling the Act to be passed unaltered. In return the Lancaster agreed not to oppose the Leeds and Liverpool's deviation when it was presented to Parliament.[12]

The new route is surveyed and chosen

MEANWHILE, Whitworth had reported on the two schemes proposed for the important matter of the new, southerly route for the canal. The first of these, via Burnley and Blackburn to above Chorley and thence to Wigan over Red Moss he had proposed himself. This line, which also passed the coal mines at Westhoughton, would have been about fifty-one miles in length. A second scheme was suggested by Longbotham, avoiding the tunnel at Foulridge and including a longer and higher summit level. Locking up to this summit at Foulridge, the line went by Colne, Marsden, Cliviger Mill, Huncoat, Upper Darwen and Rivington to Wigan, a distance of about sixty-two miles, with all the locks situated at Wigan.[13]

The earthworks on each line were about equal, making the higher one more expensive because of its extra length. The high summit level would also have needed a steam engine to supply it with water, as the reservoirs at Foulridge were too low. The final blow to this line was its distance from the developing industries of East Lancashire, only the stone quarries at Worsthorne and Haslingden being more conveniently served. Part of Longbotham's route, from Red Moss to Wigan, was considered an improvement as it reduced the distance by over three miles and this was incorporated with Whitworth's plan.

The possibility of a route somewhere between the two lines was also considered but rejected. Longbotham's southern line could not be made any lower without encroaching on the grounds and plantations round Towneley Hall which would not have been allowed by the landowner (Canal Acts normally included clauses to preserve the approaches and grounds of large houses). On the northern line, the amount of work on embankments at Burnley and elsewhere had to be set against the excavation needed to pass the high ground at Sidebeet, and this precluded any raising of this level. Variations in the route from Chorley to Wigan were also considered, but the Lancaster had chosen the only other practicable line, and it was thought difficult for the Leeds and Liverpool to use this as the canal level would then have

Looking down Barrowford Locks. The original line would have descended one more lock and swung round to the right, keeping to the valley side rather than crossing Colne Water via the Swinden Aqueduct, as seen here.

(Photo, author's collection.)

been too low for a connection to be made with the Manchester, Bolton and Bury at Red Moss.

By July 1792, Whitworth had finished the survey and plan of his lower line. The locks were to be at Blackburn and Wigan, the point of departure from the Parliamentary line being below the seventh lock at Barrowford. He had considered a level extending beyond Blackburn, but placing the locks there facilitated the crossing of the deep valleys of the River Derwent (or Darwen) and Moulden Water. If the Blackburn level had been extended it would have necessitated a long diversion to cross these valleys. The height of the level below Blackburn was designed to allow the proposed crossing of Red Moss without further lockage. This meant that the water for the Bolton branch could be supplied by the main canal, with no need for a further supply.

Opposition to the new route fell into two sections, from Colne to Heapey, near Chorley, and from thence to Wigan.[14] There was little concerted opposition to the first section. Mr. Towneley of Towneley Hall complained that the line crossed the avenue leading to his house and asked that the route be altered. Whitworth sought to find a less obstructive route and the crossing of the valley at Burnley was moved nearer the town. This increased the expense of the embankment by £8,000, but reduced the length of the canal by about one mile. Towneley agreed to this change and withdrew his objections.

Further opposition came from Thomas Whyman, agent for Mr. Shuttleworth of Gawthorpe Hall, near Padiham. He produced a pamphlet complaining of the changed route, but despite his protestations to the contrary, his opposition was based on the loss which his estates at Gawthorpe, including coal mines around Padiham, would suffer if they were not on the canal route.

The same motive was behind the opposition of Adam Cottam, Mr. Braddyl's agent at Samlesbury, who complained about what was, in effect, planning blight along the line of the canal in that area, leading to reductions in rent for land which might be needed for the canal. Apparently, a corn mill had already been built at Samlesbury in expectation of the increase in trade from the canal. Cottam's evidence to the Parliamentary committee for the deviation Bill also mentions that cotton manufacture was now the main industry on the line of the canal, an early indication of the reduced importance of the wool and linen trades in the area. Factories were still heavily dependent upon water for power and processing, and it was to protect their interests that several clauses had been added to the Bill forbidding the canal from utilising water already controlled by mills along the line, particularly at Altham and Church Kirk.

The opposition to the second section, from Heapey to Wigan, was much more organised, as this length was, in effect, a duplication of the Lancaster's line. The Parliamentary committee discussed three alternatives: could the country support two canals; if only one canal was built, should it be the Lancaster or the Leeds and Liverpool; and what form would a junction between the two canals take?

If two lines were built there would be problems with coal mining. The area served by the Leeds and Liverpool had possibly the best supplies of coal, located on the Red Moss to Westhoughton length of their line, whereas the Lancaster was more easily reached from the mines along its length, as it was constructed at a lower level, enabling the coal to be carried downhill to the canal.

In mining areas coal had to be left in the ground to help support the canal, thereby reducing the reserves and increasing costs. In this respect the Leeds and Liverpool would have adversely affected the Lancaster by reducing the amount of coal available to it. Leakage from the Leeds and Liverpool could also have caused drainage problems to mines underneath its line. As a further complication, the supply of water to the Lancaster would have been intercepted by the Leeds and Liverpool, although that available to the Lancaster would have been minimal as the Leeds and Liverpool already owned the water rights to the upper reaches of the River Douglas by virtue of their purchase of the old navigation. The close proximity of the two lines near Chorley resulted in petitions against the deviation Bill from local landowners J. Townley Parker, Richard Crosse and John Duxbury. Much of their estates would be affected, though they were particularly concerned by the destruction of timber, a valuable item at this time. They considered that any improvement in communication would best be achieved by the Lancaster.

Besides the effect upon the country through which both canals were to pass, concern was also directed towards the junction with the branch to Bolton and the implications, should only one line be constructed. The Manchester, Bolton and Bury scheme for this branch was included in a Bill which also proposed a branch from Bury to Sowerby Bridge. This second branch would have attracted some of the Leeds and Liverpool's trans-Pennine trade, which caused a certain amount of friction between the two companies, although they continued to support their respective schemes at Red Moss. The Leeds and Liverpool decided not to oppose the Sowerby Bridge scheme, as they considered that the gain in traffic from the Red Moss branch would more than compensate for any loss in through trade with Yorkshire.

Additionally, any split in their ranks would have been used by the opposition, especially the Duke of Bridgewater, who was concerned about possible loss in trade on the proposed link from the Lancaster, at Westhoughton, to his canal at Worsley. He also wanted to keep the maximum amount of trade between Liverpool and Manchester passing along his canal from Runcorn. It is unlikely that this traffic would have been affected much by a route through Wigan and Bolton, because of the excessive lockage necessary to reach the summit at Red Moss. It would, however, have affected prices by creating competition.

The Red Moss branch to Bolton would have been built on the same level as the revised Leeds and Liverpool line, with 112 feet of lockage down to the Manchester, Bolton and Bury terminus at Bolton, a distance of about fourteen miles from Heapey. As a counter to this plan the Lancaster suggested two alternatives, the first a branch from Westhoughton, keeping to the lower level of the Lancaster through to Bolton, increasing the distance from Heapey to twenty-five miles; the second, for a tunnel under Red Moss to Bolton, creating a through route to Bolton, and supplying water to the Lancaster Canal by draining the coal measures under Red Moss. Coal from these seams could also be loaded straight into boats in arms off the main tunnel.

Estimates for this tunnel were produced by Rennie, the engineer for the Lancaster. He suggested that it would be about two miles long, whereas William Bennett, the engineer for the Manchester, Bolton and Bury extension, suggested that it would need to be five miles long, and that other difficult earthworks would have to be built. The committee considered the Leeds and Liverpool Bill for six weeks and, after making a number of changes, reported to the House. There the opposition proved too strong and it was thrown out, leaving the company pondering how to progress further.

The proprietors of the Manchester, Bolton and Bury continued to put forward schemes linked with the Leeds and Liverpool, and in July 1793 some of them proposed a canal from Bury by way of Haslingden to the Leeds and Liverpool at Accrington.[15] The area through which the canal was to pass was already becoming highly industrialised, with many water-powered mills in operation. Consequently, there would have been difficulty providing enough water for a conventional canal, so the construction of inclined planes was considered. This suggests the use of tub-boats, necessitating the transhipment of goods at each end of the canal, and thus increasing costs. This scheme was tied in with the Red Moss branch by agreements over the supply of water proposed to be delivered to the Leeds and Liverpool by the two branches. The Haslingden Canal obtained its Act in April 1794, though little further progress was made and the concern was wound up in 1797. One wonders how realistic the promoters of this canal were in view of the problems of water supply. Its association with the Red Moss scheme suggests it was merely a way of achieving closer ties with the Leeds and Liverpool.

A decision on the line which the Leeds and Liverpool Canal was to take had become urgent. Work on the summit level was progressing steadily and would soon reach a stage where a start would have to be made on construction beyond the point of departure of the deviation at Barrowford.

Another approach was made to the Lancaster in an attempt to agree terms.[16] The committee suggested that the Lancaster, instead of building their southern section as laid down in their Act, should construct an extension of their canal from Preston to join the Leeds and Liverpool at Newburgh, continuing their canal to the Bridgewater from the head of the Douglas Navigation at Wigan. The Lancaster would benefit from a lowering of the Ribble crossing by 27 feet, reducing the cost of the aqueduct and embankment which would be required there. The flight of locks up to Chorley and those back down to Worsley would be avoided, the proposed canal from Wigan being on one level.

The scheme would create a better route from Liverpool to Manchester, as boats would not be involved in passing through the many locks to the Red Moss summit level, while it would provide access to all the Wigan coalfields, and solve the Lancaster's water supply problems, with all that was needed coming from the Newburgh to Wigan stretch of the Leeds and Liverpool. The canal would be constructed at a lower cost, with improved connections, leaving the Leeds and Liverpool free to build their deviation.

The Lancaster committee opposed the scheme, however, saying it would create too long a route for their traffic, and would not be convenient for the transport of coal from Haigh and Chorley, where many of their proprietors had mines, as the increased distance to North Lancashire markets meant increased tolls and prices. They suggested instead that the Leeds and Liverpool lock down into their canal at Heapey and that boats not loading or unloading along the Lancaster would be exempt from tolls. The benefit to the Lancaster would be the supply of water from the locks at Heapey. The disadvantage was the problem of the junction with the Manchester, Bolton and Bury, although the committee suggested that the money saved by not building the canal from Heapey to Wigan would more than cover the cost of a branch from the Lancaster to Bolton.

Agreement is reached with the Lancaster Canal

THE two sides continued to argue, each wanting to maximise traffic on its own section of canal. Both schemes meant that the other canal would end up being disunited, a condition that neither wanted. The Lancaster had the stronger position, having already received its Act, and when an agreement was reached in April 1794 it was based on their scheme, which was probably the better of the two. The agreement virtually put an end to the possibility of a branch from Red Moss to Bolton, though the Manchester, Bolton and Bury kept pursuing the scheme over the following years. However, it made the idea of a link from Wigan to the Bridgewater at Leigh extremely attractive.[17]

By the agreement, the Lancaster was authorised to construct a junction by means of locks with the Leeds and Liverpool at Heapey. In return they would not be obstructed in the construction of reservoirs and supply of water to their head level. They conceded that, when their canal and the extension to the Bridgewater were built, they would be able to carry goods to and from Manchester which would otherwise have used the Leeds and Liverpool and the Manchester, Bolton and Bury to reach destinations to the east of the junction – if both canals had been built. Traffic on the Lancaster, after the Leeds and Liverpool deviation and the branch to Bolton had been built, would pay one shilling per ton upon passing the junction as an acknowledgement for the loss of trade to the two canals.

As a result, both sides withdrew all opposition to their respective schemes in Parliament, the Leeds and Liverpool deviation and the Lancaster Canal link to the Bridgewater. A further agreement was entered into with the Duke of Bridgewater whereby he withdrew his opposition provided that the Leeds and Liverpool between Heapey and Nightingales, at Heath Charnock, was the last section to be constructed. He hoped to be able to concentrate traffic along his own canal to the Lancaster before the Leeds and Liverpool line was completed, thus keeping as much trade to himself as possible. Following this compromise, an Act for the deviated line was passed by Parliament in May 1794. The Lancaster, though, failed to obtain consent for their line to the Duke of Bridgewater's Canal at Worsley and twenty-five years were to pass before a link from Wigan to Worsley – the Leigh branch of the Leeds and Liverpool – was eventually constructed.

The building of Foulridge Tunnel

WHILST these problems with the deviated line were being overcome in Parliament, work on the construction of the summit level was still going forward, albeit slowly. Some proprietors were critical of Whitworth's choice of line for the tunnel at Foulridge and it was decided to call in outside advice. Josiah Clowes was chosen. His independence may be suspect, as he had worked with Robert Whitworth on the Thames and Severn Canal, where he had been responsible for Sapperton Tunnel.[18]

He reported in July 1792 that the line chosen was a proper one and that it would ensure a constant supply of water. The tunnel was constructed in such a manner that water from the surrounding water table would be able to percolate into the canal and thus improve the supply. He also stated that if two extra locks were built at each end of the tunnel to raise the level, the cost would be less and the length could be reduced by about four hundred yards. An engine would be necessary, however, to raise water into the summit level, as the input from the reservoirs would be decreased. The report exonerated Whitworth, who had encountered many problems with the tunnel, parts of which were built through shifting sand, causing the work to be continually behind time.

Much East Lancashire traffic was already being sent to and from the canal at Skipton and Kildwick, which was causing the condition of local roads to deteriorate. The company complained at Preston Assizes that the poor state of the roads around Foulridge was causing the work on the tunnel to be held up and requested that they be improved. Little repair work was done as those responsible considered that when the canal opened the traffic using the roads would diminish rapidly. In September 1791, Whitworth had informed the committee that the digging of the head level had been virtually completed except for the tunnel, and that the Greenberfield to Gargrave section was progressing well. The masonry work, though, was lagging behind, due to poor supplies of stone from the quarries, and increases in wages. Whitworth reported:

> . . . indeed the masonry in general is too far behind though I should hope it would come up as there are now upon the ground 99 masons and 75 quarriers and labourers their attendants, but there is something discouraging in this business, the wages being at least one fourth higher than they were when the works began, this with bad quarries has entirely put it out of the power of every one of the contractors to finish their several contracts without considerable loss and I believe several of the diggers will be in the same predicament.[19]

From 1880 a tug was provided at Foulridge to tow boats through the tunnel. Some boatmen continued to 'leg' their boats, however, while still claiming the cost of towage from their employers. The tug was double-ended, with a propeller and rudder at each end, eliminating the need to turn round at each end. The service was withdrawn in the mid-'thirties, as many boats had their own engines by that time. The building near the tunnel entrance was originally used by the leggers when they were waiting for boats.
(Photo, Lancs. Libraries.)

The Duke of Gloucester *emerging from the tunnel. This boat was converted for use at a boy's club in Wigan in the mid-1930s, the duke allowing his name to be used. He was apparently not so enthusiastic when the boat became derelict just before the war.*

He must have realised that his estimate for the cost of completing the canal would be seriously affected. There were also problems with the tunnel, where they had encountered mud and sand and an engine had to be erected for pumping away surplus water. Because of the unstable ground about 740 yards of the tunnel were now to be constructed on the cut and cover principle. Here, the line of the tunnel had to be excavated to form a valley. The tunnel lining was constructed and then covered with the earth which had been excavated. This work was expected to take two years to complete.

The rest of the tunnel, through solid rock, was built by conventional methods. Shafts were dug down to the tunnel level, and these were connected by a pilot tunnel, which drained the workings. The contractors were slow to complete this tunnel, and pumping engines had to be erected at some of the shafts to drain the headings. Work, which continued night and day, was also delayed by a collapse of earthworks at the tunnel entrance. When the pilot tunnel was completed, it was enlarged to its full size, the ground water having drained away down the pilot tunnel. This water was later to supply the canal, and was estimated to fill at least fourteen locks per day.

By September 1793, work at each end of the tunnel was virtually complete and it was suggested that a temporary canal could be built over the top, so that traffic to Colne, Burnley etc. could be forwarded without transhipment at Kildwick.[20] Later, a tramway was proposed but neither plan seems to have been taken up. In August 1794 the canal was completed as far west as Foulridge and the company allowed its horses to be used, when available, for hauling goods to Burnley and beyond. These were probably the ones used for the construction work, not boat horses.

The tunnel was finally opened for traffic on 1 May 1796. A timetable for entering the tunnel had been drawn up, with boats allowed to enter for an hour every four hours, the times at each end being staggered by two hours. This allowed a maximum of one hour to 'leg' a boat through the tunnel. This cannot have been enough, as the time for entering was reduced a few weeks later to just half an hour, thereby allowing a minimum of one and a half hours for the passage. With the opening of the tunnel, boats could now reach Burnley, though the embankment there was not to be completed for some years. To accommodate trade, a warehouse was built where the Colne Road crossed the canal just outside the town, and a small canalside community developed, with a dry dock for the repair of boats.

Further money was needed before work could continue and in September 1794 it was decided to raise an extra £100,000 to complete the canal to Grimshaw Park in Blackburn. This was achieved by issuing 575 new shares at £180 per share, available to existing shareholders at the rate of one new share for every four old shares. With this money Whitworth was able to start work on the deviation line, which now had the consent of Parliament.

Burnley and Bentley Brook Embankments

THE valley at Burnley presented the most difficult outstanding obstacle. By March 1795 Whitworth had set out the specifications for the work. In 1792, he had produced schemes for crossing the valley above and below Burnley. One of these entailed an embankment over eighty feet high at Royle which would have cost £28,690 and they would have encountered problems finding enough earth for its construction.[21]

The plan which was adopted, after Mr. Towneley had arranged for the position to be altered as previously mentioned, was estimated to cost £13,266, and involved the creation of an embankment about forty

Right: Burnley, 1845, from the first edition O.S. map. Burnley Embankment is immediately visible on the right-hand side of this section of the map.[1] It was a major engineering achievement, although it took a long time to settle, and later suffered from subsidence because coal was mined underneath it – note the collieries not far to the east of the embankment.[2] At this time Burnley was the principal canal town on the Leeds and Liverpool, as well as an important centre for boat-building.[3] When the canal was first built as far west as Burnley in 1796, a warehouse was constructed to deal with traffic until the embankment had settled,[4] and several other boatyards were established later. After the embankment opened, a toll house and warehouse on Manchester Road were built,[6] and the main maintenance yard for this whole stretch of canal was set up at the end of the embankment.[7] Here they made lock gates and built maintenance boats, as well as having stores and a timber yard. Note also the aqueduct over the River Calder.[8]

This map was drawn just before the railway was built and the clear influence of the canal on the industry of the town can be seen, with large-scale development already well established along the canal to the south of the town. At this time all the major factories were either along the River Calder or in the Weavers' Triangle along the canal. There is also a limekiln on the Halifax road,[5] which was owned by the canal company and leased out. (see page 151.)

(Reproduced by kind permission of the County Archivist, Lancashire Record Office.)

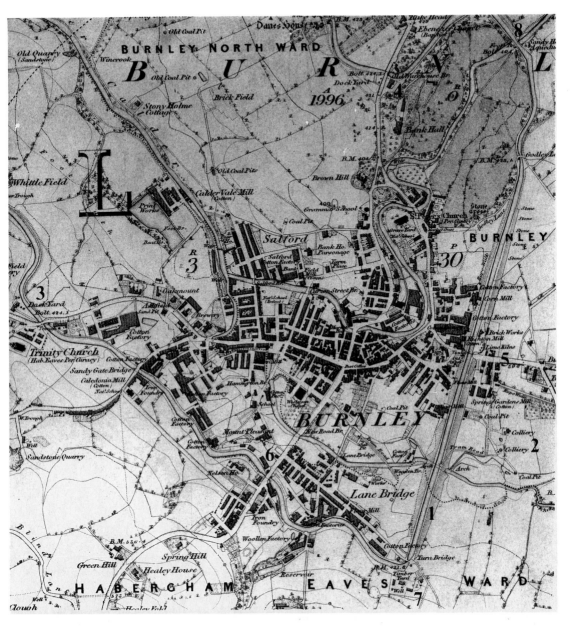

feet high and almost one mile in length.

Most of the earth for this major embankment came from the canal cutting north of Burnley and was carried to the site in short narrow boats. The spoil from the tunnel at Gannow was not used to any great extent at Burnley, as it was needed for the other large embankment in the area at Bentley Brook, between Burnley and Hapton. It is now difficult to appreciate the sheer size of Bentley Brook Embankment, as it has since been enlarged on the south side for the turnpike road from Accrington to Burnley, and the railway has been built immediately to the north, effectively filling the valley.

The canal inches westward to Henfield

WHITWORTH, one of the country's foremost engineers, was continually in demand for work on other canals. In 1795, once the more difficult work of setting out the levels had been completed, he asked for his salary to be halved, as he was engaged on several other projects.[22] These included the Herefordshire and Gloucestershire, the Dearne and Dove and a canal from Chester to the Ashby Canal. He died on 30th March 1799, the committee recording later that they:

Above: *A modern view of the 'straight mile', or 'Burnley val' as the boatmen called it – by far the longest embankment on the Leeds and Liverpool.*

Left, top: *Yorkshire Street was quite congested by the 1890s and the original roadway was very narrow. The Corporation therefore decided to bore two new footpath tunnels through the embankment on either side of the road. To avoid the chance of a major and catastrophic breach during this work, the water was drained and this temporary wooden channel was built, into which the canal was allowed back, thus allowing the canal to resume work while the tunnels were completed below. Note the very early use of electric lighting to allow the work to go on round the clock.*
(Photo, Lancs. Libraries.)

Left, bottom: *In 1927 it was further decided that the old bridge under the embankment was too small and it was completely replaced by this wider and grander bridge. The side arches constructed in the 1890s have already been removed and both the new and old road arches can be seen here.*
(Photo, Lancs. Libraries.)

... had the greatest confidence in the established abilities and integrity of their deceased engineer and in his particular attachment to this undertaking and that their declarations shall be made and entered in their proceedings as a tribute to his memory and of their esteem.

Samuel Fletcher, who, the previous year, had been promoted to inspector of the state of the canal and director of repairs, was put in charge of the works, though Whitworth's son, William, was to advise him when required. This arrangement may have ceased the following year, when William Whitworth was paid for work undertaken since his father's death.

The Fletcher family had a long involvement with the canal. James Fletcher, from Bradford, became overlooker of masonry, in 1790, at the same time as Samuel, possibly his brother, became overlooker of digging and, by 1801, another brother, Joseph, was also employed. Early in 1804, Samuel Fletcher died, and, as the committee considered they no longer needed a professional engineer, they appointed Joseph, and Samuel's son, James, as joint principal overlooker and surveyor, paying them £350 per annum. They were based at Gannow, where a house was provided, and reported directly to the committee, though they were nominally under the control of Joseph Priestley.[23]

The money raised by the last share issue had been almost exhausted, the treasurer having only £6,630 on hand in July 1797. In view of the dire state of national finances at this time, the economy having gone into recession, there was little chance of raising further capital.

The following month Priestley presented a report, produced with the canal's engineers, suggesting the canal should be completed from Burnley to Henfield, near the junction of the turnpikes to Blackburn and Accrington, thus serving both towns.[24] This was agreed, its estimated cost being a further £34,000, which was obtained from the income of the canal and from loans raised as the country's finances improved. However, the number of men employed was reduced, and their wages cut to conserve money. The work progressed slowly as a result, with problems in the stabilisation of the embankment at Burnley. This was now the main obstacle to the next stage of the canal's opening. Samuel Fletcher's report in September 1800 gives further reasons for the slow progress:

> The number of men proposed to complete the work in the report above mentioned February [1800] could not possibly be kept upon the work on account of the scarcity and dearness of provisions as they could not get sufficient subsistence with such wages as was in the power of the undertakers to give them.
>
> Secondly, the uncommon dryness of the season hath deprived the works of all water and most particularly in that part of the country where the canal must be lined with puddle both bottom and sides, consequently a great part of such work hath been stopped for a considerable time back and cannot be carried on until there is water for boating and puddling.[25]

Despite all these problems the canal was opened on 23 April 1801 to Henfield, where a warehouse 60 feet by 35 feet was built to accommodate the traffic.

Continuing problems

BESIDES the difficulties they encountered obtaining permission for their new route through East Lancashire, the committee had much to contend with in the operation of the length of canal already open. Several problems had appeared and considerable work had to be done to overcome them. For example, the Rufford Branch had suffered from the flooding of surrounding land and from the shallowness of the channel up to Sollom Lock, which loaded boats were only able to use for a few days at spring tides. In 1790 it was proposed by the local landowners to obtain an Act for the improvement of the drainage of the Rivers Douglas, Yarrow and Lostock. Whitworth met Thomas Ecclestone, one of the largest landowners, and John Gilbert, the engineer for the scheme, when safeguards for the protection of the navigation were agreed. However, no improvements were made at this time, though Whitworth did produce a plan for an extension of the canal to Tarleton.

The continuing problem of supplying the north end of the Lancaster Canal and Preston with coal and other goods revived interest in this extension and, in October 1796, a Mr. Bamford suggested that if it was constructed, then a canal could be built from Lytham to the Lancaster at Salwick. Whitworth estimated the cost of the branch to be £6,771, the price being kept down by using the stone of the old Tarleton Lock for the construction of the new one.[26]

In May the following year, another report revealed that because of insufficient depth of water in the river, the lock at Sollom could only be used by boats carrying thirty to thirty-six tons for eight days at spring tides. There were worse problems of insufficient water at Peg Hill, on the Ribble, restricting the supply of coal from the Douglas to Preston.

To overcome this the Lancaster Canal surveyed the ground between their canal at Wards House and the Ribble at Savick Brook for a

A rare and early view of the stationary steam engine near the end of Bushell Place in Avenham, Preston, which pulled tramway wagons up the steep incline from the tram bridge across the Ribble. There were many schemes for linking the two ends of the Lancaster Canal by a waterway but this tramway was all that was ever built. It worked from 1803 until the late-1850s. A re-construction of the original wooden tram bridge and a long length of the tramroad across the floodplain south of the Ribble can still be seen today, although all remains of the canal tranship-ment basin and warehouse at Walton Summit have disappeared. Some traces, including the tunnels, of the branch of the old Southern Lancaster Canal from this basin to Johnson's Hillock, however, can still be seen. (Photo, Harris Museum, Preston.)

railway, for the interchange of coal and lime-stone. Another proposal from the Lancaster was for crossing the Ribble at Preston on the level, so as to be able to join the Douglas Navigation, by a canal across the country to the south of the river – a similar scheme to the one they had rejected during the Parliamentary proceedings in 1793.

Whitworth examined the proposal and reported in Nov 1799 that although the line, twenty-two miles long, would be very crooked, it would be feasible to join the Leeds and Liverpool by a junction nine feet above the canal level at Liverpool, possibly at Appley Bridge.

However, no further action was taken. By this time the Lancaster Canal had been completed except for the aqueduct over the Ribble and the flight of locks up to Clayton Green. There were discussions over how to link the northern and southern sections of the canal, and as a temporary measure a tramway, with inclined planes, was built in 1803 between the two termini, cargoes being transhipped at each end. The Lancaster was never to achieve enough financial success for the missing section to be built, though schemes to join the northern section to the rest of the canal system have been put forward at various times, none having materialised yet. Perhaps they should have built the link to the Leeds and Liverpool at Newburgh when it was first suggested.

The plan to improve the drainage of the Douglas and Yarrow at Croston, was resurrected, however, and in April 1800 the committee received notification of the new scheme from Mr. Addison of Rufford. Priestley negotiated with the drainage proprietors, who proposed to construct a new course for the river from above Sollom Lock to Tarleton Bridge. The canal was to use the old river between those points, and an extension to the canal was to be built to a place just above the old lock at Tarleton. The negotiations led to the drainage proprietors giving the company £500 towards their costs, in return for their support. In spite of this agreement they appear to have been somewhat obstructive and altered clauses without notification.[27]

It may be that the hand of Sir Thomas Hesketh, the largest landowner in the area, can be seen here, as he was no friend of the Leeds and Liverpool. The canal company were negotiating with him at the time for land to build a towpath along the canal at Rufford. This section had been built in the 1760s by the Douglas Navigation when boats were hauled by men, no towpath being required under these circumstances. Hesketh had complained that Mr Bromfield of Preston and Richard Dobson of Sollom, coal carriers to Preston, had demolished fences on his ground to allow their horses to tow boats. Both these negotiations and the construction of the drainage scheme seemed to the company to have been prolonged unnecessarily to the detriment of their trade. The canal to Tarleton finally opened in July 1805, having cost £10,156.

Improvements to the canal

MANY improvements were made to the canal as the pressure of traffic exposed inadequacies. At Liverpool, in 1790, it was suggested that the terminal basin be enlarged, while in the following year the committee suggested a waggon way and shoots, as a link to the new docks. The Mayor and the Dock Committee, however, thought that a canal branch should be built. Problems continued in 1792, with lack of space at the terminal basin causing arguments among the flat masters. To overcome this a new basin was approved in September.

At the same time it was decided to build two locks at Appley Bridge to bypass the single deep lock there, which used large quantities of water and caused shortages higher up the canal. The need for improvements for the coal trade to Liverpool could have been behind a proposed canal to Manchester by way of Winstanley, Bickerstaffe and Rainford. Priestley reported that it was being surveyed in September 1793, though he thought it unlikely to be made.[28] The scheme was probably intended to keep pressure on the company to reduce the tolls on coal to Liverpool, always a sore point with the merchants there.

The trade had previously caused disagreement centred around the vexed question of the amount to be charged for the carriage of coal on the canal. About this, the Lancashire and Yorkshire wings of the operation had different priorities and needs. Since 1775 the tonnage charge on coal for the twenty-eight miles to Liverpool had been

A modern view of Dean Lock, with the imposing viaduct of the M6 high above. The first lock on this site was the old river lock which can just be seen blocked off at the right of the picture. From 1774 until 1781 it gave access to the Douglas Navigation as the only route to Wigan. Thereafter the lock allowed access across the river to the coal wharfs from the other side (see pages 78 and 81), and regulated the flow of water from the river to the canal. At that time there was a weir on the river, which was therefore at a higher level than the canal. The main water supply for the Liverpool length was transferred to Wigan (see page 199) and this lock became redundant for that purpose. It was finally blocked off about a hundred years ago.

The original (1781) lock on the new canal to Wigan was the one seen in the centre here. Pressure of coal traffic to Liverpool on this section led to several locks being doubled up in the middle of the last century and the lock on the left dates from that time.

(Photo, author's collection.)

reduced from 2/4 to 1/6 per ton so that coal brought by the canal could compete with that from the Sankey Navigation until it had an established market, a reduction which had been allowed on condition that the coalowners did not increase their price. Despite this, the price had advanced 6d per ton some years previously. As a result the Yorkshire proprietors argued that the tolls could be increased with no detrimental effect to the amount of coal carried, a view vigorously refuted by the Liverpool proprietors, many of whom were involved in the coal trade.[29]

At the same time a reduction in tolls had been suggested for the Yorkshire end of the canal to increase the amount of coal carried from mines near the Bradford Canal in competition with that coming from the Aire and Calder Navigation. Not surprisingly, the Yorkshire committee supported this, not least because many were involved in the Bradford coalmines. It was eventually decided at the General Assembly of proprietors on 13 April 1787 that the rate in Lancashire should be increased to 1d per ton per mile, the same as that charged in Yorkshire. Despite this, however, the problem of tolls for coal traffic was to continue for some time yet.

Additions continued to be made at Liverpool and, in 1797, it was agreed that Mr Bromfield, a carrier to Preston, should have a warehouse there to encourage traffic, now going by sea or land carriage, to use the canal. There were yet further improvements in 1800, with new coal yards and an extra basin for the timber and manure trades. The latter traffic was to become one of the most important on the canal, with street sweepings and household refuse being transported, particularly to the Burscough area, for use as a fertiliser. A new warehouse was needed at Wigan, but it was decided to wait until the canal was complete so that it could be built in the best situation for trade.

When the canal opened to Henfield, it was decided to move the warehouse at Burnley to a site on Bury Road. It was opened in 1803, when William Chaffers was appointed keeper. He had to keep an account of the boats passing and the goods sent or received, for which he was provided with a house and paid 7/6 per week. The boatyard, which had been near the old warehouse site on Colne Road, was moved to Gannow, the canal engineer living in a house nearby.

In January 1796, to improve the supply of limestone, the company authorised a branch to Rain Hall Rock limestone quarry, near Barnoldswick. The following year James Priestley was appointed to check the work there. He also looked after the tunnel, feeders and reservoirs, supervised the lockkeepers at Barrowford and Greenberfield and the warehouse at Foulridge, for all of which he was paid 70 guineas per annum. The importance of the limestone traffic can be gauged by the expansion at Rain Hall at a time of financial stringency.

The quarries at Haw Bank were also being developed and the Springs Branch had been extended by 1797, to improve the loading site. In 1792 permission was sought, and obtained, to take the wagon way from the quarries through the castle yard. It had wooden rails and reached the canal through a short tunnel under the castle walls, the staithes and chutes for delivering the limestone into boats being high above the end of the canal. In 1802 the decision was made to replace

Rain Hall Quarry at Barnoldswick. Here a canal branch was built through two tunnels into the limestone outcrop and the canal was simply extended as the limestone was removed. Eventually the branch was around 600 yards long by the time the quarry was worked out in the 1890s. The site has now been used for tipping household refuse and almost all sign of the branch has disappeared, although one can still see the tunnels.
(Photo, author's collection.)

Right, top: Icebreaking between Gargrave and Bank Newton. Here three horses are being used to draw the icebreaker. The boat was triangular in section and its keel was made of 15-inch greenheart; the boat was ballasted so that the bow would rise out of the water and break the ice by crashing downwards through it.
(Photo, author's collection.)

Right, bottom: Rather more powerful equipment was available by the time this photograph was taken in the 1930s. Here steam tug no. 57, whose crew normally operated a dredger on the canal removing rubbish, silt and leaves from the canal bed, is breaking ice near Skipton. Note the iron frame bolted on to the bow, which actually broke the ice. The bows of wooden boats were often covered with thin steel sheet for protection against ice, which could quite easily hole an unprotected boat. In this picture, there is also a rope stretched out forwards. Although it appears to be pointing slightly downwards, it could be a towrope from some horses giving the steam tug a helpful pull.
(Photo, John Aldritt.)

the rails with iron ones, allowing the use of trucks able to carry two tons. The quarry was sub-let to contractors, and a certain level of output stipulated, the company taking over if production fell below this tonnage. In 1803 the contract prices were 11d per ton for getting and delivering, with 7d per ton being paid for baring the rock.[30]

Traffic in Yorkshire had increased greatly by 1799, which caused problems with wharf space at Leeds, and regulations were introduced for the control of trade there. Overcrowding was caused by goods being loaded here for passage down the Aire and Calder and to discourage this a minimum toll equal to eight miles was placed on all traffic passing downwards through Leeds Lock. Orders were given for the wharfs to be tidied up, so that timber floating in the basin could be stored on the bank.

John Hammond, the company's agent at Leeds, was told to arrange mooring so that boats did not impede passage, and regulations were brought in to control the warehouse, open from 6am to 8pm in the summer months, in winter from 8am to 6pm. To reduce the risk of fire, candles could only be used in a lanthorn, and goods not consigned to a particular carrier were to be placed on the first available vessel. This helped to overcome favouritism when the company's agent was also employed by a carrier, as sometimes happened.[31]

April 1796 brought a change in the carrying trade in Yorkshire. Until then Mr. Whitaker and Sons had an agreement with the company allowing them a virtual monopoly of the general cargo trade. They also controlled the company's warehouses, with the company agent at each warehouse sometimes being employed by Whitakers as well. However, from that date the company decided that it ought not to favour any single carrier and the monopoly was withdrawn. This led to the Leeds and Burnley Union Company being formed, an amalgamation of individual carriers based on the Yorkshire end of the canal. A similar concern, the Liverpool Union Company, was operating in Lancashire.

These union companies were formed on many canals by small carrying firms to reduce the difficulty of creating a large carrying fleet. Although the canal company was not allowed to carry on its own account, they did have boats built for others to operate, in order to improve the service. The company also collected money from those to whom goods were consigned, on behalf of the carriers. This was only done for long-distance cargoes, consigned to places beyond the canal, when the money was collected by the warehouse keeper, as otherwise the boat would have been held up until the bill had been paid.

A report by Joseph Priestley, presented in July 1793, gave estimates of traffic on the canal when completed, with some figures for the trade already being carried. 20,000 tons of merchandise was delivered annually to Kildwick from Leeds and Hull, where it was transhipped to road carriage for transport to the Burnley and Blackburn areas. A further 10,000 tons came from Liverpool to Wigan for forwarding to East Lancashire, the same tonnage travelling there by way of Manchester or the Calder. The increased income from this traffic, when the canal was completed, would be £10,750 with a further £18,250 coming from coal, stone and limestone. This increase was equal to the total income which the canal was already receiving.

The completion of the canal from Gargrave to Henfield had cost £336,753, bringing the total expenditure on the canal to £554,569, exclusive of the cost of the Douglas Navigation. By 1804 the canal income was £51,838, which, after expenses and interest charges had been deducted, left £23,018 to be distributed as dividend of £8 per share. The income was derived as follows: Yorkshire side £14,622, an almost threefold increase from the £3,824 obtained in 1788, Lancashire side £23,652 and Douglas Navigation £11,376, the rest coming from rents, packet boats etc. The biggest rise in traffic in Lancashire had been in coal delivered to Liverpool. This had risen from about 100,000 tons per year in 1788 to 176,000 tons in 1804.

One of the best photographs ever taken of a working horse-drawn barge. The quintessential Leeds and Liverpool Canal scene, with the general cargo boat Tiger *seen here with her crew and the boatman's wife. Everything is in its place – towing masts and lutchet in the upright positions, sheets tidily fixed over the hold, water barrel and vent cover smartly painted and decorations adorning the stern. It would be difficult to beat this as an evocation of a way of life and method of transport long since lost.* (Photo, B.W.B.)

Chapter Five

'A pleasant and beautiful scene'

The canal is completed
1804 – 1820

Y the end of 1804 the Rochdale Canal had been completed, becoming the first trans-Pennine canal to be fully operational. The effect was felt immediately by the Leeds and Liverpool. Mr Townsend, the clerk at Wigan, reported in July 1805 that, during the previous three months, between 160 and 200 tons of goods destined for Leeds and Yorkshire, which had previously been sent through Wigan, was now going by the Rochdale. He suggested that four packet boats should be introduced between Liverpool and Wigan, but the committee did not agree. Perhaps they realised that the future of the canal now lay more in the servicing of the cotton, textile and other industries which were developing along the banks of the canal, than in cross-country trade.

At this time, before weaving had been mechanised, there were many spinning mills in East Lancashire, and the transportation of raw cotton was an important part of the canal's trade. As the century progressed the area became predominantly involved with weaving, with a consequent reduction in the importance of the transport of baled cotton by canal. Wool, though, was always a major cargo, with bales imported at Liverpool being carried to Yorkshire, while spun yarn was brought back to East Lancashire, particularly during the first half of the century, for the use of handloom weavers.

The cotton industry was able to mechanise the spinning and weaving processes far sooner than the woollen and worsted industries of Yorkshire because cotton fibres withstood the hard usage given by machines much better than wool. As a result, steam-powered factories developed in Lancashire at a faster rate than in Yorkshire, where hand spinning and weaving of woollen cloth continued well into the nineteenth century, though in Bradford, factories were being established for the worsted trades, as machines were soon developed to cope with the long fibres used for this type of material. This was a time of rapid expansion in Bradford. In 1801 only one 15-horsepower steam-powered mill was to be found there, but by 1815 there were ten, using a total of 250hp. This development continued throughout the century, and by 1850 there were 129 steam-powered mills using almost 3,000hp.

The two main requirements of steam power are coal and water, both of which could be supplied readily by the canal. Water was used to condense the steam used by the engines, thereby improving the efficiency. March 1808 saw the first request for condensing water for a steam engine used in textiles, when Robert Hargreaves approached the company with regard to the one at his mill in Habergham Eaves, near Burnley. The company allowed him to use their water, provided that it was returned to the canal after use, charging him a shilling a year for the privilege. These conditions had also been stipulated in 1791 when Bateman, Greaves and Co. of Liverpool had been granted similar rights for a steam engine, though theirs was not a textile factory. The supply of water for condensing was later to become a profitable sideline for the company, with the added advantage that the warm water returned to the canal made ice less of a problem in winter.

The Leigh Branch is proposed

THE need to supply the Lancashire textile industry became a major factor in the canal's future development. The completion of the Bridgewater Canal extension from Worsley to Leigh tempted the committee, in 1800, to approach the Duke of Bridgewater, suggesting a branch from Wigan to his canal.[1] This would create a valuable link between East Lancashire and Manchester, the commercial centre of the cotton industry.

After visits by Priestley and Hardy, (he had been the company's law clerk for many years) the Duke agreed, in October 1801, to the connecting branch, although stipulating that there should be an agreement with the Lancaster respecting the junction of the two canals at Heapey. As we have seen, the Lancaster had already approached him proposing a wagon way from their canal at Westhoughton to his canal terminus at Leigh. For the use of this through route to Manchester, the Duke had set them a rate of 2/6d per ton for the use of his canal, which he now also suggested to the Leeds and Liverpool. He further proposed that they should charge a minimum of 1d per ton per mile for goods passing between Liverpool and Leigh. The Duke was concerned to make the toll uneconomic to restrict the competition with his canal for traffic from Liverpool to Manchester.

As the company was probably more interested in traffic to East Lancashire, they agreed to these conditions and Fletcher surveyed the line, proposing that the canal at Wigan be raised fourteen feet by two locks, which enabled the River Douglas to be crossed and reduced the amount of excavation necessary. A further two locks would then be needed to lower the level to that of the Bridgewater. These were to be built at Dover, and near the road from Leigh to Newton. The cost of the whole branch was estimated at £29,826.[2] A Bill was then drawn up for presentation to Parliament, including the rates agreed with the Duke, and with clauses allowing the Lancaster's tramway to Leigh.

The Bill was progressing satisfactorily through Parliament, during April 1803, when the Duke died. His agent R. H. Bradshaw, who took over control of his affairs as trustee, expressed concern over the rates which had been agreed, and suggested that the Duke had also had second thoughts about these before he died. He then proposed that the Bill should be postponed until the following session, giving time for further discussions. This the committee would not agree to, so Bradshaw withdrew his support, forcing the Leeds and Liverpool to remove their Bill from Parliament.

The Red Moss scheme is aired again

THE failure of the Leeds and Liverpool to gain access to Manchester via the Bridgewater Canal led to the Red Moss scheme being resurrected by the Manchester, Bolton and Bury Canal. After an approach in February 1797, to which the committee sent a very non-commital reply, the Manchester, Bolton and Bury suggested in July 1799 that they were about to start work on the flight of locks needed for the branch at Bolton (despite not having obtained the Act of Parliament necessary). The Leeds and Liverpool replied that they would be unable to start work on the section of the deviation at Red Moss for some time, as only enough money was available to them to complete their canal as far as Henfield.[3]

Following the failure of the Leigh Branch Bill, however, a new survey and estimate of the Red Moss line was authorised in May 1805. The Henfield to Red Moss length of the main line was now expected to cost £245,275, whilst the relatively short but difficult section down to Wigan, including the 279 feet of lockage, came to £101,725. By September the route from Wigan to Red Moss had been agreed, and the committee arranged to meet the Manchester, Bolton and Bury committee, who now declined to start work on their branch from Bolton to Red Moss.[4] Because of this the committee, in April 1806, agreed that it would be more beneficial to continue work on the line from Henfield to Blackburn and to improve their communication with Yorkshire, instead of commencing construction from Wigan, in the hope that Manchester could be reached when, or if, the Manchester, Bolton and Bury built their branch to Red Moss.

One wonders how enthusiastic the Leeds and Liverpool was about using the Red Moss scheme for traffic between Liverpool and Manchester. Over 500 feet of unnecessary lockage would be needed and, having agreed to the Lancaster's line being built before their deviation, there would be serious problems over the water supply to the summit level at Red Moss.

With work starting again at Henfield, several small deviations from the line agreed in the 1794 Act were suggested to the company, but only one was of any significance. In 1800 they were approached by Jonathan Peel, whose textile printing and dyeing works at Church were one of the most important factories in Britain at that time. He requested that the line of the canal be altered such that, instead of being carried up the valley of the Hyndburn towards Accrington, where the junction with the Haslingden Canal had been proposed, the canal should pass to the west of his works, rejoining the Parliamentary line at Church.

Here we are looking up the deviated line from the sharp bend at Church Wharf; the original line was to have continued off to the right towards Accrington.
(Photo, author's collection.)

The reason for the deviation was probably Peel's concern over maintaining the supply of clean water, essential for textile printing, to his works. This would have been considerably interrupted by the construction of the canal across the valley above his works. The deviation was agreed, despite the increase in size of embankment needed for crossing the Hyndburn lower down the valley. A decrease in the length of the canal to be built was some compensation. This is the reason for the unusually sharp, right-angle bend in the canal at Church wharf. The permission of Lord Petre, the landowner, was needed for the deviation, which he granted, provided that on the length of canal next to the grounds of Dunkenhalgh Park, the towpath was built on the opposite bank, to reduce the opportunities for poaching and other interference to his lands.[5]

Blackburn is reached

THE canal was opened as far as Peel's works at Church by 1808, but the three large embankments between there and Rishton took several years to consolidate sufficiently before they could be filled with water. Work was not helped by continual wet weather in 1808 and 1809, and the excavation through the high ground between Rishton and Whitebirk was affected as well. The nine miles to Blackburn were eventually opened in June 1810, the *Blackburn Mail* reporting:

> Never since this publication was first started has it been in the power of any of the editors to record so pleasant a scene as was exhibited on Thursday last, viz. the opening of the Leeds and Liverpool Canal. There is now a direct communication between this town and Hull; and should the Corsican Tyrant ever consent to peace, and free trade with the Continent, Blackburn may with facility send her manufactures by water to most of the sea ports of Germany. If a person who had been absent from this town five years were to come to it from Burnley, he could hardly recognise that he had ever seen this place before . . . the canal has caused so great an alteration in the south-easterly part, where many new houses are erected.

A procession of 27 boats left Henfield for Blackburn to celebrate the opening, carrying vast numbers of people including the committee and many of the canal proprietors, the newspaper continuing:

> All the vessels, except the coal flats, had flags and pendants flying; this tended much to beautify the scene; and the bands alternately playing, rendered it a treat both for the eye and ear. When the procession passed Messrs. Peels' print-works, it was greeted by a number of ladies, who stood upon a temporary balcony, and, in return, repeated cheers were given them from the barges.
>
> When the procession approached near Blackburn, the vessels were much crowded by persons forcing themselves on board under the different bridges. On its arrival at Eanam, we suppose were not less than 7,000 persons on the water. Multitudes kept pace with the vessels all the way from Henfield; which, when joined to the great number of spectators assembled at Eanam, formed a concourse of at least 25,000 persons, besides the persons on board the different vessels . . .
>
> . . . We are happy to say, no fatal accident occurred . . . A man on board one of the vessels at Eanam, imprudently thrusting a red-hot poker into the mouth of a small cannon, which was charged with powder and wadding, had his hand most dreadfully shattered. Two children and three men fell into the water during the passage from Henfield. These were the only accidents worthy of notice.

The celebrations continued into the evening when, after a suitable repast, there was dancing and martial music. The opening of the canal to the town must surely have been a memorable occasion.

Linking up with the Lancaster Canal

HAVING reached Blackburn the committee now realised that a final decision must be made regarding the link with the Lancaster and the continuation of their line from Heapey to Wigan. Yet more negotiations were entered into with the Lancaster, who had already purchased the land necessary for the locks and junction at Heapey, and a final agreement was made whereby the Leeds and Liverpool would be built to join the Lancaster at Johnson's Hillock, near Heapey, and would make use of the Lancaster's cut from there to Kirkless (basically Top Lock at Wigan).[6]

The two companies were to complete the work required within three years. The Lancaster had to build the locks at Heapey and to extend their canal about half a mile to Kirkless, while the Leeds and Liverpool were to complete the canal from Blackburn to Heapey, and build the considerable flight of locks from Kirkless down into Wigan. All the locks were to be built to the dimensions of the Upper Douglas Navigation, which at that time would accommodate boats of sixty-two feet in length. The water supplies of each company were protected; in particular the Lancaster was not allowed to use those of the Leeds and Liverpool for supplying the locks which they proposed to build down to the northern section of their canal at Preston. The tonnage charged for merchandise on the Lancaster was reduced from 2d to 1½d per ton per mile, the same as that charged by the Leeds and Liverpool, with the proviso that no junction with the Manchester, Bolton and Bury should be made, thus effectively destroying any possibility of the Red Moss extension now being built.

Both canals profited by the agreement. The Leeds and Liverpool was able to complete its trans-Pennine link with far less financial outlay, while the Lancaster would at last have a regular water supply for its southern end, on which coal traffic had been continually disrupted during the summer months, with boats often being forced to carry less than half their full load; on occasion the canal had closed for weeks at a time due to lack of water. Much of their water came from coal mines, which were allowed to pump drainage water into the canal. This was no replacement for a regular supply, unobtainable because the Leeds and Liverpool owned the rights to the water of the River Douglas, whose head waters were crossed by the canal.

Work on the canal from Blackburn to Heapey was soon underway, and by April 1812 they were employing 45 masons, 26 quarrymen, 18 labourers, 20 horses, 10 carts, 141 diggers, 31 daymen and 21 carpenters. By June the line from Kirkless to Wigan was also set out, work starting there in October. There were problems with the contractors on this stretch, however, and there were delays because of lack of capital, possibly caused by the rapid rise in wages at this time. Loans were arranged by the company in an effort to reduce the interruption to work.[7]

All the usual difficulties were evident, with the embankments over the River Darwen and at Roddlesworth taking longer than envisaged to become stable, poor weather retarding the consolidation of the earth banking. By June 1816, the Lancaster wrote to the committee requesting that the Blackburn to Heapey length be opened immediately. They had good reason to complain, as it had taken almost two years longer than the three agreed for the canal to be completed. The committee replied that the opening would take place as soon as possible, though the Liverpool to Wigan length needed to be cleaned out beforehand.

The canal is completed

THE canal was finally opened on Saturday 19th October 1816, when one of the company's barges, together with one belonging to the Union Company, set out from Leeds for Liverpool, the *Leeds Mercury* reporting:

> . . . On entering the first lock, the band struck up the national air of 'God save the King.' The barge of the proprietors bore a flag, in which was inscribed the name of 'John Hustler', the engineer, under whose superintendence a considerable part of the work had been completed. It was intended that another barge belonging to the proprietors, called the 'Joseph Priestley' should have taken part in the procession, but some mischance which happened to it on its voyage to Leeds defeated this

part of the plan; all the sloops in the basin were decorated with streamers, and the whole formed a truly animated and delightful scene.[8]

By Monday, after overnight stops at Skipton and Burnley, they had reached Blackburn, where the bells were rung upon their arrival. The next day the two barges, together with a number of other vessels, set out along the new section of canal. At Johnsons' Hillock locks near where the two canals meet, they were joined by the Lancaster Canal committee for a celebratory lunch. After this, they proceeded to Wigan. On passing Haigh Hall, Lord Balcarres saluted the procession with cannon, joining the party for the descent of the locks, followed by a dinner laid on by Col. Clayton. Liverpool was finally reached at five o'clock on Wednesday afternoon, to another tremendous reception.

O'er hill and down dale – the building of the canal

AS we have seen, many problems were encountered during the construction of the Leeds and Liverpool. Foulridge Tunnel and Burnley Embankment both created considerable headaches for the engineers and navvies, and other aqueducts, locks and embankments had presented difficulties. In many respects, the planning of the Leeds and Liverpool illustrates all the various phases of canal thinking, as well as the advances in civil engineering that took place over the forty-five year period of its construction.

Engineering features, warehouses, stables, reservoirs and feeder streams on the Leeds and Liverpool Canal.

The first sections to be built, from Gargrave to Leeds and from

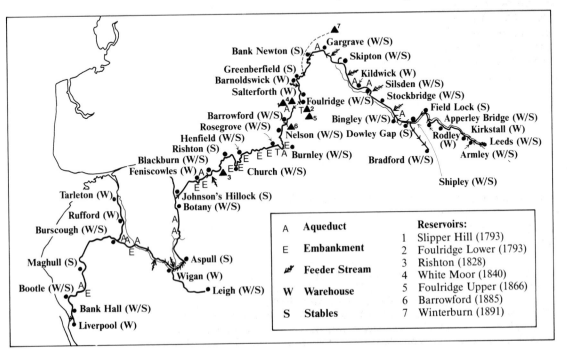

The Newburgh Aqueduct, one of the main engineering features on the Liverpool length opened in 1774. The River Douglas was weired to form the navigation and would have been much deeper then than now.
(Photo, author's collection.)

Liverpool to Newburgh, were fairly straightforward. On the former section the canal followed the River Aire and only a small number of aqueducts was required to carry the canal over obstacles as it moved up the valley. On the latter, the canal took a circuitous route so that only a short embankment and aqueduct were required to carry the canal over the River Alt near Aintree. Similarly, the canal was built along the contour lines from Gargrave to the summit level, as can be seen from the winding route around East Marton.

Having said this, early schemes for the canal tended to minimise the problems that major obstacles could cause, while some engineers seemed to enjoy planning huge engineering works. Thus the intended aqueduct at Whalley was only the grandest of several huge works that would have been needed on the original Parliamentary line. By intending to build the canal further north, each of the valleys that had to be crossed was deeper – for example, the Darwen Valley at Hoghton would have needed an embankment or a long, high aqueduct rather like the impressive railway viaduct that can still be seen there today.

By the latter stages of construction, engineers seemed to be more realistic but also more confident. The decision to lower the summit level and build a tunnel shows not only a more confident approach to the construction, but also a more realistic view of the water supply needed. The higher the summit level, the less water would be available.

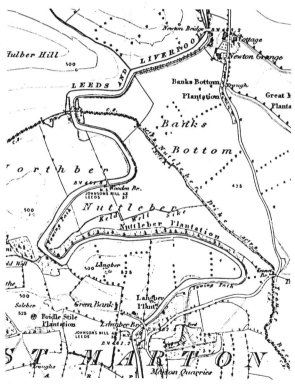

What better illustration of a contour canal than this section of the Leeds and Liverpool at East Marton, where the canal meanders around the hills without a single lock in sight.

This balance between the ease and cost of construction, the supply of water and the expected volume of traffic, was the canal engineer's prime consideration.

As we have seen, Foulridge Tunnel had to be built in two sections through the sand and rock and all sorts of problems with soft ground, excessive water and poor stonework had been encountered. Nevertheless, it was a major achievement and still the most important engineering work on the canal.

The route chosen between Barrowford and the Lancaster Canal shows how the confidence of civil engineers had increased. There were many valleys to be crossed, which were boldly traversed by large embankments. Besides the well-known embankment at Burnley, there were eight others, some higher, though none longer than 'the straight mile', as it is known locally, or 'Burnley val' as the boatmen called it. The other embankments were at Swinden, Bentley Brook, Altham, Church (where there were three), Blackburn and Roddlesworth. The line of the canal at Church may seem tortuous, but an embankment to avoid this detour would have had to have been at least 120 feet high. This would have been prohibitively expensive, even if the technical problems could have been overcome.

The navvies must also have had their problems. Tunnelling in particular was dangerous, and many deaths and injuries occurred. As a result of the collapse of scaffolding in the tunnel, George Clark and Hugh Frazer received one guinea each for their injuries, while Alexander and James Frazer were paid half a guinea. The company also settled the surgeon's bill of one guinea. Besides danger at work, the navvies could be subjected to intimidation by the local population. The riot at Barrowford and Marsden in 1792 is one example. It was only stopped by the intervention of Captain Clayton, a local justice of the peace. The company threatened to prosecute any person inciting further trouble, and five hundred notices to this effect were distributed in the area.[9]

The numbers of men employed on construction varied from 250 to 500. Fewer were employed at harvest time, and Whitworth took care to set out the line after the harvest had been collected, to reduce damage.[10] During September 1796, when Gannow Tunnel and the embankment at Burnley were under construction, 217 men were employed. There were eight miners, twenty-five diggers and twenty-seven stone getters and masons working for contractors on the tunnel, with seventy-four diggers, thirty-six masons and ten labourers working elsewhere. The company provided a further thirty-six carpenters and labourers. The engineer reported progress monthly to the committee, with details of those employed, even noting the numbers of horses and carts used. Surveying the route and negotiating with landowners were further aspects of the engineer's work. A good example of this can be seen in 1796 when, as the line progressed westward, it had to be marked out and agreement reached for land purchase.

Major Clayton, of Little Harwood, the committee member responsible for obtaining land in East Lancashire, wrote to Lord Petre, regarding his land in Rishton:

> We have always appreciated so much friendship from your Lordship, in support of that project, that you are strictly entitled to every information,

respecting its progress; and the more so, when we are advanced so far westward, as that it shall become necessary to begin to trespass upon your Lordships property. We have taken the liberty to order the surveyor to set out the line, in one part of the township of Rishton, where there is some deep cutting and difficult work. It is the rule with us, never to break the ground until we have settled with the owner thereof. Your Lordships property in Rishton happens to be in life lease, therefore separate bargains must be made, not only with your Lordship, but with the tenants who hold separate leases.[11]

The deep cutting mentioned was from Whitebirk to Rishton, where the canal crossed the high ground between the Rivers Darwen and Calder.

Although the line appears to have been set out in 1796, it was not until 1807, with construction about to begin, that the price for the land was agreed. Mr A. Cottam had assessed the land for George Petre the previous year and the canal company obtained their own valuations from Mr Eccles and Mr Brandwood of Blackburn. When prices differed, they were settled by one Mr Binns of Gisburn. The price paid for the land was based upon its yearly rental, usually being equal to the income over thirty years. Rents here varied from twenty shillings to 155/- per acre, dependent upon whether it was pasture or arable, and whether it had been regularly limed or used for industry. The highest valued was for that containing housing; the lowest for mossland. The tenants agreed to accept the value which was arranged with George Petre.[12]

The price agreed, work could commence, and the canal through Rishton was completed in 1810. The damage done to the land not used for the canal was then assessed. Payment had to be made for stone obtained from local quarries, and the repair of fences. Where soil had been removed, the company had to pay the equivalent of twenty years' rent, while half that was sufficient for the slopes alongside the canal. In these cases, the landowner retained the land and was in effect being paid for the time taken for it to recover.

An initial payment of £2,000 was made to Petre in 1807, and a further £902 in 1811 for the land used. A final payment of £981 for damages was made in 1812, following a letter from Petre's agent, John Harper, demanding a settlement.[13] Petre's tenants' rents had already been reduced by an amount equivalent to the land taken by the canal, and he had already paid them for damages during construction; the canal was open, and earning revenue for the proprietors, so he was the only party not receiving any benefit from the canal. There were still matters outstanding in 1822, when he complained to the committee about repairs needed to fences and watercourses. He was also worried about trespass, saying that:

> Persons employed by the canal proprietors bring men from Blackburn or other places with nets and dogs pretending to fish in the canal through Rishton etc.[14]

The company tried to keep on the right side of large landowners like Petre, from whom they rented land for their reservoir at Rishton and their warehouse at Henfield. In 1851, John Croasdale built a cotton mill alongside the canal at Rishton, on land belonging to Petre. When Croasdale tried to obtain access for carts to his mill along the towpath, he was only granted its use as a footpath for his workmen on payment

Above: One of the most famous features of the Leeds and Liverpool, the five-rise at Bingley. This is a particularly sharp photograph from the 1890s, when there was a carpenter's shop at the bottom. Swing bridges were usually constructed on the spare land on the right.
(Photo, author's collection.)

Right: A recent photograph of the three-rise at Bingley. Although their heavy use of water made riser locks like these suitable for river navigations, this was a considerable disadvantage on a canal like the Leeds and Liverpool, and later sections of the canal were built with flights of single locks instead. It did mean, however, that the section below Bingley was never short of water.
(Photo, author's collection.)

121

Top left: *The dramatic setting of the Bingley five-rise is seen from this recent photograph, which was taken from the top of the three-rise nearby.* (Photo, author's collection.)

Left: *Originally the floors of the locks were wooden (now replaced with concrete). Lock gates needed to be replaced occasionally, as shown on both pictures (left). In the bottom picture a new lockgate has just been delivered by boat and is being lifted into position by sheer legs.* (Photo, B.W.B.)

Top right: *Obviously the water would be drained out while the work was undertaken. Here the cills, which were fitted to the bottom of the lock to create a seal when the gate was closed, are being repaired (see also page 169.)* (Photo, author's collection.)

Right: *The company owned several steam launches for use by the committee during inspections of the canal. The* Alexandria *seen here was mainly used on the Yorkshire section. Her engine and hull still survive at the boat museum at Ellesmere Port.*

Right: *If a section of canal had to be drained, stop planks would be placed at each end of the length. They were also inserted at many points overnight during the Second World War as a protection against flooding if the canal was bombed. Originall,y automatic stop planks were installed at either end of embankments to reduce problems if there was a breach; some still remain, although they have been inoperative for many years. Here a coal boat waits at Red Cote Bridge near Leeds for the canal to be reopened.* (Photo, Leeds City Libraries.)

An early photograph of the spoon dredger Sir Robert at Kildwick. The spoon was raised and lowered by the crane being operated by the man on the left. When it was on the bed of the canal, the man on the right would fill the spoon with rubbish by manipulating the wooden handle which he is holding. When it was full it would be raised and emptied into the boat. Note also the crane on the towpath.

Steam power was used for dredging from the end of the nineteenth century. Here dredger Noll, together with its mud hoppers, is tied up at a dredging tip. The steam crane behind was used to unload the hoppers.

Today diesel and hydraulic power are used. This recent photograph shows a section of canal being piled to protect the canal bank from erosion. (Photo, Ben Shaw.)

A section of the first edition O.S. map showing the area around Crook. There were dozens of tramroads and inclined planes from collieries to the canal throughout the Douglas Valley and the Wigan area in general. Here we can see a major one from Standish Colliery down to the canal near Crook Hall. Another joins the opposite side of the canal nearby. Of greater interest, however, is the Crook 'Tunnel Canal' marked here running northwards. This was a branch which led into a tunnel and on to a large colliery just off the map at the top. The end of the branch is now used for moorings, while the staithe opposite is still just visible.

(Reproduced by permission of the County Archivist, Lancashire Record Office.)

of five shillings per annum. He appealed to Petre, who approached the committee, which granted Croasdale the required access for one pound per annum, provided a suitable fence was built along the canal bank.[15]

Branches and tramways

WHEN the canal had first been promoted it had been intended to build branches to serve towns and industries not on the main system. Some small branches had been built, such as that at Rain Hall Rock for the supply of limestone, and arms off the canal were constructed by collieries at Hapton and Altham in 1805 to reduce interruption to traffic on the main line from boats loading and waiting to load.[16] A longer branch in the same area had been suggested in 1799, to connect Mr Shuttleworth's collieries in Ightenhill Park to the canal east of Gannow Tunnel. The branch was mentioned in the 1794 Act, probably to appease the opposition of Mr Shuttleworth, whose agent Whyman had campaigned against the deviation plan. Fletcher laid out a line for the branch and Whyman was to contract for the purchase of the land

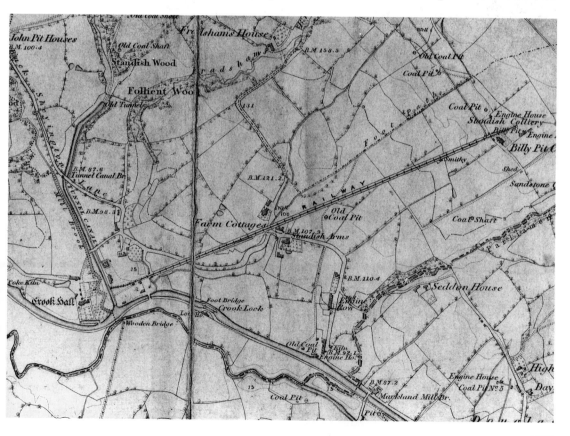

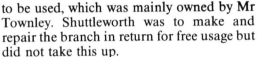

to be used, which was mainly owned by Mr Townley. Shuttleworth was to make and repair the branch in return for free usage but did not take this up.

In 1821, some of the Yorkshire proprietors proposed that a branch could be built to Keighley. The work was to have included a twelve-arch aqueduct across the River Aire and an embankment over half a mile long and was to be financed locally at a cost estimated at £31,455. Perhaps this was too expensive as no further action was taken and the canal warehouses at Stockbridge continued to serve the town.[17]

There were several other short branches or arms built from the canal, mainly to coal mines in the Wigan area. A tunnel into a coal mine at Crooke, which worked from 1798 to around 1850, was particularly notable, where narrow boats, similar to those at Worsley, entered the mine to load.[18] The old lock into the Douglas at Gathurst continued to be used as access to the tramway staithes used by mines around Orrell to the south of the river. One of these tramways, from Clarke's colliery in Orrell to the canal at Crooke, is particularly notable as it was here that the first steam locomotives in Lancashire were operated. Robert Daglish, the colliery's manager, arranged for three locomotives to be built at Haigh Foundry under Blenkinsop's patent. They were similar to those used on the Middleton Railway in Leeds, the first one being built in 1812. To provide traction, Blenkinsop's design used a toothed gear on the engine, which engaged with lugs cast into the side of the rails. These engines used steam at the then high pressure of thirty-six pounds per square inch, and could draw up to thirty wagons, each carrying three tons, on the level.[19] Despite their success, horses and stationary steam winding engines were used on other tramways in the area, and steam locomotives did not become widely used until the latter part of the nineteenth century. By this time many of the lines serving the canal had closed. Wigan was the main centre for such tramways, but they could also be found at many other places, mainly where collieries or quarries fed the canal.

The company in financial difficulties

THE canal had cost £877,616, including the purchase of the Douglas Navigation and the construction of the branch to Tarleton, a sum far in excess of Brindley's original estimate of £259,777. For this, the company had built a canal 116 miles in length (excluding the Lancaster) at a cost per mile of £7,500. Finance had been procured from three sources – the issue of shares, the income from tolls and by borrowing money against the future income of the canal.

In 1812, before the canal had been completed, some of the proprietors, particularly a group from London, were concerned that, by using the income from tolls in this way, the dividend paid to them by the company was reduced. They considered that a greater return could be provided by increasing the number of shares, and using the money so raised in paying off the company's debts and completing construction of the canal. All the income from tolls could then be used to pay what they considered a reasonable dividend.[20] There was considerable opposition to such a scheme which was overruled.

A couple of years later Priestley produced a report on methods of liquidating the company's debt, which at that time amounted to £400,000. He suggested three solutions. The first involved creating about 1,951 new shares, in addition to the 2,880 which had already been issued. In the second, the debt would be divided among the existing shareholders in proportion to their shareholding. As the income from the canal increased, the dividend paid to each shareholder would vary, depending upon which of these two schemes was adopted. His final solution was to create a sinking fund into which the income would be paid, using this to discharge the debt. The payment of a dividend would be suspended until the debt had been extinguished. He thought this last would be inconvenient for those who held shares for life only and relied upon the dividend for their income.

Instead of adopting any of these schemes the committee decided in November 1815 that they would apply to Parliament for an Act to raise more money and to enable them to increase the tonnage rates allowed in the earlier Acts. The rates per mile which the company charged had not been increased since the 1770 Act and were still at the original level of ½d per ton for bricks, limestone etc, 1d per ton for coal and lime, and 1½d per ton on timber and merchandise. They hoped to raise these to 1d, 1½d, and 2½d per ton respectively. The rates charged by other canal companies were generally higher than those on the Leeds and Liverpool – in fact, many were above the proposed increased rates. For example, the Rochdale charged 4d per ton per mile for merchandise and 2d per ton per mile for coal; the Bradford Canal charged 3d for merchandise and 2d for coal. And the increases would only bring the Leeds and Liverpool into line with tolls charged on the Lancaster.

Despite this there was considerable opposition from the traders on the canal. That from the coal dealers in Liverpool was especially fierce. They complained that they already paid above the rate stipulated in the original Act because they used the Upper Douglas, where the rates allowed to the Douglas Navigation were still in force, resulting in charges of 3/9 per ton from Wigan to Liverpool, instead of the 2/6 per ton which should be paid under the 1770 Act. They were also concerned as to the effect of the increases on the Irish coal trade and on return traffic through Liverpool, such as yarn, corn and beef, which could develop when the canal was opened completely.

Opposition from the ironfounders of Bradford was almost as strong. They implied that the opening of the canal had been put back for a year by the junction with the Lancaster being obstructed by a mound of earth placed in the canal by the company's workmen.[21] Because of this opposition the company was forced to withdraw their Bill from Parliament following its second reading.

However, the company's income still needed to be increased and in June 1816 various alterations to the financial arrangements were suggested. The price of limestone sold by the company was below that of other producers and so they raised their price, though realising that this would reduce sales. In compensation they expected that the reduction in this trade on the summit would ensure a better supply of water for the increase in merchandise traffic which they expected when the canal was opened throughout.[22]

Under the 1783 Act they had been authorised to charge a minimum tonnage equal to 20 tons on all traffic. This had only been charged occasionally but was now introduced universally. The yards and staithes at Liverpool which had been let at low rents to encourage trade now had them increased, as were the tolls on slack and merchandise sent to the town. The advanced rate charged on the Douglas, which was to have been repealed when the canal was completed, was retained. Legally, the reduction need only be effected when the Parliamentary line was finished. By using the Lancaster from Heapey to Kirkless, the canal had technically not been completed, and the higher charge could remain. These increases must have gone some considerable way to compensating the company for the loss of its Bill. They certainly annoyed the coal traders, who continued to complain over the high rates to Liverpool and Preston, though the loss of trade which they complained about was probably a result of the national depression, following the end of the Napoleonic and American wars in 1815. Not all the traders on the canal were unhappy as, with the opening of the canal across the Pennines, the partners in the Leeds Union Company of Traders said that they would remove all their boats and trade from the Rochdale to the Leeds and Liverpool.[23]

A junction with the Bridgewater Canal at Leigh

WITH the completion of the canal, thoughts again turned towards a branch to the Bridgewater at Leigh. After the initial attempt to obtain an Act had failed in 1803, a further application was made in 1809. Bradshaw, for the Devisees of the Bridgewater Estates, had agreed to the junction provided that the minimum tonnage charged on merchandise from Liverpool to Manchester would be one penny per ton per mile and that a branch canal or railway be provided from the canal at Platt Bridge to the Duke's collieries at Low Hall. These conditions were soon agreed. Further clauses were included to vary the tonnage on coal, depending on its quality; to increase tonnage rates; and to borrow a further £500,000 to complete the main line and the branch to Leigh.

The Bill encountered considerable opposition, and the clauses relating to tonnage had to be withdrawn. Bradshaw then insisted on a clause restraining the company from making a junction with any other canal which would enable them to obtain an alternative route to Manchester. The Rochdale Canal initially opposed this clause, bringing it to the attention of the Manchester, Bolton and Bury, who complained that they already had an agreement to construct such a junction with the Leeds and Liverpool, at Red Moss, dating back to 1794. Following this agreement, they had constructed their canal with broad locks, at an additional expense of £20,000.[24]

The Leeds and Liverpool retorted that the application in 1794 for an Act to construct the Red Moss branch had failed and that subsequently, at a joint meeting of the two companies, the agreement respecting the exclusive approach to Manchester by such a branch had been ended. The decision of the Manchester, Bolton and Bury to construct a broad canal postdated this meeting and so could not have been influenced by the Leeds and Liverpool. In an attempt to placate the opposition and to save their Bill, the Leeds and Liverpool then tried to have the possibility of reaching Manchester by the Manchester, Bolton and Bury included in the offending clause. None of the

The Leeds and Liverpool Canal warehouses at the junction with the Bridgewater Canal at Leigh. The smaller stone building on the left is the original warehouse and the building to the right is an extension built when improvements were undertaken to the canal in the 1880s.
(Photo, author's collection.)

parties would agree to this, and suspecting that it would fail, they withdrew the Bill. With the Manchester, Bolton and Bury and the Bridgewater arguing between each other, the Lancaster approached the Leeds and Liverpool and agreed to withdraw their clause for the wagon way from their canal to Leigh. This was replaced, as mentioned previously, by an agreement for the junctions at Heapey and Kirklees, once the two companies had come to terms concerning their respective interests.

Discussions continued with Bradshaw about the Leigh branch, and, in July 1814, another attempt was made to come to some arrangement. This again ended in failure. Finally, in September 1818, a draft agreement was set out, and application made to Parliament, where the Act was quickly passed, without opposition, and assent given on 21 June 1819. Tolls similar to the main canal were authorised, though 4d per ton was allowed on all traffic carried on the proposed railway from Platt Bridge to Low Hall, near Hindley. However, all goods passing the junction at Leigh were subject to a toll of 1/2 per ton, except for flags which only paid 2d per ton, payable to the Bridgewater, although payment of this toll exempted those goods from the compensation toll paid at Castlefield if they were destined for the Rochdale Canal. It also allowed the use of the Bridgewater wharfs and warehouses at Manchester for four days without payment. In the original Bill the Bridgewater were to be entitled to wharfs on the Leeds and Liverpool though, in lieu of this, they eventually agreed to a payment of £5,000. Several clauses related exclusively to the Leeds and Liverpool, changing clauses in previous Acts. There were two of significance, the first concerning empty boats and the payment of the twenty-ton minimum toll. The company had been taken to court to decide which boats had to pay this minimum, and empty boats were to be exempted. Instead they had to pay 5/- when passing through the first lock which they came to. The other major clause empowered the company to raise a further £280,000 either by borrowing, loans from shareholders or by creating new shares. Work went ahead speedily and the branch was opened in December 1820, having cost £61,419. The previous June, Fletcher had informed the committee that the Leigh to Worsley section of the Bridgewater was not as deep as the Leeds and Liverpool. A complaint was sent to Bradshaw but improvements were not undertaken until after the branch was opened when, in the following March, the traders on the line also complained.

With the completion of the Leigh Branch, the Leeds and Liverpool was connected to the rest of the canal system. There was a desire on the part of some traders to use narrow boats on traffic to and from the narrow canals around Manchester. The Act had foreseen this and allowed two narrow boats to be charged the same toll as for one wide boat, the tonnage carried being approximately equal. Unfortunately, the locks had been built 62 feet in length and in November 1821 Pickfords wrote to the committee asking for them to be lengthened to 72 feet so that their narrow boats could use the canal through to Wigan and Liverpool.[25] Fletcher made an estimate of the cost, initially supposing that an extra pair of gates would be added at the lower end to extend each lock. The shorter Leeds and Liverpool craft could then use the original gates and thus save water. It was soon realised that gates just ten feet apart would cause difficulties and in March 1822 the committee agreed to lengthen all the locks to Liverpool without retaining the original bottom gates. The work was completed by the following September.

Improvements at Liverpool

THE committee in Liverpool kept an eye on the various proposals for new docks as they were presented to Parliament to preserve their right of access to the river granted in the 1770 Act. In 1804, a Bill for the improvement of Queen's Dock was proposed, this being the most southerly of Liverpool's docks. The canal company were somewhat concerned about the expansion at this end of the docks as it was considerably further away from the canal terminus. An Act had been obtained in 1799 for a dock, which was to become Prince's Dock, between George's Dock and the Fort, which would have been a much more convenient site with regard to the canal. Improvements and enlargements to the wharfs and warehouses at the basin were carried out in the expectation that this new dock would be built first, as laid down in the 1799 Act, and so the company opposed the new Bill. Opposition also came from the merchants of Liverpool, who were annoyed about the increased dock dues proposed, and the Bill was lost.

Relations with the Dock Committee had improved by 1811 when the canal company gave their support to a Bill to complete Prince's Dock and for alterations and extensions to the southernmost docks. Two years later, work on Prince's Dock had commenced and the Dock Trustees were asked by the canal company to sell them land for a connection, though the price suggested was considered too high.[26] The following month, after discussions about the insertion of a clause in the next Dock Bill confirming the right of the canal to a free communication with the Mersey, Mr Foster, the dock engineer, was consulted regarding a canal link with Prince's Dock. He told the company that the engineer, Mr Rennie, would be in Liverpool soon and suggested that he be approached to set out suitable lines for such a junction. Rennie must have been too busy, as the report, presented in December, was produced by William Chapman, a London engineer.[27] The guidelines he had been given show that the canal company's main reason for such a connection was to increase their export coal trade by enabling such cargoes to be transhipped directly from barge to ship. Coal storage provision also needed improvement as vessels in this trade were often held up by contrary winds. It was expected that 120,000 tons would be exported annually, of which 90,000 tons would be loaded into boats exclusively carrying coal.

Chapman suggested four schemes, two from the canal basin at Liverpool and two from places on the canal near to the town boundary. The latter two he rejected, as they would connect directly with the river where the boats would be exposed to adverse weather

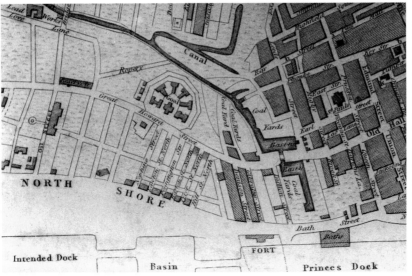

Liverpool canal basin in 1824. The canal ended at the appropriately named Leeds Street for many years until the branch to the docks was built in the 1860s. The importance of the coal trade is immediately apparent from the number of coal yards shown around the basin. For many years, until they were moved to Pall Mall, the canal offices were built over a part of the basin, shown here between the two words 'basin'. The building with the semi-circular plan is the borough gaol.

(L.R.O. DP 175. Reproduced by permission of the County Archivist, Lancashire Record Office.)

conditions whilst transhipping cargo or in reaching the dock system. Of the remaining lines, one was unsuitable as there was insufficient space between the far end of the basin and the new Prince's Dock for the flight of locks required. He therefore recommended a plan which involved a separate dock, 270 feet by 110 feet, for the use of colliers and which would be built to the north of Prince's Dock above Strand Road. Four locks would join the canal to the new coal dock where six 200-ton vessels could load at one time without impairing access to the other docks by barges from the canal. By April 1814, estimates for this scheme were presented to the committee, but it was rejected as the cost was considered too great, probably because they considered completion of the canal itself to be more important.

This was a time of rapid expansion of Liverpool's docks, and the increased trade required improvements in the accommodation at the canal basin. Albinus Martin, who had been appointed in May 1824 as engineer for the section of canal from Kirkless to Liverpool, reported on conditions there in 1825.[28] He considered that the coal merchants were well provided for by the new coal yards, but that, besides more water space, warehouses were required for the merchandise traffic, where loading and unloading could be carried out under cover. The former could be arranged by building arms off the main basin and by widening and walling the canal banks on the approach to Liverpool. This would also reduce the erosion of the banks caused by the wash created by the passage of packet and fly-boats. Regarding the latter, he recommended several situations for new warehouses, which were either to be constructed over arms off the canal or alongside the canal so that awnings could be built out from the warehouses to cover the loading and unloading operations. It seems strange that it had taken so long to realise the need to keep merchandise cargoes dry, especially as dampness could cause cotton bales to combust spontaneously. There was a variety of warehouses already at Liverpool, some for particular traffics such as the trade to Preston and those serving the packet boats, whilst others were occupied by particular companies, such as the various Union Companies of traders. Pickfords, when they commenced carrying from Manchester to Liverpool in 1821, arranged with the company for a new warehouse, but they seem to have vacated this by 1825. Possibly they had not been able to compete with John Kenworthy and Sons who continued to operate a packet service to and from Manchester.

Improvements at Leeds

A map of the centre of Leeds, showing several features which date from the early- to mid-nineteenth century. The weir above the river lock prevented access to the upper reaches of the river until a lock was built in 1845 from the canal basin up into the river above the weir. This allowed boats to have access to several mills, such as that at Bean Ing, on the river; later a power station was reached by the same method (see page 224). The route of the Leeds and Bradford Railway (1846) is marked (see also pages 165-6); it crossed land belonging to the canal and the company retained ownership of the land underneath the arches.The railway viaduct remains a very prominent feature today and a weekend craft market is held under the arches.

IMPROVEMENTS were not confined to the Lancashire end of the canal, with the basin at Leeds being enlarged between 1818 and 1820. An increased number of stables was provided, besides extra housing for canal staff. A new carrying concern was established with the formation of the Craven Navigation Company in 1809. They requested the provision of a counting house for the organisation of their trade, and the company allowed them to use an office at Leeds. They must have found competition with the established Union Company difficult at first as they complained in 1810 that there was partiality by warehousemen in the dispatching of goods, though the poor service offered by the Union Company could have been the reason for the new company being formed. Earlier, in 1806, a letter between two Aire and Calder proprietors refers to the Leeds and Liverpool saying:

> . . . They find their trade decreased so much at this end and think that the Union Company, the present carriers, manage so ill, that they have come to a resolution of commencing carrying themselves and I am to meet their principal agents Mr. Priestley and Mr. Peckover at Leeds on Wednesday to give them the best information I can for their books and business . . .[29]

The Aire and Calder had been the principal carrier on its navigation for many years and would thus be able to advise the Leeds and Liverpool in these circumstances, though no company carrying fleet was set up until after the Canal Carriers Act had been passed in 1845.

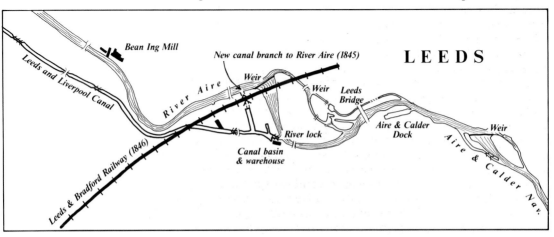

The canal had now been in operation for upwards of forty years and many of its servants were reaching old age. Mr Peckover, who had taken over as treasurer on John Hustler's death in 1790, died in 1810, though the family connection was maintained as his brother and nephew took over control of the company's finances, with their firm, Peckover, Harris and Co. of Bradford, being retained as bankers.

Three years later, on being notified that Joseph Priestley was ill, the committee sent their best regards, and in September the following year presented him with a piece of silver worth 100 guineas inscribed:

> From the Company of Proprietors of the Canal Navigation from Leeds to Liverpool, To their Superintendent Joseph Priestley, Esq, In token of his long, able and faithful services and of their individual Esteem and Regard.[30]

He died on 14 August 1817, aged 74, having worked for the company for 47 years. Initially employed as book-keeper, he had progressed through being accountant and secretary to become superintendent, which post was in effect general manager; he had even taken control of the engineering work after Whitworth's death, though here he was assisted by Samuel Fletcher and his son. Always careful over money, he had been paid £170 per annum since 1796, a salary less than that paid to Fletcher in 1804 and he had even refused to have an assistant in order to save the expense. His son, after working on canals in the South, became chief clerk to the Aire and Calder in 1816, a post he kept until 1851, while his grandson, to whom the Leeds and Liverpool in 1818 gave 500 guineas in trust till his twenty-first birthday, also continued the canal tradition, being employed to work under Albinus Martin and Mr Benson at the company's Liverpool office.

By 1824 the total income from tonnage had reached £94,423, with £32,346 having been earned on the Yorkshire side, including all traffic carried east of Johnsons' Hillock. The returns for merchandise traffic show that about an equal tonnage was carried on each end of the canal, with a total of 271,692 tons carried. 241,422 tons of coal passed between Wigan and Liverpool (including the Leigh and Douglas branches), with 94,042 tons carried in Yorkshire. This again emphasises the importance of the Liverpool coal trade, especially when the tonnages are compared to those for other traffics. 17,156 tons of limestone were carried from Rain Hall Rock, 68,033 tons from the Springs Branch and 2,287 tons from other sources, the main destination being the Bradford Canal. To set against this income, £15,051 had been spent on repairs and the purchase of land at Liverpool, which, after paying £19,703 for interest on money borrowed, had allowed a dividend of £15 per share to be paid.

Chapter Six

'Betwixt the east and west seas'

Trade and the arrival of railway competition 1820 – 1850

EFORE moving on to look at the later history of the canal, it is worth pausing to consider how its trade had developed since it was first conceived. The *Summary view of the proposed canal from Leeds to Liverpool* published in 1768 before building work was begun, contains estimates for the anticipated income, from which the reasons for constructing the canal can be deduced. If the anticipated incomes from the various traffics are divided by the tolls charged, a figure is obtained for the volume which the canal's promoters hoped to achieve annually. As we have seen, limestone, flags and brick head the list with 4,080,000 ton miles, followed a long way behind by merchandise traffic, with 1,300,000 ton miles, and coal with 840,000 ton miles. If the average distance travelled by each cargo was twenty miles, this would suggest the promoters expected about 300,000 tons to be transported annually. How wrong they were! At its height, the canal was carrying eight times this amount – almost two and a half million tons – the largest traffic being coal, though merchandise was just as important because of its higher toll. The extensive limestone traffic which the promoters expected never materialised, and it only reached 130,000 tons by the mid-nineteenth century.

The most valuable traffic – merchandise

BECAUSE of its profitability, the company was to spend much time and money on the promotion of their merchandise trade, and it is this

Flyboats tied up at Gargrave. On the Leeds and Liverpool merchandise boats seem to have been designated flyboats not from any specific way of working, but to indicate that they had priority over all other kinds of cargo. Some of the flyboats had two crewmen and worked for about eighteen hours before resting. Others had three men and could work round the clock. The boatmen would become practised at working locks and negotiating bridges in the dark, without the aid of artificial light. Here the boats are probably held up because of engineering works or possibly a drought affecting the summit level.

(Photo, author's collection.)

we shall look at first. As we shall see, the company did not become directly involved in carrying until after the Canal Carriers Act was passed in 1847. Before the canal was completed, of course, carrying concerns had to restrict themselves to one side of the Pennines. In Lancashire, the most important was the Liverpool Union Company, formed when the canal first opened, and which continued until it was taken over by the canal company in 1848. Union companies operated on many canals and seem to have developed from amalgamations of small carriers and boat owners, enabling them to afford agents at depots along the canal and to build up a sizeable fleet without it costing too much. A Preston union company also worked on the canal from Liverpool; while in Yorkshire there was the Leeds Union – later called the Leeds and Burnley Union Company – following the extension of the canal.

In Yorkshire, John Whitaker and Co. was the most important carrier until 1796, when the owners retired. They had controlled the canal warehouses, besides operating their own boats, which enabled them to monopolise much of the traffic. Following their retirement, many of their boats were purchased by the Leeds and Burnley Union, though the family's links with the canal were not severed, as some of the warehouses continued to be managed by them.[1] Shortly afterwards, there were complaints that the Leeds Union Company was not promoting the canal sufficiently, which may explain why the Leeds and Liverpool purchased two boats in 1799, for hire to those keen to improve canal carrying.

On occasion, the union companies sent in false bills of lading, hoping to reduce their tolls.[2] Most boats were 'gauged' after they had been constructed. By loading them with known weights, the boat's depth in the water could be observed. The lock keeper then reported each boat's freeboard, as it passed their lock, to the company's office, where the toll could be calculated from the chart produced when the

The canal basin and warehouses on Victoria Street, Shipley in 1937. This warehouse had only recently been built to cater for the woollen trade and we can seen here three boats probably engaged on that trade. The Tweed was built in 1936 and was a motor flyboat operated by Canal Transport Ltd. The Omega was an older horseboat dating from 1905. The warehouses and basins can still be seen today (1990).
(Photo, W. F. King, Shipley.)

This boat is a Mersey flat, one of many that worked from the estuary and the docks into the canal. This is the Heathdale unloading what looks very much like pottery (which would be packed in soft material and held together in bales with wire mesh) at a warehouse in Liverpool. Note the hatch covers, necessary for boats working regularly on tidal waters.
(Photo, Merseyside County Museums.)

boat was gauged. False declarations could be discovered, and the union company would be charged the full tonnage, plus a penalty.

The early canal carriers were also involved with road transport, so they often advertised through conveyance of goods to places beyond the canal. In 1801, for example, flax imported from Europe via Hull was being delivered to Kirkham following transhipment to road at Burnley; and baled cloth was sent from Leeds to Liverpool, travelling by road between Burnley and Wigan.[3] Many towns were served by road from the canal, and John Parnaby and Co. advertised in 1796 that they would deliver to Settle, Blackburn and Rochdale, from Leeds.

It is often difficult to find out what was carried, but, in 1810, following the opening of the canal to Blackburn, the local paper reported arrivals for about six months. During the last week of July, the following were delivered:

Boat *Victory:* beans, raisins, gunpowder, malt, porter, hops, packages.
Boat *Duncan:* malt, yarn, pots, hops, soap, linen yarn, tow, cast iron pillars and boskins for stables, eight packages.
Boat *Industry:* molasses, malt, flour, yarn, pots, oil, woollen cloth.
Boat *Speedy:* weft, linen yarn, flax, flags, snuff, raisins, paint, rushes.
Boat *Nancy:* tallow, calico pieces, hemp, flax, nuts, powder, molasses, staves, packages.

A further 223 tons of coal, 693 feet of timber and sixty-six tons of road stone were delivered by ten more boats. Unfortunately, no list remains of the goods that were sent from Blackburn.

Much of the goods were carried in small amounts. This was to remain so throughout much of the life of the canal. Some of the items were for onward delivery, and the flax and tow noted above may well have been for the linen industry based at this time around the West Lancashire coast. The cloth could have been for export from Liverpool, though the hops and malt were probably for use by breweries around Blackburn. Groceries were another important cargo, which continued right up until carrying finished. Even though the canal was still incomplete, its importance as a trans-Pennine route can already be seen.

Such a wide variety of goods must have proved a temptation, and, in 1814, the company paid towards the costs incurred when Liverpool Union prosecuted a person who had stolen linen and clothes from a Wigan warehouse.[4] The organisation of the company warehouses seems to have been defective. On one occasion a quantity of cheese had been left in a warehouse without any payment having been made and, as the owner could not be found, it was sold to defray expenses – three years later! Despite, or perhaps because of, such inefficiency, there were continual requests for the enlargement of the canal's warehousing.

After Blackburn had been reached, further extension was delayed because the embankments over the Darwen and Moulden Water were taking some time to settle. Beyond them, the canal had been completed to Johnson's Hillock and the Lancaster Canal. In order to be the first to operate a service on this length, in December 1810 the Craven Company transported its boat *Speedy* by road from Blackburn to Radburn Wharf. Sixteen horses were used to pull the boat on the eight-mile journey. At the Moulden Water Valley, three more horses had to be attached, but even then they still could not move the boat. Fortunately, the event had attracted great attention, and with the help of the large number of onlookers the boat eventually reached its destination.[5]

As trade became established, the number of carriers seems to have diminished. Only two are listed as working on the Leeds and Liverpool in Baines' 1822 directory of Leeds, though boats serving York used the canal basin. Two years later, the directory for Liverpool lists nine carriers based there, reflecting the expansion following the opening of the main canal and the Leigh Branch over the preceeding ten years. By

Top: Although dividends never reached the heights that they did on some canals, due to the length of time and the high cost of building the canal, they were fairly consistent throughout the nineteenth century, only falling with the passing of the 1891 Act and the introduction of toll controls under the 1888 Railway and Canal Act. A marked fall in dividends just before the period of the railway lease is indicative of the cut in income that was experienced during the late 1840s, when both the canal and the railways were cutting tolls to try to capture as much trade as possible. The favourable terms of the lease, as far as the canal company was concerned, is reflected in the relatively high dividends of that period. Judged by these figures, the decade before the arrival of the railways was the canal's most successful period.

Bottom: Traffic receipts also reached their maximum during the canal's monopoly before the introduction of the railways, with a spectacular fall during the intense competition before 1850. Income remained steady throughout the railway lease, but the canal's success in revitalising its merchandise traffic can be seen in the increase in receipts from 1880. This should be set against the reduction in income from coal traffic resulting from toll reductions to enable the canal to compete with railways. Individual receipts are not available after 1910, but the large variations suggest increasing difficulties in competing with other forms of transport. By the 1930s, as road transport improved, the canal was becoming less and less competitive. Immediately striking is the minimal income that derived from the carrying of limestone. There is an irony here, for while the canal's promoters clearly miscalculated on a grand scale when they assumed that limestone would be the most important traffic, the railways made almost as big and potentially a more serious blunder when they assumed that merchandise would be their most profitable and important trade, little knowing how well the canal would be able to compete and how much they underestimated their own success at carrying passengers.

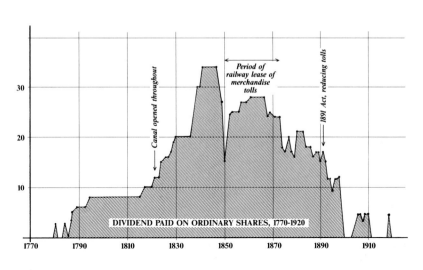

DIVIDEND PAID ON ORDINARY SHARES, 1770-1920

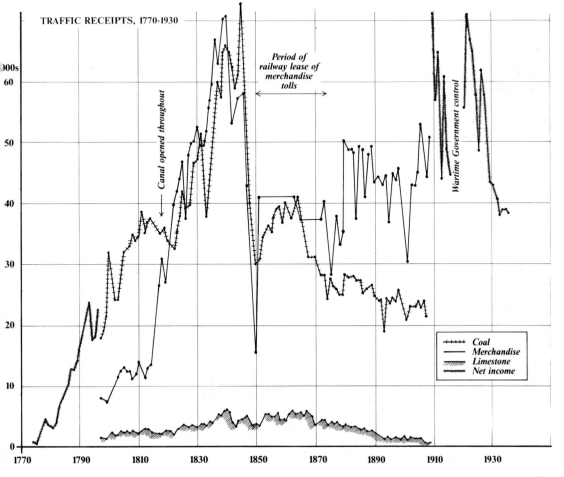

TRAFFIC RECEIPTS, 1770-1930

1847, when much of the merchandise carrying was taken over by the company, only four major carriers were operating. The Union Company, the Liverpool Union Company and Tyrer and Glover were amalgamated to form the canal company's fleet of forty-five boats, while Crowther and Dixon, the lessees of the Bradford Canal, maintained their independent existence, relying on agents to obtain traffic. We shall consider the subsequent history of the merchandise trade later, since after 1850 it became inextricably linked with another great theme of the canal in the mid-nineteenth century – competition with the railways.

The most important bulk traffic – coal

AS we have seen, coal was regarded as a relatively insignificant cargo in 1768; indeed, its main use was seen as being for burning limestone in order to produce lime for agriculture and building. During the following decade, the first stretches of canal were opened and coal quickly developed into the main cargo, with industries expanding because of the regular supply which the canal could provide. Many proprietors became involved in coal mining, changing from seeing the canal as part of agricultural development, to realising its potential for increasing manufacturing production. This change really marks the beginning of the Industrial Revolution, and the Leeds and Liverpool was a significant catalyst. The coal traffic on the Leeds and Liverpool can be divided into four sectors: Yorkshire, East Lancashire, from Wigan to the Ribble, and from Wigan to Liverpool, the last being the most important. Here we shall look at each of these routes in turn and assess their importance over the entire history of the canal.

Coal in Yorkshire

THE early coal trade of the Aire Valley was supplied by mines at Bradford and around Keighley and Shipley. These collieries had been restricted by the difficulty of transporting coal to their various markets. Not surprisingly, therefore, their owners were among the most enthusiastic promoters of the canal. Originally, they had hoped to increase their sales indirectly through the expansion of the limestone trade, then the largest user of coal; and, indeed, the supply to lime kilns on the canal banks did become a major business. It also enabled boats to be loaded in both directions, since limestone was brought down from Craven and coal supplied in return. Because the industry had been well established before the canal opened, the full toll was charged, of 1d per ton per mile, while in Lancashire, where coal mines only developed following the completion of the canal, the toll was halved to encourage trade.

The years following the opening of the canal saw Bradford expand rapidly. The availability of cheap limestone and the improvements in transport brought about by the canal were important reasons for the development of the ironstone deposits to the south of the town. In 1788, Low Moor Ironworks was established by the partnership of Preston, Hird, and Jarrett, who were also involved with the Bradford Lime Kiln Company. Many others were involved, nearly all of whom were also shareholders in the canal – men like Hustler, Balme and Hardy. These new works rapidly took all the available coal supplies around Bradford, leaving the expanding textile industry short. Coal was essential to them, not to drive steam engines, which were still in their infancy, but for the processing of raw wool and cloth. They had to look further afield, and coal was obtained from mines to the south of Leeds.

The Yorkshire coal trade changed as the local mines became less productive at the end of the nineteenth century, with more and more coal coming via the Aire and Calder instead. There was greater variety of coal available from the South Yorkshire collieries, and to obtain a certain type boats often worked to collieries as far away as those on the Barnsley Canal.

No one firm came to dominate the trade, and many small businesses were established, each serving their own town. Walter Holden of Skipton, James Glover of Bingley and De Barr's at Armley were typical. They supplied not only the domestic market, often being the local coal merchant, but would also deliver to the mills and gasworks which had been constructed along the canal banks. Most used horse-boats, though some firms operated steamers after the First World War. On the heavily locked length from Leeds to Bingley, little time would be lost by using horses, as they were able to start a boat moving faster out of a lock than a motor. Each boatman would have his own horse, which would tow the boat all the way to the colliery. On the River Aire at Leeds, there was no towpath between River Lock and the Aire and Calder warehouse. Here, the tug would be used or, to save money, the boat could be poled up or down the river while the horse was walked round to the start of the towpath.

The accounts of Riddlesden coal merchant William Oldfield, for the early-twentieth century, remain. They owned three boats, supplied the horses, and paid their boatmen about £2-10-0 per trip, which covered the wages of two men, and expenses. They averaged about two trips per week, though this depended on which colliery they were to load at. About £10,000 worth of coal was purchased annually, while wages, tolls and carting cost around £800. They ceased using the canal after the Second World War, when, along with the other coal carriers, they found road transport to be more convenient.

Leeds City Electric Department operated boats to their Whitehall Road power station, reached through Arches Lock, under the railway station. The canal basin was six-feet deep, allowing cargoes of up to ninety tons to be carried. With the expansion in demand for electricity, a new power station was built at Armley in 1931, the canal being deepened to five feet to enable loads of about seventy tons to be carried. These, and the other coal traffics in Yorkshire, continued after nationalisation, but had virtually ceased by 1960.

Coal in East Lancashire

IN East Lancashire industries were supplied
with coal from numerous collieries between
Rishton and Burnley, augmented by deliveries from Wigan and Adlington. The
collieries at the eastern end of this length
also competed with Yorkshire boats to
supply the area between Barnoldswick and
Gargrave. As late as 1920, five boats from
Burnley were working over the summit into
Yorkshire. The coal mining industry had
two phases in East Lancashire. The early
pits, located near the embankment at Burnley, at Hapton, Altham and Church, opened
soon after the canal, but had ceased production by 1880. They were replaced by new and
larger pits at Rishton, Moorfield near Accrington, and several in the Burnley district.
The first two were alongside the canal, while
those in Burnley, some of which were over a
mile from the canal, were connected by
ginny roads.

Besides these pits, Blackburn was also
served from the Wigan coalfield, with deliveries mainly from collieries at Adlington,
Arley, Aberdeen and Haigh, all on the old Lancaster Canal. Boatmen
who worked this length were known as 'Haigh cutters'. Coal was also
brought from below Wigan locks according to demand. In the latter
part of the nineteenth century, much traffic above Wigan was operated
by the Wigan Coal and Iron Company, based at the top of the locks,
who provided a steam tug, *Wales,* for towage on this length.

Although household coal was supplied by the canal, the largest
single market was for the textile industry. Indeed, many mills were
deliberately built alongside the canal, especially in Blackburn and
Burnley, so that they could be easily supplied with coal. Delivery of
raw materials, and the availability of cooling water for condensing
steam used by their mill engines, were added advantages.

At the collieries, the coal was tipped straight into the boats, but it was
unloaded at the mill by barrow and shovel, often having to be wheeled
some distance to the boiler house. Three or four men would unload
about ten to fifteen tons per hour. These primitive methods continued
to be used into the 1950s. A crane was used for unloading at the Star
paper mill at Feniscowles, while the Sun paper mill nearby had an
inclined tramroad down to the works, though unloading of the boats
was still done by shovel. There were two sets of coke ovens adjacent to
the canal, at Gannow and at Moorfield. The former dates from before
1850 and must have supplied the canal, but by the end of the century,
railways were better able to serve the coke market, and little was sent
by canal.

*Coal being loaded into a barge
at a staithe, possibly in the
Burnley area. The coal would
come from the pit via a chain-
operated ginny road – a steam
engine, usually situated near
the pit, would operate an
endless chain and wagons
would be attached to it. Some
ginny roads were over a mile
long. Women (pit head girls)
were often employed in the
Wigan area not only in
operating the machinery, but
also ensuring that the boat was
loaded evenly, as we can see
here.*

(Photo, author's collection.)

Whitebirk power station, which opened in the 1920s, created a regular traffic that increased further with modernisation in the 1940s and after. There were three carriers involved. Dean Waddington and Co. Ltd. of Blackburn brought coal from below Wigan locks. Some of their boats were fitted with a series of six boxes, each containing seven tons. This enabled the boats to be unloaded very quickly. The drawback was the weight of the boxes, which reduced the carrying capacity by about five tons. Maypole colliery, on the Leigh branch, was Waddington's main loading point. Crook and Thompson Limited, also of Blackburn, were the other main contractor, delivering coal from the colliery at Bank Hall in Burnley. Both these firms delivered to other sites, and were merchants for household coal as well. Following the 1951 moderni-sation, additional coal was delivered by Henry Crosedale, from the tip at Rose Grove. These firms were taken over by Hargreaves (Leeds) Ltd. in the 1950s. The Wigan run finished in 1958, and traffic ceased completely in 1963, when the remaining boats were transferred to the supply of fuel to Wigan power station.

Scenes like these were particularly common around Wigan. This photograph was taken at Rose Bank Colliery at the 12th Lock at Wigan.
(Photo, Wigan Record Office.)

Coal from Wigan to the Ribble

COAL sent down the River Douglas supplied three markets. The most

important was the Irish export trade, but coal was also sent to the Fylde district and Preston. This latter market expanded with the opening of the Lancaster Canal, allowing North Lancashire to be supplied through the town. These three markets had been established by the Douglas Navigation, and were supplied from the Douglas Valley coalfield, which was not fully exploited until the construction of the Leeds and Liverpool. During the 1770s, several canal proprietors invested considerable sums in the mines here, resulting in a dramatic

Loading boats might have been mechanised but unloading certainly wasn't. Both these photographs show Crook & Thompson's coalyard at Blackburn. The door on the bottom photograph led directly through onto the wharf.
(Photos, Lancs. Libraries.)

144

Above: *Coal staithe at Crooke, in the mid-'50s, loading boats directly from railway wagons. One of Dean Waddington's boats is being loaded with coal brought from John Pit for Wigan Power Station. John Parke & Sons' boat* Sarto *is waiting to be towed to Liverpool by their tug* Leo *(extreme left) while beyond Ainscough's horse-boat* Parbold *waits to load. The much older tunnel canal was just through the bridge on the left.*

Right: *John Parke & Sons' boat* Mario *waiting to unload at Lineacre Street Gasworks in Liverpool.*
(Photos, Jack Parkinson.)

increase in production.

About 10,000 tons of coal were shipped down the old Douglas Navigation each year, and this continued after the Leeds and Liverpool took over the navigation. As we have seen, boats continued to use the river until the canal branch to Rufford was opened in 1781, when 11,973 tons of coal were carried. Over the following ten years the tonnage doubled. Limestone was the return load, having been brought as ballast by ships in the coal trade; 3,747 tons were carried in 1781. Competition for the Preston market came from coal carried by road from pits around Adlington and Chorley, and increased significantly with the opening of the Lancaster Canal in 1798.

Initially, the coal from the southern end of the Lancaster Canal had to be carted to Preston by road from the canal terminus at Walton Summit, making it more expensive than that from the Leeds and Liverpool. Alexander Haliburton, the agent at Haigh, complained in 1801:

> A Lancaster company (chiefly of the canal committee) have got in the way of carrying large quantities of coal and cannel by the Douglas Navigation to Preston, to the exclusion of the coal and cannel from their own south end.[6]

It was not until the tramroad from Walton to Preston was opened in 1803 that the Lancaster was able to challenge the Leeds and Liverpool effectively for the Preston market, and even then water shortages on their southern section caused the supply to fluctuate. The opening of the Leeds and Liverpool in 1816 at last provided the Lancaster with sufficient water to allow boats to carry their full tonnage regularly.

By the following year the merchants selling coal from the Douglas were asking for a drawback of one shilling and sixpence on their tolls, to compete with the Lancaster at Preston. They also complained that their trade from Freckleton had greatly diminished as alternative sources of cheaper coal were supplying their markets. The Irish trade was supplied from Cumbria and Cheshire at prices almost one third lower, and farmers in the Fylde were buying coal delivered by the Lancaster Canal. Demand at Ulverston had also declined, the dealers there purchasing coal instead from Cheshire. The canal committee set up an inquiry, and reported in 1818 that the coal trade generally was suffering from the depressed state of the economy, but that the loss of trade by the Leeds and Liverpool was not significant. They did, however, allow a reduction of sixpence per ton on coal passing down the Lower Douglas.[7]

The coal dealers petitioned the company again in 1822, claiming that the high tolls on the Lower Douglas were ruining their trade. They stated:

> That owing to such a cause a number of vessels formerly employed in that trade, are now rendered useless, some being sunk, and others laid up; and that the present vessels in that trade are rapidly wearing out and going to decay . . . that where several of your petitioners residing in Preston formerly discharged twelve vessels every spring tide, they do not now on an average discharge more than three or four.[8]

In the following year, the committee asked George Leather of Bradford to report on the Lower Douglas coal trade. Coal shipments were declining, having fallen from 54,239 tons in 1800, to 32,235 tons in

1822. Of the forty-one vessels regularly employed, thirty supplied the Irish Sea trade, and the rest Preston and the Fylde. The Irish trade was increasing, though Leather envisaged more competition when the Lancaster opened their branch to Glasson Dock, which afforded a much better anchorage than the Ribble. Alterations to the customs boundaries on the Cumbrian coast had affected supply to the Ulverston area; Douglas coal now had to pay a duty of four shillings per ton for crossing from the Lancaster district to Carlisle. Whitehaven coal, which was taking over this market, did not have to pay as Ulverston and Whitehaven were now both in the Carlisle district. Leather considered that the main problem with the Lower Douglas coal trade was that there were too many people involved: the coal owner, the canal carrier and the coal merchant, all wanting their profit. They were competing with coal sent by the Lancaster, which was owned, carried and sold by the same firm. The committee decided that, to encourage cheaper prices, they would reduce the toll on coal costing less than six shillings, from two shillings to 1/6 per ton, the old rate remaining for the more expensive coal.[9]

Another petition was presented in 1828, which claimed that the Lancaster had drastically reduced tolls on their southern section, from 1/8 to 5d per ton, and did not charge for coal sent from Preston to Glasson Dock, though it was later discovered that the toll from Preston was in fact 8d per ton. It seems that carriers took advantage of these rates, and coal from the Douglas Valley was supplied to Preston via Wigan locks and the Lancaster, rather than via the Lower Douglas. This caused problems with water supply above Wigan, and the Lancaster agreed to charge the full rate, of 1/8 per ton, on coal which had ascended the locks during April, May, June and July, together with August and September when there was a drought. Coal continued to be carried this way, since it was more reliable than the Ribble, which was only navigable on spring tides. The number of boats unloading at each spring tide had decreased from between thirty-five and forty in 1815, to between twelve and fifteen in 1829, despite increased demand from industry.[10] A canal from Tarleton to Preston was proposed, but was considered too expensive by the canal committee.

A further petition, in 1840, complained of the possibility of competition from the North Union Railway. There had been little change in the Lower Douglas coal trade, and the introduction of the railway virtually put an end to the Preston traffic. Freckleton wharf, however, was rebuilt at this time, and continued to be used regularly. In the 1870s, only about 4,000 tons of coal reached Tarleton each year, and by the turn of the century traffic had almost disappeared, with just one flat per week delivering to Freckleton. Tarleton itself continued to be supplied by canal, but even this traffic had ceased by the 1930s.[11]

The Liverpool coal trade

IN terms of tonnage, the most important traffic on the Leeds and

Liverpool over its entire period of operation was the Liverpool coal trade, mainly supplied from collieries in the Douglas Valley. These were relatively small before the canal was built, and concern was expressed by the committee as to the quantity of coal available.[12] A committee member, Mr Hardcastle, was sent to inspect them, and his report was so positive in its findings that several committee members began to invest in the mines. It was a combination of the cheap transport provided by the canal, and this extra finance, that enabled the mines to develop so rapidly. In the early 1770s, about 10,000 tons of coal was transported on the canal. This had increased to 31,400 tons in 1781, and to a staggering 137,790 tons by 1790.

During the late-1780s, the old division between Lancashire and Yorkshire proprietors re-emerged, with an attempt to bring the Lancashire tolls, of ½d per ton per mile, up to the one penny charged in Yorkshire. The Liverpool merchants argued successfully that they had considerable opposition from the Sankey Navigation, the collieries at Prescot and from Cheshire, while in Yorkshire there was a virtual monopoly, and the trade could stand the higher charges.[13]

Although much of the coal delivered to Liverpool was for local consumption, the export trade was not neglected. In 1789, Lord Balcarres proposed a wagon road from his collieries at Haigh to the canal. He anticipated exporting 30,000 tons of cannel annually to Paris, but his request for a drawback on tolls was rejected by the committee.[14] Several committee members were also coal owners, and they may have been more concerned to protect their markets from competition from Haigh. Paris was supplied by Lord Balcarres, but the company's attitude soured relations and he was to become a supporter of the Lancaster Canal. The Irish trade was also important, and in 1796 a drawback of fourpence per ton was allowed on coal sent to Dublin via Liverpool, provided that more than 50,000 tons were delivered annually.

By 1800 over 200,000 tons of coal were being delivered to Liverpool each year. The Liverpool committee was concerned to ensure the supply and suggested that the company should purchase its own mines. The Yorkshire committee pointed out, however, that they did not have powers to do so under the canal's Acts. The Liverpool traffic was now well established, and despite considerable opposition from the coal dealers, the tolls from Wigan to Liverpool were raised, eventually reaching 3/9 a ton in 1815. Until 1823, annual tonnages remained fairly static at about 200,000 tons. By this time the Leigh Branch had opened, enabling Liverpool Docks to be supplied with Wigan coal via the Bridgewater and the Mersey. Sailing flats sometimes worked this traffic, though they were horse-drawn on the canal. The coal was advertised as delivered to the docks in one bottom, this reducing the breakage caused by transhipping to road when the coal was supplied via the canal at Liverpool. This traffic continued even after the dock branch was built in 1846.

By 1832, the canal was carrying 270,753 tons to Liverpool, which represented almost half the coal consumed there. Of the 584,000 tons sold in the town, steamships were being supplied with 100,000 tons each year, while 81,000 tons was exported, mainly to foreign ports as ballast. The remaining 403,000 tons were used by industry and in

A motor boat tows the dumb boat Bruno *towards Dean Lock from Wigan in around 1963, not long before the end of coal carrying on the canal. A sign of the times is the towering viaduct of the newly completed M6 motorway high above the canal and railway.*
(Photo, Wigan Record Office.)

Bank Hall Colliery at Burnley in the 1950s.
(Wigan Education Dept.)

homes around the town. Competition from railways and other canals was beginning to reduce the tonnage carried, so in 1833 the toll was reduced to 3/4 per ton per mile. This had the desired effect, and by 1840 the annual tonnage had reached 512,579.

In 1852, there was a suggestion that coal containers be used to reduce the breakage occurring during transhipment.[15] Walmesley Stanley did not consider that much saving would be effected, and John Hartley, Liverpool's dock engineer, reported difficulties maintaining the hydraulic cranes which it was proposed to use. Containers were used by the Lancashire and Yorkshire Railway on their high-level railway at Bramley-Moore Dock. This was opened in 1857, but, surprisingly, does not seem to have affected coal traffic on the canal. In fact, between 1855 and 1858, coal delivered to Liverpool by canal

Remains of coke ovens at Aspden Colliery near Church. Note the canal arm in the foreground. There were many such coke ovens along the line of the canal in East Lancashire.
(Photo, Ben Shaw.)

increased again, from 765,065 tons to 1,205,588 tons.

The 1860s were the peak years for coal to Liverpool, with over a million tons being carried every year. In May 1871, there were 181 coal boats per week arriving at Liverpool, with Crooke colliery alone sending eighty-eight boats, Wigan fifty-seven, Douglas Bank thirty-five, and Bryn Moss twenty-three. Ince Hall Coal and Cannel Company ceased carrying at about this time, probably accounting for the reduction in tonnage from 1873, when 897,217 tons were carried. The rebuilding of the terminal basin at Liverpool resulted in the loss of many retail coal wharfs, though by then the canal was more involved with the supply of industry and gasworks.

In the twentieth century, tonnages declined slowly. The two main traffics were to the gasworks at Athol Street and Linacre Road, and to Tate and Lyle's sugar refinery, though many other places were supplied. There were two main carriers, John Parkes and Sons, and Richard Williams and Sons, better known as Dicky Billy's. Much of the coal was supplied from John Pit at Crooke, and Maypole Colliery on the Leigh Branch, the gasworks continuing to be supplied until 1964, when carrying ceased on the main line of the canal following difficulties during the hard winter in 1963.

Limestone

THE limestone traffic never fulfilled the expectations of the early proprietors. Following the completion of the canal to Skipton, and the construction of the Springs Branch, Lord Thanet's quarries near Skipton Castle were able to supply much of the available demand, and many limekilns were erected alongside the canal, particularly in the

Right: Haw Bank Quarry, Skipton, around 1890. There is a remarkable lack of machinery, much of the work still being done by hand and the stone carried to the tramway by barrow run.
(Photo, North Yorks Libraries.)

Below: A limekiln alongside Burnley Embankment. This kiln was owned by the canal company and leased out and we know that its chimney had to be heightened following complaints of pollution from residents in the 1890s.
(Photo, Lancs. Libraries.)

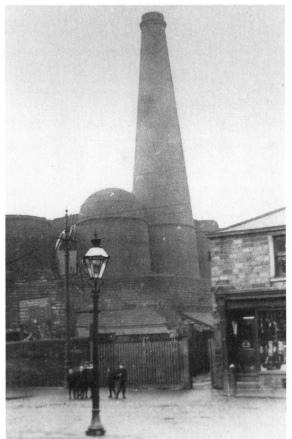

Bingley and Shipley areas. Agriculture and building accounted for about ninety per cent of the lime produced. The Bradford Lime-kiln Company was one of the largest customers for limestone, purchasing a total of 62,815 tons between 1773 and 1781, when, because of the poor state of the national economy, the business became virtually bankrupt. It was taken over in 1783 by the partnership, Preston, Hird and Jarratt, who, besides their interests in coal mining and the woollen industry, were among the proprietors of the Leeds and Liverpool Canal and also leased the Bradford Canal.

In 1785, the Leeds and Liverpool leased the quarries at Skipton, opening up a new quarry at Haw Bank, three quarters of a mile from the canal branch. This expansion was certainly fortuitous, as three years later, Preston, Hird and Jarratt formed the Low Moor Ironworks at Bradford. Considerable quantities of limestone were needed for iron smelting, and they were to become the main purchaser from the new quarries. In 1794, the Springs Branch was extended a further 240 yards, and a tramroad was built to ease the transport of stone to the canal.[16]

As the canal extended westwards, more quarries were opened in its vicinity, the main ones being at South Field bridge near Thornton, at Gill Rock near Greenberfield and at Coates and Rain Hall near Barnolds-

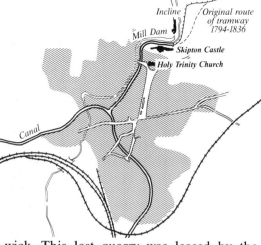

The tramway which connected Haw Bank Quarry near Embsay to the Leeds and Liverpool Canal via the Springs Branch, drawn from the 1893 O.S. map. The tramway's original line, in use from 1794-1836, is shown. The tramway's tunnel was in use from 1836 until 1896, when it was abandoned during the re-laying of the tramway to standard gauge.

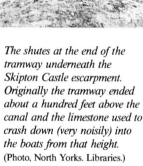

wick. This last quarry was leased by the canal, and it was agreed to build a branch into it in 1796. The working of the company's quarries was usually sub-let, with agreed prices for the different types of limestone. A minimum tonnage was stipulated, and should the contractors fail to reach this, the work was taken over by the canal company to ensure continuity of supply. Sales at Rain Hall were slow as there was little industrial use of limestone in Lancashire. In 1811, empty boats were charged at a rate equal to twenty tons for passing Barrowford locks in an attempt to encourage traders to take limestone as a return cargo, though no charge was made if there was no limestone waiting to be loaded at Rain Hall.[17] This seems to have been successful, and the workings were extended. Following the complete opening of the canal in 1816, limekilns were built alongside the canal throughout most of Lancashire, including Liverpool. The exception was the stretch of canal from Parbold to Liverpool, where there was no industry and the soil was unsuitable for improvement using lime.

At the Springs Branch in Skipton, the tramway from the quarries

The shutes at the end of the tramway underneath the Skipton Castle escarpment. Originally the tramway ended about a hundred feet above the canal and the limestone used to crash down (very noisily) into the boats from that height.
(Photo, North Yorks. Libraries.)

The Springs Branch shortly after a disastrous flood on 3 June 1908 in which the beck overflowed and flooded much of the town. Here we see the branch drained of water so that the debris can be removed. This photograph was taken from the end of the branch looking west and the limestone shutes can be seen in the background.
(Photo, North Yks. Libraries.)

originally ended high above the canal, and the limestone was dropped about 100 feet into the boats via long shutes. Not only did this damage the boats, but it was extremely noisy, and Lord Thanet, who lived in the castle nearby, asked for the tramroad to be extended to the main canal, rather than using the branch at all. The canal company refused, and the quarries were leased under the old conditions, and a new tramroad, with an inclined plane, was built. This was opened in 1836, and allowed the wagons to be lowered to a level just above the canal, and considerably reduced the noise and damage created by the old system.[18]

By the 1830s, annual production at Haw Bank was 80,000 tons. Three grades were produced – foundry stone at one shilling and twopence, limestone at one shilling and roadstone at tenpence. As there was no crushing plant at the quarry until the twentieth century, much of the better quality stone was delivered in pieces about nine inches square. These were broken down to the size required at their destination. The different grades of stone depended upon the size of the pieces, with waste being sold as roadstone.

By the 1850s, William Harrison was the largest purchaser of stone, though Crowther and Dixon, who leased the Bradford Canal, and Hird, Dawson and Hardy, of Low Moor Ironworks, also bought substantial amounts. In 1861, Low Moor complained that their stocks of limestone, run down when ice closed the canal, were not being replaced quickly enough. They paid a fixed price for the stone, and the boatmen were apparently selling it to other customers who paid more, while telling Low Moor that there had been delays in loading. This was true to a certain extent, because the reduction in trade caused by the American Civil War led many coal boats to transfer to the limestone traffic. Despite loading more than 500 tons per day, at one time there had been thirty-one boats waiting. Once loaded, the boatmen worked day and night to reach their destination, and returned immediately to claim their place in the queue at Skipton for reloading, only sleeping while they waited.[19]

The Bradford district continued to be a major consumer of limestone, providing a ready market for the company's quarries, which had now been in operation for over eighty years. Until 1877, about 20,000 tons were loaded annually at Rain Hall, but then the tonnage slowly diminished as the limestone became worked out. The lease of the quarry was finally given up in 1891. By this time, delivery by canal from Haw Bank had fallen to about 40,000 tons. In 1889, the quarry had been connected to the Midland Railway, at Embsay, though when steam locomotive haulage was introduced in 1892, most of the track was of four feet one inch gauge to suit the wagons used to supply the canal. When the Skipton Rock Company was formed to work the quarries in 1896, the canal company paid for the alteration of the railway system to standard gauge. Limestone continued to be carried almost until nationalisation, the inclined plain system being removed soon after, though stone was still despatched by rail and road. There were several attempts to revive canal traffic, the last being in 1964. Stone was brought down by lorries using the site of the old incline, and was used by British Waterways for making concrete piles. This traffic finished after only four months, though the quarry is still in production.

The arrival of the railways

LITTLE more than a decade passed between the completion of the Leeds and Liverpool Canal in 1816 and the first proposals for the building of railways to compete with it on key sections of its length. This crucial development eventually had a serious impact on the commercial viability of the canal, but for quite a time the canal was able to hold off the challenge very effectively. Here we look at the time from 1816 to 1850; for the first half of this period, the canal held a virtual monopoly of traffic along its route whereas, following this, the time and energy of its committee were taken up with trying to respond to the new challenge which the railways presented. This threat began earlier on the western side of the Pennines. The cotton merchants of Manchester were dissatisfied with the service provided by the Bridgewater Canal and the Mersey and Irwell Navigation, whose virtual monopoly of trade between Liverpool and Manchester had enabled them to charge exorbitant tolls. With the opening of the Leigh Branch linking the canal to the Bridgewater, the Leeds and Liverpool had been able to enter this trade but the greater distance by their canal made reductions in toll difficult, although traffic did increase because of the regularity possible on a still-water canal compared to the tideway.

The remains of the limestone shutes at the end of the Springs Branch at Skipton. The stone would be tipped directly into the boats waiting underneath. (Photo, author's collection.)

To break this monopoly the merchants decided that a railway should be constructed. This was first mentioned in the canal company minutes on 21 September 1822, when the law clerk was asked to protect the company's interests in view of the application to Parliament for a railway from Liverpool to Manchester and from Newton to Bolton. The company, together with the Aire and Calder and the Mersey and Irwell, was successful in opposing the Bill. Two years later a new Liverpool and Manchester Bill was presented to Parliament and a Mr Harrison was retained to oppose it. Yet another scheme for a railway, from the Manchester, Bolton and Bury Canal to the Leeds and Liverpool, was proposed in a newspaper article in December 1824. The promoters of this project included the proprietors of the former canal and their plan was that the railway should join their Bolton terminus with the canal basin at Leigh. Their ultimate objective was probably a junction with the Liverpool and Manchester.

The opposition to these two schemes was considerable, and included that from the Sankey, Ashton and Peak Forest canals. The Liverpool and Manchester Bill was lost, though that for the Bolton and Leigh received its assent after clauses, introduced by the Leeds and Liverpool and the Bridgewater refusing permission for the crossing of their canals, had been inserted, in effect making the railway little more than a canal feeder.

The following year the Act for the Liverpool and Manchester Railway was finally obtained, again after clauses protecting the canal had been inserted. Construction of the two railways was soon underway, the Bolton and Leigh being opened for goods traffic in May 1828. By the end of the year the Kenyon and Leigh Junction Railway was being promoted as a link to the Liverpool and Manchester. Agreement was soon reached over the canal crossing.[20] The bridge was to have a minimum of twelve-feet clearance, and the arch was to be thirty-feet wide, though this could be reduced to twenty-four feet if the difference in cost was more than £120. The headroom of bridges on the Leigh Branch was especially important, since it needed to accommodate the sailing flats, albeit with lowered masts, that carried coal from Wigan to Liverpool docks. As compensation for the bridge at Leigh the railway paid the canal company £500 and agreed to a charge of £15 per day for any interruption to the canal traffic during construction. In return the canal withdrew its opposition to the line. Later that year the railway enquired whether they could build a swing bridge instead. This would have removed the requirement for a large, expensive embankment on either side of the canal, but was refused. The Bolton and Leigh Railway also requested a transhipment wharf at Leigh. This was agreed and Fletcher met Stephenson to make the arrangements. The railway were to pay for piling the bank, while the canal would help towards the cost of a couple of cranes.[21]

In Parliament, many MPs were strongly biased in favour of railways, and opposition to them was becoming more and more difficult. Consequently, instead of opposing schemes directly arrangements had to be made with promoters in order to protect the interests of the canal. When the Wigan Branch Railway brought its Bill to Parliament in 1830, for example, the deputation sent to attend to the opposition had to come to terms with the promoters, clauses being inserted to ensure that adequate bridges were built with the minimum of interruption to trade, and that the water supply from the River Douglas was not diverted. In return the railway were to pay the canal £1,475 compensation upon obtaining their Act.

The canal competes successfully

THE opening of railways brought, for the first time, the possibility of effective competition to the canal for its established trade. In 1830, even before the Liverpool and Manchester had been completed, the coal traders on the Lancashire end were asking for a reduction in the rents and rates paid by them to the company and, if this was not granted, threatened to cease trading on the canal.[22] They were concerned that coal delivered by the railway was already being advertised at the low price of 8/6 per ton. However, the company realised that much work on the railway needed to be finished before they could provide sufficient coal to satisfy the demand in Liverpool and consequently refused any reduction.

Two years later the traders again applied for a lowering of the rates. Coal delivered by the railway had been undercutting their prices, resulting in the loss of some trade, and they hoped that a reduction in the canal tolls would enable them to keep their remaining traffic. Unfortunately, they had approached the company at precisely the wrong time, for at the very same meeting, a deputation from the Bolton and Leigh, Kenyon and Leigh, and Wigan and Newton Railroads requested that an agreement over rates should be drawn up, since they were making considerable losses.[23]

The following month the Bolton and Leigh presented proposals to the canal concerning the traffic to Leigh and Bolton. They offered to rent this part of the canal trade for £1,000 per annum, or at a higher figure if the company could show that the traffic warranted this. Alternatively they were willing to lease the railway to the canal for the net rental they then received of about £4,000. The railway was operated at this time by the carrying firm of Hargreaves and Co., who paid a total of £9,000 per annum for the privilege. They finally proposed that the Leeds and Liverpool should send all their Bolton trade from Leigh by the railway instead of by cart. The railway would then give up all connection with the Liverpool and Manchester and with Hargreaves and Co. and restrict themselves to the carrying trade between Bolton and Leigh. The canal committee rejected these offers but did agree to minimum rates from Liverpool of 6/- per ton to Leigh and 10/- per ton to Bolton. In 1834 the Bolton and Leigh raised their offer, suggesting a rent of £2,500 for the canal trade in lieu of tonnage on all merchandise traffic from Liverpool to Leigh, with £1,000 to cover the income received from the back carriage of coal. This was again refused by the company as they considered that it would create a railway monopoly.[24]

John Hargreaves

IN the background to all these discussions over rates is the figure of John Hargreaves, who lived at Hart Common, near Wigan. His family had been carriers from Manchester and Liverpool to Scotland for generations and he had become one of the main carriers on the Lancaster Canal. In 1830 he was reputed to own more horses than anyone else in the country, his business being the equal of Pickfords who controlled the carrying trade south from Manchester.[25]

He leased the Bolton and Leigh, and the Kenyon and Leigh Junction Railways and entered into a contract with the Liverpool and

Manchester for the exclusive right to all traffic to Leigh and Bolton, thereby creating a monopoly for himself. He also operated a daily goods service on the Lancaster and Preston Junction Railway from 1841. He even owned his own locomotives and wagons for use on the various railways.

Prior to the opening of the railways the two main carriers to Leigh by the Leeds and Liverpool were the Union Company and George Nutall, the goods being sent to Wigan by canal and forwarded to Leigh by road at a rate of about 15/- per ton. After the railway opened, Hargreaves charged a much reduced figure, forcing the two canal carriers to relinquish the traffic as uneconomic. In order to keep this trade the canal company empowered Walmesley Stanley, their engineer, and John Tatham, their Liverpool clerk, to commence carrying in opposition, charging the same rate as Hargreaves, 7/- to Leigh and 12/- to Bolton, with the company paying for the goods to be carried overland to Bolton from the canal at Leigh.

Hargreaves replied by lowering his rate to 8/- per ton and the canal company quickly followed suit. A similar battle took place with Hargreaves for the Wigan trade, the rate falling from 7/- to 5/- per ton after the opening of the Wigan Branch Railway in 1832. Hargreaves also started to compete with the canal for the trade to Chorley, Blackburn and beyond, and he constructed a warehouse at the point where the canal and railway crossed in Wigan so that goods could be transhipped easily into his boats. An arm off the canal was needed for this, though initially he neglected to ask the company for permission to construct it.

Competition with the railway was also fierce for the Liverpool to Manchester trade, with rates falling by half from an initial range of 15/- to 20/- per ton. The company, together with the Bridgewater, allowed drawbacks on their tolls of 2/3 and 1/8 per ton respectively on this traffic and when this was found to be insufficient gave further drawbacks of 8d and 4d respectively. There were also drawbacks of 6d per ton on goods from Manchester to Wigan.

In December 1832 the railways involved in the Bolton and Wigan trades met the company and an agreement was drawn up settling the rates to be charged, which were 6/3 per ton to Wigan, 6/- per ton to Leigh and 10/- per ton to Bolton. Hargreaves, however, was not happy and in 1835 obtained a *rule nisi* requiring the company to show why it did not charge equal rates to all canal users, as required by the company's Acts.[26] He thought he was being discriminated against because he was being charged the full toll for the cargoes he was carrying from Wigan to Chorley and beyond, whilst other carriers received drawbacks on goods to Wigan and Bolton. The company replied that the discounts applied to traffic on specific routes and that all traders carrying between those places would receive the reduction.

Deputations from the company and from the Liverpool and Manchester Railway met several times to discuss the problem and agreement was finally reached in September. The Bolton and Leigh Railway (or Hargreaves himself) were to pay the Leeds and Liverpool £1,800 per annum for the lease of the tolls for traffic on the canal from Liverpool to Leigh and Bolton, together with the use of the warehouse at Leigh. This was equivalent to the tolls on fifty tons per day, and had taken some time to agree. The railway considered it to be excessive, though the tonnage carried by the canal to Leigh over the previous years had increased as tolls fell below those of the Bridgewater. Any quantity of goods carried above the fifty-ton daily average was to be charged at 2/6 per ton, but there was no rebate if less was carried. Hargreaves was to be allowed to build his short canal extension at Wigan to connect with his warehouse but was only to use it for his Preston trade and was to cease altogether competition for trade to Chorley, Blackburn and beyond.[27]

As it happened this agreement worked to the canal's advantage as, by 1838, Hargreaves complained to the Liverpool and Manchester that he was paying £1,650 per annum for the Leigh trade, which had fallen to twenty-three tons per day. The railway agreed to share any losses as they suspected that any reduction in canal traffic must have been the result of an increase in that carried by rail. The arrangement continued for some years and in 1843 John Hargreaves junior requested a reduction in his charges so that he could oppose the Mersey and Irwell trade to Manchester.

The Hargreaves company finally ceased railway operation in 1845 when the railways with which they were concerned amalgamated with the Grand Junction Railway which, with further amalgamations the following year, became the London and North Western Railway. They continued to lease the Leigh traffic and in 1847 they approached the company for a reduction in the rental, presumably due to a decline in trade.[28] They also asked if they could take over as lessees of the Liverpool to Wigan trade from Atkinson and Son but these requests were refused.

The rivalry for merchandise goods was particularly intense. The canal still retained an in-built advantage when it came to bulk cargoes, though the speed of the railways gave them a distinct competitive edge when it came to light, general cargoes. The strength of competition for this merchandise trade can be seen in a request from the Union Company in 1841, for a lowering of the rate from Liverpool to Leeds so they could reply to a reduction by the Manchester and Leeds Railway. No alteration was allowed but 3/- per ton was given on all goods to compensate for the expense of collecting bale goods in Leeds. Two years later the Liverpool and Manchester Railway joined with the Manchester and Leeds in a proposal that they should be allowed to carry all the through traffic to Leeds and Bradford, leaving the canal to carry to towns in between. This was refused, together with the proposal to arrange a fixed rate for these traffics.[29]

The canal company's own carrying fleet is formed

FOR their part, two of the firms involved in the canal's merchandise trade, the Union Company and Tyrer and Glover, had approached the company several times in 1842 and 1843 requesting reductions in tolls and rents to enable them to compete with railway reductions, but little was allowed them besides a lowering of the rents of some warehouses and the provision of free porterage at Wigan. However, with the passing of the second Canal Carriers Act in 1847, which allowed canal companies to borrow money to set up their own carrying departments, the Leeds and Liverpool decided in 1848 that they would set up their own fleet. Following a reduction of tolls in 1847 to 1d a mile in response to railway competition, the company's income from merchandise traffic had fallen drastically, from £58,128 in 1846 to £15,333. The company took over the boats of the major bye-traders who had been involved in carrying merchandise, as their traffic had been most heavily affected by the railway competition. The carrying business on its own made a loss of £5,002 on its first year and a half of operation, but when this, together with Lancaster tolls and interest payments, were subtracted from the total tonnage payments received from the department, the canal actually produced a profit of £25,000 from its merchandise trade over this period.[30]

The railways are unable to compete

ALTHOUGH they had made some inroads into the merchandise trade, the railways were unable to compete effectively with the canal for the traffic in minerals used by industry, such as coal and limestone, since many of the factories using such minerals had often been built immediately alongside the canal, enabling delivery to be made without the need for road carriage. These established industries continued to use the canal for this type of material, while the railways developed their own mineral traffic by serving new factories which were built alongside their lines. It also took some time for railways to organise the use of their track sufficiently to undertake the transport of bulk goods, for the slow speed of this type of train interfered with the running of passenger traffic, which was then producing most of their income.

Following the demise of the passenger-carrying packet boat, therefore, the principal competition from railways was for the merchandise trade, which produced the largest income from tolls for the canal. Competition forced down rates, however, and the railways were finding it difficult to carry merchandise profitably. Indeed, had the railways relied solely upon this traffic for their income, as had been expected in their prospectuses, then canals would probably have been able to force their closure, especially when it is remembered that the canal's construction costs had virtually been paid off by this date, whereas the railways were still encumbered by large debt charges.

Fortunately for the railways, however, passenger traffic far exceeded the original expectations and enabled railways like the Liverpool and Manchester to survive and prosper against the competition of the canals. Surprisingly, perhaps, relations between railways and the company remained fairly amicable. For instance, in 1832 the canal supplied water for the locomotives of the railway at Leigh and later this service was also given at Liverpool, Burnley and Leeds.

Transhipment wharfs were permitted and in 1849, at Niffany near Gargrave, a warehouse was built for traffic on to the North Western Railway serving Lancaster. Transhipment facilities were also proposed at Nova Scotia in Blackburn for the use of the Blackburn, Darwen and Bolton Railway.

Railways created other problems beside that of competition. In 1837 the Bolton and Preston Railway included in their Bill clauses allowing them to purchase or rent the southern end of the Lancaster Canal, with powers to vary the tolls. The first the Leeds and Liverpool knew of this was when it was advertised in the papers.[31] They quickly approached the Lancaster, who explained that the Bolton and Preston needed to use the line of their tramway from Walton for the railway's approach to Preston, and the tolls for the trade on that section would be transferred to the railway. The Lancaster would continue to collect the tolls for the southern end of the canal and clauses were included specifically protecting the trade of the Leeds and Liverpool. They also suggested that the Heapey to Kirkless section could be adopted by the Leeds and Liverpool so that they would then control their whole line, and particularly the supply of water to the southern Lancaster, implying that this was still not all it should have been. No further action was taken, however, as the railway altered its approach to Preston and the tramway continued in operation until 1858. In 1845, the Lancaster again suggested a lease of their southern section to the Leeds and Liverpool for a rental of £7,331 per annum, which represented the net returns for 1844 plus £138-10-0 annual rental. This was refused, as was a subsequent offer of £7,000 per annum for three years, then falling to £6,300.[32]

The canal's monopoly in Yorkshire

WHILE the Lancashire end of the Leeds and Liverpool was forced to cut rates and reorganise its carrying activities in response to the railways, the Yorkshire side was in the happier position of being able to monopolise trade for at least a decade longer. There the major challenge for the canal was created by the rapidly changing and expanding industries around Bradford which, by the early-nineteenth century, was taking over from Leeds and Halifax as the centre of the wool trade.

Power-looms began to be introduced in Bradford early in the century and the invention in 1825 of the self-acting mule by Richard Roberts increased the rate of yarn production to keep pace with the mechanised weaving of cloth. The preparatory process of wool combing was also mechanised, by Peatt and Colliers in 1827, and the worsted industry, based essentially in the Airedale district, converted to machinery much more rapidly than the woollen industry of the Calder Valley, which continued to use non-automatic spinning processes and hand-weaving throughout the nineteenth century. The increase in production of worsted cloth brought about by these

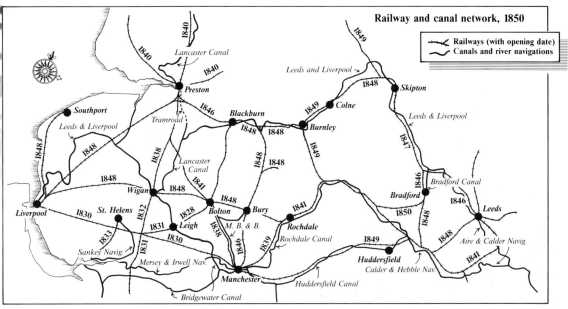

improvements put considerable pressure on the transport system around Bradford. The Leeds and Liverpool, very much a product of the needs of the Bradford merchants, had answered their requirement for reliable transport effectively, but the poor state of the Aire and Calder impeded trade.

When the Aire and Calder had first been built, in 1699, the undertakers had mainly been wool merchants looking to improve communications with Hull. By the time the Leeds and Liverpool was proposed, the descendants of these undertakers had ceased to have much connection with trade and were more concerned to maintain their income by monopolising the carriage of goods to Hull. As a result, several Leeds merchants became Leeds and Liverpool propriet-ors and looked to the canal to provide a through route to the coast in opposition to the river. They were much involved with the proposed Leeds and Selby Canal in the early-1770s which, though unsuccessful, had forced the undertakers of the Aire and Calder to improve the navigation and to build the Selby Canal.

Since then there had been little improvement to the river, though the undertakers had been involved in the Barnsley Canal, which increased the supply of coal available to the West Riding. This lack of investment allowed large dividends to be paid, which in 1817 reached 150%. Such a situation could not continue indefinitely and by 1819 the undertakers were concerned about the amount of high-value merchandise traffic which had left the Aire & Calder and was being taken to Selby by road. To counter this threat, they obtained an Act in 1820 for a canal from Knottingley to a new port at Goole, thereby avoiding the difficult stretch of tidal river up to Selby. Along with the construction of this canal, the existing navigation was improved to allow boats to carry up to 100 tons, the locks being widened to eighteen feet and the river deepened to seven feet. This improvement came about just in time to help both the navigation and the Leeds and Liverpool to compete in

Yorkshire with a new threat to their trade, the railways.

The first major railway scheme in Yorkshire was a suggestion in 1824 for a line from Leeds to Hull to operate in direct competition with the Aire and Calder. Work commenced the following year but the improvement of the navigation to Goole removed much of the incentive for the scheme and construction stopped in 1826.

Despite the building of the new canal to Goole, the Leeds merchants still felt there was room for improvement and it was a sign of the times when the idea of a railway was resurrected; the Leeds and Selby Railway received its Act in 1830. Two schemes were then suggested for railways crossing the Pennines to compete with existing canals for the coast-to-coast merchandise traffic. The first was the Liverpool and Leeds Railway, proposed by Sir John Tobin, which would have passed through the Wigan coalfield and linked up with Manchester, Bolton, Bury and other towns. A Bill was presented in 1831 but did not comply with standing orders and so was withdrawn. The other scheme followed the route of the Rochdale Canal, who successfully opposed it on the grounds that there were sufficient means for transporting goods already.

Five years later the scheme was re-introduced as the Manchester and Leeds Railway, which obtained its Act in July 1836. Another railway proposed in 1831 which was later to become a major competitor to the canal was the Leeds and Bradford. The majority of

A faded but very early (c.1860) photograph of the River Aire at Leeds Bridge. The main interest for us here lies in this very rare picture of clinker-built Leeds and Liverpool barges. The timbers on clinker-built barges, in particular the protruding edges and their protecting beading, were very prone to damage in canal locks and eventually all wooden boats were built on the carvel principle, since these could withstand wear and tear much better (see page 24.)
(Photo, Leeds Libraries.)

Another view of the River Aire below Leeds Bridge. Here we see the Mary of Bingley *being shafted down river to the head of the Aire & Calder Navigation. Owned by John Barron and Sons of Bingley, she was probably on her way to collect a load of coal off the Barnsley Canal of from collieries near the Aire & Calder.*
(Photo, Leeds Museum.)

landowners on the line were opposed to this scheme, and the canal deputation, together with the Aire and Calder, did not need to present a petition, restricting themselves to supporting the landowners, who successfully opposed the Bill.

During the 1830s the improvements on the Aire and Calder, together with the growth of the worsted industry in Airedale, began to make an impression on the merchandise traffic carried on the Yorkshire end of the canal. At the start of the decade less than 50% of the merchandise income on the canal derived from the Yorkshire section. By 1840, this had increased to nearly 66%, though this may have been influenced by the slower development of railways in the region compared to Lancashire. The coal trade did not reflect a similar pattern as, despite an increase in the tonnage of coal carried, there was no significant rise in the percentage of income from this traffic in Yorkshire, which remained around 10% of the total for the canal. There were few mines alongside the canal in Yorkshire, and most of the coal that was delivered to the towns in the Aire Valley came from the Aire and Calder Navigation and the Barnsley Canal, and the distance travelled by boats carrying this on the Leeds and Liverpool would often be less than fifteen miles. In Lancashire, coal was loaded from canalside pits which increased the tonnage carried and it often passed upwards of thirty miles along the canal to its destination, both factors increasing the income from that length of the canal.

To accommodate the increased merchandise traffic at Leeds, improvements were carried out regularly, with additions to the warehouses and wharfs being carried out in 1831, 1836 and 1839, though the eight-mile minimum toll for the use of the river lock at Leeds discouraged local traffic.

In an attempt to improve the situation John Leather, a Leeds engineer, and John Atkinson, a local solicitor, proposed unsuccessfully in 1839 to make the River Aire navigable from Leeds Bridge to Armley Mills, a distance of just under two miles, forming for the purpose the Leeds and Armley Navigation Company.[33] There were several water-powered mills in the centre of Leeds at this time which obtained their water from a weir just above the Leeds and Liverpool lock into the river. Access to the river above this weir would have been by a second lock into the river upstream from the north side of the canal basin. The depth of the whole navigation to Armley was to be seven feet, the same as on the rest of the Aire and Calder.

The canal company were not impressed by this scheme which had in fact been suggested previously, in 1823 and 1837, possibly to improve communication with the mills of Benjamin Gott at Bean Ing and Armley, though the latter was already served by the canal. The woollen industry was just beginning to mechanise and these mills were the most advanced of their time, though they were unlikely to use the Leeds and Liverpool very often because of the minimum eight-mile toll charged at the river lock. Wool did reach Armley by canal on

The river lock and Rider's Yard at Leeds in July 1960. Three Co-op coal boats are tied up in the foreground at the Co-op's coal wharf on the Aire. The boatyards at Leeds were still working and it looks as if a boat is being built near the basin (right). Note the poster advertising arches to let. When the railway was built across canal company land, the railway bought only the land for the piers of the viaduct, so the canal company retained ownership of the land below the arches. The railway and a signal box can just be seen in the background.
(Photo, Leeds City Museum.)

Steam towage between the Aire & Calder and the Leeds and Liverpool was introduced in the 1860s. Here we see a steam tug heading upstream with a coal boat, perhaps for the Co-op Wharf, in tow. Note the spectacular warehouses, most of which have now disappeared.
(Photo, Leeds Libraries.)

occasion, however, as the wharf there is known as Botany, the first wool from Australia reputedly being delivered there.

Besides the Leeds and Selby of 1830 and the Manchester and Leeds of 1836, the development of railways in the area of Yorkshire served by the canal was much slower than in Lancashire and it was not until the 'Railway Mania' of the mid-1840s that Parliamentary sanction was obtained for schemes which directly affected the canal.

The most important of these was the Leeds and Bradford, which finally obtained its Act in 1844, some thirteen years after it had first been proposed. The approach to their Leeds station was across the canal company's land between the basin and the river, and to increase the amount of compensation that the railway company would have to pay, the committee decided in September 1844 to take up Leather and Atkinson's idea and build a lock from the basin into the river above the weir, at a cost of £2,362. Initially permission was only granted for the construction of the foundations, expenditure being kept to a minimum until an agreement about compensation was reached. At the same time the irksome eight-mile charge for passing the river lock was removed in an effort to encourage traffic prior to the opening of the railway. Agreement over the price for the land taken by the railway was finally reached, and £5,734 awarded to the company for land and damages. It should be remembered that they only sold the land needed for the supporting piers of the railway, as it was carried over the canal

165

property on a huge viaduct. The company still controlled the land underneath the viaduct, which they used for storage. The lock into the river was opened for use by the end of September 1845, enabling boats to reach the industries located on the north bank of the river.

The Bradford Canal

THE influx of Australian wool from about 1820 and the repeal in 1825 of the Act restricting the export of British wool, caused a rapid increase in the wool industry. Bradford, as the centre of that trade, expanded at the same time and it is reasonable to assume that the Bradford Canal shared in the boom. Limestone was still one of the main traffics, delivered to the ironworks at Bowling and Low Moor as well as the limekilns alongside the canal. Tramways ran down into the town from these ironworks and although they did not reach the canal itself due to the press of buildings around the terminus, they enabled limestone to be carried up to the works, with iron castings and forgings being returned for export. The chemical factories of Mr Rawson were also constructed near to the canal, with cargoes of sulphur and pyrites being carried.

Water had always been a problem for the canal and the supply stipulated in the original Act allowed the use of all the streams running into Bowling Mill Beck within 2,000 yards of the head of the canal. A further Act was obtained in 1802 in an attempt to legalise the purchase by the canal of a mill and other land to improve the supply but industry was now using the local streams very heavily and a regular feed was very difficult to obtain. Eventually the waters of Bradford Beck itself were stopped by a dam, which allowed a certain amount to flow into the canal.

Over the years, with the rapid increase in the washing and dyeing industry, the water supplied to the canal became more and more

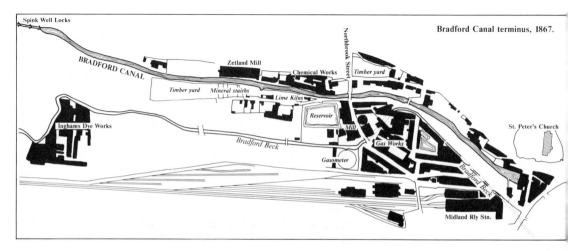

Bradford Canal terminus, 1867.

polluted, a problem exacerbated by the lack of domestic sewerage facilities. With such a supply to a still-water canal, heated by use as condensing water for the engines of canalside mills, it is small wonder that the Sanitary Committee of the Town Council had certified the canal as a public nuisance.

Matters came to a head in 1849 when a cholera epidemic in the area caused 406 deaths and there was much local agitation calling for the closure of the canal, claiming that its highly polluted water had added to the spread of the outbreak. The Council proposed an Improvement Bill, by which the lack of sanitary provision in the borough was to be remedied, and part of this Bill allowed for the purchase of the canal. £100,000 was to be raised by loans to undertake the work and permission was to be granted for the closure of the canal, the site then being sold to offset the original loans.

The canal's traffic must also have been adversely affected by the opening of the Leeds and Bradford Railway in 1846, one of whose main objects was to corner the profitable wool trade between the two towns. Small wonder, then, that the Bradford Canal committee thought that it might be the best policy to sell up. However, strong support for keeping the canal was given by the Leeds and Liverpool and the Aire and Calder, which enabled the majority of the canal's shareholders to oppose both the Improvement Bill and the suggested sale. In this they were helped by the quarry owners and iron companies who relied on the canal for the movement of their bulk cargoes. This latter group was well represented on the Council and were able emasculate the Bill, removing the clauses relating to the purchase and sale, but leaving those for closure of the canal (which was now impossible to implement), and for cleaning the beck, which would remove the source of the problem. The canal was thus able to continue in use, but little was done to improve the quality of the water.

The terminus of the Bradford Canal in 1867. This map shows the industrial and commercial premises around the canal. Other premises are not shown. Note the timber yards, lime kilns, chemical works, dye works, mills, gasworks and mineral staithes, all clustered around the canal. The canal took most of its water from the highly polluted Bradford Beck; this was technically illegal but continual usage seems to have established the precedent and it became difficult to stop the canal drawing water from that source. It is worth noting that today, 140 years after a cholera epidemic in the town was blamed heavily on the pollution in Bradford Beck, signs are still displayed prominently and starkly along the beck warning of contaminated water. As we shall see, the canal was eventually filled in from the terminus to Northbrook Street and its water supply was cut off. Water then had to be pumped up some 86 feet in all from the Leeds and Liverpool at Shipley instead (see page 194).

Problems and improvements to the canal

ALTHOUGH in a technical sense the Leeds and Liverpool Canal was fairly simple and had a good overall record of reliability, there were bound to be occasions when things went wrong on such a long canal. Particularly serious was the closure of Foulridge Tunnel in 1824 due to a partial collapse of the lining at its west end. This was the section which had been constructed on the 'cut and cover' principle and it seems possible that heavy autumn rain had raised the water table to such an extent that the stonework of the lining was unable to withstand the water pressure created, causing the bed of the tunnel to rise up. The stones forming the top arch of the tunnel had also been displaced in some areas. This may have been due to poor drainage of the surface, as Fletcher was ordered to improve this to stop the top of the tunnel from being penetrated in future.

The reconstruction work took eighteen months, and to keep traffic moving a road was constructed over the tunnel for the carriage of goods between Foulridge and Wanless, where a wharf was built on land owned by Bernard Crook, who wrote, in January 1825, to a friend in America:

> About one third of the tunnel has given way so much that a boat cannot pass through. In consequence of which the Navigation Company have taken part of the Wanless Holme as a wharf to load and unload goods from the boats. The land which they have taken I asked them £1 a perch for, but have not yet come to any settlement with them. The Navigation Company complain of my demand being far too much. I think they ought to pay a very high price for a small piece of land to make a wharf on. They have taken the new part of Laycock's house and are now occupying it as a public house (called the Grinning Rat). It takes the ale of three pecks of malt weekly to furnish the men that are working at the tunnel. There are about 500 men now at work and have been for the last three months. It is expected to be finished about next June.[34]

Fletcher was responsible for the restoration work, which cost between £22 and £25 per yard of tunnel, the whole amounting to several thousand pounds. He was awarded a bonus of 100 guineas for his attention to the work, his annual salary being raised to £400 at the same time. It was particularly fortunate that this major collapse occurred when it did. Had it happened a generation later when railways had been built, a closure of eighteen months might have been sufficient to harm the canal's trade quite severely.

Traffic was also held up at Foulridge by the time-consuming method of legging boats through the tunnel. In 1840, Fletcher suggested that it should be opened out and widened at a cost of £23,000, but this was probably more than the company could afford at a time when railway competition was beginning to be felt, as there was no further mention of the scheme. There was another collapse in the tunnel in May 1843, which was quickly repaired, but three further sections required rebuilding and the tunnel was closed for ten days in September. Ely, Pickles and Co., carriers, asked for an allowance for carting corn over the tunnel and they were granted 1/- per ton for the duration of the stoppage.[35]

As can be seen from the damage to the tunnel, too much water can be just as much of a problem to a canal as too little. This was the case in June 1838 when a sudden downpour caused the brook at Newburgh to swell to such an extent that the aqueduct there was nearly destroyed and traffic between Liverpool and Wigan was interrupted for about a fortnight. Repairs continued night and day and a temporary wooden aqueduct was constructed to allow trade to resume as soon as possible.

Six years earlier, the Liverpool length had been closed for a week while the canal between Marsh Lane and Coffee House Bridge in Liverpool was deepened. The canal had been built four feet deep, and boats now loaded up to 3 feet 10 inches draft. However, when the wind blew hard from the west the water was blown towards Wigan, where it overflowed at the by-washes and the level at Liverpool could drop by as much as nine inches. As a result between forty and fifty boats had been held up for at least a day on several occasions.[36]

Further improvements to this length were undertaken in 1844 when the cutting at Halsall Hill, where the first sod had been cut in constructing the canal, was widened to allow two boats to pass, though it has remained difficult for two loaded boats to pass here up to the present day. The same year a branch to Ormskirk was suggested to the committee by a Mr Welsby. The company would not undertake such a

Right *A dramatic photograph of a breach at Keighley Golf Course in May 1952. The maintenance boat was actually on the site at the time to investigate a known leak when the breach took place.*
(Photo, Elizabeth Gavins.)

Below: *Water is again missing from the canal here, this time for maintenance work to be carried out to the cills at the bottom of Bingley Five-Rise. The workman posing for this photograph is Noah Banks.*
(Photo, author's collection.)

plan but arranged to meet the proposers in Liverpool to see if they were willing to construct such a branch themselves. This became the company's standard response to proposals for branch canals, for by this time the introduction of railways made such schemes commercially unviable.

The terminus at Liverpool continued to be improved, with a new basin being built in 1829. New warehouses, sheds, wharfs and other improvements were carried out between 1833 and 1842, with approximately £9,400 being spent there over thirteen years. In 1846 the Liverpool and Bury Railway proposed to extend its line from its existing terminus, and to construct a new station in Tithebarn Street. In doing this they needed to cross the canal basin, timber wharf and several coal yards. The warehouse and offices occupied by the Union Company also needed to be demolished.

The company opposed the Bill and retained Mr Vignoles as their engineer, an agreement finally being reached whereby the railway crossed the canal on a bridge of 120-feet span. The remaining canal property was traversed by two arches of 112 and 70 feet respectively and a viaduct with arches of at least 30 feet, the clearance under these to be 16 feet. In return the railway paid the company £20,500 as compensation for the land used for bridge piers and for other inconvenience caused by the work, which was completed in 1850.

At last, a connection to Liverpool Docks

IN Liverpool the docks continued to expand northwards with the opening of Clarence Dock in 1830. Four years later there was a suggestion that the canal should be linked to this dock but this came to nothing and ten years were to pass before the Dock Committee again proposed a branch. These ten years saw a rapid increase in the number of ships using Liverpool, with Waterloo, Victoria and Trafalgar Docks opening at the northern end of the dock system and Brunswick and Coburg Docks opening to the south. In 1844 further accommodation was required for the port's rapidly growing trade and an Act was obtained to build five more docks at the northern end (Salisbury, Collingwood, Stanley, Nelson and Bramley-Moore).

The Dock Committee approached the canal company asking what advantages there would be if the canal was joined to these new docks. Tatham, who ran the Liverpool office, considered that the coal trade would benefit by being able to supply vessels in the docks without needing to use road transport from the existing canal basin. The Runcorn export coal traffic, which went via Leigh and the Bridgewater Canal, would be reduced, and there was the possibility of the pig iron, Welsh slate and other goods, which formed the return traffic from Runcorn, being sent by way of Liverpool. Tatham also felt that the trade in corn, flour and other goods, for onward delivery to East Lancashire, which was now using Preston, could also be regained by Liverpool.

A modern photograph of the entrance to Stanley Dock (centre) and to the Leeds and Liverpool Canal. Jesse Hartley's two original warehouses from the 1860s can be seen to right and left, with the massive bulk of the later tobacco warehouse in between. Part of the original Stanley Dock was filled in to make room for this latter warehouse which therefore fits rather tightly and uncomfortably between the two older structures. It remains the largest brick-built warehouse in the world and is the subject of some controversy as a search continues for a new use. Should it be retained, or should it be removed in order to restore Stanley Dock to its former glory?
(Photo, author's collection.)

Although the Dock Committee were themselves the instigators of this new proposal for a branch, they were not fully convinced of its usefulness, and Daniel Mason, their secretary, wrote to Nicholson at Bradford:

> It is only fair to state to you that the scheme of a communication does not meet with universal approval . . . there are parties here who oppose it, and others who do not see its advantages and who entertain strong doubts as to the traffic ever paying the interest of the cost.[37]

There had always been opposition to a branch to the docks. This may have been increased as a result of Liverpool's early involvement with railways (which since 1830 had had a direct connection to the docks at Wapping), with those railway shareholders on the Dock Committee concerned to keep as much traffic as possible on the railways.

Despite this internal dissention however, agreement was soon reached for the Dock Trustees to purchase the necessary land and construct the branch. This would then be vested in the Leeds and Liverpool, who would pay £50,000 towards the construction work. Originally the canal purchased all the land required for the canal to the west of Regent Road but some was re-purchased by the Trustees for the construction of Stanley Dock, reducing the total cost paid by the company for the branch to £42,622.

The dock engineer, Jesse Hartley, one of the foremost civil engineers of the time, laid out the works and oversaw the construction, and the locks, as built, display the massive masonry work which is so

distinctive of Hartley's designs. His first plan included three locks of eleven-feet fall between the canal and Great Howard Street, with the final lock under Regent Road giving access to Collingwood Dock. Subsequent plans produced in 1846 included a variety of schemes for a dock to the south of the canal line, but eventually one, which included the construction of Stanley Dock between Regent Road and Great Howard Street, was chosen.

The locks were built slightly longer and wider than the standard locks to Wigan in order to allow Mersey flats to reach the canal. Perhaps the possibility of vessels with fixed masts using the branch explains the lifting bridge for the railway crossing of the canal on the original plan, but the construction of a stone bridge of restricted dimensions at Great Howard Street removed the need for this and limited the use of the canal to dumb boats. Vessels using the branch were to be charged 1½d per ton for access to the docks, though this was waived if they were continuing into or from the river, as allowed in the original Canal Act of 1770. Construction started in 1846 and was completed by 1848, the same year as the new docks were opened. Use of the branch was controlled by a lock house built by the Dock Trustees at the top of the locks, overlooking the junction.

Parliamentary legislation and the canal

THE increasing amount of legislation affecting the canal resulted in a deputation from the company being sent to Parliament each year to oppose those Bills which conflicted with their interests. Naturally, Railway Bills required the most attention, with clauses controlling the height and width of bridges over the canal needing to be inserted. Bills were also introduced by Local Boards to address the health problems caused by growing urban population. These included the improvement of water supply, the provision of reservoirs, and the construction of foul-water sewers. They often attempted to appropriate the water used by the canal, and clauses had to be inserted in such Bills protecting the company's right to its water supplies. Among the other Bills investigated was one for the improvement of the Ribble Navigation, which was opposed as it interfered with the River Douglas Navigation. William Birkbeck gave great attention to the company's Parliamentary activities and was presented, in 1831, with a piece of plate worth 300 guineas for his work on behalf of the canal. He died in 1838, after serving on the committee for thirty-six years.

Public legislation also concerned the canal and following the passing of the Canals (Offences) Act in 1840 the company was able to appoint its own police force. A list of employees suitable to be made policemen was drawn up in 1841, but none were considered experienced enough for the superintendent's post, so Thomas Batho, formerly of Manchester Police, was appointed in 1842 at £150 per annum plus expenses.[38] His job, with the help of three constables, was 'to prevent depredations and robberies' and to control any nuisances along the line of the canal. The constables, who were to be paid 18/- per week, along with and all the company's agents, lock-keepers and bank rangers, were instructed to report any pilfering to the superintendent. He was soon at work, and in March 1843 he recommended that four lock keepers be discharged for stealing from boats. This was agreed, though one of them, George Priestley, was moved from Barrowford to the three-rise at Bingley in view of his 43 years' service with the company.

Other problems investigated included the use of the towpath and warehouse yard at Burnley as a 'common road' by mill hands. Eventually the mill owner was granted a right of way on payment of 5/- annually as an acknowledgement for the privilege. During the summer of 1844 when the water supply was restricted, Batho was sent to detect leakages and to check for non-return of water by mills where it was being used for condensing. Two of his assistants were also stationed at Blackburn to help the lock-keepers regulate traffic in an effort to conserve water. The canal bye-laws did not escape notice and he suggested that smoking should not be allowed in warehouses in order to reduce the risk of fire. Pilferage, though, was the main business of the police, and in a statement in support of the Liverpool and Bury Railway Bill in 1845, Lord Balcarres estimated that up to ten per cent of his coal sent by canal had been stolen.

Batho had died by September 1848 and Abraham Beanland was appointed in his place at £100 per annum. Three years later, possibly as a result of the lease of the merchandise tolls in 1850, his services were dispensed with by the water committee, and his assistants and the leggers at Foulridge were given one month's notice.

The water committee was responsible for the day-to-day operation of the canal and both the police and the leggers came under their control. At the same meeting as they had appointed Batho, they had introduced new bye-laws to control the leggers at Foulridge, noting that:

> . . . the men at present employed in assisting the boatmen are many of them discarded servants of the traders upon the canal and consequently of more than doubtful character, they would therefore submit, that for the protection of the trade upon the canal and for the maintaining [of] its respectability no other persons should be employed for this purpose except such as are of known good character and are approved by the committee.[39]

A shed for the shelter of the leggers was built at the west end of the tunnel, next to the bank ranger's cottage, and notices were displayed requesting all boat captains to use only those leggers appointed by the company.

The period from 1825 to 1850 was the most successful financially for the company and many improvements to the facilities offered by the canal were undertaken, with the warehouses being enlarged all along the line. Such alterations were curtailed during the 1840s as competition with the railways began to reduce the income of the canal. Other problems began to appear, with subsidence from coal mining causing a bridge at Grimshaw Park in Blackburn to give way in 1831.

The following year, subsidence resulted in the Burnley Embankment having to be raised to stop water leaking and to reduce the possibility of a breach. Much of the coal under the embankment had been purchased and left underground to stop the subsidence, but it was sometimes considered cheaper to allow for reconstruction of the works than to purchase the coal involved. The company employed coal surveyors to check where coal was to be removed and in 1826 Grimshaw and Co. were extending their mine at Burnley and offered the company the coal under the embankment for a price of £880. This was considered too high and arbitrators were called in, who made the intriguing discovery that the coal offered for purchase was not even under the embankment. Grimshaw mined several seams under the embankment but he did not always cause the company problems, as from 1832 he was allowed to pump water from his mine into the canal. The draining of mines in this fashion was to provide a useful source of water to the canal.

The lifeblood of the canal – water

BY the time the canal was fully operational, it was obvious that the level of trade was greater than had originally been anticipated, with important consequences for the amount of water that was needed.

Initially the canal had been supplied from rivers and streams; by the end of the nineteenth century, it was supplied by seven reservoirs, with a total capacity of 1,174 million gallons, a far greater volume than had been thought necessary by the promoters of the canal.

A longitudinal section of the Leeds and Liverpool Canal and its various branches, based on a drawing executed for the company in the 1920s. The basic structure of the canal remains like this today, except that several locks, especially on the Leigh Branch, have had to be moved because of subsidence (see also page 200). Here four locks are shown on the Leigh Branch; those at Dover and Bickershaw have been moved and today there are just two locks at Poolstock in Wigan. Crooke Lock on the main line has now been removed, and Pagefield Lock had just been completed when this drawing was compiled. In Yorkshire, the Bradford Canal, with its ten locks raising its 3½-mile length by some 86 feet, was closed in the 1920s, but has been added to this drawing. The reservoirs

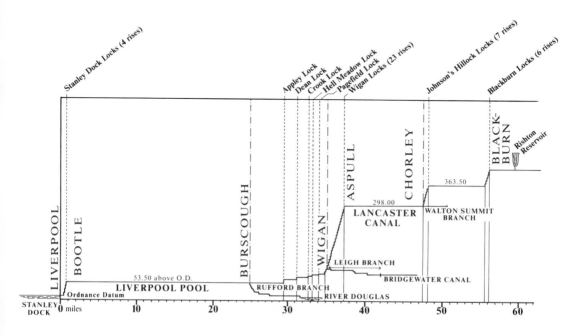

are shown at their respective heights above the level of the canal.

Before the two ends of the canal were joined, they were known quite logically, as the 'Lancashire' and the 'Yorkshire' ends. When building re-commenced westward from Gargrave in 1790, however, all the new sections, even after the building work had crossed into Lancashire, became known as part of the Yorkshire end. Because the Leeds and Liver-pool was theoretically split in two by the Southern Lancaster until the 1860s, this practice continued, with everything east of Johnson's Hillock (including all of East Lancashire) therefore being included, to the confusion of everyone since, in the accounts for Yorkshire; all bridges and locks were also numbered accordingly.

The original Act allowed the canal to use all brooks, streams and watercourses within 1,000 yards of the canal, increasing on the summit level to five miles. Reservoirs were permitted within the same distance. There were exceptions: for example, water could not be taken from the streams used by mills along the line; the River Douglas was also excluded.

According to the early plans, the main supply was to be a large reservoir (or 'basin') between Foulridge and Barrowford, which the canal would pass through. John Riley surveyed the available watercourses and considered the stream at Langrigstone Bridge, three miles from the summit, to be the best. Further supplies on the eastern side were to come from Salterforth Sough and a stream at Acrinley, and on the west from streams at Slipperhill and Ball Bridge, though these were smaller than those to the east. However, all these plans became unnecessary as money ran out before the summit was reached.

In Lancashire, a supply of water had been obtained by the purchase of the Douglas Navigation. The canal was fed from Dean, where there was a lock into the river, and an adequate supply for the Liverpool length was assured by the deep lock at Appley Bridge. The head of the navigation at Wigan had always suffered from a shortage of water, so in 1775 Longbotham arranged for Hindley and Ince Brooks to feed that section. When the new length of canal from Dean to Wigan was opened in 1780, by-passing the old navigation, a supply was taken from the river into Wigan basin (see page 199). There were water shortages above Appley lock, the locks from there up to Wigan having been built with less fall, and in 1792 two new ones, similar in depth to the others on the canal, replaced the old single lock. This improved matters considerably.

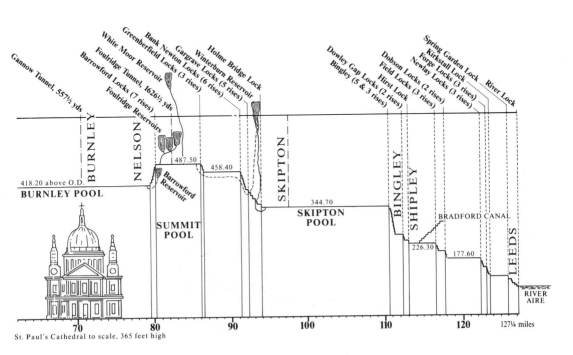

St. Paul's Cathedral to scale, 365 feet high

The sale of water for industrial purposes was to become a useful source of income, and the first such arrangement was at Wigan in 1789, when Mr Corbett was allowed to use canal water for the steam engine at his corn mill adjacent to the warehouse there. Industry also supplied water to the canal. In 1789, the Earl of Balcarres wrote to the company about his coal trade. He complained about the shortage of water at Wigan and proposed to construct a tunnel from the basin to his mines at Haigh. Not only would this facilitate the supply of coal to the canal, but it would drain his mines and supply the canal with water. He offered to build the tunnel at his own cost, but asked for a rebate on the toll on his coal. This must have been refused, as the tunnel was never built.

In Yorkshire, streams which intersected the canal between Gargrave and Bingley were used. The main feeds came from Eshton and Morton Becks, though Bradley and Howden Becks could also be diverted into the canal. The five-rise locks at Bingley used considerably more water than five individual locks, because enough water for four locks was taken from the summit when a boat going up was followed by a boat descending, or vice versa. This made a good supply of water imperative, although as a consequence it ensured that the canal below Bingley was always well filled.

In 1776, Owen, Hustler and Priestley presented a report on the water available for the summit level. They estimated that nearly one million cubic feet could be supplied daily, which, after allowing one third for leakage etc., would be equal to 120 locks with a five-foot fall. As Leeds and Liverpool locks usually had about a nine or ten feet fall, this would have meant that only thirty boats per day could have used the summit. To improve matters, Owen proposed the summit be lowered by forty feet, to create a level six miles long. This, together with the proposed fifteen-mile Settle Canal at the same level, would have provided a sufficient reserve of water without the need to construct a reservoir. Unfortunately the Settle Canal was never built, and reservoirs were necessary when the canal was extended further westward in 1790.

When building work began again, the section from Gargrave to Foulridge was the first length to be opened. The feed again came from streams, at Dauber Bridge, and at the first lock at Bank Newton. In 1792, Whitworth and Priestley surveyed the rivers and streams which crossed the canal, but they must have been too small, or already in use for industry. Consequently, sites for reservoirs were sought at Foulridge. In 1794, Whitworth reported finding two suitable places. The first was above Ball Bridge, and was capable of holding 397 locks-full of water. He proposed another reservoir above this site, though only on a temporary basis; this was eventually built in the 1860s. The second reservoir was at Slipper Hill, and was estimated to hold 289 locks-full of water. The committee agreed to both plans, which they hoped would be completed within a year.

Besides arranging for new supplies, the company had to preserve its existing rights. When the southern Lancaster Canal was being built, they feared that it would intercept the streams which fed the Douglas, and sent Priestley in 1795 to check. He reported that there had been several alterations to the natural flow of water, and the committee

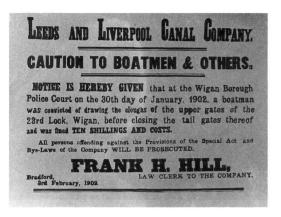

approached the Lancaster, asking them to reinstate the interrupted supplies. Priestley also found that the Lancaster had purchased land at Anglezarke, where they proposed to construct a reservoir. The waters to feed this already supplied the Douglas, so belonged to the Leeds and Liverpool. The site, however, was an excellent location for a reservoir, and Priestley recommended that they use it themselves. The scheme lay dormant for several years, but was resurrected following water shortages on the Liverpool length in 1800 and 1801. The area of the reservoir proposed was 128 acres, and it would have been seventy-four feet above the canal level at Heapey. There were to be two feeders, one to Heapey, and the other to Anderton Mill on the proposed Red Moss branch. The scheme was not mentioned again until 1814 when Fletcher produced an estimate for its construction, though again no action was taken. In 1840, the Lancaster proposed that the reservoir be built, but the committee declined. Finally, in 1847, the site was used by Liverpool Corporation for their Rivington Reservoirs. The company opposed the Bill for this scheme, though withdrew when a clause had been included ensuring an adequate supply of water for the River Douglas.

In 1800 there were proposals to enlarge Foulridge reservoir, which were revived following a water shortage in 1812, but no action was taken. In 1815, some improvement to the water supply was obtained, with the lease of the County Brook and Salterforth Brook for one hundred pounds per annum. Even so, shortages still occurred. There was obviously a problem and in 1816 John Rennie was asked to suggest improvements. He was most critical of the use of riser locks, particularly the two-rise at Greenberfield, which drew excessively from the summit level. They were in poor condition anyway, and he pressed for their immediate replacement with single locks. The five-rise at Bingley was also recommended for speedy removal, and he suggested locations for new locks here to shorten the line of the canal. More reservoirs were needed, but as no suitable site above the summit level could be found, Rennie suggested one at Salterforth Moss, with steam engines pumping the water up to the summit level. Steam engines were also recommended for returning the water used at Blackburn and Barrowford locks.

In 1817 Fletcher reported on Rennie's suggestions. He thought a new reservoir at Salterforth, at a cost £27,000 for land alone, would be too expensive. Instead, he recommended that Foulridge reservoir should be enlarged, as in wet weather there was a considerable surplus of water running to waste. This could be saved by raising the embankment two feet, at a cost of just £150. Not surprisingly, the committee immediately agreed to this, and to the replacement of the two-rise lock at Greenberfield.

Water, the life blood of any canal, remained in short supply, the main problem being the intensive use of the canal between East Lancashire and Liverpool. A reservoir had been built at Rishton, on

The Foulridge area in the mid-1840s. Here we see three of the early reservoirs, as well as the tunnel. There is only around twenty feet of ground above the tunnel, leading one to wonder why they did not just dig a cutting instead – the answer probably being that they were afraid of the reservoir breaching if it was built so close to a major cutting. Note the site of a lime kiln which has now been restored,[1] and the warehouse nearby which was in use before the tunnel opened.[2] The reservoir actually fed into a stream before it found its way into the canal, so that it could be diverted downstream to Barrowford if required.[3]
(By permission of Lancashire Record Office.)

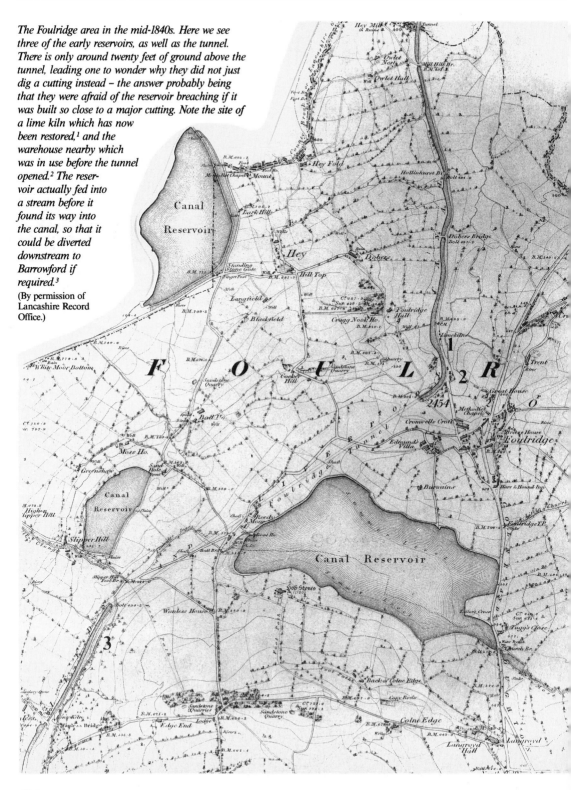

Boats tied up at Gargrave. That they are half-loaded might suggest that they are being held up because of the drought. (Photo, author's collection.)

Below: *A fleet of forty barges held up at Eanam in Blackburn for a week in October 1919 because of a drought. From left to right we see several tugs that were used in the Blackburn area – no. 56 was also used for ice-breaking; no. 55 was eventually sold to Liverpool Corporation; and no. 29 was a cargo boat that was converted and used as a tug.* (photo, author's collection.)

Lord Petre's land, in 1828, which improved matters but the summit level continued to be poorly supplied. Fletcher looked at the Salterforth site in 1824 and again in 1832, but the cost, of about £20,000, was prohibitive. Instead it was decided to raise the level of Foulridge reservoir once more, this time by a further three feet, at a cost of £4,119.

Traffic was still increasing and further water supplies were needed. A reservoir was proposed at Blackburn, but the landowners would not consent, so instead Rishton reservoir was raised, with work completed by 1839. Salterforth was again suggested as a supply for the summit, but the cost must still have ruled it out. Instead a new reservoir was built at White Moor, to the north of Foulridge, at an estimated cost of £5,354. It was completed in 1840, actually having cost £10,150. Fourteen years later the level of Rishton reservoir was raised for a third time.

Foulridge continued to be the main source of the canal's water, and in 1861 it was decided to build the second reservoir that had originally been proposed in 1794. The ground was more porous than expected and this increased the amount of puddled lining required and caused the cost to escalate. When the reservoir was opened in 1866, it had cost £14,774. Boat houses were built for two local landowners, Mr Carr and Mr Parker, with a grant from the company. These reservoirs eased the water shortage on the summit, but by 1870 the committee were again requesting a survey of additional reservoir sites, though ten years were to pass before action was taken.

————

The years of monopoly

1840 was the Leeds and Liverpool Canal's best year financially, with an income of £164,908. Out of this sum £8,000 was raised from rents. £57,882 came from the Yorkshire side of the canal, with the rest from Lancashire; results such as this enabled a dividend of £34 to be paid from 1841-7. Coal traffic continued to increase and by 1850 there were 582,728 tons carried in Lancashire and 315,132 tons in Yorkshire. Merchandise traffic receipts, however, were not sustained following railway competition and the reduction in rates in 1847. In 1840 this trade made £71,001, of which £39,020 derived from Yorkshire. By 1850 this had reduced to £15,533 and £9,119 respectively. The total canal income had fallen by more than 50% in ten years to £71,523, with that from Yorkshire being £22,364. As a result of this drastic reduction the dividend was reduced to £15 and it was certainly fortuitous that the last of the debt incurred in constructing the canal had been paid off by 1847.

From these figures it would be easy to suppose that the railway competition had finally overcome the canal. However, the reduction in tolls had also seriously affected the railway companies and in November 1848 both sides met in an attempt to agree rates. By the end of 1849 some sort of provisional agreement had been made but the railway companies amended this, suggesting that the merchandise traffic, the only traffic that the railways were really interested in, should be divided between the two sides in the proportions which had existed during the latter half of 1849. The canal was also to raise its rates so that they were equal to those charged by the railways. The canal rejected this, but continued to negotiate and eventually an important agreement on the leasing of the merchandise tolls on the canal to the railway companies was agreed in August 1850.

The rent the company received of £41,000 per annum for the tolls was probably based on the tolls paid in 1847, a year before the large reductions caused by competition. While losing control of the merchandise traffic, the favourable rate of the lease and the guaranteed income it provided enabled capital to be accumulated that was to leave the company in an excellent financial situation on the termination of the lease in 1874, allowing the company to challenge the railways once again for the lucrative merchandise traffic.

Chapter Seven

The railway lease

Financial success amid declining standards 1850 – 1874

HE late-1840s was an important period for both the canal and the railways that were competing ever more vigorously with it. As the railway network increased, more and more sections of the Leeds and Liverpool Canal came under direct threat. Many new lines were opening, and amalgamations were creating a much more organised opposition. The canal's main competitor in Yorkshire, the Leeds and Bradford Railway, now ran as far west as Skipton and Colne. It was taken over in 1851 by the Midland Railway, who also leased the North Western Railway to Lancaster from 1858.

In 1847 on the other side of the Pennines, the Lancashire and Yorkshire Railway had been formed from the Manchester and Leeds Railway, and was enlarged by amalgamation with the East Lancashire Railway in 1859. As a result, they controlled the lines from Liverpool to Blackburn, Burnley and Colne where it joined the Midland, thus providing an effective route to compete for the canal's traffic. Through traffic between Liverpool and Leeds was shared with the London and North Western Railway, who also operated lines to Wigan and Leigh.

The canal successfully competed with these railways, particularly for the lucrative merchandise traffic until 1848, when they finally entered into negotiations with the railways over rates. As we have seen, the railways in Lancashire had tried at the beginning of 1850 to force the canal to raise its merchandise rates to the levels they charged. This had been refused, but by the end of the year, after the Midland Railway had also become involved, an agreement was reached for the lease of the whole of the canal's merchandise traffic to the railway companies.

By law, the railways could not be concerned directly with the lease, and the agreement was actually made with the Huddersfield and Manchester Railway and Canal Co., the Ashby Canal Co., and the Manchester, Bolton and Bury Navigation and Railway Co., all of which were railway-owned canals. The East Lancashire Railway, not a canal owner, was made a party to the agreement. The lease stipulated that the tolls on all goods, except minerals, coal and bricks, should be raised to 1½d per ton per mile and leased for twenty-one years at an annual rent of £40,500. The warehouses, wharfs, offices, cranes and other fixtures were also leased, for £500 per annum. The carrying fleet was to be purchased outright for £13,880.[1]

Ironically, perhaps, the company's fleet had been formed as a result of railway competition only a couple of years earlier. The bye-traders in the merchandise carrying trade had found themselves in financial difficulty because of the railways, and in order to keep their boats running, the company had been forced to purchase them. As we have seen, three firms had been taken over in 1848; the Union Company with fifteen boats and forty-eight horses, the Liverpool Union Company with sixteen boats and thirty-two horses, and Tyrer and Glover who had fourteen boats and twenty-eight horses. The fleet, when it was sold to the railway companies two years later, comprised eighty-one boats, 128 horses and various lorries for deliveries by road.[2]

The railway's lease was for twenty-one years from 5th August 1850, and was passed at a special general assembly of the canal company on 1st August 1851. To overcome any problems with the Lancaster Canal, a further lease was agreed at the same meeting covering the merchandise tolls on traffic passing between Kirkless and Johnson's Hillock. This was also to last for twenty-one years, from 10th March 1851, the Leeds and Liverpool paying £4,335 annually to the Lancaster, and included the warehouse at Knowley, near Chorley. This left the Leeds and Liverpool with an annual income from the merchandise traffic of £36,665.[3]

Railway income must indeed have been suffering from the canal competition, as the terms of the lease were quite generous for the canal company. Not surprisingly, Mr Pease, who had negotiated on behalf of the company, was awarded a piece of plate worth £200 for his efforts. Dividends, which had fallen to fifteen per cent in 1850, rose to twenty-five per cent by 1856, hardly indicative of a company in financial trouble. Excess money was invested, and £10,000 worth of Liverpool Corporation loan stock was purchased in 1852. Such investment continued throughout the term of the lease, with railway stock actually forming a major part of the company's holdings.

By 1852, perhaps realising that the deal was not all that advantageous to them, the railways began to voice several complaints about the lease. They claimed the expense of working the canal had fallen from £1,678 to £968 per month, and that the carrying fleet had not been handed over until September 1851. The lessees must have reduced the size of the fleet quite quickly, as they had sold eighty horses, valued at £1,180, for only £764, while twelve horses, valued at £177, had died. They owed the canal company £10,244, and, in view of these losses, estimated at £9,926, offered £5,000. A deputation from the canal company met the railways, and a compromise was arranged.[4]

A further complaint was received in 1857, when, as a result of stoppages on the canal, the railways demanded a reduction of £706 in their rent. There had been three stoppages: at Shipley, following a severe leak; at Foulridge, where an iron casting on the boat *Emma* had fouled and damaged the tunnel lining; and at Johnson's Hillock locks. The first two claims were allowed, though that in respect to Foulridge was halved. Regarding the last, the company stated they had no control over the Lancaster Canal. They undertook to inform the lessees, in future, when maintainance work was to be carried out, should a stoppage of traffic be involved. The railways could then send their own engineer to see if the work was essential. Compensation was again claimed, in 1860, when the lessees asked for £257-18-6, following the collapse of a culvert at Saltaire. The repair, which had taken thirteen days, due to a severe frost, had been caused by work on the mills at Saltaire. The company referred the lessees to Mr Salt, the owner of the mills, for settlement.[5]

The railways had clearly hoped that, when they obtained control over the canal's merchandise traffic, some of it would be diverted onto their railways. They achieved this to a certain extent; whereas in 1840 the canal had carried about 360,000 tons of merchandise an average distance of over thirty miles, by the end of the railway lease in 1871, only 282,485 tons were carried an average of twelve miles. This despite thirty years of growth in the economy.[6]

Bye-traders on the canal continued to undercut the railway, however, particularly on goods carried a short distance. Bye-traders' boats were often used for the grain traffic from Liverpool, hired at low rates by the lessees. Under the conditions of the lease, the railways were not allowed to carry minerals, including coal, on the canal. There was no such restriction on the bye-traders, and it was the carriage of coal to Liverpool, as a return cargo, which made the grain traffic economic for them.

In 1859 the East Lancashire Railway amalgamated with the Lancashire and Yorkshire Railway. The lease of the merchandise tolls was then divided between the three remaining railways, though the Midland Railway was allowed to drop out of the group in 1864. They were slow to pay the rent due, and their final payment was not made until 1870. Following the withdrawal of the Midland, the rent was reduced, in 1865, to £37,300.[7]

The Midland was not involved when the Lancashire and Yorkshire, and the London and North Western Railways negotiated a two-year extension of the lease, from August 1871. The canal company had begun to improve its facilities before the end of the first lease, but much more was needed. This second lease extended the time for finishing the improvements, though by 1873 there was still a considerable backlog of repairs.

The railway companies do not seem to have made the most of their situation. There had been complaints in Lancashire about delays to goods sent by the railway companies, both by rail and canal, the Lancashire and Yorkshire in particular having a bad name. Memorials were sent to the canal company in 1872 from the Corporations of Wigan and Burnley, and from as many as 400 merchants and millowners in Blackburn and Burnley, requesting them to recommence carrying, independently of the railway companies. The committee obviously felt that they were in a good position to do better than the railway and decided, in April 1873, to terminate the lease from 4 August 1874.

Pros and cons of the railway lease

FOLLOWING the lease of the merchandise traffic to the railway companies in 1850, there was a change in the pattern of trade. The figures show a reduction in tonnage in Yorkshire, and on the Douglas, while that in Lancashire increased. This suggests that traffic was becoming concentrated on the East Lancashire section of the canal, with a reduction in imports and exports from Liverpool and Hull. The average journey length, calculated in 1856, shows that merchandise travelled an average of twenty-one miles, while before the railway lease it had been more than thirty miles. This confirms that the railways were finding it difficult to challenge the canal for short-haul business, though the poor reputation of the Lancashire and Yorkshire Railway service, particularly in East Lancashire, could also have influenced businesses to use the canal. Although not directly involved in carrying, the company still encouraged trade, and in 1864 authorised the construction of twelve boats, these being sold or leased to bye-traders.[8]

During the railway lease there had been a consolidation of the canal's financial situation, the dividend reaching twenty-eight per cent in the years 1861-7. Nevertheless, it must have been worrying for the company to see that merchandise traffic on the canal continued to fall, even though this was not always a result of a transfer to the railways. The American Civil War, during the early-1860s, created a cotton famine in Lancashire, and the resulting loss of traffic amounted to about 25,000 tons per annum. During the Cotton Famine, the canal paid £500 to the central committee for the relief of distress in the cotton districts of Lancashire and Yorkshire, indicating that their financial situation was still satisfactory. Other philanthropic gestures included regular donations, from the 1850s, of five guineas each to the Town Mission Society of Leeds, and the Liverpool and Wigan Boatmen's Mission for their work with the labourers and boatmen employed on the canal, while the Northern Hospital in Liverpool and the new Leeds Infirmary were each given £25 in 1861.

The company continued to operate the important mineral traffics, with notable success. In East Lancashire, the railway found competition for coal traffic difficult until the Great Harwood loop line opened in 1877, by-passing the congested junction at Accrington. Coal by canal reached its peak in 1866, when 1,897,000 tons were carried, the Lancashire end accounting for two-thirds of this. The limestone trade also reached its peak in the same decade, with 139,135 tons carried in 1862, mainly from the Haw Bank quarries in Skipton.

In 1862, it came to the notice of the Leeds and Liverpool committee that the Lancaster Canal was to be transferred to the London and North Western Railway. Mr Gregson, the manager of the Lancaster, was approached for information, and a committee set up to oppose the transfer of the southern section.[9] By the following year agreement had been reached with the railway company for the Lancaster to be divided between them, with the Leeds and Liverpool taking the southern end. The coal owners using that length were opposed and were only bought off by a reduction for coal to ¾d per ton per mile. The Bill was passing smoothly through Parliament when, at the last minute, the Lancashire and Yorkshire Railway petitioned to be included. No agreement could be reached so the Bill was withdrawn. It was passed in the next session without change. The Leeds and Liverpool were to lease the whole of the southern length, from Kirkless to Walton Summit, for an annual rent of £7,075 per annum from July 1864. The London and North Western soon closed the tramroad between Preston and Bamber Bridge, though it was still used for the supply of coal from the canal at Walton to the mills at Bamber Bridge until 1879.

'A concern uncared for . . .'

IN January 1850, Robert Nicholson, who had been the chief agent and superintendent of the Leeds and Liverpool since 1826, died. His place was taken by Mr Tatham, of the Liverpool office, at a salary of £800 per annum. To reduce expenditure, the Bradford office was closed, and the staff transferred to Liverpool. Two years later the old offices in Manor Row were purchased by the East Morley and Leeds Savings Bank for £2,850. Tatham continued to be employed as superintendent until 1869, when £17,000 was found to be missing from the previous year's accounts. He had been ill for some time, but had insisted on continuing at work, disappearing for a few days when the accounts for 1868 were to be audited. Tatham was removed from his post, but stayed on to help sort out the company's books.[10] Alas, the strain must have been too much, and he died in October 1869. The loss to the company was considerable, only £5,000 of the money

being recovered. Tatham transferred to the company several securities, given as guarantee when he was promoted to the post of superintendent, and, following his death, houses he had owned in Seaforth and Liverpool were sold by the company. Some £6,000 was raised by these means. Despite this, shares owned by the company had to be sold to pay off the debt completely. In view of Tatham's long service, in 1872 his widow was granted a pension of £25 per annum. John Thorley, of Manchester, was taken on as chief agent at £600 per annum, plus five per cent of the gross annual earnings of the company from £100,000 to £110,000. His responsibilities, though, were reduced by removing the engineering department from his control.

On occasion there has been some confusion about where the company's offices were. This building in Bradford was the original headquarters of the canal company until around 1850 when the head offices were moved to Liverpool. (Photo, author's collection.)

Charles White, who had earlier valued the limestone quarry and works at Haw Bank, was taken on as engineer at a salary of £400 per annum. In his application for the post, he reported to the committee on the state of the canal, having seen

   . . . much to be done, that was completely neglected and had the aspect of a concern uncared for, which will take a time by whoever has the management of it to work it round so as to seem and be in the eyes of the public in a prosperous state.[11]

The condition of the canal had been allowed to deteriorate during the railway lease, though the reservoirs were in a reasonable state. Later, Mr Thompson, the chairman of the company, was criticised for allowing the decline. It was agreed, however, that he had improved the dividend and enabled a capital reserve to be established.

Other improvements were needed and the lessees of the tolls were ordered to repair buildings for which they were responsible. A full survey of the warehouses was made in 1873, and it was noted that new ones were needed at Shipley and Nelson.[12] In Liverpool, warehouses were already under construction at Bank Hall and at Old Hall Street, where offices were also to be built. Despite the good condition of the reservoirs, an increase in water supply was essential, and the committee ordered a survey to be made by Bateman & Co., in 1870, to see if there were any suitable sites for additional reservoirs.

In 1864, there was a request from the Coal Association of South Lancashire that the canal from Wigan to Liverpool should be improved. They complained also about pilferage of coal. No action was taken concerning improvement, but Tatham, approached the Chief Constable of Liverpool to see if special constables could be appointed to keep a watch on boats and canal property. At this time, the Lancashire Union Railway was being promoted by members of the Association. The Earl of Crawford, who owned the Wigan Coal and Iron Company at Kirkless, a major user of the canal, took the lead in the promotion, supported by the London and North Western. The railway was to commence at Blackburn and reach Wigan by following the route of the canal. Branches were to be built to various collieries along the line. From Wigan the railway was to continue to St. Helens, where it would join the London and North Western, who were in the process of leasing the St. Helens Canal and Railway Company, creating an alternative route from the coalfield to the docks at Liverpool. Vigorous opposition ensued, resulting in the Wigan to St. Helens section being removed from the Bill. The line, which crosses the canal at five places, was opened in 1869.[13]

The Liverpool to Wigan length was dredged and deepened in the early-1870s, after a request for the introduction of steam towage for the Liverpool coal trade. This length also saw the introduction of electric telegraph, in 1861, when a line from Liverpool to Manchester was installed by the United Kingdom Electric Telegraph Company. They used the canal banking to Leigh, at a rent of £5 per mile for twenty-one years, with the canal company having free use of the line. The Post Office took over responsibility for the service in 1870.

The Liverpool office on Pall Mall, built in the 1880s, was destroyed during the Blitz. The doorway was photographed shortly before it disappeared completely (above). The building at Lock 2 near the basin at Leeds, marked 'Canal Office', was no more than a branch office, used to keep a check on traffic entering the canal, especially important in view of the eight-mile minimum charge there.
(Photo, Jack Parkinson.)

Bridging the canal

THE maintenance of bridges was initially the responsibility of the company. Although some were on public highways, many were built purely for the convenience of the landowners, linking parts of their land isolated by the canal. With increased industrialisation, many of these bridges were subjected to heavier traffic, and occasionally the

Left: A modern photograph showing the repair of a bridge on the Leeds and Liverpool. (Photo, Ben Shaw.)

Below: The re-construction of Burlington Street bridge in 1904. Many of the Liverpool bridges were replaced with more modern structures at around this time. Here we see two steam engines being used – one, on the right, is for pile driving; the one on the boat on the left was for operating the crane. (Liverpool Corporation, City Engineer's Dept.)

Riley's swing bridge at Church, looking towards Dunkenhalgh Hall, where Lord Petre lived.
(Photo, Lancs. Libraries.)

company was asked to improve them. This happened at Church, in 1841, which Messrs Haworth, Barnes and Boardman wanted re-building. John Faner replied for Fletcher:

> . . . he orders me to say that the swivel bridge at Church when first placed there was done merely for an occupation bridge, but of late years it has been used for various other purposes for which it was never intended, as such he says the canal company will not feel itself justified in being at the sole expense in the repairs of it, therefore he considers there ought to be a proper understanding about it, with you and the company, but for the present he will send over the carpenters to repair it until such arrangement can be made.[14]

From the 1850s, the growth of road traffic around the rapidly expanding towns of Lancashire and Yorkshire began to affect the canal. The stone bridges over the canal were of the 'hump-back' variety, and horse-drawn vehicles found difficulty in crossing these, particularly as loads increased. In 1858, the Corporation in Liverpool asked to be allowed to rebuild Old Hall Street and Boundary Street bridges, lowering the hump by using iron girders. This was agreed two years later, following a complaint by the Local Health Committee about the state of Liverpool's canal bridges. The company paid £250 towards a new bridge at Old Hall Street, which they were to keep in repair, though the Corporation were to maintain the road, and gave a grant of £750 towards the bridge at Sandhills, where the Corporation took over all responsibility for repairs.

In 1861, the Royal Agricultural Society's meeting was held at Armley, near Leeds. To improve access, Canal Road at Armley was declared a public highway, and the Town Clerk of Leeds requested that the canal bridge should be repaired for traffic to the show. The company reminded him that the bridge was not a public one, but allowed its use provided it was policed so that canal trade was not interrupted.

Swing bridges were used on the canal from the start. They were cheaper to build than stone bridges, though their maintenance proved problematic. Thomas Newte in his *Tour in England and Scotland* in

1799 observed:

> The bridges are made of wood, and turn on a center, by means of a circular iron, and iron wheels. These bridges are constantly out of repair, and are attended with considerable expence.

Such bridges were difficult to balance, the track was prone to blocking with stones and rubbish, and they were generally difficult to operate. In 1799, Fletcher was asked to produce a model of the swing bridge which had been recently introduced on the Sankey, with a view to altering existing bridges. It is possible that in this design the bridge swung on two convex cast iron plates, the bridge being located by a spigot in the middle of the plates. This method was used by the company, but the bridges became difficult to operate when overweight loads passed over the bridge and cracked the bearing plates. Now swing bridges are supported by large ball bearings, running in steel tracks, close to the central locating spigot.

Most of the stone bridges are of simple construction. That at Eanam, however, is built at a skew. Constructed in 1810, it is an early example of the method, though the stonework is not as complex as later skew bridges. It has been widened twice, though the original arch is still visible. New bridges were needed from time to time, and, in 1829, the canal was drained at Silsden for one week while the foundations for one were built. This may seem quick work, but foundations for wharfs were sometimes installed in just twenty-four hours.

The railways erected many new bridges, two of particular interest crossing the canal at Bentley Wood Valley, near Burnley. These were of wrought-iron box-section construction built by Mr Fairburn of Manchester, to test a design that was later used on the well-known railway bridges across the Menai Straights and at Conway. They were replaced in the late-nineteenth century.[15] The East Lancashire Railway did not always use such advanced techniques, and their bridges over

the reservoir at Rishton, the canal and valley at Church, the canal at Whitebirk and the Liverpool line over the canal at Wigan, were spindly wooden viaducts. That at Rishton was replaced in 1858, when the reservoir was drained for cleaning, while the one at Wigan was converted to an embankment in 1867.[16] This seems to me a much likelier candidate for the origin of Wigan Pier than the coal tip so named today.

Pollution . . . and manure

ANOTHER major problem for the canal, resulting from the rise in urban population, was sewage pollution. The company were well aware of this and, in 1859, the Burnley Improvement Commissioners were granted a small piece of land near the embankment on the condition that they did not erect urinals. Ten years later, as pressure for public health improvements gained momentum, the company gave evidence to the Pollution of Rivers Commission about the state of the Douglas. Little can have been done to improve conditions, and the company complained to Wigan Corporation in 1873 about sewage being discharged into the river. In the same year, the Local Boards at Nelson and Brierfield were requested to discontinue turning sewage into the canal. Improvements in sanitary conditions led to the company having to fit toilets to its buildings. Botany Bay, near Chorley, had long been considered an unhealthy area, and in 1872 the company connected their warehouse there to the new sewer which was being installed. Industrial pollution created problems, too, and in 1873 James Hacking of Enfield was told to stop emptying waste into the canal from his soap works.

Although the increase in road traffic and population caused many problems, it also brought an increase in trade. The vast numbers of horses used by road carriers produced their own street pollution. To reduce the possibility of diseases, street sweepings had to be removed from the major towns. Night soil also needed removing, and many years were to pass before mains sewers became universal in urban areas. Fortunately, manure was in increasing demand, particularly by the farmers of West Lancashire, and huge amounts were carried from the large towns for use on fields along the canal.

The 1770 Act had exempted manure from tolls, provided it was for the use on land through which the canal passed, though this traffic did not become extensive until the nineteenth century. Following the draining of Martin Mere by John Gilbert in the 1780s the reclaimed lands required improvement before they could be used for arable farming. Initially lime was tried, but the heavy ground did not respond. The soil needed breaking up, and for this, manure was particularly useful. It was provided by the rapidly growing Lancashire towns.

Throughout the first half of the nineteenth century about 50,000 tons were carried annually. Special wharfs were set up, as storage of the manure prior to shipment became a problem. In 1828, the committee

Several long, spindly wooden viaducts like this were built by the East Lancashire Railway, all of which were replaced later. One lay just to the south west of Wigan at Seven Stars and, given the known origins of the Wigan Pier legend, set upon a train heading for Southport, this seems to be a much likelier candidate for Wigan Pier than the coal staithe which receives the credit today. The viaduct shown here was on the East Lancashire line at Church and the canal passed under the far end. It was filled in to form an embankment in the 1880s, some time after the one at Wigan had received similar attention.

(Photo, Lancs. Libraries.)

ordered that no manure should be deposited on Blackburn wharf, where it must have interfered with the merchandise traffic. Grimshaw Park and a site near Robert Muir's house were to be used instead. Liverpool was the main source of manure, and in 1849 good horse dung could be bought for between four and five shillings per ton on the wharf there.[17] The toll was a ½d per ton per mile, though canalside farmers were exempted, causing considerable problems for the company deciding when the toll should be charged. Both farmers and boatmen attempted to deceive the company about the destination of manure in order to evade payment.

From 1841, guano from Peru began to be imported for use as manure, the canal delivering considerable quantities to Lancashire farmers. The import of cattle from North America also provided large amounts of manure. So that the manure could be sold in Liverpool the cattle were not cleaned out during the voyage. Consequently the wooden decks of these ships became impregnated with ordure, which leached out later whilst returning with emmigrants on their way to America, creating atrocious conditions. Eventually, regulations covering the cleaning and preparation of such ships for the emigrant trade were introduced.

In the 1880s and 1890s, the canal carried about 150,000 tons of manure annually. By this time, the amount of night soil had increased considerably, and there were many complaints about the state of

When boats were nearing the end of their working lives, many would suffer the ignominy of being used for the manure traffic. Here Ben, owned by William Knowles, is being unloaded at Tarleton. It must have been one of the most unpleasant jobs on the canal. All the usual deck furniture – dog kennel, water barrel, proven box, ventilator cover and spare tiller – can be seen.
(Photo, author's collection.)

manure wharfs. Mr Tomlinson, a JP from Burscough stated:

> It is monstrous that such accumulations should be tolerated in the midst of such a populous village. Honest horse and cow manure deserves respect, but the villainous compounds that are positively ennobled by being styled 'manure', reek with noxious odours that send one home to Sunday dinner many a time with sickened appetite.[18]

Many councils operated their own boats for removing manure, though there was sufficient traffic for a considerable number of bye-traders, who usually owned boats which were virtually worn out. Before loading, the night soil was mixed with household refuse and ashes to make it less liquid. The heat generated afterwards dried it out, and farmers often complained that boatmen dampened the manure to increase its weight and hence its price.[19] Manure wharfs were positioned at many bridges in West Lancashire, where carts were loaded for delivery to farms away from the canal. For those closer to the canal, the boat would tie up against the field to be manured for unloading. The manure traffic continued into the 1930s, subsequently declining as sanitary standards improved.

The Bradford Canal – 'seething cauldron of impurity'

THE operation of the Bradford Canal had usually been leased out to a firm involved in the limestone trade. In 1852, however, the lease was offered to the Leeds and Liverpool at £1,400 per annum for seven years. This could have been an attempt to make the canal's future more secure, following problems over water supply in 1850. The Leeds and Liverpool consulted the Aire and Calder, as much of the merchandise traffic to Bradford passed along that navigation, then refused the lease because of the poor state of the canal. The canal was expensive to operate, and they were concerned about income, badly affected by the Leeds and Bradford Railway's opposition to the canals. The lease was finally taken up by Crowther and Dixon, limeburners in Bradford. They received an annual allowance from the Leeds and Liverpool of £450 for limestone traffic and £250 from the Aire and Calder for flag and slate, provided the canal was kept in good repair. The lease was for seven years and was renewed in 1859.[20]

Litigation concerning the canal continued. In 1853 the company complained that the council had taken water from Chellow Dene Beck during a drought. As this constituted part of the canal's supply, they demanded damages and were eventually awarded £100. Despite problems with water supply, nothing was done to improve conditions. Matters came to a head in 1864 during a particularly hot summer. This had a predictable effect upon the canal which became, in the words of the *Bradford Observer*: 'that seething cauldron of all impurity.' A group of industrialists, not dependent on the canal for transport, took the company to court, seeking to compel them to abate the nuisance. They had originally asked the Council to undertake the prosecution, but in view of the complex history of the water supply, the Council declined. The canal had been supplied by Bradford Beck, illegally, for almost one hundred years. The 1853 court action had endorsed this use, and suggested that the Council was responsible for ensuring the purity of the water. The Council's lack of enthusiasm for a further court action was hardly surprising.

The case came to court in June 1865, when it was decided that the canal company was at fault in allowing the use of an impure water supply. The company appealed, but in the meantime an injunction was granted, forcing them to cleanse the basin every two weeks. This was done by opening the sluices in the locks to let out the foul water, the canal then being refilled from the Beck. In March 1866, the judgement was upheld at the appeal, and the company restrained from using their old water supply, from November of that year, on penalty of £10,000.

This most famous view of the old canal basin at Bradford, with the tower of St. Peter's Church behind the warehouses, shows the cramped nature of the facilities at the end of the canal but does not hint at the huge public nuisance that the waters of the canal represented while it was being fed from the highly polluted Bradford Beck. The area was described in 1870 as 'a plague spot'.
(From *The Centenery Book of Bradford*, courtesy Ron Marshall.)

The financial condition of the company was already poor following the reduction in traffic due to the leasing of the merchandise traffic on the Leeds and Liverpool. Railway competition over the previous twenty years had also had its effect. In an attempt to save and improve the canal, the Leeds and Liverpool offered to take over the lease for one year, but anti-canal feeling was too high and this was refused. Following this rejection, both canal companies introduced Bills into Parliament in a last ditch effort to keep the canal open.

The Leeds and Liverpool suggested that, if they could lease the canal, they could supply water by pumps from their canal at Shipley. To finance this they would fill in the terminal basin and sell the land. A counter proposal from the Bradford sought either to fill in the basin and lease the rest of the canal to the Leeds and Liverpool, or to abandon the canal completely and sell the land. Both these Bills failed. Early in 1867 the canal was dredged and, in May, the water supply shut off and the canal drained, effectively closing the navigation.

This was not the end of the canal. Among its heaviest users had been the stone quarries on the eastern side of the valley. These were poorly situated for connection to the railway system and consequently had relied upon the canal for transport. Their owners approached the canal company, who agreed to sell them the section below Northbrook Bridge for £2,500. That above was sold, for an unspecified amount, to builders. The Council was given enough land for the widening of Canal Road and £2,000 towards the culverting of Bradford Beck, which could no longer be used to supply the canal. The old company was wound up in March 1870, and a new company, the Bradford Canal Company Limited, registered in 1871.

The directors of the new company, which had a share capital of £35,000, were mainly involved in the stone, lime, and coal trades. They anticipated that the traffic, which had

been about 125,000 tons per annum before closure, could easily be increased to 180,000 tons. A Leeds engineer, called in to report on the water supply, identified three streams and two reservoirs which could provide water for most of the year. Back pumping from the lower levels, costing £650 per annum, could be used at other times. As the old terminus had been filled in, a new wharf, capable of accommodating forty-three boats, was proposed. A Bill was presented to Parliament, and received assent in July 1871. It allowed three years for construction, while the Leeds and Liverpool and the Aire and Calder were given the option to purchase, for £2,900 plus the cost of improvements, should the new company fail to finish the work.

Work went ahead quickly, and the canal was ready for reopening the following year. Half a mile of new wharfs had been built at Northbrook Bridge, and the whole length of canal restored to its original depth. As a request to the Leeds and Liverpool for a gravity water supply from the top of the five-rise at Bingley had been refused, water was diverted from two streams which joined Bradford Beck further down the valley. Steam-driven pumps at each lock supplemented the supply, drawing water from the Leeds and Liverpool at Shipley. The canal reopened on 1st May 1872, five years to the day after it had closed.

Almost a year passed before the official opening, on 15th April 1873. The steam tug *Enterprise,* renamed *Liverpool* for the day, was hired from the Leeds and Airedale Steam Tug Company for the occasion. With the directors on board, the tug towed the stone barge *Mayday* up the canal from Shipley. Unfortunately, several boats had preceded the official party, and as the pumping engines had not been worked, the water level had fallen. The two boats frequently ran aground, but finally managed to reach the wharfs at Bradford. This inauspicious opening was a portent of the canal's future.

Assessing the impact of the Leeds and Liverpool Canal

The engine house on the Bradford Canal at Spink Well Locks. This was the pumping engine at the top of the 86 feet of lockage that took the Bradford Canal up from the Leeds and Liverpool at Shipley. This engine was required simply to pump water up this flight of locks and there were other engines further down the flight. The canal runs just behind the buildings; the building on the right is the lock house.
(Photo, Railway and Canal Historical Society.)

WITH the canal now approaching its most successful period, it is perhaps appropriate to pause in order to assess the canal's overall impact. By providing the first truly effective means of conveying goods over long distances, the canal obviously was of great importance in terms of transport and, being the longest single canal in the country, the Leeds and Liverpool has a very significant place in the history of transport itself.

But the canal's impact was far greater and more diverse than merely providing a new means of transport. It influenced the development of industry, the location of new factories and in several cases profoundly influenced the entire development of towns along the route; it affected the patterns of trade on both sides of the Pennines; it even had a considerable impact on the agriculture of the areas through which it passed. On another level, the canal was important in terms of the landscape. New reservoirs and feeder streams affected drainage patterns and the canal itself, with its embankments, aqueducts, locks and scores of bridges, often altered profoundly the whole nature of the townscapes and landscapes of the areas through which it passed.

Inevitably, the most immediate and greatest impact of the canal was in terms of the much improved transport for industry and commerce which it provided. A glance at trade figures and the total volume of traffic carried gives a clear and unambiguous impression of the economic significance of the canal. The whole area around Wigan was truly opened up by the canal, with coal output increasing tremendously in the years after it opened. Liverpool came to depend on the canal for many years for virtually all of its coal supplies. As we have seen, limestone and general cargo were carried in great quantities. It is always difficult to quantify the degree to which local economic development is attributable to what cause, but it seems certain that the canal, by providing a relatively cheap, quick and notably efficient means of transport, had a consistently important impact on the scale and speed of economic expansion on both sides of the Pennines.

Evidence of that impact can be seen more tangibly in other ways, perhaps most strikingly in the way in which the canal affected the location of industry and the development of the industrial towns along its route. Blackburn provides a good example here, if one compares the

An aerial view of Blackburn around the Eanam Wharf area in the 1920s. This whole area was developed because of the canal, and industrial premises are clustered all around it. Eanam Wharf can be seen in the centre foreground and there were coal wharfs to both sides of it. The stables of the canal company were situated just to the right of the main wharf. (Photo, Lancs. Libraries.)

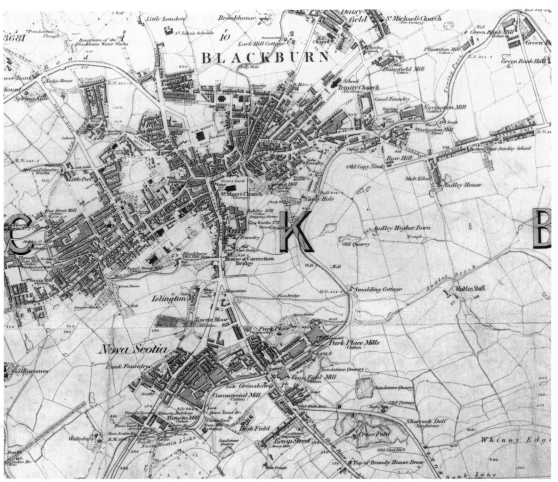

A graphic illustration of the impact of the canal is provided by the O.S. map of 1848. The new industrial areas around Nova Scotia and Eanam straddle the canal which had initially skirted around the south and east of the old town to avoid high land prices near the town centre. The town's industrial centre then moved out to meet the canal. Blackburn Locks can be seen, bottom left, and the canal works its way north-eastward to Eanam before passing Green Bank Mill on its way to Church and Burnley.

(Two sheets of the first edition O.S. map are joined together here. Reproduced by permission of the County Archivist, Lancashire Record Office.)

small market town with a strong handloom weaving trade at the end of the eighteenth century with the booming cotton town of fifty years later. The canal drew to its banks large-scale development at Nova Scotia and Eanam and maps of the period show how the whole nucleus of the town shifted towards the canal.

A similar pattern can be seen at Burnley, where in 1827 there were still only two mills at the Weavers' Triangle but where large industrial development quickly took place alongside the canal, making good use not only of the transport facility but of the useful condensing water – increasingly important to serve a growing number of mill steam engines, and which gave the canal a significant competitive edge over the railways.

A similar pattern can be seen in Yorkshire, where the pollution and congestion around the canal at Bradford led to many industrialists choosing to re-locate at nearby Shipley on the main line instead. Most notable of these was Titus Salt, who built a mill for processing alpaca wool and a factory town for his workpeople at Saltaire. The railway may have been a factor here, too, but wharfs were certainly provided and the canal was undoubtedly a major attraction for the same reasons as in Lancashire.

Left: The complete industrial landscape. A view of the top seven locks at Wigan. This photograph is taken from the top of a huge slag-heap made up from waste from Wigan Coal & Iron Co.'s ironworks and the hill in the distance is another heap of waste, this time from the collieries at Aspull. This whole landscape has been changed for ever because of its proximity to the canal.
(Photo, author's collection.)

Below: Slater's Terrace at the Weavers' Triangle in Burnley, a canalside warehouse with housing above for the workers in Slater's mills. This whole area was developed because it was next to the canal.
(Photo, Ben Shaw.)

Like the railways afterwards, the canal always tried to avoid the centre of towns, where land prices were highest. Thus the canal tended to be built around towns, rather than through them, as at Wigan, Chorley, Blackburn, Skipton and Bingley, and eloquent testimony to the attractiveness of the canalbanks for industrial development can be seen from the way in which those same towns developed out towards the canal from a very early date. It seems certain that in a rapidly expanding economy the canal was an important factor in where that development took place and at the same time a significant stimulus to yet further development, with several towns owing much of their economic growth, directly or indirectly, to the canal.

It was not only towns that were affected by the arrival of the canal. As we have seen, limestone was always envisaged as being a major traffic and the ready supply of lime allowed a great deal of land, particularly in West Yorkshire and East Lancashire, to be improved. This not only increased the harvest but the price of the land; for example, when the canal was extended from Henfield the price of land which was treated with lime was about 50% higher than the rest. More important still was the manure traffic of

A section of the first edition O.S. map of the Wigan area, dating from the mid-1840s, just after the arrival of the first railways. This is therefore an excellent date at which to review the canal's impact on this area. Immediately evident is the large number of tram-roads that feed the canal from the many collieries in and around the Douglas Valley. Prominent among these are those of the Ince Hall Coal and Cannel Company.[1] Also marked is their branch canal that used to carry coal down to the canal.[2] This firm stopped carrying on the canal in 1872 and transferred their traffic to the railway, whereupon the canal company took over their fleet of boats to cater for the increasing traffic at the end of the railway lease. It is notice-able also how all of the industrial premises are located either on the River Douglas, where water-powered mills had been situated for some time, or along the canal itself, where they used condensing water and received deliveries by means of the canal. To the west of the town can be seen a length of canal wharf which is the site of the original River Douglas Navigation basin.[3] Close by is a tramway which brought coal down to a coal tip that has now been immortalised as the supposed 'Wigan Pier'.[4] After the closure of the regulating lock at Dean (see page 106), the water supply for the Liverpool length entered the canal at Wigan. It left the River Douglas at a weir near Scholes Bridge,[5] and entered the canal nearly opposite the junction with the Leigh Branch.[6] At the side of the railway we can see the warehouse that John Hargreaves built in order to tranship his merchandise between the railway and canal.[7]

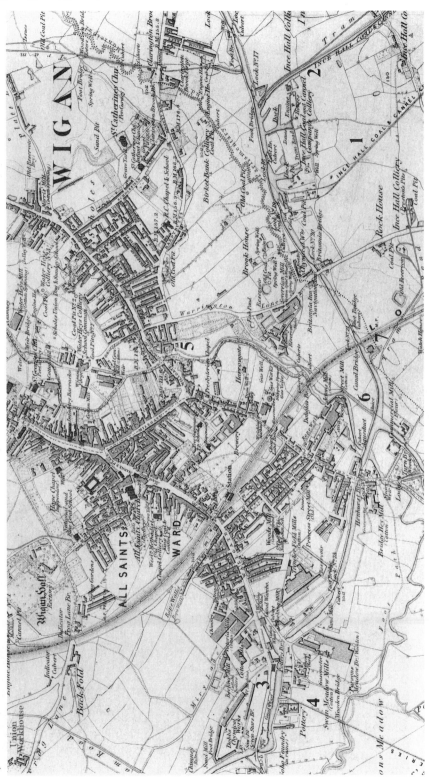

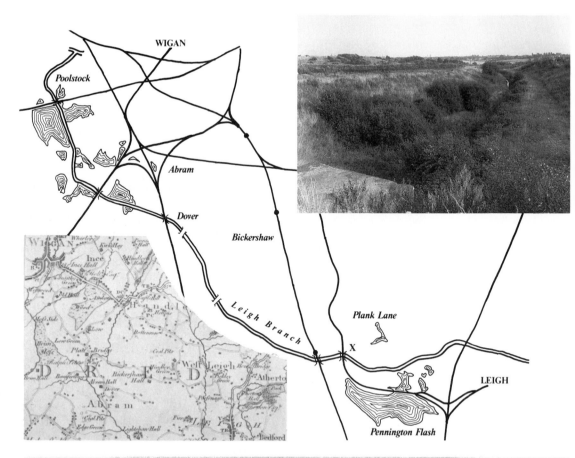

Left: The Leigh Branch, from Wigan to Leigh is a good example of almost total landscape transformation. The inset map is a detail from Yates' 1786 map of Lancashire, surveyed before any major industrialisation had taken place. The sketch map is drawn from recent O.S. maps and shows the Leigh Branch and the intensive railway network that grew up around Wigan (many now closed). Evidence of subsidence due to coal extraction is not hard to find. Not a single pond or lake appears on Yates' map but by the present day many flashes such as that at Pennington have formed as the land subsides. The main flashes are shown, showing not only the canal's importance for the location of collieries but also how it interrupted land drainage. The effect that this subsidence can have is shown graphically by the photograph (top right) of the old trackbed of one of the railways that used to cross the canal for, although it is now some fifteen feet below the canal, when the railway was operating it actually crossed above the canal on a bridge (marked X). It has been estimated that up to ninety feet of coal has been removed from this area and how much more subsidence will occur is uncertain. Already, much of the canal appears to run along embankments and during this century the locks originally at Dover and Bickershaw have had to be moved to Wigan.
(Yates' map by permission of the County Archivist, Lancashire Record Office.)

Left: A splendid nineteenth-century print of Saltaire, near Shipley, where Titus Salt established a large alpaca mill on the banks of the canal. The River Aire can be seen flowing past in the foreground, with the canal just visible behind.

West Lancashire. With hugely expanding populations, the towns of South and West Lancashire generated a need for their increasingly intensive farming systems in order to cope with demand for agricultural produce. Household refuse, horse manure and sewage from the towns was carried along the canal in great quantities to fertilise lands in West Lancashire that came to be capable of providing three crops every two years. The canal not only transported the manure, but it carried the potatoes, carrots and other produce to market.

By the 1880s, grain had also become an important traffic, the income from which was worth as much as that generated from transporting cotton. Windmills had long been found alongside the canal – the stump of one at Parbold can still be seen today – and following the introduction of steam power many more flour mills were built to be served by boat. This was particularly so in Lancashire, where they were erected at Liverpool, Burscough, Parbold, Blackburn, Clayton-le-Moors and Burnley, as well as at Skipton and Bingley in Yorkshire. Breweries were also large users of grain, with those at Blackburn and Kirkstall both being well placed for deliveries by canal.

In terms of the environment, the canal's impact is especially keenly felt around Wigan. In some places up to ninety feet of coal has been removed and subsidence has been very marked. Many early canal proprietors were responsible for the development of this coalfield and much of the coal was taken away by canal. The subsidence, especially noticable on the Leigh Branch, affected the canal in turn, with several locks having to be moved and with whole stretches of the canal ending up appearing to have been built on long embankments because the surrounding land has fallen away so much.

The construction of the canal was to interfere with drainage, not only by obstructing natural channels but also by the construction of reservoirs and feeders. Although the quality of canal water has often been criticised, the company actually had a good record of trying to keep it clean and it would appear that on the whole they succeeded. Water quality was constantly monitored and where contamination did take place, as at Bradford and with the water supply from the River Douglas, it was usually the fault of industry. Constant use of the canal ensured a fairly steady flushing of the canal as water was lost by leakage and through locks and, although the water could be churned up by commercial use and look dirty to the uninitiated, every indication is that the water itself was reasonably clean, certainly when compared to some of the streams and rivers near to the canal.

Thus, the building of the Leeds and Liverpool Canal produced what can only be described as a canal 'corridor'. Near its banks a particular kind of development took place whose legacy is still with us. Much of the industry built along the canal dates from the period of the canal's greatest success – the early- to mid-nineteenth century – and when these traditional industries began to decay and die the canal's traffic and very *raison d'être* died with it. It is not hard to find remnants of these industries: derelict land, worked-out mines and quarries, empty factories, mills and warehouses line the former industrial sections of the canal, symbols of the region's former glory. The time when 'Britain's bread hung by Lancashire's thread' has gone, but the immense impact the canal made on the area remains.

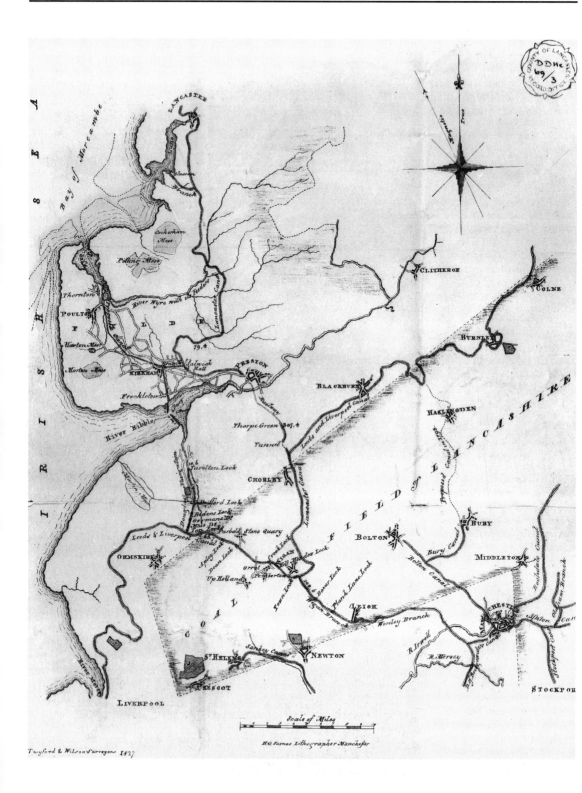

Left: *Various plans were put forward for the joining of the two ends of the Lancaster Canal from Preston to Walton Summit, which was connected by a tramway (here marked 'Railway') for much of the nineteenth century. None was more imaginative than this 1827 scheme, which included a floating towpath across the River Ribble from the mouth of the Douglas to a new canal at Freckleton, serving Kirkham and Poulton. A removeable section in the towpath would have allowed shipping access to Preston. It was never built.* (L.R.O. DDHe 69/3. Reproduced by permission of The Lord Hesketh, Towcester.)

Right: *Two excellent photographs of horse-boats. Walter was a general cargo boat and we can see here the sheeting that was used to keep the cargo dry. The side sheets, which were firmly wedged to the coamings, hang down into the hold while the top sheets are folded up on the stern deck. The three lines of iron supports for the sheets can be seen, but the wooden rails which ran on top of them have been removed. The profile of the bow section of the hull appears to be of clinker construction (see page 24), but the protrusions are protecting strips (known as 'whiskers') attached to the hull. On the other photograph the crew take an opportunity to feed the horse while they pose for the camera at Gargrave in around 1900.*

Right: *A very early drawing of a boat passing under Chisenhale Street bridge in Liverpool in around 1804. The River Mersey can be seen in the background.* (L.R.O. DP175. Reproduced by permission of the County Archivist, Lancashire Record Office.)

Left: Top Locks at Burscough, with the Rufford Branch disappearing in the distance. The houses on the right were built for boatmen. Stables were also provided with the houses, and canalside communities, such as this, are also to be found at Ring O'Bells, Burscough, Crabtree Lane and New Lane.

(Photo, author's collection.)

Right: *A steamer and dumb boat loading at Sawhills warehouse under Bankhall Bridge in around 1900.* (Photo, Liverpool City Engineer's Dept.)

Left, centre: *The canalside community at Rodley. Stabling was provided at the building, centre right; behind was a canalside pub and the company warehouse, while there is a coal wharf beyond the swing bridge.*

Left, bottom: *A maintenance boat at Bank Newton.*

Below: *The only known photograph of Liverpool basin when it was in use. It was taken from the canal warehouses on Pall Mall; the building on the left is the Bridge Inn, often used by boatmen.* (Photo, Liverpool City Engineer's Dept.)

Chapter Eight

Indian summer

Heyday and decline of the Leeds and Liverpool 1874 – 1990

N 4th August 1874 the Leeds and Liverpool terminated the railways' lease and took over responsibility again for running the merchandise traffic on the canal. Their timing could hardly have been better. Not only had the company managed to build up sizeable financial reserves during the period of the lease, but the railways, particularly the Lancashire and Yorkshire, were in no position to withstand the effective opposition which the canals were able to mount. For this was a time when the economies of Lancashire and Yorkshire were expanding faster than the railways were able to cope, resulting in poor service from their virtual monopoly of merchandise carriage. The service was often inefficient and, just as important, the railways were tending to drive rates upwards. Thus, they were vulnerable to any competition that was cheap and efficient, and it was this that the canal now endeavoured to provide.

The latter part of the nineteenth century was a time of promise for several northern canals. On the Aire and Calder, compartment boats, better known as 'Tom Puddings', had been introduced in the 1860s. To accommodate trains of compartment boats, the locks on the navigation were lengthened to 200 feet below Castleford, and 120 feet to Leeds. With improvements to their docks, they were able to compete successfully for traffic carried by railways, and by 1870 had significantly increased the tonnage of goods, particularly coal, using the navigation.

Then, in 1873, the Aire and Calder were asked by the Bridgewater Navigation Company if they were interested in a joint purchase of the Rochdale Canal.[1] Although no decision was made, it shows that trans-Pennine trade was still regarded as important for canals. The Bridgewater's interest in the improvement of canal trade is surprising, since in 1871, the company had been purchased by Sir Edward Watkin and W. P. Price, respectively chairmen of the Manchester, Sheffield and Lincolnshire, and the Midland Railways. Almost immediately, concern was expressed about railway involvement in the company. There was limited use of the Leeds and Liverpool for trade between Liverpool and Manchester, but the Bridgewater was the railway's only major competitor for that traffic. This dissatisfaction with railway monopoly of trade to Manchester was at least as important in the decision to build the Manchester Ship Canal as the expense of using Liverpool docks. The ship canal was first proposed in 1876, but not taken up due to the trade depression. The idea was revived as trade improved, and an Act obtained in 1885. The canal opened in 1894.

Work had started on improvements to the Leeds and Liverpool Canal before the railway lease ended. The introduction of steam tugs for the Liverpool coal trade had made dredging essential and in 1873 a new steam dredger was purchased at a cost of £1,045 from Sampson, Moore and Co. of Liverpool. A report presented to the committee discussed the condition of the warehouses, and recommendations were made for new ones.[2] In the five years from 1874, these were built at Bankhall, Liverpool, Brierfield, Nelson, Stockbridge, Shipley, Kirkstall, Botany and Rodley. Stables were built at Liverpool and Burscough, and a veterinary centre set up at Liverpool. Maintenance and improvement work was carried out on other warehouses all along the canal. Following the alterations at Liverpool, the Liverpool and Wigan Canal Mission were allowed to use an old office as a meeting room, and were given £10 per annum towards their expenses.

The carrying trade and how it was organised

THE carrying fleet had been bought back from the railways for £3,343, a quarter of the price paid in 1850. Then the fleet had consisted of eighty-one boats; by 1874 this had been reduced to less than thirty, many in need of repair. The inefficiency and lack of investment during the railways' control of the carrying trade is illustrated by the speed with which trade returned to the canal. Soon there were not enough boats and by the middle of August 1874 Warde-Aldam, a director of the company, noted:

> The lessees sent boats once a fortnight to Leeds, we have sent eight already . . . the lessees carried 3,250 tons last August; we in the fortnight have carried 4,250, and the wharfs are all blocked. There is now a great scarcity of boats. We depended on the Wigan Coal and Iron Company hiring us boats, but they have had a great demand, and are hiring boats themselves. We could have loaded thirty more boats if we had had them.[3]

Eight new boats had been ordered by the canal company before the carrying fleet had been taken over. They were delivered during 1874. Twelve more, at least, were needed, but the boatyards on the canal were too busy with repair work, so they were ordered in 1875 from William Alsop of Preston, who built a steam tug, six iron and six wooden boats,

for £690, £360, and £260 respectively.[4] In an effort to improve the supply of boats, the company purchased the boatyard at Whitebirk, leasing it for twenty-one years to one John Hodson. Land was purchased for the same reason at Burscough.

In addition, the Ince Hall Coal and Cannel Company's fleet of twenty boats was purchased, as they had recently ceased to use the canal. By 1875 the company owned sixty boats, though more than half the trade continued to be carried in bye-traders' boats.[5] Traffic increased steadily, and the canal was soon competing effectively again with the railways.

At this time, the canal company's boats were all named, with certain ones designated as flyboats. These had a crew of three men and operated to a daily timetable. From Liverpool, often leaving in the early evening, and working non-stop they could reach Leeds in two days and three nights. There were also daily flyboats to Bradford, Burnley and Blackburn, with other places served as required. The general cargo boats would leave when loaded and did not work to set times, though boatmen were paid a bonus for saving time. Two men operated these boats, in 1874 their weekly wage being twenty-three shillings for the captain and twenty shillings for the mate.

Steamer no. 40, built around 1910, here photographed probably at the top of Bingley-Five. In the centre of the boat is the lutchet or main mast, which was used particularly in locks for holding the boat steady. The four crewmen are all wearing the traditional 'ganseys' (from the word 'Guernsey'), a seamless jumper knitted on four needles. They also appear to be wearing the common dark blue corduroy trousers.
(Photo, author's collection.)

The steamers

IN 1880, the introduction of steam-powered cargo carrying flyboats brought about a change in the method of operation. These were able to tow three or four unpowered flyboats, and at locks horses were stabled for towing them through. This system operated at Wigan, Johnson's Hillock and Blackburn, the steamer waiting at the top or bottom for the horse-drawn boats to catch up. The dumb boats were dropped off on reaching their destination, or exchanged for boats with more urgent cargoes. On arrival at Barrowford locks, the steamer would continue on its own, leaving the dumb boats for Yorkshire to be worked by the horses stabled there or at Foulridge. Steam tugs which did not carry cargo operated to a regular timetable on the long lengths between Liverpool and Barrowford and on the Skipton length, towing general cargo boats not designated flyboats.

The flyboats would pick up, or set down, anywhere along the canal. Traffic was controlled from Liverpool, and messages were passed to the boat captains by lock keepers or agents at the warehouses, who were informed by letter or phone from Liverpool of any changes in the delivery or receipt of cargoes. Local agents could also arrange for the loading of goods by informing lock keepers. No load was too small, and often the boats would stop to take on just two or three hundredweight for delivery a matter of miles. The times when the flyboats passed were well known, and the company guaranteed the time of delivery. The system was extremely efficient, and during the 1880s the company took much traffic away from the railways, particularly in East Lancashire.

Bye traders had flourished during the railway lease of the 1850s and 60s. They were able to carry cargoes in both directions, taking coal from Wigan into Liverpool, and grain back to Blackburn and Burnley. The only unprofitable part of the journey was from the mill to the coalfield, but one hopes the boats were cleaned out properly between trips! Once they restarted carrying, the company found that most of their trade was from Liverpool and Leeds into the manufacturing districts. Return, and hence more profitable, cargoes were hard to find.

At this time, the textile machinery manufacturers were increasing their overseas market. The canal company became regular carriers for them, not only storing the machinery at their warehouses until it was needed for export, but also delivering it directly to the ships' side at Liverpool, removing the necessity for the goods to be handled on the quay. This speeded up loading, and cost less.

Empty working of boats was unprofitable and the company was always on the lookout for return traffic. In 1894 they started carrying cloth from East Lancashire to Manchester. The canal had never been a major carrier of finished textile goods, which, because of their high value and low weight, had been carried by road, and later rail. The Lancashire and Yorkshire Railway was not happy about the canal encroaching on their traffic and the local goods manager wrote, suggesting that it would lead to strained relations.[6] However, much to the railways' annoyance, in 1898 £300 was spent on providing the necessary covers and linings for the boats, allowing them to commence carrying finished goods. By 1901 the cloth trade was reported as satisfactory, saving boats coming from Manchester with grain, cotton, etc, from having to return empty. The traffic increased enough for improved craneage to be installed at Blackburn.

On occasion the company hired out boats to other carriers. In 1897, they were approached by Fellows, Morton and Clayton, the narrow boat carriers, who were tendering for a traffic from Manchester to Feniscowles, possibly for the paper works there. They required three boats, which the company offered to hire for forty pounds per annum each, and to sell them, during the three-year contract, at a price per boat of £230 plus expenses. It is surprising that Fellows, Morton and Clayton did not own short narrow boats, as several firms operated them, usually in pairs, carrying salt, chemicals and coal over the full length of the canal.

The horse marines

THE steam flyboats, although efficient, had definite disadvantages. On the Burnley length, they passed only once a day. If an urgent cargo had not been loaded by the time the steamer passed, it would be held up, creating problems, particularly if it was required at Liverpool for loading in the docks. Time was money, and ships could not afford to be kept waiting for small items of cargo. The company did have a warehouse at Birkenhead, and several lighters which acted as floating warehouses, but these were preferred for incoming cargo.

To overcome the delays, the four tugs used between Wigan and Blackburn were withdrawn in 1905 and replaced by nine horses and six marines (men who led and looked after the horses). The marines were on call twenty-four hours a day and house boats, for up to twelve men, were stationed at Wigan and Blackburn for them. While an urgent cargo was being loaded, the marine and his horse would be sent to the boat, which would then be three-handed, and could work fly to Wigan. There were several tugs working from there to Liverpool, with sailings at regular times throughout the day. If they had just missed a tug, the marine could continue with the boat, changing his horse as necessary at the company's stables. He would then return to Wigan or Blackburn by train. This system caused horses to accumulate at one depot, and marines had to be sent to walk them to the stables where there was a shortage.

By 1918, three marines were also based at Foulridge, which was where the proven and hay were kept for supplying the company's horses between Burnley and Leeds. Boats needing proven were given a sixty-pound bag, while small amounts, usually a few hundred pounds, were sent to the stables along the canal as required. This was delivered, either by the boat which brought the proven from Burscough to Foulridge, or by any other company boat that was passing in the right direction. About 1,500lbs were supplied to stables in the area each week, apart from Burnley, where about 5,000lbs were taken, mainly for the delivery horses based there.

There were twelve horses based at Foulridge, used by the marines for hauling boats into Yorkshire. Bradford, Shipley and Bingley were regular destinations, with the marines sometimes returning by train. The horses only worked as far as Gargrave or Skipton, where fresh ones were available. Besides their normal duties, the marines had to replace boatmen who became ill or were injured, enabling goods to be delivered without holdup. They were also used for unloading boats when warehousemen were not available, allowing the number of warehousemen to be kept low, and avoiding the need to lay men off when work was slack. During busy times, when extra help was needed, a passing boat could be stopped and the crew made to work in the warehouse. This was not popular with the boatmen, as apart from keeping them away from home, the wages were not as good.

The merchandise traffic, especially between Liverpool and East Lancashire, built up rapidly after 1874, as the canal successfully took trade away from the railway. The merchants and millowners of Burnley, who had asked the company to rescind the lease, were soon sending large quantities of goods by canal. A report in the *Accrington Observer and Times,* in May 1876, describes the trade at Burnley:

> It is a marked fact that the traffic on the railway from this district has fallen off considerably through the facilities offered by the canal company, and the statement is prevalent that the railway company has canvassed many manufacturers in the town to be allowed to resume their traffic, more especially to Liverpool, and that the falling off in this department has been so great of late that the railway company has been compelled to dismiss some of their servants.

The report went on to say that not only did the canal company provide better warehousing, but that their service from Liverpool was quicker than the railways'. The canal was certainly causing the railways to revise their operations and provide a better service.

Proposals for the building of branch canals

AT this time, prospects for the canal were even bright enough for proposals for several branches to be considered. In 1875, a petition was presented from the merchants and Accrington Local Board, asking for a canal to the town.[7] At one time, Accrington was to have been served by the canal by way of the original deviated line through East Lancashire, but the line had been altered and the warehouses at Church and Henfield became the centres for canal trade in the area. A Bill for the branch was presented in 1882 by the Local Board. It was to leave the main canal near to the Peel arm at Church, and follow the valley of the Hyndburn, to end just below the railway viaduct. Two industries in particular would have benefited from the scheme; coal could have reached the gasworks, and grain from Liverpool could have been delivered to the corn mill, both near to the proposed canal. Howard and Bulloughs, the textile machinery makers, who were major users of the canal for their export trade, would also have benefited. The removal of night soil to the West Lancashire agricultural area was another possible traffic. Unfortunately for Accrington, the canal company declined to make the branch themselves, even suggesting that the promoters would have to pay for the water used. Consequently the Bill was withdrawn. A branch was also proposed by Colne Local

The trees hide the only part of the abortive scheme to build a branch canal to Southport – an embankment that leaves the main canal about two miles west of Burscough.
(Photo, author's collection.)

Board, in 1880, but no further action was taken.

Branch canal schemes were sometimes designed to pressurise the railways into reducing their rates. This was the reason behind a branch to Southport, described in the *Liverpool Mercury* on 14th November 1885:

> The object of the scheme is to reduce the cost of transit of goods between Liverpool and Southport and adjacent places, and it is stated that the cost of carriage by the new canal would be cheaper than by either the Lancashire and Yorkshire or the Cheshire Lines Railways.

The canal was promoted by landowners and gentlemen from Southport. Plans were drawn up, and it was intended to hold a public meeting to canvas support. Interestingly, no official approach seems to have been made to the Leeds and Liverpool. The promoters must have owned much, if not all, of the land, as work was started without an application for an Act of Parliament. Initially the branch was to be from Scarisbrick, but this was soon altered, with a scheme to leave the main canal about two miles west of Burscough, heading almost due north. Work seems to have started with the construction of a short embankment which can still be seen today, about a quarter of a mile from the canal, to the north of Martin Lane, where there were to be two locks.[8] Perhaps this had the intended effect of persuading the railways to reduce their rates, for no further work was carried out and the embankment remains the sole monument to the scheme.

The West Lancs. Railway and Tarleton

THE traffic to and from Southport was also the object of the West Lancashire Railway. Their Act allowed them to operate vessels to ports on the Lancashire coast, to the Isle of Man and on the Leeds and Liverpool. The line from Hesketh Bank to Southport opened in 1878. Two years later they rented land, at twenty shillings per annum, from the canal, for a branch to Tarleton. Even before this, they had been carrying goods by canal, from Liverpool to Becconsall, where it was transhipped to the railway. Coal and iron were also delivered from

Wigan, but the main cargoes were groceries, grain, timber, flour and general goods from Liverpool. By 1880, they owned five boats, and a regular daily service was in operation between Liverpool and Becconsall. The opening of the railway branch to Tarleton in 1881 made the operation of this traffic much easier, as boats no longer had to use the tidal river.[9] When traffic warranted, extra boats were hired, often from the canal company. It is difficult to see how this traffic can have been profitable, however, as the canal tolls had to be paid before the railway could make any money.

The West Lancashire operated the Liverpool, Southport and Preston Junction Railway, which opened in 1887, and ran from Altcar to Southport.[10] Four years later, to reduce the cost of its independent service to Southport, the West Lancashire suggested an interchange basin at Halsall. The Liverpool, Southport and Preston was less than a mile from the canal here, and possibly it was planned to build a branch linking the railway to the canal. This scheme would have halved the canal distance travelled by goods from Liverpool to Southport, reducing the tolls by a similar amount. The railway was bankrupt for much of its existence, however, and so presumably could not afford to carry out the plan.

In 1882, the West Lancashire line was extended from Hesketh Bank to Preston, crossing the River Douglas on a swing bridge. The railway company tried to restrict the opening of the bridge to vessels with fixed masts, but the canal company was opposed, as it would interfere with their right of navigation. There were continual difficulties over the operation of the bridge. Tarleton was a port of some importance in the nineteenth century, and sailing vessels often lay against the quay wall below the lock to load and unload. Consequently it was important that an opening bridge should be provided, allowing access for those vessels. Warde-Aldam said of the port, in 1873:

> It has been proposed to make a tidal lock . . . vessels of eighty to one hundred tons come up to Tarleton, mostly with slate. Tarleton would be a second port for the canal and might be to the Leeds and Liverpool what Goole was to the Aire and Calder.[11]

It is a pity that a larger tide lock was not provided, though a scheme was suggested, in 1897, for a new canal from Tarleton to the Ribble, as an alternative to rebuilding the lock. This would have helped the Preston coal trade, but no action was taken as traffic did not justify the expense. In the nineteenth century, the level of the river bed outside the lock, was much higher, allowing cargoes to be transhipped between barges and sailing vessels while they sat on the river bed at low tide. The dredging of the Ribble from the turn of the century to improve access to the new dock at Preston resulted in the scouring out of the bed of the Douglas and, by 1910, this had made the transhipment of goods in the river at Tarleton difficult, though little trade remained.

The Lancashire and Yorkshire absorbed the West Lancashire in 1897, and, on finding that they did not own the land used by the Tarleton branch, proposed to abandon the line. The canal company eventually agreed to sell the land and the branch continued in use. By 1929, the only traffic was timber from Liverpool for James Mayor and Company's boatyard. The railway, which had complained to Mayor's about the expense of operating the branch, asked for £650 to put the line in order. Mayor's refused, as other means of transport were available, and the branch was closed in 1930.[12] Some of the rails from the branch were used by Mayor's to build slipways at their yard.

Profitable developments at Liverpool

1882 saw major changes at Liverpool. The Lancashire and Yorkshire's original station had been elevated, which made access difficult, and they wished to rebuild it at street level. This meant that the railway over the canal basin would need to be lowered as well. In addition, because of the canal basin, there were many changes in road level in the area and no through roads, so the Corporation also wanted to make several improvements. A scheme was agreed in which much of the old basin was filled in and a new road, Pall Mall, built across the site. A new basin and warehouses were to be constructed to the east of this road, allowing the railway to purchase some of the old basin site for the new approach to its station. The Corporation was not charged for the land used by the new road, though compensation was paid for the demolition and re-erection of the warehouses and other buildings.[13] After the new railway and roads had been built, the canal company still owned a large area of land on the old basin site.

During the reconstruction, traffic had to be accommodated elsewhere. Bankhall warehouse was already in operation, and new sheds were opened at Bootle in 1885. Alternative arrangements were made for the traders who occupied land around the old basin, and compensation had to be paid for the loss of their buildings. The old terminus was closed in August 1886. New offices and warehouses were then erected on Pall Mall and the veterinary department, only established in 1876, moved to Burscough, together with the main depot for stabling and provender.

Because of the alterations at Liverpool, the canal company had been able to modernise all their facilities there at little cost. More important, a large amount of compensation was paid. The company received £185,341 for land and buildings, which stood at only £21,595 in their books. There was also land around Old Hall Street, which had not been purchased by the Corporation or the railway. This was rented out and sold off over the years, providing another valuable source of income. With this influx of capital, and with the income from carrying trade increasing, the time seemed ripe for improvements to the canal.

Winterburn Reservoir and continued investment

BY 1880, an average of ninety boats were passing the summit every week. Three years later, lack of water forced the closure of the summit level for as long as a week on three occasions. Goods had to be transferred at Nelson to the Midland Railway, who delivered them to Skipton to be reloaded into boats. There was another drought in 1884, when the canal was closed for the whole distance from Gargrave to Wigan for three weeks. There was a further three-week closure the following year, but the worst stoppage was in 1887. The whole length from Bingley to Wigan was closed for over a month, and the summit section for a further two weeks, costing the company over £2,000 per week. The opportunity was taken by the engineering department to make repairs, and dredging was carried out more economically due to the low water level, but the closure was a major disruption.

The water shortages during these droughts were aggravated by the dramatic increase in traffic following the termination of the railway lease. In 1881, Mr Glaiser FRS advised the company about rainfall patterns along the canal, and Mr Filliter, a noted water engineer, suggested sites for new reservoirs. As a result it was decided in 1882 to build a reservoir at Barrowford to supply the canal in Lancashire, fed by the overflow from the reservoirs at Foulridge.

Despite these improvements, the Lancashire section was still short of water and in 1884 an arrangement was made with Blackburn Corporation for a supply from Pickup Bank and Daisy Green reservoirs at a cost of 3d per 1,000 gallons. The poor rainfall during the 1880s also restricted public drinking water supplies, and in 1885 Liverpool Corporation wished to stop the supply of compensation water to the Douglas from their Rivington reservoir, as required by their Act, and they arranged instead to increase the supply from Blackburn's reservoirs by the stipulated one million gallons per day. Blackburn suggested that the two reservoirs should be purchased by the company, but a price could not be agreed. They continued to use the supply until 1893, when the new reservoir at Winterburn was opened. Blackburn again offered to sell the two reservoirs in 1896, following another drought, but the offer was not taken up. Water was taken from Blackburn's supply for the last time in 1900.

Yorkshire also needed a new reservoir. The original site proposed in 1882 was on the Eshton Beck at Holme Bridge. This was close enough to the canal to be allowed by the original Act, so no extra powers would have been necessary. Unfortunately, Lord Hothfield, the landowner, would not agree, and other sites had to be considered. The location selected was at Winterburn, higher up Eshton Beck. The estimate for the reservoir, which was to hold 3,550 locks full of water, was £45,000. Work was soon underway, supervised by the consulting engineers, Filliter and Rose.

Conditions for the navvies was primitive and smallpox broke out in 1888. Skipton Rural Sanitary Authority complained, so the contractor erected a hospital, with furniture provided by the company. The reservoir was completed in 1891, allowing the supply to the Skipton length to be improved. The level of the reservoir was sufficiently high to allow it to feed the summit, and plans were drawn up for a pipeline feeder to Greenberfield. Besides supplying the canal, it also provided water to several houses and farms. It was completed in 1893.

Although the water supply was improved, there were still problems with the operation of the canal. The size of boats and their carrying

Bank Newton maintenance yard in about 1890. Just visible in the yard are some of the pipes that were used to build the pipeline to take water from Winterburn to the canal at Greenberfield. Note also the cow wandering among them.
(Photo, author's collection.)

capacity was considered too small, and both the Aire and Calder, and the coal merchants at Liverpool, had repeatedly asked for the canal to be improved. A report was produced in which it was estimated that the cost of upgrading the canal to allow boats to carry sixty-seven tons would be £550,000. If the cargo each boat could carry was increased to 110 tons, this would rise to £833,700. Both schemes required the locks to be lengthened. Mr.White, the canal engineer, finally recommended the less ambitious scheme, and had found ways to reduce the cost of this to £475,746.[14]

As built, Winterburn Reservoir was more than five miles from the canal, so its construction was not covered by the existing Acts. A Bill was presented to Parliament, not only for retrospective powers regarding the reservoir, but also to allow money to be raised to cover the cost of improvements. Unfortunately, to obtain the Act the company was forced to agree to several expensive clauses which, together with the new rates stipulated by The Railway and Canal Traffic Act of 1888, were drastically to reduce income. Their improvements were decided upon just too late to be financially viable.

The Act, obtained in 1891, besides authorising the work already undertaken, permitted the constitution of the company to be revised, and the company's shares to be rationalised, with permission for the issue of another £275,000. The constitution had to be changed to conform to the Companies Clauses Consolidation Act of 1888. The company's name was changed to 'The Leeds and Liverpool Canal Company', all reference to the Douglas Navigation being dropped, and the outstanding 2/36 shares finally purchased on 16 February 1893. It allowed a further £91,500 to be raised by mortgaging the old basin site in Liverpool, and they hoped to repeal the clauses in their old Acts which allowed landowners near the canal free passage for manure for their lands.

As a result of a legal battle, new clauses were also introduced to cover the working of coal mines under the canal. In the old Acts, the canal company was only obliged to purchase the coal directly under the canal if they wished to avoid subsidence. The Pearson and Knowles Coal and Iron Co. of Wigan had taken the company to court, claiming that to prevent subsidence considerably more coal needed to be left, and that the canal company should pay for all the undisturbed coal. The judgement went against the canal company, and it was estimated that this would cost them £30,000.

In Parliament, the Bill encountered considerable opposition from several quarters. The landowners obviously wanted to maintain their right to free carriage of manure; millowners were worried about the cost of condensing water for their steam engines; and West Riding County Council was concerned to keep a reasonable flow of water in the River Aire after the new reservoir was built. The principal opposition, however, came from the municipal and rating authorities along the canal. They had long considered the canal to have been under-rated, and had often attempted to obtain an increase. Under the original canal Acts, the rateable value had been the same paid for the land before its use by the canal. The company hoped to maintain this advantageous situation, while the authorities demanded increases to make the valuations comparable to that paid by railways.

As the water supply was still insufficient, a clause had been included for the construction of two more reservoirs in the Winterburn valley. Following the drought in 1896, when the summit had been closed for fifty-one days, estimates were produced for these reservoirs, together with an enlargement of Barrowford, and its connection to the Winterburn pipeline. A survey of one of the sites was ordered in 1898, but the cost of the overall scheme, estimated at £230,000, was prohibitive. The powers under the 1891 Act expired in 1906, and an Act was obtained in 1905 to extend the time for construction of the reservoirs. The work was never carried out, probably because of the cost. The company also realised that the increased volumes of compensation water demanded for the River Aire by the local authorities would significantly decrease the amount available to the canal, thus making the project uneconomic.

The Act, as in 1891, had many unfortunate features. Although the new reservoir was allowed, it also stipulated that 750,000 gallons had to be diverted daily into Eshton Beck as compensation water. Agreement over rating came too late for inclusion in the 1891 Act, and had to wait until the following year, when yet another Act was obtained. The valuation of the canal was raised, though for seven years only half of the increase had to be paid, costing the company £1,000 per annum. At the last meeting of the old committee, before the new Act came into force, it was noted that five members belonged to families connected with the company for at least seventy years, while Wheatley Balme was an ancester of Abraham Balme, who had served on the first committee, formed in 1770.[15]

Parliament slashes the canal's income

WITH the passing of the two Acts, the company was looking forward to the benefits of the reconstruction. Unfortunately, in 1893, the rates and tolls charged by the company were reviewed following the passing of the Railway and Canal Traffic Act in 1888. The canal's success may have led to the Board of Trade altering the canal tolls so that they were similar to those of the railways. The Board also attempted to abolish the empty boat charge, which raised £7,000 per annum for the company. It was opposed, but the company still had to accept a fifty per cent reduction in the rates it was allowed to charge.

Further, under this Act, they as general carriers had to take all goods offered at the rates designated. Bye-traders were under no such obligation and only took those which were highly profitable, leaving the company to take the remainder. These alterations had a disastrous effect upon profitability. The dividend had been equal to 3½% (or £15 per share) in 1890, but fell to 1% by 1900. The following year no dividend at all was paid on ordinary stock.

Despite the reduction in tolls, whose consequences were momentous in the longer term, the improvement of the canal went ahead. In 1892 two dredgers and a discharging crane were purchased for the Lancashire end of the canal. For Yorkshire, two steam spoon dredgers were acquired, following A. W. Stansfield's appointment as assistant engineer there at £400 per annum. Charles White retired in 1897, though he continued to act as estate agent, his son becoming engineer at £600 per annum. In 1902, Stansfield, previously vice-chairman, became managing director. Around the turn of the century responsibility for the different departments changed fairly rapidly, with alterations in title now making it difficult to decide who was doing what. R. H. White died on 28 May 1907, and was replaced by A. W. Stansfield, who was now designated general manager and engineer at a salary of £1,200 per annum.

Before mechanisation all the wood used for lockgates, swing bridges and boats had to be sawn by hand on the sawpit. By the time this picture was taken around the turn of the century, most of the wood would have been sawn up on the steam-powered saw at Burnley yard.

(Photo, author's collection.)

Because of the financial position, the engineer's job was now restricted to maintenance. There were innovations, though, and in 1909 a concrete mixer was purchased. This was mainly used for bank protection work. The company paid for their engineer to become a member of the Concrete Institute, so must have envisaged more advanced uses for the mixer. A decision to deepen the canal from Leeds to Shipley, by raising the banks at a cost of £99,157, was deferred. The protection of the banks between Liverpool and Wigan was carried out, but money was not available for widening the bridges.[16] Improvements continued over the next few years and by 1899 work was progressing on the Burnley length. This was estimated to cost £39,357, with a further £5,000 for work at Norden and Altham. However, the financial situation following the cut in tolls was deteriorating, and work beyond Blackburn was halted, except for £4,000 already commited.

The company was in a poor financial situation, and some of the shareholders formed an investigation committee to look into possible bad management. It was alleged that there was complacency, especially when it came to seeking new traffic. A meeting of shareholders, reported in the *Liverpool Mercury,* on 21st September 1901 noted:

> Complaints were heard, we observe, that there is no adequate canvassing for traffic, and that quotations of through rates and other necessary information are difficult to obtain. These are defects which ought to

Aspull Boatyard. This was the Wigan Coal and Iron Company's yard at Haigh, not far from the top of the Wigan flight. Here they had a large sawmill for all of the company's woodwork, as well as boat maintenance, and three slipways. The house on the right is now all that is left on the site.
(Photo, Wigan Education Dept.)

A coal boat passes Apperley Bridge maintenance yard in Yorkshire. This yard was owned and operated by the canal company and much of its work was in building and repairing lock gates. Some idea of the work involved at yards like this can be gained from the fact that in 1850 over one-third of the workmen's time was taken up just sawing wood into usable sizes; at this date all of this sawing work would have taken place in a saw pit. The canal company's yards also built coffins for company servants who had passed away. Interestingly, the workmen would get a couple of days off work after the funeral and, when the coffin was being transported along the canal, it was traditional that it had absolute priority over all other traffic.
(Photo, William Oldfield.)

The Finsley Gate Yard at Burnley in around 1900, one of the main yards on the canal. Here the length of the timber arriving appears to suggest that it had been felled locally, since it would not have fitted on a canal barge.
(Photo, Lancs. Libraries.)

have disappeared long ago. Business in these days does not drop into anyone's mouth. Even the railway companies are learning that in their own interests they must remove all hinderances from a customer's path, and render the consignment of goods a simple and straightforward matter. The Leeds and Liverpool Canal must cultivate the same methods, and there is no reason why it should be beaten by any railway company in energy and enterprise.

The directors replied with a statement comparing income and expenditure in 1890 and 1900. The toll on mineral traffic had fallen from .31d to .28d per ton per mile, so, despite an increase in coal carried, up 38,627 tons to 1,195,586 tons, income had fallen by £4,014.[17] Tolls on merchandise had also dropped, from .61d to .42d per ton per mile, and although the amount carried was at 630,271, up twenty-five per cent, receipts had fallen by £5,762. There had been a thirty per cent drop in income from tolls despite the increase in volume carried – such was the effect of the 1891 Act.

The beginning of the end?

THE company had certainly been unlucky. Their poor financial circumstances were the result of a number of unfortunate decisions, many of which lay beyond their control. Such large investment in improved warehousing and the upgrading of the canal had always been a risk, though much of this work was essential after the lack of investment during the lease of the merchandise traffic. On top of the reduction in income, there was the increase in rateable value, and the requirement to purchase coal under the canal, again both outside the control of the company. Finally, the weather had not been kind, with droughts in six out of the ten years before 1901, and a prolonged frost in 1895, when the canal was closed for two months. It was suggested that dividends had been kept too high, preventing the finance of improvements from income instead of capital. Had this policy been followed, it was argued, the company would not have been so heavily in debt.

All was not lost, though. Improvements to the canal reduced repair costs, and the deepening of the canal from Liverpool to Burnley did encourage traffic. The company still had large holdings of land in Liverpool, which were sold as the opportunity arose and the proceeds put towards reducing the debt. To increase the profitability of the carrying department, every effort was made to improve and promote the service. Further expenditure on improvements was curtailed, and the lengthening of the locks from Wigan to Blackburn to seventy-two feet, authorised in 1902 at a cost of £24,000, was postponed until finances justified the expenditure.

Despite, or perhaps because of, the financial situation, two offers came to buy the company outright. The first was in 1895, from Sir Fredrick Bramwell Bart, and was immediately rejected. A second, in 1905, came from a syndicate, acting through a firm of chartered accountants, J. H. Duncan and Co. of London.[18] The price was to be £100 per cent for debenture stock, loans and preference stock, with ordinary stock at £60 per cent. The syndicate was asked for a payment of £1,000 for the option, and for £1,500 against expenses. J. H. Duncan, who was present, declined these terms, offering £1,000 instead towards expenses, which was refused. The option remained open, though, if they would agree to the terms. The chairman and vice-chairman were against the proposal, coming when the company was in such poor shape. It is possible that the bid was actually put forward by shareholders, upset by the company's financial position.

The purchase and demise of the Bradford Canal

IN Yorkshire, the reorganised Bradford Canal was quickly in trouble. The restoration of the canal in the early-1870s had cost £25,000, and the expense of purchasing water from the Leeds and Liverpool and pumping it up to the summit level was greater than had been anticipated. Merchandise traffic, especially wool, did not return in the volumes expected, and although mineral traffic was increasing, tolls on this were low, and merchandise trade would have been the real money earner. To improve their finances, a mortgage of £5,000 had to be taken out.

In 1876, they offered to sell the canal to the Leeds and Liverpool and the Aire and Calder. A price of £27,000 was agreed and the two companies, as equal partners, split the cost and paid off the mortgage. The time limit for such a transfer, under the 1871 Act, had passed, however, and it was necessary to obtain a new Act to make the transaction legal. The canal was transferred on 1st January 1877, though the new Act was not passed until the following year. Following the takeover, water was supplied free by the Leeds and Liverpool, though the cost of pumping was still charged to the Bradford Canal accounts. The old company was wound up, and a new board set up, consisting of three members each from the Leeds and Liverpool, and the Aire and Calder. The chairman's post alternated yearly between the two companies.

With the Bradford Canal now under new management, investment came quickly. Three large warehouses were built at Bradford, along Canal Road, completed in the early 1880s, when they provided the best warehousing in the town, though the Lancashire and Yorkshire, and Midland Railways soon erected equally impressive facilities. Galvanising the railways in this way may have been the canal's best achievement, as its traffic only increased marginally. By 1892, a total of £58,437 had been invested in the canal, including the initial purchase.

The Aire and Calder suggested, in 1891, that the canal from Leeds to Bradford should be deepened to six feet. The company did not respond, being more concerned to improve the canal in Lancashire, where most of their traffic lay. There was a steady increase in trade, and the warehouses had to be enlarged in 1895. In 1900, over 9,000 tons of goods were sent to Bradford from Liverpool, with almost 3,000 tons from other places.[23] Only 2,000 tons were shipped from the canal. Income was £2,892 for the year, and expenses, including pumping, £3,192, resulting in a £300 loss. By 1902, warehousing again needed expanding, and space was rented from various other concerns to alleviate the situation. Lack of warehouse space at Bradford had resulted in boats having to wait for some time to be unloaded, which had caused a shortage of boats at Liverpool. In 1902, the Aire and Calder again asked for the canal up to Bradford to be enlarged, but, by that time, the Leeds and Liverpool was in no condition to spend the amount of money involved.

Indeed, warehousing provided most of the canal's income. In 1915, at the behest of the Aire and Calder, the warehouses were insured against aircraft raids for thirty pounds per annum, at an agreed value of £20,000. Despite the income from the warehouses, the expense of operating the canal was becoming prohibitive, especially the cost of pumping. In 1910, tonnages had begun to fall, and between 1917 and 1922 only 150 boats had used the canal each year. Because of the need to tranship at Leeds, even the Aire and Calder was finding it cheaper to send goods by road. In 1921, a Bill sought powers to abandon the canal. It was opposed by the Corporation, Chamber of Commerce, and the West Riding County Council. The preamble to the Bill was not proved, but the following year a similar Bill was passed, and the Bradford Canal closed on 29th June 1922.

It may seem surprising that the Bradford Canal never really achieved a great measure of success. It was, after all, Bradford merchants who instigated the main canal, and the head offices of the canal company were there. Despite the rapid expansion of Bradford, however, the canal was always hampered by the difficulty of its route up the confined valley of the Bradford Beck. With a fall of around eighty feet to the main line at Shipley, the water supply was never sufficient after the canal was no longer allowed to draw from the Beck and, at the end of the day, there was too little traffic to justify the high cost of pumping and maintenance.

Electric power?

THE company tried to keep abreast of the latest developments in canal engineering. In 1895, R. H. White and Mr Harris, sons of the engineer and chairman respectively, visited Danzic to see the inclined plane on the Ellring Overland Canal. On their way back they inspected ice-breaking techniques and types of boat used in Germany and Holland. In 1901, H. F. Killick, the company secretary, travelled to Belgium with Mr Bartholomew, of the Aire and Calder, to study electric traction, used on the Charleroi Canal. In 1897, electricity had been tried on the Leeds and Liverpool, when Thwaite and Cawley had been allowed to use one mile of canal for experiments with battery-powered boats.[19] A second trial was undertaken by Professor E. W. Marchant, of

Liverpool University who reported in 1907 on a system of towing boats using electric locomotives running on lines on the towpath. Trials, using two long barges, were carried out near Wigan, probably above Pagefield Lock. Marchant suggested the system could be introduced between Liverpool and Blackburn, where 2,000,000 tons were carried annually, which could repay the initial investment. The cost of the scheme, including track, overhead wire, sub-stations and eighty locomotives, was estimated at £196,635. The trial had been at Professor Marchant's request, and the company was not involved, beyond providing facilities. The results were presented to the Royal Commission on Canals and Waterways in 1908, but no action was taken to

George Clarke's brickyard at Rishton in around 1900, where firebricks for furnaces were made. There were several brickworks along the canal, especially in East Lancashire, using the canal for deliveries of coal to fire the kilns and to carry the bricks away.
(Photo, author's collection.)

Wigan Power Station in the mid-1950s. The coal for this power station came from Plank Lane Colliery on the Leigh Branch and formed the last traffic to use the canal until it finally ceased when the quality of coal from this colliery was no longer suitable for power station use in 1972.
(Photo, Jack Parkinson.)

implement the scheme.

Nevertheless, the company was extremely interested in electric power. In 1896, they proposed the construction of a generating station, for lighting purposes, to Bingley Urban District Council. Various schemes were drawn up to use the water lost at the five-rise locks. Turbines, operating on the waste water, could drive dynamos to feed a battery of 120 accumulators. One scheme involved the combined fall of the five- and three-rise locks, but was rejected as it would have affected the water level between the two sets of locks. Agreement over charges could not be reached with the Council, who improved their gas-holders instead.[20]

Foulridge Tunnel had to be closed for three weeks in 1902, when the section under the road to Barnoldswick collapsed. The repairs were carried out quickly, and Mr Bateman, the section engineer, was awarded ten pounds for his work. A further opportunity to repair the tunnel was taken during the summer drought, in 1910, when it closed for four weeks. In 1903, the lock at Ell Meadow was rebuilt, and a second lock was added in 1904. The same year plans were again drawn up for lengthening the locks to Blackburn, but no action was taken, although a new lock was built at Pagefield, near Wigan, as a result of subsidence. It included an experimental sliding tail gate, possibly to see if leakage following further subsidence could be reduced. The lock

An excellent photograph of the Whitehall Power Station on the River Aire, just upstream from the junction with the Leeds and Liverpool. In 1848 an arm of the canal was built from the basin up to the River Aire to by-pass the weirs and railway bridge. This made a stretch of the river from Leeds to Armley navigable for the first time and coal for this power station came via that arm. It actually came upstream from the Aire & Calder and boats had to come through the river lock onto the Leeds and Liverpool and lock up the canal arm in order to join the River Aire above to get to the power station. The arm has now been filled in.
(Photo, Leeds Libraries.)

walls had to be raised, in 1909, and the sliding gate may have been replaced at the same time.

There continued to be minor improvements to the water supply. Pumps were installed at Leeds in 1902 to feed the basin, and at Liverpool locks in 1934. Pumps were also proposed, in 1907, for the shaft of the old Stockbridge colliery, but the uncertainty of the reserves here prevented their installation. Bore holes at Foulridge were suggested in 1937, after it was thought too expensive to raise the lower reservoir, but they were never installed because of the cost of pumping. Closure of the canal due to lack of water continued after nationalisation, even in the 1970s. The increased pleasure use of the canal causes problems, with maximum demand in the summer when supplies are at their lowest. When the canal was used commercially, demand was more constant and, if anything, highest in winter when rain kept the canal topped up. The planning of water supply is now computerised, using information from rain gauges located throughout the watershed. From this, the flow of water from each reservoir is calculated to obtain the optimum supply. It is hoped that closure from water shortage is now a thing of the past.

There were many other requests for water. In 1801, Col. Lloyd was allowed to use the canal in the event of fire at Armley Mill. Sometimes water was taken without permission, and, in 1826, the company made Mr Houghton pay ten pounds to charity, and place an apology in the *Blackburn Mail,* when it was discovered that he was using canal water for his brewery at Grimshaw Park, near Blackburn. Water supply continued to be protected, with cast-iron notices warning traction engines not to take water from the canal, though the railway companies had been customers for many years. The Lancashire and Yorkshire were charged threepence per 1,000 gallons in 1904 for the supply of water at Wigan. Originally half a million gallons were allowed each week, but this was soon trebled. There were some odd requests, such as Mr Hulbert's for a supply of water to his kennel of hounds at Bingley. The committee agreed, charging him five shillings per annum. In 1901, the engineer complained that farmers around Skipton were washing their sheep in the canal, in contravention to the bye-laws. They refused to pay for the privilege and were polluting the canal and damaging the banks. Legal advice was taken, and the farmers were charged for the water. By 1905, only nine out of thirty-two farmers had paid, and proceedings were threatened. It was finally agreed that they could continue to use the canal, provided they did not damage the banks, and that only the sheep of canalside tenants were washed.

Warehousing continued to be improved, and new sheds were provided in 1903 at Feniscowles, for paper traffic, and at Stockbridge, for machinery. The following year a shed was built at Rufford. Better facilities were provided, and electric-powered hoists were introduced to replace the gas engines. At Blackburn, an electric motor was hired from the Corporation in 1909 for this purpose. The warehouse there had already been lit by electricity for twelve years. The operation of independent carters at the various depots had been criticised, and, in 1901, the company bought out the business of Mr Crawshaw, the carrier at Church, paying £1,500 for his horses, lorries, stables, etc. This must have proved successful, as the carting firms at Burnley and Nelson were also taken over in 1905.

Limestone traffic continued to decrease, and the lease of Rain Hall Quarry was given up in 1891, as it was worked out. Haw Bank continued to be operated, however, and the quarry had been connected to the Midland Railway in 1888. A stone quarry, Dawber Delf, was leased in 1900 at Appley Bridge. Much of the stone for the training walls of the Ribble Navigation came from here, providing a regular traffic to Tarleton.

Strikes!

INCREASING unionisation of labour was to have its effect on the company. The coal strike in 1912 cost £4,000 in lost income. The effect of the strike was reduced by the fact that the year before the company had bought 600 tons of coke, which enabled the steamers and tugs to continue operating. Closer to home, the Boatmens Union in Liverpool had tried unsuccessfully to obtain recognition from the company in 1911. There was a strike about payment for Sunday work on 15th February 1913, when 200 boatmen, mainly from Burscough, were involved. A few of the strikers were summoned before Liverpool magistrates, where they were ordered to pay one week's wages as damages, and charged two shillings costs, for ceasing work without giving a week's notice, as required by their contract.[21] The company only asked for the costs, keeping the wages temporarily to deter further action. The same year the Liverpool Shipwrights Trade and Friendly Association requested an increase in pay for the boatbuilders at Wigan and Burnley. The company refused to recognise the union, and, in May 1913, the boatbuilders at the two yards left the company's service. This may have had some effect on the company, as the carpenters and other tradesmen were recommended for wage increases.

The company's financial situation was not helped by the First World War. To keep staff, who would otherwise have left for well-paid jobs producing munitions, the company was forced to pay war bonuses. These started at two shillings per week in 1915, rising to eighteen shillings by 1918, increasing wages by more than fifty per cent. Unlike railway companies, no help towards these was given by the Board of Trade. The cost of the two shillings increase for boatmen was £2,124 per annum, suggesting that 400 men were employed in the carrying department.

Working conditions, where they were out in all weather and often away from home, made it difficult to keep men. The situation was improved when soldiers, from the Transport Workers Battalions, were sent to work on the boats. Each soldier boatman was paired with one of the company's boatmen, and acted as mate. As army personnel, they continued to wear uniform. A new munitions wharf at Salterforth, and the Ordnance Depot at Burscough, provided new traffic, but overall it was decreasing. This may have been caused in part by the difficulty in keeping staff, and in 1916 the engineer reported that repairs were held up for this very reason.[22]

An order from The Board of Trade, on 22nd February 1917, brought the canal under the Canal Control Committee. They hoped to encourage trade by canal, as railways could not cope with the traffic. Compensation for government control was to be based on the accounts for 1913, but the company complained that this had been a poor year, and a five-year average was agreed. The committee controlled all aspects of the canal. New boats could only be ordered with their agreement, and staff conditions were changed arbitrarily. For example, in 1919, they ordered tradesmen's hours to be reduced to forty-seven per week without consulting the company.

Government control came to an end on 31st August 1920, despite applications from many independent canals to the Ministry of Transport requesting a continuation of government subsidy. The Leeds and Liverpool was still in a very poor state financially, and asked for a guarantee that its expenses would be paid until the effect of post-war increases in tolls had been ascertained. Instead, the Ministry offered a loan of £6,666 for twelve months, at one per cent above the bank rate. Further financial assistance was not forthcoming from Parliament, but the Minister said he would look favourably on increases in tolls. To keep the canal going, the auditor agreed that capital money could be used, provided debenture holders were covered by the canal's assets. In the midst of these negotiations, one of the shareholders, a Mr Sing of Liverpool, offered to buy the company at market price. The directors recommended that shareholders only accept fifty per cent of the book value, which must have been too high, as the offer lapsed. Another inconclusive offer came at the end of 1923, from Messrs James Little and Co. Ltd. of London.

The company ceases carrying

THE company merchandise fleet comprised about 130 boats in the early 1900s, though the total number they had owned between 1874 and 1921, when they gave up carrying, was at least 298, including forty-six steamers. They also owned ten steam tugs. In the twentieth century, names were no longer used for boats, each one being identified by a number, with the horses suffering a similar indignity. Flyboats worked to specific destinations – for example, twenty boats were designated Bradford flys and a similar number served Blackburn. The last three boats built for the fleet were nos. 350-352, and were launched in 1920.

The company was especially concerned about the cost of the carrying department. In 1920, the traffic manager produced a scheme offering the boatmen a fifteen shillings per week increase, with a further five shillings after three months if trade improved. This was refused by the boatmen, many of whom chose this moment to leave the company. By 1921, a large number of boats were tied up for want of crews. This, on top of the company's already precarious financial situation resulted in the company giving up carrying on 30 April 1921, and the boats and carting equipment were sold off.

Continued decline on the Leeds and Liverpool

LEEDS and Liverpool assets continued to be sold in an effort to improve finances. By March 1922, £26,079 had been raised from the sale of boats, only fourteen steamers and twenty-nine boats remaining unsold. The entrance to the Rain Hall branch was purchased by the Barnsey Shed Co. Ltd. for one hundred pounds, while Rufford warehouse was removed by John Sutton, on payment of twenty pounds. More land was leased, including the canal bank at Aintree to Messrs Tophams. The King had attended the Grand National in 1924, and Lord Derby had thanked the company for the arrangements they had made.

Several power stations were built along the canal, and these provided a good source of income, since the canal supplied both coal and cooling water. There were three new canalside stations, at Wigan, Whitebirk and Armley. At Armley, an arm was built alongside the canal in 1927, at a cost of £13,806, providing a profit to the company of £2,394. Two years later, the canal in Liverpool was used as the route for a high voltage power line, and cables were suspended from gantries erected over the canal, from Lightbody Street to Litherland. In 1927, the warehouses at Pall Mall, Bankhall and Bootle were sold to the Mersey Wharfage Co. Ltd., raising £85,000. Mersey Wharfage agreed to keep the wharfs and basins open for the benefit of the bye-traders. It was not all bad news, however, and the wool traffic to Shipley was expanding, where a new four-storey warehouse was built in 1928 at a cost of £8,000. It was extended in 1931. Another warehouse for wool was built at Stockbridge, in 1934, at a cost of £6,000. Competition for this traffic was keen, and rates had to be lowered in 1931 following a reduction by the London, Midland and Scottish Railway.

The three main firms which continued merchandise carrying after 1921 were John Hunt & Sons, Benjamin C. Walls, and Lancashire Canal Transport. John Hunt & Sons had been carriers on the Aire and Calder since the middle of the eighteenth century. They had not worked on the Leeds and Liverpool before, but following an approach by Mr Garnett, the agent at Leeds, they leased the warehouse there and purchased five boats. They eventually had twenty boats, all horse-drawn, and named after animals. They carried from Liverpool to Leeds, their main traffics being sugar from Tate & Lyle for the Leeds Co-op, sugar and barley for Tetley's Brewery and cocoa beans for Rowntree & Co.. Cement formed their return cargo, and they persuaded G. & T. Earle of Hull to open depots at the canal company's warehouses. Their traffic on the canal was never very profitable, though it did increase their business on the Aire and Calder.

Benjamin C. Wall had been the Leeds and Liverpool Traffic Inspector since 1903, so knew the canal well. His fleet eventually comprised twenty boats, named after Greek letters and planets, eight of which were motor boats. They carried a wide variety of goods, but their main traffic was wool. Walls later became wool merchants, with transport only part of the larger business.

Lancashire Canal Transport was organised by Commander Dean, awarded the VC in 1918 for his bravery during the blocking of Zeebrugge; he also managed Dean Waddington, the Blackburn coal merchants. They had thirty-two boats, identified by their old company numbers, and leased most of the warehouses in Lancashire. Their trade included all those previously carried, mainly cotton, groceries and grain from Liverpool, with textile machinery taken in return.

By 1929, Lancashire Canal Transport was in financial trouble, and to extricate them the company forced an amalgamation of the three main merchandise carriers. Shares were also to be held by the Liverpool Warehousing Co. Ltd. (formerly Mersey Wharfage.). The Leeds and Liverpool owned fifty-one per cent of the new comany, called Canal Transport Limited. The capital of the new firm was set at £40,000, and the Leeds and Liverpool's general manager and engineer were to be manager and secretary of the new company respectively. New steel and wooden motor boats were purchased by the canal company and sold to Canal Transport Ltd. on hire purchase terms, a method of encouraging trade the company had used before. A model of one of these new boats, built by Yarwoods of Northwich, was presented to Liverpool Museum by the canal company and Canal Transport Ltd. in June 1934.

In 1925, Stansfield retired, though continued to act as a consultant, at £600 per annum. He was replaced, as general manager and engineer by Robert Davidson, who was to remain until nationalisation, initially at a salary of £800 per annum. In July 1929, the maintenance of the canal was rationalised. F. W. Bateman, inspector between Leeds and Blackburn, took responsibility for the supply of materials, dredging, water supply, ice breaking, etc. for the whole canal, with Albert Bateman as his assistant; he reported directly to the general manager. The canal was then divided into four sections, with a foreman in charge of each. The sections were from Leeds to Rainhall, Rainhall to Blackburn, Blackburn Bottom Lock to Appley Bridge and from there to Liverpool, the foremen being A. Turner, A. Buck, A. Rigby and R. W. Gaskell respectively. The carpenters' yard at Briars Hall, near Burscough, was closed, and the two men employed there were transferred to Wigan. A scheme was introduced at the same time to improve the canal banks, particularly in areas of high unemployment, and details of the work were sent to the government to obtain financial assistance.

It was suggested, in 1937, that more water could be saved if the locks at Wigan were equal in depth. This was considered too expensive, but it was agreed that the length above Wigan should have concrete bank protection, which could have reduced leakage. A suggestion in 1935 to lengthen the locks in Yorkshire to take two boats and thus speed traffic, was not taken up.[24] A further sign of the times came when the warehouses at Botany and Salterforth, which had not been used for some time, were demolished.

With the threat of war, A. S. Keeling, an engineering assistant, was sent on a course for anti-gas precautions, and a pamphlet was issued to all the company servants. Air raid precautions were taken, and stop planks were positioned at eighty points along the canal. ARP wardens were instructed in the use of these planks, which were put into position every night in case the canal was damaged by bombing, in order to reduce the amount of water lost. Government grants were obtained for the installation of further stop plank grooves at danger points. Air raid shelters were built at Liverpool, Wigan, Burnley and Apperley Bridge depots, and a good supply of sheeting obtained for the repair of breaches. The canal was also deemed to form one of the fall-back lines should Britain be invaded, and tank traps and gun emplacements were erected, most noticeably in West Lancashire.

Enemy action damaged the canal at Liverpool, Litherland and Leigh in September 1940, and in the following January there was a major breach opposite Sandhills coal tip. It took two months to reopen Sandhills depot and six months before the terminus and locks could be used. Because of damage at Pall Mall, a temporary head office was set up in a house in Formby, and the company's legal papers were moved to Bank Newton, where a strongroom was built. A new depot was constructed, for goods from the docks, just outside Liverpool at Gorsey Lane, where bomb damage was less likely.

Because of war work, it again became difficult to keep staff. In February 1941, tradesmen were awarded 3/6 per week increase, while the outside staff, who were more difficult to retain, were given from 5/6 to 8/3 per week. In November, following a dispute, boatmen's wages were increased by ten shillings per week. Wages continued to be increased throughout the war, and from 1945 the canal was closed on Sundays to reduce overtime payments. The boatmen were in dispute again, in May 1945, and went on strike for ten days for improvements in wages and conditions. The company had often provided pensions for long serving employees, but following an increase in state pensions in 1946, each case was looked at individually.

Maintainance work continued, and in April 1945, the depth of the twelfth lock pool at Wigan was raised by two feet, as the cill on the eleventh lock had become too shallow. It was hoped, eventually, to equalise locks ten to thirteen to help save water. On the Leigh Branch, there was a breach caused by subsidence, and the bed of the canal from Plank Lane to West Leigh was raised with 20,000 tons of rubble. This reduced water pressure at the bottom of the canal, which had become too deep due to subsidence. In 1946, Leeds warehouse was flooded when the River Aire overflowed, and some of Tate and Lyle's sugar was damaged. A raised curb was built round the basin in an effort to prevent a recurrence.

Nationalisation and 'rationalisation'

THE independent existence of the Leeds and Liverpool finally came to an end on 1st January 1948, when the canal was nationalised and came under the control of the North West Area of the Docks and Inland Waterways Executive. The last general meeting was held in Manchester, on 24th March 1948. The canal was still used extensively, particularly for the supply of coal to power stations and gasworks, and grain continued to be carried to Blackburn and Burscough, wool and sugar from Liverpool to Yorkshire, and cement from Leeds. The importance of the canal was reflected in the appointment to the Docks and Inland Waterways Executive of Robert Davidson, general manager of the company since 1925.

Initially, few changes were made, though Mr Keeling, who had been Robert Davidson's deputy, responsible for engineering, was moved away from the canal. Mr Adams became area engineer, based at Wigan, and his assistant was Mr Dawson, who had worked many years for the canal. The control of maintenance became more centralised, with offices for the whole of the North West located at Lime Street Station in Liverpool. C. M. Marsh, formerly of the Weaver, was engineer there, with his deputy, Muir White, responsible for the Leeds and Liverpool.

Morale on the canal, already low as traffic disappeared, was reduced through poor management. A new gate-making workshop and boat repair yard was established at Wigan in the mid-1950s. This was badly designed, the roof not being high enough for the new gates to be turned over during construction, and when the yard was run down, many of the machines, installed at great cost, had hardly been used. With money being spent elsewhere, little major work was undertaken on the canal. The locks and bridges were in a poor state and it seemed likely that the canal would be closed. Fortunately, this did not happen, and following the 1968 Transport Act, the offices at Liverpool were closed, and the engineering staff concentrated at Wigan, under the Area Engineer, Mr Freeman, though Northwich was the headquarters for the North West area. Since this reorganisation, lockgates are made at Stanley Ferry or Northwich, with the local workshops responsible for day-to-day maintenance. Recently there have been further changes, with Mr I. Selby appointed as manager of the canal, a position similar to the post held by Robert Davidson up to nationalisation.

During the 'fifties, many traffics had disappeared, and by 1956 working expenses had reached £260,000, with an income of only £127,500. This represented about thirty per cent of total losses from the national waterway system.[25] Many factories were turning from steam to electricity and no longer needed coal, while others simply closed. Loading and unloading facilities were often old fashioned, giving the canal a poor image, and many continued to rely on on manual labour, which was becoming more expensive. The weather finally killed trade during the winter of 1963-4, when the canal was frozen up for several weeks. Afterwards, the delivery of coal to Liverpool Gas Works, the last traffic on the main line, ceased.

Perhaps it was the triumph of the accountant, with their opposition to the stock piling of material, so essential to canal trade, that was the real cause of the death of carrying on the canal. By the strictly financial criteria of accountancy, it was easy to show that road transport was cheaper and more reliable. No account, though, was taken of environmental factors, where canal transport is undoubtably superior. There were other reasons, though, for the demise of traffic.

In 1962, the fleet of John Parke & Son Limited, which worked the Liverpool coal traffic, was taken over by the Waterways Executive. It must have been obvious at the time, that the traffic which they were employed on would soon cease. There had been several attempts in the 1950s to increase traffic on the canal by firms such as Airedale Canal Services, but they were never able to acquire sufficient boats to obtain long-term contracts. By purchasing Parkes' fleet, the Waterways Executive ensured the demise of carrying on the Leeds and Liverpool, and most of the boats were broken up immediately after the coal traffic to Liverpool finished. In 1962, the canal had lost over £200,000, and it was envisaged that such losses would continue. Because of this, and the minimal income received from pleasure craft and water sales, there was a distinct possibility that the canal would be closed.[26] Fortunately, pressure was growing for the leisure use of waterways, enabling the canal to survive, albeit in a run-down condition.

With the decline in traffic, the basin at Liverpool ceased to be used, and was filled in from Chisenhale Street bridge in 1960. The remaining traffic on the canal disappeared in the early-1960s until only the coal delivery to Wigan Power Station remained. This finished in 1973, when the quality of coal from Plank Lane Colliery became no longer suitable for power station use. There have been attempts since to restart trade. Northern Counties Carriers, David Lowe, Derek Bent and Chris Topp have all been involved, but difficulties in loading and unloading, insufficient craft, problems with the condition of the canal, and not least the closure of the canal for maintenance in winter, have all played their part in their lack of success.

The carriage of goods on the canal had lasted just two hundred years, and now leisure and recreation have taken over from commerce. Over the last twenty years there have been many improvements, and the neglect of the 1950s and '60s is disappearing, although, because of its larger dimensions, the canal did not require dredging to the same extent as the narrow canals of the Midlands. Much money has been spent on the locks, with new gates being regularly installed, though much of its original paddle gear, which was simple and robust, has disappeared, to be replaced often by more complex and slower hydraulic gear. Although more money is now being invested in the canal and its environment, much remains to be done to improve its amenity value for the community. However, recent initiatives to regenerate the canalside auger well for the future.

Chapter Nine

'For the conveyance of passengers'

Passenger traffic and leisure use on the Leeds and Liverpool

HE possibility of the canal being used for leisure had been envisaged even before it opened, and the original Act of 1770 contained a clause allowing the use of pleasure boats by owners and occupiers of land adjoining the canal. No charge was to be made, unless they passed through a lock, when they had to pay a toll equal to the carriage of fifteen tons. They were also warned not to obstruct the navigation. Shooting game and fishing from a boat was deemed illegal, however, with a £5 fine for each offence. The fishing rights were granted to the local lord of the manor, or the landowner, provided they did not damage canal property, but they were not able to prosecute company servants who took or destroyed fish in the course of their work. The towpath was not considered to be a right of way, and, as early as 1782, the canal committee was complaining about it being used to evade turnpike dues.[1]

The packet boats

AS soon as the canal opened, in 1774, passenger-carrying boats began operating between Liverpool and Wigan. These were called 'packet boats' as they also carried parcels. They were not allowed to carry merchandise, which had to be sent by a flyboat, which only carried cargo. The charge for travelling by a packet was laid down in the bye-laws, passed in October 1774, which stated:

> That every person passing in any boat between Wigan and Liverpool, or any other part of the line, shall pay for every two miles or under, one

half-penny; each passenger to be allowed fourteen pounds weight of luggage; and in case any boatman shall neglect to give a just account of the number of passengers he shall at any time carry on his boat, with the distance each passenger shall have passed, he shall forfeit the sum of ten shillings.[2]

It must have been difficult for the company to ascertain numbers of passengers travelling on the packets, as the following year an annual charge of £90 per boat was introduced. There were at least two firms owning and operating packet boats, the Union Company, and Longbotham and Co.

Later, the canal company owned the packet boats themselves, renting them out to the operators. In 1789, Jonathan Blundell and Sons of Liverpool hired the two packets for seven years. They did not take the market boat, which, presumably, carried farmers and farm produce into Liverpool. The cost had risen steeply, suggesting that this form of travel had become very popular. Blundell and Sons paid £400 per annum for three years, and £450 afterwards, though they were exempt from tolls. It was agreed that a new packet be built to Blundell's plan, either by the canal company, or by Blundell, who would be paid 200 guineas by the company in the latter case. Letters and employees sent by the company were carried free.[3] Following the building of the new packet, one boat was spare, and it was used on a commuter service between Liverpool and Old Roan, at a rental of £20 per annum.

In 1791, Gurney Pearse, one of the London proprietors, asked if he could set up a service from Skipton to Bingley. The company stipulated that his boat should be no longer than forty-five feet and was not to have sails. He was given permission to operate for seven years, at £50 per annum, though parcels over fifty pounds in weight were not to be carried.[4] The following year he was allowed to extend his service to Holme Bridge, near Gargrave, but was initially refused permission to operate a second boat from Bingley to Horsforth Bridge, near Leeds. By 1793 packet boats were working through to Leeds. Three were used, and in view of the time which would be lost at the riser locks, it is likely they operated from Gargrave to Bingley, Bingley to Newlay and Kirkstall Forge to Leeds, avoiding the three-rise and five-rise locks.

The early packet boats were not particularly well organised, and Thomas Newte commented in his *Tour of England and Scotland*, published in 1791:

> Several boats are kept on this canal for the convenience of passengers, but they are by no means so well regulated as the boats on the Duke's canal; for we were witnesses of much disorder, and very improper

CANAL PACKET BOATS
FROM LIVERPOOL,
TO
Crosby, Southport, Wigan, Manchester,
AND INTERMEDIATE PLACES,
DAILY.

THESE Boats, which possess very superior accommodations, leave the Canal Basin at Liverpool, for Bootle and Crosby, and return to the same place, Four times each day until the 1st of June next ; when the extra Boat will, *as usual*, commence plying ; from that time until the 1st of October, the communications to and from Liverpool and those places of fashionable resort, will be *Seven times each day* ; to and from Southport, Wigan, Manchester, &c. once each day.

Carriages attend the Packets at Scarisbrick to convey Passengers to Southport, where they arrive from Liverpool at 12 o'Clock.

By these Boats Passengers arrive at Liverpool, Manchester, Bolton, Rochdale, Stockport, &c. *without the risk of the Tideway, or the frequent accidents attendant on Steam Boats.*

Arrival & Departure of Packets Daily, during the Summer Months.
(EXCEPT SATURDAY AND SUNDAY.)

FARES.

ONE FAMILY.	To BOOTLE.	LITHERLAND.		To BOOTLE.	LITHERLAND.
4 Weeks	£1 4 0	£1 7 0	One Passenger, 1 Year, £7 0 0	£8 0 0
4 do.	2 0 0	2 12 0	Two do.	9 0 0	10 0 0
20 do.	4 10 0	6 0 0	Three do.	10 0 0	10 10 0
The Summer Months, from 1 May to 1 Oct.	6 0 0	8 0 0	Four do.	10 10 0	11 11 0

Subscribers to the LANCASHIRE WITCH to pay one-half additional for the use of the small Boat.

MAY, 1827.

Until the advent of railways, the canal provided by far the most comfortable means of passenger transport – smooth, peaceful and quiet. The lock-free length at Liverpool was ideal for such traffic and was used intensively, as can be seen from this timetable, for packet boats using this section in 1827. Judging from the fares at the bottom, the company was keen to attract regular customers, and those who chose to take advantage of the yearly tickets (£7 to Bootle, £8 to Litherland) could use any of the seven departures every day during the summer months.
(L.R.O. DP175. Reproduced by permission of the County Archivist, Lancashire Record Office.)

conduct, which must make those vehicles very unpleasant to females.

Besides poor organisation, there were reports in 1800 that the Liverpool packets were carrying merchandise at the lower parcel rate. The charges were increased, but the company cannot have been satisfied with the way Blundell was operating the boats, as they took away his license in 1806. Two new boats were built, sixty-feet long by ten-feet beam, to be worked by the company. By 1814, there was a daily service between Liverpool and Wigan, the journey taking nine hours.[5] There were a further two trips, of just over two hours, between Old Roan and Liverpool. A market boat ran on Saturdays, and an evening service on Sunday.

A new service was introduced in September 1816, when Silvester Bracewell began operating between Blackburn and Burnley. He was initially charged £6 per month, but the following year this became five shillings per trip. Mr Lawrence Houghton, of Altham, described this boat in his reminiscences of the Accrington district in the 1830s:

> Each boat was drawn by two horses, both of which were ridden, and one of the riders blew a bugle from time to time to give notice of the approach of the boat to would-be passengers. Between the stopping places the horses went at a trot after the boat had gathered speed. These boats, which carried mails for the Post Office, were seated for passengers on both sides, and had their decks covered over, there being windows in the sides which gave an ample supply of light. The covering, or roof, that enclosed the deck had a flat top, on which accomodation was provided for additional passengers when the interior of the boat was full. I have seen them sometimes on Sunday nights, festival occasions, and the like, so crowded with passengers that they appeared to be in some danger of being swamped.[6]

At night time the boats were illuminated inside. Mr Bracewell thought the boats, which were about twelve yards long, to be beautifully painted, but gave no indication of their colour scheme.

The opening of the Leigh Branch at the end of 1820 allowed a service to Manchester. At first it ran between there and Scarisbrick, from where Southport could be reached by road. The packet ran three times per week, though not on Sunday. A few years later this had become a through service between Liverpool and Manchester, and many Manchester people used the service to reach Southport. The following description was given by Sir George Head in 1836:

> On arriving at Scarisbrick Bridge, a little to the northward of Ormskirk, omnibuses and luggage carts were waiting for the conveyance of passengers to Southport, a watering-place near the Ribble, and distant about six miles, with which place the citizens of Manchester keep up a continual communication by means of the canal. Vehicles leave Southport at nine in the morning, meet the Liverpool boat on her way to Manchester, and remain at Scarisbrick Bridge until four o'clock, the usual time for the arrival of the boat moving in the opposite direction.[7]

It was also possible to catch the coach for Preston and the North, by leaving the packet boat at Burscough. In summer, the journey took about fourteen hours, and was completed each day, but in winter an overnight stop was made at Wigan. This caused some problems, and on one occasion a family's possessions were stolen from the warehouse at Wigan, where they had been left for safe keeping overnight. The company denied responsibility, but gave them £30 to compensate for any hardship. In 1821, a new packet was built for the local service to Old Roan, and by 1827 there were seven trips daily, with one less at weekends, though the Sunday service was withdrawn in 1830 following the presentation of a memorial to the company.[8] The local Liverpool boats were very popular. The company was approached by a Mr Miller, who wanted to run his own boats to Bootle; permission was refused, possibly because they would compete with the company's own service.

In 1833, a report on the new Lancaster Canal packets was presented to the committee.[9] These boats could average ten miles per hour between Preston and Lancaster, horses being changed every five miles. They were seventy-six feet long, with a beam of six feet, drawing five inches of water unloaded, increasing to eighteen inches when full with one hundred passengers. Despite its speed, this type of boat was considered unsuitable for the Leeds and Liverpool. They did not provide enough accommodation, particularly for families, who were the largest users of the packets. They were also more expensive to operate. At that time, income from the packets was £9-10s-4d per day. The cost of hauling the boats of £4-11s-9d, would increase to £8 with the new type of boat, reducing the profit.

By 1838, rail travel between Liverpool and Manchester had reduced demand for the packets. They may still have been operating in 1842, when Mr Gregson of the Lancaster Canal requested a donation from the company towards the cost of designing a steam-powered packet. It is uncertain when the last one operated from Liverpool, but the service between Burnley and Blackburn was still running in 1843. It was then owned by Mr Crabtree, of Burnley, who also had a fleet of cargo carrying boats. He does not seem to have been too particular about his passengers, the canal police complaining that people ran along the towpath after the boat, damaging the swing bridges and fences along the way. Often those on board were drunk, and even on Sundays there was riotous behaviour and music. The company warned him several times about such excesses, but it made little difference.[10] They finally asked the Commisioners of Excise to withdraw his licence for the sale of ales and spirits on the packet, but were informed that there were no grounds for the licence to be revoked. The boat was still operating in 1847, when the company refused permission for passengers to land at Blackburn warehouse on Sundays, after some goods that had been stored on the wharf had gone missing. In the end, the packet boat had become a pleasure boat rather than a means of transport. Crabtree had died by 1851, his widow continuing to run his carrying fleet, though by 1854 she had sold the boats.

The day tripper

EXCURSIONS were continued by some of the coal carriers. They would clean out a boat during the summer, when trade was slack, and

A faded photograph of an excursion about to return from Skipton wharf in the 1890s. The boat was owned by William Oldfield of Riddlesden, so the party may have come from Keighley.
(Photo, author's collection.)

instal benches. Many schools and churches used the boats for their annual outings. From Wigan and Blackburn, a favourite destination was the pleasure gardens at Whittle Springs, at the bottom of Johnson's Hillock locks. These excursions were sufficiently well organised for tickets to be printed, and one dated 24 June 1876 gives the price of the trip from Whittle Springs to Top Locks as sixpence.[11] Some parties may have considered the Whittle Springs Brewery to be an added attraction. The pub there was frequented by boatmen when passing through the locks. Boats supplied the brewery with coal and malt, and delivered their beer and ales as far afield as Liverpool.

In Yorkshire, Skipton was often visited by boating parties from Bingley, Keighley and Silsden, while the gardens at Saltaire were the destination for many further down the canal. Upwards of one hundred people could be carried in a boat, such trips continuing into the 1950s. They ceased when the Board of Trade brought in regulations governing passenger-carrying boats, unlicensed boats only being allowed to carry twelve passengers. Trip boats, covered by these regulations, increased significantly during the 1970s. Shipley, Skipton, Chorley and Burscough were the early centres for such boats, but other towns came to be served later.

Pleasure boating

THE earliest reference to pleasure boats in the committee minutes occurs in 1839, though they must have already been well established. In that year Mr Brown of Keighley was granted permission to keep a small boat on the canal. At the same time Mr Fletcher, the engineer, was ordered to prevent such boats being used or hired out on Sundays. In 1855, the company charged five shillings per annum for the privilege of keeping a pleasure boat on the canal. This was increased to fifteen shillings by 1870. Most of these craft would have been rowing boats, though steam power would have been introduced towards the end of the century. Motor boats were in use by 1916, when one was provided by Mr W. A. Brigg as recreation for wounded soldiers from Keighley War Hospital. The company charged him five shillings per annum, which seems petty in the circumstances.[12]

In 1920, Leeds University Boat Club approached the company, asking to be allowed to use the length from Rodley to Apperley. A one month's trial was agreed, with a charge of £6 per annum suggested. The

Right, top: This shows an outing from the Colne or Nelson area. The Board of Trade would certainly be concerned now if this number of people were on a boat, although accidents seem to have been rare. The boatman must have found difficulty in steering with so many people on the stern deck, though hopefully he controlled his language. Note the decoration on the chimney.
(Photo, Lancs. Libraries.)

Right, bottom: A party on the summit length about 1900. Although called Electric, *the boat is in fact a steam launch. Such excursions could be used for business purposes, and the canal company often invited important users of the canal, like Howard and Bulloughs of Accrington, to accompany the directors on their annual tour of inspection.*
(Photo, Lancs. Libraries.)

Left: The canal reservoirs have always been used for recreational activities. Ice skating, swimming and fishing were the main pastimes, while boating was the reserve of the more affluent. This turn-of-the-century photograph shows a group who have been sailing on Rishton Reservoir.
(Photo, Lancs. Libraries.)

Left: Hundreds of boats now cruise the canal. Almost all are narrow boats these days, however, since a narrow boat of under around 60 feet in length is not only cheaper and easier to handle, but can move onto virtually any other waterway in the country. On summer days, East Marton is a favourite mooring point and we can here see several boats tied up on what is undoubtedly one of the most attractive stretches of the Leeds and Liverpool.
(Photo, author's collection.)

success of the trial was not reported, but the use of rowing boats on a canal still operating commercially must have caused problems.

The 1930s saw the establishment of the first club for pleasure craft, when the Mersey Motor Boat Club was formed in 1932. Their first mooring was at Litherland, though after the war a club house was built at Lydiate. Membership increased, and in 1955 further moorings were taken at Scarisbrick, the site being purchased in 1973. Early on, many of the members had broad-beam sea-going boats, and after the war converted ex-lifeboats were used regularly. Such conversions were common along the whole canal, enabling families to go boating for little expenditure. Nowadays, there are few left, their place being taken by fibreglass and steel hulls, suitable also for use on narrow canals.

The fishing rights on the canal had always belonged to the land owners, and the company could do nothing about complaints such as those received in 1889 of people fishing at Marton. During the financial problems of the early-1900s, one of the shareholders suggested stocking the canal with fish, but this was considered contrary to the Act. In 1903, however, the Armley Angling Club were allowed to use the canal, on payment of one guinea per annum plus one shilling per member. By 1913, fishing must have been well established, as the Fresh Water Fish Preservation League suggested to the company that there should be a closed season. This was not accepted.

On the towpath

THE company always monitored the use of their towpath. As industry developed along the canal, access for goods and employees to the various factories was only allowed upon payment of an acknowledgement, often a nominal five shillings per annum. A yearly rental was also paid for windows facing onto the canal.

Prior to 1923 the company prevented the towpath becoming a public right of way by instituting a 'Halfpenny Day'. On one day every year, men were posted on the canal banks from 6 a.m. to 5-30 p.m. in order to collect one halfpenny from those using the towpath as an acknowledgment for the privilege. This was not always forthcoming, and one employee was attacked with umbrellas by two ladies who thought he was begging. Possibly as a result of such attacks, the company had receipts printed. This custom was expensive, and between 1911 and 1913 the company erected 200 cast-iron notices forbidding trespass and cycling on the towing path. During the Second World War many of these notices were removed, together with the mileposts, for security reasons, and were never replaced. After the canal was nationalised paper notices forbidding trespass were pasted up on one day each year. In recent years, the value of the towpath as a footpath has been recognised and access has been considerably improved, though barriers have been erected to deter motorcyclists and horseriders. Originally pedal cyclists needed a permit to use the towpath, but since 1984 the stretch from Burscough to Wigan has been upgraded in an attempt to encourage wider use by bicycles. This has been successful and further sections may receive similar treatment.

More difficult to control was trespass by so-called 'undesirables'. When the canal police were first introduced in 1842 one of their jobs was to discourage such people. Following their disbanding, the local police were usually called in. This was the case in 1888, when complaints had been received about people congregating on the towpath at Leeds, bathing, gambling and generally creating a nuisance.[13] Such goings on seem to have been common all along the canal; three youths were summoned for bathing in the canal at Burnley in 1896. They were fined two shillings and sixpence each with costs. Bathing in the canal has always taken place, with the younger inhabitants of canalside towns and villages having their favourite spots. Isolated locks, with no lock house or keeper, were popular in summer, despite the dangers of such deep water. Power stations, as well, were considered good places, with the warm water returned to the canal making bathing pleasant for much of the year. Whitebirk, in particular, was well used in this respect.

The company's desire to protect its property sometimes had more serious consequences. In 1910, the fishing and boating rights at Foulridge reservoir belonged to the local landowner, Edward Carr. To improve these facilities he had fences erected round the site, blocking off a public footpath. Many local people were upset about this, and on 30 May 1911 there was a mass trespass, during which several fences and walls were knocked down. This was repeated on 3 June. The company took the case to court, where agreement on the footpath was eventually reached in July the following year.

Reservoirs had other recreational possibilities. Skating was a popular Victorian pastime, especially during the cold winters at the end of the nineteenth century. Rishton, in particular, was well used, probably because of its proximity to the towns of East Lancashire. They were not always happy occasions; on Christmas Day 1887, the wife of William King, the carting agent at Blackburn, was drowned during a skating party on the reservoir. Rishton was also an early location for sailing, and has been used since the turn of the century. Sailing also takes place at Foulridge, but the rights for such activities belonged to the landowners, and the company was not involved, apart from ensuring water conservation.

An unusual leisure use of the canal took place in Blackburn during the 1950s and early-1960s. In the summer, tug-of-war teams from all over the town used to meet at Whitebirk, where contests were held across the canal. The site of a disused swing bridge formed an ideal place for these tournaments. On occasion there would be thirty teams involved, with the contests lasting all day.

An activity common to many canals was kebbing for coal, carried out by many boatmen and canalside residents. This involved the recovery of coal from the bed of the canal, where it had fallen during loading and unloading. A variety of implements were used, but the most common consisted of a shaft, with a D-shaped iron frame fitted to one end. A wire-netting bag was fixed to the frame, and this was drawn across the bed of the canal near to a coal wharf. The bag, filled

Left: Coal spilt during loading and unloading provided a free supply for many who lived alongside the canal. Although coal could be 'kebbed' out of the canal at normal times, it was much easier when sections were drained for maintenance, as here, near Adlington. The wire mesh basket would be thrown into the water and collected coal and other rubbish from the canal bed as it was drawn back.
(Photo, Margaret Walton.)

Below: The recently refurbished warehouses at Wigan, opposite the 'pier'. The ones shown here were built of brick during the improvements in the 1880s and '90s; the earlier stone warehouses were situated just past them.
(Photo, Ben Shaw.)

with coal and other rubbish, was lifted out, any mud being washed out through the netting. Other methods can be used – a metal bucket attached to a rope dragged over the bed of the canal is quite effective, as the author can testify from his own experience. This activity was frowned upon by the company, who occasionally prosecuted offenders, as besides damage to the canal bed, it could result in much rubbish being deposited on the towpath.

Today . . . and tomorrow

WITH the amenity value of the canal now widely recognised, many features are being restored and improved. The warehouses at Skipton were converted for leisure purposes many years ago, and have withstood the change extremely well, though it is a pity that more use is not made of the towpath and wharf opposite. The warehouse at Burnley continues to fulfil its old function, though the building materials stored there now come by road. The warehouse buildings themselves look well following their restor-

Some warehouses are still used for the storage of goods, such as these at Shipley (top) and Burnley (right). With the improvement of the canal environment, such sites are becoming more valuable for offices and similar uses, and the warehouse at Burnley will soon be vacated by the present occupiers. The site will then be developed as part of the regeneration of the Weavers' Triangle area.
(Photos, Ben Shaw.)

ation, and the old toll house has been much improved by those involved with the museum there. It is to be regretted that it took so long for Slater's Terrace to be restored, though perhaps now that the aesthetic value of this kind of older buildings is being appreciated, more of the area will be improved.

The restoration of Eanam Wharf in Blackburn has just been completed, and forms the centrepiece of the scheme to improve the environment along the canal corridor in Lancashire. The warehouses retain their character, but the improvements are spoilt by that lack of attention to detail, common to many restoration projects. Here, the old mooring rings on the wharf have been covered during re-surfacing, making it difficult for boats to tie up, when it may well have been better to have refurbished the old surface. Most of the mills by the locks in Blackburn have now been demolished. Before, the canal was cut off from the town by these mills, but now it overlooks the town and hopefully will be a major feature in the re-planning of the Grimshaw Park area.

Wigan, too, has been transformed, with the former canal terminus alive once again, though now with tourists. Yet again, lack of attention to detail spoils the improvements; the timber walkways in front of the warehouses are large enough to accommodate ships rather than canal barges. The locks have been well landscaped, however, and are certainly an improvement on the former dereliction.

The same cannot be said of the two terminii of the canal. At Leeds the old arm under the railway has been filled in, which allows improved access round the basin, and the arches have been turned into craft shops. However, little has been done to the old canal warehouse, though this may change in the near future as developments around the old Aire and Calder warehouses encourage improvements further up the river. Above the basin things have improved, with the canal and towpath used to link the city centre with the industrial museum at Armley and the remains of the Abbey at Kirkstall, while the canal at Rodley still attracts many visitors.

To a great extent, Liverpool continues to ignore the canal. The housing estates at Netherton are perhaps the finest example of how not to integrate a canal into a housing scheme. High fences cut off the waterway from the estate and provide an excellent climbing frame for children, who are thus able to reach the canal, whilst adults, who could provide some control, are effectively excluded. Lack of initiative on the part of the city planners resulted in the dropping of a scheme to reinstate the canal terminus after demolition of the Tate and Lyle works, built on the site in the 1960s. It is to be hoped their negative attitude will not blight any scheme for the improvement of Stanley Dock. One of the main reasons for lack of use on this stretch of the canal is that there are no safe moorings for visiting craft. These could be provided at the redeveloped Stanley Dock. Schemes to fill in the canal seem to have been dropped, but retention is only worthwhile if some use is made of the facilities, and every encouragement should be given to this end by improving access and amenities.

The future of the canal is probably brighter now than at any time since the war. While all attempts to resume commercial carrying have so far failed, a significant proportion of the dereliction and decay that characterised some stretches of the canal is being removed and the canal is certainly more attractive and welcoming to the public than at any time during its history. Its leisure and amenity potential is great and increasing all the time, and is beginning at last to bring back employment to the banks of the canal. In an age more and more concerned with the quality of the environment, the canal's place as a quiet, peaceful and non-polluting method of transport seems rosy. And, who knows, but that there may come a time when it is again seen to offer an economical, smooth and efficient way of transporting goods from one side of the country to another, just as John Stanhope, John Hustler and John Longbotham did over two hundred years ago.

Notes on the text

Chapter One

1. Doncaster Library Archive, DDWa/N/5/4.
2. Quoted by A. J. Lewery in G. Wheat, *Leeds and Liverpool Canal Craft*.
3. Minute books, James Mayor & Co. Ltd.
4. Doncaster Library Archive, DDWa/N/5/4.
5. E. Rosbottom, *Burscough, the story of an agricultural village* (1987).
6. P.R.O., RAIL 846/20, 4 February, 1875.
7. P.R.O., RAIL 846/15, 4 May, 1843.
8. Doncaster Library Archive, DDWa/N/5/1.
9. P.R.O., BT 41/351/2011.
10. John G. Collin, Wakefield Library.
11. G. Roberts, 'Steam haulage on the Leeds and Liverpool Canal', *R.C.H.S. Journal*, ii.
12. P.R.O., RAIL 846/29, 16 Dec. 1903.
13. North Yorkshire R.O., ZFW 9/1.
14. P.R.O., RAIL 846/29, 19 March 1903.
15. P.R.O., RAIL 846/33, 21 May 1919.
16. E. Rosbottom, op cit.
17. ibid.

Chapter Two

1. The early history of the Aire and Calder is based on C. Hadfield, *Canals of Yorkshire and N. E. England* (1972), and R. W. Unwin, 'The Aire and Calder Navigation parts 1 & 2', *Bradford Antiquary* (Nov. 1964 and Sept. 1967).
2. The history of the Aire Navigation is based on papers in the Hailstone Collection in York Minster Library, The Scruton Collection, case 1, box 16, no. 14, in Bradford Record Office, and *J. of the House of Commons*, 1 Feb. 1744.
3. Map of the Mersey and Irwell . . . by Thomas Steers, 1712, Local History Dept., Manchester Central Library.
4. *J. of the House of Commons*, 10 April 1713.

5. Lancs. R.O., DDKe/66.
6. *Journal of the House of Commons,* 12 January 1720.
7. Lancs. R.O., DP258 and DP258a.
8. Early history of the Douglas from: P.R.O., E112/1147/12, E134/7Geo2/Mich/14, E134/8Geo2/Hil/3.
9. Lewis Melville, *The South Sea Bubble* (London, 1921), 89.
10. 'Customs Letter Books of the Port of Liverpool', *Chetham Society,* iii, 40.
11. Majorie Cox, 'Sir Roger Bradshaigh, 3rd Baronet, and the electoral management of Wigan, 1695-1747'. *Bulletin of the John Rylands Library,* xxxvii, no. 1, September 1954.
12. John Rylands Library, Haigh MSS Box K1.
13. Wigan R.O., D/D Lei B2/4.
14. Wigan R.O., D/D Lei B2/4.
15. Wigan R.O., D/D Lei B2/4.
16. Wigan R.O., D/D Lei B1/C1-2.
17. Wigan R.O., D/D Lei B2/4.
18. Lancs. R.O., DDX 689/1/1.
19. Lancs. R.O., DDKe/66.
20. Lancs. R.O., DDHe 69/1.
21. Lancs. R.O., DDCa 1/47-48.
22. Lancs. R.O., PR2851 5/5.
23. Lancs. R.O., DDX 689/3/1-4.
24. Wigan R.O., D/DX Ta 34/3/1-3.

Chapter Three

1. Bradford R.O., Sp St/13/2/4.
2. Bradford R.O., Sp St/13/2/4.
3. Bradford R.O., Sp St/13/2/4.
4. Bradford R.O., Sp St/13/2/4, letter from John Hustler.
5. Bradford R.O., Sp St/13/2/3.
6. P.R.O., RAIL 846/1.
7. P.R.O., RAIL 846/1, 24 July 1769.
8. Bradford R.O., Sp St/13/2/4, letter from John Hustler, 2 September 1768.
9. Bradford R.O., Sp St/13/2/4.
10. P.R.O., RAIL 846/41.
11. P.R.O., RAIL 846/41.
12. J. Picton, *Liverpool Municipal Archives*

1886, p245.
13. Wigan R.O., D/DX A13/38 and Liverpool R.O., Binns Collection.
14. Md 335/17/7, DD49/BRA 301, Yorkshire Archaeological Society, Lancs. R.O., DDPt 20, and Bradford R.O., Sp St 13/2/4.
15. Bradford R.O., Sp St 13/2/4, n.d.
16. MD 335/17/7, MS 1186, Yorkshire Archaeological Society, Lancs. R.O., DDPt 20, Bradford R.O., Sp St 13/2/4, undated newspaper cutting, Walls Collection, Craven Museum.
17. P.R.O., RAIL 846/2, 31 August 1770.
18. H. F. Killick, *Notes on the early history of the Leeds and Liverpool Canal.*
19. P.R.O., RAIL 846/2.
20. P.R.O., RAIL 846/2, 27 Sept. 1771.
21. Wigan R.O., D/DX Ta 13/44/2.
22. P.R.O., RAIL 846/2, 29 January 1772.
23. Lancs. R.O., DDX 689/3/1-4.
24. P.R.O., RAIL 846/2, 31 May 1782.
25. H. F. Killick, op. cit.
26. Leeds R.O., DB250.
27. P.R.O., RAIL 846/2, 28 July 1775.

Chapter Four

1. D. Anderson, *The Orrell Coalfield, Lancashire 1740-1850.*
2. P.R.O., RAIL 846/3, 9 October 1789.
3. P.R.O., RAIL 846/3, 24 June 1790.
4. A. Mackenzie, *A History of the Mackenzies.*
5. P.R.O., RAIL 846/4, 24 Nov. 1790.
6. P.R.O., RAIL 846/4, 11 July 1791.
7. P.R.O., RAIL 846/4, 16 Sept. 1791.
8. P.R.O., RAIL 846/4, 11 February 1792.
9. B.W.B., Leeds and Liverpool Deeds.
10. Lancs. R.O., DDTo (canals).
11. P.R.O., RAIL 846/4, 23 March 1792.
12. P.R.O., RAIL 846/4, 1 June 1792.
13. P.R.O., RAIL 846/4, 22 June 1792.
14. For a full account, see the Parliamentary Minutes of Proceedings of the Committee, May 1793, in Rennie notebooks in the Local History Library, Manchester Central Library.
15. P.R.O., RAIL 846/5, 30 July 1793.
16. P.R.O., RAIL 846/5, 4 November 1793.
17. Lancs. R.O., DP175.
18. P.R.O., RAIL 846/4, 27 July 1792.
19. P.R.O., RAIL 846/4, 16 Sept. 1791.
20. P.R.O., RAIL 846/5, 13 Sept. 1793.
21. Lancs. R.O., DDTo (canals).
22. P.R.O., RAIL 846/5, 17 Dec. 1795.
23. P.R.O., RAIL 846/7, 24 February 1804.
24. P.R.O., RAIL 846/5, 10 August 1797.
25. P.R.O., RAIL 846/6, 19 Sept. 1800.
26. P.R.O., RAIL 846/5, 8 December 1796.
27. Leeds R.O., Birbeck Papers 8, 9 May 1800.

28. P.R.O., RAIL 846/5, 13 Sept. 1793.
29. Lancs. R.O., DDBd 48/8/4-7, Liverpool R.O., MD 58/8/2.
30. P.R.O., RAIL 846/7, 1 September 1803.
31. P.R.O., RAIL 846/6, 16 May 1799.

Chapter Five

1. P.R.O., RAIL 846/6, 3 January 1800.
2. P.R.O., RAIL 846/7, 9 April 1802.
3. P.R.O., RAIL 846/5, 25 July 1799.
4. P.R.O., RAIL 846/7, 11 April 1806.
5. Lancs. R.O., DDPt 20.
6. P.R.O., RAIL 846/8, 21 Sept. 1810.
7. P.R.O., RAIL 846/8, 2 March 1815.
8. Quoted in the *Blackburn Mail,* 30 October 1816.
9. P.R.O., RAIL 846/4, 4 December 1792.
10. P.R.O., RAIL 846/6, 21 Sept. 1798.
11. Lancs. R.O., DDPt 20, 5 October 1796.
12. Lancs. R.O., DDPt 20.
13. P.R.O., RAIL 846/119.
14. Lancs. R.O., DDPt 20, 1822.
15. Lancs. R.O., DDPt 20.
16. P.R.O., RAIL 846/7, 14 February 1805.
17. Manuscript in Keighley Reference Library.
18. Wigan R.O., D/d St C11/1/14.
19. Lancs. R.O., QAR 5/39.
20. P.R.O., RAIL 846/8, 10 April 1812.
21. Bradford R.O., Bradford, case 5, box 17, no. 2.
22. P.R.O., RAIL 846/8, 7 June 1816.
23. P.R.O., RAIL 846/8, 24 October 1816.
24. P.R.O., RAIL 846/8, 16 June 1809.
25. P.R.O., RAIL 846/9, 9 November 1821.
26. P.R.O., RAIL 846/8, 12 May 1813.
27. Lancs. R.O., DP175.
28. P.R.O., RAIL 846/11, 24 June 1825.
29. Bradford R.O., Sp St/13/2/24, letter from Wm. Rooth, 12 April 1806.
30. P.R.O., RAIL 846/8, 17 Sept. 1813.

Chapter Six

1. P.R.O., RAIL 846/5, 29 April 1796.
2. Leeds R.O., Birbeck papers 8.
3. P.R.O., RAIL 846/6, 19 February 1801.
4. P.R.O., RAIL 846/8, 30 April 1814.
5. *Blackburn Mail* 26 December 1811.
6. Haigh MSS, 23/6/44, 3 May 1801.
7. P.R.O., RAIL 846/9, 10 April 1818.
8. P.R.O., RAIL 846/9, 21 Sept. 1822.
9. P.R.O., RAIL, 846/9, 11 April 1823.
10. P.R.O., RAIL 846/11, 10 April 1829.
11. Rufford branch traffic book, (in private hands).
12. P.R.O., RAIL 846/2, 29 January 1772.
13. Lancs. R.O., DDBd 48/8/4-7.
14. Haigh MSS, 23/6/182 and 190.
15. John Goodchild Collection, letter

from Walmesley Stanley, 17 Feb. 1852.
16. P.R.O., RAIL 846/7, 9 April 1802, and G. Biddle, *Trans. Newcomen Soc.* (1967-8).
17. P.R.O., RAIL 846/8, 27 March 1811.
18. D. Binns, *The Railways of Craven.*
19. Doncaster Library Archive, DDWa/N/5/3, 13 May 1861.
20. P.R.O., RAIL 846/11, 9 April 1829.
21. P.R.O., RAIL 846/11, 11 Nov. 1829.
22. P.R.O., RAIL 846/11, 17 Nov. 1830.
23. P.R.O., RAIL 846/11, 21 Sept. 1832.
24. P.R.O., RAIL 846/11, 17 July 1834.
25. Myles Pennington, *Railways and other ways,* 20-35.
26. Leeds R.O., Birbeck Papers 8.
27. P.R.O., RAIL 846/13, 16 Sept. 1835.
28. P.R.O., RAIL 846/15, 9 April 1847.
29. P.R.O., RAIL 846/15, 19 July 1843.
30. Doncaster Library Archive, DDWa/N/5/1.
31. P.R.O., RAIL 846/13, 18 January 1837.
32. P.R.O., RAIL 846/15, 8 July 1845.
33. P.R.O., RAIL 846/13, 14 Feb. 1839.
34. Letter at Colne Public Library.
35. P.R.O., RAIL 846/15, 15 Sept. 1843.
36. P.R.O., RAIL 846/11, 14 April 1832.
37. P.R.O., RAIL 846/15, 10 January 1844.
38. P.R.O., RAIL 846/15, 26 July 1842.
39. P.R.O., RAIL 846/15, 16 Nov. 1842.

Chapter Seven

1. Doncaster Library Archive, DDWa/N/5/4, 7 May 1872.
2. Doncaster Library Archive, DDWaN/5/4, 7 May 1872.
3. P.R.O., RAIL 846/16, 1 August 1851.
4. P.R.O., RAIL 846/16, 14 February 1852.
5. P.R.O., RAIL 846/17, 7 February 1860.
6. P.R.O., RAIL 846/124.
7. Doncaster Library Archive, DDWa/N/5/4, 7 May 1872.
8. P.R.O., RAIL 846/18, 8 April 1864.
9. P.R.O., RAIL 846/17, 11 April 1862.
10. P.R.O., RAIL 846/18, 4 February 1869.
11. P.R.O., RAIL 846/18, 23 Feb. 1869.
12. P.R.O., RAIL 846/19, 4 August 1873.
13. P.R.O., RAIL 846/18, 19 January 1864.
14. Lancs. R.O., DDPt 20.
15. Newscuttings at Accrington Library.
16. P.R.O., RAIL 846/18, 6 February 1867.
17. 'The agrarian revolution'. *Trans. Lancs. & Cheshire Antiq. Soc.* lxii.
18. Quoted in E. Rosbottom, *Burscough, the story of an agricultural village* (1987).
19. Lancs. R.O., P135/1, 22 Sept. 1904.
20. P.R.O., RAIL 846/16, 23 April 1852.

Chapter Eight

1. C. Hadfield, *Canals of Yorkshire and N. E. England.*
2. P.R.O., RAIL 846/19, 18 April 1873.
3. Doncaster Library Archive, DDWa/N/5/4.
4. P.R.O., RAIL 846/20, 4 February 1875.
5. Doncaster Library Archive, DDWa/N/5/5.
6. P.R.O., RAIL 846/26, 15 Feb. 1894.
7. P.R.O., RAIL 846/20, 2 December 1875, and reports in the *Accrington Times.*
8. Lancs. R.O., DDSc 80/10 and 161/3.
9. Rufford branch traffic book.
10. P.R.O., RAIL 846/24, 16 Dec. 1891.
11. Doncaster Library Archive, DDWa/N/5/4.
12. Minute books, J. Mayor and Co. Ltd.
13. P.R.O., RAIL 846/21, 6 Dec. 1882.
14. N. Yorks. R.O., ZFW 9/1.
15. P.R.O., RAIL 846/24, 22 July 1891.
16. P.R.O., 846/25, 15 November 1893.
17. N. Yorks. R.O., ZFW 9/1.
18. P.R.O., RAIL 846/29, 21 June 1905.
19. P.R.O., RAIL 846/30, 16 January 1907.
20. N. Yorks. R.O., ZFW 9/1.
21. P.R.O., RAIL 846/31, 13 March 1913.
22. P.R.O., RAIL 846/32, 21 June 1916.
23. N. Yorks. R.O., ZFW 9/1.
24. P.R.O., RAIL 846/70, 17 April 1935.
25. Bowes Report (1958).
26. 'The Future of British Waterways' (B.W.B., 1964).

Chapter Nine

1. P.R.O., RAIL 846/2, 19 April 1782.
2. Lancs. R.O., DDBd 48/3.
3. P.R.O., RAIL 846/3, 10 October 1789.
4. P.R.O., RAIL 846/4, 16 Sept. 1791.
5. Lancs. R.O., DP 175.
6. Newscuttings at Accrington Library.
7. Sir G. Head, *A home tour through the manufacturing districts of England.*
8. Lancs. R.O., DP175.
9. P.R.O., RAIL 846/11, 12 April 1833.
10. P.R.O., RAIL 846/15, 14 Sept. 1843.
11. Wigan R.O., MMP 6/40.
12. P.R.O., RAIL 846/32, 21 June 1916.
13. P.R.O., RAIL 846/23, 4 July 1888.

Bibliography

Primary sources

Bradford Record Office:
The Spencer Stanhope papers cover the early period of the canal, from 1760 to 1814.
Papers from Bradford Public Library.
Bradford Canal Company papers.
British Waterways Board archives at Gloucester.
Craven Museum, Skipton:
Walls Collection.
Cumbria Record Office, Kendal:
Crewdson papers.
Doncaster Library Archive:
Warde Aldam papers, notebooks covering committee meetings, 1849 to 1890.
University of Durham Library:
Backhouse papers.
Institute of Civil Engineers Library:
Rennie report books.
Lancashire Record Office:
Many of the family papers here have references to the Leeds and Liverpool Canal. A handlist is available but should not be considered comprehensive.
Leeds Record Office:
Birbeck papers 8, 1773 to 1830.
Eagles papers, DB250, accounts 1771-1788.
Liverpool Record Office:
Holt and Gregson papers.
Binns collection.
Canal boat registers.
Manchester Central Library, Local History Dept.:
Rennie notebook.
North Yorkshire Record Office:
Wyvill papers, 1871 to 1907.
John Rylands Library:
Haigh MSS (now in National Library of Scotland).
Public Record Office, London:
RAIL 846, minutes, accounts etc. of Leeds and Liverpool Canal, 1766 - 1948.
Board of Trade, joint stock companies.

Exchequer Kings Remembrancer papers.
Lancashire County Palatine papers.
Wakefield Public Library:
John Goodchild Collection.
Wakefield Record Office:
Papers deposited by British Waterways, Dock Street, Leeds.
Wigan Record Office:
Information on the Douglas Navigation can be found in the Leigh Papers and in those from Taylor, Bridge, Baron and Sykes, solicitors from Wigan.
Yorkshire Archaeological Society Library, Leeds.
York Minster Library:
Hailstone MSS.

Contemporary

J. Aiken, *A description of the country for thirty to forty miles around Manchester* (London, 1795).
Thomas Boyle, *Hope for the Canals* (Wolverhampton, 1848).
A cursory view of a proposed canal from Kendal to the Duke of Bridgewater's Canal . . . with several proposals addressed to the proprietors of the Grand Canal between Leeds and Liverpool (1769).
D. R. de Salis, *Bradshaw's guide to the canals and navigable rivers of England and Wales* (Blacklock, 1918).
An explanation of the plan of the canal from Leeds to Liverpool (Bradford, 1788).
Sir George Head, *A home tour through the manufacturing districts of England in the summer of 1835* (London 1836).
Leeds and Liverpool Canal Company, *Official Handbook* (1927).
Leeds and Liverpool Canal Company, *Twixt Leeds and Liverpool* (Liverpool, c.1936).
Thomas Newte, *A tour in England and Scotland* (1791).
John Phillips, *A general history of inland navigation* (London, 1792).

Joseph Priestley, *An historical account of the navigable rivers, canals and railways throughout Great Britain* (Longman, Rees, Orme, Brown and Green, 1831).

Joseph Priestley, *A letter to the proprietors of the Leeds and Liverpool Canal, occasioned by Mr Whyman's address* (Bradford, 1793).

Abraham Rees, *The cyclopedia or universal dictionary of arts, sciences and literature*, 39 vols. (London, 1819).

A summary view of the proposed canal from Leeds to Liverpool (Bradford, 1768).

John Sutcliffe, *A treatise on canals and reservoirs* (Rochdale, 1816).

W. C. Taylor, *Notes of a tour in the manufacturing districts of Lancashire, 1842* (3rd edition, Cass, 1968).

A view of the advantages of inland navigations . . . (London, 1765).

Thomas Whyman, *An address to the Leeds and Liverpool Canal Company* (Preston, 1793).

Arthur Young, *A Tour of the North Country.*

Secondary sources – books

Donald Anderson, *The Orrell Coalfield, Lancashire, 1740-1850* (Moorland Press).

James Barron, *A History of the Ribble Navigation* (Preston, 1938).

Gordon Biddle, *Pennine Waterway* (Dalesman, 1979).

Donald Binns, *The Railways of Craven* (1974).

W. Cudworth, *Round about Bradford* (1886).

Jack Dakres, *The Last Tide, a History of the Port of Preston, 1806-1981* (Carnegie Press, 1986).

Marilyn Freear and Marilyn Sumner, *Roland, one of the fast 'uns'* (Wigan Metropolitan Borough Council, c.1988).

M. D. Greville, *Chronology of the Railways of Lancashire and Cheshire* (Railway and Canal Historical Society, 1981).

Charles Hadfield and Gordon Biddle, *The Canals of North West England*, 2 vols (David and Charles, 1970).

Charles Hadfield, *The Canals of North East England*, 2 vols (David and Charles, 1972).

John Hannavy and Jack Winstanley, *Wigan Pier: an illustrated history* (Wigan, 1985).

Harry Hanson, *The Canal Boatmen, 1760-1914* (Manchester University Press, 1975).

John Hartley, *Seets in Yorkshire and Lancashire* (c.1900).

Arthur Helps, *Life and Labours of Mr Brassey* (1872).

H. R. Hodgson, *The Society of Friends in Bradford* (1926).

W. T. Jackman, *The Development of Transportation in Modern England* (3rd edition, Cass, 1966).

J. A. James, *A History and Topography of Bradford* (1841).

John Langton, *Geographical Change and Industrial Revolution: Coalmining in South West Lancashire, 1590-1799* (Cambridge University Press, 1979).

M. J. T. Lewis, *Early Wooden Railways* (Routledge & Kegan Paul, 1970).

David C. Lyons, *The Leeds and Liverpool Canal: a photographic journey* (Hendon Publishing Co., 1977).

A. Mackenzie, *The history of the Mackenzies.*

G. G. Macturk, *A History of the Hull Railways* (1879).

J. U. Nef, *Rise of the British Coal Industry* (1932).

Edward W. Paget-Tomlinson, *Britain's Canal and Rivercraft* (Moorland, 1979).

Edward W. Paget-Tomlinson, *The Complete Book of Canal and River Navigations* (Waine Research Publications, 1978).

Myles Pennington, *Railways and other ways* (Toronto, 1894).

J. A. Picton, *City of Liverpool Municipal Archives and Records*, 2 vols (1886).

Edwin A. Pratt, *A History of inland transport and communications in England* (1912, David and Charles reprint, 1970).

E. Rosbottom, *Burscough: the story of an agricultural village* (Carnegie Press, 1987).

Peter L. Smith, *A Pictorial History of Canal Craft* (Batsford, 1979).

C. E. Stretton, *The history of the Preston and Walton Summit Plateway* (1883).

A. P. Wadsworth and J. deLacy Mann, *The Cotton Trade and Industrial Lancashire, 1600-1780* (Manchester University Press, 1931).

J. R. Ward, *The finance of canal building in eighteenth-century England* (Oxford Historical Monographs, 1974).

Geoffrey Wheat, *Leeds and Liverpool Canal Craft* (1972).

T. S. Willan, *River Navigations in England, 1600-1750* (1936, reprinted Cass, 1964).

Secondary sources – articles

Sir W. H. Bailey, 'On the use of steam for canal boat propulsion', *Manchester Association of Engineers, Reports and Papers* (1885-1886).

Joyce H. M. Bankes, 'A nineteenth-century colliery railway', *Transactions of* the Historic Society of Lancashire and Cheshire, vol. cxiv (1962).

Gordon Biddle, 'Early days on the Leeds and Liverpool Canal', *Railway and Canal Historical Society Journal*, vol. v.

Gordon Biddle, 'The Leeds and Liverpool Canal', *Waterways World* August 1981, 44-49, and September 1981, 32-37.

Gordon Biddle, 'A short history of the Bradford Canal', *Railway and Canal Historical Society Journal,* vol. iv.

Gordon Biddle, 'The Skipton Rock Railway', *Trans. of the Newcomen Society,* vol. xi (1967-1968), 171-173.

A. Birch, 'The Haigh Ironworks, 1789-1856', *Bulletin of the John Rylands Library,* vol. xxxv (March 1953).

Lilian Birch, 'Lancashire inland waterways; welfare and education of boatmen', *Journal for Industrial Nurses* (1952).

Charles Clegg, 'Our local canals', *Halifax Antiquarian Society* (1923).

H. E. Clegg, 'Some historical notes on the Wigan coalfield', *Transactions of the Institute of Mining Engineers,* vol. cxvii (1957-1958).

W. Cudworth, 'The first Bradford bank', *Bradford Antiquary,* vol. ii (1905).

T. Ecclestone, 'The drainage of Martin Mere', *Transactions of the Society for the Encouragement of Arts, Manufactures and Commerce,* vol. vii (1789).

John H. Farrington, 'The Leeds and Liverpool Canal; a study in route selection', *Transport History,* vol. iii, no. 1, 52-69.

Gary Firth, 'Bradford coal, Craven limestone and the origins of the Leeds and Liverpool Canal, 1765-1775', *Journal of Transport History,* 3rd ser. vol. vi (1983), 50-62.

Gary Firth, 'The Bradford Limekiln Company, 1774-1800', *Bradford Antiquary,* vol. xlvii (1982).

Gary Firth, 'The early days of the Leeds and Liverpool Canal', *Industrial Past,* (Summer, 1977).

M. J. Freeman, 'Road transport in the English industrial revolution', *Journal of Historical Geography,* no. vi (1980), 17-28.

John Raymond Harris, 'Liverpool canal controversies, 1769-1772', *Journal of Transport History,* vol. ii (1956), 158-174.

William Harrison, 'The development of the turnpike system in Lancashire and Cheshire', *Transactions of the Lancashire and Cheshire Antiquarian Society,* vol. iv (1886).

Prof. H. Heaton, 'Benjamin Gott and the industrial revolution in Yorkshire', *Economic History Society Review,* vol. iii, no. 1 (1931).

Robert C. Jarvis, 'Custom letter-books of the port of Liverpool', *Chetham Society,* 3rd ser., no. vi (1954).

H. F. Killick, 'Notes on the early history of the Leeds and Liverpool Canal', *Bradford Antiquary,* n.s. vol. ii (July 1987), 169-238.

Tony Lewery, 'The northern tradition', *Waterways World* (June 1975), 26-29.

R. M. McLeod, 'Social policy and the "floating population" ' *Past and Present,* no. xxxv (Dec. 1966), 101-132.

John Maffey, 'Some of the decayed families of Bradford', *Bradford Antiquary* (1888).

W. E. Preston, 'Some notes on an old Bradford partnership', *Bradford Antiquary,* n.s. vol. iii (1912), 312-325.

W. F. Price, 'Notes on some of the places, traditions and folklore of the Douglas Valley', *Transactions of the Historic Society of Lancashire and Cheshire,* vol. li (1901).

G. Ramsden, 'Waterways in the economic development of Leeds', *Leeds Journal* (1955), 81-84.

Gordon Roberts, 'Steam haulage on the Leeds and Liverpool', *Journal of the Railway and Canal Historical Society,* vol. ii, no. 3.

J. R. Roberts, 'Bradford waterways: rise and fall', *Bradford Textile Society Journal* (1962-1963).

W. Robertshaw, 'Historical links between Bradford and Shipley', *Bradford Antiquary,* n.s. vol. ix (1950), 277-292.

D. A. Roydes, 'The Duke of Bridgewater and his thirty year monopoly of the trade to Manchester', *Transactions of the Lancashire and Cheshire Antiquarian Society,* vol. lxxxiv (1987).

A. Rucklidge, 'Leeds and Liverpool Canal', *Railway and Travel Monthly,* vol. viii (1914), 25-35.

R. B. Schofield, 'Bagshawe v. the Leeds and Liverpool Canal Company: a study in engineering history, 1790-1799', *Bulletin of the John Rylands Library,* vol. lix, no. 1 (Autumn, 1976), 188-225.

E. M. Sigsworth, 'Bradford on the eve of the industrial revolution', *Bradford Textile Society Journal* (1953-1954).

Peter L. Smith, 'Steam on the Leeds and Liverpool', *Canal and Riverboat* (February, 1989), 30-31.

G. H. Tupling, 'The turnpike trusts of Lancashire. *Manchester Memoirs,* vol. xciv (1952-1953).

James Unsworth, 'Horse boating', *Waterways World* (April 1981), 50-53 and (April 1982), 50-53.

R. W. Unwin and R. G. Wilson, 'The Aire and Calder Navigation', *Bradford Anti-*

quary, n.s. vol. ix.

W. Wharton, 'Chugging along the cut', *Dalesman* (May, 1988).

R. G. Wilson, 'Three brothers: a study of the fortunes of a landed family in the mid-eighteenth century', *Bradford Textile Society Journal* (1964-1965), 111-122.

Theses

Brother Lewis Donaghy, 'Operational history of the Liverpool and Manchester Railway', Ph.D Thesis (Pittsburgh, 1960).

Gary Firth, 'The Genesis of the Industrial Revolution in Bradford, 1760-1830', Ph.D. Thesis (Bradford, 1974).

Official Publications

Royal Commission on canals and inland navigations of the United Kingdom, *Report,* 12 vols. (1907-1911).

'Canals and Inland Waterways: Rusholme Board of Survey', (British Transport Commission, 1955).

'The Future of the Waterways. An interim report', (B.W.B. 1964).

Appendix One

Letter by J. Hustler before meeting at Bradford, 2 August, 1766.

IT gave me great pleasure to observe an advertisement proposing a meeting at Bradford upon the 2nd August next to consider of the long talked of navigation betwixt the east and west seas, by the Rivers Air and Ribble, with branches to Liverpool, Lancaster and all the trading towns in the vicinity of these rivers.

And having been drawn into diverse disputes about the propriety of this grand scheme on account of the uncertainty of its answering the great expense which will attend the execution; I have been lead to consider attentively the extent of business which is likely to fall to its share and the profits attendant on it; which would appear so incredible to many that I do not think it prudent to lay it before your readers at present. But as a proper introduction to it beg their consideration of the following circumstances respecting it.

Viz:— 1st. All navigations are beneficial to the country within the reach of them, as tending (by their cheapness) to communicate the aboundings of many useful and necessary things, in one part, to the wants of them, in another, which the extraordinary dearness of land carriage renders of no value where they abound. And by doing the business of multitudes of draught and pack horses, which are always a dead weight upon trade and a great loss to the public, by consuming the produce of our lands, which would otherwise be employed in the propogation and feeding of multitudes of profitable cattle, of young horses for sale abroad, beef and mutton for the Shambles, wool and leather for the employment of our manufacturers and extending of our most advantageous branch of commerce, will be of greater emolument to this community in particular and to the nation in general than can be well conceived.

2nd. The great article of limestone which inexhaustibly abound through the middle parts of the proposed navigation and of which the eastern and western parts of it through a large extent of country is in a great want of, that it will constantly employ many vessels; and coals which abound in the country which wants limestones, and are wanted throughout the country wherein limestones abound, will plentifully supply them with back carriage and both collectively bear a toll it is believed sufficient to pay the interest of the money the whole will cost, and yet be delivered to the consumers, upon an average cheaper by one half than heretofore, which will occasion a prodigious increase in the consumption of both.

3rd. The country through which nearly the whole of this navigation with its branches will extend, not producing a fourth part of the corn consumed in it and the lands almost generally turning to better account for pasture than tillage, a saving of from three to seven shillings per quarter in the conveyance of it from the eastern coast will occasion still less to be grown there and more brought by the rivers, so as to make it also a great article in the navigation and employ the boats which bring down limestone more than coals are wanted above.

4th. Wood abounds greatly in some parts of the district of the proposed navigation, also slate and flags and particularly the black slate which are all wanted in others and through the cheapness of water carriage will find their way along the coast in prodigious quantities and furnish great employment for the boats, more than can be conceived at present.

5th. Lead from the mines to both the seas and through all the intermediate districts and the search for it encouraged by the facility and cheapness of conveying it to the markets. Wool by being to and fro in all its processes from the sheep to its being completely manufactured and sent to the eastern and western ports, for exportation to foreign nations, Ireland and our plantations in America; will furnish another very considerable and valuable article of conveyance.

6th. Also cheese, butter, ale and porter, hardware, furniture, soap, hay, straw, salt, potatoes, turnips and a multitude of other articles of our own produce will make a continual intercourse and increase of business there than can be well conceived.

7th. Goods imported as wool, yarn, linen cloth, hides, grease and a multitude of other articles wanted in this trading country in great quantities from Ireland, sugar, rum, tobacco, rice, cotton, mahogany, logg wood, fustick and other dying woods from America, wines, fruit, oil, brandy, deals, deal timber, iron, hemp, flax linnen yarn and other merchandise from the continent; will also occasion such employment for the navigation and be a great convenience and saving to the country; and in short there is scarcely any thing of general use which will not furnish its quota to the support of it.

8th. And lastly the proposed communication with the other great navigation and through it the Severn with all its branches, will open a new intercourse of great profitable business, which heretofore the expense of land carriage has prevented.

It may therefore be reasonably hoped that all noblemen, gentlemen, merchants etc. who wish the prosperity of this country and nation will give all proper encouragement to it, as a laudable and beneficial improvement.

J. Hustler.

(Bradford R.O., Sp St/13/2/4/J)

Appendix Two

Chronology of the Leeds and Liverpool Canal

1699 **Aire and Calder Navigation Act passed.**

1704 Aire and Calder Navigation opened to Leeds.

1712 Navigations proposed for the River Douglas to Wigan; and for the Mersey and Irwell to Manchester.

1713 River Douglas Navigation Bill rejected by Parliament.

1720 **River Douglas Navigation Act passed** – Thomas Steers and William Squire named as undertakers.

1731 Alexander Leigh and Alexander Radcliffe take over as undertakers for the Douglas Navigation.

1736 Mersey and Irwell Navigation opened.

1737 Robert Holt replaces Alexander Radcliffe as undertaker of Douglas Navigation.

1738 Work starts on building the Douglas Navigation.

1742 Douglas Navigation opened.

1744 Bill for the navigation of the River Aire from Bingley to Skipton – the 'Aire Navigation' – rejected by Parliament.

1757 Sankey Brook Navigation opened.

1765 Bridgewater Canal opened to Manchester.
Canal from Leeds to Preston proposed by John Stanhope and surveyed by John Longbotham.

1766 Public meeting at Bradford to discuss Stanhope's scheme and subscription opened to pay for detailed plans.

1767 Proposed canal now to run from Leeds to Liverpool.

1768 First meeting in Lancashire about the canal.

1769 Liverpool promoters suggest that the canal should pass through Burnley and Blackburn instead of through Whalley as proposed by Longbotham.

1770 **First Leeds and Liverpool Canal Act passed,** authorising a line via Skipton, Gargrave, Colne, Whalley, Walton-le-Dale and Parbold.

1771 **Bradford Canal Act passed.**

1772 Alexander Leigh's shares in the Douglas Navigation purchased.
Springs Branch Act passed.
Liverpool Canal Bill, proposing to link Liverpool with Wigan, fails to obtain Parliamentary assent.

1773 Leeds and Liverpool Canal opened from Bingley to Skipton.

1774 Leeds and Liverpool Canal opened from Liverpool to Gathurst, and then via Douglas Navigation to Wigan.
The sections from Skipton to Gargrave, and Bradford to Shipley and Bingley also opened.
Leeds and Selby Canal Bill, and the Settle Canal Bill, fail to obtain Parliamentary assent.

1777 Leeds and Liverpool Canal opened from Shipley to Leeds. Work on constructing the main line ceases, all available capital having been spent.

1780 'Upper Douglas Navigation' opened for Leeds and Liverpool Canal from Gathurst to Wigan.

1781 Douglas Navigation closed following the opening of the branch canal from Burscough to Rufford and Sollom Lock (the 'Lower Douglas Navigation').

1783 **Second Leeds and Liverpool Canal Act passed,** allowing the River Douglas Navigation to be purchased.

1785 Springs Branch leased from Lord Thanet.

1790 **Third Leeds and Liverpool Canal Act passed,** authorising the line to be altered to avoid the aqueduct at Whalley Nab.

1791 Building of the canal recommences westward from Gargrave.

1792 **Lancaster Canal Act passed.**

1793 Bill for a deviation of the line through Burnley, Blackburn and Chorley, to the canal at Wigan fails to obtain Parliamentary assent.

1794 **Fourth Leeds and Liverpool Canal Act passed,** authorising the deviation through East Lancashire. **Rochdale Canal Act and Haslingden Canal Act passed.**

1796 Leeds and Liverpool Canal opened to Burnley, following the completion of Foulridge Tunnel.

1799 Southern section of the Lancaster Canal opened from Haigh to Wheelton.

1801 Leeds and Liverpool Canal opened from Burnley to Henfield. Duke of Bridgewater agrees to Leigh Branch.

1805 As a result of the Croston Drainage Scheme, the Rufford Branch is extended from Sollom Lock to Tarleton.

1809 Bill for Leigh Branch fails in Parliament.

1810 Leeds and Liverpool Canal opened from Henfield to Blackburn. The use of the Lancaster Canal between Heapey and Haigh agreed.

1816 Leeds and Liverpool Canal completed and opened throughout.

1819 **Fifth Leeds and Liverpool Canal Act passed,** authorising the construction of the Leigh Branch.

1820 Leigh Branch opened.

1826 **Liverpool and Manchester Railway Act passed.**

1828 Bolton and Leigh Railway opened to the canal at Leigh.

1843 First trial of steam-powered tug.

1846 Liverpool Dock Branch opened after construction by Jesse Hartley, Liverpool's dock engineer.

1848 Leeds and Liverpool Canal Company takes over the carriage of merchandise.

1850 Merchandise traffic leased to railway consortium. Head office moved to Liverpool.

1858 Leeds and Liverpool Canal Steam Tug Company formed.

1864 Southern section of the Lancaster Canal leased by the Leeds and Liverpool Canal.

1867 Bradford Canal closed.

1871 Steam tugs re-introduced.

1872 Bradford Canal re-opened.

1874 Leeds and Liverpool Canal Company resume operation of merchandise traffic following the termination of the railway lease.

1878 Bradford Canal purchased by the Leeds and Liverpool Canal and the Aire and Calder Navigation.

1880 Steam-powered carrying boats introduced.

1882 Basin at Liverpool re-constructed.

1891 **Sixth Leeds and Liverpool Canal Act,** authorising construction of Winterburn Reservoir.

1892 **Seventh Leeds and Liverpool Canal Act,** altering the rating of the canal.

1893 Leeds and Liverpool Canal, Rates, Tolls and Charges Order introduced by Parliament.

1897 First trial of electric power for boats.

1903 First trial of diesel power for boats.

1905 **Eighth Leeds and Liverpool Canal Act,** extending the time allowed for the construction of further reservoirs.

1921 Canal Company disposes of its carrying fleet.

1922 Bradford Canal closes permanently.

1928 **Ninth Leeds and Liverpool Canal Act,** altering the tolls charged.

1930 Canal Transport Limited set up to undertake merchandise traffic.

1948 Following nationalisation, canal controlled by the Docks and Inland Waterways Executive.

1953 British Transport Waterways set up and takes over responsibility for the canal.

1960 Regular traffic over the summit level ceases.

1963 British Waterways Board formed.

1964 The last traffic on the main lines finishes.

1972 Regular trade on the canal ceases when the coal traffic to Wigan Power Station stops.

1985 'Canal Corridor' improvement scheme set up by Lancs. County Council and Wigan M.B.C..

Advice and guide for using the Leeds and Liverpool Canal

Introduction

IF you are a newcomer to boating on BW waterways, then this section will answer many of the common questions about putting a boat on the water and using it for the first time.

Also, it is hoped that boaters, whether novice or experienced, will read the advice given in the sections on conduct, lock use and water safety. Please follow the simple rules and guidance so that everyone can enjoy Britain's waterways.

This is a general guide which should help you to cope with most BW waterways though it is, of course, primarily intended for those using the Leeds and Liverpool Canal.

Basics

BW Addresses
Liverpool to Greenberfield Lock
British Waterways
Pottery Road
Wigan, Lancashire
WN3 5AA
Tel: Wigan (0942) 42239
Greenberfield Lock to Leeds
British Waterways
Dobson Lock
Bradford, W. Yorkshire
BD10 0PY
Tel: Bradford (0274) 611303

Locks and bridges
Twice a year BW issue an *Information Circular* regarding use of locks to cover the summer and winter periods. It gives the following important information:

- The opening times of all manned locks and bridges.
- The telephone numbers of certain key locks and bridges and their VHF radio channels, where these are available.

For further information a copy of this publication can be obtained free of charge from BW main offices.

Maximum craft dimensions
Liverpool to Wigan:
Length 21.95m: Width 4.35m: Height 2.44m: Draught 1.06m

Rufford Branch:
Length 18.90m: Width 4.27m: Height 2.44m: Draught 1.06m

Wigan to Leeds:
Length 18.29m: Width 4.35m: Height 2.28m: Draught 1.06m

Leigh Branch:
Length 21.95m: Width 4.35m: Height 2.44m: Draught 1.06m

You will need a special padlock key to use the Leeds and Liverpool Canal. It can be obtained, priced £2.50, during normal office hours from Leeds, Castleford, Burnley (please telephone Burnley, 0282-28680), Wigan and Apperley Bridge offices (please telephone the Waterway Manager's office first).

If you have a padlock key for the Ashton Canal you may also use it on this canal.

Special windlasses are needed for the canal. They are obtainable from most boatyards on the canal and during normal working hours from

Leeds, Wigan, Plank Lane Swing Bridge, Burnley, Apperley Bridge and Skipton offices.

Stanley Dock flight of locks

Please give at least 48 hours' notice to BW's Burscough office to use this flight. Telephone Burscough (0704) 893160. We cannot normally provide for passage at the weekends.

Liverpool to Aintree

Please telephone BW's Burscough office and give 48 hours' notice to use this length of canal.

Wigan Flight

Your passage through this flight will be assisted between the hours of 0900 and 1800 each day. Due to vandalism, passage is not normally possible outside these hours. Contact the Section Office on (0942) 44449.

Foulridge Tunnel

Passage through the tunnel is controlled by traffic lights. Please telephone BW's Burnley office (Burnley 0282-28680) if you want to check the opening hours for each direction.

Bingley Five-Rise Locks

We manage passage through these locks. Opening hours are 0800 to one hour before sunset.

Rufford Branch

The entrance lock is tidal. For opening hours, telephone BW's Burscough office during normal office hours or James Mayor's boat-yard on Tarleton (0772) 812250.

Leigh Branch

Plank Lane Swing Bridge. Opening hours: Monday to Sunday from 0800-1200 and 1245-1800.

If you want to use the Bridgewater Canal beyond Leigh, please contact:
The Manchester Ship Canal Co.
Estate Office, Dock Office
Trafford Road, Salford M5 2XB
Tel: 061-872 2411 ext. 2348.

Your British Waterways licence will be valid for 7 days on this canal.

Barton Swing Aqueduct

Operated by the Manchester Ship Canal. Opening hours: Monday to Thursday from 0900-1800 (closes 1900) and Friday to Sunday 0900-2000 (closes 2100).

You and your boat

Licensing

All boats whether powered or un-powered must have a valid licence or certificate issued by BW, when used or moored on their waterways. If hiring a boat on the Leeds and Liverpool Canal, this will be arranged for you, but make sure that all licences are up to date.

Pleasure boat licence

This is the standard licence which allows you to put your own boat on any BW waterway available for pleasure cruising in England and Wales. Fees are based on the length of the boat and licences can be issued for periods of one year, six months, three months, one month or seven days.

Further information can be obtained from the Craft Licensing Officer or Area Leisure Officers.

Pleasure boat licence without use of locks

If you have a small powered boat not exceeding 15ft and a 4bhp engine, you have the option of taking out a pleasure boat licence which excludes the use of locks, at a reduced price. In addition to the usual periods of issue, a one-day licence is issued.

Small unpowered boats and canoes

All small unpowered boats and canoes are issued with pleasure boat licences which exclude them from using locks. This applies to rowing boats, tenders and dinghies under 20ft, and to all canoes.

Reduced fees are available for youth organisations and licence holders under 18 years of age, and special arrangements exist for members of the British Canoe Union.

Insurance

You are not obliged by law to have your boat insured, but you are *strongly* advised to arrange proper insurance cover before you put your boat on the water.

The very minimum should be some

form of 'third-party' cover which will safeguard the owner or the person in charge of the boat in the event of claims made against you for injury or damage to other people'e property (including that of BW).

In addition, you should insure the boat itself against loss or damage and provide cover for the safety of the crew.

If you are hiring a boat, the hire company will usually organise insurance for you, but check first.

Mooring

If you are going to leave your boat afloat it will need a permanent mooring approved by BW. Normally this will be on a BW mooring site or a privately managed mooring site or marina, but approval for mooring at other locations may also be given.

British Waterways Mooring Sites
To moor your boat at one of the BW permanent mooring sites you will need a mooring permit. These can be issued, subject to conditions, for periods of three, six, nine or twelve months and they always run from the first day of the month.

A list of sites and fees, together with conditions of use, can be obtained from the Waterways office at Wigan (see above for address).

Details about availability of mooring at a particular site and application forms are available from the Waterways office at Wigan. All completed applications for a mooring permit should also go to this office.

Private moorings and marinas
Many approved mooring sites and marinas are operated commercially or by boat clubs. For details of fees and availability you will need to contact the operator direct. Waterways offices can help by providing local names and addresses.

Other moorings
In certain circumstances approval may be given for a permanent mooring which is not at a BW or private site.

You should write to BW, giving details of the location and size of your boat. Permission is needed even in cases where your boat would be moored to your own property, for example at the end of your own garden.

If your intended mooring is found to be acceptable, a mooring permit will be issued, charged at 50% of the standard BW mooring rates.

For further advice on tying up, see the code of conduct below.

Facilities

Water points on the Leeds and Liverpool Canal are as follows:;
Leeds: Leeds Basin;
Leeds: Office Lock;
Leeds: Oddy Locks;
Rodley: Rodley Boat Centre;
Apperley Bridge: BW Maintenance Yard;
Bingley: Bingley Top Lock;
Silsden: Pennine Boats;
Bradley: Bridge 182, Snaygill Boats;
Skipton: Gallows Footbridge;
Skipton: Pennine Cruisers;
Gargrave: Higherland Lock;
East Marton: Between Bridges 161 and 162;
Bank Newton: Bottom Lock;
Barrowford: Top Lock;
Burnley: BW Maintenance Yard;
Blackburn: Nova Scotia Wharf;
Wheelton: Johnson's Hill, Top Lock;
Adlington: Rawlinson Bridge, L & L Cruisers;
Adlington: White Bear Marina;
Aspull: Wigan Top Lock;
Wigan: Chapel Lane Top Lock;
Wigan: Mayor's Boatyard, Wayfarer Boatyard;
Wigan: BW Maintenance Yard;
Burscough: BW Maintenance Yard;
Leigh Branch: Plank Lane swing bridge;
Rufford Branch: Mayor's Boatyard, Tarleton.

Sanitary Station facilities on the Leeds and Liverpool Canal are as follows:
Leeds: Leeds Basin;
Rodley: Rodley Boat Centre;
Apperley Bridge: BW Yard;

Bingley: Bingley Top Lock;
Bradley: Bridge 182, Snaygill Boats;
Skipton: Gallows footbridge;
Gargrave: Higherland Lock;
Greenberfield: Top Lock;
Barrowford: Barrowford Top Lock;
Burnley: BW Maintenance Yard;
Blackburn: Nova Scotia Wharf;
Wheelton: Johnson's Hill, Top Lock;
Adlington: Rawlinson Bridge;
Adlington: White Bear Marina;
Aspull: Wigan Top Lock;
Wigan: Chapel Lane Lock;
Burscough: BW Maintenance Yard.

Code of conduct

Sound signals

■ **One short blast**
(about one second)
I'm altering my course to starboard (to the right)

■ **Two short blasts**
I'm altering my course to port (to the left)

■ **Three short blasts**
My engine is going astern (in reverse)

■ **One long blast**
To be sounded every twenty seconds when approaching a bend

Rules of the road

■ On inland waterways always keep to the right when passing a boat coming from the opposite direction.

■ If you overtake another boat you do so on the left and at a slow speed.

■ Do not overtake on a bend, near a bridge, lock or when you cannot see a clear way ahead.

■ When being overtaken by another boat slow down so as to just have steerage way.

■ You usually find deeper water on the outside of bends, but look out for other craft.

■ If you meet a deep draughted boat which has to hug the outside of the bend pass on the 'wrong side' i.e. the left: Sound your horn twice to let the other boat know.

■ There will be other times when it is not possible to pass on the right e.g. when a boat is being towed from the towing path. Pass on the left and sound your horn twice.

■ Pleasure craft should keep well clear upstream or downstream of commercial craft whilst they are manoeuvring at wharfs, staithes, in locks etc. Watch out for sea-going vessels; they have limited manoeuvrability.

Speed limits

■ Plan your trip with leisure in mind. There are speed limits on the inland waterways. Excessive speed creates a strong wake that can cause a nuisance to others, increases fuel consumption and damages the banks of the canal.

■ In shallow water your boat will actually travel faster if you reduce engine speed, as over-revving pulls the bottom of the boat deep into the mud.

■ **4 miles per hour is the set limit on most inland waterways, including the Leeds and Liverpool. This is about a fast walking pace.**

■ Use the water conditions to determine your speed and never go faster than the speed limit maximum, except where it is essential for your safety in tidal or flooding waters. Slow down before you reach bends, bridges, locks, tunnels or repair works.

■ When you are passing fishermen, moored boats and small unpowered craft such as rowing boats, reduce speed to a level at which disturbance is negligible.

Tying up

■ Always moor to the towing path when possible, in a position where your boat is not a hazard to navigation. A boat must be tied up at both the bows and stern.

- Never tie your ropes across the towing path; use rings or bollards as provided, or hammer your stakes on the canal side of the path and have regard for other towing path users, such as anglers and walkers.

- Where possible, boats should moor at approved temporary mooring places where facilities for rubbish disposal etc. can often be found.

- Never moor longer than necessary at water points or sanitary stations. Move away as soon as possible to allow others access to facilities.

- Don't moor by 'blind' bridges, in lock entrances or near sharp bends and junctions – you might be rammed.

- Do not moor on the outside of bends. That wall may look inviting, but large boats need the channel on the outside of bends.

- Usually, the bank opposite the towing path is private property. On river navigations both banks are often private property and you may need the landowner's permission to tie up.

- On river navigations it is suggested that you moor with the bows of your boat facing upstream. On tidal waters, moor with bow facing the tide and try to avoid mooring overnight.

Anglers

- Watch out for fishermen. Please slow down and keep to the centre of the channel.

- At fishing matches there is often some warning given by notices on the towing path.

Tunnels

- Do not enter the tunnel until it is clear. Switch on headlight and sound horn. Keep a lookout for small unpowered craft.

- On some tunnels there are restrictions on time of entry to allow a one-way system. Times are shown at the tunnel portal and must be adhered to. Foulridge Tunnel on the Leeds and Liverpool Canal is controlled by traffic lights.

Lift and swing bridges

- Before setting out, make sure you understand how to operate lift and swing bridges. Most are operated manually, although there are a few mechanised ones – these have instructions on the control box (secured with a standard BW yale key).

- Before operating the bridge make sure that the road is clear of approaching traffic. Use barriers where these are provided and remember to close the bridge after you.

- Extra care must be taken with these bridges. (see Safety on the Water section).

Litter

- Please keep all litter and refuse until you can dispose of it either at one of the many points that are provided at locks, moorings and boat yards, or take it home.

- Never throw bottles or tins into the water. If a disposal point is full, please don't add to the mess by dumping your litter nearby; it may only blow into the water. Don't hide rubbish in the undergrowth, as sheep or cattle can tread on it and injure themselves.

Noise

- The waterways are a haven of peace and quiet. Please don't spoil it, for example by playing radios too loudly.

Using locks

- If possible, share a lock with other boats. It is better to wait a few minutes than to close the gates on an approaching boat and waste up to 20,000 gallons of water. For the same reason always wait turns at a busy lock.

■ Always ensure that all gates and paddles are closed after you leave a lock, unless you can see a boat approaching to use the lock, when you should leave the gates open to help them.

Going up

1. Make sure the top gates and paddles are closed.
2. If lock is full, empty it by raising the bottom paddles.
3. Open bottom gates and enter lock.
4. Close bottom gates behind you and lower the paddles.
5. Open the top paddles to fill lock.
6. Open top gates and take your boat out.
7. Close gates behind you and lower the paddles.

Going down

1. Make sure the bottom gates and paddles are closed.
2. If lock is empty, fill it by opening top paddles.
3. Open top gates and enter lock.
4. Close top gates behind you and lower the paddles.
5. Keep boat clear of cill and open bottom paddles to empty lock.
6. Open bottom gates and take your boat out.
7. Close gates behind you and lower paddles.

Wide locks

■ These operate in the same way as other locks, but need to be used with extra care by narrow beam boats – especially when locking up.

■ Keep the boat to one side of the lock well back from the gates and open the paddles on the same side as the boat first. By doing this the circulation of water will hold the boat against the lock side. Then open the remaining paddles slowly.

Staircase locks

■ Do not attempt to use staircase locks unless you know the correct procedure. Passage through the Bingley Five-Rise is managed by BW staff.

Safety advice – locks

■ Always make sure that your boat is completely inside the lock and check that:
When going uphill, your rudder cannot catch in the bottom gates, and
When going downhill, that the rear of the boat is not likely to sit on the cill.

■ Secure your boat in the lock by looping ropes around the bollards provided – DO NOT TIE.

■ Make sure that nobody is standing on the roof or foredeck when entering a lock, the bump of the boat against the side may throw them in.

■ Do not leave windlasses on spindles as they could fly off if the paddles are run down.

■ Be careful not to trap your fingers in any of the mechanisms, or between ropes and bollards.

■ Always check that the previous boaters have left the lock mechanisms correctly.

■ In narrow locks be aware that a boat tends to be drawn to the upper gate when the lock is filling.

■ Do not use a lock in the dark, it is only too easy for someone to fall into the water and not be heard and seen.

■ Do not let anyone play near locks, be it running around or jumping over gates etc. It is not worth the risk of them falling in.

■ You should know exactly what to do if someone falls into the water. If this happens close all the paddles immediately and throw a lifebuoy. Then consider how to get them out – possibly this could be done by filling the lock up slowly to bring them to your level.

■ Never dangle your arms or legs over the side of the boat; they may be crushed between the boat and the lock side.

■ Beware of floating debris between the boat and the lock sides.

Safety on the water

Swimming

■ Do not swim in any BW waterway – you could get entangled in weeds or rubbish, be hit by a passing boat or be drawn into a paddle if someone uses the lock, and the results could be fatal. Swimming is an offence against BW byelaws.

Ice

■ Never walk on any ice that has formed on the waterways in winter. Ice is nearly always very thin and could easily crack with your weight.

Tunnels

■ Switch on headlight. Proceed at a moderate speed and beware of water dripping from the roof. Never enter a tunnel without making sure that your boat is equipped with adequate lights, and ensure nobody is standing on the cabin side or roof.

■ Care must be taken when using a small boat in any tunnel and other boats must be on the lookout for smaller boats.

Boats and ropes

■ Always ensure that your boat is suitable in all respect for the waterways which you are intending to navigate. Make sure that the engine and all its controls are in good order and that you have sufficient fuel.

■ When cruising there must always be at least one person on board who is competent in the handling of boats.

■ Pleasure boats are advised not to cruise in the dark and must not cruise when visibility is poor.

■ Please take care when refuelling; no smoking or naked lights. Do not store petrol below the decks. Remember, Calor and Butane gases are heavier than air and sink into the bottom of the boat. Guard against leaks.

■ Boats should always carry fire-fighting equipment, a first-aid kit, life jackets and buoyancy aids. Non-swimmers, both adult and children, should always wear life jackets and users of small, unpowered boats and boats with out-board motors are strongly advised to do the same. A life belt should also be carried aboard every boat. Whilst your boat is in motion, it is best not to allow anyone to sit on the roof.

■ Make sure you are wearing suitable footwear for boating. Whenever moving about the boat, take care, particularly on gunwhales. Check that the weed hatch is properly closed and that all ropes are coiled up so there is no danger of anyone tripping over them.

■ All boats should have at least three mooring lines made of strong, sturdy rope and these should be of sufficient length to cope with locks etc. on the waterways which you intend to navigate.

■ Always use mooring rings and bollards where these are provided. At other times make sure that your mooring stakes are driven in firmly and that your mooring ropes are not obstructing the towing path.

■ Take care not to trap fingers between ropes and bollards.

NB All information correct at time of going to press. The publishers cannot accept responsibility where information is incorrect or out of date. Contact British Waterways for up-to-date information.

Circular walks from the canal, by John Dixon

TEN superb walks have been devised by John Dixon, using the canal towpath and allowing the walker to explore some of the lovely countryside and historical sites which lie close to the Leeds and Liverpool Canal. John Dixon is the author of a series of beautiful walking books in Lancashire and West Yorkshire, copies of which are available from local booksellers.

The walks

The walks are all easy to follow and are circular, using a section of the canal towpath. The maps reproduced here are for general information only and walkers are advised to make use of the excellent Ordnance Survey Pathfinder series of maps. Please observe the country code and keep to the official footpaths at all times.

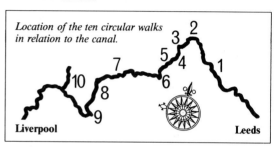

Location of the ten circular walks in relation to the canal.

Walk One
East Riddlesden — Rombalds Moor — Ilkley Moor — Addingham High Moor — Ghyll — West Riddlesden

Distance: 12 miles, circular. Allow 6 hours.
Grade: Moorland walking; good underfoot; wear walking boots.
Lunch: Packed lunch.
Evening Meal: Bridge Inn, Keighley Road.

TWELVE miles may seem rather a long walk but it is well worth the effort. The landscape we pass through on Yorkshire's most renouned moor is splendid, as are the views to be had from several points on the walk. We sample the historical delights of East Riddlesden Hall and walk through countryside heavily littered with Brigantian remains.

East Riddlesden Hall

East Riddlesden Hall is a typical large Yorkshire house of the seventeenth century. The house was built for James Murgatroyd, a Halifax clothier, in around 1642, with a new range added in 1692.

The house is first viewed across a fish pond, part of a former grange of Bolton Priory that stood on the site before the Reformation. The visitor enters the house through a round-arched doorway flanked by fluted columns with a rose window above, all topped by battlements and pinnacles. This arrangement is repeated at the rear. Inside are collections of pewter, domestic period utensils and Yorkshire oak furniture.

To the left of the entrance is a row of servants' cottages dated 1642, and near the roadway are two seventeenth-century barns. The Great Barn is of around 1640 and houses a collection of farm carts and implements. The barn and the grounds can be viewed free; entry to the Hall costs £1.50. There is a gift shop and tea room.

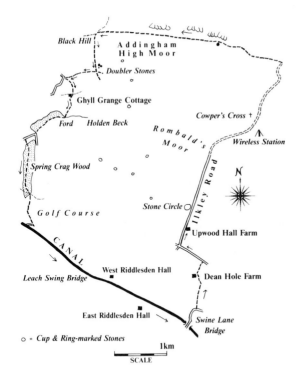

East Riddlesden Hall to Brass Castle Stone Circle

Leave by the main gateway and cross the road to walk up to join the canal towpath at the swing bridge by the Marquis of Granby Inn. Follow the towpath to the right to leave via next bridge (No. 198). Walk up Swine Lane, around the corner then left to walk up Bury Lane track to Dean Hole Farm via gates. Follow the farm lane on to roadway, left, and walk up Street Lane to go right at crossroads. Walk up Ilkley Road, past Upwood Hall, to go over wall-stile on left at footpath sign. Walk on and over next stile. The stone circle is forty yards down on the right following the fence.

Brass Castle/Bradup Stone Circle

No finds are recorded from this badly damaged Bronze Age site. The circle, which measures some thirty feet across, contains twelve stones, less than half its original number.

On to Cowper's Cross

Return to the roadway and follow it on, past Bradup Farm, and on up (notice the well on the left dated 1853 T.H.X.S.) to go through gate below wireless station.

Walk down the trackway to Cowper's Cross.

Cowper's Cross

Standing in the centre of Rombalds Moor, Cowper's Cross gives one a fine vantage point above Ilkley and on over to the Yorkshire Dales. The cross has a date of 1883 with the initials ILB IM.

Follow the track on down to the tarmack surface, then follow the left-hand track to Silver Well Cottage. Follow path on to go through wall-gate by shed and on through the ferns to join lower pathway. Follow the path on to the railed-off 'Swastika Stone' at the top of Woodhouse Crag.

The Swastika Stone

Rombalds Moor was an important area of settlement throughout the Bronze Age and into the Iron Age. Before the coming of the Romans an important Celtic political and religious centre was established at Ilkley.

It was during these later Brigantian times that the 'Swastika Stone' was carved. It represents the major river valleys in this mid-Pennine area and the major tribal centres. The NW arm shows the Craven Aire Gap and the important settlement at Gargrave Caput; the NE arm is the Upper Wharfe Valley and Grassington settlement; the SW arm is the Lower Aire Valley and the 'caput' of Leeds; the SE arm is the Lower Wharfe Valley leading over to Tadcaster and York; the loop represents the Brigantian capital at Aldborough.

Roman dominance was to break up the political confederacy of the Briganties by establishing forts and towns upon the tribal centres. However, the 'Swastika Stone' still remains mapping out those early Celtic realms that were to rise again after the fall of Rome.

Follow the cragside path on, over wall-stile and on over Addingham Moor to go over two wall-stiles (notice the boundary stone to the side of this last stile I/M – Ilkley/Morton, ILB 1893). Follow the path on to go over five stiles and on to a cairn-marked crossroads in paths of Black Hill. Take the left-hand path and walk on to go over wall-stile. Follow the path directly on down the moor to go through fence-gate below the wind eroded rocks of Doubler Stones.

Doubler Stones

The mushroom-shaped, wind-eroded rocks of Doubler Stones conjure up much in the imagination, especially when the 'cup and ring' marks are examined on their upper surfaces. There are over 250 examples of this Bronze Age carving within the few square miles of Rombalds Moor. Upon our walk thus far we have passed about thirty of the stones (use the O.S. Pathfinder map to locate them). The carvings are varied and include cups, many concentrically ringed, ladder markings and swastikas. The stones differ in size and a number are difficult to find, especially when the bracken growth is high.

Back to East Riddlesden Hall

Walk on to the farm lane and follow it on to the right, through gateway and down to next gate. Turn around and now follow right-hand wall on to go through gateway and on down the track to driveway. Walk down the driveway to go through small gate on left opposite Ghyll Grange cottage. Walk around the building and on to go through gates on right. Follow track down to go through gateway. Walk down the field to go over footbridge under pipeline. Follow path to the right to go through gateway and on following left-hand fence to go over fence-stile into wood. Walk down, across the brook and up and on, following edge of wood, to go down bridleway and to go over stile by gate onto roadway. Walk down the road to go through gate on left at footpath sign. Follow right-hand wall to enter wood via stile. Follow path into wood and after a short way take the left hand fork on up and continue on to leave wood by wall-stile up on left. Follow right-hand path down to go over stile by gate onto golf course. Follow right-hand wall on, then 'yellow staked' pathway down to join gravel trackway and on down, past the club house to go down the trackway on right and onto the canal towpath. Follow the towpath on to the swingbridge at the Marquis of Granby Inn. Walk down the road to East Riddlesden Hall car park.*

Walk Two
Skipton — Flasby — Gargrave — Skipton

Distance: 10 miles, circular. 11 miles with Kirk Sink Roman Villa. Allow 2½ hours from Skipton to Gargrave plus time to explore the Roman villa and Gargrave village; 2½ hours back along the canal. All at an easy pace.
Grade: Easy, but wear walking boots. Do not go up on the fell if the mist is down.
Lunch: Masons Arms, Gargrave.
Evening Meal: Royal Shepherd, Skipton.

IN this easy walk we take in the rugged splendour of the highlands above the market town of Skipton. To the north east rises Rylstone Fell and Embsay Moor, a great wilderness from whence the stones were hewn to build the castle and town of Skipton. To the north west, our route is marked by the pike of Sharp Haw, sentinal to the upper Aire Valley, from which vantage point the lay of Craven is overviewed. We descend quickly from the rough gritstones of Flasby Fell to the locks east of Gargrave to return by way of the towpath to Skipton town.

Skipton Parish Church to Flasby

Walk down by the church and over the bridge to turn right and walk up Chapel Hill, left at the fork and on up to go over wall-stile by gateway. Walk up the hill to go over wall-stile by gate. The Battery earthwork is over on the left. Walk on down the hill to go over stiles and up onto bypass. Cross the road and go over fence-stile opposite. Cross the field to go over fence-stile. Walk directly over the golf course to go over corner stile in section of walling. Follow the wall around to go through stone gap-stile and follow wall on to go over stile by gate. Follow left-hand fence over on the left, down to go over stile onto Brackenley Lane, left and walk up the road to the road junction. Cross the road and pass over stile opposite. Walk on directly to go over fence-stile near

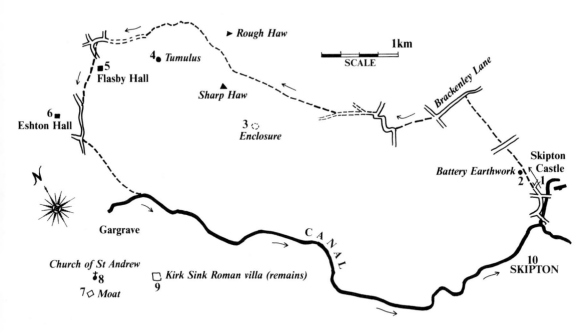

electricity pole. Follow left-hand hedgerow, then fence on, to go over stile by gate onto road. Follow road on, around two corners and on to go through gateway on left at third corner. Follow trackway on through two gates onto moor. Leave the trackway and walk up onto the moor and follow guide-posts to go through gateway. (To the left are the Craggs and the Iron Age enclosure; in front rises the pike of Sharp Haw and on the right, Rough Haw. Far over on the right Rylston Fell dominates with Norton Tower at its peak.) Our path now goes between Sharp Haw and Rough Haw, so follow the staked pathway on in the direction of Sharp Haw to veer sharply off the path to the right before path ascends to summit. Walk on to (in summer this meadow is covered in flax) go through field-gate in wall. Walk across the ling on a right-diagonal down to go over wall-stile by small gate. Walk on on a left-diagonal and follow the path down and over to the right of the clough and on to go through field-gate in wall. Walk down the field to far left-hand corner to join trackway via gate. Follow trackway down into Flasby.

Flasby to Gargrave Church

Turn left at the wall post-box and walk down the lane to go over a fence-stile on the right at footpath sign. Walk up to go over next stile. Walk on on a left-diagonal to go over fence-stile (the ruin of Flasby Hall is over on the left and the folly tower down on the left).

Follow left-hand fence on down to follow yellow marker-posts on to go up and through kissing-gate onto road. Left, and walk down the road, over the bridge (Eshton Hall is over on the right) and on to road junction. Go over wall-stile on the left and cross the field on a right-diagonal to go over stile by gate. Follow fence to the right to go over fence-stile (a magnificent view of Flasby Hall is to be had from here). Walk up the field veering slightly to the left, then directly on along the brow of the hill to go over stile by pine plantation on the left. Walk down to go over next stile. Cross the field, veering left, to go over stile then footbridge and up onto the canal. Follow the path down to the locks and cross the footbridge onto the canal towpath. Walk up the tow path to leave via the second bridge. Follow gated pathway on to the Swan Inn and on to go over the bridge to the Masons Arms and the Parish Church.

St. Andrew's Church to Roman Villa site

Walk down the lane by the side of the church and on into farmyard. (Here ask the farmer for permission to walk upon the site and section of Roman road). Follow the footpath on to Kirk Sink earthworks.

Gargrave to Skipton

Make your way back to the canal towpath and follow

it on down into the centre of Skipton (notice the swing bridges on the way).

Points of interest

1. As we walk up High Street, where the market is held, the Church of Holy Trinity is up on the left, with the round towers of the Castle entrance over on the right. The church dates back to some time before 1120, but the earliest remains today are Decorated in style and date from around 1350. The rest is mainly Perpendicular, with seventeenth-century restorations. The figures on the First Earl of Cumberland, Henry Clifford, are worth viewing, dating from about 1542. A good guide book enables one to explore the church in full.
2. The Battery is a square earthwork on the summit of Park Hill. Some suggest that it is a Civil War Parliamentary gun emplacement used during the siege of 1642. Others see it as a Roman signal station above the Aire Gap.
3. The enclosure near Sharp Haw is an Iron Age hill-top site, probably a redoubt for the capital manor of the Celtic 'cantrev' of Craven, being at that time sited at Gargrave.
4. A Bronze Age tumulus and cairn have been identified here on Flasby Fell. Also, a Bronze Age rapier was found in the clough coming down from the fell – now on display in the Craven Museum, Skipton.
5. The village of Flasby is mentioned in the Domesday Book. The central farmhouse is a seventeenth-century building; Flasby Hall is wholly Victorian. Some years ago, in the grounds of the Hall, the remains of an ancient chapel were discovered, its origins unknown.
6. Eshton Hall, now a retirement home, was built in around 1826 by the architect George Webster of Kendal for Sir Mathew Wilson, and what a splendid frontage it presents.
7. The moated manor house site to the west of the church is locally known as the Garris, once the home of the Gargraves of Gargrave, having their seat here since the twelfth century. Gargrave was a 'double' manor – on both sides of the river. The northern moated manor house site of the de Longevilers is sited above North Street.
8. The church of St. Andrew was established in Anglo-Danish times and a number of ancient cross fragments from the tenth century can be viewed inside the church. The building itself was mostly rebuilt in 1852, while the tower dates from 1521. Across the way is the Masons Arms, an excellent lunch stop – good service, good ale, all at very reasonable prices.
9. Kirk Sink Roman Villa, built upon an Iron Age site, consists of a second-century villa and bath house, two third/fourth-century houses and an administration block, all within a walled and ditched courtyard. Just outside the complex is a very good cambered section of Roman road.
10. The town of Skipton owes much to the nineteenth century, but its incremental layout and development owes more to the medieval, leaving the visitor many varied changes in streetscape to observe and enjoy. The main focus for the town is the castle of the Cliffords, first built in Norman times and added to over the centuries. The outer bailey gateway, with rotund semicircular projections, leads us into one of the finest castles to be found in the North of England. A good historical guide to the church and castle is available in the church.

Walk Three
East Marton — Bank Newton — Ingthorpe Grange — East Marton

Distance: 5 miles circular.
Grade: Easy walking, but wear light boots or stout shoes.

Lunch/Evening Meal: Cross Keys Inn, East Marton or Abbots Harbour (lunch and cream teas from 8 a.m. to 6 p.m. each day, East Marton.

Newton Hall to Ingthorpe Grange

Turn left at the junction and follow the road past the quaint wayside farmstead to go through a field-gate on the left. Follow the stream up for a short way then walk on across the field to go over wall-stile onto roadway. Follow the road on around the bend and on to go over wall-stile on left opposite hawthorne bush. Walk up the hill on your right to go through wall-gate at summit. Walk over the brow of the hill on a left diagonal and on down to go through field-gate. Walk on over the hill, bearing right and on down to go over stile by gateway over on the left. Walk over the rise on a left diagonal and on down to go over fence-stile, brook and wall-stile. Pass through the gateway over on the right and cross the field on a left diagonal to go through green wall-gate at Ingthorpe Grange barn. Left, and follow lane on to view the spectacular frontage of Ingthorpe Grange.

Ingthorpe Grange to East Marton Church

Follow Ingthorpe Lane on to the roadway at East Marton, noticing on the way the splendid views of Flasby and Rylstone fells to the north-east. Left, then cross the road to walk down the lane to the church.

Church of St. Peter to Cross Keys Inn

After visiting the church leave via stile at the top right-hand corner of the churchyard to walk directly on (notice double-arched canal bridge down to the right) to the Cross Keys Inn, via wall-stile.

Points of interest

1. Mullioned frontage cottage with a dated door-head 1698 and the initials A.A.A.
2. Abbots Harbor and Sawley House; the latter is said to incorporate within its fabric the remains of a monks' rest house established in the twelfth century by the convent at Sawley. Notice the two Early English windows with the cross above.
3. Opposite the TV mast set on the edge of the towpath is an iron milestone: Leeds 37¼ miles, Liverpool 90 miles.
4. The six locks at Bank Newton and the old lock-keeper's cottage. A further six locks are to be encountered on the way down to Gargrave.
5. A delightful seventeenth-century farmhouse at Cald Newton, surrounded by a walled garden that is a profusion of colour in the summer months.

FOR many who walk the nearby Pennine Way the three Domesday manors of Marton, Newton and Ingthorpe are passed by in the push for Gargrave. The folly of others – for not tarrying awhile – is our gain. Here, amid the rolling hillsides of Craven, we shall discover Jacobean farmsteads and monastic granges still unknown to the crowds in this splendid rural backwater.

East Marton to Bank Newton Locks

Your car can be parked on the side road by the telephone box or on the far rear Cross Keys car park as long as you check with the landlord that this is acceptable

Walk down the lane to the rear of the pub to Abbots Harbor and Sawley House, then over bridge no. 162 onto the towpath. Walk under the bridge and follow the delightfully tree-shaded towpath on through its many curves to leave via a gate above Newton Grange. Follow canalside lane on and over bridge no. 165 to pass over stile on left onto the towpath. Walk on and take in the six locks at Bank Newton.

Bank Newton Locks to Newton Hall

After viewing the locks return to bridge no. 165 and back over the stile to walk down the lane, passing Cald Newton Farm, to the road junction. The imposing gable of Newton Hall is now in front of you.

6. Newton Hall, a seventeenth-century yeoman farmhouse, once home to the Banks and Townley families. Adjoining the Hall is a small chantry chapel, now an outhouse in the garden. The aisled barn is worthy of note.

7. Ingthorpe Grange, an imposing seventeenth-century house with a chapel at the rear. Above the first-floor window of the porch is a triangular panel informing us that '**** Baldwin birth was 1671'; below the window is the datestone of the house, H.B.B. 1672. Ingthorpe was a bercary (sheep farm) established by Bolton Priory in around 1301. Before 1295 it was farmed for wheat by four ploughmen.

8. St. Peter's, East Marton. Short, broad Norman tower, but the nave, chancel and south aisle are nineteenth-century in date. Inside is a fragment of a late Anglo-Norse cross of Viking style depicting the god Thor with his hammer, defending himself against the earth serpent. South of the church are the earthwork remains of the c.1445 Hall of the Martons, lords of the manor, and the ancient fish ponds.

9. The double-arched canal bridge came about when the level of the roadway had to be raised. This spot is a haven for anglers from the Craven district.

10. The Cross Keys Inn offers a good variety of food and a fine selection of ales within 'olde worlde' surroundings – plenty of bar space, good place settings with traditional furniture and two large open fires, all add up to a cosy evening atmosphere. The day I was there I had 'fisherman's pie with veg' at £2.85 – served within five minutes – and it was very good and filling.

11. Abbots Harbor serves home-made traditional farmhouse food amid a tranquil setting. The village biscuits in particular are a must – delicious. Abbots can also accommodate two adults and two children bed and breakfast, by appointment – Tel: Earby 843207. Good food here too, and more varied than the Cross Keys which is a Chef and Brewer house.

Walk Four
Salterforth — Barnoldswick — Thornton — Earby — Kelbrook — Salterforth

Distance: 8 miles, circular. If you wish to shorten the walk, buses run every half hour between Earby and Salterforth. Allow 5 hours, including visits and lunch hour.

Grade: Easy walking, but wear light boots.

Lunch: The Red Lion, Earby.

Evening Meal: Anchor Inn, Salterforth.

Start: Anchor Inn, Salterforth, by canal bridge no. 151, but the walk can just as easily be started from Barnoldswick, Earby or Kelbrook.

THIS ramble takes us through five West Craven settlements that have their origins in the seventh century, before Craven was a Celtic kingdom in itself. Since then Angles, Scandinavians and Lancastrians, have made inroads in this land of drumlins between the southern gritstone of the Pennines and the northern limestone of the Dales. The hilly landscape of West Craven was caused by retreating glaciers depositing boulder clay over nodules on the limestone floor. With churches secreted away from the main settlements one could well believe that we are within that realm attributed to Thomas Hardy. All in all, a delightful arcadia of rural tranquility to discover at our leisure.

Anchor Inn to St. Mary-le-Gill

Follow the towpath northwards, passing Barnoldswick Marina and on past the Silentnight and Rolls Royce factories to the rural setting of the three Greenberfield Locks. After the locks the towpath changes to the opposite bank of the canal via a footbridge. From this point we follow the waymarked

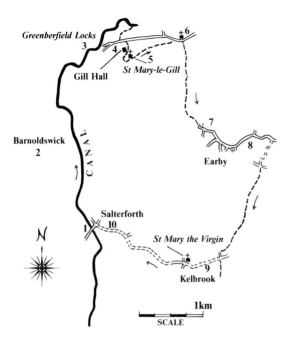

Greenberfield Locks
3
4
5
St Mary-le-Gill
Gill Hall

CANAL

Barnoldswick
2

7

8

Earby

Salterforth
10

St Mary the Virgin

9

Kelbrook

N

1km
SCALE

Pendle Way through Gill, Thornton and Earby to just above the village of Kelbrook. Even given the waymarking, the route will still be described.

After crossing the footbridge, follow the curve of the canal to the right and after it curves to the left pass over the wall-stile on your left. Follow the path up to follow the Rolls Royce factory fence over to the right to go over the stile by gate. Follow path to the left to go over wall-stile by gate onto lane. You are now standing on the line of the Roman road between Ribchester and Elslack. Cross the main road and walk down the grass verge to go through a small gate opposite factory entrance. Follow path up, passing Gill Hall, to enter churchyard via gated stile.

St. Mary-le-Gill to Thornton Church

Follow the path on the outside of the south churchyard wall down to go over Gill Syke up onto the golf course. Cross the course directly to go through kissing-gate after gap in conifers. (As we leave the golf course the tower of Thornton Church comes into view along with the southern Dales, Pen-y-Ghent, Bowland Fells, Pendle and the summit of Weets above Barlic. To the right of the church tower can be seen the start of the wild Pennine 'Bronte' Moors). Walk directly across the brow of the hill to go over fence-stile, and on to go over hedge-stile onto roadway. Cross the road and walk on to Thornton Church.

Thornton Church to Earby Mines Museum

Pass over the stile opposite the church porch and walk across the field (notice the field-well on the left) to go through kissing-gate and on to go through wall-stile. Cross the field directly to gate at bend in road. With your back to the road cross the field on a left diagonal to go through stone-gap stile in fence. Cross the field to go over stile by gate, then walk directly on to go through stone stile. Cross the field in front of The Grange on a left diagonal to go through stile by gate. Walk down the field on a right diagonal to go over fence stile, and on to go over wall-stile into lane behind All Saints Church. Walk down to the roadway and across into School Lane, then along and down to Earby Mines Museum on the left.

Earby Mines Museum to Red Lion Inn

Walk along the road, passing Wardle Storeys mill, and on into Water Street to enter Old Earby. Walk on along the road to the Red Lion Inn.

Red Lion to Kelbrook Church

Continue along the road, past the Youth Hostel on Birch Hall Lane and on up to go through stile by gate set back on the right. Follow right-hand wall on to go over wall-stile, and on following right hand fence/hedge to go through stone stile into old Mill Lane. Walk on to the roadway, turn left and walk up to go through stile on right. Walk on to go through gateway, and on following trackway to go over wall-stile. Cross the field directly and follow Moor Hall farm track up to go through stile by gate. Walk on, across the stream and on to follow right-hand fence to go through field-gate. Follow old track on to go over stile by gate. Cross the field directly to go through gateway. Walk on, veering right, to enter old lane via stile. Walk on to the junction. (The eighteenth-century Tunsted Farm is just on a way, over the stile on the right.) Turn left and walk on to Heads Lane. Here we leave the Pendle Way to follow the lane down to the top of Kelbrook. Follow the riverside trackway on to the church of St. Mary the Virgin.

On to Anchor Inn, Salterforth

Walk across the bridge and on to the Craven Heifer. Walk up the track on the right of the inn and follow it on to go over a stile. Follow right-hand hedgerow on to go over stile at wall. Down the steps to cross the line of the old railway and on to go over stile. Follow left-hand fence for a short way to go over stile on left. Walk down *to go over footbridge (two large stones set on piers). Walk on to go through gateway and on, following hedgerow, to go through gate. Follow track on, over stile, to follow goit on, over stiles to Salterforth. Cross the road and walk up by the bus stop to the Anchor Inn.*

Points of interest

1. The Anchor Inn. Stalactites have formed in the cellar by water seeping through the limestone.
2. Barnoldswick's social and economic development can be traced through its architecture. It well deserves its title of 'Lancashire's best kept secret'. Good and varied shopping, good pubs, clean and tidy streets and very friendly folk, as one would expect from 'old Yorkshire'.
3. Greenberfield Locks, within a rustic setting second to none.
4. Gill Hall is a late-sixteenth-century building built by the Banisters, the first grantees of the Manor of Barnoldswick after the Dissolution. As can be seen from the east gable, the house was once much larger.
5. The Cistercian monks from Fountains Abbey first came to Barnoldswick in 1147 to establish a convent here. But at that time, during the reign of King Stephen, the house suffered from robbers, poor land and a bleak site, and in five years the monks had moved to their new site at Kirkstall. The main fabric dates from the rebuilding of 1524, though the roof and lancet east window belong to the thirteenth century. The interior is laid out with Jacobean box-pews and a complete three-decker pulpit with octagonal sounding board. A leaf-shaped sword of the Late Bronze Age was discovered near the church on Swilber Hill.
6. St. Mary's, Thornton. The tower is Perpendicular and contains several carved stones within its fabric. In the churchyard stands an octagonal well-house of 1764.
7. Earby Mines Museum is housed within the old grammar school of 1658, itself sited upon the foundations of a Cluniac Priory of c.1145. The museum contains over 600 lead mining relics from the Yorkshire Dales and other mining areas, plus a reconstructed crusher and many working models of mining operations. Open from the last Sunday in March to the last Sunday in October and Saturdays June to September. Opening times: Sundays 2 p.m. – 6 p.m; Thursdays 2 p.m. – 9 p.m; Saturdays 2 p.m. – 6 p.m. Small admission charge.
8. The Red Lion Inn is a typical working village pub serving good meals and good ale in very good company.
9. Kelbrook, along with Earby, Thornton and Barnoldswick, is mentioned in the Domesday Survey, but the village reflects more of the eighteenth and mid-nineteenth centuries. A noisy little river flows through the centre of the village, giving it a romantic air.
10. Sited upon an ancient salt way, Salterforth is a seventeenth- and eighteenth-century hamlet. In Domesday it is referred to as 'the other Earby' and even today Old Earby and Salterforth have much in common.

Walk Five
Foulridge — Blacko — Barrowford — Foulridge

Distance: 8 miles, or two walks of 4 miles each, using the southern end of Foulridge Tunnel as the mid-point in the 'figure-eight'. Allow 4 hours, excluding lunch and Heritage Centre visit.
Grade: Easy, but wear light boots.
Lunch: Cross Gaits Inn, Blacko.
Evening Meal: New Inn, Foulridge/White Bear, Barrowford.

Start: The walk begins from Foulridge Wharf, but you may choose to start at Park Hill Heritage Centre at Barrowford. Both have parking facilities.

AN opportunity here to explore the highest section of the canal, as well as gaining a glimpse of Pendle. The route follows sections of the Pendle Way, but we stray off to visit gems that the route planners have missed. A walk that you will want to return to many times.

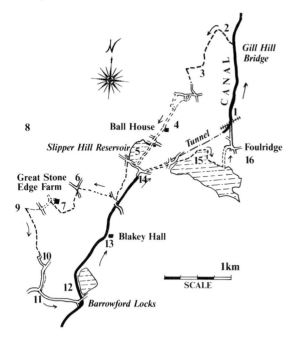

Foulridge Wharf to Slipper Hill Reservoir

Follow the towpath northwards to Mill Hill Bridge No. 149 (milestone Leeds 44¼ miles, Liverpool 83 miles). Walk over the bridge to go through right-hand gateway, then follow trackway on to go over stile by gate into Country Brook Mill yard (listen to the clatter of those Lancashire looms). Walk up the yard and on up the leafy lane (notice mill lodge on right) into the tiny hamlet of Hey Fold. Continue on to Mount Pleasant Chapel. Pass over a stile on the left just before the Chapel and cross the field to follow the track to the road junction at Hill Top. Turn right and walk up the road for a short way to go through waymarked gated wall-stile on left. Cross the field on a right diagonal to go over fence-stile. Walk a few yards down into the farmyard to go over stile on right and cross the driveway to go over next stile. Follow wall around to the left and on to go through wall-stile. Walk down the old lane, passing the rear of Ball House (we will be viewing the front of the building later), to pass over a stile at the bottom. Walk on to enter tree-lined pathway via wall-stile, and on to Slipper Hill Reservoir.

If you wish to return now to Foulridge, then follow the reservoir path to leave by waymarked stile at corner and walk down to the southern entry to Foulridge Tunnel.

Follow directions to Foulridge Wharf and New Inn.

Ridge Wharf

For the longer walk follow the path around the reservoir to leave by white gate. Cross the road and walk over the bridge to go over stile on right, walk on to go over next stile and on to go over stile by gate. Follow house fence on, then hedgerow, over stile and on, through gateway to follow right-hand hedge on to go through old wall-stile. Cross the field veering left to go through stile by gate. Follow wall down to Lower Wanless farmyard gate. Pass through gap in hedge up on the right and walk across the farm lane to go over footbridge. Follow the ancient trackway up, via stiles, to the Cross Gaits Inn where a surprising offer awaits you!

On to Park Hill Heritage Centre

Come out of the pub and walk across to a house dated J.H. 1860 to go over stile at side of house. Cross the field to go through stile by far left-hand gateway and on to go over wall-stile, then down to go over fence-stile (before this stile a path on the left leads to the front of Lower Stone Edge Farm if you wish to view). Follow the fence up to go over corner stile and walk directly on to go over stile by gate (Great Stone Edge and Blacko Tower now come into view, while over on the left the great Lion of Pendle rises above Stang Top). Walk on, over stile by gate, and on to go over next stile. Turn left and pass over stile, then follow wall down to roadway via stiles. Pass over stile by gate opposite and walk down the field on a right diagonal to go over fence-stile. Follow path through the wood and over stiles onto Water-meetings Farm Lane. Cross the bridge then turn immediately left into pathway. Follow the riverside path down, via gates and stiles, into Higherford to go over the old pack-horse bridge on the left. Follow the cobbled lane on to cross the roadway. Walk down, past the Old Bridge Inn, to go through stile by bridge. Follow path on into the Heritage Centre car park.

Heritage Centre to Foulridge Tunnel

Follow the road up from the Heritage Centre on the right-hand footpath to go over stile by gate near motorway. Follow trackway down to go over bridge No. 143 onto towpath. Follow the towpath up Barrowford Locks, passing the ancient Blakey Hall over on the right just before the bridge, to the entrance of Foulridge Tunnel.

From here you can return to Barrowford by walking above the tunnel, over the bridge and on to the roadway.

Left, and walk up to the entrance of Slipper Hill Reservoir. Follow earlier directions.

To Foulridge Wharf/New Inn

Walk above tunnel, over the bridge and on to the roadway. Right, over line of old railway, then left to walk along a trackway to roadway. Cross the road and walk up onto Lake Burwain Marine (Look across at the hillside for a view of Ball House). Follow the path around the lake to leave by waymarked lane on left. Walk up to cross the road and walk down next track into Sycamore Rise Road. Walk directly on to enter trackway on the right at Ivy Cottage. Follow it on down to the road. The New Inn is up to the left across the main road. The Wharf is directly down to the left.

Points of interest

1. Foulridge Wharf and warehouse were built in 1815. Raw American cotton was brought up from Liverpool to supply the local mills. Today converted barges run canal trips from here. In 1912 a cow fell into the canal at the Barrowford end of the tunnel and swam the distance to Foulridge. A photo of the swimming cow can be seen in the Hole in the Wall pub nearby.
2. Country Brook Mill stands on the boundary of Lancashire and the old West Riding of Yorkshire. A number of old Lancashire looms still weave cloth here today.
3. Hey Fold is an early-eighteenth-century hamlet, at that time the home of Mary Barrit, the first woman evangelist in the area. Mount Pleasant Chapel was originally two cottages, converted by the Rev. John Barrit in 1822.
4. Slipper Hill Reservoir is one of six feeder reservoirs used to top up the canal at this, its highest point. The house across the water was once used as a shooting and fishing lodge by the directors of the canal company.
5. Ball House was built by the Quaker, 'Blind' John Moore, in 1627 and is possibly the smallest gentry house in the Lancashire Pennines.
6. 'Good ale tomorrow for nothing', an offer that has been open to all since 1736 at the Cross Gaits Inn. A highly recommended lunch stop.
7. Great and Lower Stone Edge are two farmsteads displaying much of their seventeenth-century origins.
8. Blacko Tower, built in around 1890 by Jonathan Stansfield to obtain a view over Ribblesdale. A much-loved landmark.
9. Here, where Pendle Water meets Blacko Water, stands the whitewashed seventeenth-century farmstead of Watermeetings, built by the Hargreaves family, who were among the principal tenants after the deforestation of 1507. The spur of land above where the waters meet is the haunt of local modern witches ('white' witches, so I am informed) who ply their craft and frolic naked in the nocturnal hours at the time of their pagan festivals.
10. Higherford's buildings owe much to the seventeenth and eighteenth centuries. The 'Owd Brig' is a packhorse bridge built between 1583 and 1591 on the old Gisburn to Colne road. From the apex of this bridge, John Wesley preached to the folk of Barrowford in the 1770s.
11. Park Hill, Pendle Heritage Centre, contains exhibitions on local farming and weaving, local history and architecture, and a video story of the Pendle Witches. Outside is a walled eighteenth-century herb garden and the frame of an early-sixteenth-century cruck barn. Opening times: Easter to last Sunday in November – Tuesday, Wednesday, Thursday, Saturday, Sunday and Bank Holiday Mondays, 2.00 p.m. to 4.30 p.m. Admission charge. The Heritage Centre has produced a book *A Walk through Barrowford* that allows you to explore this delightful village in full, a good buy at £2.00.
12. Barrowford Locks and lock-keeper's cottage.
13. Blakey Hall, rebuilt in the eighteenth century, re-using many late-sixteenth-century features of the original house of Simon Blakey (c.1690), a devout Catholic who suffered heavy fines for his recusancy.
14. Foulridge Tunnel, 1,640 yards long. Barges were 'legged' through the tunnel – men lay on planks fixed to the boat and 'walked' along the tunnel walls. The horses were walked along a path above the tunnel.
15. Foulridge Reservoir, now renamed Lake Burwain, was constructed in 1793 to supply the summit level of the canal. It is now also used for leisure purposes – boating, fishing and walking and contains within its environs a great variety of wildlife, including the great-crested grebe.
16. Foulridge is centred around a village green surrounded by old weavers' cottages. The New Inn makes for a good lunch or evening meal stop – the pub even has a resident ghost; the landlord will tell you all about it over a pint of good ale. Across from the pub stands the seventeenth-century Breeze House, built by John Holgate, and records show that bull-baiting took place here at one time.

Walk Six
Weavers' Triange, Burnley — Brierfield — Queen's Mill — Towneley Hall — Burnley

Distance: 10 miles circular; allow six hours with lunch at Harle Syke.
Grade: Easy walking, but wear light boots.
Lunch: The Craven Heifer or the Commercial, Harle Syke.

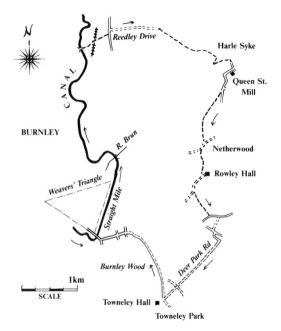

WITH the industrial revolution and the building of the Leeds and Liverpool Canal, Burnley grew to become the world's leading cotton cloth producer. Though 'King Cotton' has all but gone, the legacy of that age lingers on to intrigue those who have a fascination for a wealth of historical, cultural and industrial heritage that has gone into the making of this town on the banks of the River Brun.

The Weavers' Triangle

Within the 'Triangle' are to be found former spinning mills and weaving sheds, engine and loom foundries, canalside warehouses and the homes of the former weavers. The Weavers' Triangle Visitor Centre, on Manchester Road, is housed in the former wharfmaster's house and canal toll office. Displayed inside are all aspects of Burnley's former industrial age, and with the restored canal wharf it provides an interesting setting. The centre is open to the public free of charge, on several afternoons each week during the summer months and on most bank holidays. Tel: (0282) 30055.

Visitor Centre to Queen Street Mill Museum

Go through the white gate opposite the Visitor Centre and follow the towpath on, passing British Waterways dock then above the town along the 'Straight Mile' (notice Pendle Hill over on the left and the Cliviger Gorge over on the right) to pass by the side of Thompson Park (once part of the Bank Hall Estate) and over the River Brun. The towpath now winds its way into the Forest of Pendle and we leave the path by way of the field access bridge after road bridge No. 134. Follow the path on to go over the railway bridge then cross the football fields to the top left-hand corner to go through iron gate and on to the road. Cross the road and walk up Reedly Drive, over on the left, to the very top. You come out on a new estate over on right. Cross the road and go through the Victorian gateway opposite and follow track on and round to the main roadway. Turn left and cross the road to footpath sign. Follow the pathway on past the rear of the houses to go over fence-stile. Walk on to follow right-hand wall on, through wall-stile and on to go through next wall-stile.. Follow footpath on by side of houses to go over stile and on down the trackway, right and down through the farmyard onto the roadway. Turn left and walk along the road, past the Craven Heifer and The Commercial, past the post office to turn right into Queen Street. Walk down to the Mill Museum.

Queen Street Mill

This is the only surviving steam-powered cotton mill in Britain, built in 1894 at the height of the cotton industry. The working mill gives one an insight into the conditions of Victorian factory life. During viewing hours the magnificent steam engine, 'Peace', powers over 300 deafening Lancashire looms in the imposing weaving shed. Cotton cloth is produced by staff in authentic 1890s' costume. The mill houses a coffee shop and a craft shop selling 'steam woven' goods manufactured at the mill – in particular the famous Union Shirt, a traditional garment of working men from the nineteenth century up until the mid-1950s.

Queen Street Mill to Rowley Hall

Walk back onto Queen Street, then left along the side of the mill to go left down a trackway to the gateway of Musty Haulgh Farm. Go over the stile on the right and walk on to go over fence-stile. Walk on and over to the left to go over stile in wall. Walk down and over to the right to go over fence-stile into wood. Follow the path on and down to cross the River Don by footbridge. Follow path on, over stile and on up the steps to cross the field to corner of wall. Walk on to enter the seventeenth-century farmstead of Netherwood via gate. Walk past the front of the cottages to entry gateway, then go over the stile over on the left. Walk down the narrow enclosure to go down stone steps, over stile to brook. Take the right-hand path, then over the footbridge on left. Follow path up by the side of the River Brun to enter the driveway of Rowley Hall via stile.

Netherwood displays some seventeenth-century mullioned windows on the gable, typical of a farm cottage of that time. Rowley Hall is a much grander building, having been built before 1610 by the family of Halstead of gentry/yeoman status. The house and grounds are private, so content yourself with looking at the outside from the driveway.

Rowley Hall to Towneley Hall

Walk down the drive, over bridge and on to go into trackway on the left above the play area. Follow track on, take higher track at fork to roadway at the Thornton Arms. Cross the road and walk down to go over corner stile just before the bridge. Follow the path up to the top roadway. Left, and cross the road to walk down Springwood Road, then left into Deer Park Road and on, around to the right and on down into Towneley Park. Follow the driveway on to the front of Towneley Hall.

Towneley Hall was the home of the Towneley family from the early-fifteenth century until 1902. It is now Burnley's Art Gallery and Museum and admission is free. The Hall contains a fine collection of English oil paintings and watercolours and a large collection of Pilkington Royal Lancashire pottery, as well as some splendid Jacobean oak furniture, glassware, militaria and a local history and archaeology section. There are also period room settings, street scenes from the late-nineteenth century and displays of former local trades. The nearby Natural History Centre houses many live specimens and an aquarium. Wild flower and geological gardens have been developed outside.

Towneley Hall to Weavers' Triangle Visitor Centre

Walk down the main driveway, past Towneley High School and out onto roadway. Cross the road and walk along Parliament Street to join the canal at bridge. Follow the towpath back to the wharf.

Walk Seven
Feniscliffe — Pleasington — Hoghton — Riley Green — Feniscowles — Feniscliffe

Distance: 7 miles, circular. Allow 5 hours with lunch.
Grade: Easy, but wear walking boots.
Lunch/Evening Meal: Butlers Arms, Pleasington/ Royal Oak, Riley Green.
Start: Witton Country Park.

DURING the 1950s, before the advent of popular motoring, this walk was a great favourite with the Blackburn mill workers. Today it is relatively quiet, but well worth exploring. The walk heads for Hoghton Tower via Pleasington Priory and returning via the canal towpath.

Witton Country Park to Pleasington Priory

From the Park Cafe follow the westerly path along the edge of the wood, over stone footbridge and stile, then cross the field to go over stile and footbridge. Cross the playing fields to the roadway and follow it on to enter the road up to the cemetery. At the duck-pond follow the trackway to the left to enter lane. Left, and follow the lane on to the Priory and the Butler's Arms.

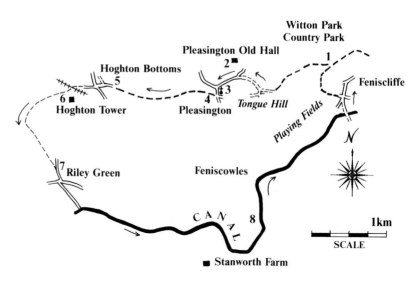

Pleasington Priory to Hoghton Tower

Follow the track to the right of the pub to go over stile. Over the hill, following left-hand fence, over two stiles, down to go over wall-stile. Follow right-hand wall to go over stile and on down to river bridge. Cross the bridge and walk up the lane to roadway. Right, and over stile on left to follow path up to cross the railway. Follow the path to the right to go over stile. Follow wall round, over stiles, to Hoghton Tower driveway.

Hoghton Tower to Royal Oak

After visiting the Tower, walk back down the driveway to the lodge house, turn left and go through kissing-gate. Follow left-hand fence up to go over stile. Walk down the field directly, over stile, straight down and over stile into farm lane. Walk on to Riley Green.

Riley Green to Witton Country Park

Upon leaving the inn, cross the road and follow the Chorley/Belmont road on to join the canal towing path. Follow the towpath on, passing Feniscowles paper mills, Livesey housing estates, to leave the canal at Cherry Tree Bridge. Walk down the road to cross the main road. Right, then first left after the shops to join a pathway into Pleasington playing fields. At the end of path cross the road and follow the trackway on into Witton Park, via bridge over the River Darwen. Right and walk on to the cafe starting point.

Most likely, you have taken your lunch at the Royal Oak. This being so, may I suggest a short drive to the

Butler's Arms for an evening snack or meal, children are catered for and the service and food are the finest for miles around.

Points of interest:

1. Witton Country Park has been developed from a former mill owner's country estate and holds many fine attractions. A Visitors' Centre has been developed from the Fielden Coach House and Stables: facilities include stables, harness room and coach house, with displays of harness, farm tools, horse-drawn farm machinery and several horse-drawn carriages. The Natural History Room displays the wildlife to be found on the many nature trails within the park. Also included is a lecture room and changing exhibitions are held there. Sports facilities are also numbered among the park's attractions.

2. Pleasington Old Hall is dated 1587, and above the doorway is a carved panel bearing the arms of the Ainsworth family, with the initials of Thomas de Hoghton and John Southworth of Samlesbury, who were the chief owners of land in Pleasington. The hall stands upon the site of an earlier moated manor house and remains of the moat can still be made out in the grounds of the house. To the rear of the hall is a wildlife and butterfly garden, opened in 1987 by the botanist, David Bellamy. The hall is reputed to be the home of the 'White Lady' ghost that wanders the lanes around the Great Hall at Samlesbury. The ghost is claimed to be that of Dorothy Winckley of Pleasington Hall, who

married first a Southworth, then a de Hoghton and finally Thomas Ainsworth.

3. The Roman Catholic church of St. Mary and John the Baptist, known locally as Pleasington Priory, affords a proud landmark

    The church was built in the years 1816-19 as a thank-offering of John Francis Butler of Pleasington Hall. According to tradition, he had met with a serious accident while hunting and was very nearly killed. He resolved to erect a church there in thanks for his escape. Considering that it was built before Catholic Emancipation in 1929, it is an astonishing edifice, with its frontage modelled after that of Whalley Abbey before the Dissolution.

4. The Butler's Arms, named after the Butler family of Pleasington Hall, is a true country inn standing amid a delightful rural land-scape. The Gothic frontage blends well with the setting. The inn serves a good selection of local ales and beer and bar lunches are served from mid-day, all at very reasonable prices. A well maintained bowling green and beer garden are further attractions.

5. Thirty years ago Hoghton Bottoms was a much frequented place; tea was served by a local farmer's wife and the old mill still had its water wheel. Today, the hamlet has few visitors, the water wheel has gone and the mill stands as a relic to unwise conversion. A walk along the mill-race, through the gorge, with its towering railway arches, up as far as the weir is most rewarding. Wild garlic covers the ground and broadleafs fall to meet the river – in all, a very restful setting.

6. Hoghton Tower, a large and spectacular castel-lated stone mansion stands upon a spur of hill overlooking the township of Hoghton in Gunnolfsmoors – a Hiberno-Norse settlement within the Leyland Hundred. The Tower has only seen action once, leading to its fall and capture by local Parliamentarians, during February of 1643.

The Hoghton family, one of Lancashire's oldest and most famous (and infamous), can trace their ancestry back to Hamon le Boteler who married a daughter of Warine Bussel, Norman Baron of Penwortham and holder of large estates in Lancashire.

The highlight of the family's history came in 1617 with the knighting of 'Sir Loin' by King James I on a visit to Sir Richard Hoghton, High Sheriff of Lancashire, known at court by the title of 'Honest Dick'. Sir Richard's son, Gilbert, also rode into the pages of history with his ill-fated 'siege' of Blackburn during the Civil War, which led to the sequestering of his estates in 1646. However, his son, another Richard, supported Cromwell and the estate was returned to the family, the decendants of whom still live on the estate today.

The Tower is open to the public: Easter Saturday, Easter Sunday, Easter Monday from 2.00 p.m. to 5 p.m; every Sunday until the end of October; Saturday, Sunday, July, August and Bank Holidays. Admission charge.

7. We would have to travel far to come across a finer wayside inn than the Royal Oak. With the inn's whitened frontage and blackened corner stones it cannot help but bring back memories of the old coaching days. Inside, beneath the low beamed ceiling, you will find many a cosy nook in which to rest, chat and enjoy good ale.

8. The canalside walk here holds great interest for the industrial archaeologist and layman alike. As the canal enters the very western edge of industrial Blackburn, the first nineteenth-century mills begin to appear. Notice the loading and unloading facilities for the former coal barges as you pass the former mill sites.

Walk Eight
Chorley — Rivington Country Park — Anglezarke — Chorley

Distance: 8½ miles, circular.
Grade: Easy walking, but wear light boots.
Lunch: Bay Horse, Anderton or a light snack from Rivington Lower Barn.

THIS walk takes us into the Lever Park at Rivington to discover the many delights within. We return along the banks of Anglezarke Reservoir and back to the canal towpath at Chorley.

Chorley

Chorley is a small Lancashire market town. Cotton and coal formed the original economic base. The town has two markets. The covered market is open on Tuesday, Friday and Saturday, whilst the open 'Flat Iron' or cattle market is held on Tuesdays. The parish church of St. Laurence is supposed to have contained relics of the saint brought back from Normandy by Sir Rowland Standish in 1442, and the tower and parts of the chancel are from this period. The Standish and Parker pews are early- and late-seventeenth century respectively. Chorley's best known figure from the industrial revolution was the sugar manufacturer, Sir Henry Tate, who gave the nation the magnificent Tate Art Gallery in London. The best of Chorley's houses are Georgian and stand on Hollinshead Street, one having a handsome tripartite doorway with segmented fanlight.

Chorley Bus Station to canal

Walk down Union Street, left along Clifford Street, then right up Stump Lane to Eaves Lane. Right, and cross the road to walk down Froom Street to the canal towpath.

Froom Street canal bridge to Bay Horse Hotel

Follow the towpath on to leave by the second bridge after passing under the railway. Walk up the track and cross the railway. Follow lane to the right to go over stile on right of farmyard entrance. Walk on to follow left-hand fence to go over stile onto golf course. Follow yellow stakes up (around the wood) and on to follow right-hand tree-hedge to end, then walk up to club house to go over stiles on right up onto lane. Walk down the lane to go over stile by gate at corner. Walk on to go over stile by gate on left, then follow right-hand wall on to go over stile by gate. Follow lane to the left to go over stile on right onto Stacks Farm drive. Follow drive onto go over stile by gate and on to go over next stile. Follow path on, over next stile and on up to the main road. Right, and walk on to the Bay Horse.

On to Rivington Lower Barn

Take the Rivington road, across the motorway and round to the right to go left down trackway after Major Bottoms Cottage. Follow track on, through gate and on into Cuncliffe farmyard (notice the weavers' workshop

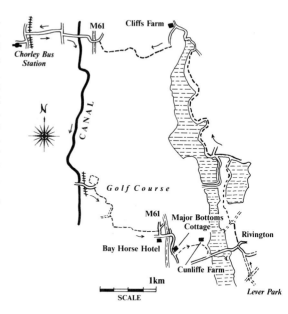

windows on ground floor). Follow farm lane down to road, left and across the reservoir. Take the lane on the right, past the old school, and on following lower path around to the Lower Barn.

Rivington Country Park

This is one of the best of Lancashire's country parks. Here one can hike or merely stroll on the numerous trails that lead one around the park or up on the high West Pennine moors. The dovecote, the ornate gardens, Rivington Pike and the replica of Liverpool Castle by the lake, are only a stride away. So are a number of sites set aside for nature conservation (we shall be walking through one soon). Lower or Great House Barn, was built in the late-sixteenth century and is constructed of large oak crucks, each side being taken from the same tree. Today it houses an information centre for visitors to the West Pennine moors, a cafe and local book shop. The adjacent stone building was once Great House Farm. This has now been converted to provide a craft shop, Ranger's office and toilets.

Lower Barn to Rivington Village

Walk down the roadside pathway, down into the village.

Rivington village

A few cottages, post office, two churches, school and village stocks – what a romantic setting to greet the eye!

The first building one notices on approaching the village from the west is the school of 1714. It was built on the site of the old free grammar school founded by Bishop Pilkington in 1566. The church across the way was built around 1540, but only a few windows remain from that period. For the most part, the church represents the rebuilding of around 1666. Inside is a monument to John Shawe, who died in 1627, in the form of a large brass plate with a skeleton on a mattress at the bottom.

Across from the village stocks stands the Unitarian Chapel of 1703. The inside is furnished with box pews and the pulpit is in the middle of the north side. By the churchyard gate can be found a collection of dated doorheads from old houses lost to the reservoir.

Rivington to Cliff's Farm

Pass through the kissing-gate opposite the Chapel gates and follow the path on and down, over stile, and on to go over stile. Take the left-hand track up to lane and to follow gated metalled trackway on the right up and onto roadway via kising-gate. Left, and walk down the road, right at the junction, on into picnic area and through kissing-gate. Follow the lane on for some way to enter nature conservation area at footpath on left. Follow path on, keeping left all the way, over stiles and onto roadway. Left, and follow road on to Cliff's Farm.

Cliff's Farm presents an interesting face to the inquiring eye. The house is dated 1696, with the initials T. A. and R. M. with a single M above. The building is a very good example of farmhouse building which can be seen in the Chorley and Heapey area.

Cliff's Farm to canal/Chorley bus station

From end of barn, follow the track up past the quarry to where paths cross. Walk up the right-hand path to go over stiles and on up to cairn. Take the left-hand path on down, across other path, and on down to go over stile. Follow path down, and along the edge of field to go over stile. Follow path on to the right to go over stile onto mill driveway. Left and on over the motorway and canal bridges to walk up Froom Street. Cross Eaves Lane and walk down Stump Lane, on over the railway to go left along Clifton Street. Turn right into Union Street and walk on to the bus station.

Walk Nine
Wigan Pier — Haigh Hall Country Park — Wigan

Distance: 8 miles, return.
Grade: Very easy; walking shoes.
Lunch: Kirkless Hall Inn, Top Lock.

FROM the major heritage development of Wigan Pier up through the impressive Wigan flight of 21 locks to the wild and romantic Haigh Hall Country Park, this walk passes through some fascinating landscapes and shows the visitor the best that Wigan has to offer and the contrasting aspects of Wigan Borough. A return can be made from the country park by local bus, allowing one a greater freedom of time to discover what is on offer.

Wigan Pier

The name Wigan Pier was first coined as a joke by the music hall star George Formby Senior at the expense of the seaside resorts of Southport and Blackpool. Later, George Orwell, in his book *The Road to Wigan Pier,* in his search for this wonder, used it as a symbol of decay for the falling fortunes of the industrial North.

Today the 'pier' stands at the heart of a unique complex of canalside warehouses and mill buildings. Concerts and conferences are housed at 'The Mill at the Pier'. In the 'Schools Centre' and on floating classrooms, guided by resident tutors, children study their heritage. The Pier boasts the largest working steam engine in the world, the Trencherfield Engine, and the 'Way We Were' Heritage Centre, with exhibitions of local life in the late-nineteenth and early-twentieth centuries.

Wigan Pier is open from 10 a.m. to 5 p.m. every day except Christmas Day and Boxing Day. General enquiries (0942) 323666.

Wigan Pier to Top Lock

Join the canal towpath at the rear of the Wigan Pier Information Centre and follow it all the way up to the Kirkless Hall Inn at Top Lock.

Kirkless Hall

Kirkless Hall stands in a field to the left of the towpath just before Top Lock. The building is of brick with a mock-timber framed entrance porch. A datestone to the left of the porch records a date of 1663, but I doubt that this refers to the exterior.

The inn looks out onto the canal locks, and on a fine day tables are placed outside so that folk can enjoy the view of water traffic. The food and beer served are to a very high standard, and very reasonably priced too.

Top Lock to Haigh Country Park

Follow the towpath on to leave by the third bridge after Top Lock, situated in the wooded section. Walk up the drive to Haigh Hall and on to Stables Visitors.

Anciently, Haigh Hall, of which place only the moat still survives, was the home of the Earls of Crawford and Balcarres.

A curious tale is handed down through history referring to the hall's residents in the early 1300s: Sir William Bradshaigh and his wife, Lady Mabel, were dwelling at the hall when in 1315 Sir Adam de Banastre of Shevington and Charnock Richard called upon Sir William to rise up against Thomas, Earl of Lancaster. Along with other local landowners, they set forth. The two forces clashed at Deepdale, near Preston, and the Banastre Rebellion was crushed. Sir Adam and others were executed, but Sir William fled into exile and was later presumed dead. After this time Lady Mabel remarried, but after the death of Thomas, Earl of Lancaster, Sir William returned and slew the usurper. Mabel was reunited with her former husband, and by way of penance her confessor bade

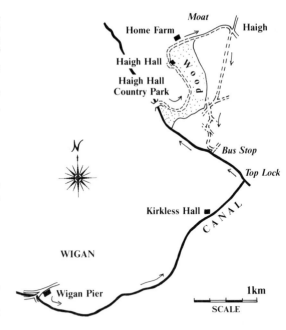

her to walk 'onest every week barefoot and bare-legged to a cross near Wigan from the Haghe'. The cross stands in Standishgate and is known today as Mab's Cross.

The last of the Bradshaighs died in 1770 and the estate passed to Alexander Lindsay, 23rd Earl of Crawford. He started an ironwork foundry building colliery machinery, as well as investing heavily in the Leeds and Liverpool Canal.

Today, Haigh Park provides plenty to attract visitors. There are woodland walks and nature trails, a small zoo with a variety of exotic animals and an eighteen-hole golf course. For the children, there are model and miniature railways, a model village, playground and picnic areas. The Stables Centre includes a cafe and offers a good starting point for exploration.

On to Wigan (via canal or bus)

Coming out through the Stables Centre archway, follow the drive round to the right and walk down the main drive to Haigh village. Turn left into the trackway opposite the pub and follow it on to enter pathway. Follow the path down to trackway, go right and walk on to go left at roadway, over the bridge and on down to go into signed footpath on right. Walk down to go over footbridge. Follow path up to trackway, left, and walk on to roadway. Turn right, and on down to the canal to return to Wigan Pier, or you may catch the bus from here to the town centre – a five-minute ride.

Wigan

Wigan first came to light as the Roman town of Coccium, built upon the summit of the elevation in the centre of the town, on which the parish church of All Saints now stands. Sadly, little remains to be seen today, but inside the church there is the head of a Roman altar. At nearby Dalton a headless statue of Cautopates, one of the attendants of the god Mithras, was found, possibly indicating the site of the Mithraic Temple. This now stands in the

Ribchester Museum. Meaningless away from its true context, it should be returned to where it was found, in Dalton.

During the post-Roman, Celtic period, Wigan was the capital of Greater Makerfield, later re-formed into the 'hundreds' of the northern Lancashire plain.

Today, Wigan is undoubtedly one of the finest towns in Lancashire. The old city centre street pattern has been maintained, offering a selection of shops and inns hard to find anywhere north of Chester or Manchester. All in all, well worth a visit.

Walk Ten
Rufford — Croston — Rufford

Distance: 7 miles circular.
Grade: Very easy walking; light boots.
Lunch: Croston: Lord Nelson, Wheatsheaf or Crown Inn on Station Road.

HERE we follow rivers, a canal and field ditches through the crop growing lands of the Lancashire plain. All manner of vegetables grow in the rich soils of Croston Moss, and in the villages of Rufford and Croston the agrarian tradition in village life lives on. Truly a glimpse back to a former age of rural life.

Rufford Old Hall

Rufford Old Hall, built by the Heskeths in the late-fifteenth century, with seventeenth-century additions, is a very picturesque half-timbered house. The interior of the house is overpowering, with an exuberance of decoration matched nowhere else in the county – the decorated hammer-beams, the great monster of a screen with its barbaric shapes are only two of the impressive features that compete for the eye.

On the lighter side, some evidence exists that a William Shakeshaft was a young member of the Hesketh Company of Players in around 1585, coinciding with another player's absence from

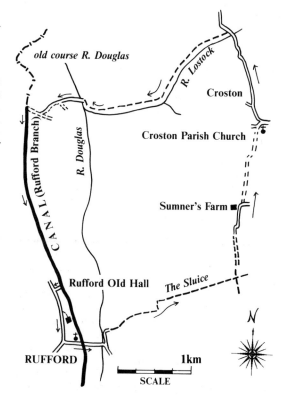

Stratford due to a bout of deer poaching from the park of Sir Thomas Lucy of Charlecote.

You can view the hall, with its collections of sixteenth-century arms and armour, oak furniture and period costumes from 24th March to 5th November, every day except Friday, 1 p.m. to 5 p.m., Sunday 2 p.m. to 5 p.m. Admission charge.

Rufford Old Hall to Croston Church

Leave the Hall grounds and follow the main road to the left, to go left again down the Parbold road, past the Parish Church of St. Mary, over the canal and railway bridges to turn into track on left after road bridge. Follow the track on, over flat bridge then right to follow sluice up to go left at corner and directly on to ditch boundary. Right, and follow ditch boundary on, across field road, and on, through hedgerow and on to field lane. Left, and follow the field lane on up, past Summer's Farm and on along the lane into Croston. Cross the stone footbridge, right and down Church Street into the churchyard.

St. Michael, Croston

The approach to the church is flanked by terraces of brick cottages of around 1704, the entrance of which is home to the village cross, mounted upon steps. It is from the cross that we first notice the slanted church tower (most of the buildings in Croston are leaning this way due to the marshy nature of the ground).

The church itself is late-Gothic, with strange additions and rebuilding work done between 1577

and 1823.

The north doorway displays leaf spandrels (late-fifteenth-century) and the window above (mid-sixteenth-century) is straight-headed, with un-cusped arched lights. Worthy of note inside the church are a thirteenth-century double piscina, a fifteenth-century aumbry and a font of 1663.

Croston village

The village displays many periods of cottage architecture, all leaning one way or the other, that date from the sixteenth century onwards. The almhouses, a long, low building on Station Road, has a datestone of 1692 that informs us that they were endowed by Henry and Isabel Croston at that time. Near the church we find the Yarrow Bridge which is dated 1682, and nearby the Rectory gateway, a tripartite Gothic piece with ogee arches, which is apparently meant to appear ruinous. The classic view of the village is one looking down Church Street with the cross in the foreground.

Croston to Rufford

From the parish church, walk up Church Street, left and follow Town Road through the village and on into Station Road (the almhouses are over on the right). Follow road on, over railway bridge and on to go over stile on the left after crossing Lostock Bridge. Follow the riverside path on to cross Red Bridge. Follow the lane on to the canal towpath. Left, and follow the towpath on to leave by the third bridge. Walk on to the main road, left and on to Rufford Old Hall.

Index

Numbers in bold lettering refer to illustrations